Survival Skills of Native California

SURVIVAL SKILLS
of Native California

Paul Douglas Campbell

GIBBS·SMITH
PUBLISHER
Salt Lake City

To my son Joseph Ara and the memory of my son Razmig

First Edition
03 02 01 00   3 2 1
Copyright © 1999 Paul Douglas Campbell

All rights reserved. No part of this book may be reproduced by any means whatsoever without written permission from the publisher, except brief portions quoted for purpose of review.

Published by
Gibbs Smith, Publisher
P. O. Box 667
Layton, Utah 84041
Web site: www.gibbs-smith.com

Cover design by Forth Gear, Layton, Utah

Interior design by Roderick C. Burton - Art & Design, Bellingham, WA

Printed and bound in the U.S.A.

Library of Congress Cataloging-in-Publication Data
Campbell, Paul, 1942–
    Survival skills of native California / Paul Campbell.
p. cm.
Includes bibliographical references.
ISBN 0-87905-921-4
    1. Indians of North America—California Life skills guides.
    2. Indians of North America—Industries—California.
    3. Indians of North America—Material culture—California.
    4. Survival skills—California.
    5. Wilderness survival—California.
    I. Title.
E78.C15C32   1999
613.6'9' 08997—dc21   99-24412
                                                                        CIP

Contents

Preface: The Wisdom of the California Hunter-Gatherer VII
Introduction: Secrets of Indian Survival XIII

Part One: Basic Skills, Tools of Gathering and Food Preparation, Implements of Household and Personal Necessity

How Coyote Brought Fire to the Karok
    The Fire Drill 4
    Fire—Some Indian Tips 11
Shelter: A Continuum of Simplicity
    Minimalists 16
    Wickiups 18
    Willow-framed Dome Houses 20
    Location 30
    Water 31
    Chumash Water Bottle 34
    Indian Travel 41
    California Cordage—Fibers and Technology 47
    Traps 57
    California Digging Stick 67
    Acorns and Other Bitter Nuts 80
    Mortar and Pestle 92
    Soaproot Brush 98
    Acorn Storage Basket 100
    Closely Twined and Coiled Baskets 103
    A Breakfast of Sweet Acorn Mush with Boiled Shank of Venison 113
    Southern California Pottery 119
    Greens, Beans, Flowers and Other Vegetables 136
    Sugar and Salt 146
    Berries, Cherries and Other Fruit 149
    Pine and Other Not So Bitter Nuts 157
    Seeds and Seed Beater 162
    Mats 169
    Carrying Nets 173
    California Survival Basket 183
    Household Brushes 188
    A Strange Baja Basket 190
    Wooden Bowls, Buckets and Vials 196
    The Technology of Good Grooming 202
    Native California Clothing—An Overview 208
    Rabbitskin Blanket 213
    Elderberry Bark Skirt 218
    Yucca and Agave Fiber Sandals
        of Southern California 223
    Yucca Slab Survival Sandals 228
    Moccasins 231
    Diegueño Rawhide Sandals 235

    Plaited Yucca Sandals 236
    California Elderwood Flute 239
    Filtered Cigarette 244
    Indian Stick Game 246

Part Two: Hunting and Fishing

California Indian Bows
    The Northern California Wide-limbed, Sinew-backed Bow 254
    The Sierra Nevada Hook-ended Sinew-backed Bow 258
    The Southern California Plain Wood Bow 262

And Arrows
    Northern California Arrows 277
    Southern California Arrows 283
    Quivers 295
    How to Shoot an Indian Bow 298
    Bowguard 305
    The California Atlatl 307
    The Atlatl Dart 312
    Throwing the Atlatl Dart 318
    California Knapping 320
    Glue 332
    Stalking 335
    How to Stalk, Kill and Eat a White-throated Woodrat 340
    California Hunting Magic: Split-twig Figurines 346
    California Rabbit Sticks 349
    Sling 362
    Snowshoes 364
    Brain Tanning 369
    Meat Preparation 374
    Twined Bags and Hide Sacks 378
    Wooden War Club 381
    Insects: Small Quarry, Big Protein 385
    How California Indians Made Tule Balsas 390
    Tule Serving Tray 396
    Twined Double Basket Pomo Fish Trap 397
    Fishing Nets 405
    Harpoons, Fish and Sea Mammals 416
    Indian Angling 423
    Fish Poison 433
    Fish and Shellfish Preparation 435
    Bibliography 440

Preface: The Wisdom of the California Hunter-Gatherer

Ignorance keeps primitive people locked in a hunter-gatherer way of life. Once exposed to the bounty of agriculture and the wonder of civilization, they quickly join the inexorable march of progress. It is heretical for moderns to imagine otherwise. But is it true?

Word spread fast among the bands and tribelets of aboriginal California. On nearly every stop along the California coast in 1542, Indians made known to explorer Juan Cabrillo that Spaniards had arrived some days' journey to the east, referring to Coronado's expedition which had reached the Colorado River. The river Indians grew corn and the hunter-gatherer coast Indians told Cabrillo of the existence of much corn to the east. Most of the groups of southern California, northern Mexico and the Southwest had strong long-standing trade relations; they were connected by an extensive system of trails and undoubtedly were aware of what the other fellow picked and ate. It was not for ignorance California Indians clung to the old ways.

Recent studies reveal even the simpler bands of California to have been consummate horticulturists: they burned fields to optimize the growth of edible seed plants, kill pests, and open hunting grounds; they cut back bushes of willow and sourberry and cleared around them to bring forth new straight withes for winnowing and storage baskets, and some groups diverted rivulets of rain water or ponds for thirsty greens in their camp or for roots of cattails nearby. While most California Indians did not practice agriculture, we know the Diegueño transplanted wild onions and tobacco seeds to improve the strain, and from the Colorado River Yumans the Imperial Valley Diegueño learned to plant small plots of corn, beans, and melons on recently flooded banks. But clearly, even for them, agriculture was a secondary choice: word of abundant game or an area rich in useful plants would send them off, ignoring the harvest of their domesticated crops. Agriculture did not become important for the Diegueño and others until Europeans made it necessary by inhibiting the traditional hunter-gatherer patterns, until the newcomers put up fences, cleared forests and overgrazed fields. Agriculture was born of necessity.

A review of southwestern archaeology lends perspective. Evidence of corn introduced from Northern Mexico to the Southwest dates to over three thousand years ago, during a period of increased rainfall. However, it was not until the middle of the first millennium B.C. that a significant number of people began to settle into permanent villages and base their lives on the growing of the new grain. And the reason for that, speculate archaeologists, was not because of corn's supposed superiority over wild foods—in fact, the early Chapalote varieties of the Southwest bore small cobs and required great care—rather they turned to agriculture as a *last resort*. With population growing along the coast and perhaps causing a ripple effect in the hinterland, other groups finding deteriorating climate in the highlands of Mexico and pushing north during the period 3000 to 1000 B.C. and the Southwest itself experiencing a population increase during times when the climate there was more favorable; wild foods were overharvested, and this stress on the environment after 1000 B.C. was exacerbated by a climate turned significantly drier. In other words, as the supply of wild food declined, more and more groups were *forced* to look to domesticated corn. Wild foods were always considered better when they had them.

Archaeology reveals wild foods continued to be significant again when they could get them, even after the introduction of corn. Many other groups of the Southwest, like those of California, rejected agriculture completely—refusing temptation in their Garden of Eden—right up until European contact.

Wherever we have not despoiled the world or overpopulated it, the harvesting of natural bounty is easier than artificially growing crops. It was not ignorance but logical priority based on nutritional value, effort and availability that determined a food's place in a diet, and Californians clearly chose the fruits of hunting and gathering over agriculture. Who was happier? The handful of Paiute who in January 1844 feasted explorers John Charles Fremont and Kit Carson from the seemingly limitless supply of Lahontan trout in Pyramid Lake—their flavor was superior "to that of any fish I have ever known," wrote Fremont, who described them "of

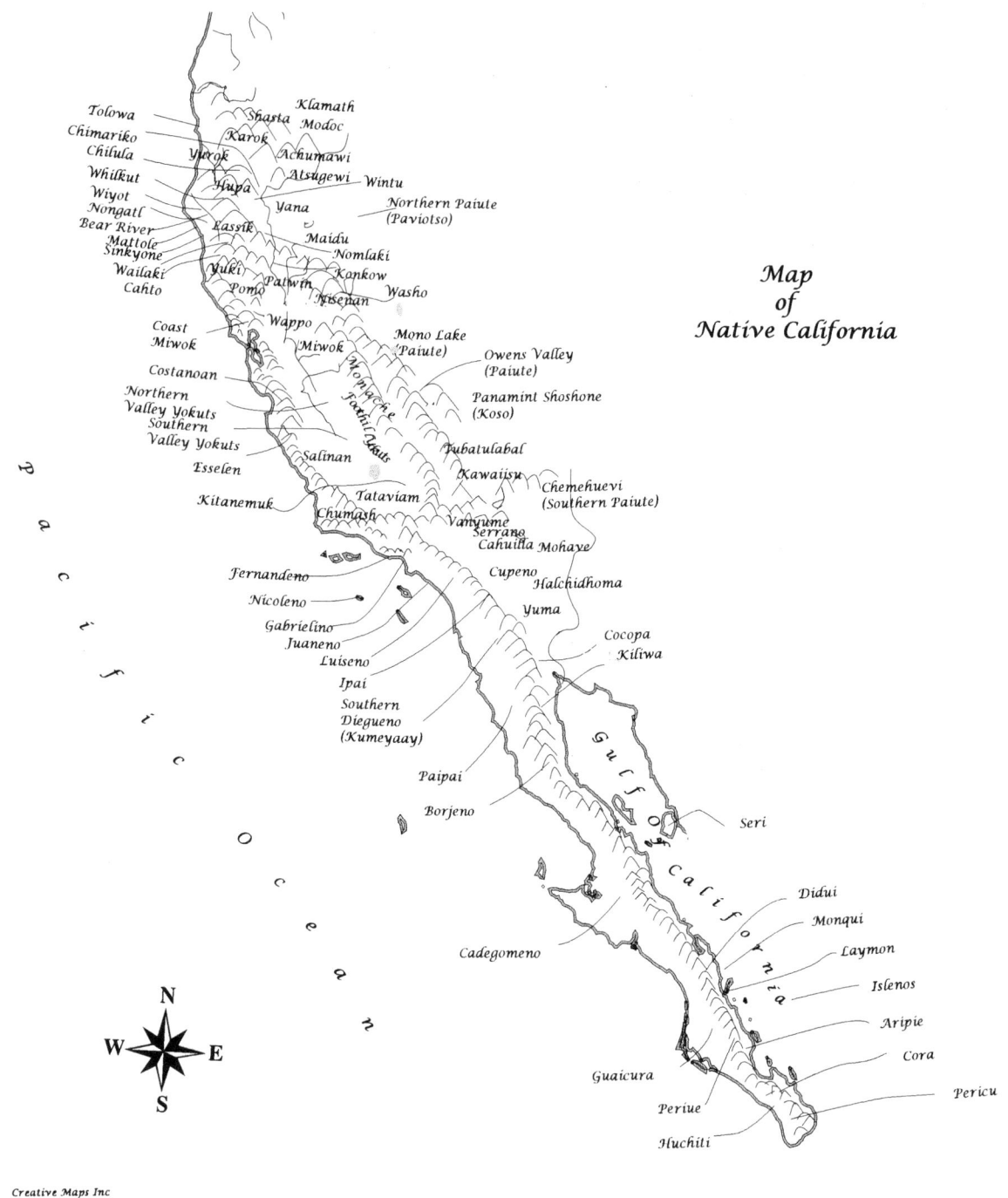

Map of Native California

Creative Maps Inc
Cartography by Zain

extraordinary size—about as large as the Columbia salmon—generally two to four feet in length." Or the thousands who now drudge long hours to maintain the dam that destroyed the native trout and work vast mind-numbing fields of monoculture fed from its waters (while hatcheries plant much smaller nonnative fish in the lake)?

Once freed, the genie of the agricultural "revolution" seems to obey our every wish, and we lose track of costs. Most ancient cities of the Middle East overpopulated and over-tilled the land, destroyed the environment around them, and disappeared. When wetter conditions returned to the Southwest, the Anasazi and others, now full-blown agriculturalists with improved strains of corn, prospered mightily. In Chaco Canyon the Anasazi went from small groupings of mud and thatch pit houses to massive multileveled, multiroomed apartments (up to four stories and over 800 rooms) built of masonry and decorated in veneer. Six thousand may have lived in the canyon itself by the middle of the eleventh century, supported by a hinterland of scores of communities spread over more than 25,000 square miles. The population of Mesa Verde Anasazi and the Montezuma Valley may have reached 30,000 in A.D. 1100, with 25,000 at Mesa Verde alone. At the same time, Mogollon populations soared at sites along the Mimbres River in settlements of single-story adobe and stone apartments of over a hundred rooms. The Hohokam of the Gila River increased greatly in numbers under the impetus of irrigation agriculture at Skoaquik (Snaketown), which became an important regional center similar to Chaco Canyon. But suddenly it all ended. The climate turned dry once again; the great centers were abandoned.

The Chaco Canyon phenomenon collapsed after A.D. 1130 when a prolonged drought struck the San Juan Basin. The Mimbres people moved on about the same time. At Mesa Verde they held out a little longer, but around A.D. 1300 Mesa Verde and the entire San Juan drainage were deserted by the Anasazi. Today the wind through the canyons haunts the spectacular cliff houses they left behind. In the 1400s Snaketown, too, was finally abandoned.

It is ironic that a dry period, which earlier had made domesticated corn an acceptable addition to an archaic diet for many, now put a sudden end to the overextended way of life evolved from reliance on domesticated crops. We cannot be certain climate acted as the catalyst for the great abandonments, but whatever the reasons—climate, the farming of marginal fields, overtilling and loss of soil fertility, warfare, or population stress—the fact remains that the land, any given region of the Southwest, was no longer sustaining indefinitely large groups of agriculturalists. After A.D. 1300 we see them occupying an area for a hundred years or so and then relocating. At the time of Spanish contact, the great Pueblo edifices of the Southwest were noteworthy as much for the absence of people as for their presence. Modern, mechanized agriculture—computerized tractors directed by satellites, chemical fertilizer, synthetic insecticides, and massive pumping of groundwater—perhaps only forestalls the process.

Where population pressure and agriculture had not absorbed them, the old archaic hunters and gatherers continued their way of life as they had for thousands of years. California was such a place. Except for the limited agriculture of the Colorado River, nature needed little nudging in California; the garden had endured.

Many Californians lived in bands of a few families, exploiting the garden in seasonal rounds. The apparently simple material culture of such groups is misleading. The frequent movement of bands restricts the size and complexity of the tool kit, but as Ralph Michelsen discovered, it does not restrict the skills needed to fabricate and use the kit; in fact, this is exactly where the energy goes. To think of these people as ignorant is to be truly ignorant. Furthermore, in band societies intimate knowledge of survival skills is universal. Since they live in small groups and frequently find themselves alone, traditional skills are indeed a matter of survival. All adults must know everything, the distinction between man's and woman's work blurs. Absorbing traditional wisdom and knowing intimately the natural world around them took Native Californians a lifetime of intelligent listening and observation.

As among all peoples, Californians tended to seek foods that gave the most calories (and presumably vitamins and minerals in addition to proteins, fats and carbohydrates) for the least effort, forming a kind of prioritized list, moving down the list as foods near the top became unavailable seasonally or with changing climate patterns or depletion from overharvesting. Big game hunters had followed the great herds and megafauna out of Siberia over 12,000 years ago; they continued into historic times hunting buffalo on the American Great Plains. In California the huge animals became extinct much earlier, and by 9,000 years ago, archaic Indians had turned to smaller game, sea mussels, and the gathering and milling of calorie-rich seeds. Environmental change—the inundation of the heavily seeded coastal plains—and growing population eventually left fewer and fewer seed-producing grasses. Another calorie- and protein-rich food, still high on the list but requiring greater preparation, came to prominence—the acorn. California Indians are today identified with the acorn. Mortars and pestles for their processing came into use in southern California around 6,000 years ago. In the same region sea mammals and deepwater fish began to be exploited with elaborate gear and boats. In northwestern California the harpooning and netting of salmon became a way of life. Throughout California Indians dug nutritious, starchy tubers and roots; harvested flowers, berries and greens; and hunted and trapped deer and rabbits. In the Great Central Valley, tule roots and freshwater fish, waterfowl, antelope and elk supplemented the staple acorn. Indians of the basin and range areas of California often lived near marshes where they ate the flesh of ducks and fish or the rhizomes of cattail, but as these areas became flooded during epochs of greater rain or desiccated during prolonged droughts and the cost of catching and gathering became too great, they turned to pine nuts harvested from the sides of mountains in the late summer and fall. Mountain sheep provided meat for many desert people. For those of the low deserts east of Los Angeles, rabbits, mesquite pods, and the leaves and stalk of agave were foods of choice.

If one cuisine epitomized the Native California diet, it might have been the Tubatulabal's, whose name means piñon gatherers but who utilized the acorn and many other California foods as well. They lived and today still live along the south fork of the Kern River at the confluence of five great natural regions of California: the Sierra Nevada, the Central Valley, the Great Basin, the Mohave Desert and Southern California. Erminie Voegelin, who collected ethnographic material from knowledgeable elders in the early 1930s, concluded that roughly 40 percent of the aboriginal diet came from meat, fish and fowl; acorns and piñons made up another 40 percent, and the rest was garnered from small seeds, stalks, roots, berries and other wild plants. During spring and summer the Tubatulabal ate a varied diet including many plant foods, but by fall fresh vegetable foods had declined, and during winter, as eighty-six-year-old Steban Miranda put it at the time, they "just ate acorns, piñons, and meat of any sort they could get, and dried and fresh fish . . . more acorns were eaten than piñons," he remembered.

Beyond the California paradise, Indians often depended on a single food, and when the salmon or the buffalo or the corn failed, they went into a tailspin of starvation. A. L. Kroeber emphasized that Californians, unlike so many others, almost always had options. The seasonal round, that took them from semipermanent winter villages in the valleys or foothills to the deserts and mountains for gathering and hunting in spring and summer and, for many, from there to the important fall acorn harvest, was not rigid and exclusive. Deer could be taken at any time and there were always fish in mountain streams and valley lakes and rivers. Even loss of the acorn crop did not spell disaster: because of the complexity of the terrain and weather, failure of one variety or on one mountain did not always mean failure of another acorn or another area; and if they already did not have stored a two- to-three-year supply, as they often did, they could always find substitutes in the buckeye of the north and wild plum in the south, whose kernels were gathered, hulled, dried, ground, sifted and leached in a manner similar to that of the acorn.

In fact, the emphasis on process more than specific foods seems to have sustained the California Indian. The process of gathering acorns could be extended to pine nuts and other vegetable foods and from there it is but a small step to the picking of caterpillars, snails, mollusks, crayfish, turtles or grasshoppers. Acorns were pounded in mortars. Earlier, they had milled seeds on the grinding slab. Eventually not only seeds and acorns but dried salmon, vertebrae, berries (which in southern California are generally dry and seedy), nuts, fruits and whole small rodents were pulverized and eaten or stored. A digging stick unearths edible worms as well as bulbs and can cut the heart from the agave as the stalk from the yucca. It was even used to plant seeds by the Mohave. The basketry that beats seeds from bushes or transports acorns from the harvest can be adapted to trapping fish or eel in mountain streams. Nets that carry goods also catch rabbits and fish. Loop snares took quarry ranging from mice and ducks to coyote and deer. Processes, which were often slow and repetitive and entailed great patience, extended seamlessly from one food or area of life to another.

Everything was connected to everything else. Life was whole. The same elderberry tree that gave berries to eat lent bark for clothing and wood for a flute. Yuccas produced edible flowers as well as a stalk, which could be harvested for food or saved for a quiver, and leaves, whose natural fiber might be woven into a sandal or twisted into cordage for nets and bows. It is this unbroken vision that gave the California Indian such wonderful integrity with the world. Ultimately, it is a question of value. The final hedge against starvation and misery was generosity. Stephen Powers found in the 1870s: "No Indian is despised so much as one who is close-fisted; nothing is more certain than that, if an Indian comes along hungry, they will divide with him to the uttermost crumb." Sharing was an important California Indian value, even between distinct groups as when Miwok would go and live with Mono during lean times. This recognition of the interconnectedness between people as between processes and resources is a wisdom that must be restored if we want to find our way beyond the

Above, site of old Hupa village on the Trinity River in northwestern California. Below, salmon, freshly netted by Yurok fisherman, roast for a Yurok and Hupa feast on a bank of the Klamath River at Weitchpec, where the Trinity meets the Klamath, July 1998.

badly fractured state of inequality, regimentation, misinformation, frustration and corruption to which we have descended. The lesson of the twentieth century is clear: *primitive* lies not at the bottom of a linear progress but represents the youth, vigor and hope of our species.

We all have some practical understanding about the world. Refined to the point of science, this knowledge becomes data and short-range predictions of how things work, a probability of what happens when two chemicals mix or what the weather will be like tomorrow. However, even at its most ambitious in the form of complex computer models, the relevancy of its prognostications in the real everyday life decrease rapidly as they are extended in space and time. A corporation might, for a while, control the hydrology of a valley perfectly as it turns it into a reservoir or megafarm but miss entirely the downstream or long-range effects on the beings who live in the valley or in the larger world. That is where a "primitive" folk wisdom should become important, an intuition of the heart refined over the ages of right and wrong. Folk wisdom goes beyond practicality and science and encompasses the whole. It consists of value and determines choices. Bemused by the glitter of technology and almighty dollar, unattached to the land, transnational megacorporate groupthink ignores these warnings of the heart. Apologists extol the global economy and human evolution as upward and noble and in defense point to the agricultural revolution and the *progress* of civilization.

Biologists speak more sanely. They describe adaptations to various environments, evolution as never-ending process. In that sense, first, agriculture and later, civilization were simply human adaptations to ever more degraded and overpopulated environments. The exploding population of today's California continues to bring proportionately more civilization in the form of more laws, order, regimentation, restriction, costly technology, class inequality and toil.

To forget the lessons of the past is to not only endlessly repeat its horrors but to lose its most magnificent possibilities. Knowing how to do something does not mean we should do it. The early inhabitants of California had that folk wisdom, almost a gut intuition built over millennia, of what was good and bad, a sense of value that allowed them to make what must seem to us an astounding choice: they rejected progress—the tilling of soil—in favor of a hunter-gatherer way of life.

> "Grandson, listen to the river and the sky, watch the seabirds and smell the smoke of my blood that now runs through your veins. The raven and the bear already know of your footprints in the sand and the salmon will sing for you because they know you are of me and I live on in you."
>
> —*from a poem by Mel Smith, Yurok*

Introduction: Secrets of Indian Survival

This book undertakes the task of restoring what we have methodically destroyed: California Indian survival skills. From the scattered bits and parts it seeks a critical mass of essential detail on each representative skill to recreate a whole technology.

Not an end in itself, California survival lore unlocks a paradise too long maligned as mere unused land marked for development. Beyond the sprawl, the asphalt, the final orchard gate, the very end of the last dirt road, looms the mystery and vitality of California wilderness. The stars there still glitter like ice, the sun burns more brightly. Valleys, mountains, streams, deserts and sea—not long ago all of California was wilderness. The first Californians lived in harmony with that untamed place, using skills refined over 10,000 years. For those who believed in the sacredness, it was a garden, carefully tended. Conquest, greed, the mercantile juggernaut of Western civilization, in a few short decades crushed a marvel but weakly understood. California native skills were lost, buried beneath highway and city without end.

The mindless backhoes continue unabated. Modern technology beguiles us. We extol the good and blithely ignore the bad, or we meet the hell it spawns reflexively with more industrial technology, merely to survive. We buy expensive computerized treadmills and stay indoors because our manicured parks are polluted and dangerous. We make love to Virtual Veronica in cyberspace because the parameter of our existence is a sterile suburban box, magnificent forest clear cut and turned to ticky-tacky. We fear the wildness beyond the asphalt and lights.

"Only to the white man was nature a wilderness," pronounced Chief Luther Standing Bear of the Oglala Sioux, "and only to him was the land 'infested' with 'wild' animals and 'savage' people. To us it was tame. Earth was bountiful and we were surrounded with the blessings of the Great Mystery." Native survival skills allow us to enter the Mystery and truly make wildness a blessing, to recognize it as home and lead a richer and more fulfilling life, to relieve the monotony and slow death of cynical corporate greed.

Though often extolled, Native American survival skills, in particular those of California, are aptly termed survival secrets since in most cases the details were obliterated in the holocaust that took the people who knew them, remembered now only brokenly by a surviving elder on a remote reservation or shattered and strewn through a myriad of histories, adventures, government accounts and ethnographic tomes. In a sense, the headlong rush of academia to categorize and compare general traits, often superficially and from a distance, killed in its own way just as certainly as smallpox and bullets, the theft of land and gift of TV, did in another. Significant about the Indian was not the quaint terminology for a second cousin on the male side, not the blood types or the shovel incisors, not even the mythology, but how they lived with the earth, which was the genesis and underpinning of the mythology, the oneness with nature. Animals were people and human existence apart from earth and sun, inconceivable.

Survival skills comprise that knowledge that allows living in the wild free from the destructive effects of industrial technology. Paradoxically, Indian skills often must be gleaned from the writings of the very people who little esteemed them. From the beginning of European contact, fragments of Native California technologies were gathered by the shock troops of industrialization, by those who came to conquer; these early explorers kept journals or wrote books. For that we are indebted. Few, even very few anthropologists, however, preserved details, the somewhat tedious, technical manual-like procedures that are the skill. Witnessing and describing an end product is not enough. I have seen a thousand televisions but cannot build one. Much of the problem stems from the chronicler's aim to titillate with exotic adventure or the scholar's aloof interest in culture as an abstract evolutionary process. Both attitudes result in the tracking of skills but devalue the skill itself. Bow, Yuman. Rabbit stick, Diegueño.

The magic in making a hook from bone, wood and fiber and catching a fish with our primitive outfit is not captured by the abstract knowledge that the Sinkyone possessed bone hooks. Luckily, but so rarely, a prescient few described how Indians made and used tools. Where they did not portray the whole skill, another independent observer occasionally provided key pieces; or overlapping parts of a skill were recorded from neighboring groups and by juxtaposition of these complementary observations on the page, the ancient know-how coalesces and lives.

A bookish approach does not necessarily render a stilted picture of Native California, a hit-and-miss selection; for, unlike language or ritual, which could change abruptly from this valley to the next or from that grove of oaks to another on the far side of the mountain, California survival skills stayed surprisingly the same. Nature herself kept them honest: what worked, worked. Accounts of early observers generally describe gradual differences in skills—long stretches in which they were essentially the same—and as they moved from one natural province to another, skills simply adapted, more dependent on environment than, say, linguistic affiliation of which there were so many in California. The Cahuilla, largely a desert people, in the mountains built tipi-like wickiups of incense cedar bark similar to those of the Miwok of Yosemite 400 miles north. Because of the greater snowfall in the Sierras, the cone of the Miwok bark house was steeper, less flat than the Cahuilla structure, in order to shed the deeper snow. Blankets of twisted rabbit fur were ubiquitous, but where fox, beaver, sea otters or ducks were abundant, the pelts of those animals were similarly used. The technique of starting a fire with two sticks or rolling cordage of natural fiber on the thigh changed little from the Great Basin to Baja. Only the materials gradually shifted, Indian hemp giving way to fiber of agave. Acorn technology, as the others, varied but was similar throughout California.

We find in the search for the essence of the skill its variety. Bows transformed significantly from northern California forests to the southern deserts but were surprisingly similar within each region. Yet no two individuals did everything exactly the same. The idea of survival skill itself is an abstract concept. Survival technology was a whole; skills blended into each other almost imperceptibly. The making of a snare, for example, involved the making of cordage, which involved the cutting and processing of a fibrous plant with stone tools and on and on. Categories are for books, which are for convenience. Would that we might have followed and observed the elders themselves who truly lived the forgotten ways.

Admittedly, there is much of Native California not in the old books. For that reason Ralph Michelsen in the 1960s sought remnant bands of Yuman speaking Indians in the mountains of northern Lower California—the Southern Diegueño or Kumeyaay, the Paipai and Kiliwa—who retained knowledge of traditional California Native skills. Some families still depended heavily on hunting and gathering; many employed these skills during economic hard times, such as loss of wage labor on ranches or during droughts. Forced to move from his adobe house to a year-round spring during the dry spell of 1963, Southern Diegueño Fernando Cuaja built an old-style A-frame hut of two forked cottonwood poles, a ridgepole, sycamore side beams and sotol thatching. The sotol leaves were laid butt-end up, the tips of the first course buried in a shallow ditch around the structure. A throwing stick, skillfully employed, protected the nearby garden and furnished the family fresh rabbit meat.

In 1775 these same Diegueño Indians, frustrated with strict sedentary mission routine and disruption of their hunter-gatherer rounds (cattle grazing on coastal food seeds for example), had revolted and burned the Franciscan Mission of San Diego. Fearing retaliation, some Indians escaped to mountain redoubts; others later drifted south to live with relatives in northern Baja California. There in the later years of the eighteenth and early nineteenth century, Dominicans established a chain of missions. These suffered the same fate as the one in San Diego. Near the middle of the nineteenth century, Diegueño Indians from Nejí destroyed Misión Guadalupe del Norte and their neighbors the Paipai burned Santa Catalina Virgen y Mártir. Unlike the San Diego mission they were never rebuilt.

Despite new roads near their territories and increasing pressures on their remaining land from Mexican ranches, some of these Indians still in the 1990s—thirty years after Michelsen knew them—possess and use the old skills. Most graciously by allowing me to follow and observe them, they taught me many details of California Native survival skills overlooked in the archives, and they fleshed out others only sketched from more northern areas of California.

In some cases where books failed and Indians who knew how had long ago passed on, careful analysis of museum and archaeological specimens yielded secrets of manufacture.

In all cases I have tried to make clear the source or author of my information (while avoiding the horror of footnotes). At times even this may seem a bit tedious or academic but it is a correction to the endless run of bogus Indian skill books available. It permits refinement of the information and it is just good to know and honor those who remembered and knew how.

Ultimately, the book's intention is to equip one to survive by one's own wits in the woods, a book of survival skills, not an encyclopedic listing of the infinite resourcefulness of Native California. It is necessarily selective, hopefully of some of the best, most accessible and useful from the full range of indigenous California, past and present, Upper and Lower.

The goal is to recapture something of the vigor of the youth of our species and of the tranquility and warmth Thomas Jefferson Mayfield experienced among Indians, still traditional, in California of the 1850s. Raised from the age of six by the Choinumne Yokuts while they followed the timeless ways, Mayfield years later recalled the allure of the end of a day in that life:

After the evening meal they would all lie around the fire on the ground through the long evening and tell stories and sing until as late as ten or eleven o'clock. This was the finest part of their lives. Here was the real family circle. The long evenings were spent about the fires in the most pleasant way imaginable. Every night was a bonfire party. The old sages would tell stories about their own experiences when they were young, or about the history of their tribe, or just simple stories they may have made up. We youngsters would sit around with our mouths and eyes and ears open and listen until we had to go to bed.

The Indians of California bequeathed us a paradise they had been stewards of for 10,000 years. Skills such as the percussion of rock to make tools stretched back to the very beginning of Native California and along with many other skills were adapted to the changing land and climate and perfected over millennia. Paipai elder Benito Peralta once told me that Indian survival skills seem unimportant to most people, but there surely is going to come a day, he said, when we will need these skills again. Not even the most corrupted urban booster can believe that given the present rate of progress (or decadence) and population growth under Western technology and values over the last 200 years, there will even be a California a few centuries from now. Gross overconsumption has been a jolly good party but the obese revelers must go home. We must change our direction to survive. Indian California was not just a quaint anomaly, another way, but taken in its largest meaning, I believe the only way.

Traditional stick game between Hupa and Yurok youth in natural outdoor stadium on bank of Klamath River, 1998.

Part One
Basic Skills, Tools of Gathering and Food Preparation, Implements of Household and Personal Necessity

How the Coyote Brought Fire to the Karok

Far away toward the rising sun, somewhere in a land that no Karok had ever seen, the creator Kareya made fire and hid it in a casket, which he gave to two old hags to keep, lest some Karok should steal it. But coyote befriended the Karok and promised to bring them some fire.

He assembled a great company of animals, one of each kind from the lion down to the frog. These he stationed in a line between the home of the Karok and the far distant land where the fire was, the weakest animal nearest home and the strongest near the fire. Then he took an Indian with him and hid him under a hill and went to the house of the hags who kept the casket and rapped on the door. One of them came out, and he said, "Good evening," and they replied, "Good evening." Then he said, "It's a pretty cold night, can you let me sit by your fire?" And they said, "Yes, come in." So, he went in and stretched himself out before the fire and reached his snout toward the blaze, and sniffed the heat, and felt very snug and comfortable. Finally he stretched his nose out along his forepaws, and pretended to go to sleep, although he kept the corner of one eye open watching the old hags. But they never slept, day or night, and he spent the whole time watching and thinking to no purpose.

So next morning he went out and told the Indian whom he had hidden under the hill that the Indian must make an attack on the hags' cabin, as if he were about to steal some fire, while he, the coyote, was in it. He then went back and asked the hags to let him in again, which they did, since they could not believe that a coyote could steal fire. He stood close by the casket of fire, and when the Indian made a rush on the cabin and the hags dashed out after him at one door, the coyote seized a brand in his teeth and ran out the other door. He almost flew over the ground, but the hags saw the sparks flying and gave chase, and gained on him fast. He was out of breath by the time he reached the lion, who took the brand and ran with it to the next animal, and so on to each animal, barely having time to give it to the next before the hags came up.

The next to last in line was the ground squirrel. When he took the brand, he ran so fast with it that his tail caught fire, and he curled it up over his back and burned the black spot we see to this day, just behind his shoulders. Last of all was the frog, but he couldn't run at all, so he opened his mouth wide and the squirrel chucked the fire into it, and he swallowed it down with a gulp. Then he turned and gave a great jump, but the hags were so close in pursuit that one of them seized him by his tadpole tail and tweaked it off, and that is the reason why frogs have no tails to this day. He swam underwater a long distance, as long as he could hold his breath, then came up and spit the fire into a log of driftwood, and there it has been ever since. So now, when an Indian rubs two pieces of wood together, the fire comes forth.

(A Karok fable adapted from Stephen Powers, 1877)

Karok Indian Fritz Hanson makes fire as a medicine man does, rubbing the two sticks of the fire drill.

Photograph by J. P. Harrington, spring 1926
(Smithsonian Institution National Anthropological Archives).

The Fire Drill

There is no machine on earth so potent, yet so simple and elegant, as the two sticks of the Native American fire drill; a hearth piece, the female element—according to Ishi, who emerged in 1911 from forty years of concealment in the California bush as the last "wild Indian" of North America— and the drill itself, an approximately 1/2-inch by 2-foot-long rod, the male element or "man piece." With these, a little tinder and much skill, the Indian created fire.

On the other hand, no aboriginal California Indian ever made fire from a bow drill. At least there is no convincing evidence for this. Eskimos and some nearby groups used the bow drill with a two-man cord system for increasing the spin of the drill. Some Canadian Indians and a few in the northern United States also knew the bow drill. Paul Martin described a complete bow-drill kit—including yucca fiber cord, hand piece and fire drills—taken in 1890 from a cliff house in Grand Gulch Canyon, Utah. Likely of the Pueblo III period, the Field Museum had purchased the set when Martin published his account in 1934.

But this "improvement" (more people are able to make fire with the bow drill), or modernization, entails more pieces and complexity than the simple hand drill: one must spend hours making cordage and finding and fitting a top hand-hold piece and finally the bow itself. Something is lost. The bow drill is just too modern.

The hand fire drill was universal and ancient. Mayan hieroglyphs of the fire-making hand drill extend back in an unbroken line to the Olmec iconography of San Lorenzo—the first American Indian civilization—some 3,000 years ago. Undoubtedly the skill is thousands of years older, lost in the Paleolithic. Fittingly, it was the Olmec god of the north and darkness who made compensatory fire with the sticks. The Aztec started their new year by drilling for new fire at night on a hill outside of Tenochtitlán. Should the drill have failed, it was said the demons of darkness would descend to eat men and the sun would be destroyed forever. Much later, Indians such as the Karok of California made new fire with the sticks to begin a new year. So important was the drill, young Aztec men had it burned onto their wrists in the form of the fire drill constellation (the belt and sash of Orion). The ancient Maya ritual of the Bakabs exhorted, "To be charmed, the fire is always kindled with a fire drill."

It was the simple two-piece hand drill the ancients revered. At the time of European contact, the fire drill could be found everywhere in California. The ability to make fire in the wild is perhaps the most important survival skill one can possess—literally the difference between a dark shivering death and a hot meal in the glow of a warming blaze. It cannot be taught by theory. Only through familiarity with the range of materials and techniques the Indians actually used in a variety of environments and by practice does the fire come forth.

Variety of Materials and Manufacture of the Machine

Simple and elegant perhaps, but despite myriad ethnological descriptions and survival-book explanations, almost nobody today is able to make fire with the hand fire drill. Somehow significant details get left out. Styles were many yet basic principles are few. For the Indian, every detail counted and preparation was paramount.

Theodora Kroeber brought together the accounts on Ishi, the only survivor of his Yahi band. Recognizing him as the last culturally pure Native Californian, Alfred Kroeber and others had taken pains to record his skills, which included fire making. The lower, or female, element was flat, of wood somewhat softer than the male shaft, usually willow or cedar, seasoned and dry, but not so old to be brittle. With an obsidian knife, sockets were bored or gouged out about 1/4 inch deep and notched at the side into a shallow channel to the hearth's edge. The drill, about the length of an arrow but larger at the lower end, fit the socket. Ishi preferred buckeye, but sagebrush, poison oak or any fairly hard wood worked.

The Southern Diegueños, at the other end of California, sharpened the point of the fire drill—which for them was a foot long—by rubbing it on a stone. One hundred years ago, Walter Hough, the great student of the Indian fire drill from the National Museum, cautioned that shaping the lower end of the spindle was to allow contact with the bottom of the shallow depression or socket lest it bind against the edges of the hole and defeat the object. To start a fire by friction, the point had to be shaped to avoid contact with the sides of the hole but be dull. That is, it had to be wide enough to make surface contact with the bottom and not sharpened to an acute point. Otherwise, the speed—which increases on the edge of a circle or wheel with distance from its center—would be minimal, and sufficient friction and heat would not be produced when the drill was spun.

Smeaton Chase recorded the Palm Springs Cahuilla fire-making technology in the early years of the twentieth century. Dry palm fruit stems of the California fan palm (*Washingtonia filifera*) made both hearth and drill, the former about 1 inch broad and of any length, the latter less than half as thick and about 1 foot long. In the hearth they cut a hollow with a little groove that led to a small heap of dry leaves. The drill was trimmed to a *blunt* point, placed upright in the hollow of the hearth, and rolled rapidly between the open hands of one Indian while another steadied the hearth. The hands moved down as the firemaker spun the drill and returned again and again to the top. A stream of wood powder fell from the groove upon the leaves. Smoke arose from the hearth in less than two minutes. A coal fell on the tinder and blowing on it produced a flame. All this was completed in under three minutes of hard work and at much risk of failure in blowing the ember into fire.

The Tubatulabal of the Kern River in the southern Sierras employed dry Fremont cottonwood root for a hearth and the shredded cottonwood roots for tinder. Erminie Voegelin noted a 2 to 2 1/2-foot stalk of mule fat (*Baccharis glutinosa*) for the drill. The Kiliwa of the Sierra San Pedro Mártir in Lower California also used a drill of mule fat, called in Spanish *guatamote*, or the stalk of a nolina (*Nolina parryi*), 1 1/2 feet long. The Kiliwa split the guatamote, or nolina, and made a half-round hearth an inch or more across. They started the hole near the center with the drill itself, then cut a notch to the edge.

Similarly, the Luiseño generally employed a single wood for both drill and hearth, in their case, *Baccharis douglasii*. The Yana, Maidu and Miwok often used well-seasoned buckeye for both pieces. The Kawaiisu used sagebrush (*Artemisia tridentata*) with the drill piece lashed to a common reed (*Phragmites*) main shaft. The Yurok used willow root for both.

The Chumash, too, used guatamote for the vertical stick but *romerillo*, Spanish for coastal sagebrush (*Artemisia californica*), for the hearth, reversing the idea of a harder wood for the drill and a softer one for the hearth. In the early years of this century the Chumash Fernando Librado told John Peabody Harrington *(field notes, see E. Mills, 1981-91)* of a Fernandeño friend who also used guatamote and romerillo for the drill and hearth. The Chumash were centered around present-day Santa Barbara and the Fernandeños were a branch of the Gabrielinos of the Los Angeles area. Other informants agreed that these woods were used by the Chumash. In addition, willow was mentioned for use as both drill and hearth (split willow) as well as guatamote for the drill with a cottonwood hearth. Apparently the Chumash drill could be especially thin. Hudson and Blackburn quote early Sespe residents Henley and Bizzel who described the drill of guatamote as very dry and as thick as a lead pencil. A presumed Chumash fire-making set was discovered in a cave in Salisbury Canyon. Both pieces were blackened by fire. The hearth, 7-1/2 by 3/4 inches, had a small hole near the edge, a V-notch opening from it. The drill itself was a mere 11-5/8 inches in length and 1/4 inch in diameter.

Hough examined many aboriginal fire sticks and found that besides dryness, softness from incipient decay was common. Often the pieces were riddled by worms. Such wood powdered easily and retained the heat generated by friction until the accumulation of heat ignited the powder. Vascular, starchy flowering stems were favorites. The Maricopa flattened the soft inner wood of the giant cactus for a hearth and made a drill of peeled, straightened arrowweed 15 to 18 inches long and 1/4 inch in diameter.

Some groups, as indicated, made composite drills. The Klamath used reed for the main shaft and a short piece of hard greasewood set in and lashed with sinew for the point. The Modoc and Klamath Lake, according to S. A. Barrett, also made fire with a very dry willow root bound at its end to any straight piece of wood for the shaft. This was twirled in a hearth of cedar. The canoe paddle, always of cedar, often served as a hearth. A small cup was cut near the end of the handle or near the juncture of the blade and the handle but above the line water would reach as the paddle would dip into the water. Leslie Spier, on the other hand, reported that the best Klamath drill was made from sagebrush (*Artemesia tridentata*), but could also be the dried tip of the bull pine or willow; it was 2 feet long and 1/2 inch in diameter. Others were told that a dry, dead, yellow pine branch about 1/4 inch in diameter, seasoned and softened by the weather, worked. Black sagebrush bark was the tinder. Men carried the drill

Northern Maidu hearth and drill. Hearths were usually of cedar, observed Dixon, 30 cm. or more in length (this one measured 59 cm.), 3 to 6 cm. wide, and 2 cm. thick. Drills of buckeye were about 45 to 50 cm. in length (the one depicted was 69.5 cm.) and 7 to 15 mm. in diameter. Maidu Indians held the hearth on the ground with the knees and spun the drill in a small scraped out hole at the head of a notch which had been cut from the edge of the board. Dry grass or punky wood served as tinder. A piece of punky wood also carried a smoldering fire while traveling; the Maidu rarely permitted fires to go cold (Dixon, 1905).

in the quiver, *women* in the cradle. The Klamath believed that they could coax the drill by telling it of the animals the firemaker would kill and cook when the flame arose.

The Utes of the Southwestern Plateau would use the yucca flower stalk for a hearth, like the Apache and Navajo, and the reed for the drill shaft set with a greasewood head. Undoubtedly this was because greasewood was difficult to obtain in long straight sections. Ute women were also firemakers.

One of Barrett and Gifford's Miwok informants stated that the block was of cedar and the stick of elderberry; the Field Museum has a Central Miwok set in which both elements are made from cedar. Rotten buckeye wood, dry pine needles, shredded cedar bark or finely shredded grasses were the Miwoks' choice of tinder, although the Central Miwok of the mountains preferred the dry white punk of a rotten hollow tree.

According to Spier, the Southern Diegueño of Campo used dry sagebrush bark for tinder. It was pounded until the fibers were loose and then placed around the point of the drill. Tachi Yokuts dancing and medicine man Bob Bautista still lived around Tulare Lake when he told J. P. Harrington in the early years of the twentieth century how they made fire. The hearth consisted of three pieces of cattail leaves lashed together. An unspecified stick was the drill. The leaves would soon begin to smoke and glow, he told Harrington, suggesting perhaps that hearth and tinder were one and the same.

For the Pomo, as witnessed by Barrett, the drill was sometimes made from a relatively soft wood and the hearth from a harder wood, usually buckeye. Elderberry, buckeye or mountain mahogany were specified as some of the woods used for drills. Hearths viewed by Barrett were flat-bottomed to sit firmly on the ground and had from four to ten holes for the drill, which was 2 to 3 feet long with a diameter about the same as an arrow. In making fire, it was important that the twirling drill never lose contact with the hearth. Materials such as the pith of elderberry, certain fungi or very fine dry grass served as tinder. One informant told him that the best method was to catch the fine hot wood dust, which trickles through the notch, on a leathery dry fungus (one which ignites easily) and blow the tiny incandescent dust into a glow to ignite finely divided dry grass or very dry outer bark of wild hemp. Once it took flame small sticks were added. Fire making was not an easy task. Only a few could do it quickly. The firemaker usually perspired freely by the time he had achieved the tiny glowing ember. It was essential for success, the Pomo believed, not to have too many spectators observing as the firemaker spun the drill.

Exact Technique of Spinning the Drill

Ishi placed dried moss, thistledown or finely shredded inner bark of willow along the channel of the hearth and onto the ground where it led off the board. T. Kroeber described how he began. Squatting, Ishi either held the ends of the hearth steady against the ground with his toes or knelt on it. He placed the drill, larger end down, into the socket. Between the palms of opened hands he twirled the stick back and forth, all the while bearing downward into the socket. From photographs of Ishi's position we see him with his elbows directly under his shoulders. The drill was near his right knee which was on the ground. The left knee was raised up and his left arm was to the inside of his knee. The drill was close in, permitting maximum downward force with his trunk, shoulders, hands and arms.

The downward pressure of the hands on the drill brought them closer and closer to the hearth. Just before they touched, they were returned to the upper end of the stick, the drill motionless for an instant. If motionless for too long, the dull contact point where all friction and force was focused would cool, prolonging the process or preventing success altogether. Hough (1890) warned against allowing air to get under the drill and recalled that Barrett (1952), when writing of the Pomo, stressed the importance of maintaining contact between the drill and hearth. Returning the hands to the top of the drill was a deft motion requiring practice.

Edward S. Curtis's dramatic 1914 motion picture of the Kwakiutl Indian making a spiritual quest fire with sticks underscores the importance of preparing materials and, once the actual process begins, the importance of downward pressure on the spindle and the proper method of returning the hands to the top of the drill. The Indian's shoulders and head lean heavy over the downward-moving hands, but unlike any other ethnographic source of which I am aware, we learn from the Curtis film exactly how to return to the top of the drill. As descending hands near the hearth, one hand clasps and steadies the drill while the other returns quickly to the top portion and grabs and steadies the drill at that point. This allows the bottom hand to release and return to the top of the stick where the other hand opens to meet it and together they resume at once the downward back-and-forth twirling of the stick. It can be seen that the hand grasping the stick at the bottom (as the other returns to the top) slips slightly downward in maintaining strong pressure on the drill. In order to catch this, I had to slow the film.

Both strength and coordination are needed to maintain firm and continuous pressure of the drill into the hearth. It demands a subtle balance. The fire-maker must not expend too much energy at the outset. As wood powder, ground off the bottom

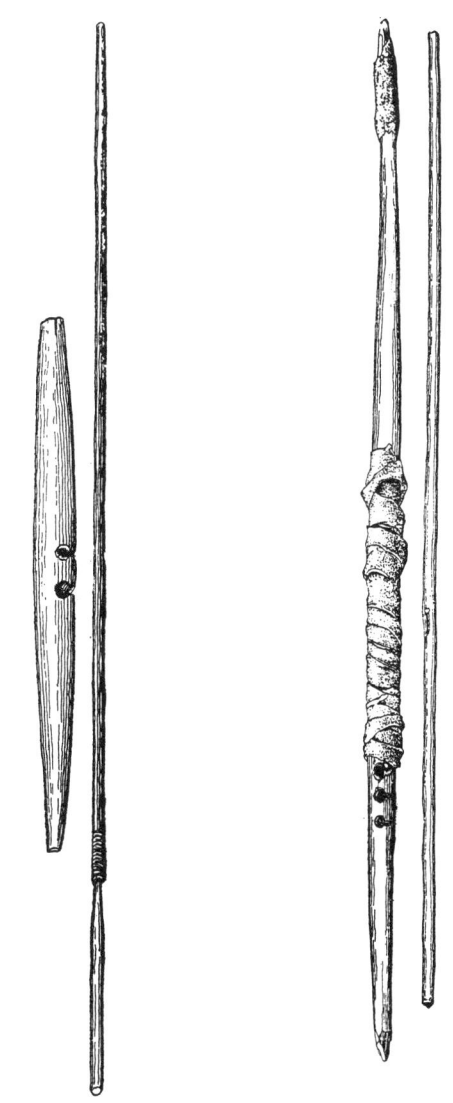

To the left, Klamath Indian fire-making set collected by L. S. Dyar in the nineteenth century. The hearth is rounded, likely of cedar, 13" long. Unusually small holes, less than 3/8" in diameter, have slots cut into the rounded edge which widen below, allowing the coal to drop down and receive air on the tinder. The 26" drill is an arrow-stick with a hardwood point set in with pitch and served with sinew (Hough, 1890).

On the right, a Washo Indian fire-making set collected by Stephen Powers during the nineteenth century. Hough described the wood of the hearth as soft, well-seasoned pine. It has eight rather small holes, all blackened by drilled fire. A 1" wide strip of buckskin has been wound around the fire holes to keep them dry. A mass of pine pitch at one end suggested to Hough the hearth had been the property of an arrow-maker who used heated pitch to fix arrowheads to shafts. The drill is of hardwood (Hough, 1890).

margins of the socket and the drill, begins to turn brown, to form a wisp of smoke, to turn darker and into charcoal, and to smoke even more, the accumulating mass begins pushing out of the socket into the notch, along the channel and off the hearth. It was only at this point that Ishi gave it his all, twirling the stick furiously to form a tiny glowing ember outside in the notch. Had he spent his energy earlier, this would not have been possible.

The spark does not form in the socket, where it might have been suffocated, but just outside, where it follows the open channel into the tinder on the ground. María Solares, one of J. Harrington's Chumash informants, told him that the hearth had a notch so that the dust made by the motion of the drill would find a place to catch fire. The full-blooded Chumash Librado said that they called the notch or channel a word that meant "tear of the fire." Hough wrote that everything depends on keeping the dust together in a kind of pellet form at this time. Without it, no fire is possible. At first dark, a thin line of smoke rising upward from the speck, it quickly begins to glow.

Adding a small handful of dry grass and courser shavings to the tinder, Ishi blew softly into the bundle holding the glowing ember and it burst into flames. According to T. Kroeber, patience, perseverance and delicate control were the important qualities Ishi brought to the making of fire.

Great dexterity and quickness were demonstrated by Indians in starting fire from the glowing coal, recorded Hough. This part of the process required as much care and skill as getting the spark. The selection and preparation of tinder was extremely important, everything had to be ready.

Refinements

In photographs, Ishi could be seen heating his drill over a fire and bending and sighting it for straightness. Fire-straightening would have helped dry the drill as well. Traveling in rainy weather, Ishi kept the drill and tinder in a protective cover of buckskin. Some groups, such as the Havasupai, even made short sets of fire sticks especially for traveling. Dry tinder and dry straight wood for a drill in the wild could be a matter of life and death.

Apparently to increase the difficulty, the Zuni actually made new sacred fire at the beginning of each new year with wood that had purposely been made wet. Generally, they made fire sticks from agave stalk, a soft pithy wood. In the late nineteenth century, Colonel James Stevenson witnessed the Zuni sprinkling a bit of fine sand on the shallow concavity of the hearth socket before drilling for fire. Increased friction, or the wearing away of damp wood, may have compensated for any wetting it had recently received. Afterwards, a piece of decayed wood acted as punk and preserved the fire that was produced. The Apache of the Southwest and the Washo of California employed sand to increase friction, and the Yumas dipped their 2-foot by 1/2-inch drill in sand before drilling on a soft agave or yucca stalk that they held under their feet. The sand technique was known to the Owens Valley Paiute of California, who made their drill sets of a black willow or sage (*Artemisia tridentata*) hearth and cane or hardwood drill with sagebrush tinder. Julian Steward recorded that fine sand was placed under the drill to make powder to catch the spark. The importance of this was observed by Ralph Michelsen among the Kiliwa of the remote deserts and mountains of northern Baja California. Rufino Ochurte preferred sotol (*Nolina parryi*) for the drill and hearth, but soon after he began rotating his drill, the end of the drill and the hearth pit often became fire-hardened. When this happened, the heat-blackened powder needed for the coal ceased to be produced. His remedy was simple: a pinch of fine sand or dry earth in the fire hole.

Other tricks or ways thought to improve performance of the standard drill have been devised. The Tlingit, who notched the fire hole nearly to the center, charred the whole hearth in fire, thereby reducing moisture and creating a more porous substance. In the same vein, Hough noted that the effectiveness of the drill and hearth increased with use and age and those charred by the making of fire generally gave a spark in half the time. This fact was brought out for me by the seventy-six-year-old Kiliwa Cruz Ochurte. His teacher had been fellow tribesman Vicente Espinosa, who died about 1935 in his late seventies. Ochurte described Espinosa as the most traditional Indian he had ever known. It was said that he wore only a breechclout into his teens and could not change his ways after that. Indeed, over sixty-five years ago, ethnographer Peveril Meigs III described Vicente Espinosa, his principal informant on Kiliwa material culture, as possessing a conservative scorn and downright fear of horses, not to mention automobiles, which he would not even approach. He went everywhere by foot, shod only in leather sandals. Ochurte learned many things from

Mohave drill and hearth (Kroeber, 1925).

Espinosa, but making fire with sticks was one of the most useful. As a youth, Ochurte called on this skill many times in the San Pedro Mártir Mountains, out hunting rabbits with bow and arrow and without matches. (*E pah' a'ow he partoo*, "to bring fire with the stick," was how Ochurte said it.) Any very dry wood, not too hard and not too soft, could be used. Best of all, however, was a hearth of ancient pine heartwood, a piece that had taken years to wash down an arroyo from high in the mountains. The weather and the years would have washed and weathered it clean and dry. An old branch of mule fat or arrowweed would work as the drill. To improve the chances further, the hearth and stick could be set to warm in the rays of the sun, the more warmth and sun the better.

The Bella Bella from British Columbia scored the drill near its point, perhaps to cause the wood to wear away more rapidly as fuel for the ember. The Kiowa left the sides of the socket and the end of the drill slightly rough and put yucca charcoal dust directly into the socket. The Owens Valley Paiute sometimes put charcoal on the drill point, because fire had already been there.

The Quinaielt of Washington made drills that bulged slightly in the middle, slowing the downward slippage of the hands. Alden Mason found that the California Salinan Indians, who made fire with a drill of poison oak and a hearth of willow like Ishi, often needed two men to make fire by friction. They traded off and relieved each other with the drill.

In some parts of the Americas, it might be noted that hand drills were extended to other purposes. The Eskimo bored holes with the hand drill. Haida carpenters used it in woodworking. With sand the drill even pierced stone for Indians of the Amazon.

How It Works

To understand in modern scientific terms the various facets of fire making with the fire drill, engineer Dick Baugh conducted experiments. He found that too high a level of volatile substances such as water or resin in the wood, through evaporative cooling, prevents the charred powder, which is being rubbed off the wood, from reaching the critical temperature of ignition for the glowing coal to begin to form. Friction heats the wood but tarry material carries heat away or may even condense on the powder, transforming it to a coarse gritty substance that is impossible to ignite by hand friction.

Wood must be light (a poor thermal conductor, like good insulation), otherwise the firemaker works twice as hard. In fact, for a person with limited muscle power, low density wood is critical for igniting a hand-drilled fire.

Using a thermostatically controlled soldering iron, Baugh also discovered that fire-drilled charcoal powder merely gives off a little smoke below 800 degrees but above 800 degrees it smokes, then ignites, taking off on its own, and glows. He ran trials with various grades of charred wood powder and found that the finer the powder, the lower the temperature needed for ignition. Woods that easily disintegrate do not pulverize sufficiently. Once good powder reaches the critical temperature, it simply takes off, spontaneously oxidizes, and raises its own temperature, increasing the rate of oxidation, which is finally limited only by available air. It is at that point of equilibrium a glowing ember appears. Combined with tinder properly prepared and the skill and delicate control of an Ishi, fire is made—a miracle.

The Final Secret

In the summer of 1880, George Redding went fishing for trout and salmon on the McCloud River. The Wintu had a *ranchería* upstream from his camp on the opposite bank. Crossing by dugout canoe at sunset, Redding found the trail to the village, arrived and entered a large semi-subterranean meeting hall. Inside, male dancers who wore only eagle feathers about their loins and a narrow band of woodpecker feathers over the forehead, blew whistles and stamped on the ground around a subdued fire as women in a semicircle turned from side to side, singing in a monotonous low tone. Later, outside, Redding met Sarah, who had been raised by a family in Shasta and spoke English, but had chosen to return to live the life of an Indian among her people. Sarah was the daughter of Chief Consolulu. Redding asked her to tell her father he wished to see an Indian make fire as they did before the coming of the whites to California. Redding's unusually detailed account that follows adds to our awareness of the variety of styles, and at the same time, exhibits clearly the essential principles of making fire with the hand drill. It includes what for me was the final secret of getting the thing to work—spit.

After long negotiations, and the exercise of considerable diplomacy, an Indian came to me, bringing his beaver-skin quiver filled with arrows. From among these, he took a dried branch of buckeye (Aesculus californica) about as long as the shaft of an arrow, but much larger at one end. From his quiver he also produced a piece of cedar (Librocedrus decurrens). This was about 18 inches in length, an inch thick, and 2 inches wide in the center, but tapering to a rough point at each end. Its general appearance might be described as boat-shaped. In the center of this piece of cedar, on one side, he had made a circular hole 1/4 of an inch deep with a piece of obsidian, and from this hole he had cut a channel extending to the edge of the wood. He now gathered a handful of dry grass, and some fine dry, powdered wood from a decayed pine. Each end of the boat-shaped piece of cedar, with the side containing the hole and channel uppermost, was placed on a couple of stones and held firmly by another Indian. The dry grass was piled loosely under the center, and on it was scattered the fine powder of the decayed wood. The fine powder was also scattered in the channel leading to the hole in the center of the boat-shaped piece of cedar. He now took the branch of buckeye and placed the largest end in the circular hole, and spitting on his hands, commenced revolving it back and forth rapidly between his palms, and at the same time bearing down with considerable force. This constant exercise of pressure, while revolving the buckeye, caused his hands to be rapidly shifted to the lower end of the stick, when he would remove them to the top again and renew the process. At the end of five minutes he was perspiring from the exercise, and no fire had been produced. He stopped a few seconds and said something. I asked Sarah to translate his speech. Sarah told me he was saying, 'Fire, why don't you come to me now as you did when I was a boy?'

He repeated these words several times, and commenced work again. In another five minutes smoke made its appearance where the two woods were in contact. In a few seconds the powdered dust of the decayed wood took fire and the fine coals communicated this fire to the dust in the channel, and rolled down to the dust scattered on the dry grass. He now took the bundle of grass in his hands and, carefully blowing upon it, soon created a blaze.

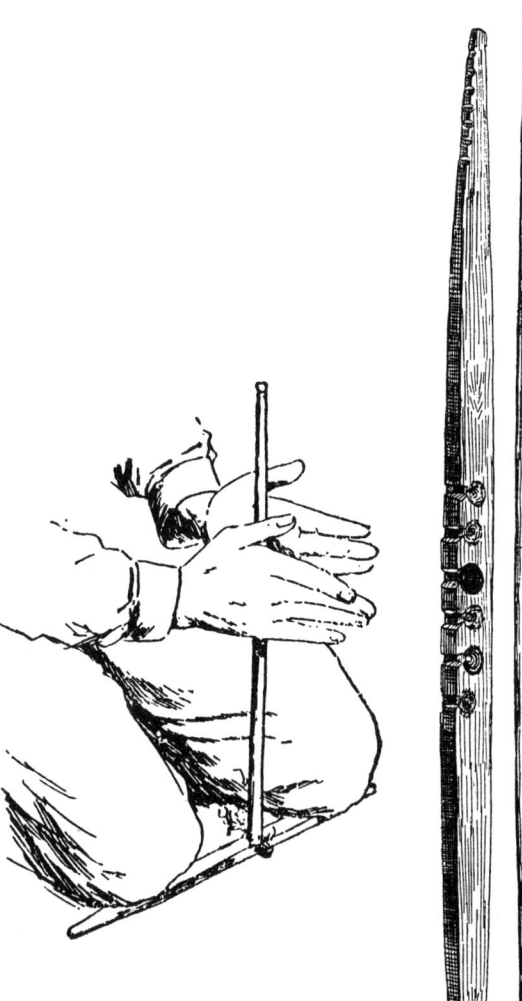

Hupa fire-making set collected by Lieutenant P. H. Ray, U.S.A., nineteenth century. In the reddish wood of the 18" hearth, fire has been drilled from one of the holes while the others are rough, carved out starts awaiting the drill. Notches at the ends may have been to tie the pieces together when not in use. They were wrapped to keep them from dampness. The 21" long drill shows charring at the base (Hough, 1890).

Fire—Some Indian Tips

Fire cooked food and warmed the body. With fire, Native Californians hardened pottery or softened wood to bend into a bow or rabbit stick. It could transform the land by clearing undergrowth to improve future hunting and gathering, or encircle and drive game for the communal store and feast. The Western Mono, for example, set fire around the base of a small conical hill when game was needed quickly for a festival. As rabbits, skunks, deer or even bear (which often bit men before they had a chance to shoot) broke through the ring of smoke and flames, posted hunters stopped them with bows and arrows. Trees for houses, *ramadas,* canoes and many other purposes were secured by means of fire. Once fire had been achieved with the drill, the original Californians nurtured, fed and carried it about almost with the tenderness usually reserved for a child. Fire was a precious tool.

Felling Trees by Fire

California Indians took down trees with fire. Philip Drucker in his surveys of southern California was told by all groups that in aboriginal times fire was the *only* method for cutting trees.

The Southern Diegueño felled a tree by building a fire around its foot. If already weakened by rot, it came down quickly. For a hard, healthy wood, the Diegueño piled bark in a chimney-like shape over the fire to create a draft and focus the flames. They constantly poked at the fire with a branch to keep it alive and hot. If it began to climb the tree beyond the desired spot, mud was packed on it at that point. Large boughs were burned off in the same manner after the tree was down.

Old or dead trees were easiest in all seasons, but younger, live trees were taken in winter by the Yokuts men when the trees were drier and there was less danger of a brush or grass wildfire. The men dug a hole around the base of the selected tree, filled it with wood chips and dry grass and set it ablaze. As the tree began to burn, several glowing oak-stick brands were pushed and wedged into the trunk. Charred areas of trunk were knocked off from time to time and the burning brand wedges were rekindled and adjusted. They beat back flames about to reach the upper trunk but they did not look up, believing that if they did, the fire, too, would ascend. Fire also broke up the downed tree into portable pieces for men and women to pack.

Selecting Firewood

Not all wood burns the same. Kiliwa Indian Sam Ochurte, when out on a hunt, starts fires with tinder of fast burning juniper bark and kindling of its twigs before he lays on heavier branches of mesquite that reduce to coals for broiling meat. Even today, the Paipai distinguish carefully between the woods they burn in the hearth. In the summer, Benito Peralta and his sister, Josefina Ochurte, prefer the nearly smokeless manzanita and in the winter, the smoky but very hot chamise *(Adenostoma fasciculatum).* Josefina fires her pots in a pit with dried trunks of yucca. In wet conditions, one must take what dry wood one can find. Benito looks on the inside and beneath any brushy older plants for old dry leaves and parts, dry dead mescal pieces for example, for fire tinder or wood.

The Pomo burned only wood for fuel—any at hand—although black oak or white oak were said to make the best coals for cooking. The coals of slow-burning oak bark were selected for parching seeds. For broiling fish, bark of the black oak was preferred. Manzanita wood, which burned quick and hot, was not used for most cooking, but along with willow, it stoked the fires of dance-house sweating contests.

Creosote bush *(Larrea divaricata)* made a good firewood for both the Cahuilla and the Southern Diegueño and probably all those in between and beyond. Ironwood *(Olneya tesota)* and Fremont cottonwood *(Populus fremontii)* also made excellent firewoods for the Cahuilla. They preferred redshank *(Adenostoma sparsifolium)* for roasting since it burned very hot. Wood for the earth oven depended on altitude, explained the Cahuilla elder Alvino Siva. In the low desert, mesquite provided the fire to bake agave but higher in the mountains oak or redshank was the first choice. Redshank burned especially hot and so, with that, the agave baked faster. As a boy, he sometimes made the mistake of collecting willow for firewood, a wood only appropriate when no other could be found. The old ones would laugh at him and say, "That's coyote's wood. Leave it for coyote."

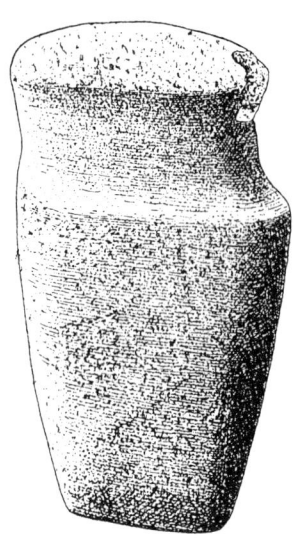

Stone axe, 13.5 cm. in length. Northeastern Maidu told Roland Dixon they did not make the stone heads but found them and then hafted the artifact between two sticks or in the cleft of a split stick with sinew and pitch. They used them in war and for woodcutting (Dixon, 1905). A. L. Kroeber had declared the axe foreign to aboriginal California. The substitute was the wedge driven by a stone. Northwestern California drove an elk-horn wedge with a shaped, hand-held maul to split wood to be carried back for the fire. Chimariko Indian Lucy Montgomery told John Peabody Harrington in 1928 something he marked in his notes "important." She described to him two other firewood tools: not only an aboriginal axe but a sledgehammer as well, and how they made them was even more astounding. They would take a young spruce tree (or sugar or yellow pine), about 4' high, and with their fingers split it from the top; at the desired thickness they put in a stone axe head or, if a sledgehammer, a big, blunt rock. Then just above and below the stone they tied hazel withes around the tree. They waited two or three years. After that time they chopped the tree off above and below to free the hafted tool. The tree had grown together and held the stone tight. With the sledgehammer that had taken three years to create they came down heavy on dry wood to break it off and in that way obtained firewood, noted Harrington. The patience of a three-year wait may stretch credulity. A Cahuilla once recalled to me a Luiseño friend whose grandfather had told of a technique to bend a branch into a rabbit stick. They hung a heavy stone from the limb of a living tree and waited for it to grow into the proper curve. Patience was a California Indian virtue.

Gathering the Firewood

Naturally, dead wood on the forest floor provided the usual firewood source, but sometimes, a short stick bound at an acute angle to the thinner end of a long pole was used by the Pomo to pull down dead branches still up in the tree. On rare occasions, a sapling was leaned against a tree as a ladder for procuring some special piece.

For carrying the firewood, the Pomo took an openwork burden basket or they fashioned a backpack from a pair of forked sticks, most often of manzanita. The sticks measured about 1 yard long and one side of each was straight so that when the wood was laid in the forks, the straight sides rested flat against the back of the bearer. The pack was bound up and carried by means of a tumpline. Sometimes, wood was bundled and carried by a tumpline alone. If without tumpline or cord, the ingenious Pomo improvised one from tule, grape vine, a bull pine limb or a young white oak shoot.

A white oak sapling was placed on any large, suitable anvil-like stone. With another smaller stone—whatever was available—they repeatedly hammered and mashed the sapling until it flattened out into a pliable band 2 to 3 inches wide. This quick, field-expedient tumpline grew even tougher and stronger as it dried out and could be used repeatedly. Wild grape vine, whole or split, in addition to binding house frames and tule bundles for the balsas the Pomo made on their lakes, served as makeshift tumpline for carrying firewood. A bull pine branch was split and used the same way. Barrett's Pomo consultants insisted that only a *side branch*, coming from a primary branch, which, in turn, came out of the main trunk of the bull pine tree, would work in this way.

Hearth Fire Technique

Spier's account of Diegueño customs at Campo contains good fireside tips. The stone supports for cooking vessels were not placed directly in the fireplace, but to one side. This helped maintain an exact level of heat to what was being cooked by permitting one to easily shovel coals from the fireplace under the vessels or take them back. It allowed separate adjustments of the fire for warmth and of the coals for cooking. Manzanita roots were the preferred fuel as they did not produce much smoke. At night two short logs entered the hearth from opposite sides, the ends pushed together as they were consumed. In a similar manner, to feed the fire the Wintu laid a log directly over the fireplace. It burned in half and the ends were shoved into the flames as they burned down. Day or night, the domestic fire of the Diegueño was not allowed to go out; something a modern camper should not emulate, of course, but surprisingly, a custom that still seems to endure among Diegueño of Lower California. I have found that even on hot summer days, their cast-iron stoves continually burn with the wood of oak or the roots of *chamiso de colorado* (redshank).

Maintaining the Fire

María Solares told J. P. Harrington the Chumash usually did not need the fire sticks that they kept on the wall of their home. They maintained fire by means of a glowing oak bark buried overnight. In the morning they would dig it up still hot and start a fire. Trying this in the woods, of course, one must be wary of dried-up underground root systems so as to not set in motion a slow-burning fuse to a forest fire.

In the Wintu household, hearth coals were preserved by covering them with ashes. They had the usual northern California cedar hearth and buckeye drill, which they twirled to ignite dry grass tinder when they needed a new fire. But generally, they kept the apparatus wrapped safely away and protected from moisture in fawn skin. It wasn't often removed. If fire in a hearth burned out, they normally just borrowed fire. Fire could be carried in a smoldering white oak limb or a small bark bucket with an earth hearth.

The Northern Maidu rarely allowed their fires to go out and even while traveling, they carried a smoldering fire in punky wood. The Pomo, too, took care to not allow the household fire to go out. But if it should, they borrowed fire from a neighbor, carrying a firebrand back to the dead hearth. When transporting fire for a long distance, they used a "slow match," usually of oak bark.

The last woman of San Nicolas Island (the farthest seaward of the southern California islands) understood the importance of preserving fire. This Shoshonean speaker, linguistically related to the Gabrielino of the Los Angeles area, survived eighteen years abandoned and alone on the island. A ship had taken her relatives and sailed off without her while she searched for a baby she never found. She wept and fell sick, and had nothing but leaves to eat. Gradually she recovered her strength and with great difficulty made fire with the sticks. She carefully kept the fire from going out. On trips around the island, she carried firebrands, and coals from the home fire she covered with ashes to slow the burning and preserve them.

Over two hundred years ago, Pedro Font recorded that the Yumas would carry a burning firebrand and use it for warmth, bringing it near whichever part of the body felt cold. Pieces of resinous wood hung over the Yurok hearth fire (which was never permitted to go out) and, when dry, splinters were bitten off these pieces for use as matches.

Torches

Bound stick torches are known from 3,000-year-old Olmec stone icons, which later became Maya and Aztec hieroglyphs preserved in parchment books. Decipherment has shown the Maya torches were of the *ocote*, or pitch pine. The California Atsugewi men harpooned fish at night from a canoe. A torch, often held by a woman, was made from four mountain mahogany sticks about 2 feet long, tied together at one end, with pitch placed between them. For a portable light, the Klamath Lake and the Modoc Indians made a torch of dry sagebrush bark. It was about 28 inches long and tightly bound along its length with spirals of more strips of sagebrush bark. The Miwok made a torch, used mainly for night travel, from dry pine needles. Bound tightly to a stick with a split withe, the needles burned 15 or 20 minutes before a fresh bundle was attached.

Klamath Lake and Modoc sagebrush bark torch (Barrett, 1910).

Traditional double-pitch Yurok houses at Patrick's Point, California, made by modern Yurok. Planks that enclosed the interior were the basic structural supports as well. Poles and grapevine root or hazel withe lashings held the planks together. Wedges of elk-horn split redwood logs and planks for this semi-subterranean house. (The Hupa and Karok made very similar houses of cedar planks.) A. L. Kroeber observed that wedges measured from a few inches to a foot and a half; some were nearly flat, others sharply curved; rubbing them on stone made the edges sharp. Cone or bell-shaped mauls drove the wedges in succession as they were set in a row on the end of a well-seasoned drift log or fallen redwood that had been burned to the desired length. Mauls were 6" to 8" in height, of basalt or mottled metamorphic rock, smooth, symmetrical, narrower in the middle, knob-ended on top and heaviest on the bottom, striking portion. Split wood was finished with an adze blade of heavy mussel shell lashed on top of the straight part of a smooth cylindrical stone handle, 6" to 10" long; the handle tapered and curved down 90 degrees 2" to 4" from the butt end. The heavier working end was slightly cut away to receive the blade; grooves in the stone held the lashings from slipping.

Houses tended to be placed on the southward slopes of hills to catch the sun and avoid the north winds. Inside was excavated a round cellar, 4' or 5' deep and 12' to 15' in diameter, where they ate and slept around a fire. They stored their dried foods and tools on the bank above, next to the wall. (Men of the village usually slept in a sweathouse.)

The Yurok plank house of northwestern California was large and skillfully built. "Southward and eastward from the Yurok this house becomes smaller and more rudely made," wrote Kroeber. "Bark begins to replace the split or hewn planks, and before long a conical form made wholly of bark slabs is attained."

Shelter: A Continuum of Simplicity

Johann Jakob Baegert, a German Jesuit who served at Mission San Luís Gonzaga in southern Baja California from 1751 to 1768, described life at a geographic and cultural extreme.

The Californians themselves spend their whole life, day and night, in the open air, the sky above them forming their roof, and the hard soil the couch on which they sleep. During winter, only, when the wind blows sharp, they construct around them, but only opposite the direction of the wind, a half moon of brush-wood, a few spans high, as a protection against the inclemency of the weather . . . when it rains, they resort to the clefts and cavities of rocks, if they can find such sheltering places, which do not occur as frequently as their wants require.

"The Californians Baegert referred to were the Guaicura. In the chill and foggy northwestern corner of California at the other extreme, Indians, such as the Wiyot, constructed houses of carefully hewn redwood slabs, split from fallen trees with elk-horn wedges sharpened on stone. According to Powers, who saw them in the 1870s, the structures were raised over deep warm pits, and shaped like modern frame houses."

Large earth-covered semi-subterranean lodges, extremely well insulated, in which a dozen people might live, and assembly houses 50 feet in diameter, supported by heavy oak columns, were constructed by the Miwok of Central California. Barrett and Gifford list more than ten different shelters they made. In this, the Miwok were typical. A considerable variety of shelters could be found within the same California group. One's abode depended on status, purpose, environment and the time of year. A Miwok man of importance in the foothills, for instance, might pass the winter covered by a bearskin robe within a carefully insulated earth lodge, while his son, on an early spring collecting expedition to the mountains, might sleep nearly naked near a small fire in a quickly crafted, open-sided cedar-bark wickiup. In many parts of California, willow frame huts were home for the colder months, while a temporary brush enclosure served when exploiting resources of other environments during the warmer seasons. Native California shelters ranged all the way from a bed of pine needles under the stars, to plank houses, earth lodges and public round houses of substantial timber construction.

The simpler California Indian shelters can be built by an adventurous spirit in the wilderness of today. California Indians lived in nature without destroying her. Unencumbered, they saw the wilderness itself as home. It could simply be the warmth of a fire, or a very simple enclosure, a wickiup or the modest willow-frame dome house found nearly everywhere in California a mere 200 years ago.

Minimalists

The Yuman-speaking Halchidhoma of California fled the lower Colorado River between 1825 and 1830 to join the closely related Maricopa of the middle Gila River. One hundred years later, Spier did fieldwork among the combined groups. He learned that when traveling, they built no temporary dwellings whatever. In the summer, the usual time of travel for collecting various foods, shade was most desirable and they simply camped under the overhanging bough of a large tree. In the winter, when preparing for sleep, they shoved hot ashes into a hole, covered them with dirt, and made the warm surface their bed.

Jedediah Strong Smith (Brooks, 1977), the first white American to make the overland trip to California, found the Mohaves (another Yuman-speaking group of the lower Colorado) using similar techniques in 1826. "When they become cold they draw the sand out from under fires and spread it where they sleep," he wrote. He noted as well that, during cold weather, they built many small fires and slept in the intervals between them. When camping without shelter, the Southern Diegueño of Campo, California, built a fire on either side. Barrett and Gifford recorded that a Miwok with insufficient bedcovers might lie with his face to the central fire, while a small oak-bark fire smoldered behind him. The coals of oak bark retained heat for an extended period. So effective were they, one's back could become purple from the warmth.

Tubatulabal men hunting deer in the mountains sought natural rock shelters, camping under an overhanging ledge or beneath a natural gable formed by the meeting of the tops of two huge boulders. Families gathering pine nuts simply leaned poles along the two sides of a horizontal tree limb. The downward and outward sloping sides were then covered with brush and, over that, slabs of pine bark. Mike Miranda told Voegelin in the early 1930s that they were from 4 to 6 feet high and used for storage or for sleeping during thundershowers. Otherwise, on such expeditions, they all simply ate and slept in large circular brush enclosures with an entrance on the east side.

Margaret Wheat learned from Northern Paiute informants that in the mountains, women made temporary shelters from sagebrush pulled up by the roots and pine boughs broken from trees. They piled these in a circle to the height of a man's shoulders and built a fire in its center, giving them protection from the wind and reflective warmth from the fire. Slender willow withes could also be woven into tight circular fences for protection from wind and sand. A single Paiute on a journey made a shelter simply of brush spread over one bush to the next, or leaned against whatever was at hand. Barely enough space remained to crawl into the nest. It gave shade in the summer and warmth in the winter. Students of outdoor skills find the interiors of such shelters, packed thick with brush and leaves and constructed with minimal space for the occupant, sufficiently warmed, even on a cold night, by body heat alone. A small area to heat and enough brush for effective insulation are the key factors.

It all seems too simple for those of us weaned on weighty tents and pots and pans lugged over exhausting trails where the best part of the trip is settling in behind the wheel and driving home. What about rattlesnakes and other reptiles that might be attracted to the warmth of our sleeping space?

During hot, dry, summer camping trips, the Miwok would construct a rectangular flat-topped sunshade of brush, grass or tule, propped up on poles. In fact, almost all groups in the sunnier portions of California made ramadas or shed roofs for shade as the Southern Diegueño, Paipai and the Kiliwa of Lower California still do. Every home in the Paipai village of Santa Catarina has one to this day, often with leafy branches of mule fat piled on the top. They are simply four upright posts sunk in the ground, with supporting poles, and branches, willows or other shrubs laid or thatched over this, creating a living and workplace beneath. Voegelin found them in use among the Tubatulabal in 1933. They were about 6 to 8 feet long, almost as wide and 4 to 6 feet high. Two willow poles rested lengthwise in the forked posts, and willow branches were simply piled at right angles across these to a depth of 3 to 4 feet. Women worked under them in hot weather. Larger, more elaborate versions served as eating and sleeping quarters. These had three walls for protection from the wind with an open side to the east. Willow poles, about 1 inch in diameter with the branches left on and stuck upright in the ground in a closely packed straight line, formed the walls. Bands of willows on the inside and outside were attached horizontally every 1 to 2 feet for stability. Fernando

Miranda remembered them as being built large enough for several families during fiestas at the hot springs near Kernville. The women cooked at separate fires in the open front of the shelter.

In much the same way, the Miwok worked and slept under their sun shades. But because the simple structure was open-sided, and they feared rattlesnakes and a certain lizard, they laid the stems of the California thistle around the temporary dwelling as a barrier. Modern controlled experiments to test the efficacy of thistle-stem barrier technology have not, to my knowledge, been undertaken. I can vouch, nevertheless, that such activities improve sleep tremendously.

Wickiups

The widespread American Indian wickiup, which finds apotheosis in the elegant teepee of the Great Plains, makes a perfect survival shelter. Simple, easy to construct, great reflector of fireplace heat, even as a crude cone of sticks, without the beauty and sophistication of the buffalo hide teepee, it can save a life and quickly turn the wild into home.

Maidu

"Little circular Lodges made of old trees and bark," was how Jedediah Smith saw the Maidu homes on the American River in the oak-covered foothills of the Sierras in 1827. These were the *hübo* which Kroeber described in his *Handbook of the Indians of California* almost 100 years later. He wrote that a Maidu conical hut was made of several poles "leaned and tied together over a shallow excavation," and covered with "bark, sticks, slabs from dead trees, pine needles, and leaves in any combination. . . . The disturbed earth was banked up the sides as far as it would reach, some two or three feet." The northeastern Maidu went even further and built a low doorway of two stakes with a stick across them and other sticks sloping from this to the poles that formed the main body of the structure. Powers recorded that this style of wickiup served to protect the occupants from the snow in the High Sierras and had the fire built within, while in lower regions and warmer seasons a side would be left open to the north or east, shading the interior from the sun. The fire would be outside in front of the door to keep the lodge smoke free.

According to A. Kroeber, valley Maidu inhabited large earth-covered log-frame houses, extremely well insulated, on the scale of those of the Pomo, Winton and the Miwok. In the foothills and higher sierra, these substantial structures gave way to the wickiups or conical huts described. Pine, rushes or other soft material served as Maidu beds. Both wickiups and large earth-covered houses were essentially winter dwellings. When the rains and snows ended, the Maidu often simply lived under open brush roofs or shades that appear to have been similar to those of the Miwok.

Miwok

Most elegant of all California wickiups was the Miwok. Though poles were used, covered with long strips of incense cedar bark, brush, grass or tule (these latter overlapped and bound on with grape vine withes); and though poles served as the frame for a portable, conical house covered with tule mats and a tule-mat door (the mats were fastened to sticks for ready rolling and transport); frequently in the mountains no frame of poles was employed at all. Long bark slabs, leaned together, offered mutual support and became at once both frame and covering. Old photographs show these bark-slab wickiups pitched very steeply, perhaps 60 degrees or more, perfect to shed the heavy rain and snow of the central sierra. Cracks between slabs were overlaid with other slabs, the walls reaching a thickness of three or four pieces. This effectively weather-proofed the structure, which extended 8 to 15 feet in diameter. The doorway, simply an area left open on the side,

Miwok bark wickiup (drawing based on early photos and depictions).

was covered by a large bark slab that rested against the wickiup when not in use.

The Miwok preferred incense cedar bark *(Libocedrus decurrens)*; however, bull pine *(Pinus sabiniana)*, ponderosa pine *(Pinus ponderosa)*, sequoia *(Sequoiadendron giganteum)* and other conifer bark were also used. Barrett and Gifford noted that the bark was always taken from dead trees. Earth might be piled against the outer lower sides.

In the center, a shallow depression held a fire for warmth, light and some cooking. Next to it was the earth oven, a foot deep, a foot across, or slightly larger. Barrett and Gifford explained that here with hot stones, the Miwok baked and steamed acorn bread, greens, bulbs, corms, meat and fish. The long needles of bull or ponderosa pine covered the floor of the Miwok wickiup where mats or skins, usually of deer, were spread as bedding. A man of means might even have a bed of willow poles, 15 to 18 inches from the floor. A hunk of wood or stump was a stool. Leaves of a cypress became a seat, indoors or out, and piled-up pine needles or a rolled coyote hide served as a pillow.

Galen Clark, who first visited Yosemite Valley (the heart of Miwok territory in the Sierra Nevada) in 1855, wrote that in the summer months the Miwok generally lived outside in brush arbors and used their *o'-chums* (pole and bark wickiups) for storage.

How to Build a Cahuilla Mountain Wickiup

Harry C. James, in a letter reprinted in Bean and Saubel's *Temalpakh*, described the making of a mountain wickiup covered with the bark of incense cedar. Calistro Tortes of the Santa Rosa Cahuilla was James' informant and teacher. Tortes stated that his own people and the Mountain Cahuilla sometimes built such houses. On viewing a photograph of the Miwok bark shelters of Yosemite, Tortes found them smaller and more steeply walled than those of the Cahuilla, whose more southern location with lower snowfall may have accounted for the difference.

To begin, they stripped bark from dead trees, which is much easier than from living trees. Cedar bark resists rot and remains in good condition for years after the tree's death. To take it from living trees requires considerably greater effort and would kill the tree. Slabs of all sizes were collected, from 6 inches by 36 inches, to 2 feet by 14 feet.

Next, three slender poles about 16 feet long were tied together about 1 foot from the top, the bottom spread out to about a 15-foot diameter and embedded in the ground. A dozen or more poles were then laid against these, forming a cone to support the bark. For an entrance, which should be kept as small as possible, a short branch was secured horizontally across two of the poles about 3 feet from the ground.

Beginning at the bottom they placed the slabs of bark against the supporting poles around the structure. A second round overlapped the tops of the first and, where necessary, a third round overlapped the tops of the second. Short pieces of bark covered any remaining holes, except for a small smoke hole left at the very top. Stones were placed against the outside bottom round of bark. James noted that as the work progressed, Tortes would sing "snatches of Cahuilla song," which he refused to explain.

In the center of the wickiup a tiny fire pit was dug and lined with stones. A slab of wood served as a table near the fire pit. Pine needles and oak leaves were heaped between small-diameter logs and three sides of the shelter for beds. Tortes told James that in the old days, strips of rawhide fastened the first three poles together and also secured the short pole across the doorway. A piece of hide served as the door itself to protect the occupants against inclement weather.

A note on a possible substitute for rawhide in Cahuilla house construction: David Prescott Barrows, in his fieldwork during the last years of the last century, described the Cahuilla *jacal* (a Mexican word from the Aztec *xa-calli*, "house of straw") as a rectangular dwelling. It was likely influenced in form by the earlier Spanish presence. Material and construction methods were undoubtedly local, however, and Barrows discovered that the beams and rafters of the jacal were bound in place with leaves of the Mohave yucca. Strips of yucca work for many jobs where rope or rawhide might otherwise be employed.

Boys from a camp had helped Tortes build the wickiup, which was in the San Jacinto Mountains. James wrote that they all were astonished at how weatherproof it was and that, despite wind, rain and snow, the bark had remained in place and had lasted for years at the time of his writing. He attributed this to Tortes's insistence that the wickiup be built in a sheltered location facing east or southeast.

Willow-framed Dome Houses

Usually more spacious than the wickiup, but still easy and quick to construct, the pliable willow pulled and tied into a rough dome shape and covered with any natural insulating material at hand was a very common semipermanent dwelling. They were at times elaborate and permanent. They could be huge and high among the Chumash, made from long willow poles tied and spliced with willow bark, covered with tiers of tule, wild grass, cattail, fern or *carrizo* with a large smoke hole left at the top. Diligent people used tule mats as a first layer before additional thatching, according to Fernando Librado, the elderly full-blooded Chumash who spoke to J. P. Harrington in the early years of the twentieth century. Diligent Tubatulabal, on the other hand, used tule mats as an *outside* covering to their dome houses, after plastering thatch with mud or clay.

Early explorers found many villages of thatched dome houses, especially in the southern part of the state, along the warm coastal valleys and through the Great Basin. Juan Cabrillo saw them in 1542 along the California coast near present-day Santa Barbara. Round and covered to the ground, the ship's log recorded them.

Edward Curtis gave a more ample description 350 years later when he wrote of Diegueño dwellings as small elliptical huts of poles, thatched with brush, grass and earth, in which beds of grass were covered occasionally with rabbit-fur blankets. Although we have an idea of how they looked, complete detailed accounts of willow-frame, dome-style house construction steps were few. The following descriptions of very simple houses from the Great Basin Paiute and remnant Yuman-speakers in Lower California make the technology clear.

A Cattail House

In April 1958, Wheat observed and recorded in detail the construction of a small temporary willow-frame house of the Northern Paiute. It could have served as living quarters for one or two people, or for storage of food and implements or even as a sweat house. Jimmy and Wuzzie George and Daisy Aster had made many of these, and they were assisted by Lily Shaw, who had lived in one, and Dora John. This house, judging from Wheat's photographs, was about 7 feet in diameter and about 7 feet high. Larger, more substantial houses of this type were for families and would last five or more years, according to Wuzzie George.

Southern Diegueño camp with willow hut east of San Diego, California, October 23, 1849. Pencil sketch by John Woodhouse Audubon (in Dentzel 1957).

A dozen long willow posts, perhaps 1 inch thick, were set, heavy end down, into small holes that had been dug with sticks and knives, the dirt pushed back in around them. This formed a circle of upright sticks.

Around the base, about 2 feet from the bottom, a line of thin willow poles was run perpendicular to the posts and parallel to the ground. Strings of sagebrush bark secured the light poles to the outside of each post. An opening was left for a door that always faced east toward the rising sun. They venerated the sun each morning as the people and the sun rose together. East also happened to be away from the prevailing wind.

The first round of willow poles brought the posts slightly together toward the center, and the second round, about 2 feet above the first, drew the frame tighter still and defined the top of the doorway. The third, about 18 inches above the second, pulled the willows sharply together, forming the ceiling of the house, which had a somewhat pointed but essentially half-spherical shape. An opening in the center of the roof became the smoke hole.

They preferred cattail leaves to cover the frame because the flat surface of the cattail would shed water best, but tule or grass could also be used. The cattails were made into crude mats, about 4 feet square. They did this by placing three slender willow sticks on the ground parallel to each other and about 1 foot apart. An armload of cattails covered the willows crosswise. Over these, three more willows were laid (directly over the first) and tied through the willows from the bottom every few inches, clamping the cattails between them. Leaves were included in the knots themselves to prevent splits in the protective cattail sheath and keep the wind out.

The mat, with leaves upright, was tied to the frame with the bottom edge touching the ground. More mats were made and positioned. The second round of mats, above the first, overlapped

Eight pole willow framework for traditional California dome house. Angel Quilpe, a Northern Diegueño thought to be 100 years old when John Peabody Harrington commissioned the project in 1925, came from an area of northern San Diego County, California, where the territories of the Luiseño, Cupeño, Cahuilla and Diegueño met. According to Harrington's notes, two Cahuilla men assisted Quilpe in building the willow-framed shelter. After the ground was cleared and leveled, a string of the desired radius tied to a stake was used to inscribe a circle in the earth. A digging stick excavated post holes along the circumference, each a short step apart; dirt scooped out with the hands was carried away in an Indian basket. The initial eight slender willow poles, 15' to 20' high, were lashed in the form of a Greek cross. Photograph by J.P. Harrington, 1925. (Smithsonian Institution National Anthropological Archives)

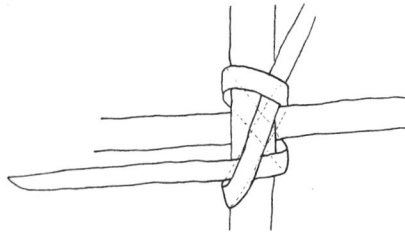

Detail of lashing of horizontal pole to vertical frame. Binding appears to be a leaf of yucca (Yucca whipplei). Sketch above based on one in Harrington's notes; it is the backside of the view in the photograph. Apparently, the two ends in the drawing were brought up in crisscrossed fashion and tied behind the vertical pole above the horizontal pole (or tied on this side after encircling the vertical pole above the horizontal). Harrington's notes simply read, "crisscrossed it twice around and tied in overhand knot." Photograph by J.P. Harrington, 1925 (Smithsonian Institution National Anthropological Archives).

enough to weatherproof the house. They also made one for the door. As weaknesses occurred over time, mats were added.

Wuzzie George said that such a hut was used as a sweat house by her father, Sam Dick. He made a fire outside and placed rocks in it. When hot, the rocks were taken inside and cold water was placed on them to create steam. They would rub themselves with their hands. Men and women took these baths together or separately. When people didn't feel well, when they had rheumatism or a cold for example, they would sometimes take a sweat bath. They would put straw on the floor and they prayed to the sun.

Paiute Grass Hut

The Paiute grass hut had a frame similar to that of the cattail or tule house but with minor differences. In the one made for Wheat by Mable Wright, two of the upright posts terminated, or perhaps had been cut, about 2 feet from the top. These were brought together over the doorway that they framed in a long triangular form. Another difference was that after the basic frame had been constructed, many additional (but more slender) poles were set in the ground and secured vertically *over* the horizontal willows. Equal in length to the substantial upright posts, there were perhaps five of these thin willows placed between and parallel to them.

Great loads of grass were collected. Small bundles of grass were twined together with native cordage about 5 inches from one end like hula skirts. Row after overlapping row of these sections were tied to the frame and secured with horizontal willows running along the outside and tied to the frame about 5 inches from the bottom of each row of grass. More skirts of fringes were added as the grass dried and thinned and as holes appeared. Eventually a thick insulating cover protected the hut. In the winter a small fire burned in the center of the floor beneath the opening in the roof, while piled grass and rabbit-skin blankets offered comfort for sitting and sleeping.

A Diegueño Example

In 1993 I happened upon a willow-frame house of the Kumeyaay (Southern Diegueño) at the site of the old Mission of Guadalupe in Lower California. It had been built two years earlier by Gloria Castañeda, a well-known Kumeyaay basket maker of the region. The thatching on the house was secured with long willow branches, much like the Paiute grass house, except here, not only was the frame of willow, the insulating material was as well. Hundreds of long very thin branches of willow with the leaves simply left on were fastened with horizontal willow withes running around the frame every foot or so with the first at the very bottom. The underlying frame was in the fashion of the Northern Paiute cattail house, except that this was a larger structure, perhaps 12 feet in diameter by 8 feet high.

The poles overlapped at the top, wickiup fashion; the horizontal structural willow poles were placed approximately every foot and the high door opening was two thirds of the way to the top of the house.

A Kiliwa Wa'—Step by Step

I wanted to see the construction of a traditional California dome-shape willow-frame house for myself. Meigs (1939) had found them still being made in the 1930s by a handful of Kiliwa who had retreated to the vastness of the San Pedro Mártir Mountains in Lower California. The Kiliwa speak a Yuman dialect and once roamed widely over the deserts, along the coast and in the great antelope-filled valleys of northern Baja. The Europeanized, land-hungry mestizo farmer and rancher, anxious to profit on sky-rocketing consumer populations and American tourism, eventually drove them into the remote wilds of the highest mountains in Baja. I sought out the Kiliwa in 1994, exactly 200 years after the founding of Misión San Pedro Mártir de Verona. The mission failed to bring these freedom-loving mountaineers under its control, but today, pressured from the outside world, very few traditional Kiliwa remain. Ralph Michelsen learned much from Rufino Ochurte some thirty years ago. I found his nephew, José Ochurte, living with his older brother, Teodoro, beyond the Kiliwa mountain village of Arroyo Leon.

By accident I had discovered the Kiliwa five years earlier while exploring for a hidden Baja trout stream. At that time they were living in *jacales*, rectangular thatch structures of Mexican form made from local materials. In five years, these had become

Angel Quilpe stands before the completed framework of willow poles. Examination of the photograph reveals that many of the joints were not "crisscrossed" but merely lashed diagonally and others not lashed at all. Distance between horizontal members around 1', diameter of floor about 15'. Photograph by J.P. Harrington, 1925 (Smithsonian Institution National Anthropological Archives).

milled-board and tin-roof shacks, infinitely less pleasing to the eye, but not so prone to leaks. José and his brother had built one just a few months before my visit. Their brother Trinidad had died in the summer of 1994. Following tradition, they burned the old thatched house and abandoned the area. I was skeptical when Ochurte strongly assured me that he remembered well how to build a traditional willow-framed wa'. It had been more than thirty years since he lived in one. But as he and fellow tribesmen Tito Ochogo and Ricardo Albañez began gathering materials at dawn on a wet November morning, his knowledge and expertise became evident. For convenience, the work may be divided into seven stages:

1. The wa' was built various ways and in various sizes, depending on circumstances. A willow frame might have been covered with tule *(Scirpus)*, cattail leaves, sedge, sotol, arrowweed or other brush at hand. That morning, as three Kiliwa men set out to hunt deer farther up the mountain, José, Tito, and Ricardo descended a canyon to chop long (8 to 10 feet) thin, leafy stems of arrowweed *(Pluchea sericea)*. Due to the cold damp weather and the chill in the cattail marsh, Ochurte had chosen arrowweed over what he felt was the superior cattail, found in a tarn-like area of the canyon. Arrowweed grew farther down the same canyon and required a tiring tote to the house site. Along the way, near a fall of water from the recent rains, they cut structural poles and withes (about 28, each 10 to 12 feet long) of arroyo willow *(Salix lasiolepis)*—the very best for framing a wa', according to José.

When they returned, Teodoro, who was too old for house building, selected out a few branches of the arrowweed and began carving arrows which would require no straightening in the fire. They would stay straight indefinitely, José said.

The house site had been chosen for its good drainage on a gentle slope, eighty strides or so above an upwelling of clear water from a dry arroyo. Around the site and on other nearby knolls grew the long stiff leaves of the Mohave yucca *(Yucca schidigera)*. With the yucca the house would be bound together. José carefully instructed his helpers to avoid the thick leaves at the top center of the plant and to take the leaves nearer the base. They were older and thinner, but still green and free of any blight that might weaken them. Thick strips of yucca such as were found in the top of the plant would not hold a knot. Later, José demonstrated this fact.

The carefully selected leaves were thrown a few at a time on a fire made from six or seven handfuls of dry twigs from the weather-darkened desert brush in the immediate vicinity. The fire was allowed to burn down for only minutes before leaves were placed on the blazing deadwood and rapidly forming coals. The men moved the long leaves about the small fire for a few minutes in an attempt to warm them evenly, and then, as the leaves began to brown, they removed them and replaced them with others. Warming the stiff yucca leaves in this manner softened them and made them more pliable, but did not weaken them. Next, they dug their fingernails into the center of each leaf as they doubled the leaf lengthwise, splitting it into two strips from which, in turn, were torn in the same manner tough cord-like strands around 3/16 of an inch wide.

2. All the freshly gathered and prepared materials were neatly stacked at the house site. Holes about 6 inches deep were dug a little over 1-1/2 feet apart around the circumference of an 8-foot-diameter circle. This would be a house for one person or a temporary structure for a family. A greater distance was left between the holes on either side of the projected doorway. They purposefully faced the door away from the prevailing wind that came down the arroyo from the south. This was the paramount consideration in the doorway placement. But to catch the morning sun and perhaps overlook the arroyo they settled upon a northeasterly direction.

Posts on either side of the entry needed to be the thickest. To begin the actual construction, the men placed a 1-1/2-inch-diameter pole to the left of the doorway. At its thinner end they overlapped about 2 feet or more another thinner end of a willow pole. After adjusting the height of the hut (about 6 feet) to the hole on the opposite side of the circle, they bound them together with multiple wrappings of yucca leaf strips that they tied off in square knots. The foot end of the second pole was placed in the hole opposite the doorpost hole. The two branches formed an arch that measured about 8 feet from the ground level along the arc of willow to the pinnacle. The poles themselves had been cut fairly straight, 10 to 12 feet long, trimmed of their side branches. The operation was repeated with two willow poles, slightly thinner, placed perpendicular to the first arch at the pinnacle and secured to it. This formed a four-legged frame. Further, similar arches were added around the circle, tying everything together at the top. In some cases, single poles were simply laid from a posthole to the pinnacle

I. Stages in construction of the Kiliwa Wa'

II. Stages in construction of the Kiliwa Wa'

where they were tied in. Upper ends of the willows that extended above the center of the forming dome, wickiup-like, were later broken off. As the frame began to meet José's satisfaction, postholes were filled in. Occasionally new holes were dug when additional poles were deemed necessary to make the frame tighter and more complete.

    3. Finished with the vertical pole or dome phase of construction, the structure still looked rather ungainly and irregular. The poles were not perfectly alike or straight; some were arched and some tied on, wickiup-fashion. José now began placing the horizontal ribs. Generally, these poles were somewhat thinner than those used vertically, roughly between 3/4 of an inch and 7/8 of an inch in diameter, and in one instance, José substituted an arrowweed withe, apparently because the remaining willows were too thick and inflexible. He formed a joint with the first horizontal willow rib. A point near the thicker end was placed outside and up against the left doorpost about 4 inches off the ground. The end extended less than 1 inch into the door space. He double-wrapped a yucca strip diagonally around the joint, and tied the two ends tightly with a square knot. He continued around the outside of the hut, making two tight diagonal wraps (in the same direction) with a single yucca-leaf strip around each joint, and tied the ends of each in a square knot. The horizontal rib poles, nearly the same length as the vertical, were spliced together with yucca wrapping in order to completely reach around the circular frame and end on the right doorpost. A second tier ran about 28 inches above the first. As men double-wrapped diagonally and tied these joints off, some of the straighter and irregular vertical poles pulled into the overall dome-like shape of the wa' and one could

Angel Quilpe leans against completed house, thatched with grass in tiers. (Other thatching material which could be used: tule, carrizo and various brushwoods.) Horizontal poles lashed opposite the inner ones held the grass firm. The thatching was four inches thick, said to be impervious to wind and rain. A fireplace and pot resting stone were in the center beneath an ample smoke hole. Small willow twigs woven in an oblong frame of willow poles made a door. Loosely tied to the opening, it signified no one should enter while the occupants were away. Door could also be made of a tule mat stood on end. Long mat of tule left of doorway was for sitting and sleeping. Photograph by J.P. Harrington, 1925 (Smithsonian Institution National Anthropological Archives).

see the house taking a pleasing regular form. The third tier was placed about 33 inches over the second. To this point the door had been left open—a triangular shape to the top of the structure.

    4. Beginning again just to the left of the doorway, bundles of arrowweed were lifted from the well-organized pile—stacked with trunk ends of the plants all in one direction—and placed vertically on the frame. Some bundles were laid as they grew—top up; others were the reverse, top down. If the trunk was too long and had no leaves, it was broken off before being placed on the structure. Bundles were spread out a bit to completely blend and cover the dome. The wickiup appearance grew with the laying on of these straight arrowweed branches that extended over the top of the structural dome as much as 1 foot. Once in place, they were left uncut. The arrowweed was in constant danger of falling or blowing away, and sometimes it was necessary to hold it in place on one side or another of the wa'.

    As soon as the house was completely covered to a thickness of a few inches, darkening, but not blackening, the inside of the hut from the sun, a horizontal withe of arroyo willow about 3/4 of an inch in diameter was fastened over the thatching. It began again on the left doorpost at the level of the third tier of structural horizontal poles at approximately 65 inches from the base of the wa'. At least two tight diagonal turns of the yucca strip together with a square knot held it in place. They ran the withe horizontally around the entire hut, splicing another into it by overlapping the ends when necessary, until it reached the right doorpost where it overran, as with the left, about 1 inch. Ties along the horizontal withe, every couple of feet or so beginning from the left doorpost, were made by carefully reaching through the arrowweed and winding a strip of yucca preferably around a *horizontal* frame pole. The yucca was pushed back through the arrowweed and the process was repeated to double-wrap the horizontal binding withe and the structural willow branch together, sandwiching the arrowweed brush between them. The wrapping was pulled tight and tied in a square knot. José carefully tucked the loose ends of the ties into the thatch. At times two of the relatively short yucca strips were tied together in a square knot to make a strip of adequate length to reach through the arrowweed and double-bind the two willow poles.

    In the same fashion, Ochurte tied in the bottom horizontal withe. It was repeatedly double-wrapped about every 2 feet to the structural horizontal willow, 4 inches off the ground. To get the yucca bindings extra tight, he placed his knee on the withe next to each binding and pushed in forcefully, compressing the arrowweed between the two horizontal willow branches. With both hands he pulled back the ends of the yucca strip and tied it off. Another withe, around 28 inches from this, was tied in the same way, using his knee and fastening it to the structural horizontal pole beneath. Loose ends were tucked into the thatch. Any thin or open spots in the thatch were filled in with additional arrowweed pushed under a binding withe. This also served to tighten the withes and increase their holding power on the thatch. José said this process might be repeated many times over the years, as thatch wore away and as greater protection and warmth might be desired. (Meigs had been told that a house could be used for ten years before it had to be replaced.)

    5. The apex of the doorway opening was crossed with a section of willow at the level of the third-tier withe. The piece was a few inches longer than the width of the door at that point and was secured to the doorposts with lashings of yucca leaf. Small leafier lengths of arrowweed were laid over this, upside down, to the top of the hut, filling the opening completely. Another willow withe was bound over the first section of willow with yucca strips to hold the arrowweed in place. A final forth-tier withe was added around the entire top of the hut, approximately 16 inches above the third. Since remaining willow poles were thick and inflexible, a thin arrowweed branch was stripped of leaves and used. It was bound with yucca to various of the vertical-frame poles, including the two doorposts. Finally José neatly broke off all arrowweed branches jutting into the doorway below the level of the cross-beam.

    6. Employing the same technique as for the house, Ochurte made a door. He cut six willow rods, each about 1 inch in diameter, their length measured across the doorway itself. About 4 inches from the top, he cut a horizontal piece which overlapped both doorposts. He dropped down about 10 inches and repeated the procedure. He continued this until he had six pieces; the last measured at about 4 inches from the bottom. Two willow poles 1-1/2 inches in diameter were cut to extend from the ground to about 3 inches above the doorway. They were laid on the ground in the shape of the doorway and the six rods were placed over them in ladder fashion and in order.

    José positioned the uppermost rung about

7 inches from the top and the last about 4 inches from the bottom of the two poles with the others spaced more or less evenly between them. The rungs slightly overran the poles on either side. He bound each of them to the poles with split yucca wrapped diagonally one way and frequently crossed the other way over the first diagonal as well. Lengths of yucca were tied together as needed. Over this he laid the last remaining arrowweeds, bottom ends up (toward the narrow end of the trapezoid). The thatching completely covered the door frame. Three willow withes were cut and placed to hold the thatch; one over the top rung, one over the bottom, and one a little over 2 feet down from the top rung. They more or less coincided with the withes of the house itself, making the door almost undetectable when in place. Rungs, thatching and withes were all on the outside of the two door posts. Withes overran the door posts very slightly and were secured at these joints with wrappings of two joined yucca strips. A slip loop was pulled through the square knots so that they could be undone if desired. The finished door frame was loosely joined to the right doorpost by means of a yucca strip tied about 1 foot down from the upper right corner. To this point; all the material collected had been used up. Nothing remained. Nothing more was wanted.

    7. To prevent runoff from flooding the house, a trench approximately 1 foot from the wa' and extending out another foot was dug around it to a depth of a few inches. Ochurte piled and packed the excavated dirt along the outside bottom of the wa' just reaching the first-tier withe. Then he walked the trench, packing down the loose dirt. He swept the inside of the hut and declared it finished.

    It was two thirty in the afternoon. He had worked with incredible speed and skill and had given masterful direction to the others. It seemed he had made a hundred such willow-framed houses. I asked Ochurte about the wind. He just laughed and suggested that I shake the structure. It proved to be unbelievably sturdy. I asked about animals entering the wa'. He said he would lay cholla cactus (which grows abundantly in the area) around it.

    Meigs had written that every wa' had a small fire near the front next to the door that was the only smoke outlet. (Indeed there was no smoke hole in the wa' we had built.) Eventually the inside would become blackened by the smoke. The fire was primarily for warmth at night, but an older lady would keep a few sticks smoldering during the day through the summer to keep out the flies. Food, clothing and tools were hung from the ceiling or wedged into the walls. Interiors were smooth and well finished but with brush, boughs and yucca trunks piled on the outside, the wa' sometimes took on the formlessness of an untidy trash pile. In fact, such accretions would have improved insulation and, as Meigs also mentioned, made the house almost impossible to see, so perfectly it blended with the natural environment.

A Paiute Hybrid

    Like a wickiup in its cone shape and like a willow dome in thatching, the Moapa Paiute winter wickiup would have been lost to history if it had not been for an old lady's desire to live her last days "in a house like her mama lived in," and Frances Watkins' 1945 description of it. When the old lady died the house was burned, as was the custom, and there were no more.

    The floor measured 9 feet wide by 10 feet 4 inches long (from the doorway to the back). It was excavated to about 10 inches deep, and the dirt removed was later banked around the outside circumference of the structure. Twelve willow poles placed at regular intervals against the sides of the excavation were tied together at the top, 9 feet above the floor. The five back poles were slightly longer than the others and slanted at a greater angle. Smaller willow poles were woven horizontally through these, over and under, around the dwelling, row upon row, with considerable but unspecified distance between the rows. The space left for a doorway was low so that one would stoop on entering and it generally faced east toward the morning sun or away from the prevailing wind. A thatch of arrowweed was woven vertically through the horizontal willows, again, over and under, with the bottom ends toward the top and the leafy ends (which were not removed) toward the ground. An opening or smoke hole was left at the peak. The fire pit was almost halfway from the center toward the front. This remarkably simple yet sturdy structure would withstand the fierce winds that swept through the valley and the placement of the arrowweed leaves, pointing downward, would shed the rain.

Location

Elder Jim McCarty told Leslie Spier at Campo, California, over half a century ago that the Southern Diegueño selected campsites on the basis of accessible water, adequate drainage, protection from weather and ambush (often placing the camp near boulder outcrops), and abundant wild edible plants and animals. As in modern real estate, for the American Indian, the key was location, location, location.

Primitive technology expert Errett Callahan took a lesson from old Ute wickiups found preserved into the 1990s on the flat bottom of a draw beneath the Medicine Bow Mountains of Colorado. An early homesteader left an account of how a band of Utes would hunt buffalo there in the summer. One year, in the early 1880s, they overstayed into the fall. Unexpectedly, their horses ran off and the men chased them all the way to Yampa Valley, fifty miles to the west. At the same time a severe early snowstorm came up and separated the men from the women and children. It was the women who likely built the wickiups that allowed them to survive until the men returned with their horses in the spring. The wickiups were made of aspen poles, but what Callahan found significant was their location. The exact spot was no arbitrary matter for the Indians. The doorways faced north away from prevailing winds and toward an open sage-covered hillside about 500 feet above the valley floor. They were deep in a grove of aspens, perfect protection from the harsh winter and a fact that allowed their continued existence even to this day.

Survival depended on a good campsite. Powers wrote that California Indians had to reconcile the need to live near water with the desire for security against surprise attack. In the mountains they selected a sheltered open cove where an approaching enemy could be seen before he was within the range of a bow and arrow and where there was a knoll with good drainage. The Great Basin Paiute made camp on hilltops and carried up their water in basket jugs. Powers emphasized the importance of protection by referring to Kit Carson who blamed the deaths of many early settlers on their penchant for camping down next to streams. Today, the backwoods camper does not have to fear an attack by enemy Indians, but there are still many good reasons not to camp in a stream bottom where mosquitoes, flash floods or noisy hikers might find you.

Campsites should be continually refined. During a recent visit to the Kiliwas, I found José and Teodoro Ochurte planning a short move down their arroyo to a point where an embankment afforded increased protection from the ferocious winds they faced in their present, more exposed location.

Placement of the camp was often contingent on the effects of the sun. Still today, the Navajo go and live in the cool shadows of the Canyon de Chelly to escape the summer heat. The warm rims and flat open country outside of the canyon entrance become home in the winter at a time when solar heat is welcome. Similarly, many California Indians faced the door of their shelters toward the east for natural air-conditioning. Needed warmth from the sun came in the cool of the morning and the shade during the hot afternoon. They often moved to the mountains in spring and summer to hunt and exploit mountain resources. They knew enough to stay out of the high country in the winter and made their semipermanent village in lower warmer climes. Ironically, Kit Carson was the one who flouted this practice. "Snow upon snow," an apprehensive Washo Indian was said to have remarked, as Carson, John C. Fremont and their party set out to cross the Sierra Nevada in the winter of 1844. But Carson and Fremont traveled more like a modern army than a band of nearly naked Indians. Conquering the wilderness was the aim of the new Americans. Finding a home in nature was the way of the Indian.

Teodoro Ochurte, Juan Espinoza, Ricardo Albañez, Tito Ochogo (kneeling) and José Ochurte rest around completed willow-frame wa'.

Water

Water sustains life. Many seem to have forgotten that simple fact. The modern city dweller's cavalier approach to water does not stop at the forest's edge. Dirty dishes, detergent, leftover food, human waste, beer cans and old fishing gear are all dumped in the sparkling brook. Ten thousand years of living at the source taught a different lesson. Thomas Jefferson Mayfield's account of the Choinumne Yokuts, Indians of the foothills of the Great Central Valley who raised him from early boyhood in the 1850s, gives even the tidiest camper pause.

Indians were very careful about polluting a stream near their ranchería or camp. If they had to wade in the stream they would do so below the camp, or they might cross on rocks above. The sweat house was located below and all bathing was done there. They would very seldom wash their hands and face in a stream. When drinking from a stream they would arise with their mouths full of water. They would allow this water to run over their hands and would in that way wash their hands and faces away from the stream. One mouthful of water would wash hands and face and leave some to spare. To wash was shoom-lú-suh.

Few Indian encampments, historical or archaeological, are found far from sources of water. It would have been a terrible risk to rest beyond known streams, springs or rain basins, especially in southern California and most particularly in the deserts of southern California. Yet there were times they ventured beyond the familiar, times when knowledge of landscape and the likely location of hidden water meant survival. The Cahuilla traveler saw the willow as an indicator of groundwater near the surface. It signaled life for the California hunter-gatherer. I have come upon dozens of spring-fed arroyos lined with willows within walking distance of my home in La Crescenta, a Los Angeles suburb in the foothills of the San Gabriel Mountains—*Hidakupa,* as they were known to the Gabrielinos of Los Angeles. When Indians left the security of known water, they often carried ceramic ollas or canteens or basketry water bottles. Water was always a consideration.

The Seri Indians of Tiburón Island in the Gulf of California lived in an especially arid land and their ways with water are instructive to us today. In a desert, the location and accessibility of water, more than anything, determines the placement of camps, their duration and the activities of the inhabitants. Richard Felger and Mary Moser studied the Seri for many years and recorded these activities. The Seri generally went for water early in the morning when camped any distance from it, especially in the heat of summer. They prevented water from sloshing over the top of the ollas that they transported it in by stuffing sweet-smelling or odorless plants into the ollas' openings. A mule deer stomach or bladder, cleaned, inflated and dried, then tied off with a tendon or strip of gut, became a canteen. To be safe, long journeys in groups, especially when children accompanied them, were undertaken immediately after rains. Permanent water sources were exceedingly scarce, but after a big rain, temporary catch basins or playas held considerable water. In order to store water, large pottery ollas were sometimes filled with water, sealed with a top, covered with brush and buried. This was often done near a hole about to go dry. Depressions where water might collect were enlarged. Holes were dug in the dry lake beds to catch water from the next rain, and channels were cut through carrizo to allow the water to flow, as well as to gain access to it. Small wells a little over a meter in depth, were dug after rains. Barrel cactus *(Ferocactus wislizenii)* sometimes supplied an entire camp for weeks, especially during the long dry season of late spring and early summer. The barrel cactus liquid taken on a full stomach avoided the diarrhea they might experience if they had gone without eating. Resting after drinking the juice was also helpful. The liquid of cooked century plants, on the other hand, was used only in a survival situation when all else had failed. Cactus-fruit juice was another source. The blood and body fluids of a large turtle were drawn and left for a few hours until the redness settled. The resulting clear liquid (serum), they drank. This was only an emergency source of water.

Like the Seri, the Kamia or Southern Diegueño of Imperial Valley, California, dug wells. With a sharpened mesquite digging-stick-shovel, they dug vertical-walled wells in the subsea-level floor of the valley, recorded Gifford. The wells were not for irrigation but just deep enough to dip water with a pottery bowl. They poured the water into ollas for drinking and cooking.

Paipai elder Benito Peralta, living in the Sierra Juárez Mountains and the Sonoran Desert of northern Lower California, told me how to get water from the large, cylindrical, prominently ribbed barrel cactus (*Ferocactus acanthodes, gracilis* and others). All one needs is something sharp to cut it open and get beyond the spines, ribs and skin. A broken stone will suffice. A piece of pulp is cut out, placed in the mouth, chewed, and the water sucked from it. Later the remaining dry fibrous mass is spit out. This is a common practice while traveling in the desert. Peralta laughed at the idea that it might cause stomach upsets or intestinal problems—never in his experience.

Kiliwa Indian Sam Ochurte recounted how they would burn the spines off of a barrel cactus which they then sliced and ate like watermelon, spitting out not the seeds but the pulp fiber as they trekked over the desert.

Bean and Saubel recorded that in emergencies the Cahuilla often made a natural reservoir from the barrel cactus. They found the cactus growing on gravelly fans and slopes in the desert, especially abundant at the openings of canyons. The top of the plant was sliced off and some pulp removed to make a depression. In the cavity they then squeezed the pulp by hand to make a large liquid-filled bowl. On occasion, with the addition of water and hot stones, such a hollowed barrel cactus was even used as a cooking pot.

The fruit of the barrel cactus, indeed the fruit of nearly all cacti, was a ready source of

Southern Diegueño Raúl Sandoval cleans the spines from a cactus fruit with the twigs of a broom plant.

moisture for the Cahuilla. Buckhorn cholla *(Opuntia acanthocarpa)*, pencil cactus *(Opuntia ramosissima)* and prickly pear *(Opuntia megacarpa)* are common examples. The spines of the cactus fruit, or tuna, were brushed off with a handful of grass or brush. In the Santa Catarina region of Baja California, the Indians still use a low-growing bush for this purpose; its Spanish name means "broom plant" *(hierba de escoba)*. The fruit must be knocked from the cactus, or, as Southern Diegueño Raúl Sandoval often does it, plucked with tongs made from a bent section of yucca leaf. As an alternative to brushing the tuna to remove the spines, Sandoval sometimes shakes a bunch of tunas in a small agave-fiber net bag. Sam Ochurte takes no provisions when out hunting in the desert for a day. Cacti quench his thirst.

Cactus joints or pads of nearly all species were an important food source for the Cahuilla. Prickly pear and the young and tender joints of beaver-tail cactus *(Opuntia basilaris)* were cut into small pieces and eaten, usually boiled. Buckhorn cholla *(Opuntia acanthocarpa)* is a common cactus found on dry mesas and slopes from the Colorado and Mohave deserts of Alta California to northern Baja California. Indians traveling on the desert consumed it as a survival food because of its high moisture content. Some decades ago Michelsen described the ease with which Kiliwa Indian Rufino Ochurte, Sam's father, prepared it. He first cut a number of young shoots from the cholla. Next, using a pair of sticks as tongs, he placed the shoots in a small fire. After the spines had been well singed he pushed the fire to one side and excavated a shallow hole in the hot sand. In this he buried the cactus and replaced the fire above. A half hour later the food was cooked. He pried it out with a short stick and roughly scraped and peeled it. Michelsen called the flavor "not disagreeable" and noted "the food was heavily laden with moisture."

Yuman-speaking groups of the lower Colorado River gathered from beneath the sand the succulent flower stalk of the rare parasitic plant known as sand food *(Ammobroma sonorae)*. They baked it in ashes, peeled the thin bark away and ate the fleshy water-filled stalk. Sand food appears on the surface of the sand as a small, tan, semi-globular cluster of hairs and purple flowers. It blooms from April to May in dunes and washes of the southwestern United States and northern Mexico. Under the sand the stalk can be over 4 feet in length.

Chumash Water Bottle

In the pluvial Northwest, California Natives rarely found themselves more than a few steps from a natural water source. The Great Basin and arid South were different. Indians carried a water jug and provided the home with a special container for water. Shoshonean peoples from the Great Basin to the Tehachapis twined willow or sumac splints diagonally into conical or round-bottomed vessels. Lugs on the sides held a soft buckskin tumpline. To seal them completely these most durable of portable water jugs had the entire inner and outer surfaces smeared with melted pine pitch. Along the southern California coast, the Chumash and Gabrielino twined more stationary, flat-bottomed basket jars. Hot asphaltum swirled over the inside and spread on the outside at the mouth and bottom kept them watertight.

Beginning in the early seventeenth century, explorers along the California coast left a record of these asphaltum-coated basketry water vessels. In 1602, Father Ascención referred to a flask of water and other water containers made of reeds. Pedro Fages in the eighteenth century wrote of water bottles coated with tar, and Miguel Costansó described them as made of rushes and shaped like Spanish jars. More recent studies by Albert Mohr and L. L. Sample delineated in detail the sizes and shapes of over a dozen twined Chumash water bottles found cached in sandstone caves of the remote Sierra Madre Mountains. The containers ranged from small globular bottles to large, tubular, barrel-shaped vessels. All had narrow, short necks (diameter 4 to 7 cm.; height, 2.5 to 5.1 cm.) and slightly flared rims (4.5 to 7.5 cm.). Heights ranged from 22 to 48 cm.; diameters, from 15 to 31 cm.; estimated capacity, from 2.6 to 29.9 liters. They were not perfectly symmetrical nor evenly shaped.

The Sierra Madres are near the Santa Barbara coast and they drain into the Cuyama River on the north and the Sisquoc to the south. Given the excellent state of preservation and presence of European trade items in some of the caches, it appears that basketry bottles found in these mountains were made near the historic epoch.

Materials

The elderly Chumash consultant Fernando Librado Kitsepawit told J. P. Harrington in the early years of the twentieth century that *'esmu' (Juncus acutus)* was twined whole and unsplit into a water bottle immediately after it was cut. Alexander Taylor noted in the middle of the nineteenth century that

Large juncus water bottle found in Castro Canyon, Cuyama area of Santa Barbara County. Diameter, 20 cm.; height, 45 cm. Four rows of simple twining over single warps alternate with three or four rows of simple twining over two warps. The twining over two warps is continuous from the shoulder to the rim, as seen on detail next page. Interior, neck, rim and base are covered with asphaltum.

Chumash water bottles were sometimes made of tule. Lawrence Dawson and James Deetz studied the corpus of Chumash basketry and found that juncus and tule rush (*scirpus*) were used for twined basketry water bottles. The tule was split and twisted for the weft, or weaving strands, and made into two-ply cordage (S-twist, according to Mohr and Sample) for the basket's warp, or foundation. Chumash María Solares told Harrington that *suna'y* (sumac or *Rhus trilobata*) was another material employed in making water jugs. Dawson and Deetz found only one Chumash vessel of this sort, twined of split sumac shoots on a peeled shoot warp. The slant of the twining twists was upward and to the right in a twill pattern much like a piece from the Gabrielino to the south, suggesting that it may have been a trade item. Mohr and Sample pointed out that twill or diagonal twining, and coiling of a splint around the last course of twining to finish the rim (found in this particular Chumash bottle), were also characteristics of Great Basin water jars.

The historic record suggests that the Chumash twined juncus while it was still green. In my experience (though apparently not in the record for tules), thin dead tules still standing in moist soil and not weakened by rot, work well. The damp base areas of these light brown rushes with a thickness about that of an arrow are tough and pliable. Fine strips of the cortex can be twisted into strong, stiff cordage for warps or twined very tightly as wefts.

Another large juncus water bottle from Cuyama area— found in Floom Canyon—on loan from Snedden Collection to Santa Barbara Museum of Natural History where it is on display in a diorama. Double and triple rows of simple three-strand twining form bands on a ground of four or five rows of simple twining over single stem warps. Asphaltum-covered, as on previous example. Detail of Castro Canyon bottle shown upper right, Floom Canyon bottle, lower right. (Photographs taken at Santa Barbara Museum of Natural History with the assistance of Janice Timbrook, Senior Associate Curator of Anthropology.)

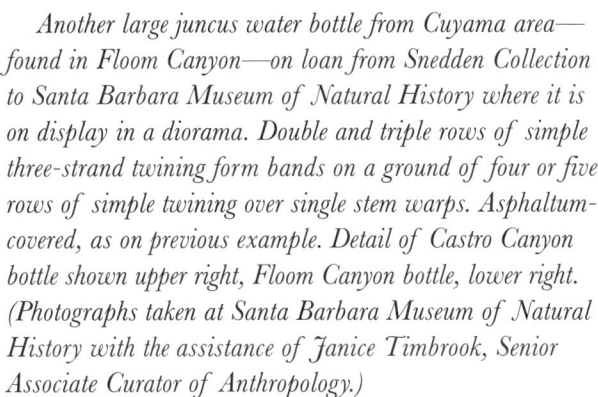

Warps, Beginning Knot and Wefts

Travis Hudson and Thomas Blackburn (1983) pictured and described a representative sample of Chumash water bottles from the Sierra Madres and beyond. Where it could be determined, most warps were of two elements, occasionally more than two, but sometimes only one. Based on work with Chumash consultants, Harrington determined that the bottom starting knot of close-work twining consisted of two pairs of warps. These were likely placed parallel, side by side, as in the three pairs of warps (or six simple elements) found as a start in the one Chumash bottle where Mohr and Sample believed they could see the beginning. Other starting knots were obscured by asphaltum. The center of the entire bunch of starting warps was undoubtedly encircled by a weft and at that point the twining began. Patricia Campbell, a staff associate in the Anthropology Department of the Santa Barbara Museum of Natural History, spent hours poring over the starting knots on Chumash basketry water bottles and fragments of bottles. From the clues of the asphaltum-obscured bottoms and fragments, and by experimenting with different starts, she was able to determine that the most common starting knot consisted of a bundle of eight stems of juncus tightly wrapped in its middle by a single juncus weft. The weft strand encircled the bundle once and was staggered so that the two starting weft strands that were produced would not be of the same length. This insured that two weft splices would not occur at the same point. After encircling the bunched warps, the juncus strands were twisted about each other 180 degrees and four warp stems were encircled by the two ends and the next twining twist was made. Groups of four warps were gathered and twined like this for one turn around the knot. Two warps were twined together for a few subsequent rounds and then one warp was twined for the remainder of the basket.

Harrington noted that the twining went from left to right and the outer weft leaned downward. That is, looking in the direction of twining, the two wefts twisted clockwise about each other. In Mohr and Sample's measurements of the various jars, the wefts crossed as few as five and as many as twenty-four warps per 5 cm. From nine to twenty-eight weft courses were stacked every 5 cm. Weft splices were largely hidden and must have consisted

Simple twined water bottle from Wellman Canyon, Sisquoc area, part of neck and rim missing. Diameter, 24.5 cm.; height, 24.5 cm. Juncus weft, two-stem warp. Interior, some of neck and base, asphaltum-coated. Bottom view shows concave dimple. (Photographs taken at Santa Barbara Museum of Natural History with assistance of Janice Timbrook, Senior Associate Curator of Anthropology.)

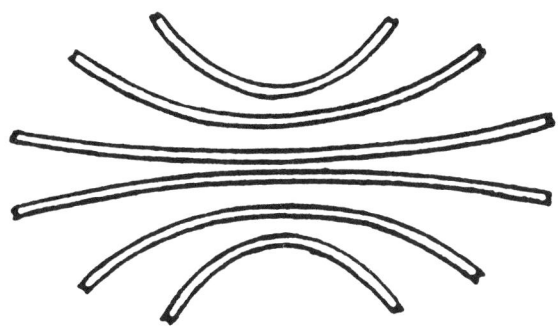

Diagrammatic sketch of primary warp arrangement (Mohr and Sample, 1955).

uncovered. Campbell found common in the jars she studied what might be termed the "V" or "U" method, where a stem (or two stems for a two-element warp) is simply bent in the middle and immediately twined in as two warps. Another technique in the single-warp baskets was simply to stick a new warp in the twist alongside an old one and use it as a single warp on the next round.

When the projected sides of the vessel were reached, the warps were bent at near right angles and the introduction of new warps slowed considerably or stopped. Approaching the neck, the process of adding warps reversed, as strands were cut off and warps recombined. In one bottle pictured by Hudson and Blackburn, warps of the neck, mouth and rim were made up of significantly more elements and thus of greater diameter than those of the body of the vessel. Since rims flared slightly from the constricted neck and mouth, a few additional warps were introduced when approaching the rim. Rims were finished by simply cutting the warps even with the last round of twining.

While two-strand simple twining, generally with a downward slant, comprised most of the body of each water bottle; decorative weaves, up to three styles on a single piece, could be found in bands just below the neck to the base. They occurred in rounds of one, two or three, separated by regular bands of simple twining of around four rounds in some bottles to as many as ten or twelve

of simply burying the new end between a warp and the last of the old weft and running the new one over the old one to the next warp where the new weft held the old end against this warp (as the old held the new to the previous warp) and continued on. In another method I found, the tail of a new weft was pinned up along the right side of a warp by the twining twist, which also pinned the last of the old weft to the left side of the next warp.

Since the base of the basketry bottle was flat (actually, most were slightly concave, a few gently convex) the initial expanding spiral of twining required the addition of warps at a rapid rate. They were commonly introduced by separating the two strands of a double warp and adding a new strand to each of these. Mohr and Sample illustrated this along with three other less frequent methods they

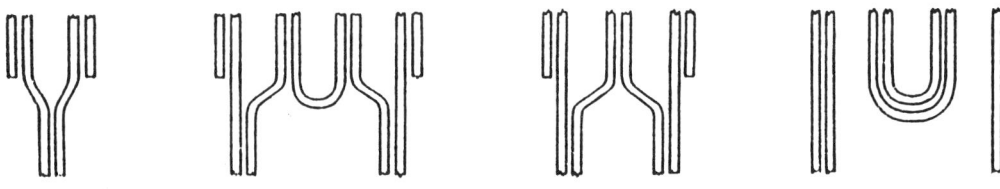

Diagrammatic sketch of the methods of inserting new warps when warps are of two-elements each (Mohr and Sample, 1955).

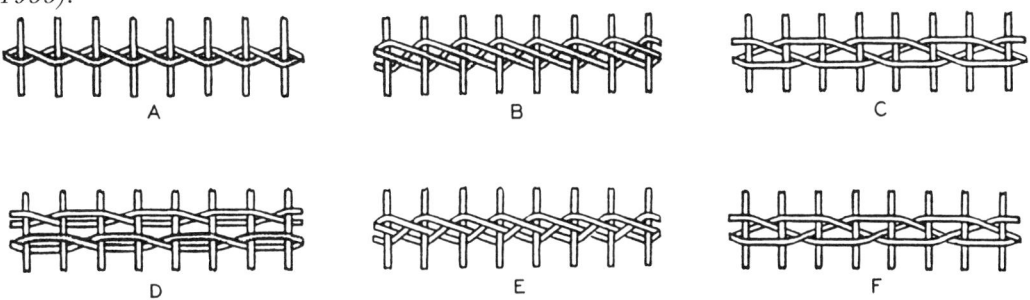

Twining techniques of Chumash water bottles. Basic weaves in top row, variations on each below. A) Two-strand simple twining. B) Simple three-strand (diagonal) twining. C) Three-strand parallel twining. D) Two-strand twill (or diagonal) twining. E) Three-strand braided twining. F) Three-strand herringbone twining. First five found in Mohr and Sample, 1955, last identified by Dawson and Deetz, 1965 (drawings adapted from Mohr and Sample, 1955).

in others. The decorative twined bands were of two-strand diagonal or twill, simple three-strand diagonal, three-strand parallel, three-strand herringbone, and three-strand braided twining. Reversing the slant of the twining in the decorative band, or doubling the warps twined (to contrast with twined single warps), gave further variations.

Sealing Tar

Bottles were made watertight with asphaltum gathered from natural seeps in Chumash territory. Many upwellings of natural tar can be seen to this day along Santa Paula and Sespe creeks. The inside of the vessel was completely coated as well as the exterior rim, mouth, neck (to a point 4 to 5 cm. below the neck) and bottom. Librado told Harrington that they first covered the basket with thick mud so the tar would not leak out. Then they put pulverized tar in the jug, followed by six heated rocks, each about 2 inches in diameter, dropped in one by one. They kept the rocks rolling about until the tar cooled. Some Chumash recounted that later the mud was washed off. Librado said they left it in place.

In his 1853 voyage to San Nicholas Island, George Nidever discovered a lone woman, abandoned there many years before. He observed this incredible lady making a basketry water bottle. She spoke a tongue more closely related to Gabrielino than Chumash, but the technique of tarring was undoubtedly similar. Several heated stones about the size of walnuts were dropped on the pieces of asphaltum in the jar. Then, "resting the bottom of the vessel on the ground, she gave it a rotary motion with both hands until its interior was completely covered with asphaltum," Nidever wrote. Librado added that a newly tarred bottle was filled with water

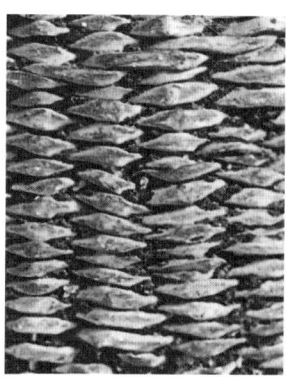
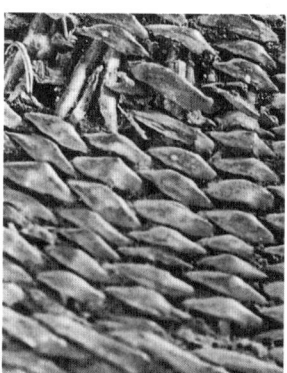
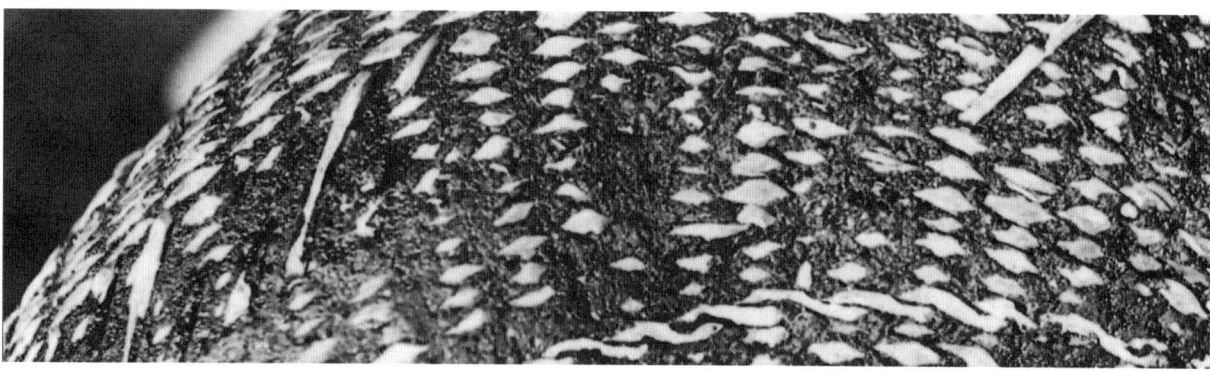

Chumash water bottle found in Santa Barbara County cave, some of neck, mouth and bottom missing. Simple two-strand twining with widely spaced bands of single-row, simple three-strand twining. Asphaltum-coated on the inside. Double juncus stem warps can be seen in damaged upper left portion in detail photograph to the right. A warp bundle of two is split and combined with those on either side—three warps reduced to two—as the neck of the bottle is approached.

Detail in the center shows likely introduction of new wefts (near middle of picture). Beginning of new weaver was slipped between last warp and end of old weaver, effectively pinning and hiding the tip of the new (not always with complete success) against the warp and pinning under the new the very end of the old to the next warp.

Bottom: detail shows remnants of what appears to be additional juncus stems sewn over a number of rows near the bottom of the basket to strengthen it in this vulnerable area. (Photographs taken at Santa Barbara Museum of Natural History with assistance of Janice Timbrook, Senior Associate Curator of Anthropology.)

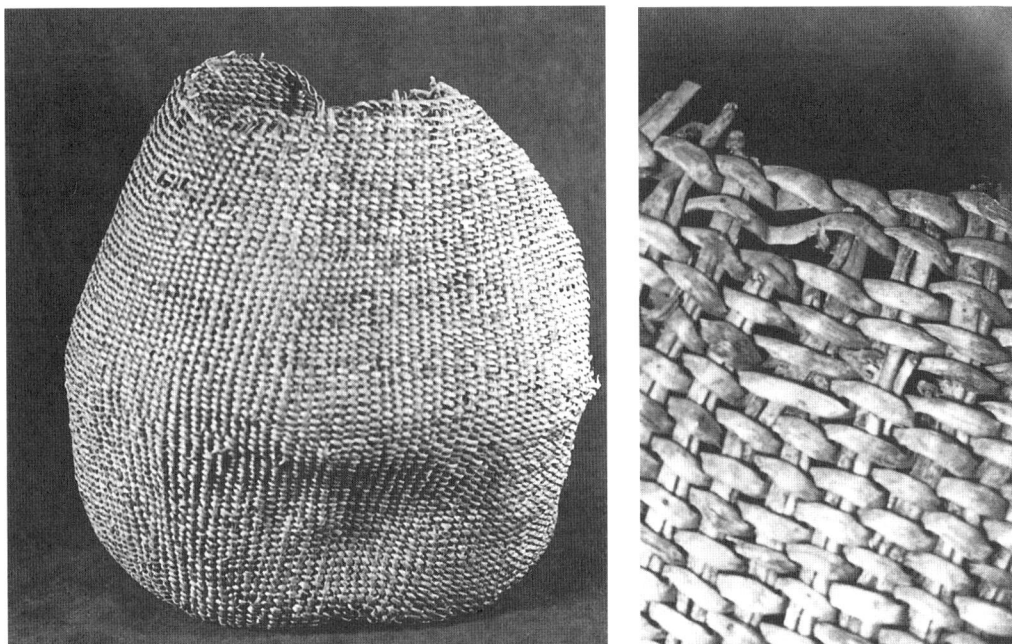

Untarred, close-twined juncus basket about 1' in height, discovered in Mono Canyon, Santa Barbara County, reveals construction techniques. In detail at right, a weft splice is effected (seventh tier from top, second column from right) by bringing up the end of the old weaver, after the twist, to left of the next warp. The other, downward slanting weft holds it in place. The tail end of the new is inserted from below just before the twist and next to the previous warp where it is held by the twist. Both loose ends extend up into the next tier of twining and are grouped with the warps. (Photographs taken at Santa Barbara Museum of Natural History with assistance from Janice Timbrook, Senior Associate Curator of Anthropology.)

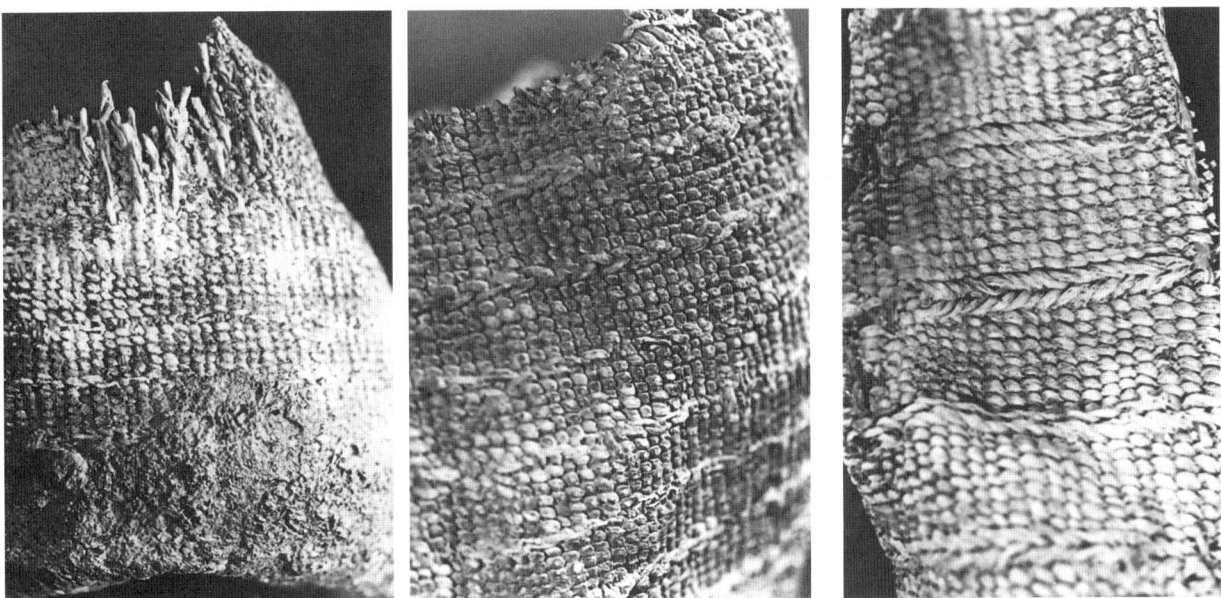

Details of baskets and fragments that reveal Chumash water bottle twining techniques. Left: twisted two-ply tule cordage warps exposed by damage in basket of Cuyama area twined of fine, twisted tule strips. Center: basket twined of extremely fine tule strips (five columns equal 14 mm., five tiers, 10 mm.) with decorative rows of three-strand herringbone twining. Right: fragment from Salsbury Canyon, Cuyama area, also of tule strips, showing decorative bands consisting of a three-strand downward twined row followed by a three-strand upward twined row. (Photographs taken at Santa Barbara Museum of Natural History with assistance of Janice Timbrook, Senior Associate Curator of Anthropology.)

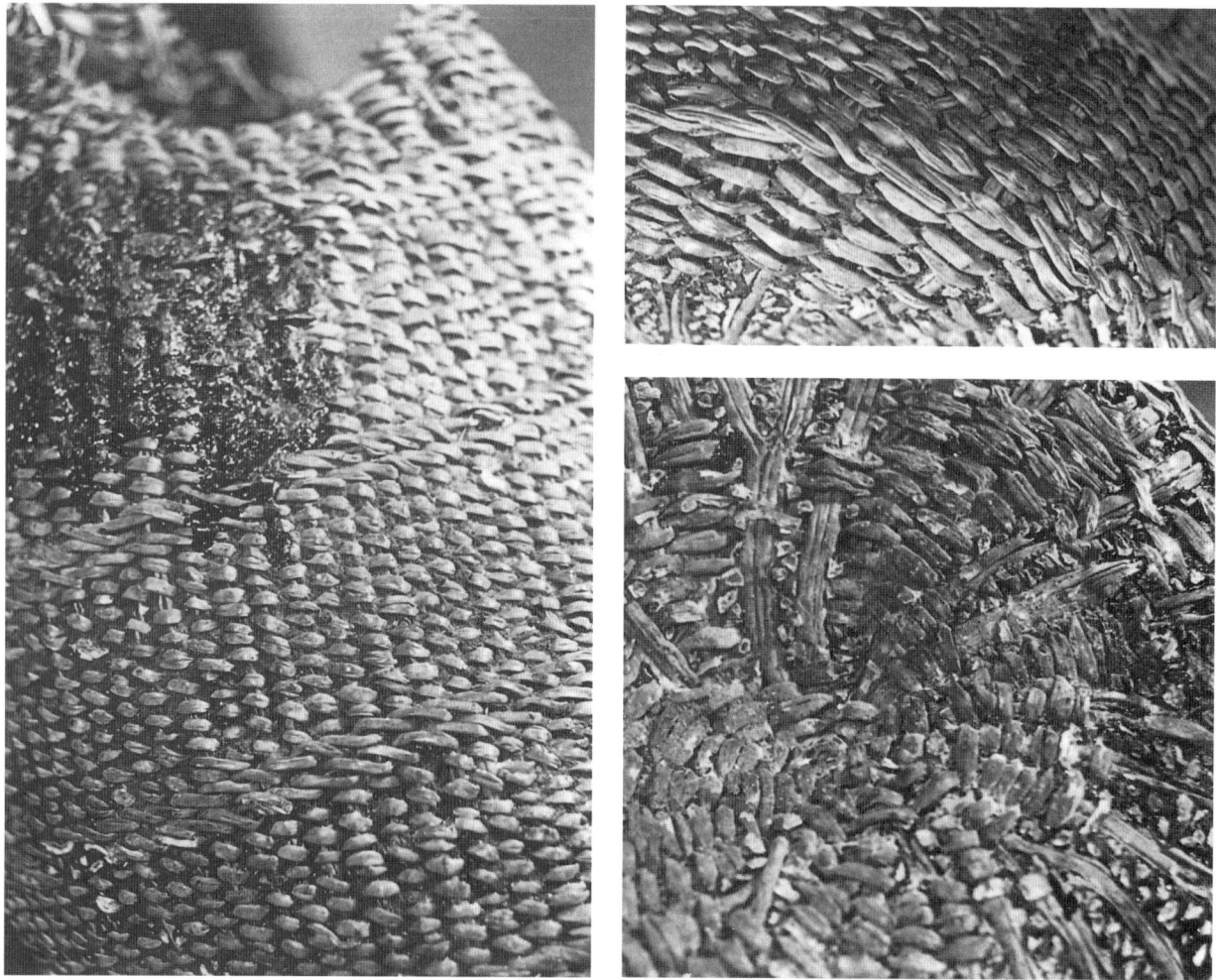

Basket detail above has two consecutive rows of three-strand downward twining for decorative bands. This asphaltum-lined basket is of juncus, found in a dry cave in Wellman Canyon on the Sisquoc River of Santa Barbara County. The last two photos show the worn bottom of the basket, not covered with asphaltum, and the primary warp arrangement. Multiple-strand warps apparently were made thick before the circumference of the base and then on the edge, marked by a three-strand twined row, each warp was split into two thinner warps of two juncus stems each. (Photographs taken at Santa Barbara Museum of Natural History with assistance of Janice Timbrook, Senior Associate Curator of Anthropology.)

from the river and left until the next morning when fresh water replaced the old. On the third day of refilling the vessel, the taste of tar was gone and the bottle was ready for use.

Nidever noted that the basketry jug held water well and if full, could even be safely placed in the hot sun. At home the bottle rested on a flat stone. Librado remembered that when they went to fetch water, if a little remained in the jug they poured it on the stone. Again, when they returned with water a little was poured on the stone, perhaps to cool the stone so as not to melt the tar, reasoned Librado. They drank from the basketry water jug. But first it was filled from the river with a gourd or small basket dish used as a dipper. Stoppers of tar or tule plugged the mouth of the jug. The top end of the stopper was wider, like the head of a mushroom. The stem portion entered and blocked the neck. The tule for the stopper had been doubled many times and wrapped with additional tule. Willow leaves or twigs stopped the mouth for those who were less diligent. The inverted gourd or basket cup used for dipping was placed over the mouth and neck for convenience or to further protect the contents. Chumash María Solares told Harrington that as the asphaltum lining of the bottle aged it imparted a good flavor and made the water fresh. Pine nut shells adhered to the asphaltum on the interior of some archaeological examples, suggesting a secondary function of storage container for the twined Chumash water bottle.

Indian Travel

Rapid travel was a California phenomenon even before we paved the land. A surviving narrative from Sir Francis Drake's 1579 anchorage in Drake's Bay north of San Francisco recorded of the Indians (likely, Coast Miwok): "They run very swiftly and long, and seldom go any other Pace." Not all travel was rapid, of course; age saw to that. The elderly walked with canes.

Canes or walking sticks, generally for use by the old or infirm, have been made by the Paipai Indians of Lower California since time immemorial. Elder Benito Peralta still makes them. He told me that a s*hutát* can be carved from any wood. He prefers willow or scrub oak (whose knots detract somewhat from its appearance, he felt). The one he made for me was of willow. A straight stick (3 feet 3-1/2 inches in length) was cut, side branches removed, and the pole stripped of bark. The narrow end of the stick (7/8 of an inch in diameter) was further narrowed from one side (to 5/8 inches diameter) for 5 to 6 inches from the top. On this narrowed side a 1/8-inch-deep V-cut was made about 3-3/4 inches from the end of the cane, and it was further narrowed from about 1 inch above and below the cut and descending to the bottom of the V. After soaking this end for a short time in water, it was heated in the coals of a small fire and then slowly, carefully and repeatedly bent as they did in making a bow, toward the V-cut, until a straight handle angled out from the cut at almost 45 degrees.

Fellow villager Andres Albañez made a walking stick of willow (about 1-1/4 inches thick by 3 feet long, not counting the handle). A thick natural side branch (1-3/4 inches by 6 inches) that jutted straight out at 90 degrees from the stick formed the handle.

The Pathfinder

I wondered aloud about getting lost. A walking stick was fine, but how did Peralta find his way and keep his orientation when traveling? He told me it was not a problem in his day because they seldom went so far that a familiar mountain was not always in sight. It is this emphasis on familiarity, I came to discover, that most characterized Indian travel. In a sense, they were always home or close to a worn trail.

The Mohaves were great travelers. Men went up and down the Colorado River. They crossed west over the Mojave desert, followed the Mojave River to the San Bernardino Mountains and beyond to trade with Indians on the coast, reaching the Chumash at present-day Ventura and Santa Barbara. They traveled for war and exploitation of resources and trade, or for visits or the pure love of travel. They were reputed at times to cover nearly 100 miles in a single day. When they traveled, they ran—a steady trot—often without food for days in the desert. Most important, when they traveled they remembered where they went, the significant features of the landscape, every spring and stream, and how much water they could expect to find. And though they occasionally traced maps in the sand, the truly important map was in their head.

Of the northern California Kato Wailaki, Powers wrote:

> It is wonderful how these Indians have all the forest and plain mapped out on the tablet of their memory. There is scarcely a bowlder, gulch, prominent tree, spring, knoll, glade, clump of bushes, cave, or bit of prairie within a radius of ten miles which is not perfectly familiar . . . he will conduct you to the desired place with the absolute infallibility of the sun's rays in finding out the hidden corners of the earth.

Here Powers encapsulates the essence of the hunter-gatherer mind-set: focus on the natural world and the enormous practical knowledge and sense of belonging such intense focus brings. John Wesley Powell expressed it again in describing two Kai'vavits guides who took him in 1870 from Utah into Arizona over dry, seemingly impassable volcanic terrain, cut by deep ravines at the heads of small canyons running into the Grand Canyon:

> There is not a trail but what they know; every gulch and every rock seems familiar. I have prided myself on being able to grasp and retain in my mind the topography of a country; but these Indians put me to shame. My knowledge is only general, embracing the more important features of a region that remains as a map engraved on my mind; but theirs is particular. They know every rock and every ledge, every gulch and canyon, and just where to wind among these to find a pass; and their knowledge is unerring. They cannot describe a country to you, but they can tell you all the particulars of a route. . . . Shuts, the one-eyed, bare-legged, merry-faced pygmy,

walks, and points the way with a slender cane; then leaps and bounds by the shortest way, and sits down on a rock and waits demurely until we come, always meeting us with a jest, his face a rich mine of sunny smiles. . . . At dusk we reach the water pocket. It is in a deep gorge on the flank of this great mountain. During the rainy season the water rolls down the mountainside, plunging over precipices, and excavates a deep basin in the solid rock below. This basin, hidden from the sun, holds water the year round.

Arizona, Utah, California—the entire West was crossed by Indian trails. They linked all of the Californias, north, south, east and west. Not only local trails, but super pathways traversed and bisected the region and reached trails far beyond, leading to what would become adjoining states such as Arizona and Nevada. And no matter how forbidding the trails may have seemed, they always led to water—stopovers where the weary wanderer could rejuvenate.

The Cocopa of the Colorado River Delta exchanged goods and intermarried with the Kumeyaay and Paipai of the peninsular mountains to the west. Daniel MacDougal traveled among the Cocopa in the first decade of the twentieth century. His description of the intertribal trails still in use at the time exemplifies the importance of water on the ancient routes. There were two main trails. One crossed the Cocopa mountains near Borrego Peak, leaving the delta through a long canyon southwest to Agua de Palmas, the first watering hole. The main ridge of the range was crossed through a low pass, and from there the way led through granite, volcanic and clay ridges, to Agua de las Mujeres, a seepage in a sand wash among the badlands. At that point, a blind trail passed straight as a line due west across the valley to the south of Laguna Maquata (Salada), thirty miles across a baking desert plain to the mouth of Palomar Canyon. Friends watched for their safe arrival, signaled by smoke, or they carried a water olla. This

Above: Ancient east-west trail along a ridge through the Chuckwalla Mountains in the Colorado Desert, southeastern California. Next to the trail, areas cleared of rocks, or "sleeping circles," are of the kind Malcolm Rogers linked to the earliest distinctly California culture, the San Dieguito, dating back perhaps 10,000 years. Much later, the trail formed part of a trade route between the Hohokam people to the east and Shoshonean people to the west. M. J. Harner used datable pottery from trailside shrines in the California section to demonstrate travel on the trail during the last thousand years. Francis and Patricia Johnston, beginning at animal and human ground relief figures north of Blythe in old Halchidhoma domain along the Colorado River, documented the footpath through Desert and Pass Cahuilla, Luiseño and Serrano territory into the San Bernardino Valley. Others followed evidence of its continuation to the Pacific Ocean. The Johnstons noted that the trail is rarely a single trail but consists of subsidiaries as well, running parallel to a main trunk. Trails are truly footpaths and vary from six to twelve inches in width and are about one inch deep; often, when enough stones are present, they have a rim or ridge of stones on each side of the trail.

leg was reckoned entirely by the directions and distances of obscure topographic features and required much experience. Three miles up Palomar Canyon, a favorite Indian camp and meeting place with running water and a shade of palms awaited the dehydrated wayfarer. Agave grew on nearby slopes.

The second trail began near the Hardy River floodplain and passed over the southeastern spur of the Cocopa Mountains down to Pozo Coyote, south of the main range. (As long as this water was constantly used, the black alkali content would be proportionately low and the water potable. But when the water stood and evaporated, the alkali level rose to dangerous levels.) From that stop the trail ran again across the flat barren plain, farther to the south of the Laguna Maquata, either to a *tinaja*, or small water-filled basin, at the northern end of the small Tinaja Range, or up the wide valley of the Arroyo Grande, still farther south. The Arroyo Grande route was much traveled. Its grades were the easiest from the Colorado River into the backbone of the Baja Peninsula and consisted of short legs from water to water.

As mentioned, the Mohave were travelers who would often go the great distance to the Chumash at Ventura. There they traded southwestern textiles for *olivella* shells and beads. In 1776, on route from the Colorado River to the San Gabriel Mission, Fray Francisco Garcés met groups of Mohave traders along the old Mohave trail. The trail began at a Mohave village on the west bank of the Colorado River just north of present-day Needles, California. It went northwest, linking a series of three springs as it made its way across the Mojave Desert to Cedar Pass Spring between the New York and Providence Mountains. At Marle Springs the trail turned southwest toward dry Soda Lake, the sink of the Mojave River, whose underground flow came to the surface at Afton Canyon. In wet seasons it had water for much of its length. They followed the river almost to the Cajón Pass where the trail forked; one branch went south through the mountains to the headwaters of the Mojave River and down tributaries of the Santa Ana River into the San Bernardino Valley. The other skirted the northern edge of the San Gabriel Mountains through the Antelope Valley. Punctuated by various springs, it headed northwest through the Castaic Valley to link with a trail going north from the Santa Clara Valley to the San Joaquín. Two trails headed southwest off the Antelope Valley trail through the Soledad and San Francisquito canyons, which had seasonally running streams, to the Santa Clara Valley itself. From there a trail followed the Santa Clara River all the way to the Chumash at present-day Ventura on the Pacific Coast.

The branch of the Mohave trail that headed south near the Cajón Pass split into three branches south of the pass, one going west to the Cahuilla through the San Bernardino Valley. Another continued south and a third passed west around the San Gabriel Mountains in Gabrielino territory and northwest through the Newhall Pass into the Santa Clara Valley where it came together with the four previously mentioned trails that entered the valley. Malcolm Farmer, who briefly described the Mohave trade routes in 1935, recorded that the archaeologist Richard F. Van Valkenburg had traced the old trails entering the Santa Clara Valley and determined that they all followed the ridges, not the floors of the canyons.

The Tubatulabal of the southern Sierras traveled for various reasons—to hunt, fish, gather food, play games, see a shaman or trade—and like the Mohave, they went as far as Ventura. They set down piñon nuts for the Chumash who took what they wanted from the pile and left fixed amounts of shell money in return. Shell cylinders and steatite were also obtained by the Tubatulabal on these journeys and, while at Ventura, they fished the ocean and collected lumps of asphalt from the beach. The

Sleeping circles with diameters a little more than the length of a man, are often found in groups and are presumably distinguishable from much later circles demarking a thatch hut with cleared doorway openings on the east or south. In the photograph the circles are part of a group of seven next to a trail that bisects the above east-west trail perpendicularly and leads to Aztec Wells in an arroyo on one side and to another large arroyo just below the mesa of the circles on the other.

trails to and from Ventura and other distant destinations followed various topographic features, but within Tubatulabal territory, as Voegelin noted, trails lay chiefly along ridges.

Indians had blazed numerous trails in the mountains that naturalist John Muir called "more rigidly inaccessible than any other I ever attempted to penetrate." These were the San Gabriel Mountains of Los Angeles County. Years ago, Will Thrall traced the main Indian routes that crossed the San Gabriel range north from the Los Angeles Basin to the Mojave Desert beyond. In analyzing them it becomes apparent that water was an important criterion. Streams and springs are encountered with just the frequency to obviate a need for packing water even on a fast strenuous journey. In the San Gabriels routes were also as direct as possible, and on the few faint old footpaths I have trod, ridgelines and spectacular commanding views were preferred to rock-strewn streambeds or arroyo bottoms. It made no sense to meet up with the impenetrable steep head of a box canyon when, on one side or the other, a moderate grade spur could be followed over the mountain. There may also have been a desire to not spook game that had gone down to a stream or catch basin to drink but to maintain the commanding features and keep them under surveillance. There were other reasons.

In the early 1870s Powers complained that the Indian trails of northern California always seemed to seek the high ground.

> *Time and again I have wondered why the trails so laboriously climb over the highest part of the mountain; but I afterward discovered that the reason is because the Indians needed these elevated points as lookout-stations for observing the movements of their enemies. They run the original trails through the chaparral. . . . When the whole face of the country is wooded alike, the old Indian trails will be found along the streams; but when it is somewhat open they invariably run along the ridges, a rod or two below the crest—on the south side of it, if the ridge trends east and west; on the east side, if it trends north and south. This is for the reason, as botanical readers will understand, that the west or north side of a hill is most thickly wooded. The California Indians seek open ground for their trails that they may not be surprised either by their enemies or by cougars and grizzly bears, of which beasts they entertain a lively terror.*

It seems there was no natural feature too daunting for the California Indian to cross. Muir, in his travels through the high passes of the Sierra Nevada, encountered barefoot Paiute women carrying immense loads with men leading the way. They crossed from the Great Basin in the east to trade with the Miwok and other Indians on the west of the range. They would feast on trout in Yosemite Valley, hunt deer and bring back acorns in exchange for pine nuts and shore fly *pupae* gathered around Mono Lake.

Miwok trails, wrote Barrett and Gifford, were "almost airline in their directness, running up hill and down dale without zigzags or detours." An obscure trail, however, might be marked so that a stranger could find his way back by throwing down sticks for him. Pine needles marked trails over the granite of the treeless alpine regions of the high Sierra Nevada. Less rarefied, but undoubtedly effective, was the Miwok use of the sense of smell for finding their way. On trees along difficult trails they sometimes hung the carcasses of skunks. Powers had the opportunity to experience this during his travels among them.

Often the old well-worn Indian trails are no longer visible because, first, wagon roads and then the highways that followed, obliterated them. Nature

Benito Peralta, Paipai, walks with his shutát, fall 1997.

herself has reclaimed some. Others, especially in the deserts and mountains, can still be found, now more used by deer and coyotes than men. Justin Farmer, while hunting deer, would follow an old Indian trail just below a ridgeline through the mountains out of Napa County into the Sacramento Valley. At a certain point the trail simply stopped and became lost in the chaparral. One day, a great fire swept through the region and cleared the brush. There on the ground once again appeared the old foot-worn path.

Pliny Earle Goddard noted that along Hupa trails there were traditional rest stops, special trees they shot arrows into for luck, and piles to which they added a stick or stone and gave a prayer for a safe journey. These good-luck piles seem to have been a common California Indian practice. Malcolm Rogers, during his ramblings years ago in the western deserts, found piles of such stones bearing the patina of the ages along the most ancient trails of the San Dieguito, the earliest distinctively California Indian culture.

Magic clings to Indian trails and to those who ran them. The Chemehuevi George Baird told the story of a fellow tribesman of the southern California desert named Rat Penis, who died young but who was the last of his tribe to possess an ancient knowledge. Friends tried to track him one morning when he left from Cottonwood Island, Nevada to go to the mouth of the Gila River in southern Arizona. At first his steps looked like staggerings in the sand, the stride was long and irregular; then the footprints became ever farther and farther apart, lighter and lighter, over the sandy desert. Upon inquiring at his destination, his friends learned he had come into Fort Yuma on the Gila River at sunrise the same morning he left!

Peter Nabokov also wrote in his book about Indian running of Yurok trail runners described to him by anthropologist Thomas Buckley. Sons of influential families received esoteric training in running. The emphasis was on coming into harmony with the earth's natural forces. They were taught to sing to the earth, to address it and open themselves to it and receive it as a being. The trail should dictate the run as though *it* were doing the running under the runner and out behind him. One might practice by running with eyes closed, trusting the trail, or see the air that rushed past as a rope by which one could pull himself along with special breathing techniques and hand motions. The feet should be felt as not hitting the ground so much as the ground pushing up against the feet. Ultimately, the runner went into a light trance where the running just happened and where it was of no importance who was doing it—earth or runner. This inspired great power.

While the runner may have been a mystic, basic Indian orientation on or off trails was cosmic. The Mohave reckoned how long each day's travel over the desert would take in terms of the sun's position at the day's beginning and at its end. They measured the total distance in numbers of days. Truly encompassing markers for the California Indian were in the sky. From them, they oriented not only in space but time.

Basic Orientation

Despite exceptions (the Yurok placed everything in terms of the river on which they lived, up river or down river were their directions) most Indian orientation, east and west, north and south, came from the sun. The sun was a god, *Kakunupmawa* for the Ventureño Chumash, "the radiance of the child born on the winter solstice." His position on the horizon was carefully watched. Observatories such as Condor Cave were set up with reference to markers on peaks on the eastern horizon over which he would first appear on the winter solstice. This was a time of particular anxiety, since the sun had been daily descending lower and lower in the sky to the south. The solstice marked rebirth, renewed warmth and life, and it brought rejoicing. Travis Hudson and Ernest Underhay sought out all the old sources on Chumash knowledge of the skies. They learned that special painted and feathered sticks with a stone disk at the top represented the sun and were set up by the sun priest during solstice ceremonies to pull the sun back and ensure survival. Radiating red lines on these disks likely represented the horizon directions of the solstice, encompassing east and west, as well as the directions north and south. Similar painted circles and radiating lines found in Chumash rock art seem likely to have been similar solstice symbols. The sun stick and offerings to the sun for bountiful harvests also formed part of a summer solstice ceremony when the sun reached its most northern point in the sky.

But the sun was only the brightest orb that guided the ancient Californians. Fernando Librado told Harrington that the sun is opposite the North Star at midday. Both the star and the sun stick carried the name *Miwalaqsh* "to divide or separate in the middle." Polaris, the North Star, was known by the Chumash and other California Indian groups as the star that never moves.

Constellations were important too, particularly in southern California. The three stars of Orion's belt marked the month and the approach of the summer solstice for the Juaneño, Luiseño, Diegueño and undoubtedly others. This asterism, along with the Pleiades, appeared to be linked in many songs of the Southern California Indians and was represented in sand paintings of the Diegueño. The two asterisms together signaled the summer solstice for the Juaneño and Luiseño and indeed the Pleiades immediately preceded and heralded the sun's rising on the summer solstice (about June 22) at the sun's very location on the eastern horizon.

Antares marked the position on the horizon of the winter solstice (around December 22) for southern California Indians. It presaged the winter solstice sun rising just before sunrise on that date. Antares is the main star of the constellation Scorpio, which the Diegueño called "a boy with bow and arrow." The three stars of the belt of Orion were mountain sheep to the Cahuilla. The three stars of Orion's sword represented an arrow shot at the mountain sheep by a hunter who was the bright star Rigel. The Pleiades were three sisters. Awareness and knowledge of such familiar fixtures in the night sky, which could be related to the position of the sun in the daytime sky, must have made it seem like home wherever one might have wandered. The Milky Way th Ventureño Chumash called "Journey of the Piñon Gatherers"; the Barbareños and Ineseño Chumash said it was the "Night's Backbone"; and the Cahuilla declared it was dust raised in a foot race between Isil and Tukut (Coyote and Wildcat). Most California Indians saw the Milky Way as a ghost's road. The Luiseño linked it to the spirit of a dead man as well as to the sacred cord of life. The Chumash recognized its changing seasonal orientation.

Phases of the moon gave Southern Californians twelve months (or thirteen on occasion, when the lunar year began to fall too early for the solar). Star markers anchored the months to their general positions in the year and the year generally began around the winter solstice. The Diegueño and Cahuilla had six named months that repeated each half year—a division created by the solstices. Stars also delineated special seasons. August Lomas of the Cahuilla Martínez reservation told Lucile Hooper about the eight seasons that were focused on the cycle of the mesquite bean but signaled the arrival of other food plants as well.

The old men used to study the stars very carefully and in this way could tell when each season began . . . when a certain star finally appeared, the old men would rush out, cry and shout, and often dance. In the spring, this gaiety was especially pronounced, for it meant they could now find certain plants in the mountains. . . . They never went to the mountains until they saw a certain star, for they knew they would not find food there previously.

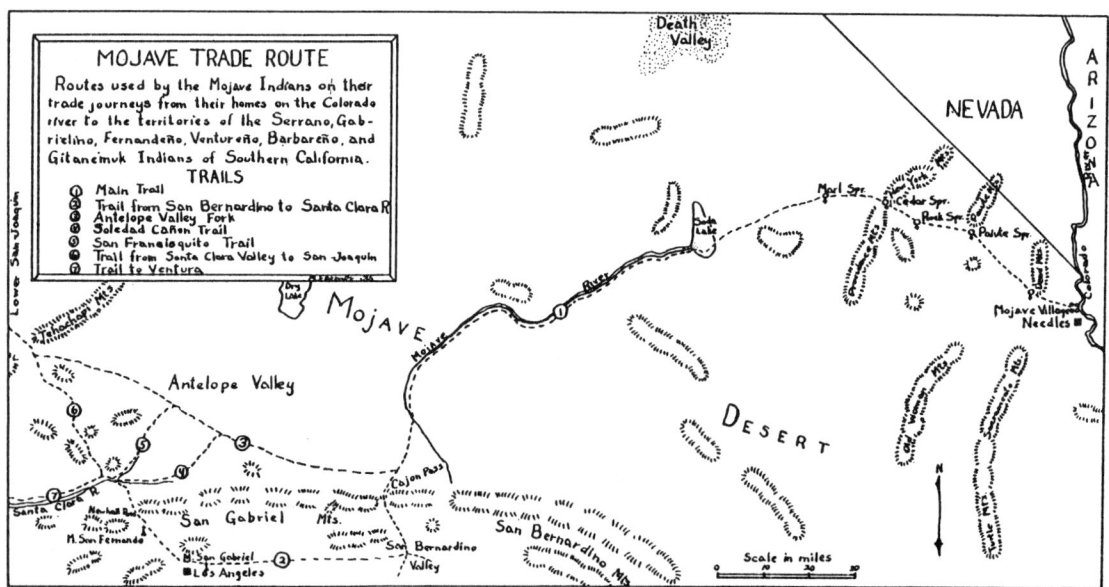

The principal intertribal "Mohave" trails (Farmer, 1935). Note that map shows trail going through the Cajón Pass, but earliest records indicate it ascended the San Bernardino Mountains by the Mojave River slightly to the east. Routes of a few local Gabrielino trails, crossing the San Gabriel Mountains north and south but not shown above, are found in Robinson, 1977.

California Cordage—Fibers and Technology

> *. . . the Paiute Indians tied their world together. They tied their wood and willows in bundles to carry them into camp; they tied small game onto their waistbands; they tied the tules to make boats, and cattails to make houses; they tied babies in baskets, and arrowheads to shafts. They used cords in place of buttons and safety pins, to make traps, to catch fish and hang them to dry. In addition to the tough rope of cattails and sagebrush bark, they made strong string of sinew and human hair. They also used supple young willow withes for tying. But the finest cordage of all was made of Indian hemp, or dogbane.*

Margaret Wheat described the traditional survival skills of the Northern Paiute of western Nevada in the late 1940s. But the territory of these bands extended into the northeastern corner of California and their technology of cordage-making was not so different from the rest of California. It reminded me of what I saw nearly a thousand miles away on a remote ranchería of Yuman-speaking Indians in the mountains of Lower California in 1994. To appreciate the similarities and, at the same time, to capture a variety of material and skill, let us pass through old accounts and ethnographies of representative groups along this great swath of California, and conclude with a detailed eye-witness description of cordage making still practiced among the Kuatl lineage (Southern Diegueño) in isolated villages of Baja.

The making of cordage underpins California Indian technology. Snares, sandals, bows, fish lines, fishnets, carrying nets, pole house frames and tule boats are only a few of the survival tools that were not completed without some form of twisted plant fiber or sinew cordage. Sinew held feathers to arrows, and, rolled into one-, two- or three-ply string, was used on most Native California bows. The Paipai of today still twist a strip of rawhide into a serviceable bowstring. The Gabrielino made ropes from the hide of sea lions. But perhaps most useful to California Indians were the cords made of vegetable fibers, since they did not expand or loosen when wet and the raw material was virtually everywhere, available to everyone.

For those brave few who dare to leave the coastal megalopolis and actually get out of the car, native fiber, though often greatly diminished, still grows wild and can still be rolled into cordage the old way. The effete finger-twisting techniques of modern survival books and classes are tedious and slow and assume that we are all too citified to learn what every Native Californian knew well: the hand rolling of cordage on the thigh. The old Indian methods were best. Once mastered, they comprised a liberation and a long step toward making the wilderness home.

Fiber From a Flower— a Northwestern California Technique

The Karok and Yurok moored a boat with a grape vine, just as it grew. They twisted smaller grape vines into rope. The Northwest California Indians used strips of willow bark and hazel withes as bindings, and with willow bark they even made a temporary net. But, far and away, the preferred cordage material in northwestern California came from a small species of iris *(Iris macrosiphon)*, commonly called bowl-tubed iris because of a bowl-like enlargement at the top of a very long corolla tube. Groups such as the Tolowa, Hupa, Yurok, Karok, Coast Yuki and Shasta tediously extracted two silky thin, but tough fibers, from each leaf to make an unusually fine even cord. Iris fibers were twisted into cordage by rolling them between the palm and the thigh. I have seen old Indian nets tied with iris fiber string so perfectly regular and exquisitely made that any attempt at illustration would be futile.

The Hupa claimed that fiber taken from iris plants growing under oaks was superior to that growing under pines. Leaves were gathered in the fall when fully mature. Early accounts by Gifford reveal that Karok women gathered the leaves, sometimes with the help of men. The leaves were 1 to 2 feet long and they gathered them with bare hands, leaf by leaf, from plants in the lower mountains. They formed them into bundles as they went along, one of the leaves wrapped around each bundle, and put them in a burden basket. At camp or at home, the bundles were hung out of the reach of smoke so that the fiber might be extracted the next day without breaking. Should the bundles dry before processing, however, they were dipped in water and laid in a basket for a day to make the leaves damp and pliable.

The bundles were opened and each leaf was split from the far end with a thumbnail. The index finger followed in the split to complete the longitudinal halving of the leaf. A. Kroeber's 1909 field notes indicate that the leaves were held in the left hand by the Yurok and other northwest California Indians, and the thumbnail that did the splitting was an artificial nail worn on the right thumb. Gifford describes it as a false thumbnail of mussel shell, the edge of which was sharpened with the stem of the giant horsetail *(Equisetum)*. It was often made from the end of a woman's mussel-shell spoon. A hole was drilled on either side of the shell to hold the concavity to the thumb. The apex or hinge was toward the base of the thumb and the opposite end extended over the nail.

Each half-leaf was scraped, wrote Gifford, by being drawn between the end of the middle finger and the mussel-shell scraper. A. Kroeber noted that the green pulpy material of the half-leaf was stripped away by drawing the shell thumbnail from the middle of the half-leaf out, first toward one end, then toward the other. They turned the half-leaf over and did that side the same way. The result was a single silken white fiber—two from a whole leaf. Sometimes the Karok simply scraped the leaves directly on the sharp edge of the mussel-shell spoon.

Woman's work done, the men twisted the fibers into string on their bare thighs. A bunch of fibers was folded over to make two groups that were rolled into two-ply string having a right-hand twist. Also referred to as an S-twist by ethnographers because the direction of the two elements of the cord went in the direction of the center section of the letter "S," a right-hand twist resulted when each of the two individual elements was twisted first in the opposite direction, becoming the so-called "Z twist." This put the strands in each group under tension and caused them to spring back together into a two-ply S-twist cord.

California Indians did this on their thighs. Seated and holding the cord with the left hand as the two strands draped over the leg side by side, they rolled the strands with the palm of the right hand over the thigh twisting them away from the body. Each was kept separate and slightly apart for S-twist tension in each, then, after a momentary release of the left hand, rolled back toward the body, tightening the two strands together in a Z-twist. The pattern was reversed, the two separate strands brought toward the body for Z-twist tension in each, then together, away from the body, for a single S-twisted cord. More fibers were added or spliced in as the end of a strand was approached.

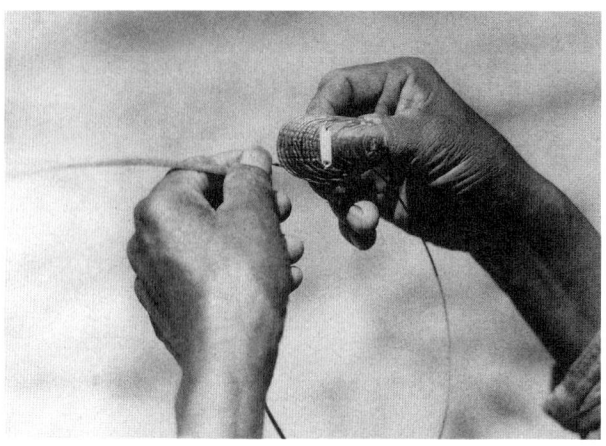

Karok Indian Fritz Hanson wearing artificial thumbnail of mussel shell grasps split-iris leaf. Photographed by J. P. Harrington, 1926 (Smithsonian Institution National Anthropological Archives).

Sometimes the thigh would get sore, the Chimariko told J. P. Harrington, and they would rub some grease on the thigh and rest for a time. Or, to prevent soreness, a 6-inch-long rectangle of fawn skin with a cord from each corner was tied over the thigh and they rolled the string on that. (Detailed accounts of thigh-rolling methods follow in sections on the Western Mono and Rancho Escondido.)

Two-ply cords can be rolled together on the thigh into larger cords and rope. Two original Z-twist cords, for example, are rolled toward the body then away into a combined S-twist "rope." Two of these in turn are combined by rolling away from the body then back into an even thicker Z-twist piece of cordage. The Karok, having made a sufficiently long cord, wound it over the hand and flexed elbow, removed it, and bound it at the center into a hank. It was rewound from this onto a shuttle when needed to make a net.

Nets of many forms and sizes for salmon, sturgeon, lampreys and other species along with bags, snares and many additional items were made from the iris fiber cordage. Most of the string was two-ply and very thin but three-ply and four-ply were also rolled. In cords collected by A. Kroeber among the Yurok in 1907 the basic strands measured .5 mm. They had been twisted into two- and three-ply cords which in turn were rolled together into cords that measured from 2.0 to 2.6 mm. In one case two three-ply cords had been twisted together and then three of these rolled together into a cord 4.4 mm. in diameter and 20 meters long. Iris-fiber snares for deer, and harpoon and tow lines for sea lions, measured up to 1.3 cm. thick.

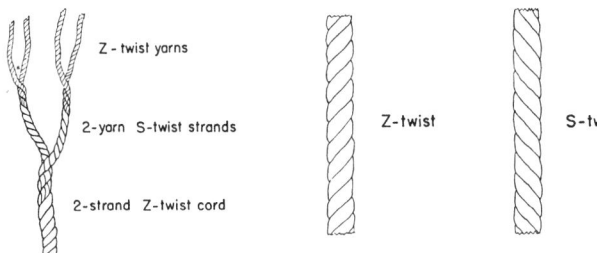

Alternating twists to produce ever-thickening cordage. The basic forms: Z-twist and S-twist (drawings by Gustaf Dalstrom in Martin, 1954).

Karok Grapevine Root Rope

It could be 15 or 20 feet long. When not in use, it lay in a 10-inch diameter coil at the bottom of the canoe. It remained strong and supple a long time for the tying of the canoe moored at the edge of the river. The Karok explained everything to J. P. Harrington many years ago.

A long grapevine (*Vitis Californica*) root, mostly around 3/4 of an inch in diameter but part of it, 1/2 inch or less, had been dug from a patch of grapevines along the river. Since the roots were both underground and on top, something for cutting was all that had been needed to remove them. Section by section, on all sides, the root was next warmed thoroughly over a small fire. While still hot, and in a sunny place, they twisted the root between the hands to make it flexible and cause the bark to break away. Then, section by section, it was pounded with a stone maul on an anvil for the entire length. In the pounding strokes, the maul was raised only seven inches and fell mostly on the knots of the root. Finally, the vine root was again twisted throughout the length. The rope was ready.

As a by-product, bark of the grapevine root was made at times into fairly strong cordage about the diameter of medium iris string but much inferior. The bark fibers were twisted on their thighs. The process worked best if the bark had soaked in cold water for three, four, or more days.

Notes on the Modoc

In his early studies of the Modoc and Klamath Lake Indians, Barrett found that the most common string from the region came from the nettle (*Urtica*) fibers. A brown milkweed string was used to a much lesser extent. As in most areas cordage was two-ply. Fish were taken with string nets but also hook and line. The main part of the line was of gray nettle string while the leader was of the brown milkweed that was thought to be stronger and less visible in water.

Paiute Indian Hemp Cordage

Wheat wrote that growing in moist soil or along the banks of streams, Indian hemp (*Apocynum cannabinum*) might look like a willow or a milkweed with thin pods. The Paiute sought out the tallest plants with the fewest branches. New stalks appear reddish-brown and it was these they chose, for as the color faded over the years and the stalk became shaggy, the fiber weakened.

In the early days they would scrape off the thin reddish skin with a crescent-shaped obsidian. However, when Wheat knew them in the 1940s, a knife was good enough. Next they pressed the stalk between thumb and forefinger, or even used their teeth to split it lengthwise from the tip to about 6 inches from the base, exposing the hollow and pithy center. The unbroken end functioned as a handle and kept the fibers untangled while stored.

Johnny Dunn, whom Wheat observed, held the pithy side of the split stalk against his left wrist and arm as he went along with his right hand, bending the stalk and cracking the pith at short intervals against his left arm (the pith would break easily if dry). This loosened the pith from the fiber and the broken pieces of pith were scraped or brushed from the fibers with his fingernails. Finally, the fibers were gently rubbed between the fingers to separate them and complete the cleaning.

To make cordage, Dunn took two bunches of a few fibers each in his left hand and rolled the first bunch in a pushing motion with his right palm on his right pant leg. Next, he did the same to the second bunch (both were about 2 feet long). With a rolling return stroke toward his body, the palm then twisted the two plys together into string. Splicing fiber in as needed, the process was repeated over and over as completed cordage was wrapped on a stick. Edna Jones told Wheat that her grandfather, Captain Wasson, whose rabbit nets of great workmanship were still in existence, wore no clothes when he made string because the fibers rolled better on bare skin.

For traps and fish lines, for most purposes, string made of Indian hemp sufficed but sometimes ropes were needed. Tule and cattail boats of the Paiute were held together with ropes of twisted cattail. Long unbroken leaves were thoroughly soaked. The tips of two small bundles were then overlapped—far enough to stay—and then the whole length was simply twisted hand over hand (preferably with two people) into a strong short rope that held even when dry.

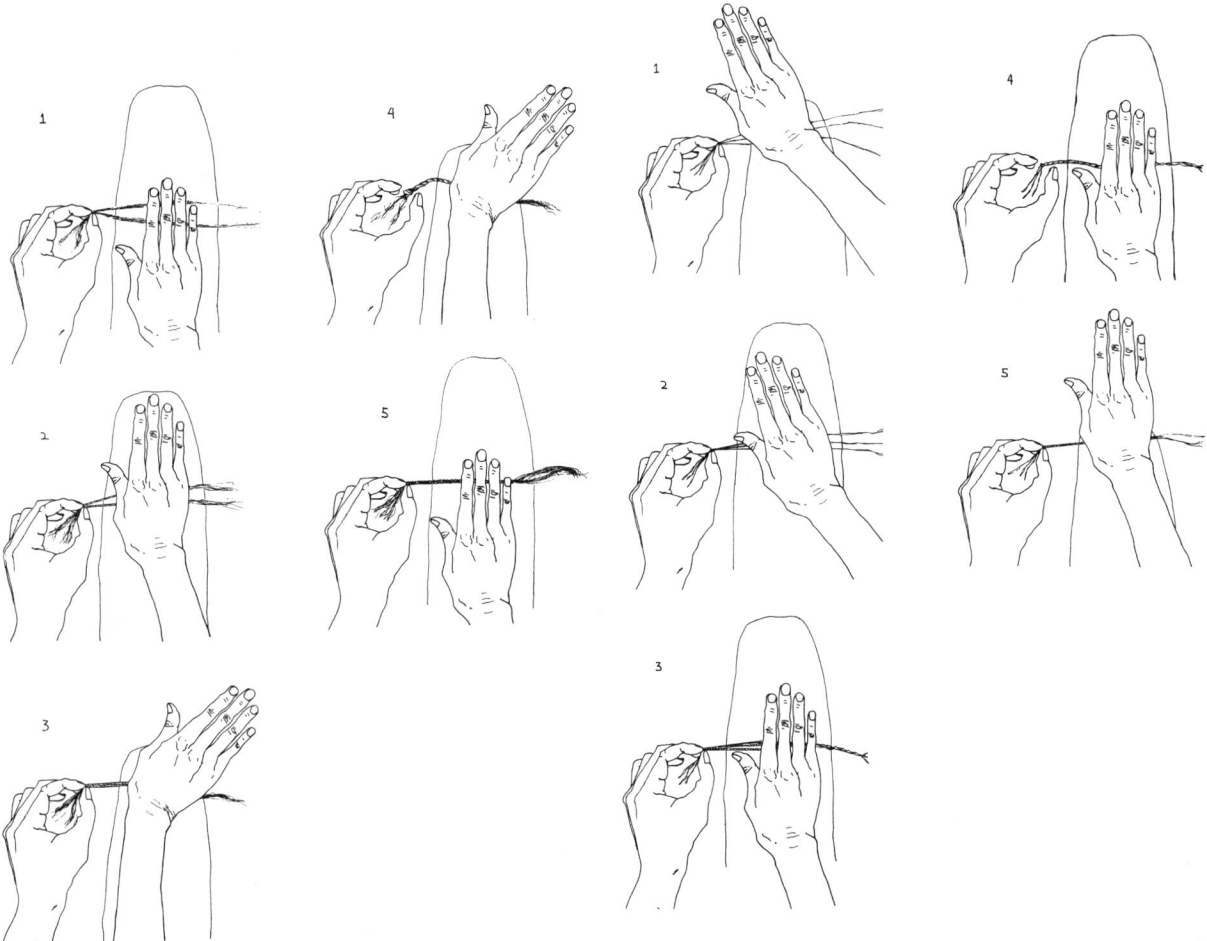

(1) First position for Z-twist cord (2-ply). (2) The hand pushes forward on the thigh; the strands are rolled under the palm into two S-twist yarns. (3) As the hand reaches the end of the roll, it abruptly pivots clockwise near the right side of the palm, swinging the left side in an arc which catches the lower strand more forcefully and carries it up against the upper strand. (4) At the very moment of reversing the direction of the right hand for the return roll, the left hand momentarily releases its grip; the two S-twist strands automatically spring into a Z-twist cord toward and under the left margin of the right hand. (5) The right hand returns, tightening the Z-twist under pressure of the left portion of its palm. (After this, the left hand moves its grip down to the end of the newly completed Z-twist portion of the cord; the remaining strands are untangled and the process continues.)

(1) First position for S-twist cord (3-ply). (2) The hand, angled to the left, pulls back on the thigh; the strands are rolled under the palm into three Z-twist yarns. (3) As the hand reaches the end of the roll, it straightens and pivots clockwise near the left side of the palm, swinging the right side in an arc which catches the upper strands more forcefully and carries them down against the lower strand. (4) At the very moment of reversing the direction of the right hand for the return outward roll, the left hand momentarily releases its grip; the three Z-twist strands automatically spring into an S-twist cord toward and under the left side of the right hand. (5) The right hand returns outward, tightening the S-twist under pressure of its palm. (After this, the left hand moves its grip down to the end of the newly completed S-twist portion of the cord; the remaining strands are untangled and the process continues.)

Miwok Milkweed Cordage

For the simplest matters the Miwok bound things with a grass stem or grape vine. The Central Miwok used the stem of the sedge *(Carex)*. Barrett and Gifford recorded that both Miwok men and women at times made cordage from flannel bush *(Fremontia californica)*. But especially esteemed were the milkweeds: the showy milkweed (*Asclepias speciosa*), the purple milkweed (*Asclepias cordifolia*) and Gifford's milkweed (*Asclepias giffordi*, perhaps a hybrid of *speciosa* with *eriocarpa*).

Milkweed gathered in summer was dried by laying it flat on the ground, but when Milkweed was gathered in the fall and winter it was already naturally dry. The dry stems were combed through a loop of green willow held in the right hand to release the fiber that was found just below a very thin skin and above the pithy core. They wound the fiber into a ball to await the manufacture of cordage.

To make cordage, two bunches of fiber were tied at one end and the two groups rolled outward on the thigh by the right hand that was moistened with spit from time to time. The left hand moved down and secured the lower end of the twisted portion of the strings as the spinning proceeded until acceptable lengths had been twisted this way. Then the left hand returned to the tied end and the right hand rolled back toward the body, combining both strings into a cord and tightening the twist. As with most groups, detail on splicing of fiber to make longer cords is lacking.

Some Yokuts Cordage Techniques

Milkweed *(Asclepias)* was also the most common string fiber among the Yokuts. The stems were collected in early winter. They peeled off the bark after it had been shredded by rubbing it between their hands. The thin outer covering that remained was then removed from the fiber by drawing the shredded bundle over a wooden stick. The resulting fibers were not disentangled but rolled together—twisted—just as they were. To make cordage, two of these rolls would be taken and each was twisted tight on itself and then combined in a reverse roll with each other. They did it on their thighs with spit in their hand. Indian hemp and nettle were used for making cordage as well.

Yokuts men made rope from the inner bark of the "button willow" *(Cephalanthux occidentalis)*. In the fall they ringed trees with an obsidian blade at intervals of 3 to 5 feet, depending on whether one or two sections could be taken from the tree. The bark was stripped and the inner bark easily peeled from it. Without waiting for the inner bark to dry they laid it out on flat rocks and pounded it with a stone. It was rolled on their thighs into a two-ply cord or rope.

A Western Mono Sinew Bowstring

Western Mono men sometimes made three-ply sinew cord for bowstrings. Dried sinew that had been taken from the leg and back of the deer was soaked in water and pounded between two stones. A man might use a stone arrow straightener for this process. He then worked the pounded sinew with his fingers and smoothed and separated it into threads.

Anna Gayton recorded the Western Mono process of twisting the resulting filaments into cords in some detail. Three fine strips of sinew, each of a different length, were tied together evenly at one end. With the knot held in the left hand and the three threads of sinew well separated and on the right thigh, the palm of the right hand was placed over them. The left hand kept the strands taut while the right palm rolled them over the thigh *toward the body* in a kind of rotating movement. The thumb side of the hand moved hardly at all while the outside of the hand described an arc, twisting at once each of the separated strands.

The left hand loosened its grip on the knot and the three strands sprang together in a single cord; the right palm maintained pressure. The left hand again gripped the knot securely and, keeping the strands taut, the right palm now rolled the single three-ply cord over the thigh away from the body *toward the knee* in a straight outward motion. This firmed up the twist of the three-ply cord section of the sinew strands that measured about 6 to 12 inches.

The left hand then grasped the cord just above the point where it separated into three parts and the process continued. Since the strands were of different lengths, only one would be spliced at a time. When needed, a new piece was overlapped and twisted into the shortest of the three existing fibers. The splice was always made the center sinew of the three as they were rolled and twisted toward the body over the thigh.

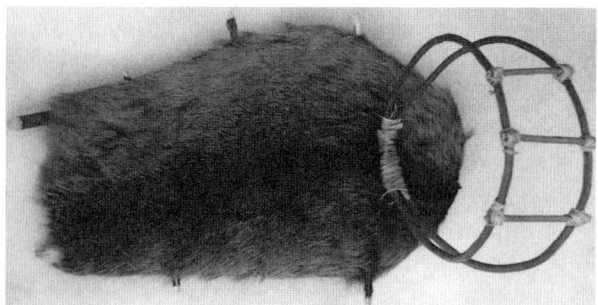

They tied their world together. Raw inner bark of willow bound three willow braces across a willow branch looped into a U-shape frame for a Paipai cradle board. The same willow bark joined two willow branch ovals separated above by three sticks also bound with the inner bark of willow to form a framework for a blanket sunshade over the baby's head. Thigh-rolled, 2-ply agave fiber cordage passed through untanned deerhide to secure the sunshade to either side of the top willow brace. Additional agave cordage across the bottom and at the top sides held the deerskin to the board (Santa Catarina, 1994).

Tubatulabal Rope

The outer bark of the flannel bush (*Fremontia californica*) was peeled from the long branches and trunk and, while still fresh, softened between the hands. Three bunches of this were then braided into rope. They used such ropes for lashing bundles of tule into rafts, tying the crook on staves for harvesting the cones of piñon, bundling firewood for transport, as pack straps and for who-knows-how-many other purposes.

Chumash Fibers and Methods

Indian hemp, sometimes referred to as red milkweed or dogbane, was the cordage material preferred by many California groups including the Chumash who called it *"tok."* Many years ago the Chumash Indian Candalaria Valenzuela told Henley and Bizzel (in Hudson and Blackburn,

1987) that tok could be found growing at *Si-top topo*, the range north of Ojai. The specific place where tok grew was *Si tok tok*. "Fine as flax," Valenzuela described it, and good for nets and fish lines. Chumash consultant Fernando Librado told Harrington they used tok string for holding together boats of wood or tule. Unlike deer sinew, it did not rot and lasted much longer. Tok was gathered near Saticoy in September but it had reached a usable state even in June, according to Librado.

The tok plant easily pulled from the ground. The top and all the leaves of the plant were removed and the bundles of stalks were brought down to camp. They dried the stalks for eight days (or sometimes they were cut dry) and pounded each bruisingly with a stick. (This was according to Harrington's consultant in the early years of this century. In the late-nineteenth century Henry Henshaw recorded that they rolled the stalk on stones to separate the fibers.) They then cleaned the fiber with their fingers removing and discarding the pieces of the tok stick. Other fibers rolled into cordage by the Chumash included milkweed (*Asclepias sp.*, also called white milkweed), nettle (*Urtica*), yucca (*Yucca whipplei*), seagrass (*Phyllospadix*) (found in sites on offshore islands) and human hair.

Yucca leaves were boiled and pounded, then rubbed and twisted to release the fiber. Luisa Ignacio Nut'u told Harrington that her mother would gather the white central leaves of the yucca and boil them in a stone mortar in an arroyo behind Mission Santa Barbara. After boiling she laid them on rocks in the arroyo and pounded them to extract the fiber for string that she used in making tule mats.

Both Chumash men and women made cordage. A few strands of clean fiber could be rolled on the fingers into a single string, but for a durable cord, two (or sometimes three or four) strands would be twisted together on the thigh.

To begin, a bunch of the fiber was doubled over, forming two strands that were then placed on the thigh and, with the hand on top of them, given a one-way motion to twist each of them at once. Next, as Librado told Harrington, the hand returned, twisting the two strands together. Sometimes they would spit on the hand or wet the hand in a dish when making the cord. As the end of a strand was reached they spliced in more fiber. Two or three of the two-ply strings in turn might be twisted together into even thicker cords or ropes. A knot was tied at the end of a finished piece of cordage to keep it from unraveling.

Luiseño Techniques

The Luiseño made line from the fiber of the Mohave yucca (*Yucca schidigera*) for use with bone or shell hooks in the ocean. The leaves were soaked in water, allowing the pulpy part to rot away.

The best fiber came from Indian hemp. One method was to pull the bark off whole and soak it in boiling water. After that, the fiber easily separated from the bark. (The Cahuilla soaked the whole stem, the fiber and bark then easily stripped off; further washing cleaned the fiber of bark.) The stems of a milkweed (*Asclepias eriocarpa*) the Luiseño soaked in boiling water to separate the fiber from the pulp. Late in the year the pulp would decay and basting the stems alone did the job of separating out the fibers. Fiber was kept rolled in a ball until needed. Nettle (*Urtica halosericea*) was also used but little esteemed.

Southern Diegueño Mescal Cordage

Jim McCarty was over eighty when he described the process to Spier at Campo, California, in the early 1920s. He knew the ways of his people well. They pounded the dry mescal (*Agave deserti*) leaves on a rock and soaked them in water to free the fibers of connective tissue.

Dampened bundles of fibers, now clean, were rolled on the thigh into loose single-ply strings almost 2 feet long. In making two-ply cord, sticky mescal juice was smeared over the thigh to bind the fibers. Two of the single-ply strings were layed on the right thigh side by side, the heavier end of one next to the tapering end of the other. And while these two ends were held in the left hand, the right palm in a single movement rolled the two strands, separately twisting them for the second time on the thigh. When the left hand was released, the two separate strands sprang into a single two-ply cord. New bundles of fibers were added as strands ran out. Pulling the finished cord back and forth around a post broke off loose protruding fibers. Spanish bayonet or yucca was not used for fiber, according to McCarty, but unprocessed strips served as rope to tie poles in house or granary construction.

An Expert from Rancho Escondido

Books record skills buried by the spreading refuse of the modern throwaway world, and we

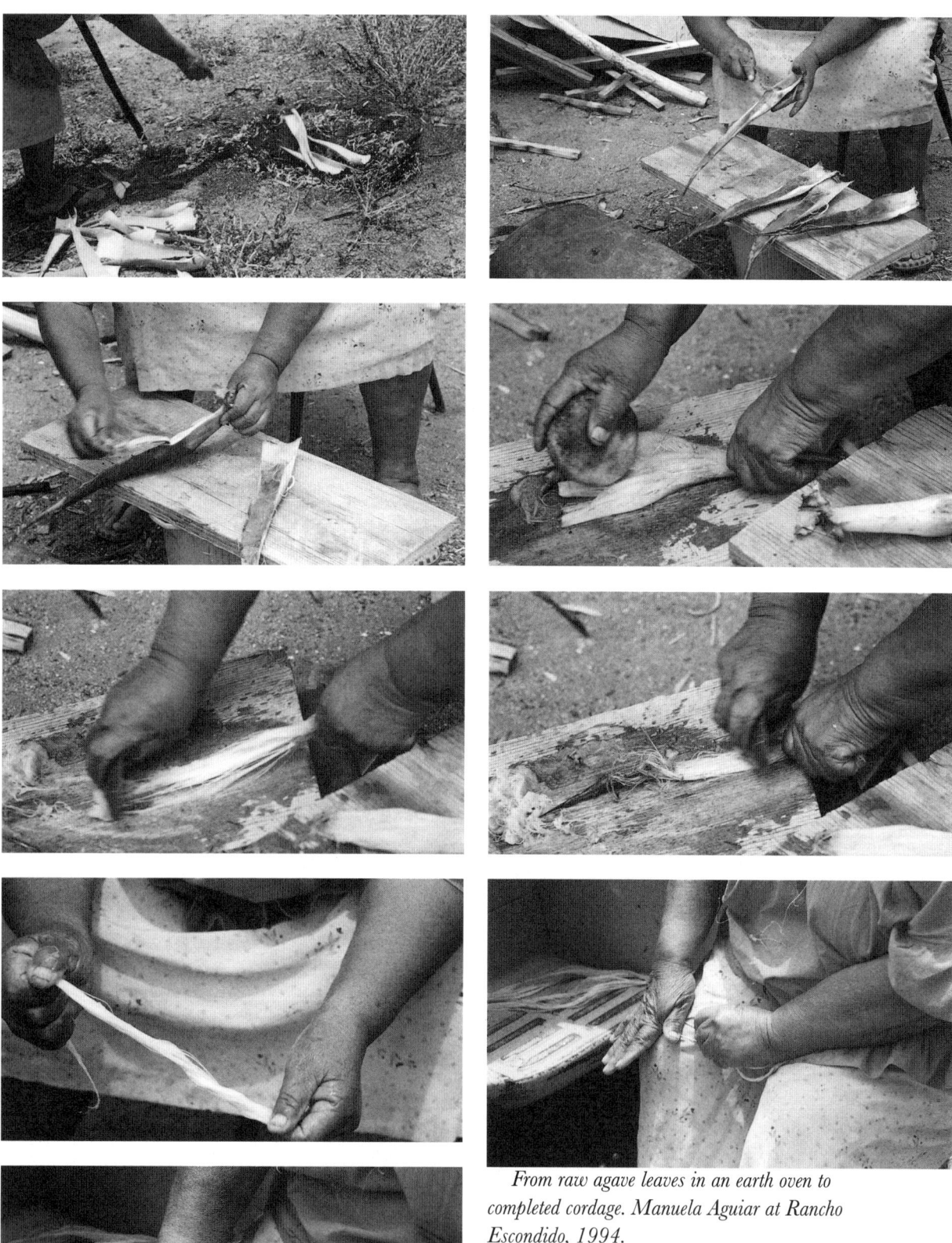

From raw agave leaves in an earth oven to completed cordage. Manuela Aguiar at Rancho Escondido, 1994.

would be much less without them. Yet books seem a weak substitute for the living tradition. Watching Manuela Aguiar roll cordage from the short rough fibers of the thick-leaved desert agave *(Agave deserti)*, I felt the sadness that comes in reducing to a few abstract lines the richness of reality.

Manuela had been making the last strings to draw together the traditional southern California carrying net. The raw white fiber had been extracted from the agave leaves after baking them for nearly half an hour in a shallow, hastily dug earth oven. Earlier, the plant's heart had been cut off at its base and carried to her home. Each of the sharp, heavy, light green leaves had been pulled off and, after wood scraps had been burned to coals (which took close to half an hour), about six leaves were placed in the 6-inch-deep pit and covered with a thin layer of the hot sandy soil. On top of this, additional scraps of desert wood were set ablaze.

More time would have been required for more leaves. In the late 1960s, Michelsen (1970) photographed elderly Petra Higuera, of Kuatl Kwepai lineage, cutting and processing agave leaves in the nearby Paipai village of Santa Catarina. Higuera used a scrub oak digging stick to remove the central leaves from a living agave plant. She removed them by stabbing at the base of the leaves with the stick and prying them. Older and tougher as well as tender and unopened leaves were discarded. With a stone she trimmed off edge spines and the sharp tips of the selected leaves. She transported the leaves to her home laid crosswise in an agave-fiber carrying net. She built a fire with creosote brush in a shallow pit. Since she was processing nearly two dozen leaves, she left the brush to burn about two hours into a deep bed of coals. Small logs of scrub oak added toward the end were removed, partially burned, and the coals pushed to the ends of the pit. The agave leaves were laid in the pit in two rows with the base of the leaves in each row meeting at the central axis of the pit. Primarily, over this central line, the leaves were covered with coals and buried with hot sand. The still-burning scrub oak logs that had been removed and additional brush were laid on top. Higuera left the leaves in the oven overnight.

Once uncovered and removed from the coals, Manuela Aguiar slipped a knife beneath the softened but tough skin of a darkened agave leaf to begin the process of removing the husk. She worked the knife back and forth, freeing large strips that she peeled off with her fingers. What remained of the leaf was soft, green, translucent pulp and strands of strong fiber that came together at the spiny tip, left intact for convenience. All the leaves were brought to this point. She then grasped each in turn by the spine end, and, resting the bulk of the leaf on a wooden board, gently pounded it with a smooth, rounded, flattish stone that fit nicely into her hand. With the stone she mashed the leaf and squeezed and pushed the liquid pulp out and away from her so that it ran down the slightly inclined board. She next scraped the remaining pulp from each bunch of fibers with an old-fashioned metal cooking spoon (explaining that as a girl she used a seashell for this) still grasping the leaf by the spine as a kind of handle. She pushed the spoon away, pressing the fiber between the edge of the spoon and the board, the concavity of the spoon facing her. She finally reversed the bundle and scraped away even the last green bit of spine that had served as the convenient handle. All she held now was a fistful of fiber.

After a short soaking in a bucket of water (Higuera would throw a palmful of ashes in a pot of warm water for this) where she rubbed one end of a doubled bundle against the other and squeezed and twisted them, each bundle in its turn, the thick strong agave fibers shown white and clean. She let the fibers dry a little in the sun.

Later she sat rolling the cordage on her right thigh as cool breezes wafted up through the ravines and hills covered with prickly pear cactus, cholla, agave and manzanita as far as the eye could see. From her brother's nearby thatch-covered house, a thin silent plume of smoke rose like a slow-motion whip against the clear blue sky. Rancho Escondido is a place beyond time. Manuela Aguiar is Southern Diegueño (Kuatl) reflecting, perhaps, the original mountain inhabitants of the area. She lives among the Paipai—the desert wanderers the Spanish missionaries brought in almost 200 years ago. The Paipai and Kuatl, both of whom speak a Yuman language, have remained together, but the Spanish missionaries who united them were sent running when the Indians destroyed the mission not long after it was built.

She took a short (perhaps 13-inch), thin bundle of agave fibers, and dampened it with a hand dipped in a little water. While holding it at one end with her left hand, she rolled the fibers away from her on her right thigh with the palm of her right hand. She would repeat the rolling process, if necessary, until the fibers were tightly twisted into a short, one-ply string. The moistening helped hold the twist and, now, she set it aside and rolled a second bundle the same way. (Higuera, to protect herself from the abrasiveness of the fiber, wrapped a piece of deer hide around her shin where she rolled the cordage and kept a jar of ashes to her left that she used as a lubricant to shield her hands. Aguiar rolled the cordage on her bare thigh, unless I was present, in which case modesty required that she use her skirt. I have seen a Yurok man roll cordage on blue jeans—generally my own preference.)

Step-by-step rigid order seemed not to dictate. Manuela Aguiar was not following rote routine, but engaged in working toward an ideal. Each bundle of fibers was unique. *One* might require a little twist with the fingers, another, an extra roll at one end with a little more moistening.

She held the two twisted bundles together in her left hand at the same end as before. She placed the strands on her thigh, keeping the two yarns perhaps an inch apart and rolled again forcefully with her palm away from her body with both strands side by side, at once tightening the twist of each. (If the previous twisting had loosened too much she might first do the two strands singly again while still holding them together in the left hand.) As her hand reached the end of the roll it abruptly pivoted clockwise, swinging the left side in an arc that caught the lower strand and carried it up against the upper strand. Then, with the two strings close together on her thigh, she released the hold with her left hand on the left end, maintaining her hold on the right between palm and thigh and watched the two strands twist together into a single string. Again, gripping at the left, she returned or pulled her right palm toward her over the two-ply string, increasing its twist. She might even repeat this latter motion or take the string in both hands and give it an extra twist or two with her fingers, always working toward the ideal cord.

As the two strands were rolled into one on her thigh, the dangling ends of strands on her right often twisted together in the opposite direction; Manuela had no special trick to avoid this. She simply had to insert her fingers between the completed cordage and the counter-twist and gently pull it back out into two strands before proceeding.

She grasped the string firmly between the thumb and forefinger of her left hand about 5 or 6 inches farther down where the two strands diverged from the single two-ply cord she had made, at once separating the two yarns and preventing unraveling of the single cord that was completed. She straightened the single-ply elements and repeated the rolling process with the remaining portions of the two strands.

The short agave fibers became absorbed into the growing two-ply cord and more were spliced in. As in the beginning, each new bundle was first moistened and twisted separately on her thigh. The fibers of a new bundle were then intermeshed or overlapped a little (an inch or two) with one of the existing strands and twisted tight with a firm palm roll away from her body on her thigh, thus joining the two sections. The process was repeated with the second strand and then both were twisted further at the same time, parallel and an inch or so apart, with a roll of the palm away from her body as in the beginning. They were then joined into the single two-ply cord by the abrupt pivoting of her right hand, the release of the grasp of her left hand, and in the return roll toward her body—a roll sometimes repeated to tighten the cord. Finally, Manuela gave the spliced area of the completed cord a smart test jerk with both hands.

No special attempt was made to stagger the splices. Each was grafted onto a strand firmly by itself in the tight twist given in the palm rolls away from her body. In fact, bowstrings of single-ply agave fiber made by Manuela for her brother Celso's bows held perfectly, even under great tension, over long periods of time. (I have had one of his bows tightly strung with single-ply agave cordage for over two years.)

The growing cordage was wound into a ball. Importantly, the pivoting of the right hand and release of the left hand continued to join the strands into a single cord, enabling the return roll of the palm to tighten the two-ply string. Otherwise, the return roll would simply reverse or undo the twists just given each yarn. The roll might be repeated. Sometimes a repeated roll was used to tighten up a length of a foot or more. When Manuela's thigh grew red and raw, she shifted to the other thigh and finally to her shin, continuing to roll the cordage there. It was all toward the end of completed perfect string. Protruding short fiber ends were cut off with small scissors, although Aguiar was aware of the method of singeing the cord that had been used by Higuera.

Traps

Selecting some trail where the deer passed frequently, they would, with no other implements but fire-hardened sticks, excavate pits ten or twelve feet deep and carry all the earth away out of sight in baskets. Then they would cover the pits with thin layers of brushwood and grass, sprinkle earth all over, scatter dead leaves and twigs on the earth, restore the trail across it, and even print tracks in it with a deer's hoof; then back out and conceal their own tracks.

The pitfalls, described by Powers over one hundred years ago, were so numerous along the banks of the river where the deer came down to drink that the early European-American settlers of northern California called it the Pit River. They dubbed the people the Pit River Indians, also known as the Achomawi. Traps of the California Indian ranged from heavy rope snares and huge pits for deer and antelope (the Kiliwa trapped migrating antelope in pits) to nets 4 feet high by over a thousand feet long (employed by many in tribal rabbit drives), to the simple rock deadfall on the unsuspecting squirrel and the light-string bird snare. The larger traps were obviously communal undertakings, but the construction of small rock deadfalls and string snares still today might be useful to the intrepid deep woods adventurer seeking an alternative to freeze-dried quiche.

Indian traps were simple only in their elegance for they exhibited considerable mechanical sophistication, required intimate knowledge of animal ways, and demanded uncommon patience. A trap works on the principle of probability. Though the odds were much better than with the remote longshot of the modern California lottery, traps were always a gamble. Expert craftsmanship and deft placement improved probability. So did numbers. It was said that a Miwok hunter could set out 200 snares in a single day. Not an easy task, but many well-placed traps insured a catch. Cordage, twigs, a springy sapling, bait—from these the snare was set. To lay a deadfall required even less.

Snares

Barrett and Gifford illustrated and briefly described the Miwok bird snare. The noose, formed by the cord passing through a loop, had a trigger stick tied a few inches from the loop (on the loop end of the string lest it tangle in the loop when the trap was sprung). When set, the trigger rested on an acorn in the center of the noose that was held spread on the ground by means of four small vertical sticks driven in the dirt. A fifth small stick, notched as shown and driven into the ground, held the trigger until it was dislodged by the pecking of a bird at the acorn. The far end of the string was tied to a bent spring pole that, when sprung, would catch the bird in the constricting noose and hoist it into the air.

The hunter visited his traps frequently and removed all of his ensnared birds before nightfall. If he did not, coyotes would eat them and destroy the traps in the process. Pigeons, jays, red-shafted flickers and a red-breasted bird were generally found in the traps—a basketful in a day if enough snares had been set.

Miwok spring snare and brush fence snare (Barrett and Gifford, 1933).

The Yokuts set a spring trap on the trails of quail, cottontail rabbits, ducks and geese. Sam Garfield explained to Gayton that they tied a string of Indian hemp to the tip of a supple limb that either grew naturally at the side of the trail or had been stuck in the ground for that purpose. They made a noose at the end of the string and tied the cord to a horizontal bar pegged about 6 inches from the ground. (Presumably, two pegs were driven into the earth securely at either side of the trail. Slight notches to hold the horizontal crosspiece under tension from the bent-over sapling would have to be cut in the pegs—small protuberances might also work. The ends of the bar would be placed in the notches or under the protuberances that, most advantageously, would face the trail so the bar could be dislodged by a creature going in either direction.) The struggling of the quarry caught in the noose while running the trail released the horizontal bar and the animal flew upward with the bowed branch.

Quail or band-tailed pigeons were taken in a brush fence snare by the Miwok. The fence was built to suit the situation but generally stood 3 feet high and was constructed of stakes driven into the ground with brush and twigs woven among them. It was often built close to a spring or around one, in which case a brush roof was built over the spring, and other nearby sources of water were concealed with fine grass or pine needles. To reach the water, birds were forced to pass through openings in the fence that were 5 to 10 feet apart. In these openings the Miwok set their snares.

They were made of human hair twisted into a fine strong thread. The snare had a small loop at one end through which the other end passed to form a noose. The noose hung from a pair of crossed sticks. It was lightly tied to the point where the sticks crossed, or to just one of the sticks, or looped over slight notches cut on the sides of the sticks. The purpose was only to spread the noose and keep it open until it was pulled away by the quarry. The other end of the snare cord was firmly tied to a nearby branch or stake. The head, wing or foot of the bird would get caught in the noose and as the animal tried to escape, it closed ever tighter.

Many other slip-noose traps of various cordage materials—with or without triggers, bait or bent spring saplings, for rabbits, squirrels, packrats, wildcats, quail and other game—are mentioned in early California ethnographies. Unfortunately, they were either poorly remembered or inadequately described and most cannot be exactly reproduced from the information given. However, the principles remain fairly constant with only the size of the trap varying according to the quarry.

The Southern Miwok, for example, took deer in snares similar to those for quail only much heavier and stronger. They made a V-shaped brush fence with a small corral at the angle of the V. In the corral, three or four openings were made. Snares were set in these openings and anchored to a tree or heavy log (which allowed the deer to run a short distance). The men concealed themselves in small pits near the entrance of the corral and jumped out to cut off retreat as the deer entered. When the deer bolted for an opening it became ensnared. The snare rope was long enough to allow the deer to move about a little, lest it pull apart with so powerful an animal panicked in close confinement. At any rate, men were present to quickly kill the ensnared deer with arrows or clubs before the animals could break loose and escape.

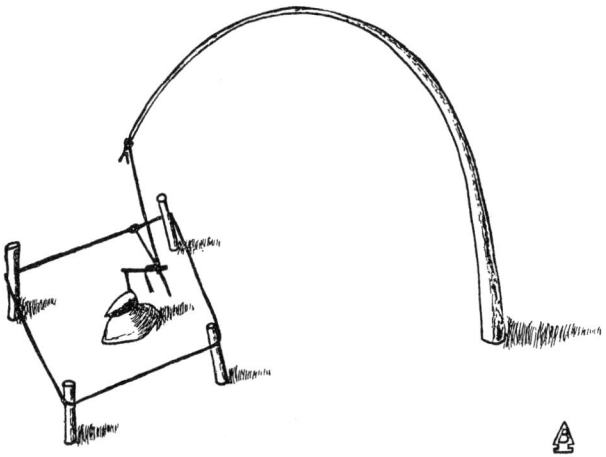

Pomo string snare. Used without a fence. Small arch held trigger, which was attached to drawstring. Four pegs spread the noose. The end of the trigger rested on a small vertical stick atop an acorn or other bait, often supported in turn by a small mound of earth. Birds such as bluejays pecked at the bait and were hoisted in the air by the neck. J. P. Harrington photographed a similar snare among the Karok. Width of the arch was over three times larger than and outside a small noose that was not pegged; the noose encircled a small depression in the ground. A fairly large trigger stick, held by the arch, pushed downward on an upright vertical stick pin, under which in the depression would have been bait. None was discernible in the photograph unless it was salt. To get to the bait, the critter would have had to stick its head in the noose. When sprung, the noose, attached to the trigger stick as in the Pomo trap, was pulled under the arch and into the air (drawing from Barrett, 1952).

Michelsen recorded an interesting trapping trick used among the Kiliwa and Paipai who frequently followed the common California practice of setting nets to catch rabbits. They made artificial rabbit trails. A file of Paipai or Kiliwa Indians marched through the grass and brush to the trapping area. Rabbits, in turn, followed the new trails unsuspectingly into the traps. Many clever ruses there must have been to put meat on a hearth before cattle trampled the land.

Smoke

The Yokuts most commonly used smoke to catch ground squirrels. They forced them out or stupefied them by plugging the entries of their burrows with grass that was set ablaze. They kept the grass burning with air from a feather fire fan. The animals tried to escape or get air at openings and were dragged out with a flexible stick about 50 inches long with a hooked end that was used for rodents in general. The squirrels were seized and their necks were broken.

Gayton's recording of the Monache technique is more complete. The vegetation was first removed from the entrances to the runways. Dried grass or weeds of any kind were tightly stuffed in the holes. A large area would be treated like this with about six holes left open in the center. The grass was lit and men or boys went around fanning the holes with feather fire fans made of hawk or buzzard tail feathers on a foot-long handle. Soon smoke would waft from the open holes and squirrels staggered out to be seized and have their necks wrung. The hunters heard squeaks and commotion underground—then silence. At that point the holes were excavated to remove the squirrels that had suffocated. The same method was sometimes used for cottontails.

Deadfalls

The Monache smoked ground squirrels out of their burrows or, in the manner of the Yokuts, pulled rabbits and rats out with a flexible hooked stick. But as Gayton recorded, the most frequent method for taking weasels, squirrels, packrats, mice, cottontail rabbits and almost any

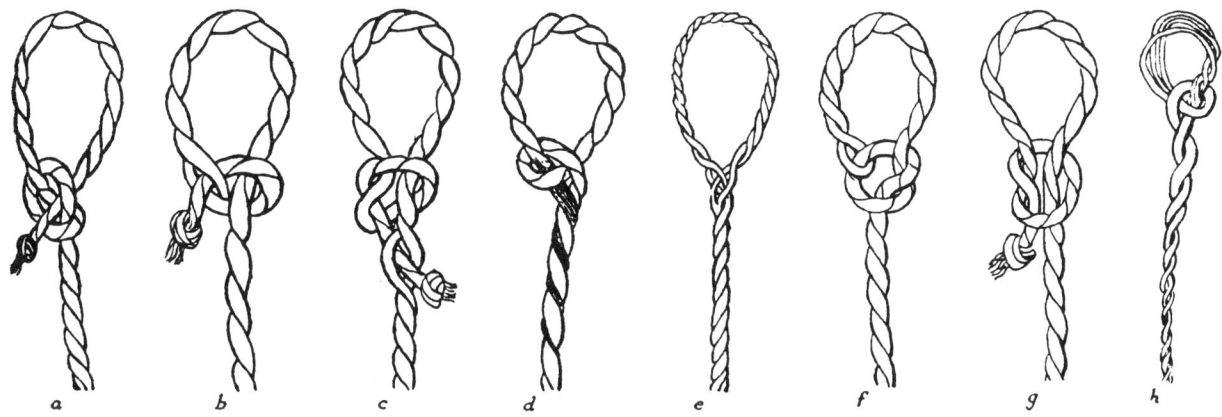

Loops of cord snares preserved in caves of the Southwest. C. B. Cosgrove found them during the Harvard Peabody Museum archaeological campaigns of the 1920s and early 1930s. From Basketmaker through Pueblo and even into modern times—the sliding-noose snare was of great antiquity and wide distribution. Those from Chávez Cave in southeastern New Mexico were of yucca fiber while those from nearby Ceremonial Cave were of Indian hemp (Apocynum). Lengths varied from 3 feet 3 inches to 4 feet 9 inches with center diameter from 3/32 to 5/32 of an inch. (Type "h" was from Ceremonial Cave, had a very short length and may have been some sort of trigger cord.) In 1877 E. Palmer found 121 noose snares in a Pueblo III corrugated olla in a cave near Johnson, Utah. With the exception of types "a" and "h," all of the above loops were represented; half had type "e." Lengths were from 6 feet 3 inches to 11 feet 2 inches. As in the other snares found, the ends were completed with an overhand knot. Fragments of a species of hair-like Cuscuta (possibly denticulata) were tied to nearly every one, likely as "spreaders" to suspend the loops from brush or sticks set in the ground; fresh, the fragments would have easily broken away when the trap was sprung. Forty-eight sliding-noose snares from a Basketmaker II cache in a cave in Adugegi Canyon in northwestern Arizona had attached to each a wooden toggle. Palmer collected a snare from the Paiute in 1875, knotted at the ends (as in the archaeological examples) and with a type "a" loop. Note the running-noose loops of "b" and "g"—perhaps to tighten after the trap has sprung to keep the noose around the animal (Cosgrove, 1947).

other small game was the simple deadfall trap. The Monache version consisted of utilizing four parts: a large, flat, upper stone propped at an angle by a forked stick whose bottom end pressed against an acorn on a flat stone base. The trigger was the acorn. When the little critter nibbled at it, a delicate balance was upset and the sky fell.

Spier described the same trap for the Southern Diegueño but did not mention a stone base. The Luiseño also took woodrats and ground squirrels with the deadfall of two flat stones baited and triggered with a short stick on top of an acorn. Mice and other smaller mammals were taken with the acorn alone. Once the acorn was gnawed through by the little rodent the stone would fall. The Luiseño described a mouse as but two mouthfuls.

In the Yokuts version of the acorn and stick deadfall the acorn was roasted. Further variations of the deadfall are reproduced here from the Western Shoshone (baited with pine nuts) and Southern Paiute (sprung by a person in hiding).

The famous Northern Paiute deadfall brought refinement. It positioned the bait at precisely the most deadly point in the crushing zone, displayed it so that it could not pass unnoticed, and collapsed at a whisker's touch—completely free of the braces that held it up. (A deadfall that comes down on its own braces has less impact on the critter beneath.) It would have been an honor to know the great trapper who invented this ingenious device. Wheat, in 1949, had the good fortune to watch Jimmy George set one. He baited it with pine nuts threaded on a trigger similar to one Captain J. H. Simpson described in 1859, as "a spear of dried grass or a delicate piece of wood." The trigger held a small stick in place under tension against the back of the main support. A string went from the center of the

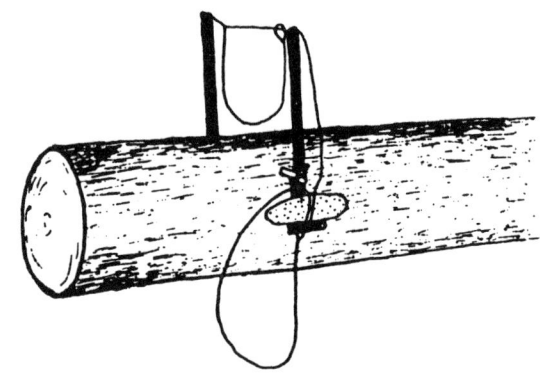

Atsugewi weighted snare. A noose was set with a trip string between two uprights on either side of a log laying across a stream. The noose ran to a heavy rock resting on a stake at the side of the log. The rock was attached to the log by a length of cord. When a coyote, fox, raccoon or other animal got caught in the noose, it would upset the rock; as the rock fell, it drew the noose tight and pulled the quarry into the water to drown. The Chumash made a weighted snare, according to J. P. Harrington's notes, in which a rock also substituted for the spring pole: the struggling quarry, caught in the noose, caused an elevated boulder tied to the other end to fall. The string had been draped on something overhead and the animal was hoisted into the air (drawing from Garth, 1953).

little stick around the front of the main support to the end of the top brace. Jimmy George still caught squirrels this way in the 1940s when he went out to gather pine nuts. As a young man he often set deadfalls for small birds and animals.

The Havasupai variation (as illustrated by Spier) had the upright support perpendicular and more distant from the rock. It was set on rodent trails with wings of brush guiding the quarry to the kill.

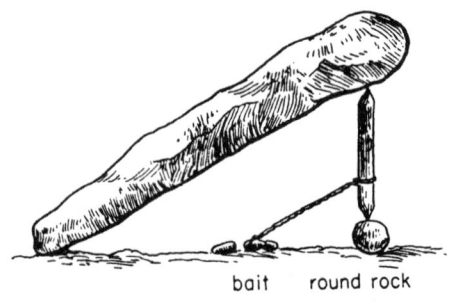
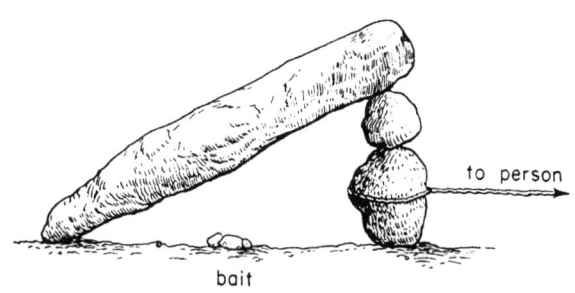

Deadfall traps: First has stick support on round rock with cord to pine nut bait. Western Shoshone. Second is made to fall by a person in hiding. Southern Paiute (after Steward in Fowler, 1986).

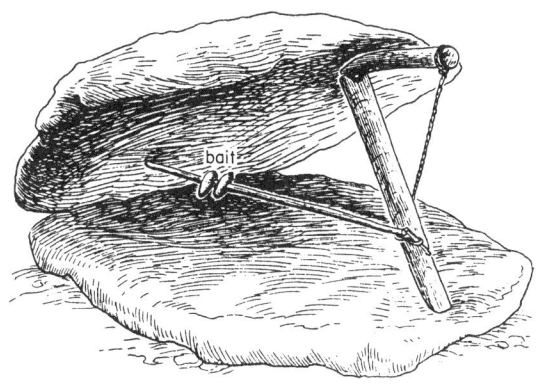

Paiute deadfall. Drawn from Jimmy George's trap, which was like this, but without the base rock and with the trigger on the opposite side. Rock should fall free of braces (Fowler, 1986).

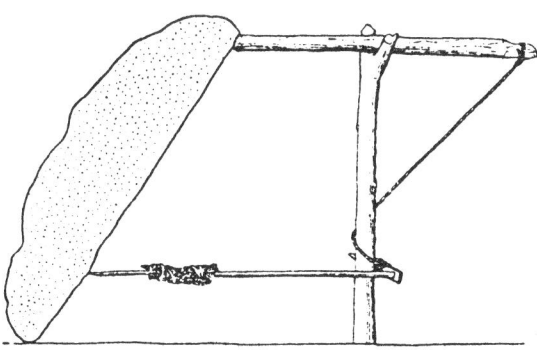

The Havasupai deadfall (Spier, 1928)

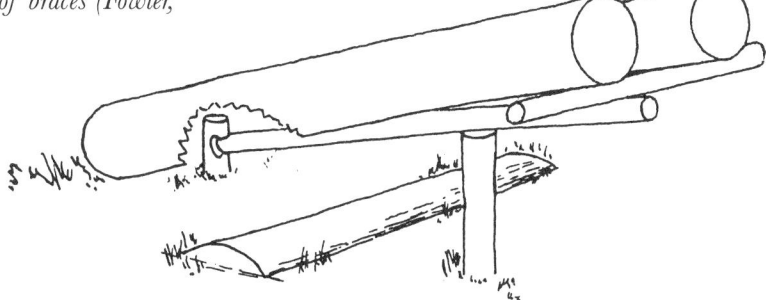

Mohave log deadfall. Heavy logs rested on a cross bar that in turn rested on a trigger pole set on a short post or fulcrum. A coyote or fox, tugging at fish bait tied to the lower end of the trigger pole, would dislodge the pole from the notch of the stake between the logs on the ground. A half-buried transverse log made certain the animal would be crushed (Spier, 1955).

The box trap for quail. Made of elderberry, mulefat or arrowweed sticks. Split prop has scarf joint at middle. Benito Aldama Jat'am, Kumeyaay of La Huerta, remembers his uncle Antonio Vaquero Aldama telling him that sometimes so many quail become trapped under the box they fly away with it. The Maricopa and Mohave also had this trap, according to Spier and Stewart. Spier found them made of arrowweed with the ends of a single string tied to the two lower corners and the middle stretched over the lower prop piece at about its midpoint. Seed beneath the box baited the trap. When the birds tripped the string, the unstable prop split and the box fell and trapped the birds. Andres Albáñez, a Southern Diegueño (Kumeyaay) of Santa Catarina, said that the string could be tied to the prop and the other end held by someone in hiding; it was pulled when the birds were under the box. The Pomo caught quail in a similar manner with a net pegged to the ground on three sides. The fourth was held open by a string that looped over a bush or limb and ran to a nearby brush shelter where the trapper hid. If one quail went under the net, soon all would follow. The string was released and the net fell on the quail and entangled them. Box trap above built by Kumeyaay María Elena León Aldama of La Huerta, 1996. Mulefat tied with yucca strips. She learned how to construct the trap from a boyfriend taught by his Yaqui grandfather. The trap is identical in form to one depicted by Spier for the Maricopa, which was said to be like that of the Mohave.

Mescal pulp tied firmly to the trigger baited the trap. Another form was known to the Tubatulabal of the Kern River in the southern Sierras of California. The ingenious Tubatulabal deadfall kept the meat fresh and safe from scavengers. It was exactly the same as the Havasupai deadfall except that a shallow hole 3 to 4 inches deep excavated between the upright post and the base of the rock imprisoned the woodrat, squirrel or bird without crushing it. Ethnographer Voegelin found that an acorn was the usual bait. As among the Northern Paiute, traps were set out during the piñon harvest (as many as twenty). Steban Miranda, near ninety when he described them to Voegelin in the 1930s, said they were checked every two days. But Voegelin forgot to ask him how he got the critter out when he found the trap was sprung!

María Elena sets the box trap.

Scissor and Vertical Noose Snares

The scissors snare is a slip-noose spring snare with mechanical advantage. Going beyond mere constriction of the prey, two loosely joined sticks turn the "noose" into a neatly levered nutcracker. Not without reason, the Mohave called the trap *cökta'vam*,— "to pinch them." The greatest pressure occurs closest to the fulcrum, or hinge, and perhaps this is why the Mohave set them vertically with the hinge on the ground as shown. Because of the lever advantage a relatively light spring pole would create deadly pressure at the hinge vertex. Spier, who did field work among the Mohave in the early 1930s, found that they used the scissor snare for large mice, rats, or kit fox.

Mechanical advantage is also accorded the trigger that acts as a lever against the fulcrum of the bar above. Since the weight of the taut string from the spring pole tugs next to the fulcrum, the far end of the trigger requires little pressure from the bait or bait stick that leans against it to hold the trigger in place. It is an easy trap to set.

An entire trapper's line of fifty-five scissor snares was found in 1971 at the Ord shelter in the south-central Mojave desert. Philip Wilke, who described and analyzed them, generously allowed me to examine the near-mint-condition traps. Judging from their appearance, one expects at any moment the trapper himself to return and claim his property, yet they have been radiocarbon dated to around A.D. 180. Likely made of chamise (*Adenostoma fasciculatum*), the 18.1 to 25 cm.-long scissor sticks were stripped of bark and, in some cases, corkscrew striations were left by a deep-biting scraping tool. The sticks measured from .4 to .6 cm. in diameter. In contrast, the triggers were often unpeeled and made from various woods. They were 7.4 to 10.1 cm. long and 2.5 to 4.0 mm. in diameter. Draw cords were tied at the end of the trigger sticks just below a natural node to prevent their slipping off. Unlike the historic Mohave snares that have the trigger stick placed about midway along the draw cord, the Ord shelter triggers were tied at the end of the cord. To be set in accordance with Spier's description of the Mohave trap, and for the same effect, the Ord shelter draw strings must be fastened to the spring pole about midway along the cord's length. The small Ord alcove, a hollowing of the underside of a huge boulder and adjoining bedrock is in an ecotone or mergence of creosote bush-low desert scrub and higher elevation sagebrush scrub. Desert cottontail, black-tailed jackrabbit, white-tailed antelope ground squirrel, desert pack rat, Merriam kangaroo rat, and various mice are common in these areas.

Cordage for the snares was two-ply, from about 1.5 to 3 mm. in diameter, and the material was, according to Wilke, divided between Indian hemp (*Apocynum sp.*) and Mojave yucca. Some snares actually had draw cords from one fiber and slip loops from the other. Many of the draw cords had snapped and been rejoined with square knots. The scissor sticks were scored a turn or two near the hinge end to hold binding that consisted of multiple turns of untwisted fiber around the two sticks, followed by more turns of fiber between the two sticks perpendicular to the first wraps until the hinge stayed open and the bindings were tight. When finished they measured about 6.5 mm. to as much as 1.1 cm. apart.

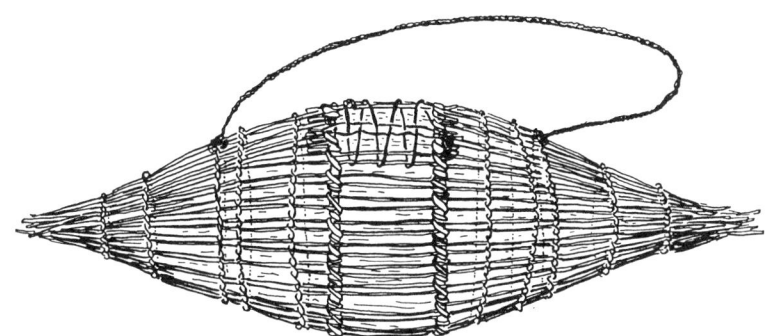

Pigeon cage twined of dogwood (sketch from Gayton, 1948). Michahai, Waksachi, Yaudanchi and other Yokuts kept up to three tame pigeons in a cage. They fed the birds cracked acorns and water and took them out as decoys, especially in late fall when pigeons flew south. Large numbers were caught with a noose about 4" in diameter, attached to the tip of a 6'-to-8' light pole they used from a blind. Michahai Yokuts Sam Osborn explained it all to Anna Gayton.

They usually placed a booth, which served as a blind, near water where the birds gathered at sunrise. It was about 8 feet long by 4 feet wide with the floor excavated about 1'. Poles of dogwood set butt end down along both 8-foot sides were tied above in a series of arcs just high enough to permit the trapper to kneel within. The arcs became lower toward the front to draw less attention. Withes tied horizontally gave the structure stability. Brush was tied on, and over this more brush and green boughs tied or thrown on, and grass laid all around the booth on the ground. Along the 4'-wide arched front, long twigs were set in the ground and the tips fastened to the arc above. One or two spaces about 12" wide were left in the front and opened directly to a circular platform 4' in diameter and 18" high of stones and earth topped by a layer of smooth sand. Manzanita brush was positioned around the edge of the platform as a barricade.

From the booth the trapper let out through the openings about six live decoys with strings tied to their legs—four from either side would be best but three per opening was sufficient, Osborn told Gayton. The birds had been kept hungry and now fed on the cracked acorns that had been scattered on the platform sand. Wild pigeons were quickly lured. The tame pigeons might be poked or jerked to cause them to flutter and draw the attention of the wild ones. Stealthily the trapper lowered the noose over the head of a bird and quickly jerked it into the booth, where he wrung its neck. They would usually catch ten to twelve birds this way. They carried them home on a stick forced through the loose skin under the necks. The decoys were carried in their cages.

Decoys might be sold but game birds never were though they might be given away. Game birds were cooked unplucked, either boiled in a pot (not a basket) or roasted in ashes.

If without decoys, a man might catch one from a blind in a tree frequented by pigeons. Leafy branches were tied in any manner possible, given the nature of the tree to make a crude blind. A beam for sitting was essential. Noose-poles were laid out in various directions, and at dawn or dusk, as the birds came to roost, one was snared with the pole most convenient. The bird now could be used as a decoy from the blind on the ground.

Waksachi Yokuts Bob Osborn said some people kept doves in these cages as pets as well as for decoys. They tamed them by holding them between the knees and pulling out a few tail feathers. They set the feathers afire and by the feet held the bird head down in the smoke for a few minutes. After this, the bird was fed acorn meal, which it at once vomited. "Then that bird was always tame," said Osborn.

A draw cord measured from 64 to 112 cm. in length. It emerged from beneath multiple wrappings of cordage around 2 cm. from the top of one scissor stick in each pair and passed through a cordage loop emerging at the lower end of similar multiple turns near the top of the second stick. There was no scoring at this end of the sticks and the loop and draw cord were held by the wound cord alone. Close scrutiny revealed that generally the draw cord was simply tied near its end in a tight overhand knot on the stick and the short end wrapped around and up the stick a half-dozen turns or so and secured with at least one half-hitch. The loop of the second stick was made by lowering a long loop or U from one end of a short cord down from near the top of the stick, then, with the other end of the cord, wrapping round and round, from near the top, covering the loop with perhaps a half-dozen turns, working down, until approximately 1 cm. of the extended loop remained (it had an approximately 2 cm. circumference). At this point, the windings were terminated again by tucking the cord under the last turn. The ending of the cord on both this and the draw cord stick was difficult to distinguish because the cordage thinned and, often, for most of the helix, it had been the mere untwisted fiber commonly found at the termination of unfinished or unknotted cords. I discovered through experimentation with this sort of knot, that after completion, twisting the last turn of the stack in the direction of the wind tightens and secures the whole knot.

The Ord shelter snares came in two joined bundles. One consisted of seventeen scissor snares and one noose snare; the other had thirty-eight scissor snares and one noose snare. The snare sticks in each bundle were collapsed; the snare had been laid on the bundle and the draw cord of each snare wrapped around all the sticks in the bundle to that point. The trigger was inserted under the wrappings of its own draw cord. Snares were added and taken off one at a time as would be expected on a trapline. The hinged ends were all on the same side in each bundle so that, when the bundles were joined, they were reversed to even the combined bundles, and the whole was wrapped with heavy yucca cordage. Another bundle from the cache, wrapped in bark, contained three larger scissor snares around 35 cm. in length.

Similar-sized scissor snares, from a cave in Castro Canyon in the Chumash area of California, described by Hudson and Blackburn, utilized a natural "Y" or fork in one stick of each pair in place of the loop found at the end of the Mohave stick. The Y was closed off with cordage to form the "loop." These forked sticks averaged 38 cm. in length and the other of each pair a bit longer—43 cm. They were about 1 cm. in diameter. Near the bottom, grooves provided a grip for three slack loops of two-ply cordage, likely of Indian hemp, around both sticks. On the fourth turn the string was brought perpendicular between the sticks for a series of close frapping coils tightening the loose wrap and terminating in a half hitch.

Barrett found that the Pomo set a double arch trap not bent at right angles in the Mohave fashion but simply two arched parallel sticks in the runways of ground squirrels and field mice. Instead of the scissor snare between the arches, a vertical slip noose was tied with very weak fiber (such as tule bark so that the ties would break when the trap was sprung) at various points to one of the arches and to two small pegs between the arches on the ground. A horizontal bar was held just off the ground to the outside of one of the arches by the pressure of a vertical trigger stick. Pulling against the bar, and a side of the arch just above it, the trigger was fastened

Maggie Icho, a Wukchumni Yokuts, carries a pigeon cage. Photograph by Clifford Relander, 1945 (Southwest Museum).

at its center to the draw cord as the cord left the loop of the snare and continued to the end of a spring pole. An animal passing through the arches depressed the horizontal bar tripping the trigger pin. The slip noose tightened and choked the animal against the two arches whose resistance permitted the spring pole to maintain a continuous deadly pressure, as in the Mohave trap. Size of the trap depended on the animal sought. Arches for the ground squirrel, for example, spanned five inches.

The importance of small mammals, such as ground squirrels, as an aboriginal food source may be underestimated. Since the whole animal was used, including bones that were often pulverized, Joel Janetski concluded that rodents and other small mammals may be underrepresented in archaeologists' reconstructions of early Indian diets. Janetski emphasized that the sheer numbers (as many as 4,600 per square kilometer in western Nevada, according to some experts) and their peak seasons (early spring to middle summer for ground squirrels), which coincide in some areas, such as the Great Basin, with depleted winter stores, suggest likely high utilization of this easily gathered meat.

In tule wetlands the Pomo trapped waterfowl with the slip noose, trigger, bar and spring pole but utilized only a single arch. They planted a tule fence in the mud and made frequent openings for basketry and snare traps. The light horizontal bar in the snare was held on the surface of the water by the near vertical trigger stick placed well to the side and under pressure from the spring pole as before. The upper end of the trigger met the arch; the lower pressed on the horizontal bar. The arch, projecting 4 or 5 inches above the water with a width of 10 to 12 inches, had been planted in the mud and tied to the tule. The slip noose was attached at several points to the arch with weak tule bark fiber. When a bird swam from either direction against the crossbar and depressed it, the trigger pin released and the pole pulled the pin and slip noose up (which easily broke from the arch), catching the bird by the neck.

Treadle Snare

With the perpendicular trigger stick nudged to the center of the crossbar and to the top of the arch, the basis of a Pomo treadle snare was created. It lacked only the treadle bars to complete it. As in double- and single-arch traps, tension from the bent pole pulled the drawstring which, in turn, pulled the trigger against the crossbar and arch. This held the crossbar to the arch. The Pomo arch was 4 inches high and 5 inches wide.

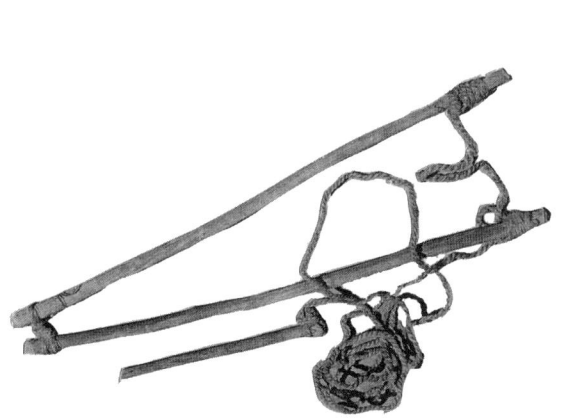 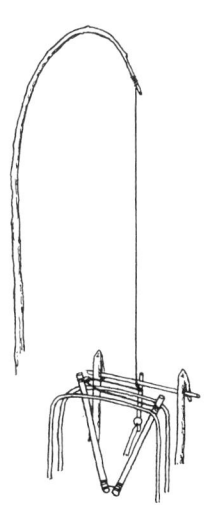 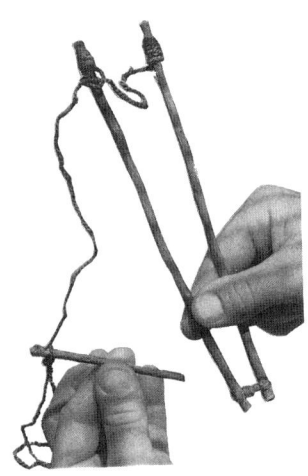

Mohave scissor trap. A pole spring, a couple of bent branches to guide and hold the snare vertical, a small stick for a trigger bar and some nearby stakes or bushes to fix the bar, bait—a little imagination and natural materials at hand will produce these or equivalents. The Mohave completed the setup with an arrowweed fence on either side of the trap (which was placed directly in the animals runway) forcing the quarry through the arches to the bait. The small slanting bait stick held a pumpkin seed on its pointed tip. This, along with the trigger and the horizontal rod and two stakes, had to be close to the two arches so the animal would be between the scissor when it nibbled the morsel and upset the trigger stick. The snare would jerk closed and upward and squeeze the animal between the scissors and against the top of the arches. The scissor trap kills by incremental squeezing, suggests Philip Wilke. When sprung, it likely catches the animal behind the front legs, and with every exhalation of the critter, the trap tightens its grip, not relaxing what it has gained. Drawing is of a Mohave trap in Spier, 1955. Photos are of an Ord shelter trap.

Treadle bars inclined from the crossbar to the ground on the same side as the end of the spring pole. The noose was formed from the draw cord after it came off the trigger where it was firmly tied. Four pegs spread the noose on the treadle and guarded against its being dislodged by a breeze. They slanted inwardly to allow the noose to slip off when the trap was sprung. The treadle snare, along with basketry and net traps, were generally set in openings of a long brush fence about a foot high. The fence followed the natural line of the brush where valley quail regularly descended into lower regions. In angles or Vs and at other points, traps were placed. The treadle bars (about 9 inches long) inclined directly opposite and *parallel* to the opening in the fence. To step on the treadle was to step inside the noose. The treadle bar depressed the crossbar and sprung the trap, hoisting the bird by its legs.

Barrett learned that the trapper visited his traps about mid-forenoon and again after sundown. It was the habit of valley quail to leave the brush in early morning and early evening. Sometimes other birds got caught in the traps and frequently so did cottontail rabbits or various other small mammals. The treadle snare, along with regular vertical snares, only rarely occupied gaps of the long rabbit brush fence that was built out in the open and had acute angle wings at either end to turn animals back into the trapping zone. The Pomo treadle was adequate for cottontails but not considered strong enough for jackrabbits.

Rabbits, quail, raccoons and beaver were taken in the treadle snare by the Mohave. Spier recorded that they used a dry willow for the spring pole. Six treadle bars were needed for quail and cottontail rabbits. Larger animals required only four. Fences guided the quarry to the side of the treadle platform.

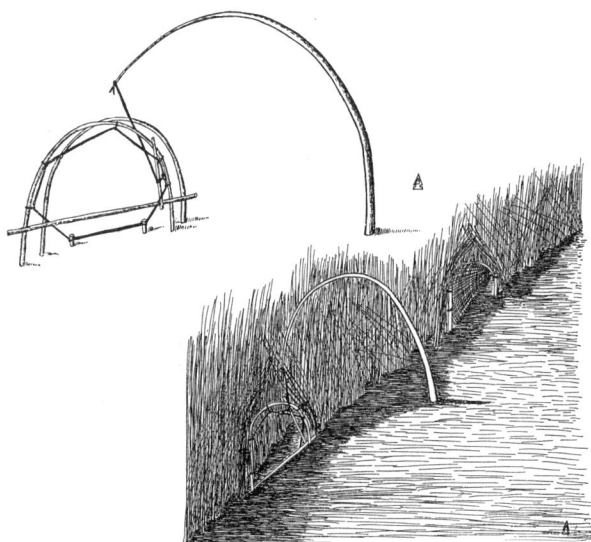

Pomo double-arch snare for ground squirrels and field mice (Barrett, 1952).

Pomo single-arch snare and basketry trap in tule fence (Barrett, 1952).

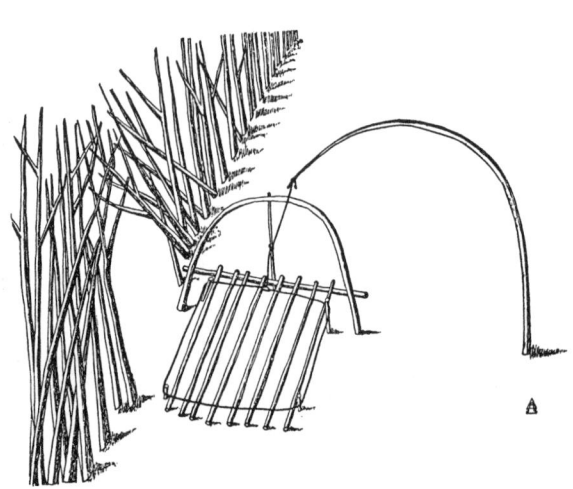

Pomo treadle snare (Barrett, 1952).

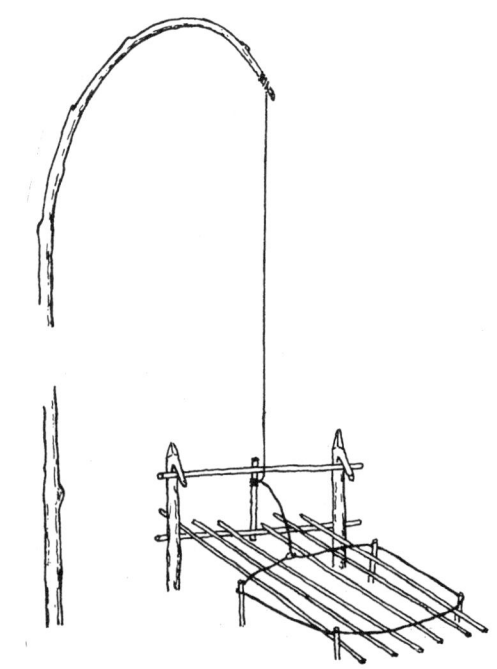

Mohave treadle snare (Spier, 1955).

California Digging Stick

Europeans who encountered the original inhabitants of the far west laughed and called them "diggers." But the simple sharpened stick with which these Indians dug ovens, postholes, and graves, and harvested roots, bulbs, corms, and mescal was a staff we might well reconsider. By merely loosening and aerating the soil a little to free a useful root, the digging stick provided for an easy renewable collection of wild food for millennia. Sodbusting plows and back-breaking labor destroyed all that. The seemingly endless birds and wildflowers, the great valley lakes and forests, the antelope and elk, the soil itself, are now largely gone. To feed ever growing masses, California's Great Central Valley even drains northern rivers in the limitless pursuit of cheap mega crops. Millions of tons of lethal herbicide, insecticide and fertilizer, and tens of thousands of impoverished workers, who drudge from sunup to sundown, complete the modern picture of European progress. Future historians will unlikely laugh at the Native California men and women who gently dug and maintained their natural garden for so long.

In northern California the digging stick was largely the province of women, who would sit or kneel, Walter Goldschmidt wrote of the Nomlaki, as they stabbed the sharpened mountain mahogany stick into the ground to uproot a plant. In the South, with the harvesting of mescal and planting of corn and other agricultural crops along the Colorado River, men were the primary users of the stick. Barrows, in his work of a hundred years ago, discounted the southern digging stick entirely. He wrote that among the Cahuilla, the woman's seed-fan or beater "takes the place of the pointed fire-hardened digging stick of the North." He held strongly to the idea that "as among all Indians, the woman is the getter of vegetable foods." Though perhaps the stick dug fewer roots in the South and the seed-beater harvested more seeds, the digging stick had not lost importance. It had simply been adapted to other environments. Its use by the men to harvest mescal and dig fields of corn led the stick itself to undergo a transformation.

From northern and central California to southern and Lower California, California's Natives fabricated and held the stick in similar ways, and even the different products of the digging stick were often baked similarly in an earth oven. The continuum from the manufacture of the stick to the breaking of soil and the collecting of plants for the preparation of food will be explored from north to south among representative California tribes. It suggests a unified process applied to changing biological regions and reveals some most surprising applications of this ancient tool.

Hupa

Hupa women of northern California dug bulbs with a pointed stick. Goddard found that men would sometimes accompany them to keep the point sharp with stone knives. The largest and most plentiful bulb was the soaproot *(Chlorogalum pomeridianum)*, which they cooked in an earth oven for about two days. A large pit was dug, lined with rocks and a fire built and maintained until the oven was well heated. Then they removed the fire and lined the pit with the leaves of wild grape *(Vitis californica)* and wood sorrel *(Oxalis oregana)*, which they also intermixed with the bulbs. More leaves were placed on top and the oven was covered with earth. Over this, a big fire was built. The leaves were said to improve the flavor of the soaproot bulbs, described as an agreeable and nourishing food.

Andres Albáñez and grandchildren.

Additional bulbs used by the Hupa, according to Goddard, were mariposa lily *(Calochortus maweanus)*, Ithuriel's spear *(Triteleia laxa)*, ookow *(Dichelostemma pulchellum* or *congestum)*, wild hyacinth *(Dichelostemma multiflorum)* and *Brodiaea*. These were roasted in ashes or boiled in baskets. Not mentioned for the Hupa but included in a list by Thomas Garth for the Atsugewi, who lived to the east, were the bulbs or roots of Lewis's lomatium *(Lomatium triternatum)* and the leopard lily *(Lilium pardalinum)*. They were baked between layers of pine needles in the earth oven.

Pomo

A little farther to the south, the Pomo digging stick that Barrett described was usually made of a hardwood such as mountain mahogany *(Cercocarpus betuloides)*—about the size of an ordinary walking stick, nearly a meter long, about 2 cm. thick. It was somewhat rounded at the handle end and at the bottom and sharpened and hardened by burning.

As a general utility implement, the digging stick was used mainly by women for digging roots, bulbs, tubers and corms. "The superabundance in aboriginal times, of this class of plants in Pomo country provided the Indians with an inexhaustible supply of these foods," wrote Barrett, and they could be gathered with relative ease by use of the digging stick. Many were eaten raw, while others were cooked in the ashes and coals of the fire, and separated from the ashes with an openwork-basketry sieve. The favorite method of preparation was baking items in an underground oven. Barrett lists the so-called "Indian potatoes" of the Pomo.

Anise *(Carum gairdneri)*: Tubers and fleshy roots were eaten raw, made into pinole or cooked like acorn bread. The seeds were also used as pinole and the top of the plant when fresh in the spring was eaten as a green.

Snake root *(Sanicula tuberosa)*: Tuberous roots were eaten raw.

Arrowleaf or duck potato *(Sagittaria latifolia)*: Potato-like tubers were eaten from this plant.

Snake lily *(Brodiaea volubilis)*: Bulbs were eaten.

Cattail *(Typha sp.)*: Roots and the bases of stems were eaten.

Wild onion *(Allium unifolium)*: Bulbs and bases of leaves were usually eaten raw like salad but sometimes they were baked in an underground oven alone or as seasoning with other bulbs.

Cat's ears *(Calochortus sp.)*: Corms were eaten.

Globe tulip *(Calochortus albus)*: Corms were eaten raw or roasted in ashes.

White mariposa lily *(Calochortus venustus.)*: Corms, said to be very sweet, were excellent "potatoes."

Shooting star or mosquito bill, probably padre's shooting star *(Dodecatheon clevelandii)*: Roots and leaves were roasted in ashes.

Harvest brodiaea *(Brodiaea coronaria)*: Corms roasted for a day were very sweet.

Blue dicks *(Dichelostemma pulchellum)*: Corms were eaten raw but were sweeter when cooked in ashes.

White brodiaea *(Triteleia hyacinthina)*: Bulbs were either eaten raw or cooked.

Blue flowered brodiaea or wally basket *(Triteleia laxa)*: Bulbs were an excellent "potato."

White-flowered brodiaea or long-rayed hyacinth *(Triteleia peduncularis)*: Bulbs were eaten.

Camas *(Camassia quamash)*: Bulbs roasted in an earth oven made an excellent food.

Gold nuggets *(Calochortus luteus, var. oculatus)*: Bulbs were eaten.

There were many other "wild potatoes." Some were considered unsafe to eat because they caused an emetic effect.

The Pomo digging stick also provided roots for making baskets, and it could even pry abalone off rocks, although a special chisel might be made from whalebone for this purpose. An ordinary digging stick or a slightly larger version was also used to make the excavation for the semi-subterranean dance house and sudatory. Young men loosened the dirt with the stick while women and older men carried the loosened soil out in baskets. With the digging stick men also dug roots for luck in hunting and fishing, but especially in gambling after their luck had been bad. They believed that the angelica root held special powers for the gambler.

The ordinary digging stick could be employed for gathering angleworms, but one much larger was preferred. The sharp point was inserted into the earth and woven back and forth and around. This agitated the soil for some distance causing the worms to crawl out onto the surface. To the north, the Bear River people made a soup of angleworms. Sometimes black caterpillars were added and sometimes the two were used separately for soup. The Yuki, neighbors of the Pomo, made a rich angleworm soup and undoubtedly the Pomo did as well. They added hot rocks with wooden tongs to the soup in a cooking basket so that it would boil, constantly stirring with a paddle to prevent burning. This is how the Pomo generally made soup, gruel or mush.

Yuki

Stephen Powers, California's first ethnographer, best described angleworm collection and soup among the Yuki in the early 1870s.

"When rain falls in autumn enough to give the earth a good soaking, and the angleworms begin to come to the surface, then the Yuki housekeeper turns her mind to a good basket of worm-soup. Armed with her 'woman-stick,' the badge of her sex—which is a pole about six feet long and one and a half inches thick, sharpened and fire-hardened at one end—she seeks out a piece of rich, moist soil, and sets to work. Thrusting the pole into the ground about a foot, she turns it around in every direction, and so agitates the earth that the worms come to the surface in large numbers for a radius of two or three feet around. She gathers and carries them home, and cooks them into a rich and oily soup, an aboriginal vermicelli, which is much esteemed by the good wife's family."

Washo

The digging stick was used as a weapon—at least once. Jedediah Strong Smith (Brooks, 1977), the first American to enter California overland, upon descending the Sierra Nevada through Washo territory in 1827, surprised two Indian ladies by coming so close to one of them that "she could not well escape such an expression of fear I had never before seen exhibited," wrote Smith. "She ran toward me screaming and raising the stick with which she had been digging roots . . . as though she were a frantic mother rushing to scare away some beast that would devour her child. . . ." Smith avoided the formidable weapon and tried to calm her, but in vain, "for when she went off her screams were still heard until lost in the distance."

Miwok

For a 3- to 4-foot-long digging stick, the Miwok, with a sharp-edged stone, hacked off a branch of mountain mahogany, or, less frequently, buck brush *(Ceanothus cuneatus)*. They scraped it with a flake of flint, and they hardened the point in fire. Barrett and Gifford recorded that they held it like a quarterstaff; the left hand grasped the stick 8 to 10 inches above the point, the right hand a foot or more above the left; and they jabbed the stick into the ground close to the bulb or root to be excavated. It was said to be more effective in hard, sunbaked soil than a steel spade because the digging stick extracted the bulb by removing less dirt.

The digging stick also excavated the Miwok earth oven to bake bulbs. They dug a hole 1 to 1-1/2 feet deep by 3 feet across. A fire was made next to the pit and stones were heated in the fire. After it burned down, the coals, followed by hot stones, were pushed into the pit. They completely covered the stones with the broad leaves of gray mule ears *(Wyethia helenioides)*. Bulbs were poured over this for about 6 inches, then more leaves over the bulbs, followed by more hot stones. They covered everything over with earth. Finally, water was poured around the perimeter of the pit, which drained down to the hot stones and coals and steamed the bulbs.

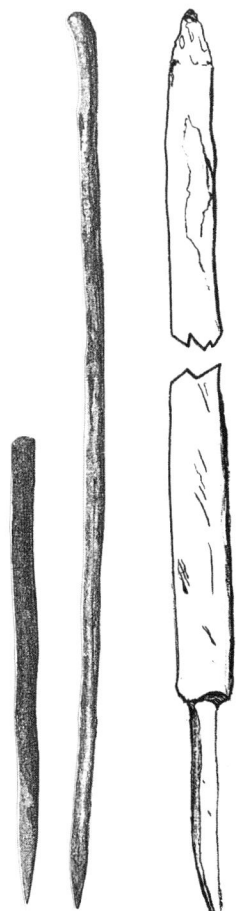

Digging sticks. First, Pomo, a little over 1-1/2' by less than 1"; following, also Pomo, a little over 3' by 3/4" (Barrett, 1952). Next, lower Colorado River style stick collected by J. P. Harrington from a Chemehuevi on Colorado River Indian Reservation in 1911 (redrawn at angle between front and side from Castetter, 1951).

After an hour the bulbs were ready and were removed to an openwork-basket tray. If many bulbs had been gathered, batches would be steamed in sequence. Barrett and Gifford listed some of the bulbs and corms utilized by the Miwok.

Harvest brodiaea *(Brodiaea coronaria)*: Together men and women dug the bulbs around the beginning of May, when the shoots began appearing above ground. They would go for four days of digging and then transport the bulbs in burden baskets to the earth oven where they were steamed and eaten without salt.

Ookow, wild hyacinth or blue dicks *(Dichelostemma pulchellum)*: Corms were steamed in the earth oven and eaten in the same way as harvest brodiaea.

White brodiaea *(Triteleia hyacinthina)*: Bulbs were dug around the same season as harvest brodiaea and white mariposa lily and steamed in the oven with harvest brodiaea.

Golden brodiaea *(Triteleia ixioides)*: Bulbs were eaten.

White mariposa lily or square mariposa tulip *(Calochortus venustus)*: Bulbs were dug from the time that buds appeared in April until the flower no longer marked the location. Bulbs did not keep more than four to five days. They were roasted in ashes of a dying fire for about twenty minutes until they were soft like boiled potatoes. Sometimes they were cooked in the earth oven with harvest brodiaea.

Yellow mariposa lily or gold nuggets *(Calochortus luteus)*: Bulbs were prepared and eaten like those of the white mariposa lily.

Yampa *(Perideridia gairdneri)*: Roots were boiled and eaten like a potato.

Anise *(Carum kelloggii)*: This was eaten.

Soaproot *(Chlorogalum pomeridianum)*: Bulbs were wilted and rubbed to remove their outer parts then baked in the earth oven. Bulbs could be dried unbaked for winter, then soaked and baked. (Note: poisonous saponin is only removed by prolonged baking.)

Queen Anne's lace *(Perideridia bolanderi)*: Bulbs were eaten raw or stone-boiled in a basket for ten minutes, peeled and eaten—mealy, like the potato. This bulb could substitute for acorn as their stores ran out in June. In such cases, they were washed then dried in sun for three or four days with their skins on. After that, they were pounded in a bedrock mortar. The resulting white meal was cooked in a basket, like acorn soup or mush, which could be eaten as it was or made into biscuits. Bulbs were preserved by mashing, drying and storing in baskets. They were repulverized and cooked as desired.

Scouler's St. John's wort *(Hypericum formosum)*: This was eaten fresh from the ground or dried, ground, and cooked like acorn meal.

California corn lily *(Veratrum californicum)*: This was roasted in hot ashes, peeled and eaten, it was not stored.

Yokuts

The Chukchansi, a northern group of Yokuts from the Sierra Nevada foothills to the south of Yosemite and the Miwok, made the woman's digging stick from a straight limb of mountain mahogany—3 to 6 feet long and 1 to 2 inches thick. It took a point that rarely became dull. They used it in a paddling motion to dig roots, postholes, graves, or anything else.

In foothills farther south, Gayton found that the Wukchumni Yokuts made the woman's digging sticks of manzanita or young white oak. They charred the tip and rubbed it down on a rough stone to sharpen and fire-harden the point. Voegelin found that, just to the south, a Tubatulabal digging stick made from a dry, straight length of oak 4 to 5 feet long was sharpened to a point on one end by rubbing it on a rock. A Yokuts woman who liked a short stick (around 4 feet) would sometimes coat the upper end with boiled soaproot and tie a piece of buckskin over it to create a knob.

They also used the bulbs of a small variety of soaproot as food. They baked the bulbs between layers of a sweet-smelling flower and coals in an earth oven. Mariposa lilies were dug with a stick when the flowers bloomed in April and May. To remove the skin the bulbs were rubbed across an open-twined basket. They were then boiled and eaten.

Owens Valley Paiute

The Owens Valley Paiute used the digging stick to harvest and incidentally till the soil around underground parts of wild plants they had encouraged through irrigation—a form of agriculture. According to Harry Lawton, Philip Wilke and others, the corms of wild hyacinth or blue dicks *(Dichelostemma pulchellum)*, harvested in the spring, and the tubers of yellow nut grass *(Cyperus esculentus)*, also known as *chufa*, gathered in the fall, were the principal crops. Chufa tubers are an ancient crop in the Old World and have been found in the intestines of Egyptian mummies as far back as 6,000 years. They continue to be consumed around the world. An analysis of the yellow nut grass from Owens Valley conducted by J. G. Waines found that tubers with the fiber and rind removed had a protein content of 8 percent. Oil content was also fairly high. The Paiute used the tubers for food and to extract a "milk" (the exact preparation is not known). Powers discovered the Yokuts on Tulare Lake of the 1870s eating "grass nuts" (which he identified as "a *Cyperus*"— "a plant with a triangular stalk") as well as the seeds of this plant.

Chumash

The Chumash digging-stick tradition seems to be transitional between the sharply pointed sticks used mainly by women to the north, and the wedge-shaped or chisel-tipped sticks used mainly by men to the southeast. Three digging sticks discovered in dry caves of interior Santa Barbara County, now in the Santa Barbara Museum of Natural History, have slightly rounded blunt points at one end, and tapered, flat, chisel-like edges at the other. Another (a fragment found in a dry cave of the Cuyama area and now in the Halford Collection) has a sharp pointed tip.

Both types (sharp-pointed and chisel-edged) are known from collections to have had, in some cases, a polished hard stone ring slipped over them. This was a practice that appears to have been unique to the Chumash. One stick, from a cave on Santa Rosa Island, has its limestone ring weight secured with asphaltum and there are indications of use at both ends of the stick. J. P. Harrington's Chumash consultants told him that rock rings were twisted on to add weight for collecting wild food. They were twisted as far as they could go and according to the depth they wished to dig. Fernando Librado told Harrington that the weight was fixed about 1 foot from the bottom. They used the digging stick for soaproot and other roots. Some informants described small stones wedged in from below to hold the circular weight. Sometimes a simple unperforated chert stone was attached with tar and lashed with rush strips. This was to make the stick heavier for digging house posts. The loosened dirt was removed with large abalone shells. (Kitanemuk neighbors of the Chumash told Harrington that the men dug graves with digging sticks and removed the earth in beautiful little baskets.) Chumash Éstevan Pico of Ventura, told Henry Henshaw in the 1880s that a hole was occasionally sunk in the bottom of the digging stick and a stone was put in for added weight. Chumash informants told Harrington that sticks could be used with or without weights. Hudson and Blackburn note that those Chumash sticks with weights are generally thinner than those without, and this may imply a difference in function.

Librado said that both men and women used digging sticks—men the heavier ones. Women employed a lighter stick for bulbs of brodiaea or blue dicks (*Dichelostemma pulchellum*). When one dug, the dirt was thrown out. Digging sticks were made from Catalina ironwood (*Lyonothamnus floribundus*) or toyon (*Heteromeles arbutifolia*), according to Librado. Others mentioned mountain mahogany (the preferred wood among groups to the north). First, the tip was held in the fire, then it was cut to a point and again held in the fire. After this, they put it in water and yet again in the fire to make the point hard.

Cahuilla and the Desert Agave

Known as mescal, century plant, or agave (*Agave deserti*), the leaves were useful for their fiber, but even more important was the plant's value as food. Bean and Saubel wrote that among the desert Cahuilla, the agave held a place in the native diet normally reserved for the acorn and piñon. Although harvested at specific times of the year, like the acorn and piñon, agave plants had the advantage of always being available for food, even during a drought.

The individual plant grows for years on arid, gravelly desert hills and slopes from 500 to around 4,000 feet all through the western Colorado Desert, from southern California to the mid Baja Peninsula. Suddenly, after about seven years, it matures, quickly sends up a stalk, flowers, and dies. The base of the stalk—referred to as the crown, head or heart of the mescal— weighs several pounds and is surrounded by a rosette of fleshy, gray-green leaves with teeth along the margins and sharp terminal spines. Some of the agave plants matured every year and began a buildup of rich sap in November and December, when they were often harvested since little else was available at that time. Around April or May the juices of the mature plants were at their richest and a slender flower stalk arose from the base many feet into the air, producing a profusion of yellow flowers at the top of the long stem. These sugar-laden blossoms were parboiled, according to Bean and Saubel, to rid them of any bitterness, then eaten at once or preserved by drying. Barrows recorded that they could be stored this way for as long as five years. The dried flowers were reboiled for consumption as needed.

The best part for the Cahuilla, however, was the stalk. It had to be harvested at 3 to 5 feet, prior to blossoming and before all the sap was consumed. This included the head, which, judging from early photos, was often separated from the rest of the stalk for baking. The leaves were cut from the head after it had been cut from its root. They were baked together with the head and stalk. Leaves were best from November through May but were edible all year. Yellowish leaves and those nearest the ground were bitter and generally discarded, unless put through a special process to reduce the bitterness. Larvae of the agave skipper butterfly *(Megathymus stephousi)* often found on the leaves, were left in place and roasted along with the leaves, then picked off and eaten as a delicacy. Not all stalks ascended nor could they all be harvested at once. There might be various harvests during the season. Agave-gathering was an activity of the men. Agave was also prepared for eating by the men.

A great pit or oven about 3 feet deep and 5 feet long was dug by hand, or with an agave shovel, in the sand of the same area where the agave grew. It was lined with stones. Mesquite wood, if lower in the desert, or oak, if higher in the mountains, was set ablaze in the oven, according to Cahuilla singer and elder Alvino Siva. Red shank *(Adenostoma sparsifolium)* might be used for a particularly hot fire requiring a shorter cooking time. The fire was maintained until the stones were thoroughly heated, observed Barrows one hundred years ago. Then mescal heads were placed in the pit together with their stalks and leaves. The pit was covered with grass and earth and the contents were left to roast from one day to as long as two days and three nights.

Barrows described the cooked heads as "fibrous, molasses-colored layers, sweet and delicious to the taste and wonderfully nutritious," and noted at the time that "pieces will keep for many years." Six decades later he revealed in a lecture recorded by Bean that a piece of agave he had saved all that time was still edible. To preserve agave the usual Cahuilla process was to pound the baked stalks and leaves and form them into cakes that they then dried in the sun and sealed in clay pots.

But something has been left out. To cook and eat agave it first had to be harvested. For that, they needed the digging stick. Bean and Saubel give much information on the preparation of agave as food but little on the implements of harvest, perhaps because modern tools replaced the aboriginal ones very early. A. Kroeber merely recorded that "the digging stick of the Cahuilla calls for no special comment, being as elsewhere merely a sharpened stick of hardwood." One he obtained was 4 feet long and 1-1/2 inches in diameter. I have seen modern Cahuilla using a long iron rod, sharpened chisel-like on one end, to harvest the mescal head. Bean and Saubel noted that a long pole of screwbean mesquite *(Prosopis pubescens)* made a mescal cutter to sever the agave leaves and that the heart was removed from the plant base with a sharply pointed hardwood pole, usually of oak or ironwood. The "shovel-shaped" cutter of leaves had a sharp fire-hardened edge and would surely have done the job, but in my experience a sharp pointed pole alone is not enough to sever the head.

Drucker's Cahuilla informants told him in the 1930s that they used a "planting stick" for agricultural purposes. The Cahuilla crops, which included corn, beans and squash, and their techniques of planting in small patches (mainly by men while women did the harvesting), storing seeds in ollas and crops in large baskets of intertwined willow branches and the cutting into strips and drying of pumpkin and squash, all make it likely that small-scale agriculture had diffused from the Yuman-speaking groups of the lower Colorado River, probably in aboriginal times. Artesian flows for water, and planting under or adjacent to mesquite or arrowweed to protect against frost, were probably local innovations. Old Cahuilla digging sticks on permanent display at the Southwest Museum in Los Angeles are sharp shovel-shaped or chisel-like at one end, about 4 feet long, and dully pointed at the other. They are much like the planting or digging stick of the lower Colorado River tribes and exactly like the digging stick still made primarily for mescal by the Paipai and Southern Diegueño of Santa Catarina in Lower California. These sticks effectively sever the head of mescal from its root.

The Sierra Juárez mountains and desert of the Diegueño and Paipai are very similar to the Santa Rosa mountains and desert of the Cahuilla. The mountains are both of the Peninsular Range, and the desert is of the Colorado. Alvino Siva of the Cahuilla tells how the mountain sheep made yearly migrations from mountain to mountain across the desert before urban sprawl blocked the route. The Paipai describe similar regular movements of mountain sheep between mountains and across desert in their territory today. The agave grows abundantly in both areas and was harvested extensively by both groups. Like the Cahuilla, the Paipai prefer oak or ironwood *(Olneya tesota)* for their digging or "agave" sticks. Screwbean, the other wood mentioned by Bean and Saubel, is favored by the lower Colorado River Yuman tribes for digging or planting sticks.

Yuman Speakers of the South

Native Californians controlled their environment by clearing undergrowth, killing infestations and enhancing seed production with fire, and by selective pruning of useful shrubs. But they generally rejected traditional Southwestern agriculture. The Colorado River Yuman-speaking tribes and their neighbors were different. On their flood plains, they planted corn, beans, pumpkins and other crops. The primary tool of their agriculture was the digging stick. The Mohave would take one step from the last hole and ram the somewhat flattened sharp end of the stick 6 to 12 inches into the ground, and insert six kernels of corn. A shorter, wider stick, sharpened flat at one end, was used to scrape away weeds from the seedlings. To the southwest of the Mohave and to the south of the desert Cahuilla, whom they bordered, a branch of the Southern Diegueño in the Imperial Valley, known as Kamia, fashioned digging sticks of screwbean or honey mesquite. According to Gifford, the sticks were around 4 feet long and 2 inches in diameter, sharpened to a point by burning. Generally held with the right hand below the left, men used them not for agriculture but to dig out and kill beavers. However, a stick slightly thinner, about 1-1/2 inches in diameter, was shoved into the ground to a depth of 6 inches for planting crops, such as beans or corn. In the manner of the Mohave, they did this after the natural inundation of land by an overflowing river. Behind the man who did the digging followed a woman who would drop five seeds into each hole. Over the seeds she crumbled fine earth. The Cahuilla of Coachella Valley dug wells and the Kamia reportedly did this with a mesquite shovel shaped by a sharp stone. Likely, until influenced by European steel shovels, this would have been a chisel-ended digging stick.

The valley-dwelling Kamia did not cut mescal—which grew at higher elevations—but they obtained dry, fibrous, baked agave cakes from other Diegueño in the mountains to the west and south.

These Southern Diegueño groups, as well as the Paipai even farther south in Lower California, possessed a chisel-ended digging stick used to cut the head of the mescal from its roots. Drucker's culture elements lists, obtained from elderly informants of the 1930s, show they also fashioned wooden chisels that were driven by cobbles for cutting the mescal heads.

It would be difficult to reconstruct the exact form the digging stick took for each Yuman-speaking tribe near the lower Colorado River. However, trade and social patterns of these groups suggest that digging-stick technology must have been shared throughout the area. Though their territories were far flung, all these Yuman-speaking groups south of the Cahuilla came together amongst the Cocopa in the Colorado River Delta. The Paipai, Diegueño (including Kamia) and the Kiliwa (from south of the Paipai) even had small settlements in the Delta. The Paipai, whose delta ranchería was mentioned in various accounts of early explorers through the region, likely had been residents for hundreds of years in the Colorado River Delta next to the Cocopa. Intermarriage among these groups has been continuous and common up to the present. Despite occasional killings, when certain gathering places were contested, there seems to have been little conflict, and the spirit of cooperation predominated.

Some visited the Delta only seasonally, or to trade agave for agricultural products since the Cocopa, though they gathered and pit-baked agave in the Cocopa Mountains beginning in April, did not find the plant extensively in their home territory. The Cocopa and River Paipai, in turn, made regular trips across the dry Laguna Salada up into the Sierra Juárez. At times they carried water in large ollas, and at other times, they did not. Friends would wait at the last watering hole for a smoke signal that the group had arrived safely at the next water. In the Sierra Juárez they visited the Diegueño and mountain Paipai, trading their agricultural products for baked agave, tobacco and wild mountain sheep skins from the Santa Catarina region. About the middle of September, they made the journey to the Sierra Juárez to gather pine nuts and hunt deer, often camping with Southern Diegueño neighbors. To this day, the Diegueño of Rancho Escondido near Santa Catarina make the trip. Historically, the interaction would have led to much shared culture.

The digging stick of the Cocopa and other lower Colorado River tribes was primarily an agricultural implement used to open the ground for corn, beans and pumpkins—their original crops.

Edward Castetter and Willis Bell described this most important tool as about 4-1/2 feet long and 2 to 2-1/2 inches in diameter, usually of screwbean wood, the lower end having been flattened like a chisel with a rough stone for about 1 foot so that the stick appeared truncated at the point the flattening began. The flattening allowed it to loosen and lift more dirt. The handle end was smoothed, when necessary, to accommodate the user's hands. One of Castetter's consultants said that willow fiber was wrapped around the stick—which was cut green—to allow gradual curing and to prevent splitting. The stick was thrust into moist earth by the man to pry and loosen the soil into a small 6-inch-diameter hill. In the center the stick was thrust perpendicular and turned in a circle to make a hole for the seeds. Dirt was scooped out with the fingers. In William Kelly's accounts of the Cocopa, women and older children placed four to eight seeds in each hole, 4 to 5 inches deep. Plantings were a pace or two apart for corn and beans, and 6 feet apart for pumpkins, but never in rows. The three crops were in separate fields. Informants told Castetter that in ancient times a short willow stick, about 1 foot long and 1-1/2 inches in diameter and flattened like a chisel at one end, was used only for tepary beans. It made short planting grooves in wet soil. While kneeling, a stick with a flattened, sharp, board-like lower half was swung in a sidewise scraping motion at ground level to cut weeds or loosen soil around the hill of a plant.

In contrast to northern California, the digging stick generally was not employed for edible roots. At least Gifford ruled it out in this regard for Kamia women. Yuman-speaking men of the lower Colorado River, however, did use the stick for the tuber of the arrowleaf plant *(Sagittaria latifolia)*, which matured in midsummer and was useful before the fall harvest of grass seeds and agricultural products. The thumb-size tuber could be dug through the winter as well. The Cocopa baked it in coals, rubbed off the skin, and ate it at once, whole or mashed. We recall that in northern California, Pomo women generally dug these tubers.

Yuman-speaking groups of the lower Colorado also gathered the large bulbs of the desert lily *(Hesperocallis undulata)* whose flower stalks grow in March and April. The bulbs were eaten raw, baked in ashes or boiled. They gathered and ate the long succulent underground stem of the sand food *(Ammobroma sonorae)*, according to Castetter. It was baked in ashes, the thin bark peeled away and eaten. The baked stem also could be dried and later reconstituted through boiling and eaten.

Fleshy cattail *(Typha latifolia and angustifolia)* rhizomes were pried out with a pole and along with the young shoots, eaten raw by the Mohave, Yuma and Cocopa. Sometimes the rhizomes were broken into pieces and dried in the sun to be stored. Later, they were pounded in a mortar and boiled with fish. The tender sprigs could also be dried and later pounded to be used with corn or tepary meal for mush. Cattail pollen was an important food.

Another Mohave and Yuma plant called *alalyk*, described as a small potato-like tuber growing in moist places (the tuber was milky if not mature), was likely yellow nut grass *(Cyperus esculentus)* or *C. ferax* or both. The tubers were parched, pounded in a mortar and eaten.

Castetter identified the "wild potato" or *achek* of the Cocopa (also utilized by the Mohave and Yuma) as likely hog potato or *comote de ratón (Hoffmanseggia densiflora)*. The 1/2-inch-long tubers on strong slender roots are found 6 to 12 inches beneath the earth's surface and are common in flooded areas of the lower Colorado River. They were described as sweet but tough. In sum, the pointed digging stick of the north generally had taken a flat chisel-edge in the south where it was employed mainly by men for agriculture and mescal but could still occasionally root out a wild Indian potato.

The Southern Diegueño and Paipai Digging Stick in Action

Andres Albáñez, whose father was Diegueño and mother Paipai, only had to walk a few paces from the leafy ramada at the side of his home to demonstrate how to cut a head of mescal *(Agave deserti)* from its root with the southern chisel-end digging stick. Agave grows abundantly throughout his village of Santa Catarina in the Sierra Juárez Mountains of Lower California. He had made his digging stick, or *yieltqechow* in Paipai, of live oak. It measured over 5 feet in length, averaged 2-1/4 inches at the top to more than 2-1/2 inches in width at the bottom chisel end, and began about 9 inches from the bottom to taper to the chisel-edge that, when viewed from the side, curved slightly, more wood having been rasped from the back than from the relatively straight front. It weighed a hefty eight pounds, giving it an almost pile-driver effect when in use. The top of the stick had been left blunt. Others he made were slightly pointed to make holes for seeds in planting, according to

Albáñez. While Albáñez preferred oak for a digging stick, Paipai elder Benito Peralta averred that ironwood made the very best.

Andres said that the branch for the digging stick could be protected against splits that occur with natural drying by laying it beneath the coals of a fire before the bark was removed. The bark protected the wood itself from burning and kept the stick from splitting as it dried. Moved about from time to time to avoid catching fire and to even the heat, it remained in the coals as long as the bark still protected it. This quick-dried the wood. Andres did not know about fire-hardening the sharp flat edge of the stick. As it dulled from use, it was simply rasped on any rough nearby stone to resharpen it.

With the stick, one accomplished many tasks from cutting mescal or knocking over a barrel cactus to digging a pit oven. It was a man's tool that a woman sometimes used. Indeed, thirty years ago, Michelsen photographed and described Petra Higuera, a Kuatl lineage Southern Diegueño from Santa Catarina, using a scrub-oak "chisel" or digging stick to remove the central leaves of agave. She employed stabbing blows and a prying motion to separate the spine-edged leaves from the living upright plant preliminary to the manufacture of agave-fiber cordage. Michelsen also photographed Petra with a somewhat short chisel-edged, ironwood digging stick on her knees, digging clay for her ceramics. She appeared to use the stick in a stabbing, paddling motion. Short sticks from northern California were used similarly in a kneeling position.

Agave heads were ready for harvest from February through May, but mostly in March, when the stalks were about 2 or 3 feet high. However, some upper stalks were cut off short in this season just at the top of the head as they began to rise, Albáñez told me. This was done to suspend the maturation process conserving all the liquid in the heart or base of the stalk that was then cut in July or August, giving a second agave harvest.

Held in the middle by one hand and near the top with the other, Albáñez jabbed the digging stick repeatedly somewhere just above the lowest dry unpalatable leaves, above ground level. There was normally a slight shoveling curve to one side of the

Albáñez demonstrates how to excavate earth and cut a head of mescal with digging stick.

chisel end and the flat or opposite side of the chisel was upward during these strokes. The cut itself sliced down into the lower heart at the same angle that the stick was held while stabbing—about 45 degrees. As soon as the juncture between root and heart was weakened, the agave was worked back and forth by hand or levered by the stick to snap it off. The whole process might be accomplished in as little as a minute. Andres demonstrated this for me. But for larger agave, the process could take a considerably longer amount of time.

Because of the angle, some roots might remain attached opposite and beneath the cut after the head had broken off. These were removed from the opposite side of the original cut while the head lay on the ground using additional stabbing motions of the chisel end. If leaves were removed to make this cut, or if dry leaves still remained at the base of the harvested "cabbage" head, they were severed at the bottom outer side of each leaf with the agave head inverted using the same stabbing motion of the digging-stick chisel. Thus, the heart of agave that remained came from slightly above the root and did not include the lowest, the driest or yellowed, leaves. The rest of the leaves were left attached. The flower stalk shooting up over the leaves was broken off just above the base or head. Similar methods of cutting mescal appear to have been extensive in the Southwest. Castetter, for example, found that the Papago used a hardwood digging stick with a chisel-shaped end to hack mescal plants off at the ground.

In a slightly different approach, the Paipai and Southern Diegueño sometimes made a thick shortened form of the chisel-end stick and used it as other Californians used a wedge. A. Kroeber had written that the California substitute for the ax was the wedge, usually a deer antler driven by a stone. It occurred as far south as the Luiseño—an antler that was as straight as possible, according to Philip Sparkman.

Stone-lined mescal pits below a ridge near Rancho Escondido, Sierra Juárez Mountains, Lower California, 1997. Great loads of wood were burned to coals and ashes in these ovens to store heat for baking mescal.

Top, a relatively small oven next to Raúl Sandoval's boyhood home (only the foundation rocks of the sotol thatch hut remain nearby). Raúl squats in the perpendicular-sided oven now half-filled with soil; sand from rodent burrows cascades into the pit. Raúl and his mother, Manuela Aguiar, last used the oven five years ago. Right: much older oven down the trail from the last, not used in Raúl's lifetime; sand from water-eroded gully filling it up.

Below: different perspectives on mescal pit near Raúl's boyhood home. Note the close fit of the boulders that line the walls.

The Shasta split logs with elk-horn wedges driven by stone mauls without handles. They were simply large handheld stones. The Klamath drove elk-horn picks with hardwood mauls. The pick, though used like a wedge, was simply an unworked elk tine cut off by laying a fire at the desired spot on the antler. The maul was made from a knot of oak or mountain mahogany with the limb attached. Paipai Benito Peralta told me that a shortened form of the chisel-end stick with the opposite end blunted (a veritable chisel) was used with a heavy cobble as a hammer to harvest the mescal heart—a two-man job. This was the easiest way to separate the heart from the root. Andres Albáñez made them from scrub oak, like a thick wooden chisel, one side slightly curved as with the digging stick. Instead of a cobble, he employed a maul of catclaw or mesquite. The mauls he made and demonstrated for me came from thick branches of mesquite that terminated in huge bulbous knots. It was a two-man job that Albáñez did alone: a seven-pound maul in one hand, the handle gripped next to the head; the 2-1/2-foot by 3-inch wedge or chisel in the other hand, positioned much like the digging stick had been positioned.

The long digging stick that cut mescal also dug the pit oven. It was held and used with stabbing strokes into the soil in the same way as into the agave. The primary purpose was to loosen the earth that they then removed by hand. Ideally, a stick with a widened chisel end was made expressly for the purpose of excavating the oven. Andres indicated that it was a bit wider than the mescal stick. Manuela Aguiar, of the Southern Diegueño Kuatl lineage, said that the end was considerably wider and more like a shovel.

Albáñez described the earth oven. It was made by excavating a huge hole in the ground and lining it with boulders. Mesquite or other wood, such as chamise, was put in, lighted and allowed to burn down to coals and ashes, then removed. Agave heads with leaves attached were packed neatly into the bottom of the pit, one immediately next to the other, as they grew with severed end on the ground. As many as thirty to fifty hearts of mescal might go into a single oven. The stalks were laid on the hearts and leaves. Over all of this the coals and ashes were pushed back so that they fell in amongst the leaves, followed by a layer of sandy earth, not too thick, that covered everything. Finally, on top, a huge mesquite fire was lit. It would take a long time to burn down. A second fire was begun before the first had cooled so that fire burned over the oven for two days. After that time the oven was opened and the contents were removed and eaten or stored.

From correspondence with Malcolm Rogers, Castetter recorded sixty years ago that the desert mountains of eastern San Diego County (former territory of the Southern Diegueño) had a tremendous concentration of well-constructed mescal pits. They were laid out on ridges in series like a trapline. Where the lines were staggered and in less even country, small stones resting on nearby boulders marked the positions so that the ovens would not be overlooked. Pits were around 6 feet in diameter, 9 feet maximum, in sandy soil and lined with boulders, often forming a raised rim on the circumference. According to informants, after the rocks were heated by a hardwood fire, agave leaves were laid in and upon the rocks, then the stalks or crowns and another layer of leaves. All this was banked over with sand and left for a day. It was reported that food left more than twenty-four hours

Albáñez transports a freshly cut head with its rosette of leaves.

Albáñez makes a stabbing blow to cut head of mescal from its root (top left). He levers the head off the root (top right). Cuts any adhering root from the plant (bottom left). Trims undesirable leaves from the bottom, head inverted.

in the oven would be overbaked. (In my experience a mere twenty-four hours results in a bland vegetable-like product. Leaving the mescal for three days produces a rich, sugary molasses or caramel-like food easily preserved.) The mescal ovens were used year after year. Waste and fire-cracked boulders cleaned from the pits had piled up to the side of many of them.

Albáñez said the leaves came off easily after the agave was baked. They were peeled and eaten. (The spines burned off.) To conserve what could not be consumed at once, the richest part of each leaf was taken and pounded into a paste, then formed together into a large cake or flattish ball perhaps 8 inches in diameter by 4 inches high. These cakes were put in the sun and stored when dry. They lasted indefinitely. Later, pieces of a cake were chipped off when desired and mixed with water to make a rich mealy drink. The fruit or tunas of cacti were peeled without cooking, pounded and formed into cakes, dried, stored, and eaten in the same way.

Manuela Aguiar added some details for me. She said the pit was covered with about 4 to 6 inches of soil, just enough to seal in the steam. On top they burned trunks of Mojave yucca and juniper bark and kept the fire going. The agave was sweetest, best, if left in the oven for three days. To serve, the hearts were cut crosswise in thin slices like cheese. They could be stored indefinitely and were often kept around the house in large ceramic vessels topped with a pottery lid. She still makes these.

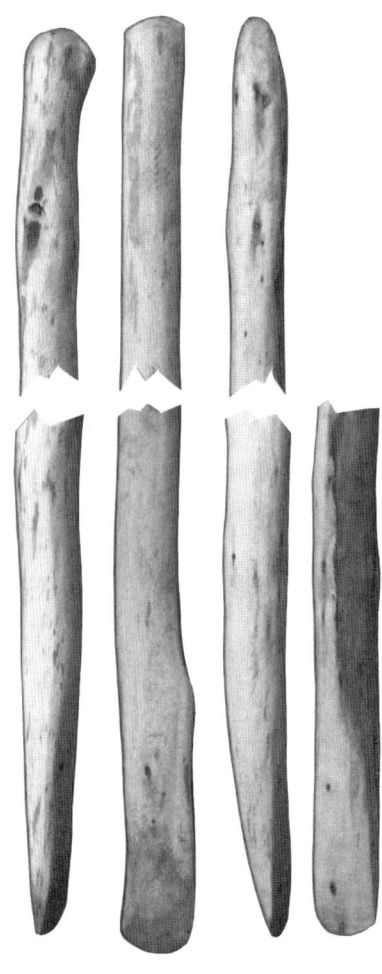

Tools of the trade: Andres Albáñez and grandchildren, Santa Catarina, Lower California, 1996. Albáñez uses scrub oak chisel and mesquite maul to separate agave head from root.

Andres Albáñez's Paipai sticks, around 5' by 2-1/2". First seen at slight angle from side, next directly from the front; last, both side and front.

79

Acorns and Other Bitter Nuts

In the time long past of the bird people, Bluejay, who lived on acorns, stored them in the woods. He knew where oak trees should grow and planted an acorn at every spot. They are growing there now. Bluejay is the reason that acorns are plentiful.

The above story from the Pomo reflects the tremendous bounty and richness of the acorn crop in California. So plentiful were they that most California Indians rejected traditional Southwestern agriculture in favor of gathering acorns. Why till fields when nature provides? Even where oak trees were few or where acorn crops in a given year might have been lean, the Indian would obtain them by traveling to more productive regions of neighboring tribes or by trading with those tribes. The acorn was the most important staple of the California Indian.

One can explore almost any area of California in the late fall and still see the great variety of oaks left everywhere by Bluejay. Each tree has adapted to a particular environment—valley, canyon, chaparral, foothill or mountain—and all are laden with rich nuts. They sustained and characterized Californians for thousands of years. Sadly, no one will pick these acorns. The laughter of boys and girls who climbed the trees to knock them to the ground, comes no more. This year acorns not gathered by birds and squirrels will fall to the earth and become food for deer and worms. Only wind disturbs the silence in the acorn-heavy boughs.

Acorns are rich in fat, which is difficult to come by in the wild. Yet the body needs fat and evolution has given us a taste for it, so we seek it out. True, in the glut of modern consumer society, that taste, unrestrained by wise discipline, has led to an unparalleled crisis of obesity and coronary disease. But in primitive society, where fat was not abundant, the concentrated calories it contained had great value. Acorn meal typically contains from 9 to 20 percent fat. It is also high in carbohydrates, about 60 percent; and protein, about 5 percent; with the rest of the nut consisting mainly of water, ash and fiber.

Something so desirable had to have a catch. The flaw was tannic acid, a bitter, potentially poisonous substance. For that reason, the bitter acorn was not universally utilized as food by the Indians of the West. The indigenous people of California, however, discovered that tannin could be removed through leaching, which was made easier by first pulverizing the acorn into meal. Grinding of other seeds had long been practiced, and the ancient and widespread process was likely extended at some point to the acorn as a prelude to leaching.

When acorn crops failed, many Indians turned to the less-desired buckeye *(Aesculus californica)*, the wild nutmeg *(Tumion californicum)* or hollyleaf cherry *(Prunus ilicifolia)* known as islay. The poison of these nutritious nuts also had to be leached before the nut meat could be consumed.

It is true that some acorns could be eaten without leaching. Canyon live oak *(Quercus chrysolepis)* acorns are not as bitter as others. The Shasta Indians of northern-most California customarily buried them whole in mud for several weeks before eating them. But sometimes, they simply roasted them in ashes and ate them as they were without any leaching process whatsoever. The southern-most lineage of the Southern Diegueño skipped the leaching stage when processing the emory oak *(Quercus emoryi)* acorn—a sweet acorn almost completely free of tannin.

But leaching was generally a necessary step in California acorn processing. In all, there were seven stages: gathering, drying, storing, hulling, pulverizing, leaching and cooking. A review of representative groups shows that these could be accomplished in a variety of ways.

Gathering

Acorns are not all alike. In fact, the Southern Diegueño Indians I know do not have a generic term for acorn. They use distinct words for each species. In collecting, processing and eating them, I learned to appreciate the distinctions.

The most popular acorn of northwestern California tribes was that of tanbark oak *(Lithocarpus densiflorus)*. Elsewhere, groups such as the Shasta, Southern Maidu, Miwok, Luiseño, and Northern Diegueño, preferred acorns of the black oak *(Quercus kelloggii)*.

Among the Pomo, where the range of the black and tanbark oak species overlapped, tanbark acorns rated highest because of their agreeable acid taste and large amount of oil. The abundant harvest of huge acorns from the enormous valley oak *(Quercus lobata)* surpassed both of these, however, in the sheer amount gathered. Other species utilized by the Pomo, and recorded by V. K. Chesnut and by Barrett, were mountain white oak *(Quercus garryana)*, blue oak *(Quercus douglassii)*, canyon live oak *(Quercus chrysolepis)* and California scrub oak *(Quercus dumosa)*—the latter described as extremely bitter. Gifford included the coast live oak *(Quercus agrifolia)* as a preferred acorn of the Pomo.

In addition to black oak, the canyon live oak and interior live oak *(Quercus wislizeni)* were Northern Maidu favorites. The Central Miwok graded oaks beginning with the black, which they most esteemed, followed by interior live oak, then white or valley oak, interior live oak in its scrub-oak form, an unidentified bushy little oak, a small bushy scrub oak (also unidentified) and, finally, the blue oak. The blue was least desired because soup from it was watery and the bread fell into pieces. The people of the lower foothills and plains gathered blue oak acorns in quantity because they were available. They traded some of them with the Indians of higher elevations for acorns of other species. Valley oaks placed third because the acorns were difficult to hull. They tended to mash when held on end and struck with a stone, so the shell had to be broken with the teeth.

For the Cahuilla, the black oak was again deemed best for its outstanding flavor and gelatin-like consistency when cooked. This was important for good acorn mush, wrote Bean and Saubel. The black oak is particularly high in fat content. It was mixed with other varieties of acorn meal to make them congeal. To a lesser extent, the Cahuilla utilized the acorns of canyon and coast live oaks. The California scrub oak acorns were not usually used alone but were added to other types of acorn meal when necessary to augment a short supply. To the acorns of the Cahuilla, the Luiseño added the acorns of the interior live oak and Engelmann oak *(Quercus engelmanni)*.

In the fall the Northern Maidu men and larger boys climbed the oak trees and beat the branches with long poles to knock down the acorns. Women and smaller children picked them up, put them in burden baskets and transported them to granaries in the village or large storage baskets in their houses. Thomas Garth wrote that men and agile girls among the Atsugewi were the ones to climb the trees and knock the acorns down with sticks or else they would stand on the ground with long poles and beat them from the tree. Women gathered the acorns from the ground, preferring the dark-colored nuts.

Julia Parker, a Kashia Pomo who carries the tradition of her husband's Miwok-Paiute grandmother, Lucy Telles, still gathers her acorns in a burden basket even as the twentieth century draws to a close. She told Bev Ortiz those acorns that fall from the tree first are the bad ones, often worm-infested. The good acorns fall around late September or early October in the central Sierras and they are heavier than the others. Parker leaves acorns with bumps or holes for the squirrels, the birds, and the earth itself. She used to gather the large acorns but learned from other Indian women that smaller acorns dry more quickly.

In southern California, the Cahuilla traveled to their oak groves in October or November before the first rains of winter. If it rained, acorns on the ground turned black and then were only eaten during food shortages. The Cahuilla camped in the groves from three to four weeks to allow the gathered acorns to dry.

J. P. Harrington was told by a Northern Diegueño informant in the early years of the century that when Indians gather acorns they always let them fall from the tree, implying that some groups, at least, simply let them fall naturally before harvesting them. Indeed, many years later, Ken Hedges learned from the Northern Diegueño at Santa Ysabel that acorns were allowed to drop and were then gathered from the ground. They believed that if acorns were picked from the trees, they would be watery when pounded.

Southern Diegueño elder Jim McCarty of Campo told Spier some eighty years ago that women gathered acorns in their carrying nets and dumped them unhulled into storage baskets set on posts 1/4 m. off the ground. The baskets, usually made from willow boughs with the leaves left on and so closely woven that rodents could not gnaw through them, stood in the acorn groves on the hills. Among California groups of whom we have record, men spent much time hunting and trapping while at the acorn-gathering grounds, leaving the acorn-processing largely to women and children.

By springtime acorns not gathered had rotted or been consumed by deer, rodents and birds. However, acorn woodpeckers stored some acorns in pecked holes in the thick soft bark of large trees such as the Ponderosa or in dead oak limbs. Jays and gray squirrels hid others and even the woodrats cached them in their nests. Barrett and Gifford, whose ethnography bequeathed us much of our knowledge on early Miwok ways, found that in times of shortage, Miwok Indians took the woodpeckers' stored acorns for their own use. The birds had pounded them in tightly to keep them from the squirrels. The

Miwok pried out the acorns with a pointed deer antler. Barrett also noted that the Pomo made a special pole for securing acorns from dead limbs full of woodpecker acorn holes. The pole, 15 feet or more in length with a short stick bound at an acute angle to the narrow end, hooked the dead branch and broke it off. The same pole was used for the gathering of firewood. Woodrats were no more fortunate; when hunting them, the Pomo usually stole their winter store of acorns from the chambers of their dome-shaped brush houses.

Drying and Shelling

Generally, acorns were dried whole and stored for use during the year. But drying and shelling were processes that occurred variously and on either side of the storage stage. Voegelin found, for example, that the Tubatulabal spread out the freshly gathered acorns on deerskins or tule mats to dry for three to four days to prevent them from sweating when cached for the winter. The Northern Maidu, on the other hand, after gathering the winter supply, removed the shells. The women placed each acorn point-down on a stone and, with another stone, struck the bottom end of the shell with several sharp blows. The acorn would split into halves, observed Roland Dixon, and the shell of each half was then separated from the nut meat with the teeth. The split meats were spread and dried a short while in the sun. Those not pounded into meal for immediate use went to storage baskets in their homes.

The Atsugewi often dried acorns unshelled on slabs of bark. Shelled acorns, however, they dried on platforms of branches and pine needles supported by four posts around 3 feet high. If it rained, a fire was built underneath the drying racks. Young people would make a contest of shelling by seeing who could shell ten acorns the quickest. They also struck the upended acorn with a stone while it rested on a flat anvil rock or they simply used their teeth. Sometimes one cracked the shell and another took it off. Boys and girls together participated in acorn-shelling.

Parker told Ortiz that acorns were inspected during the drying stage just as when first gathered and any showing insect damage, such as holes and bumps, were removed. Most were stored for at least a year before shelling and pounding. Black oak acorns could keep ten to twelve years. When the time came, Parker held the pointed end of the acorn against a flat rough stone and struck the other end with a small oblong rock. They were then hulled with the fingers. Mildewed, molded or insect-damaged acorn meats were returned to the earth unless the damage was slight, in which case the affected area was cut away. Of those used green, Parker cracked the shells and let them dry in the sun for two to seven days, covering them at night. Then she shelled and dried them completely. If needed immediately, green acorns were cut open with a knife, the shell removed, the tight skin underneath scraped off with much difficulty, and the meat sun-dried. Parker loosened the skin of the black oak acorns by inserting a knife into the folds of the meat and splitting them open. The longer the acorns were dried before hulling and skinning, the easier it was to remove the skins. Handfuls of dried hulled nuts were rubbed between the palms and against themselves; the abrasion would loosen the skins. Sometimes, again in the winnowing basket, they were rubbed against each other and against the basket with one hand as the other hand on her lap supported the bottom of the basket. Shaking in the basket also helped remove the skins. The mixture was winnowed by tossing it into the air in the scoop-shaped basket. Those whose skins refused to be dislodged and blow away after all of this were taken out, sprinkled with water, and dried in the sun to shrink and loosen the skin. They were then winnowed again. Some were saved until the next time she winnowed if the skin needed to loosen even more.

Barrett and Gifford recorded that the Miwok of the central Sierra Nevada cracked the shells on an anvil of an unworked flat stone, or in several small pecked cuppings found either on a special stone or on the underside of the portable mortar. The hammer stone was a natural pestle. The Cahuilla, Chumash and others of southern California also placed the acorn in a slight indentation of a flat rock. They struck it with a smaller rock to crack the shell. After hulling, the Cahuilla wiped off the bitter fibrous material that clung to the outside of the nut with handfuls of grass. Or they wet the nuts and rubbed the skin off with their fingers. The Shasta and the Pomo also rubbed this membrane off by hand. Finally, they placed the nut meats in the sun to dry.

Some of the freshly gathered acorns the Diegueño of southern California hulled and pounded into flour immediately. Gloria Castañeda of the Southern Diegueño village of San José de la Zorra told me they cracked the shells of those for immediate use and let the acorns dry in the sun for three days before hulling them. Acorns destined for granaries were left unhulled in the sun for as long as a month before storage. The Southern Diegueño of Campo, who harvested acorns in October, placed most of them in granaries, one for each variety of acorn—black (*ku'phral*), interior live oak (*isnyau*) and scrub (*ixwûp*). They were left there until February when it was warm and the nuts had dried. Women and old men would then crack the nuts between two convenient stones to extract the kernels. They stored the meats in clay pots cached in the rocks. Hedges observed that the Northern Diegueño of Santa Ysabel also shelled the acorns dry. Otherwise, the hulls clung to the meats. Then they rubbed the kernels with a pestle in the mortar or by hand on a flat basket to free the papery membrane covering the meat. They winnowed the resulting mixture on the flat basket. The clean acorn kernels were ready to be pounded.

Storing

It was storage, of course, that for animal and man alike made acorns more than a mere seasonal glut and gave stability to lives. The Atsugewi constructed a granary with a framework of four posts, one or two of which might be slender trees. Bark slabs tied with buck-brush withes shaped a kind of box, 4 by 6 feet at the base and 5 feet high. Before adding the acorns the floor of bark was covered with a thick layer of pine needles.

General food storage containers 10-feet-square were sometimes constructed of bark and poles and serviceberry withes in the higher branches of juniper trees where there were few limbs. Bark stripped from the trunk to make it smooth kept out mice, or, with similar intentions, the tree might be blazed around it so that the sticky pitch would form a barrier to ants. Sometimes food was simply put in sealed baskets and hung from a tree. A small tree with branches leaned against a food-storage tree served as a ladder.

The Atsugewi stored food in pits as well, 4 or 5 feet wide and around 3 feet deep, lined with bark and pine needles. Acorns or other food were protected from burrowing animals by covering the cache with a layer of pine needles, another of bark, then dirt and stones. In contrast, the Pomo, also of northern California, generally stored acorns in very large openwork baskets placed in a dry location within the house.

Acorns not processed by the Cahuilla of southern California were stored outdoors, sometimes for a year or more, in basketry-like granaries woven from branches into a circular shape. The air circulated freely through these large baskets placed in trees or on posts to keep them from rodents. Acorn meal as well as whole acorns were stored in ollas—large narrow-necked jars—with a flat rock cover. The ollas were hidden in dry caves or clefts as an emergency supply of food. Acorn meal could be formed into cakes and dried. It would keep this way for a long time before it was reground and cooked. Generally, for daily use, meal was kept in a covered olla or another pot for a short time.

The Tubatulabal cached acorns gathered near home in granaries located nearby. Others were stored in more distant acorn-gathering grounds. The granaries were constructed around a framework of four large posts 6 feet high set upright in the ground 3 feet apart and at the corners of a square. The bottom was 2 to 4 inches off the ground. Smaller poles fleshed it out. It was lined with sagebrush, filled with acorns, covered with a layer of brush and, finally, bark slabs to keep out the rain.

The Southern Diegueño possessed a circular granary roughly woven from coiled branches of willow with the leaves left on, similar to that of the Cahuilla. They also had a granary molded within a framework of four posts like that of the Tubatulabal. The posts, around 4-1/2 feet high, were set in the ground in a square with the corners 3 feet apart. A platform about 1-1/2 feet off the ground was made of two rails attached to opposite posts and crossed with other sticks. The upper extremities of the posts were connected by four short rails. Other poles were placed vertically between the posts and tied to the horizontal rails above, to each other and to the platform below. This made a rectangular box of poles above the ground. Leaves of the Spanish bayonet (*Yucca whipplei*) were used for all bindings. In the openings between the poles and inside the box they rammed a mixture of tanglefoot grass and chamise (*Adenostoma fasciculatum*), leaving a granary hollow in the shape of a cylinder. The acorns were poured in whole and unshelled. Care was taken to insure that they were completely dry before too many were stored. Those with worms they discarded. Spanish bayonet leaves tied in several directions across the top and tanglefoot grass stuffed in from above sealed it. Diegueño granaries were found in distant oak groves and near the houses of their small villages.

Pulverizing

Powers wrote of the silence of the long sweltering days in a Maidu village broken only by the "eternal thump, thump" of a woman pounding acorns. Much later Dixon preserved the details. To make acorn meal from dried acorn meats the Northern Maidu woman used a flat rock or boulder, or a flat stone sunk in the floor of her house, with a stone pestle. She spread out a couple of quarts of dried acorn meats in a circle on the flat stone. With one hand she held the pestle and struck regularly in the center of the circle of nuts, while with the other she continually gathered and swept back the fragments that scattered with each fall of the pestle. The functions were interchanged from time to time between hands to rest the muscles of the arms and hands while maintaining a continuous effort.

Occasionally an open-bottomed milling basket was used by the Northern Maidu. Its sloping sides kept the acorn meal from scattering and avoided the constant sweeping back of the fragments. The Atsugewi used such a hopper on a flat-topped rock that was about a cubic foot in size, buried until almost level with the ground. The woman held the hopper in place with half-bent legs pressing on the rim. She also exchanged hands, alternating between the oblong pestle and brushing back the particles to the center of the hopper. A small (about 5 inches long) soaproot brush swept flour from the hopper and the flat rock. Over time, a depression developed in the flat rock base, and when it reached an inch in depth the rock was discarded. The Atsugewi had no true mortars, although bedrock mortars were used to grind roots and other materials. They used milling stones for seeds, pushing a mano across the stone surface.

When the acorn meats had turned to fine meal the Maidu woman took a few handfuls and placed it on a flat winnowing basket or tray, where she tossed and caught the meal several times. She then held the tray on the palm of the left hand, tilted at about a 40-degree angle over the flat rock, and, as the fingers of the left hand slowly revolved the tray, she tapped the edge with a wooden or deer-bone tapper, causing the coarser particles that had largely separated from the finer flour to separate further and roll off over the edge of the tray. This left behind only the fine flour. A soaproot brush whisked the flour from the tray into a nearby soup basket. Dixon observed that the Maidu women, as an alternative to the tapper, sometimes held the basket tray at its edge in both hands, tilted it and dexterously shook the coarser particles off over the rim.

The particles, returned to the center of the meal on the flat rock, were pounded into a greater fineness. The sifting with the basket was repeated again and again. From time to time more acorns were added to keep the amount of meal under the pounding pestle about the same. The process continued until the desired quantity of flour had been produced. The Atsugewi, like the Maidu, used a flat basket plaque for sifting, but, as an alternative, a board about 1-1/2 foot-square was made from a hollow section of a tree ground to the desired thickness with stones.

Acorn meats were pulverized into meal in bedrock mortars by the Miwok. At first the mortar was nothing more than a slight natural depression in a granite boulder. Over time, when it became inconveniently deep (over 5 inches), they began a new one just inches away. With no bedrock mortar nearby, a flat, portable rock placed in the floor of the home served the same purpose. A natural smooth stone of approximate oblong shape from the bed of a mountain stream was the pestle.

Southern California Kitanemuk Indian Angela Lozada pounding acorns, apparently on flat rock mortar with a hopper basket. Note the heavy pestle and soaproot brush. Photograph, J. P. Harrington, circa November 1916 to September 1917 (Smithsonian Institution National Anthropological Archives).

With legs spread to either side, the woman lifted the pestle with both hands to about eye level, bending back at the waist, then forward as the pestle descended onto the peck or two of acorn meats on the mortar. No hopper was used and the meal spread out in a 1- to 2-foot-diameter circle 4 to 5 inches deep. Coarser meal naturally jarred into the meal crater under the descending pestle over the cup of the mortar. Particles to the outside were swept into the crater with the hands every fifteen or twenty strokes, and every so often a general sweeping with a soaproot brush consolidated particles that had flown even farther. The process continued until the meal had been pounded fine.

With those acorns believed to be too oily, they pounded in green leaves of Spanish clover *(Lotus americanus)* to absorb some of the oil. To whiten the acorn meal, they occasionally mixed in pulverized root of the umbrella plant *(Peltiphyllum peltatum)*. Neither of these additives changed the flavor of the meal, according to Barrett and Gifford.

Wind could easily blow away fine flour. Therefore, they chose a still day, if possible, to pound and sift the acorn meal. The closely coiled, round, slightly concave sifting basket was held at an approximate 45-degree angle toward the worker over the mortar and shaken up and down, the upper edge moving more than the lower. By this action coarse particles rose to the surface, rolled down and off the edge of the basket. The fine flour tended to form into a mass and stick to the basket. When the action ceased to bring more of the larger particles to the surface, two or three fingers were passed through the meal to loosen it. The shaking up and down then continued. More coarse particles rose to the surface and fell off the edge. The loosening of the flour was repeated, perhaps three or four more times, followed by the shaking until only fine flour remained. It was then poured into another basket. A couple of deliberate taps with the fingertips on the sifting basket loosened any stuck meal. A thorough brushing of the sifter with the soaproot brush completed the processing of each few handfuls of meal.

Voegelin noted that among the Tubatulabal of the southern Sierras, women, when pounding meal on a hot day, made piles of scrub oak or willows 4 to 6 feet high around the mortar bed to provide shade. This was important if the work was to go on for any length of time.

The southern California Cahuilla pulverized the dried acorn meats in mortars, portable and bedrock (sometimes they ground them with a mano on a metate). Each woman had her own. They often used basketry hoppers with portable mortars, especially when the depression was still slight. The hopper was attached with tar or pitch to prevent loss of meal when pounding with the pestle. Brushes of yucca fiber, soaproot or grass cleaned the mortars after grinding. Mortars were left turned upside down and the pestle placed underneath. The pestle remained in the bedrock mortar after use and they covered the depressions with grass to keep small animals out of them.

In remote areas Indians still eat acorns as a daily fare. I first visited the Kumeyaay, or Southern Diegueño, of Nejí in June 1993. Andrea Cota described the preparation of acorn mush as she picked up a dried acorn, cracked the shell with her teeth, shucked it, and with a few quick movements of her hand removed the clinging membrane and split the kernel into two clean, nut-like parts. She popped one into her mouth and gave me the other,

Kitanemuk Angela Lozada sifts acorn meal. Photograph, J. P. Harrington, circa November 1916 to September 1917 (Smithsonian Institution National Anthropological Archives).

explaining that they were bitter when not leached, but if a person does not eat too many it is not a problem. "Acorn mush goes well with meat," one of the men of the household offered. Andrea said they processed and used islay the same way but that she preferred acorns. Acorns were still a high priority item in their diets despite an array of easily obtainable modern foods, many of which they grow themselves. Large numbers of coast live oak trees in the village and on surrounding hillsides and along the stream below suggested one of the reasons this village site was chosen.

Andrea's grandmother, Pabla Mata, still coiled traditional winnowing and sifting baskets for acorns. She made them of juncus gathered deep in the mountains. She dried, then soaked the juncus prior to use. Juncus reeds formed both the coils and the warp of the nearly flat, circular basket, about 10 inches in diameter. Her baskets were utilitarian and not for gifts or show. The warp spiral of five or six or more juncus reeds was wrapped with a juncus that had been split lengthwise, then trimmed a bit with a knife. (The Gabrieliño of Los Angeles also wrapped juncus around a juncus base in their coiled basketry.) The fag, or loose tail end, of each new split juncus was left at a 45-degree angle and wrapped under the next coil of the remainder of the strip in the so-called mission style peculiar to the Indians of southern California. However, unlike classic mission baskets farther north, Pabla worked both her spiral warp and coiling weaver counterclockwise. That is, each coil stitch encircled the warp above to the left as it moved left and passed down and away from her through the top two or three stems of the expanding spiral below. Unlike tightly coiled cooking baskets, the stitch did not touch the preceding coil but left a single space.

The Seri Indians of Tiburón Island in the Sea of Cortez described such an open-stitch basket as one with eyes, referring to the exposed checkerboard of spiral and coils. The Seri used the technique to save time and materials.

I asked Doña Pabla to demonstrate the basket's use. She took it to the mortar depressions found in the granite bedrock at the heart of the village. She poured water into one, stirred it around, emptied it with her hands, and repeated this until it was clean. Acorns had been previously dried in the sun, stored, cracked with a rock and hulled. Left again in the sun (to weaken the bitter membrane covering the nut) and cleaned (by rubbing the acorns together with the hands) they were finally winnowed of debris by using the same flat juncus basket, tossing the kernels in the air and gently blowing through them. With these acorn kernels she filled the mortar hole that was about 3 to 4 inches wide and deep.

She grasped a rounded elongated stone on opposite sides with both hands and pounded the acorns rhythmically up and down. At times she would tire, change her position from sitting to kneeling, or use only one hand. It was a pleasure to watch this eighty-year-old woman in black shoes, long dark wool stockings and flower-print dress work with the litheness and spirit of a girl. Her long hair had only slightly grayed and there was no stoop to her thin body. Her dark brown face remained calmly absorbed in a task she knew well. Before long, the bulk of the acorns had been reduced to a fine meal. She took a large handful and spread it over the surface of the basket sifter.

With a hand on either side, Pabla shook the basket gently, rhythmically, up and down, holding it at an angle of about 40 degrees over the

Kitanemuk Angela Lozada cleans sifting basket with soaproot brush. Photograph, J. P. Harrington, circa November 1916 to September 1917 (Smithsonian Institution National Anthropological Archives).

mortar hole. The larger pieces of acorn rose to the top and slid off the edge of the basket back into the hole. After perhaps thirty seconds of this, she returned the basket to an even plane and, holding an edge in her left hand, struck the opposite edge from above with the tips of the fingers of her right hand, a quick snap. The flour jumped slightly into the air. This loosened the flour and brought less refined pieces again to the top. Coarser particles near the margin landed toward the center. All of these were quickly and lightly shaken into the bedrock mortar as she brought the basket again to an angle of 40 degrees over the mortar depression. Fine flour now clung to the coils of the basket that she inverted over a large bowl and shook to release the flour. She gave the basket a final tap from above to free any that was caught in the juncus weave.

Reaching well into the mortar hole for another handful of pounded flour, Pabla repeated the process. After a few more sifts, she returned to pounding, then sifted, then pounded again. She must have felt the meal was very dry because occasionally a little water was added to the mortar. Hedges' Northern Diegueño informants at Santa Ysabel indicated that they added water as they pounded to prevent too much oiliness.

Pabla Mata spoke Kumeyaay, some Spanish, but no English, and she had little or no contact with outsiders. She called the acorn *sinyaú*, and the mush she later cooked, *chaweé*. The purity of her acorn-sifting skills, practiced and refined over millennia, was a vision of time past. Modern Indians mill acorns in a blender.

Leaching

Dixon observed that in soft sandy soil the Northern Maidu scraped out a circular depression about 5 to 7 cm. deep and about 1/3 to 1 m. in diameter, then banked the earth up in a little wall around the excavation. An approximately 5 cm.-thick layer of dampened acorn flour was spread over the entire bowl-like hollow. Over the meal a few cedar sprigs or boughs were laid. These prevented the meal from being splattered, as warm water that had been heated in baskets with hot stones was poured gently on the boughs to trickle onto the meal and fill the hollow depression. Similarly, the Northern Diegueño poured water through their fingers to break its force onto the acorn meal. The little lake of water slowly soaked through the meal to the soil. As soon as it had passed completely away, a second basket of water, slightly hotter than the first, was poured into the depression. This continued until fully boiling water was used. Toward the end the Maidu woman tasted the flour from time to time until she found that it was no longer bitter. Ready for cooking, it was taken in pieces from the hollow, any adhering sand on the underside carefully removed, and placed in a basket for boiling. The Maidu leached with both warm and hot water, whereas the Atsugewi poured cold water through the meal two or three times, then allowed warm to seep through until it tasted right.

For large quantities of acorn flour the Miwok either scooped out a shallow sand basin, 3 to 4 feet in diameter, from a natural sandy spot or spread an inch or two of sand over a layer of boughs. The boughs were put down in the form of a basin and covered with fine grass to hold the sand. The meal was spread over the basin from the basket in which it had first been mixed and steeped in cold water. Next, a bundle of twigs from Douglas fir, white fir, incense cedar or tamarack was placed over the meal or held in hand to break and dissipate the flow of water onto the meal. Cold water was used for the first two or three applications, then lukewarm, increasing the temperature until the water was quite hot. In all, perhaps ten applications were needed to leach the tannin from the meal. Once it had become thoroughly wet, small furrows were made in the meal, usually with fingers, to conduct water from the center to all parts. Meal was tested by tasting it and by poking a hole in it to the bottom of the basin in several places and observing the color of the meal, which should be white—no longer yellow or brown.

Leached meal was removed from the sand basin by placing the hand, spread out full, palm downward, on the meal, which then stuck to the palm and separated easily from the sand. The very small amount of sand that might have clung to the meal was cleaned off by pouring water on that portion and catching the water in a second container. They used the same water to clean sand from successive handfuls of flour. Finally, the small amount of meal that incidentally collected in the cleanings was allowed to settle. The water was poured off and the meal recovered.

Barrett stressed the degree of care taken by the Pomo in preparing a similar sand basin. They sprinkled the lining of sand just enough to thoroughly dampen it, patted it down firmly and made it smooth, then deftly placed the acorn meal and trickled cold water very gently through a water breaker over the surface. Taking up and cleaning the meal was even more delicate. The palm pressed down on the surface of the acorn meal and came up with the meal adhering to it. The very thin layer of sand clinging to the meal was removed by the Pomo expert, either by holding the hand and surface of sand as nearly vertical as possible over a basket and gently pouring water over the surface, washing away very little meal in the process, or, even more simply, by holding the hand palm down in a basket of water, the sandy surface just below the surface of the water, and gently moving the hand back and forth. The sand was dislodged and settled in the water. Sometimes the Miwok leached a small amount of meal on a coarsely woven basket covered with a layer of broadleaf lupine leaves *(Lupinus latifolius)*. Water was poured through the meal as in the sand basin.

Chumash Indian Fernando Librado Kitsepawit described to Harrington trays 2 feet in diameter made expressly for leaching acorn meal. They were twined of unsplit fresh juncus *(Juncus acutus)* in a fine mesh. Chumash informant María Solares described leaching baskets shaped like a dish or basin of the same twined weave as the water bottle. The basket or tray was placed on three washed rocks, each about 6 inches in diameter. They spread the meal two fingerbreadths thick on the inside of the basket and poured water slowly over the meal until the basin was full. They left it that way to leach, occasionally covering it with a tray to keep the meal clean. Three times water was poured on and each time it was allowed to drain fully. Only two rinsings were needed if the quantity of meal was very small. Often, if they had only a little meal, they would merely put it in a wooden bowl, slowly stir in water, let the meal settle, and pour off the tannin-bearing water. Librado told Harrington that after a second or third rinsing like this the meal was ready to boil.

The Cahuilla believed that the creator, Mukat, had turned acorns bitter in anger toward his people. Cahuilla children sometimes husked and ate the bitter acorn nut without leaching. Canyon oak acorns were least unpleasant, it was said. But generally, as in northern California, the Cahuilla made an indentation in the sand to leach acorn meal or made a loosely woven leaching basket more characteristic of the southern people. A lining of grass or leaves or some other fibrous material prevented loss of meal in the basket. Warm or cold water (they considered warm to be faster) was poured through the meal until ridding it of the tannin taste. Once warm water was used, cold should not be substituted, Juan Siva told Bean and Saubel. The acorn meal was shaken about to speed the leaching. Whole acorns could be leached by putting them in a fine net bag, tied and placed in a stream. The running water eventually split the acorns and released most of the tannin. They dried the resulting nuts and ground them into meal. The Yurok of northern California were also known to have put whole acorns in water for long periods of time to leach them.

Sometimes a combination of the basket and sand techniques was employed. Barrows described a loosely woven shallow basket covered with sand for the Cahuilla. Ruth Benedict observed that the Serrano neighbors of the Cahuilla leached acorns in large tub-like baskets of willow twigs lined with sand. Hot water was run through until it became clear. Meal was separated from the sand by letting it adhere to the palm of the hand.

Spier preserved the Southern Diegueño method. After reducing the acorn meats to meal in the bedrock mortars located at every camping place, and sifting it in a flat coiled basket, the Southern Diegueño leached the meal by heaping it into a shallow twined basket set on a pad of twigs. Cold water was poured through the meal as a pot of water warmed. Warm water was then used. The process took about half an hour.

Leaching the Other Bitter Nuts

A. L. Kroeber recorded that the Shasta, who normally leached acorn meal on an elevated platform of sticks covered with pine needles and a layer of sand, sometimes buried live oak acorns, shell and all, in mud until they turned black; then they cooked them whole and ate the acorns or roasted them in ashes. The Northern Maidu prepared wild nutmeg *(Tumion californicum)* in a similar fashion. After the shell was cracked and removed, the Northern Maidu buried wild nutmeg nuts for several months in the ground for leaching, after which they were dug up, roasted in the ashes and eaten.

The bitter principle of buckeye nuts *(Aesculus californica)* also had to be removed before they could be eaten. The Atsugewi gathered them ripe, shelled and pounded them and put the pieces into a loosely woven basket where they soaked until the bitter juice was gone. They squeezed the mass dry. It could be eaten as it was without cooking.

The Miwok ate buckeye nuts in times of scarcity when the acorn crop failed. The nuts were collected in the autumn after they had fallen to the ground and could be stored unroasted until the next autumn. To prepare them, they were first roasted in ashes or boiled. Then they broke the husk with their teeth and peeled them. They mashed them in a basket of water by hand and the mixture was poured through a winnowing basket that strained out the coarser pieces. The basket with larger pieces was set to leach in running water for eighteen hours or more, after which the processed buckeye could be eaten without further cooking. The finer meal was leached with cold water in a sand basin for eighteen hours, often until noon the following morning, working by torchlight during the night. The meal was then taken up with the hands, mixed with water in a small basket, and drunk.

The Pomo processed buckeyes a number of different ways. In one, the fleshy outer coating and the brownish inner skin were removed and the white meat of the nuts were boiled in a basket with hot rocks. They became mealy and were then ground or stirred into flour. The flour was sifted and the finer grade leached in a sand-lined basin like the acorn flour. The coarser grade they formed into lumps or balls with the hands and placed them in a rough woven tule basket that was lowered into a stream for a considerable amount of time until the running water leached out the bitter poison. In another method recorded by Barrett, the thick outer hull was removed and the nuts soaked in very hot water until the leathery brown inner skin softened. They bit the skin with an eyetooth and peeled it away with their fingers. In a hot, rock-lined pit oven on a layer of buckeye hulls covered by a layer of grass, the peeled kernels were placed followed by a second layer of grass, hulls, and more hot rocks. A final layer of earth sealed the oven. Nuts baked from four to five hours and became very mealy. They were mashed and stirred with a stick, then leached in a sand-lined basin like acorn meal, except the surface was gently stirred. It took several hours to rid the flour of its bluish tint and leave a pure white, savory and nutritious food similar to baked potatoes. They were eaten without further preparation and went especially well with freshly roasted pepperwood nuts.

Large quantities of wild plum *(Prunus ilicifolia)*, known as hollyleaf cherry or islay, whose shiny, holly-like foliage crowds the canyons and chaparral of southern California, were gathered by the Cahuilla in August, according to Barrows. The fruits were spread in the sun until the slight pulp, which could be eaten fresh, had shrunk and dried. Then the thin shells of the large pits were easily cracked and the kernels removed. These nut meats were pounded in the mortar, like acorns, and leached in a large shallow basket of thin branches covered with carefully selected sand. As with acorns the meal was spread over a depression in the sand and water poured through it. With the poison removed, the Cahuilla boiled the meal into mush.

The Southern Diegueño cracked the wild plum *(ixkai)* on the milling stone with a mano, spread the meats in the sun to dry, rubbed them between the hands and tossed them in a coiled basket to remove the hulls. Then they ground them in the mortar and leached them as they did acorns, except only cold water was used. They were cooked into mush in the same manner as the acorn.

Cooking Acorn Meal

For the soup that was commonly made, the Maidu women added about three gallons of water to one half gallon of acorn dough. The mixture was stirred and, by means of two sticks, hot stones from the fire were put in until the soup boiled. It could be eaten hot or cold. Sand or ashes were frequent inadvertent ingredients, but the cedar sprigs used in leaching left a pleasant taste. A leaf or two of California bay or mint might be introduced toward the end of its cooking for additional flavor.

Mush was made the same way but with less water. Bread could be baked from the dough after the leaching by forming it into a loaf around 15 cm. in diameter that was then flattened and a hot rock wrapped in oak leaves placed in the center. The dough was folded over and pressed down all around the leaf-wrapped rock. Over the whole, more oak leaves were wrapped and it was baked in the ashes or under a pile of hot stones.

The Atsugewi made mush in a basket with hot stones from the fire. The stones were quickly dipped in water to remove the ashes before adding them to the mush. They stirred the mush with a plain uncarved stick and ate it from small individual baskets using their index and second finger since they had no spoons. Acorn bread was made from the meal, water, and a bit of earth. They formed it into biscuits or larger loaves and wrapped them in sunflower leaves. The bread baked all night in an earth oven. It would keep for a week and the men often took it on hunting expeditions.

The Miwok, as described by Barrett and Gifford, brought an array of baskets to the boiling of the acorn meal. In one of about 30-quart capacity, set in a depression 2 to 3 inches deep to maintain stability, they boiled water by means of cooking stones. About a dozen near white-hot stones were taken from the fire with a pair of long sharpened wooden tongs, one stone at a time, dipped in a second basket of water to clean them, then placed in the large basket of water. (The tongs used by Julia Parker were 5 feet long, of incense cedar or oak, and the stones were of steatite or basalt, rounded and fist-size, tested first in a fire to be sure they readily absorbed heat but would not break or explode.) In a third but smaller basket, about two quarts of freshly leached acorn meal was mixed by hand with six or seven quarts of warm water from the big basket. Most, but not all of this, was poured into a fourth basket and hot stones, rinsed as before, were added to boil and cook the meal. (Parker soaked her baskets at least two hours before cooking to make them less likely to leak or burn. They were placed in a shallow depression for stability. Moist, leached meal was smeared on the inside of a new basket up to the water line to further seal it prior to adding the meal for cooking.) Constant stirring with a paddle of oak or manzanita, or a looped stirrer, kept the baskets from burning. Looped stirrers were made from a withe of oak, hazel or, preferably, young black oak, doubled in figure-eight fashion and tied where the two halves crossed to make the distal end loop and near the tip of the handle. When the stones had served their purpose they were dipped out with the paddle or looped stirrer, scraped off with the fingers, and dropped into a fifth basket containing cold water. Mush that had stuck to the stone hardened and was peeled off or fell to the bottom of the basket. After the water had been drained the pieces of congealed mush were eaten or returned to the cooking basket.

The meal mixture from the third basket, or hot water from the first, was added to the cooking basket as its contents boiled to achieve the right consistency—more meal than water for a thick mush, more water for a gruel or soup. Ten to twelve quarts of acorn soup could be made from the original two quarts of meal. A gelatin-like pudding, or even a biscuit, could be formed by cooking thick mush longer, then further thickening the mixture by scooping up boiling mush in a small dipper basket over and over and letting it flow down from a height of 2 feet back into the cooking basket. When it had cooked and thickened enough, the basket dipper with the pudding was immersed for a minute or two in cold water. A pool in a running stream was most desirable. The contents cooled and loosened from the basket, which was then inverted.

The congealed loaf slid into the hands under the water and was further cooled all the way through so that it would not fall to pieces when lifted from the cold stream. The pudding-like bread was eaten daily or at feasts. Dried on a rock, it hardened into a kind of hardtack biscuit.

In the earth oven the Miwok baked a plain white bread made simply of a loaf of acorn meal (with the pulverized root of a pond lily or cattail occasionally mixed in) and a dark brown bread made from the meal of the blue oak leavened with a small amount of ashes from the blue oak bark, which made the bread sweeter but did not cause it to rise. Bread was also made from freshly leached acorn meal baked on a hot stone and turned until it browned.

Gayton described the rock lifters and mush stirrer of the Wukchumni Yokuts. The rock lifters, or tongs, were a pair of pine sticks flattened at one end. The best were obtained in trade from the Eastern Mono. Because they frequently became charred from lifting hot stones from the fire into the cooking basket, the sticks themselves were not allowed to touch the boiling food. Julia Parker soaked the tapered, flattened ends of her rock lifters in water for one and one half hours before use to prevent them from burning. The mush stirrer (so-called because one must stir about in the mush to find the cooking stones) actually had as its primary function the retrieval of stones from the basket. A young oak withe was peeled, heated over the coals and bent around the foot in the form of a loop (about 3 inches across by 4-1/2 inches long). Then it was crossed and the two sides (perhaps a foot or more in length) were brought roughly parallel and tied with a milkweed-fiber string, a thong or the inner bark of the oak. A lighter, quicker version was made of a wild grape-vine withe that could simply be peeled, looped while green and flexible, and tied. The Tubatulabal made mush stirrers from willow and bull pine as well as oak.

A Cahuilla woman's status was affected by her skill in preparing acorn mush. She distinguished fine acorn meal used for meal cakes baked in coals for several hours from coarse meal used for mush. In pouring meal that had been well mixed with water into the leaching basin, the finer meal tended to suspend and settle above the coarse meal. Adan Castillo told Harrington that mush had to be constantly stirred with a palm-frond stem paddle (2 feet long, 3 inches wide at the bottom and 1-1/2 inches at the top) to prevent scorching in the ceramic cooking pot. Unlike groups in northern California, the Cahuilla and other groups in the south possessed pottery. The thickness of the mush was tested by letting it drip from the paddle. Water was added slowly until the consistency was just right. If it was too thick, it would harden when cold. According to Bean and Saubel, it should double in volume and turn a pale pink or tan as it cooks and gel like a pudding as it cools. The flavor could be adjusted by mixing varying proportions of the four types of acorns used by the Cahuilla. For a special taste, chia seeds, berries or a bit of pulverized dried meat might be added.

Like the Cahuilla, the Southern Diegueño mixed acorns of several varieties to achieve a desired flavor. They stirred the dough into a pot half full of cold water on the fire. More cold water was added as the mush thickened until the cook felt it was right. A Northern Diegueño informant told Harrington they ate acorn mush with their fingers.

The Pomo in northern California also ate thicker acorn mush with their fingers but took gruel or soup with a spoon of mussel shell or freshwater clam. For individual service, they drank acorn soup from a small basket. Barrett preserved many unusual bits of acorn technology from the Pomo. To achieve a distinct flavor enjoyed by some Pomo but not others, acorn meats were sprinkled with water and allowed to stand and become moldy. They were then thoroughly dried, ground, leached and rock-boiled into the usual soup, gruel or mush. Acorns of the black oak could be reclaimed after unintentional and apparently prolonged molding. They were dried, shelled, washed thoroughly, placed in a tule basket, and soaked for many days in running water. This removed not only the mustiness but the bitterness as well. They were then thoroughly dried in the sun, ground and without further leaching made into the usual Pomo flat bread baked in an earth oven.

When the acorn meats were taken from the water after the prolonged soaking described above, they were often eaten at once, without further processing. They were found to be soft and sweet. In fact, a delicacy was made from what Barrett called "mush" oak or valley oak acorns soaked whole in running water for as long as two weeks, after which they were baked in the pit oven, hulled and eaten—said to be "just like candy." One consultant told Barrett that they first dampened acorns to make them moldy then soaked them in muddy water for a week or longer and they were ready to eat.

The Pomo made an interesting black bread from acorn meal fresh from the grinding, without being leached in the sand basin. The finely ground meal was thoroughly mixed with red earth—1 to 2 quarts of earth to 5 gallons of meal. All species of acorn could be used this way but only the valley oak and mountain white oak were used without leaching. Formed into flat loaves and baked in the earth oven, the bread turned very black and sweet and was much preferred to the ordinary white acorn bread because of its sweetness. When dried, the black bread became extremely hard and kept indefinitely. It was reconstituted with a short soaking in water.

Bluejay had left his mark on California. I remember the acorn mush Pabla Mata and Andrea Cota cooked for me. They adjusted the pot by adding an acorn flour-and-water mixture as the mush softly boiled, constantly, steadily, slowly stirring, until it thickened just enough. The bland, slightly nutty taste and texture had been life itself to Native California. After it cooled, the mush jelled into a most agreeable pudding. Pabla and Andrea insisted I carry it home.

Maggie Icho, Wukchumni Yokuts, demonstrates use of the mush stirrer in retrieving a stone from the cooking basket. Likely photographed by Clifford Relander, 1945 (Southwest Museum).

Mortar and Pestle

"Sharp stones and perseverance were the only things used in their manufacture," wrote Hugo Reid in 1852. He referred to the Gabrielino manufacture of stone mortars. Unlike the swift, skillful removal of long graceful flakes from fine-grained stone (Ishi, the Yana Indian, could knap an arrowhead in half an hour), pecking a mortar proceeds in endless repetitive blows, removing bits of material by crushing or crumbling tiny fragments from coarser-grained rock.

Pedro Fages (Priestly, 1937) recounted in 1769 that the Chumash used flint with great skill to cut out mortars, crocks and plates of black stone. Picks of flint pecked steatite into various objects, according to J. P. Harrington's Chumash informants. In this way they made ollas or bowls, for example. They also told him that they used other sharp fragments of stone, sometimes the first stone they might pick up.

Outside my kitchen door rests an amorphous piece of limestone I purchased for fifteen dollars from a rancher in the Tehachapi Mountains twenty-five years ago. He was making a wall of this and generally similar, large, shapeless rocks. Surprisingly, close inspection revealed a small mortar hole pecked into every one. Well-shaped, fine-grained sandstone pestles, oblong but heavier at the bottom end, lay strewn about nearby. Those stone mortars of the Tehachapis reminded me of so many other stone mortars, even the larger, deeper bedrock mortars found everywhere in Native California. Someone once described to me a rock in the Tehachapis that had perhaps 100 mortar basins pecked into it (covered over in recent times by road construction). I have seen similar outcroppings in old Miwok villages in the Sierras. Three years ago, on a trip into the mountains of northern Baja California, I was amazed to find in an ancient Kumeyaay village an eighty-year-old woman still pounding acorns with a stone pestle in a bedrock mortar. There were many mortar depressions in the extensive outcropping of granite where she worked. She represented the end of a line of mortar users that archaeologists estimate had begun some five to six thousand years ago in California. Over time, the varieties of mortars became almost endless. The materials of their manufacture came to include even wood, and not only acorns and other staple seeds, but roots, flesh, bones, tobacco, and mesquite pods were all pounded in a mortar.

Manufacture and Function of Stone Mortars

In contrast to rough-rock and bedrock mortars, naturally round, beach-worn cobbles were fashioned into mortars by the Gabrielino on San Clemente Island. In the 1870s Paul Schumacher discovered there what appeared to be a workstation for the manufacture of stone mortars. At the site were large numbers of surf-worn basalt boulders of different sizes. Some of the rocks had been broken in an apparent attempt to split off a section of the globular mass to make a flat surface on which to begin the mortar basin. Other rocks were already of a semiglobular form and bore marks of a pick, in one instance, a circle outlining the intended size of the basin. Still others had been broken and discarded while the craftsman was excavating the mortar cavity. Schumacher explained that the initial work of shaping the cobbles was done with a hammer stone, simply a chunk of hard rock. Well-aimed blows would have detached even large pieces with sufficient accuracy to give the rough form. The more exacting work on smoother surfaces was done, in Schumacher's opinion, with picks, vertically against the face of the rock. Even hard basalt would crumble under the pecking of a pointed stone.

In 1960 researchers from the Southwest Museum discovered on San Nicolas Island a partially worked mortar, a circle outlining the intended size of the basin, like the one described by Schumacher. Close to the sea and on the surface of an ancient midden, the wind had recently uncovered the spherical sandstone boulder which stood a little over 12 inches high. From this and two other sandstone mortars, found on the same island in 1926, Bruce Bryan reconstructed the likely steps of manufacturing a stone mortar.

First a groove was pecked around the top, marking the lip of a completed vessel. A large lump of rounded rock remained. Instead of trying to break this off and risk splitting the entire stone, it was pecked into quarters for large mortars or a single nodule for smaller ones. These, then, were easily knocked off without fracturing the main body of stone. The two mortars found in 1926 exemplified this stage. The technique saved time and energy. To break knobs of rock away with a few blows was much easier than removing the same amount of material through pecking. The process was repeated. The area just inside the rim was pecked away with more nodules created and broken off and so on until it was no longer possible to do this. Finally, of course, simple laborious pecking would complete the piece. The smooth finish seen on some stone bowls likely resulted from rubbing with a lump of sandstone.

One hundred years ago Barrows described Cahuilla mortars as roughly shaped from large, nearly round boulders with a slightly flattened bottom. The cavity was perhaps not over 3 inches in depth. A hopper just fit over the hole. The pestle was a thick heavy stone around 10 inches long, bluntly rounded at both ends. A double handful of seeds was placed in the depression and the woman, seated with a leg to either side, would take the pestle in both hands and drop it heavily into the mortar. Bean and Saubel recorded that the Cahuilla made mortars by first heating the area to be removed and then pecking it with a sharp rock. The pestle itself completed the manufacture by grinding the depression deeper. The basket hopper was attached with tar or pitch when the bowl was still shallow to avoid spillage of the acorn meal.

A naturally worn cobble would serve as a pestle. The Miwok found such pestles in the beds of mountain streams. The Tubatulabal also found them in river beds. Tubatulabal pestles, for both stone and wood mortars, were simply rough, cylindrical granite or slate rocks picked up from river beds and used unmodified, according to Voegelin. They were from 5 to 20 inches in length and 2-1/2 to 5 inches in width, depending on the size of the mortar. A. Kroeber noted they were somewhat shaped, partly by pecking with the edge of a flat cobble and in part by continued usage. In contrast, the 2-foot-long but very slender stone pestles used by the Cahuilla in deep wooden mortars for mesquite pods required definite dressing of the stone.

Incidentally, grinding slabs preceded mortars in the California archaeological record and they continue to be used. Like stones for pestles, slabs of granite or black slate were also easily found by the Tubatulabal. They used them on one side only with a small ovoid rub stone that was flat on the top and bottom. The slab slanted away from the person who was grinding, with the lower end resting on a basketry tray and the upper on a flat rock about 2 inches thick. Most often seeds were ground on them.

For pinion expeditions the Tubatulabal made portable stone mortars. They could be as small as 6 inches in diameter to as large as 35 inches. They were made by pecking out a depression in a round, soft, gray stone with a hard pointed rock.

Though generally associated with acorns, pounding in a stone mortar made tough, fibrous vegetables and meats palatable as well, especially for the very young and old. The process turned even bones into an accessible food. Luiseño people would bake venison and rabbits in an earth oven and what they could not immediately consume they crushed in a mortar, including the bones of the rabbit. The resulting mash, they dried and stored. The mortar was, in short, a convenient food processor. In northern California small mortars were used to crush tobacco or meat. Thirty years ago, Ralph Michelsen observed Rufino Ochurte, a Kiliwa of Lower California, grinding the cooked spine of jackrabbit in a small, rough-pecked mortar. The hole was about 1-1/2 inches deep, flaring out to a diameter of about 6 or 7 inches. The ribs of the animal had been removed and the 3-inch-diameter by 6-inch-long pestle ground small quantities of rabbit spine into a thick paste as generous amounts of salt were added. Michelsen described the result as "quite tasty," like unspiced liverwurst were it not for bits of grit and bone. He was told of an old woman who would pass an entire day grinding deer bone to a fine paste in a mortar.

Thomas Jefferson Mayfield preserved an interesting example. His father had entrusted a band of Choinumne Yokuts to raise him from the age of six, beginning around 1850 after his mother had died. This was a time when some Indians of the Sierra foothills and San Joaquín Valley still followed their traditional round. In his reminiscences Mayfield described an Indian woman digging up her mortar and pestle by the side of Lake Tulare where she had buried them the year before. The Indians had come down the river by tule boat in the spring. The lake had been a great attraction for them, Mayfield recalled, with its almost unlimited amount of game, before American settlements destroyed it all. Women waded into the water and, with pointed sticks, dug out great quantities of the young tule roots that were soft and sweet and could be eaten at once. Other women assisted by pulling them from the lake and cutting the roots from the stalks. Those not immediately consumed, the women made into an almost pure starch by first pounding the roots into a soft mass in the stone mortar. Then, in a large cooking basket, the roots were covered with hot water and stirred with a looped stirrer for about an hour. Next, fibrous parts were discarded. After an hour or two the starch settled and the water was poured off. It left a cake of starch 2 inches thick by 8 or 9 inches in diameter with little taste but very rich, according to Mayfield.

Yoimut, an elderly Chunut Yokuts lady who had lived on the northeast shore of Tulare Lake, told Frank Latta that they had not used acorn mush a great deal. They used tule roots, eating the tender roots raw (the Northern Paiute ate the white base of the stem raw) and pounding up the old roots. Latta also learned from her that a portable stone mortar could be turned into a bedrock mortar. She and Wahnomkot, a Wukchumne Yokuts, pointed out that it was difficult to pound with a heavy pestle in a mortar on top of the ground. That's why they buried them. "Uncle Bud" Akers told Latta that he had actually seen Indian women under sunshades on the shores of Lake Tulare in 1853 pounding tule seeds and roots in stone mortars buried with the rim even with the surface of the ground.

Kroeber recorded that the Yokuts denied they made the stone mortars themselves, though they found and used them. The Chukchansi Yokuts claimed all mortar holes were made by coyote, "who employed an agency of manufacture that decency debars from mention," wrote Kroeber. Small stone mortars were kept by toothless persons for pounding up whole gophers or ground squirrels that younger relatives might give them. Small mortars might also be used for processing tobacco or medicines.

The Cahuilla ground the pea-size fruit of a fan palm in a mortar. They gathered them from summer through late fall and if the thin date-like pulp was not eaten fresh or soaked in water and taken as a beverage, the whole fruit—flesh and seed—was dried in the sun and stored in clay ollas. Later, they were ground in bedrock mortars into flour (including the flesh and seed), mixed with other flours and water and made into mush.

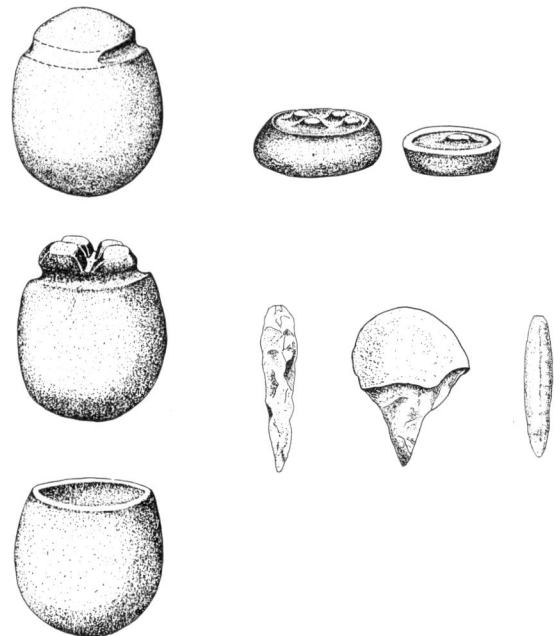

Above, partially completed San Nicolas island mortars: first, found by Southwest Museum, shows groove and likely progression that would have marked the lip of the newly begun mortar; next two, shorter than first, found by Los Angeles Museum, show further progression in pecking mortars—the remains of raised knobs, created by pecking away material around them and breaking knobs off with a hammerstone. Below, hypothetical grooved mortar, a continuation or next stage of the one above, with four raised knobs ready to be broken off; and completed mortar, knobs having been repeatedly created and broken away and interior finely pecked (drawings by von Winning in Bryan, 1970).

At right, picks from southern California Islands: first, hard-stone cobble pick, shaped by percussion, found by A. Barnard, 1882, San Miguel Island; next, percussion-shaped porphyry, found by León de Cessac, 1877, San Nicolas Island; last, of fine grained material, possibly ground or polished, also found by de Cessac in 1877 on San Nicolas Island (drawn from photographs in Hudson and Blackburn, 1987).

Wooden Mortars

Though obviously perishable and not common in the archaeological record, wooden mortars were employed in both northern and southern California. Portable wooden mortars were used by the Yokuts on the alluvial planes, according to Kroeber. The Tachi Yokuts made a mortar of white oak, flat-bottomed about 1 foot high and 1-1/2 feet in diameter. Bordered by a narrow rim, the upper surface was excavated a few inches by fire and then a smaller pit was sunk in the center of the excavation. The pestle was the same as that used on bedrock. The Chukchansi and Choinumne Yokuts also made wooden mortars.

Yoimut, whom Latta described as the last of the Chunut, knew the wooden mortar. Her mother had a big one when she was a little girl. Especially interesting were the non-portable tree-trunk mortars. When an oak tree fell they would take the bark off and with coals make mortars in the top portion of the tree. Many fallen trees had three or four mortar holes in them. The women would sit on the tree trunk and pound acorns and seeds.

Along with the Yokuts and others, the Tubatulabal made mortars of hardwoods such as oak and juniper. They burnt out the interior then smoothed it with a rough stone. It was used com-

Mortar with basket hopper and pestle. Southwest Museum records indicate that the set was in use when obtained many years ago from an Indian lady in mountains of southern California. The pecked stone mortar is 11" in diameter with a shallow circular depression about 6" in diameter. The open-stitch, coiled juncus hopper measures 15" in diameter, 6" deep, and is attached to the mortar with asphaltum. Notice how the added reinforcing stitches around the rim and mending stitches on the body of the basket have the fag or tail end of new weavers sewn under at a 45-degree angle. Black, dyed juncus zigzag pattern near the top. Photographed by George Clifton (courtesy of the Southwest Museum).

monly with a basketry hopper that kept the acorn meal from falling away. A photograph in Barrett's work on the Pomo shows a wooden mortar in the manufacturing process. A Pomo man blows through a 12- to 15-inch elderberry tube, used as a bellows, onto glowing coals in the cavity of a burl.

The desert-oriented Cahuilla made wooden mortars to pound mesquite beans *(Prosopis glandulosa)*. The pit was deep and pointed, observed Kroeber, unlike the broad, bowl-shaped wooden basin with a shallow excavation in its center used for acorns by northern groups such as the Winton and Yokuts. They fired the center of a cottonwood or mesquite stump and cut the hole with a stone ax, according to Bean and Saubel. Cahuilla Indian Adan Castillo said those of mesquite were considered best. Harrington noted that they were 30 inches high with a mortar depression around 15 inches. They buried them in the ground for the bottom 15 inches of the stump and slender pestles of stone or mesquite, 2 to 3 feet long, were worked in a standing position. In addition to mortars of cottonwood and mesquite, the Yuman tribes of the lower Colorado River sometimes employed just a simple hole in the ground as a mortar. Oblong mesquite or lava pestles pounded the mesquite beans.

Mesquite was a staple of the desert tribes of southeastern California. The mature dried bean could be broken into small pieces and eaten at once but processing in a wooden mortar was the usual way. Green pods were collected from early to mid-summer—the season comes sooner as one moves south—and the mature and dry pods three weeks after that. Tunnels were made into the thick mesquite groves by breaking or cutting out branches. The green pods were placed in the sun to ripen and dry (a hedge against leaving them on the tree to ripen, fall, and be eaten by animals or lost to floods), or immediately crushed in the wooden mortar. The crushed, pulpy mass was mixed with water for a refreshing summertime drink, common to every Cahuilla household. The Yuman tribes, according to Castetter and Bell, gathered the ripe beans from the ground, picked them from the trees with a wooden hook, and even robbed rodents' nests of the beans. Men generally went along on these expeditions to protect the women and children, who did most of the gathering, or to hunt rabbits. But in periods of high floods, men became the principal gatherers.

Mesquite and screwbean pods were transported home in large carrying nets. Green mesquite pods were prepared at once as described but groups such as the Mohave and Maricopa dried the ripe beans at least three or four days on rooftops. They stored the beans in large, tightly twisted and interwoven cylindrical willow or arrowweed baskets made by the men and set on platforms 4 or 5 feet above the ground. To utilize as food the dried beans were also crushed in the mortar for the pulp. The heavier fiber and seeds were removed from the mortar during the pounding and again, immediately after, by shaking the ground meal in a basket. Fiber and seeds were always discarded. Steeping the crushed pods in water made a sweet nutritious beverage. Castetter and Bell report that occasionally it was allowed to ferment. The Mohave, Yuma and Cocopa enjoyed the mildly intoxicating drink.

Rough-rock mortar and pestle, found with many others on a ranch in the Tehachapi mountains.

Sometimes the mortar-ground meal was made into cakes. Bean and Saubel record that the meal was put into baskets or clay vessels, dampened and left to harden for a day or so. The hardened meal could be formed into round balls, but more commonly the Cahuilla made cakes from it 2 to 10 inches in diameter and from 1 to 3 inches thick. The larger size was more common. Pieces were broken off from the cakes and eaten, boiled into mush, or mixed with water for the usual drink. Hunters and travelers especially esteemed the cakes. A bit mixed with water made a substantial meal. Cocopa Indian Sam Spa told William Kelly that cake meal was sweeter than freshly ground pod.

Studies cited by Bean and Saubel indicate that mesquite pods are high in carbohydrate and sugar with a fair amount of protein and fat. Larvae-infested beans seem to have been commonplace wherever beans were gathered, and generally this made no difference to the groups that ate them. Worm infestation may actually have made the beans more nutritious.

Unlike mesquite pods, the closely related screwbeans *(Prosopis pubescens)* were not made into cakes as the pulp did not stick together. However, this characteristic made them easier to winnow. Seeds and fiber floated to the surface when the mortar-ground pods were placed in a bowl of water and they were easily dipped out. Screwbeans ripened later than mesquite beans. In Mohave territory, for example, mesquite beans were plentiful in July and screwbeans in August. A nutritious beverage was made of screwbean pulp in the same manner as mesquite. Occasionally the fully ripe pods were dried and pounded into meal, but Castetter and Bell reported that screwbeans tasted bitter at maturity. To overcome this, the lower Colorado River tribes pit-cured them. In sandy soil they dug a large basin with sloping sides, 3 to 15 feet in diameter and from 3 to 5 feet deep. This basin was lined with arrowweed, filled with mature screwbean pods, and covered with more arrowweed. They sprinkled water on the arrowweed covering and buried the pit with dirt. Treatment could last for a week to sixty days but usually thirty days. A quick treatment of only a few days could be effected by heating the pit and sprinkling the pods directly with water before covering with arrowweed and earth. Pit-treated pods turned reddish brown and were soft, moist and sweet. They were then dried, stored, and utilized as the mesquite pods, or immediately pounded in the wooden mortar and the pulp mixed with water for the standard beverage.

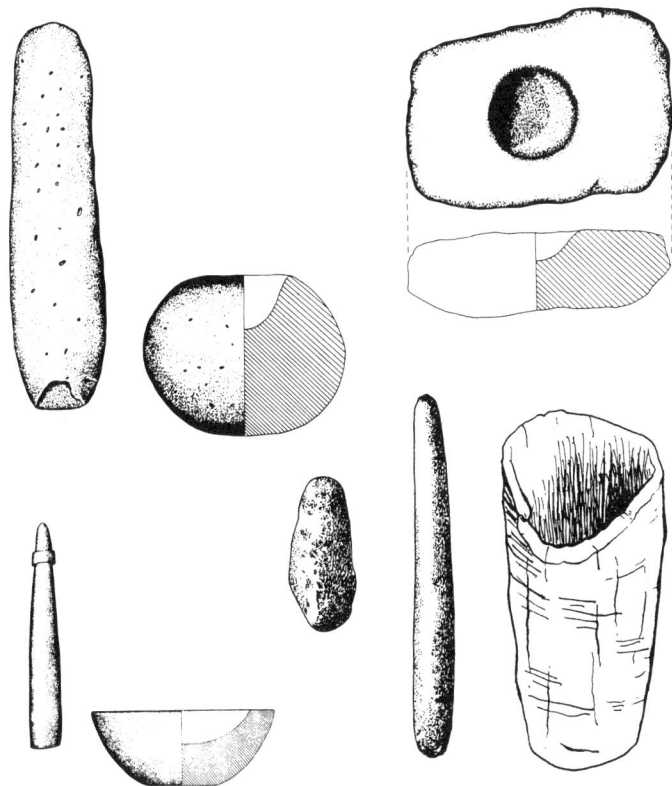

Diagrammatic sketches of southern California mortars and pestles: top, pestle, stone bowl mortar and slab mortar, coastal area from about 2,000 B.C. through A.D. 500; bottom left, ringed pestle and stone-bowl mortar, coastal area around A.D. 500 until European contact (Chartkoff, 1984). Bottom middle: Cahuilla stone pestles, first, for stone mortar; second, for wooden mortar (Kroeber, 1925). Bottom right: Cahuilla cottonwood mortar for mesquite pods (drawn from photographs in Bean and Saubel, 1972).

Soaproot Brush

The most difficult part of making a soaproot brush is finding the soaproot plant *(Chlorogalum pomeridianum)*. Look for a rosette of long thin leaves along the ground with a yard-tall stalk at its center. In the spring or early summer, branchlets from the stalk bear wispy white flowers that open in the evening. By late summer and fall the plant becomes scraggly and parched but still very noticeable among the fallen leaves of the foothill forests. I searched for months in Los Angeles for the elusive soaproot, then stumbled on an army of them buried on a pine flat between two small streams above Big Tujunga Creek.

The early Californians excavated the root with a digging stick, and after a few frustrating attempts with a shovel in the rocky soil, I, too, found the pointed end of a digging stick most effective. With a little help from bare hands, the deep, hairy bulb pulled out easily. The contrast with the delicate flowers it sustained surprised me. I shook it clean but, like some strange brown-red beast that had been pulled from his lair, it seemed angry. Julia Parker, a Kashia Pomo Indian, learned the old ways at Yosemite where she lived for many years with her husband's grandmother, Lucy Parker, of Paiute Miwok lineage. Julia recites a prayer of thanks or makes an offering while gathering soaproot, and that is a good idea. I felt I had taken a life. But not without purpose, for the uses of a soaproot brush are many. The Chumash were typical and they employed the brush for grooming hair as well as for cleaning metates of meal when grinding, or even in cleaning the floor of their home. The Miwok used it for a hairbrush, for scrubbing cooking baskets, and for returning particles of acorn for the steady pounding of the bedrock mortar.

The many dry fibers of the outer layers of the soaproot are long and durable. They readily separate from the bulb and one can make a brush from a single plant. However, most examples appear to include the fiber from three to five plants—some even more. I wanted to use the natural curvature of the fiber—the ends that wrapped around the bulb—as the handle leaving the very straight ends as the brush proper, like plastic store brushes. But for the California Indians the strong curved ends were used to advantage and the other straight ends became the handle.

Barrett and Gifford did fieldwork among the Miwok around 1906. They recorded that the dry outer fibers of soaproot were laid so that these natural covers nested together and all faced the same way. The fibers were then bound temporarily with a withe about the middle. Next, soaproot juice was thoroughly worked into the handle end. The soaproot bulb was scraped to make this mucilaginous glue. At the same time the handle was wrapped tightly, round and round, with string. Examples have the handle almost pointed, a wedge that enlarges into the bristles at the base. Exposure to the sun and air for a day or two made the handle very hard. Pine pitch sometimes substituted for the soaproot juice.

Fernando Librado, the aged Chumash Indian, told Harrington in the early years of the twentieth century that after being tied fine with *tok* (Indian hemp) cordage and cut across the top to trim

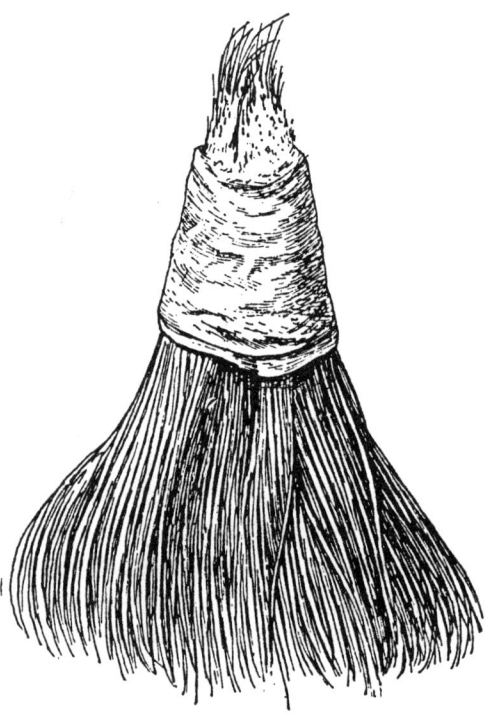

Maidu soaproot acorn-meal brush, length 14 cm. (Dixon, 1905).

it, the handle of the Chumash soaproot brush was coated with asphaltum. An oak brand burned the bristles of the brush to make it even.

The Wukchumni Yokuts soaproot brush could be as short as 4 inches to as long as 9 inches. Larger brushes were for the hair and had coarse bristles and hook-like tips. To make it, they dug the root after the flower had faded and the fibers were at their toughest. They carefully removed the fibers and boiled the bulb in water until, according to Gayton, it became a plastic cream-colored mass. The fibers were formed and tied into a brush, the bulb mass pressed and shaped over the end as a handle and tied in place with wrappings of string.

Thomas Mayfield, who had been raised by the Choinumne Yokuts in the 1850s, told of common household brushes made from a dried goose or duck wing, but he also described brushes of soaproot husks. The latter, he said, were tied with milkweed-fiber string and the handle covered with the mashed pulp of the soaproot bulb.

The Chukchansi Yokuts, recorded Gayton, used the soaproot brush for everything: cleaning acorn meal, washing and scrubbing baskets, even for sweeping the floor. They made them in various sizes, from 1 or 2 inches in width to 1 foot wide. July was when women went out with their digging sticks and came back with sackfuls of soaproots. There was no need to dry them. They removed the outer fibers and put the remaining bulbs on a bed of coals that were then buried and the bulbs left to roast at least half a day. After removal from the coals a soapy substance from the inside of each onion-like layer was scraped off with the teeth and chewed. (In later times a knife was used.) The material, which turned white, was put into a basket to await use as a handle for the brush. The bottom, coarser ends of the fibers would become the bristles. They were brought together and bound temporarily with sticks in the manner of the Miwok. The upper handle end was squeezed and twisted tight and bound up. Three layers of these, side by side, were used in an average brush and all were bound firmly together, likely with milkweed cordage. The handle was wrapped round and round with cordage. The soapy glue was smeared on the handle and smoothed. From the small temporary sticks that had held the bristles together, the brush was hung to dry in the sun or in the house. It took a week for the handle to completely harden.

In contrast to the Yokuts, the Tubatulabal dug the soaproot in March and April when the plant was green. Bunches of fibers, each 3/4 of an inch in diameter by 4 to 5 inches long, were twined together, side by side, at one end with string (three bunches for a hairbrush, four in a mealing brush). This made the brush flat and narrow. A Tubatulabal museum specimen mentioned by Voegelin was apparently wrapped at the handle end with sinew and had a characteristic triangular shape (when viewed from the wider side).

An account by Bev Ortiz describing Parker's methods elaborates on some brush-making concepts. The bulbs were gathered by Parker in late spring. She boiled them for thirty minutes with hair or fibers left on. She let them cool and removed the outer fibers. Next, she rubbed the bulbs against the back of a winnowing basket or any open-twined basket, continuing until all the pulp had been extracted and squeezed through the coarse weave of the basket. She spread a thin layer of this pasty pulp over the handle that had been bound with Indian hemp and allowed it to dry for a day. Additional thin coatings followed, one for each of five or six days. One layer had to dry before the next was applied and a layer could not be too thick or the handle would crack. After the last coat she wet her hand and rolled it over the handle, molding it to the final shape. It dried dull white or slightly tan in color.

Parker made water-resistant handles from heated pine pitch and charcoal dust. The pitch was heated to boiling, then the heat was lowered and charcoal added, enough to insure that the pitch should harden. The handle was dipped into the melted pitch and charcoal. As it cooled, but while still soft, Julia shaped it into the desired form.

All of the above methods likely produced good brushes. Using the Miwok account from Barrett and Gifford, in a few hours, I have made serviceable soaproot brushes with handles wrapped in native cordage and hardened with the raw pulp of its own bulb. A glued handle left exposed on a rock in the hot sun dries very quickly.

Acorn Storage Basket

Leslie Spier bequeathed us a description of the acorn storage basket from his observations at the Southern Diegueño village of Campo in the early 1920s:

The storage basket (cikwi'n) is made of any material, usually a willow (halasi'), but sometimes of a tougher wood (inkx ai, "coffee berry") through which the rodents cannot readily gnaw. The basket, usually made by a man, resembles a huge bird's nest, with flat bottom, fairly straight sides, but narrower at the mouth than near the base, into which the sides gradually round. Of two specimens seen, one is the largest size made, and measures seventy centimeters in height, seventy-five centimeters diameter across the rim, with a maximum diameter of one meter near the base; the other, fifty-five centimeters in height, fifty centimeters rim diameter, eighty-five centimeters maximum diameter, with walls four centimeters thick. These baskets are truncated cones: sometimes the basket is conical, and the tip must then be pried open with a sharp stick. The basket is coiled counterclockwise, working on the near side, mouth up. The green leafy twigs are cut diagonally, leaving a sharpened butt. Two are twisted together and the coil for the base started. The butt of a new twig is thrust into the mass beside one of the two elements to lengthen it. The elements are twisted once (near element moving over and away from the workman), a new twig added to the opposing element, and so on, each new twig introduced fastening the coil to the existing structure. In rough work the butt ends are permitted to project on the interior surface, but for a fine finish they should not protrude. Such graneries are set out of reach of rodents on platforms (a crib of poles, for example) near the house, never inside it.

Justin F. Farmer, a transportation engineer with a corporation based in Fullerton, California and of Ipai or Northern Diegueño descent, learned long ago how to make Diegueño acorn storage baskets (called *hekwiin* or *haqueen* in Northern Diegueño) from Dave Osuna, an Ipai Indian of Santa Ysabel, California. Traditionally, granaries were made in the late fall to store the acorn crop harvested at that time. Almost any kind of willow worked for their manufacture, Farmer told me, whatever was handy. The Cahuilla used arrowweed for similar granaries. Hedges found that the Northern Diegueño of Santa Ysabel sometimes even used branches of scrub oak (*Quercus dumosa*) along with willow in the construction of acorn storage baskets. Leaves were left on the branches used, explained Farmer, in order to repel rain, plug up interstices through which rodents might enter (they find the willow leaves distasteful) and to conceal any error in craftsmanship.

Farmer pointed out, however, that he is far and away the best traditional Diegueño granary maker in the world, perhaps making the problem of poor craftsmanship moot in his case were it not for the fact that he is also the *only* traditional Diegueño granary maker left in the world. Dave Osuna and his sister Christina Osuna Beresford, who could also make these baskets, have passed on.

Justin Farmer, left to right: beginning the coil; pointing out the emergence of the early inserted branches on side of coil; holding the granary and two groups of willow boughs as he inserts a sharpened branch into the rim.

Drawing from a large pile of fresh arroyo willow boughs (they must be gathered fresh before their leaves have fallen), Farmer selected six or seven approximately 3-foot lengths and aligned them in a tight bundle. All of the branches were thin but those selected for the start of the basket had to be especially thin and pliable. The tapered tops of the plants pointed toward his left and these he rolled toward the opposite, thicker side of the bundle. He bent the left 2 or 3 inches back once, twice, perhaps four or more times completing two or three rolls toward the thick side of the bundle, keeping very tight the small, flat, leafy disk he began to form.

Next, with the fist-sized, coiled, vertical disk gripped firmly in his left hand, his right hand separated the loose branches, that extended off the top of the disk toward the right, into two bundles bent slightly to either side of the coil. He kept them separated with his left thumb, his fingers maintaining a grip on the coil. Then his right hand reached under the first or nearest bundle to grasp the second near the point of bifurcation. With his right thumb extended, his right arm twisted clockwise catching the first bundle with the thumb and turning the two bundles about each other 180 degrees. The far bundle passed underneath the closer one as the closer bundle was carried over the far one with his right thumb. Both moved counterclockwise about each other in the direction of the growing coil or disk. They had, in effect, changed places and the thumb of his right hand held them in their new position.

Just in front of the twist in a clockwise direction on the rim of the coil, the thick end (rarely over 1/4 inch) of a new branch was inserted into and through the coil. The thick or bottom end had been cut at a sharp angle to facilitate penetration of the coil. It passed all the way through and could be felt on the other side. This tied the roll together and fixed the coil. The remainder, or opposite, thinner end of the branch, was combined with the closer bundle. Once again, his right hand reached under to grasp the far bundle and twist it underneath the closer one as his right thumb carried the closer bundle over the far one. The twist laid on the rim of

Northern Diegueño woman inserting willow branches as she coils acorn granary. Photograph by J. P. Harrington, November 1925 (Smithsonian Institution National Anthropological Archives).

Christina Osuna Beresford with acorn granary made by her brother, Dave Osuna, at Santa Ysabel. (Photograph by Justin Farmer, 1975.)

the disk and was held by his left thumb which kept the two bundles separate.

The spiral had rotated a little. Another branch was inserted in the middle of the rim just after the last twist, again all the way through. The thinner, leafier top of the new branch was again grouped with the closer bundle and the bundles were twisted. Essentially this insertion of leafy withes and twisting of bundles would be the pattern for the rest of the basket.

The function of skewering the coil with branches was to at once bind and augment the coil and maintain the girth and length of the two bundles as they were twisted in the process of coiling a flat base for the granary. In contrast to the starting coil, the thicker ends were always to the left and first inserted into the coil which proceeded in a clockwise direction.

After the first few branches had been inserted through so they could be felt on the far side of the disk, or as deeply as possible, securing the base of the basket, new sticks continued to be inserted on the outer edge of the rim but angled in the direction of the coil and toward the inside bottom of the basket (the side of the disk away from the basketmaker) where they might emerge slightly. This latter angle was done to put them under tension as they were bent back to the plane of the base and eventually bent upward to form the sides of the basket. The tension made them less likely to pull free and this strengthened the basket. The angle of insertion in the direction of the coil was also important. If perpendicular (like the spoke of a wheel), there would be little advance to the coil, but the coil would be thicker. If flat (on the rim) or too far in front of the twist, the coil would advance a great deal but would be thin and weak. About 45 degrees in the direction of the coil just in front of the twist seemed right.

At this point, Farmer was using leafy branches 3 to 4 feet long. Bigger branches could be used for bigger granaries. Longer branches would give the granary greater strength. The thickness of each bundle was about three to six branches. If one bundle became too thin, more than a single branch might be inserted in front of the twist on the edge of the rim and grasped with the thinner group when it was the nearer bundle. Soon the thickness and tightness of the basket made the entry of new withes difficult. The sharp angle at which they were cut became more important and pushing the basket against something eased the entry.

Size depended on the maker. Northern Diegueño granaries were as much as 2 feet across and 3 feet high but generally smaller, according to Farmer. He began to change from a disk form to a bowl shape as he began his way up the sides of the granary. He did this by gradually changing the point of insertion of new branches. Instead of being centered on the outer rim the point slightly shifted toward the inside, which faced away from the basketmaker, and aimed toward the inside bottom of the basket. The sharp butt end penetrated through the rim coil to the coil beneath and, if possible, toward the inside of the basket, continuing to give tension to the branches as the basket curved up and inward. Farmer watched for openings in the coiling, and when he came to those spots he pushed them down and closed them. If a branch broke and stuck out of the coil, he simply incorporated the loose end in a bundle of the next coil.

To finish, he cut off all but about 8 inches of the two groups of branches and folded them down into the concavity of the basket in the direction of the coil. They held nicely there and, when dry, would not unravel. The leafy granary looked like a large beautiful nest. As a last touch, Farmer pushed and molded it into a more symmetrical shape. Only the flat rock that traditionally would have covered the granary to keep out the squirrels was lacking.

Closely Twined and Coiled Baskets

Except for twined openwork among the Pomo, which was man's work, women by and large were the weavers and sewers of California baskets. In the northwest, twining was their exclusive technique. To the south coiling was most common, but everywhere in California basketry centered around the gathering, preparation and cooking of acorns—women's work. Shapes and sizes of baskets followed this function and were similar from one end of California to the other. Aboriginal California baskets, often decorated with great skill for aesthetic pleasure, status, gifts or ceremony, found greatest importance in their practicality. They stored acorn seeds, sifted acorn meal, boiled acorn mush, and served this food to a hungry people.

Nowadays, California Indian baskets sit mostly on shelves or pedestals. The Gold Rush was about commercialism and getting rich. Newly arrived Europeans did not extol the "savages" nakedness, their ability to quickly throw together a well-insulated hut of sticks and straw, dig roots in the woods and live on wild weeds and grasshoppers. But art as investment they eventually understood and Indian basketry at its most artful was encouraged. A. Kroeber wrote, "These people have always been reckoned among the most backward of American Indians in the general level of their attainments; but there is also a unanimity of agreement that their baskets excel those of most other tribes, in fact are probably preeminent on the continent, if not in the world" (1932).

Indian arts adapted to the European market. California baskets from caves and rock shelters tend to be more modestly decorated than those we see behind glass in late historical collections and museum boutiques. The only basket I ever came upon in actual use, by an isolated elderly woman among the Kumeyaay of the Sierra Juárez, was a plain coiled sifting basket in a crude open stitch, like those from some caves of southern California. But she was the last. Decorated basketry of only the highest quality has come to define Indian even for the Indian. In a sense, artfully made baskets linking with the past and creating a modern identity may be seen as *the* transcending survival skill. It is difficult to imagine basketry as it must have been, as something varied and beautiful but just as often practical, arising in response to a naturally evolving world.

A wide range of basketry materials was available in every part of California, while local traditions narrowed the number used in any given region to only a few. California Indians were not dilettanti but survivalists, and knowing a few materials well seemed to work best. Optimum time for collecting and treatment varied. Many plants were collected in the spring, others in the fall. They were split, cleaned and dried for future use. Reconstituting by soaking a short while in water seemed to cause

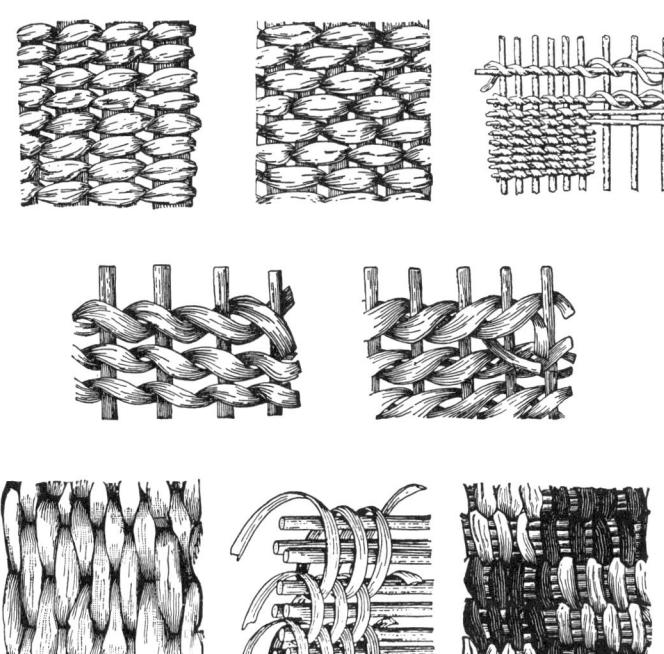

Twining and coiling. Top row: first, plain twining; next, diagonal twining; finally, the lattice-twined weave peculiar to the Pomo. In Pomo lattice-twined weaving the horizontal or extra warp was on the exterior of the basket. It made the basket rigid and strong, often used on hoppers for acorn mortars. Second row. Twined borders: first, simple twined Pomo border; next, 3-strand twined border. Bottom row: first, single rod coiling; next, diagrammatic sketch shows 3-rod foundation and coils; last, multiple strand foundation and coils (Mason, 1904).

less shrinkage than employing the material fresh. Cutting the plant back in the summer or fall or burning an area—both common practices—increased production of long straight shoots during the next couple of years. But this was only the beginning. What follows is something of the complexity of preparation of materials and making of baskets from three large areas of California, emphasizing the sewing of southern California coiled baskets.

Northwestern California

In the tightly and exquisitely twined baskets of northwest California, warps were of thin, peeled, carefully sized hazel sticks *(Corylus californica)* or, if unavailable, willow *(Salix)*. The roots of willow, cottonwood or red alder *(Alnus oregana)*, cut from the edge of a river and often split, could be made into wefts. More commonly twined as wefts were the roots of the yellow or sugar pine *(Pinus ponderosa or lambertiana)*. They were boiled, split, coiled, stored and boiled again, scraped with a mussel shell to release fine strips and split even finer with the fingernail. Wefts turned upward in northwestern California basketry. That is, they revolved counterclockwise as they moved from left to right in their upward spiral.

For designs, wefts were often faced or overlaid during the twining process with bear grass or sour grass *(Xerophyllum tenax)* for a white pattern,

Hupa twined processing baskets. Left to right and down: Openwork basket for harvesting acorns and another for carrying the crop to the village. A tightly twined granary basket. A hopper basket and another in place on the mortar with pestle and broom for sweeping the meal. Large, flat basket stored under the mortar is for catching and sifting meal. Next, a cooking basket to boil mush or fish with hot stones (overlay designs confined to the upper body, lower of split, pine-root weft alone), and an open twined tray for draining food, such as boiled fish. A smaller version of the cooking basket is used as an individual serving bowl. On opposite page, enlarged details of Hupa basket borders. First, common finish: warps are simply cut flush with last round; the twining is so tight it does not unravel. (In twining, one weaver was held taut in the mouth as the other was twined with the right hand and then exchanged for the one in the mouth.) Notice the splice, on the left; end of old weft folds over start of new and turns up along right side of warp. Second, finish used on some granary baskets, the one drawn collected by Lieutenant P. H. Ray, nineteenth century. The ends of the warps have been bent down and wrapped with willow splints (Mason, 1904).

especially lustrous if rubbed on a piece of soft wood. Split maidenhair fern stems *(Adiatum pedatum)* were overlaid for black, and a section of the two leathery inner strands from the pounded and twisted stalk of the giant chain fern *(Woodwardia spinulosa)* for red. These latter light green strands were dried and then dyed red with the inside layer of white alder bark *(Alnus oregana)*. Sandra Corrie Newman described the process. The bark could be chewed and the strands simply run through the dye bath in the mouth, or the bark was pounded, put in water and brought to a boil by some; not boiled by others. The strands were steeped in this until the proper depth of red was achieved and then wrapped to allow the color to set. The strands were dried quickly in the sun. Porcupine quills steeped in a yellow decoction of lichen *(Evernia vulpina)* sometimes added a final decorative touch to northwestern California baskets.

The Pomo

In the more central part of California, the Pomo made both open and tightly twined basketry and they brought coiling to a high state of art in their gift and funeral baskets. Closely twined baskets of the women were without overlay but decorated in fine patterns of split redbud branches *(Cercis occidentalis)*, cut in the last days of October so that the red bark would adhere. These were conical burden baskets for gathering acorns; large storage baskets with gently rounded sides; flat, bowl-shaped winnowing and sifting baskets; baskets for holding acorn meal; and deep, bottomless baskets with flaring sides that were secured over a mortar by a woman's legs stretched straight out in front of her and over the basket as she pounded acorns with a pestle. In large watertight twined baskets mush was stone-boiled. In smaller versions food was served and some small baskets were used as drinking cups. In central California beyond the Pomo these closely twined baskets were generally undecorated.

The Pomo foundation warp for twined or coiled baskets was built from slender willow stems *(Salix argyrophylla* and others) and in the northern Pomo area, often from hazel branches. They were sized with a sharp obsidian held in the palm as the rod was passed through. All were made even and of the same size. Wefts for either tightly twined or coiled baskets came from gray pine, juniper or willow root, bracken root, bulrush root *(Scirpus pacificus* and others) and sedge root *(Carex barbarae)*. These could be treated and along with redbud branches, produced striking effects.

Sedge and bulrush roots, often gathered in October, were split lengthwise while fresh. One side of the incipient split was grasped in the left hand, which pulled away as the other side of the split was held between the teeth. The right hand guided and evened the split. The outer covering was stripped away, the root split again, then coiled and dried in the shade. They were stored until ready for use, then soaked for about 15 minutes in cold water and the pith core stripped out. The edges were evened with a knife, followed in the case of sedge, by running a tight loop of the discarded core back and forth over the root. The end was sharpened and the strand became the coiling weft.

All materials were soaked and kept wet while making a basket. The coiled basket began with a simple overhand knot tied in the center of three or four pieces of rough split root 6 to 8 inches long, twisted about each other. The basketmaker coiled the split sedge weft through the center of the knot, over and over, until the entire circumference had been covered. After a few additional stitches, remaining ends of the rough root foundation bundle were severed and sharpened tips of willow rods were inserted into the bundle. One or three willow rods formed the foundation, which spiraled outward and upward and back inward to produce the pleasing flattened globe that was the Pomo

 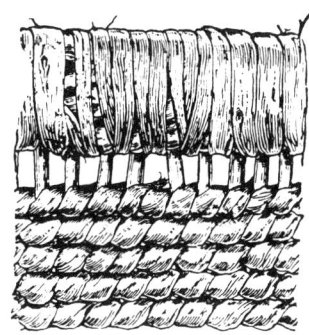

coiled basket. Designs were in the red of redbud or the black of bulrush, dyed whole for weeks in a solution of such things as black walnuts, ashes and iron oxide. Coiling went counterclockwise as the basketmaker faced her work.

Southern California Basketry Materials and Their Preparation

In contrast, as the maker faced her task, baskets of southern California almost invariably coiled clockwise. Juncus and deergrass replaced sedge and willow. Juncus *(Juncus textilis)* was the main stitching material of coiled baskets. Shredded, it was formed into a tight spiral or knot to begin the foundation. For the Chumash, another thinner juncus (likely *J. balticus*) served as the subsequent foundation in three-rod bundles.

He pulled the juncus *(J. textilis)* up and out whole, leaving the spiral-shaped juncus and taking only the good ones, Chumash consultant Fernando Librado told Harrington. He cut the rusty colored bottoms from the juncus and made a bundle of these "pure red ones" for use as decoration in the stitching. The rest of the juncus was spread in the sun to dry. Librado seemed to know all aspects of his culture, including basketry. After about a month juncus blanches to the tan or sand color desired, according to Justin Farmer, a Northern Diegueño or Ipai man who almost a century later, like Librado, carries on the basket-making tradition of his female ancestors. The Chumash stored the bleached juncus in the shade wrapped in a mat.

To ready it for use, Fernando split the juncus stem from the base. If there was a natural bend near the base, he would begin there. He inserted his awl at that point, perhaps four finger breadths from the base, and split it back to the base. Next, he grasped one half in his teeth and the other in his left hand, the thumb on the smooth outer side of the stalk. With his right forefinger in the split and his hand just beneath, the left hand moved away and began splitting the juncus. His right followed the stem, guiding the angle to make the split go straight. Some Indian women did this very quickly, the head bending back in the process. As the split grew during these divisions of the juncus, the half held in the teeth was gripped farther down. Each of the two halves was also split, dividing the juncus into four.

Chumash Candalaria Valenzuela, who split most juncus in much the same way as Librado but from the pointed end, told how she would split juncus stems which were crooked. She bent the bottom end first, then, with her right hand, she made bends at 2-inch intervals going along the stalk. Her left hand followed in the split these bends created.

She next cleaned and evened the juncus strips. She bit the edge off a small clam shell (held in buckskin according to Librado) to make a sharp edge on the shell (best if it is even and slants inward, the cutting edge on the inside). A buckskin glove that covered only the right thumb protected her skin as the juncus weaver was pulled between the shell, held by her index finger, and her thumb. The pith side faced the shell. All pith was removed. Fernando described beginning at the end opposite the base. It would be the same width until near the base when, by tilting the juncus a little, he could trim the somewhat wider edges; but they usually employed a smaller shell for that.

Even before cleaning the pith, some juncus strips were dyed black for use as design elements. Valenzuela tied them in a coil about a foot in diameter and buried them 6 inches deep in black mud, rich in humus. She would leave them for two to three weeks, but even longer would be better. Some added a special smoking process after the usual burying in mud. After digging up the blackened juncus, Librado made a fire in a pit and when it had burned to coals, he put in leaves of *ya'y* (probably *Lotus scoparius,* identified in Hudson and Blackburn's work on the material culture of the Chumash and from whose massive compilation Harrington's notes on Librado and Valenzuela have also been extracted). On top of this went the juncus, then more *ya'y*. The pit was covered with sand and left for eight days. One informant told Harrington that urine made dyes and paint stronger.

To make juncus white, the whole stem was treated while still green. On a bed of cold ashes another fire was lit and allowed to burn down. Single stems of juncus were run back and forth through the lower heated layer of ashes until they turned white. Special care was given to prevent burning. They were dried in the sun.

Among the Chumash at Ventura, quartered stems of sumac *(Rhus trilobata)* provided both round foundation rods and flat, pliable coiling material. Long thin stems without a knot were collected. Librado squared off the end of one and split the stem in half lengthwise, raising it against his knife that he held in place. These halves in turn were split. He peeled them, scraped the pith and made them flat by shaving them with a shell. With handling, the light waxy sheen of sumac developed an attractive patina seen in decorative elements on many southern California baskets. Farmer pointed out that only the first-year growth was harvested: a shoot about the diameter of a lead pencil after the leaves of the shrub had fallen in Autumn. While still fresh, he divided the 1/4-inch-diameter by 3- to 4-foot-long stem into three parts from the base of the shoot. He grasped one split section in each hand, another between his teeth, while the unsplit vertical stem was tightly held between his knees. His hands pulled gently outward and apart, maintaining nearly equal pressure in all directions. A soft arch in each one third segment produced three exactly equal withes.

If one segment was more vertical than the others in this process, it would become too thick, the others would be too thin and they may have even been stripped off. To maintain the arch in the segment held in his teeth, his hands had to pull out and away. If one segment became too thin, pressure was reduced on that side so that it became vertical and began to thicken, perhaps putting that side in the mouth and bringing the head forward. A new bite farther down may have been necessary as the splitting proceeded, but care needed to be taken not to damage the shoots with his teeth.

The core had to be removed from each piece. Farmer bent the thicker bottom end over his right index finger. The tension caused the core to break. He split it away, holding the cambium side with his right thumb against his right index finger that extended to hold the unsplit portion against his left middle finger. The left thumb and index finger grasped the core side as the two thumbs stripped the pieces apart, again maintaining the requisite equal gentle curves. He continued slowly working his way down the splitting stick.

At that point the cambium—with bark intact—was often coiled, tied off with a piece of the core and saved. As it dried, the bark came off easily by gentle rubbing with a piece of buckskin. Bark that remained could be removed with a thumbnail when the sumac was soaked just before use.

If the strand checked or cracked when wrapped around a foundation coil, it was not thin enough and a final splitting was necessary to remove more core material. Extra pressure with the thumb-

Fernando Librado coils a storage basket at Ventura, California, 1913. (Photograph by Gerald Cassidy, courtesy of the Southwest Museum.)

Pomo girls twine a basket on the Russian River. (Photograph by Carpenter, 1934, courtesy of the Southwest Museum.)

nail likely would be needed to force another break in the remaining core. With the thumbnail the break was opened and splitting accomplished as before. The object was to leave the strand thin but unbroken. The weaver strands were trimmed and made consistent in width. A section 1/2 to 1 inch from the end was reduced by half to make a point on the running end of the weaver.

Split sumac served as foundation, coils and decoration on southern California baskets and it could also be used to repair them. Dawson and Deetz noticed that old Chumash baskets often had been repaired with patches of basket fragments glued on with asphaltum and sewn with sumac strands.

The Ipai, along with many groups in southern California, the San Joaquin Valley and Sierra Nevada used bunches of deergrass flower stalks *(Muhlenbergia rigins)* for the foundation of coiled baskets. The Kawaiisu gathered the stalks in November.

The dark maroon-colored portion of the roots of the Joshua tree *(Yucca brevifolia)* and Mohave yucca *(Y. schidigera)* were coiled as pattern elements by some groups. The outer coating was pounded free and the core split off as with sumac. Joshua tree and yucca root were also used as the foundation start for the first couple of rounds of some baskets. A brown color slightly paler than the root of the Joshua tree came from the root of prairie bulrush *(Scirpus robustus)*. Maurice Zigmond learned that the Kawaiisu split the inner root into strands and coiled it as pattern material in the same way they did the Joshua tree root.

Dawson and Deetz, who did an extensive analysis of Chumash basketry, also mentioned the rare use among the Chumash of split sedge root *(Carex sp.)*, split bulrush root *(Scirpus sp.)* and a fern root dyed black for sewing strands in coiling and possibly peeled willow shoots as twining warp. It should be noted the Tubatulabal in the southern Sierras employed willow shoots *(Salix laevigata, lasiolepsis and others)* split for coiled basketry starts, whole shoots in foundations, and finely split willow roots as a light-colored weft in coiled baskets. Zigmond identified western bracken *(Pteridium aquilinum)* as the black pattern material in coiled basketry of the Kawaiisu who lived in the Tehachapi Mountains to the east of the Chumash. He surmised that it was the stipe which was used—it naturally turns black in the fall. One of his informants told him that the part used was the root. Farmer pointed out that the inner root is brownish-black, colorfast, tough and leathery, and good for pattern material in an Indian basket. At first glance the root appears very angular and inappropriate but after being split and the husk peeled away an inner core of slime appears. After it too is stripped off there remains an inner strand; it is washed and "lo and behold . . . bracken fern weaver material."

Within the memory of Zigmond's oldest informants, bracken had been replaced by devil's claw *(Myrtinia probosis)*, a Great Basin plant worked as design material by some southeastern California people. The black leathery skin of the horns of the inner pod was stripped off after an overnight soaking. The deep black color could be further enriched, Farmer explained, by baking the pod in a fire pit.

The Cahuilla sometimes made coiled baskets of California palm *(Washingtonia filifera)*. I

Plain, round, practical open-stitch juncus sifting basket coiled, unusually, counterclockwise by Pabla Mata, Kumeyaay from Nejí in the Northern Sierra Juárez of Lower California. Fag ends were bound under on the face and leading tips of old weavers on the rear.

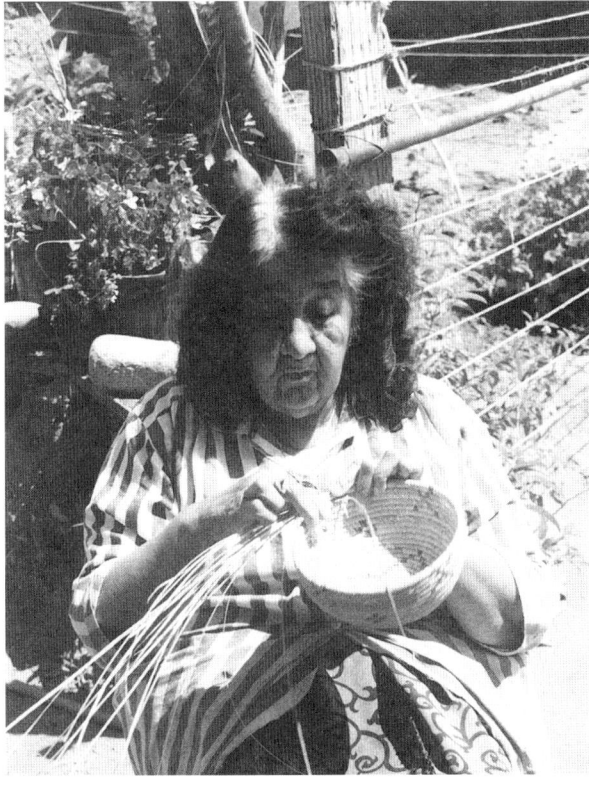

Celia Silva, Kumeyaay, coils a hat from juncus (Juncus textilis) she has split green, tied in loops to dry, and soaked to reconstitute. The start was a simple overhand knot of a few juncus strips twisted together; they had been shaved from the sides of the weaving strands as those strands were evened before coiling. The foundation is split juncus (probably J. mexicanus, although balticus and other juncus also are employed in basket-making by the Kumeyaay), dried straight and used without soaking. Below, close-up shows the fag end of the new weaver being sewed under. Notice that she ends the old weaver by inserting the tail in the hole of the previous coil. In contrast, Virginia Melendrez, Celia's daughter, begins a new coiling strand in the last hole of the old (whose lead tip does not end in the previous stitch). Thus the end of the old is buried under the new and the pressure of the old helps hold the new. The fag end does not show but is broken off close or pulled partly into the foundation. The natural brown-red decorative coils from the base of the juncus can be seen in the basket Virginia holds (upper left). Ipai Justin Farmer splits sumac into three parts (bottom right).

have seen Southern Diegueño Manuela Aguiar sew coiled baskets of split palm fronds.

Making the Southern California Coiled Basket

The Chumash started the coiled basket with a bunch of split juncus (*J. textilis*). Candalaria Valenzuela explained her way of doing it to Harrington. The coiling began about an inch from the end of the bundle. She included one inch of the juncus weaver in her bundle of ten split juncus starting strips and coiled over this end to hold it securely down as she completed the inner revolution of the basket. This was doubled over, or coiled, to begin the spiral. Valenzuela began the second revolution inserting the weaver through the hole in the center, up and over the core and back toward herself. She apparently stitched over the first round of the spiral or core, coiling over what already had been coiled. Her very sharp bone awl was not used until the third revolution. She worked from left to right.

Even before she began to sew, she evened all the juncus coiling weavers and dipped them, loosely coiled, into a wooden bowl of water placed beside her. She had the basin of water close by to wet the juncus a little so they would not break when bent. They had to be damp but not soaked or they would become too soft and pull apart. From time to time either the strand or her fingers were dipped into the water. The wet fingers would run along the strand to dampen it. She sat on a mat, legs outstretched as she sewed her basket.

Coiled baskets of southern California more commonly began with a simple overhand knot. Librado would take a few strands of split juncus, even the ends and put them around his left finger and on top of the long ends; then he pulled the tips through in a simple overhand knot. He put his awl into the center of the knot and began to sew with his weaver. All the sewing coils or wraps of the first revolution went through the center of the knot, generally without need of the awl. He had sharpened the heavier bottom end of his juncus weavers and with that end he would sew. The knot was held in his left hand, the long loose ends coming from the top of the knot were always to the right and held down on the knot by his right hand as he coiled over them. On inserting the first weaver through the center of the knot, he left exposed about four finger breadths of the tail end of the weaver. After two, three or four stitches, which he held tight with his left forefinger, this projecting end was inserted about three times into the coil to fasten the weaver tight. Or, he simply sewed the end under in coiling around the knot.

After the knot had been completely wrapped, Librado began sewing with his awl,

Wintun twined carrying basket collected by Livingston Stone on the McCloud River, nineteenth century. Designs in overlay of grass and fern are visible both inside and outside the basket in contrast with Yurok twined basketry in which ornamentation does not show on the interior. The Wintun twisted the overlaid weft to achieve the effect. The Yoruk kept overlaid wefts from twisting. The cup-shaped bottom is in three-strand twining for 3 to 4" before it switches to two-strand twining. For greater strength a coil of rods has been sewed around the bottom. Bending down the warps along a strong hoop and coiling over them with splints reinforced the top border (Mason, 1904).

emphasizing that all wrapping and sewing are always done with the weaver strand moving away from himself below and towards himself above. The dangling long end of the knot formed the beginning of the foundation of the second round or revolution. He held the awl between forefinger and thumb of his right hand, inserted it in the foundation coil beneath and left it there as he ran his right hand along the weaver to the tip. He transferred the tip to his left hand, holding it between thumb and forefinger. Then he pulled out the awl and placed it in his mouth and, with his right hand, took the tip of the weaver and slid it through the opening created by the awl. Next he grasped the weaver on the far side and pulled it tight and smooth. He proceeded piercing the foundation coil with his awl from the front (the working face of the basket) and before the hole closed inserting the leading tip of the juncus weaver.

He encircled the foundation strands above and pulled the weaver through the hole created by the awl in the spiral below. The stitch went between the completed wrappings of that spiral into the outer edge of the foundation but did not catch or interlock with the wrappings.

Fernando observed that some hold the awl in the right hand (not the teeth) as they poke the strip through, while others never leave the awl sticking in the basketwork at all but maintain it in the right hand the whole time. They are able to do this and still have all fingers free by sliding the pointed end up over the last two fingers of the hand. The dull end rests on top of the thumb while the bottom portions of the index and middle finger naturally clamp and hold the body of the awl from above.

Some women like a lean awl, some a fat one, Librado told Harrington. Hudson and Blackburn pictured awls collected by León de Cessac during the nineteenth century (1986). Robert Heizer categorized their form and material: whole whale bone, heavy mammal bone splinter, bird bone splinter, small complete bird bone—all four sharpened—split mammal bone and split bone rib. Other bone awls pictured by Hudson and Blackburn from the Santa Barbara Coast had asphaltum handles. These awls were exceptionally short and ranged from about 6 to 10 cm. Pedro Fages described the Chumash basketmaker awl in the eighteenth century as a bone from a deer's foreleg next to the shinbone. Gerónimo Boscana wrote of fish-bone awls. Voegelin discovered that among the Tubatulabal the awl from the leg bone of a deer was a man's tool for sewing buckskin while the woman's awl for coiled baskets was a spine from the barrel cactus with a small lump of asphaltum on the end as a handle. The Kawaiisu made awls for coiled basketry from the spines of the Mohave mound cactus *(Echinocactus polysephalus)*. Zigmond's informants told him that they were topped with a globular handle of insect lac from the creosote bush or sagebrush.

The Cahuilla detached the hard agave thorn *(Agave deserti)* at the end of the agave leaf with a length of fiber connected for use as a needle and thread. The fiber was also used as foundation material in Cahuilla and Diegueño baskets. Set in a wooden handle with asphaltum, the thorn became the point of an awl for making coiled baskets, recorded Bean and Saubel. It could also prick the skin and with ashes from burned agave stalks made a tattoo.

Within two or three rounds, Librado began inserting the *tash (J. balticus* and another slender juncus he described, shorter than *balticus* and *textilis)* into the core. Valenzuela used split juncus for the entire foundation but Librado inserted three unsplit juncus stems. Fineness could vary depending on the size of the basket. Consistency, however, was important. One kept the same foundation thickness throughout. The base of the whole juncus stem was inserted in the foundation core of split juncus. In the process some of the strips might have to be cut to keep the foundation even and not bunchy. Gradually the second and third stems were inserted into the core, the number, diameter and size maintained. When the foundation core thinned, he pierced it head-on with his awl, then removed the awl and stuck in the sharpened end of a new whole juncus stem. The other end of the stem was cut off square and not left tapered.

The coiling continued. Valenzuela said that for every few stitches it was necessary to place one stitch on top of another (the wraps would emanate from the same hole) to keep the coils from becoming diagonal and leaning too far to the left. Sometimes it was difficult to poke the awl over the first stitch and a second stitch was made just to the side. The awl never split a stitch encircling the coil below. "I always put the awl between two stitches," remarked Valenzuela. It only passed through the foundation coil. (Inspection of actual Chumash baskets shows that this is true for the working face of the basket but split stitches on the back were common.)

From time to time, while she worked, Valenzuela would press the coil with her hands or handle of the awl to flatten and straighten it. As he sewed the basket, Librado trimmed strands of uneven width with his fingernail. Most Indians had their clam shell handy, he said, and used that. Raw clam shells were always used, never boiled ones, since that made them brittle.

Eventually the sewing strand ran out. Librado left the end protruding an inch or so and, after going two or three rounds with the new weaver, cut it off close with his thumbnail. (Valenzuela stuck it under subsequent coils.) The new weaver, which would hide the end of the old, was inserted in the last hole of the old one. Although the hole was opened a bit by the awl, the new weaver completely filled the opening and made a tight fit. He tugged it through slowly, and the little that was left sticking out he cut or cracked off with his thumb. He did this only after going a few rounds (making new holes with his awl) lest it pull out. The end held and it was not necessary to sew it under.

To the south, beyond and to the east of the Gabrielino, they did sew the tail end under the subsequent weaver coils. Farmer described the "bound-under fag end stitch" used by the Northern Diegueño and many others. The stub, or fag end, of the new weaver was turned up at about a 45-degree angle to the right and bound down by the subsequent stitch or stitches of the weaver.

Fernando made his stitches close together, touching each other. They could be made apart as well, he advised Harrington. Coarsely coiled juncus baskets on a foundation of deer grass with a mere four to six stitches per linear inch were made by the southern Chumash, Kitanemuk, Fernandeño and Gabrielino, Harrington wrote. At the other extreme the Tubatulabal stitches could be as many as 20 to 22 per inch. Dawson and Deetz found common Chumash decorated baskets averaged around 70 stitches per square inch. The finest Chumash trinket baskets could reach 240 stitches to the square inch, but Tubatulabal and Kawaiisu coiled baskets frequently attained 200 to 300 stitches per square inch. To the south of the Chumash, the average approached 55 stitches to the square inch. When soaked, a tightly coiled southern California cooking basket held water. Gift baskets were most intricately woven. Large storage baskets were of heavier, looser coiling.

The sides of a basket were begun by slightly rotating the stitches' points of entry and exit on the foundation coil. A decision had to be made by the basketmaker after the flat bottom had been completed. Librado observed that some had the working face (where more care had been expended) on the inside and some on the outside. A globular trinket basket would be worked from the outside and a flattish, gently rounded serving tray from the inside.

The coiling wound down gradually at the very end. Librado said that they cut the core slantingly to finish it neatly—first just one *tash* at a slant, then another perhaps four finger breadths past the first and then the third. There was no unevenness at the top of the coiling. Dawson and Deetz confirmed that the ending was usually simply tapered and the stitches ended, although sometimes one or two reverse stitches were at the very end. The Southern Diegueño described by Farmer might end with six herringbone back stitches made by the coils reversing and going back to the left, coiling counterclockwise and slipping under the six previous stitches.

A Breakfast of Sweet Acorn Mush with Boiled Shank of Venison

Manuela Aguiar had long extolled the sweetness and lack of bitterness of the emory oak acorn *(Quercus emoryi)*. Her ancestors had taught her how to prepare it without the tedious leeching well known and necessary for other oaks. She comes from the southernmost lineage of Southern Diegueño Indians and lives in the vastness of the Sierra Juárez about a day's walk south of the high mountain arroyo where the emory oak trees grow. Family members make the journey around the middle of August. They travel by horseback nowadays through a mountain pass visible from the village.

The small, 3/4-inch nuts must be fully ripe. To ensure ripeness, they are not picked or knocked off the medium evergreen tree from which they come but are collected after they have fallen naturally to the ground where they dry. A rare rain at this time of year quickly ruins a crop left laying on wet soil. The acorns rot and the meat turns black. But this does not happen often. From her cache of almost one year earlier, Manuela and her son Raúl Sandoval showed me how to shell the emory acorn *(hoeel')* by turning it between the incisors and lightly biting a circular cut around the circumference. The top and bottom of the shell were then easily removed. They ate acorns in quantity that way like nuts. I tried a few and enjoyed the richness and hint of bitterness. But on this morning, the sun having just risen over Rancho Escondido, Manuela was about to prepare sweet acorn mush.

The Traditional California Indian Repast

We might wonder how California Indians arranged meals or took their food. Highly prejudicial accounts from early Spanish missions in southernmost Baja California reported instances of extreme gluttony among local Indians on the occasion of encountering uncommon quantities of food. But A. Kroeber recounted for the Yurok from northernmost Alta California that the old custom would have them eat but two meals a day, and in theory even those should be sparing. Men (and we might suppose women) attempted to accomplish their day's labor before breakfast because it came late. Kroeber noted that in his day old men still professed to be unable to properly work after eating. They took supper toward sunset.

The Miwok of the Sierra Nevada, like most California Indians, did not worry about working before their first meal but ate breakfast at sunrise. Otherwise they ate when they felt hungry, not at any regular time. River mussel shells occasionally served as spoons.

The Yokuts of the Great Central Valley and foothills of the Sierras were even more typical. Along with the majority of Native Californians, they ate two meals, the first around sunrise and the second just before sundown. Breakfast was hot acorn mush and a little meat. Supper was also mush and meat, Gayton recorded, but included the bounty the day might provide as well, such as greens, fish, pigeons or seed cakes. Deer meat was cut into chunks with an obsidian blade and boiled in a clay pot. One claimed that it was eaten with salt but others indicated that aboriginally, salt was only eaten in tiny pinches with vegetable foods, especially greens. More often the deer meat was not boiled but roasted by the men. Men and women snacked and one informant spoke of a lunch. Children ate as frequently as they desired.

The Tubatulabal, who lived along the forks of the Kern rivers where they flow from the Southern Sierras, also ate two meals. The first was around sunrise and the other before sunset. When available, meat was eaten at both meals. Eighty-six-year-old Steban Miranda told Voegelin in the 1930s that during the winter they ate acorns, piñons, meat of any sort, and dried and fresh fish: "Old-timers ate acorn mush with deer meat, like bread," said Miranda. Some informants spoke of antelope horn or wooden spoons. Others said that the acorn mush was eaten with the fingers. Women gathering seeds or tending tobacco took a lunch with them that they ate around ten or eleven in the morning. Children snacked between meals.

Grinding the Sweet Acorn

Manuela was preparing breakfast. She selected a milling stone from the many she has laying about her place. One she found some years ago in a cave—a gift from the past. Milling stones have been used by Indians in the Californias for some eight thousand years. Like most of her others, the flat granite slab had soft, smooth depressions from grinding on both the top and the bottom. The slight concavities would draw the seeds or nuts toward the center where they could be ground with

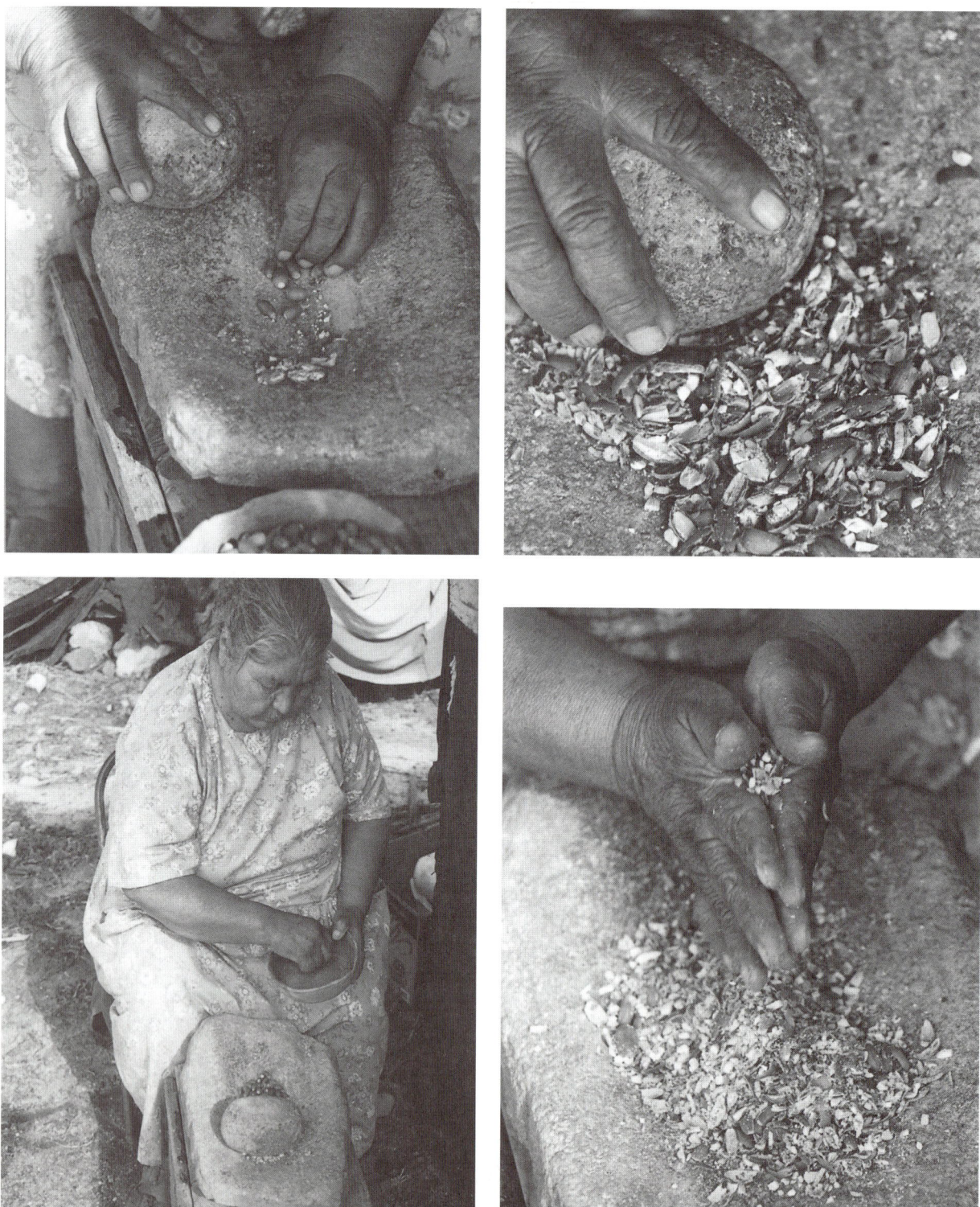

Manuela Aguiar cracks sweet emory acorns with a stone mano on a milling stone and rubs the broken bits between both palms (bottom right) to loosen shells from nuts.

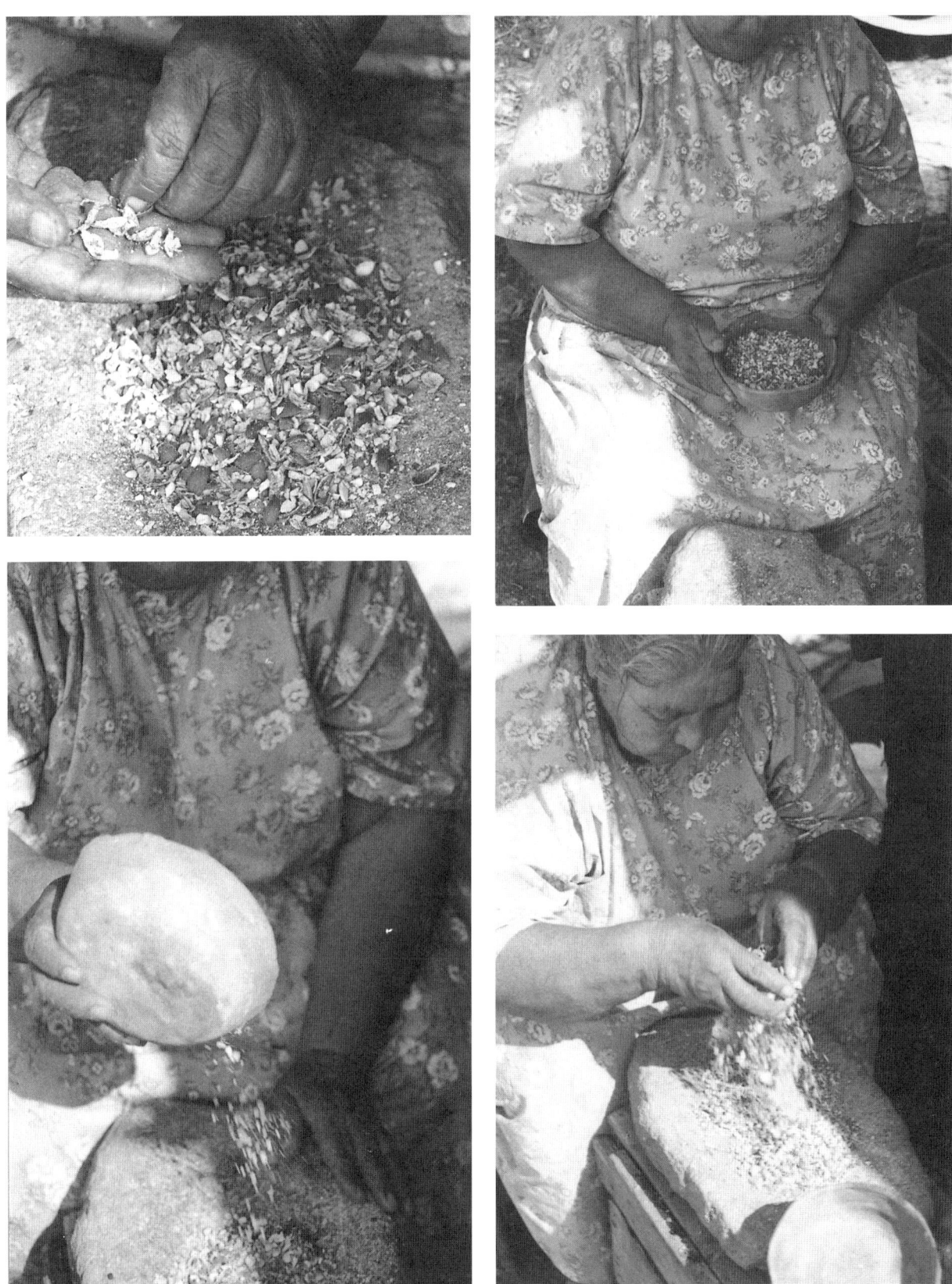

Manuela picks out and discards large pieces of shell. She then tosses and shakes batches of the mixture in a bowl—bits of husk rise to top and are plucked out. What remains, she winnows by tossing in air from the bowl. She pours cleaned mixture onto milling stone for further winnowing with her hands.

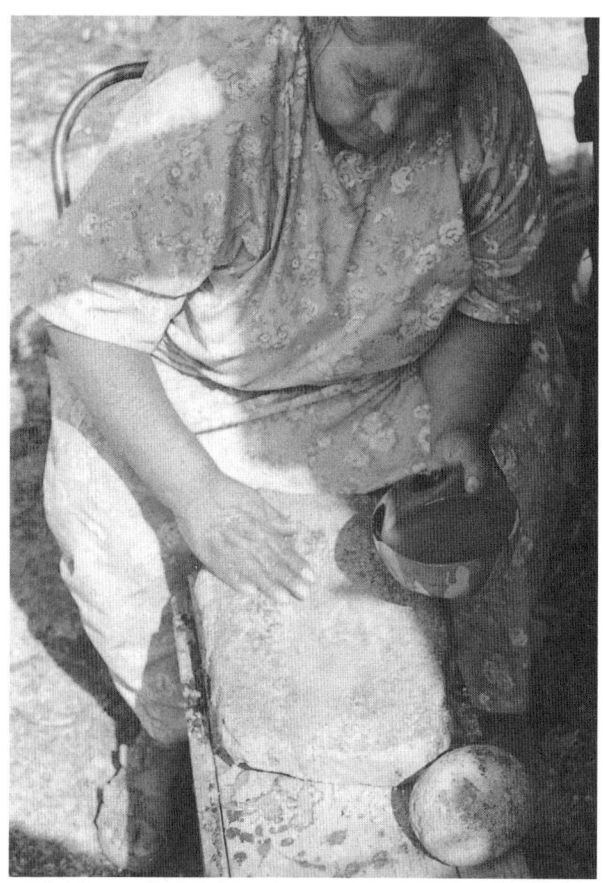

the mano, a small, even, loaf-shaped stone. "New manos are easily found," said Manuela. The milling stone itself is more difficult. She recalled that a few years ago someone passed through the village buying all the milling stones the Indians had. "It did not matter. I still make them," she smiled. "A flat stone of good consistency works. Granite or another stone which is very easy because it is soft (perhaps sandstone). Then I find a hard, somewhat pointed rock, a little bigger than a hand, usually dark colored. I peck repeatedly over the center of the slab, covering a large oval surface in the center. Soon, a slight depression forms. Now I rub it back and forth with the side of the hard stone or any hard stone, abrading the surface until the milling depression is smooth. That is all. Use will wear and smooth it further," she said.

Manuela grabbed a couple of handfuls of small emory acorns, plopped them into the center of the milling stone and began to lightly pound with the bottom of the mano she held in one hand. The beat was regular and just hard enough to crack the shells open but not so hard to pulverize the shell or contents. Handful after handful was produced and placed in a ceramic vessel until the batch was complete.

Manuela rinses milling stone. The broken acorn nuts were placed in a large bowl of water where remaining bits of husk floated to the surface and were poured off. She now forcefully grinds small batches of the dampened nut meats with back and forth movements of the mano. As wet acorn flour or dough accumulates in front of the mano, it is placed in a bowl.

She then poured a large pile of the broken shells and nuts into the middle of the milling stone and taking one large handful at a time rubbed the broken bits between both palms. The pieces fell back into the pile. She stirred the pile and repeatedly took handfuls until the shells and nuts had thoroughly separated from one another. Then she picked out and discarded large pieces of hull. She did this again and again as she continued the rubbing and separating process.

Next she transferred batches of nut kernels and the remaining smaller shells into a small, open, parallel-sided, clay eating bowl. She tossed and shook the mixture causing bits of husk that weighed less than the broken nuts to come to the top. These were picked off and discarded with her fingers. The process was done repeatedly until most of the visible husks had been cleaned from the mash.

Dough is mixed with a little water and added to boiling water in clay pot on a tripod of stones. A small juniper-wood fire maintains heat as mush cooks. Mush served in a clay bowl with a wooden spoon.

Finer pieces of shell wafted away as she tossed the broken acorns into the air off the bowl's far edge and caught them again at the near edge of the bowl. Small batches were treated in turn until all had been done.

She further winnowed the acorn mix by pouring a few handfuls at a time onto the milling stone as a soft breeze took away the chaff. She lifted some in her hands and let it fall in a stream a foot or so onto the surface of the stone. As the breeze subsided she blew gently through the cascading bits. When cleaned enough, after repeated winnowings, the few handfuls on the stone were placed in a bowl with others that had been winnowed in the same way.

Into another larger bowl, half filled with water, she dumped all the winnowed broken acorns. Except for the continuous picking of bits of hull from the mass as she saw them, this was the final cleaning stage. (She had also plucked out any black, rotten acorn meats, explaining that some people preferred to leave them in.) She stirred the honey-brown soupy mixture with her hand. Many previously unseen little pieces of husk floated to the surface (seemingly all that remained) and were poured onto the ground. She left the broken acorn nuts to soak in the water (whose volume was perhaps four to five times or more that of the mash) a short while as she wetted and cleaned the milling stone. Then she carefully poured off the water. This was as close to leaching the acorns as Manuela came.

She took a handful of the wet acorn meats and placed the meats in the center of the ancient milling stone. With the mano held firmly in both hands, she pressed and ground the nuts forward and backward in short hard strokes on the stone. Slowly, with the to-and-fro grinding movements, a fine wet dough appeared in front of the mano. The bits and pieces at the rear came little by little under the same grinding motion. When thoroughly pulverized they were pushed forward into the wet dough. Completed batches were put in a small clay food bowl.

Boiling Mush in a Clay Pot

The milling having ended, Raúl prepared a fire. He dug a very shallow, 1-inch-deep, 8-inch-diameter pit, rubbed strips of juniper bark between his hands until they frayed, then placed them in the center of the slight depression. Over the bark small splinters of dry juniper wood were laid in a rough teepee shape. The fire was lit.

Three rocks, approximately 7 inches in diameter, were set around the fire, close enough to hold a large, freshly rinsed, globular clay pot. Into the pot Raúl poured water to boil. More space had been left between two of the rocks in order to feed the fire some small split juniper sticks that kept flames on the pot.

The acorn dough was thoroughly mixed with a little water to the consistency of a very thick soup. It was then poured into the large clay pot as the water began to boil. For mush, the boiling water should have equaled less than twice the volume of the thick acorn soup that was poured into it. Raúl had set a bit more water to boil and the mush would be accordingly thin or gruel-like. Manuela said that this was all a matter of taste. With a handmade wooden spoon she stirred the boiling mush every few minutes to prevent its scalding on the bottom of the pot.

Because the grinding process was wet and there was no sifting to produce an extremely fine flour, cooking had to be long—the longer the better. Manuela and Raúl boiled the mush for twenty to thirty minutes or more. The result was a rich, sweet nutty soup—the very slight tannin taste that remained only added interest. After two large bowls I could not have felt more content.

Traditionally, Indians of California ate venison with acorn mush. Manuela had a surprise. It was a shank of venison she had boiled with a little salt the night before until the meat fell off. To my eyes, accustomed to beef nicely browned or hidden under a rich sauce, unadorned boiled deer flesh was not very attractive. To Raúl and Manuela it was mouthwatering. After I tried some, I agreed it was delicious. Eaten with sweet acorn mush, with the meat dipped or dropped into it as the Indians did, the meal was superb.

Meat and mush—boiled venison and acorn atole, the traditional California Indian breakfast.

Southern California Pottery

Pottery is the miracle of turning raw earth into sophisticated vessels. Pottery-making was not universal in the Californias. Boiling with hot stones in a container of animal skin, a tightly woven basket, or a pecked and ground stone bowl was the lot of most. Except for some archaic clay boiling stones, figurines and crude crockery, a well-developed ceramic tradition only arrived in California from the east during the last one thousand years. A. Kroeber and Malcolm Rogers suggested that an early Puebloan-style pottery entered east-central California from Nevada. It became the ware found historically among the Mono and Yokuts. Another independent style that employed a paddle and anvil had likely evolved in central Mexico, spread to western Mexico and southern Arizona, and flourished among people of the Yuman stock, principally along the Colorado River where they practiced limited agriculture. From there, the style passed to other Yuman bands in the deserts and mountains and to their Shoshonean-speaking neighbors of southern California: the Chemehuevi, Serrano, Cahuilla, Cupeño and Luiseño. This was not the tediously painted pottery of collectors' boutiques and pictured in eye-dazzling coffee-table books. It was the practical ware of people who hunted and gathered from the land and needed strong pots for cooking, bowls for eating, and large ollas to store seeds and water. Rogers noted that for thinness and hardness, the best prehistoric Yuman wares exceeded the famous Puebloan pottery of Arizona and New Mexico and in certain areas even equaled it in per-capita production. Mexican California used this ware extensively. Many sherds have been found at places such as the Sepulveda adobe hacienda near Newport Bay. Though not overdecorated, the soft functional curves of the vessels and the mysterious fire-clouding of the brown-red surfaces were beauty enough.

When Rogers conducted a study of Yuman ceramics in the late 1920s, the craft had already gone into decline. He found purity of technique best preserved among the Southern Diegueño (Kumeyaay) at Manzanita in San Diego County. The tradition was mainly in the hands of one potter, Rosa Lopez (Owas Hilmawa), whose procedures he recorded, supplementing his monograph where appropriate with archaeological and ethnographic data and the memories and practices of other potters of Yuman stock. Rosa Lopez died in 1930 and many would say that today, on the brink of the twenty-first century, Yuman pottery is also dead. But in Lower California, in the mountain village of Santa Catarina and in the surrounding rancherías, the pottery lives much as Rogers described it at Manzanita more than sixty years ago. During Rogers' time, only women engaged in pottery-making. That is true of the Santa Catarina area today. Paipai Josefina Ochurte still sits in the sun and coils her pots on a summer's day as her ancestors did for countless generations. Some of the other local potters also have Paipai blood but learned their craft from Southern Diegueño Kuatl mothers and grandmothers and speak both Paipai and Kuatl Yuman dialects. Some belong directly to the Southern Diegueño (Kumeyaay) Kuatl lineage.

In rendering Rogers' account of the process of making a Yuman food bowl with a recurved rim (one of an eight-piece batch made by Rosa Lopez), I will add significant information from Michelsen's notes taken in the 1960s, a study by Gena Van Camp in the 1970s, observations by Michael Wilken in the 1980s, and experiences of my own in the 1990s. Rogers wrote, for example, that clay pipes were no

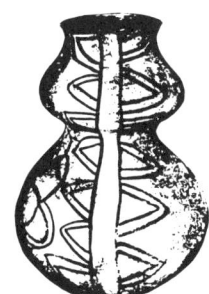

Kamia seed jar at left in Rogers, 1936. To the right of seed jar are Mohave motifs: bowl with rain pattern, ladle painted in fish backbone design and stylized cottonwood leaves on bowl from Kroeber, 1925.

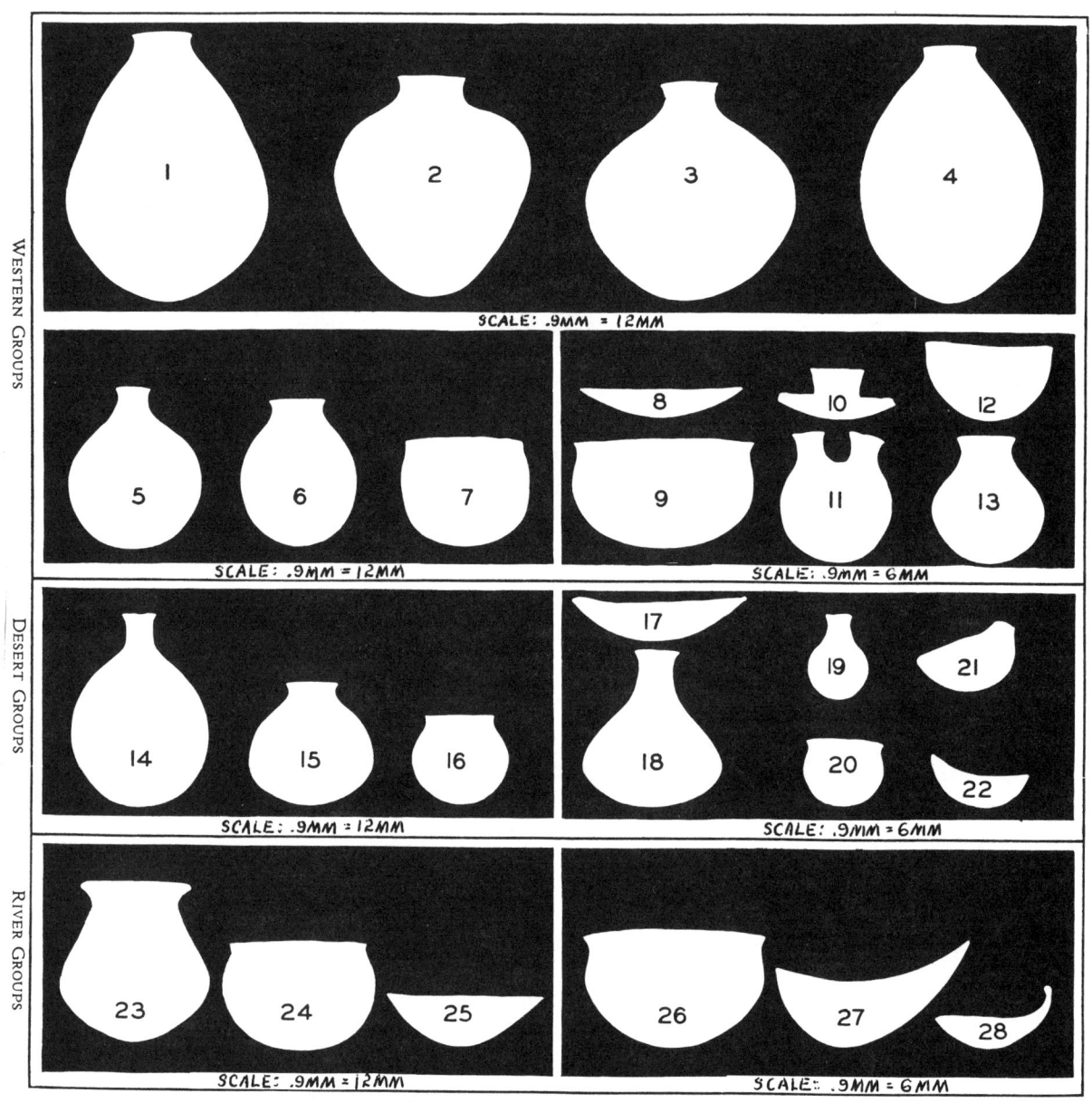

Yuman and Shoshonean pottery shapes (Rogers, 1973).

longer made by the Southern Diegueño in the 1920s but their construction was still understood. He described them as always bowed, with a flat triangular projection on the outer side of the arch and midway between the ends that served as a handle. A small hole through the handle allowed for the insertion of a carrying thong. These pipes were still made at Santa Catarina in the 1990s. I have watched them being made and have smoked native tobacco in them. For convenience, the process of Yuman paddle and anvil ceramics can be broken into ten stages, beginning, of course, with finding the clay itself.

1. Gathering Clay

Rogers divided the combined area of southern California and Lower California into a desert region, where mainly sedimentary but some residual clays resulted in a buff-colored ware, and a mountain area with only residual clay that yielded a reddish-brown pottery. Residual clays accumulated from weathering and decomposition of granite outcroppings in the southern California batholith, the underlying rock of mountains extending south from the transverse ranges of Orange County to the tip of Baja. These clays built up in pockets or layers near springs and along streams, both old and recent. They

Yuman-style pottery followed natural shapes, suggested Gena Van Camp, in particular the gourd. Bottles were gourd-like; a few, asymmetrical (21) like certain gourds; others bilobate as are gourds; the scoop was but a gourd cut in half, and pottery rattles were like the gourd ones. Other pieces took the shape of the baskets which preceded them (8). Forms, of course, were always functional: the bottoms of pots rounded, for example, so they could be carried in a net or placed in sand or balanced on three rocks of the hearth; the necks of water ollas were constricted to prevent spillage and evaporation.

Forms were not random in distribution. Semi-globular food bowls (26), plate-like parching trays (17) and ladles (28) stood out among the agricultural Colorado River Yuman groups while the desert Kamia favored graceful, long-necked water ollas (14). The slender water olla neck was often only an inch in diameter on the inside; they came in many sizes; small ones (19), sometimes with a thong strung from two holes just below the rim, were used as portable canteens. Kamia food storage ollas, on the other hand, were infrequent and not often of great size. In contrast, large storage vessels (1-4) typified the seed-gathering mountain groups to the west.

Southern Diegueño (Kumeyaay) storage ollas, with a maximum height around 33" and capacity of 27 gallons, no two exactly the same shape, were filled with seeds or other dry food or even cordage, sandals, ceremonial paraphernalia or anything else that would not spoil and was not for immediate use, and cached in caves, among rocks or buried near villages. A flat ceramic lid, small bowl, a lump of unfired clay or wad of grass sealed the top. Pitch or unfired clay held the pottery lids to the ollas. Some ollas were made with guttered or collared necks likely to provide a seating for a bowl lid. Large ollas were important vessels and meant to last. A pitch plug or cemented potsherd patched holes; infrequently, fresh clay was applied and the area refired. Mesquite or elephant-tree gum mended a crack; or cracks were repaired by means of adjacent drilled holes, with cordage or rawhide thongs to lash the sides together.

Buried to its mouth and the mouth left open, an olla became a trap for small animals. All groups used medium-sized jars at home or in temporary camps to hold food or water for immediate use. The Kumeyaay water olla (5) averaged 17" in height. Canteens (11) sometimes had multiple necks, two, three, or even four. A grass stopper secured the contents. Cooking bowls varied in size, some as small as cups. Earlier forms were straight-sided (12), later developing recurved rims (7). Shallow bowls were often painted and used for serving food, winnowing or parching seeds, as scoops and dippers or as lids for ollas. Cooking pots (6) were about twice the height of the cooking bowl and had a smaller mouth.

Yumas (Quechan) made "mixing" bowls (26), parchers (25) and boat-shaped ladles (27), sometimes with a small cylindrical handle from the rim or a tab-shaped handle at a right angle to the rim (28). The handles of such ladles occasionally were molded with curved parrot-shaped noses and coffee-bean eyes— "quail heads" as the Mohave called them. Yuma water-storage ollas (23) were Piman in profile and flare of the rim. Older ollas had smaller openings and rounder bodies; one for young girls who were not adept at carrying them on their heads was still more slender-necked and small-mouthed. Yuma food-storage ollas also had somewhat smallish mouths. A potsherd ground to disk shape was pitched over the mouth to seal the contents for a long storage.

The rare floating bowl—a shallow bowl over 3' wide in which women placed perishables and babies—was pushed ahead of a swimmer to cross a river; very few could make such a large piece.

Cooking bowls (24), squat, wide-mouthed with recurved rims, were given a special protective finish by the Colorado River tribes and desert Kamia. A stucco of coarse sand or crushed rock, or coarsely crushed potsherds, added to clay mixed with water was plastered over the outside of the bowl after it had been sundried and before firing. They applied the slip and tamped it down with the palm of the hand, thickest on the base—up to 1/4"—tapered on the sides and discontinued a few inches below the rim. It was said it kept the inner wall of the bowl from cracking. As pieces of stucco came off through use, fresh patches were applied.

The Mohave made a special temper for the cooking ware clay itself of a course white sandstone, easily crumbled; they added two parts of this to three parts of clay. They sun-fired the cooking pot for two days, applied stucco and fired it an entire night in a pit kiln. (Mohave ware not intended for cooking had a potsherd temper and were fired one at a time on the surface of the ground; they were placed upside down on three burnt pieces of clay and the fuel stacked in a cone around the pot.)

In the end, function followed need: the Kumeyaay and Paipai, Michelsen discovered, may have made a vessel for one purpose but readily used it for another—a cooking pot could store seeds, a seed-storage olla could hold water—practicality governed the small band, hunter-gatherer mind-set.

The miracle of pottery: Josefina Ochurte turns unbroken clods of earth into finished household ware. Mano and clods, above left. Pulverizing with mano on the grinding stone, above right. Below, she stands by the pit kiln and recently fired canteens and winnowing bowls.

122

came complete with their own temper, particles of quartz, feldspar, and mica (which was of two kinds: biotite and muscovite). The mica could often be seen shining on the surface of the pottery made from this clay. Generally brown, impurities of iron compounds or carbonaceous material or more complete oxidation gave the fired clay a dark, reddish color. Van Camp found that sherds made from residual clays were thicker than those of sedimentary clays.

Sedimentary clays (whose fired pots went from buffs, pinks and light reds to lavenders and grays) developed from fine particles of soil carried along and separated out from coarser particles by water that then deposited them on the banks of the Colorado River, in ancient desert lakes and over other alluvial areas of the Colorado desert. To avert cracking, coarse tempering material had to be added to this clay before firing. Salts were often found in sedimentary clays and would form a scum on the surface of the fired pot or cause a vessel to crack. To prevent this, the potter would actually taste the clay. Those with high salt contents were avoided, especially for a cooking pot.

Women from the Manzanita area often traveled into Northern Diegueño territory to obtain a highly micaceous clay to make cooking pots. Their local clay, widespread in the region on the sides of canyons and valleys, was a coarse decomposed granite that seemed an unlikely raw material for ceramics, but it was much used. By weight, 85 percent of the substance was quartz, mica and partially altered feldspar crystals. Before modern tools, quarrying was with jagged rocks and sharpened sticks. The Southern Diegueño and Paipai of the Santa Catarina region still dug clay with an ironwood digging stick in Michelsen's time (Michelsen and Smith, 1972).

Michelsen noted that Petra Higuera, an elderly Kuatl woman of Santa Catarina, unlike many other local potters, would travel as far as 20 miles to procure clay having less coarse foreign matter. The result was superior pottery. Some obtain clay today in Santa Catarina almost at their doorstep from the valley floor near the local stream.

The Mohave dug sedimentary clay from the Colorado River bank at the base of Parker Mesa, a clay found nearly everywhere along margins of the broader areas of the Colorado River valley, according to Rogers.

Except in cases of special necessity, clay was gathered and pottery made only during the summer months when fuel and ground were driest. As one moves south, summer in effect begins earlier. In the mountain desert of Santa Catarina, potters are at work by springtime, rising early in the morning and working throughout the day directly in the sun so the pot will dry rapidly and the finished piece can be placed in the kiln. Wilken described Santa Catarina and the quarrying of local clay, recognized in finished vessels by its many flecks of shimmering mica:

> *At dawn on a clear spring day, an Indian woman sets off across the desert to a place where her grandmother taught her to gather clay, followed by an assortment of children, grandchildren, and*

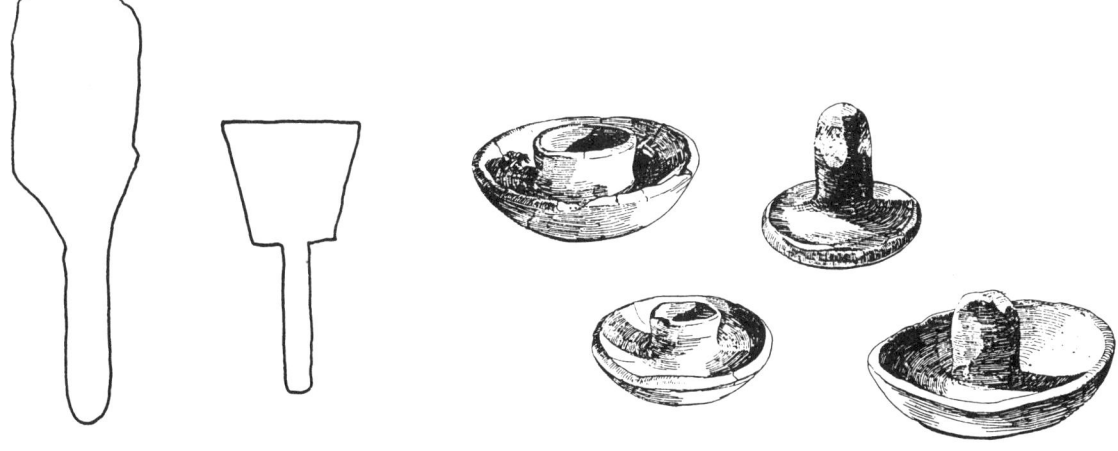

Old-style Southern Diegueño paddle on left, new on right. (Drawn from Rogers, 1936.) Next, two pottery anvils of the Cocopa in the University of California collections. At right, early Southern Diegueño pottery anvils from Campo, California, Museum of the American Indian, Heye Foundation. (First Diegueño anvil, about 9 cm. in diameter.) These are virtually identical with those made by Josefina Ochurte in Santa Catarina in 1994 (drawings in Gifford, 1928).

dogs. She walks along a well-worn trail through manzanita, yucca, and juniper bushes. Making her way up the low hill at the base of Red Rock Mountain, she comes to a clearing and begins to dig into the dark red veins of earth, looking for clods with just enough sand and not too many rocks (Wilken, 1987).

II. Crushing the Clods

The gathered clods were then crushed. Sometimes at Rancho Escondido, where a small band of Southern Diegueño live a little ways down a trail beyond Santa Catarina, Manuela Aguiar's son would do this for her on the bare ground with a metal tool. Any rough rock that fit the hand served to smash the clods on the ground or on a flat stone. A mortar or a grinding stone with a pestle or a mano worked well. Large, unbreakable pieces were picked out and discarded. The resulting crushed material was dried in the sun for a day.

III. Grinding and Sifting

Once dry, on a grinding slab or in a mortar, the crushed clods, including small chunks of mixed clay, mica and other minerals, were completely pulverized, pounded and ground into powder. Josefina Ochurte's slab was simply a flat rock about 1 foot long and a little under 1 foot wide. It had worn down somewhat unevenly through prolonged use. Her mano was a stream-worn oval boulder that nicely fit her hand. With both hands she pushed it back and forth over the forward edge of a pile of crushed clay on the slab. Little by little finely ground clay began to appear in front of the mano. Coarse clay particles not reduced during this stage and allowed to remain in the clay would lead to shrinkage cracks in fired vessels. For that reason the pulverized clay was thoroughly sifted.

The old way, as demonstrated for Rogers by Southern Diegueño Rosa Lopez, was done on the surface of a parching tray—a nearly flat basket about 16 inches in diameter. With a few scoops of dry clay powder in the center, the tray was flopped up and down. Large inclusions came to the surface and were picked out. Then the tray was moved to and fro, concentrating coarse particles in the center of the tray, where they were again plucked out. A rotary movement left the fine useful material in the center and carried the remaining coarse bits and pieces to the edge where the flat of the hand pushed them over and away.

Rogers analyzed this method and compared it to a more modern screening. Virtually identical in results, either method increased the clay ratio of Rosa Lopez's raw material, from nearly 16 percent to slightly more than 20 percent. It was now ready to use, complete with its own quartz, feldspar and mica tempering.

Rogers noted that archaeological evidence and early observations showed that the Serrano and the Desert Cahuilla did not add coarse tempering. Sufficient coarse inclusions were already in the residual clays they used. This was true for Rosa Lopez's clay and undoubtedly for the residual clay of the Santa Catarina potters, although some of these added potsherds, ash or even steer manure to the clay to assure that the pots would not crack.

Yuma Indians, who employed sedimentary clays from the Colorado River flood plain and upper terrace, added a scant handful of ground potsherds to a heaping handful of ground clay. This applied to everything but cooking bowls. For cooking ware a handful of decomposed granite, burnt and pulverized, was mixed in with two handfuls of clay.

IV. Adding Water and Kneading

Bunches of yerba santa *(Eriodictyon californicum)* with leaves left on the twigs were soaked in water for twenty-four hours. This liquid, when mixed with the clay, was believed to increase plasticity and to help bond the coils. Rogers referred to a study where tannin (thought to be the substance involved) had this effect and reduced shrinkage as well, while increasing hardness and tensile strength of sun-dried and burned clay. The roasted stems of a cactus *(Opuntia occidentalis)* were used in the same way. Petra Higuera added a handful of wood ashes to her water.

On a metate or flat rock, the prepared water was poured into the center of a ring of the pulverized clay. Water and clay were mixed and kneaded like dough. It should not be too wet nor too dry. Some pounded it with their fists. Others slapped it between their palms or squeezed and manipulated it. This stage could not be hurried or shrinkage cracks would appear in the pot while drying and certainly when it was fired. Bubbles would cause the pot to explode when fired.

In earlier days, loaves of the prepared clay were wrapped in wet grass and buried in the ground for as long as possible to improve plasticity (through reduction of organic matter). The Yuma would bury

Left to right and down: With large mano Josefina Ochurte flattens ball of clay into tortilla-shaped base for new pot. She paddles it out on cloth-covered bottom of old bowl. A coil is placed and attached with finger tabs. She wets a polished stone and with it smoothes the new coil onto the base.

Before paddling and thinning the new attached coil, she allows some time for drying by working on a clay pipe. She shapes the bowl of the pipe and the stem with her fingers. A smooth stone polishes the exterior of the pipe. She then paddles the coil already attached to the bowl and rolls out a new coil which she places as before.

small pats of prepared clay in the wet ground for at least two days in order to ripen. At the time of Rogers' study, Lopez wrapped her clay in wet rags and used it almost at once.

V. Forming the Vessel Base

Josefina Ochurte took a lump about the size of two fists and mashed it like a tortilla on a flat, cloth-covered surface with a smooth, somewhat flattened, large round stone she could just grasp with her fingers. This flat disk of clay was then placed on the bottom of an inverted pot and molded to it. Rogers wrote that Rosa Lopez began with the lump directly on an inverted cooking pot. Such a pot was favored because the wide mouth kept it steady on the ground. Other pots would be used, depending on the vessel intended. Ochurte covered the inverted bowl with an old cloth to prevent sticking. Some potters at Santa Catarina today, and Rosa Lopez in 1928, rubbed wood ashes over the surface for the same effect. When a vessel was unavailable, the potter began a new piece on her flexed knee or on an appropriately shaped basket. Small bowls or jars 4 inches in diameter or less were made from a single or several slabs of clay and were not coiled.

From the lump or disk, a symmetrical base was beaten or tapped out on the mold with a flat wooden paddle about 8 inches long. The blade was about 4 inches square for Lopez but, according to Rogers, older more traditional paddles had a blade twice as long as wide, with the base curved into the handle at the sides instead of forming a right angle. At Santa Catarina, Josefina Ochurte used the new-style paddle, while Margarita Castro still employed the old. Traditionally, paddles were cut and ground from the flat splinter of a fallen tree. The kind of wood mattered little but cottonwood was preferred. Sometimes the scapulae of a deer or mountain sheep served as a paddle.

VI. Coiling and Paddling the Walls

A sausage-shaped clay hunk was held vertically between the palms and rolled back and forth. In this way it lengthened until it reached about 12 inches at a uniform diameter of about 1 inch. This formed a coil. (Coils were sometimes thinner on prehistoric pots.) As Rosa Lopez's right hand laid the coil clockwise on the base, still inverted on the mold, her left thumb pushed small sections of the coil over and onto the base at intervals of 1 inch to fasten it. Each coil was a concentric unit (unlike the Pueblo spirals). If necessary, extra pieces were spliced in to make it complete. The thumb tabs were rubbed over with a moistened thumb and the entire line smoothed with wet fingers to bond it. Josefina Ochurte laid her coils counterclockwise with her left hand while her right middle finger pulled out the little connecting tabs. A small smooth flat stone dipped in water replaced wet fingers to bond the seam.

Blows directed downwards with the paddle flattened the coil, pulled it out, thinned it, and increased the height of the pot's wall. It was removed from the mold and held upright in the lap. Moistened fingers bonded and smoothed the inside seam as they had the outside.

Before placing the next coil, irregular rims were trimmed level. A moistened flake of stone or wet agave fiber cord, used in a sawing motion, traditionally did this, but in Rogers' time and more recently at Santa Catarina, a steel knife was used. The joined tips of the thumb and first finger formed a right angle which swept clockwise around the cut rim to smooth it. The bowl was lifted and turned counterclockwise after each stroke.

Returning the bowl to the mold, the coiling continued until it reached the vertical side of the mold. After this, additional coils were placed with the bowl maintained upright on the lap. An anvil held against the inner wall opposed paddling on the outside. A water-worn cobble served as anvil, bonding, thinning and giving curvature to the wall. A small bowl, mano or, as an expediency, a small basket would work. A hollow or solid-stemmed mushroom-shaped ceramic anvil was also employed. Such anvils are still made in many sizes by Josefina Ochurte at Santa Catarina. The paddle struck *upward* against the wall to lengthen and thin it and prevent lateral distention. Any cracks were quickly filled by the fingers with a thin clay soup and then paddled.

To bring a wall in, the rim was beveled acutely inward and the new coil placed on its outer margin. Bonding took place on the inside first, the reverse of the earlier procedure. (Sometimes the tabs pushed out with the thumb were not completely obliterated, but could be found on the finished vessel.) To recurve the rim, coils were placed on an outward beveled rim, the reverse of bringing the wall in. Paddling continued upward until the desired thinness of the wall was achieved. At Santa Catarina, finished pots varied from around 1/8 to 3/16 of an inch in thickness.

To make the small water-olla-style neck, the paddle was reversed and the paddling done with the narrow handle against the first two fingers of the left hand inserted in the neck of the pot. The coils were also thinner at this stage. Sweeping upward motions of the paddle drew the clay out and gave height to the neck. Because of its delicacy, irregularities of the rim were nipped off with the teeth. Finally the potter filed pits and cracks with daubs of wet clay and, using the wet palm of her hand in a circular motion, rubbed and smoothed the entire surface of the vessel.

VII. Drying

Next the light cinnamon-colored or buff-brown pots were dried in the sun. Only a few hours might have passed between the completion of the last piece and the preliminary baking that followed the drying. Rosa Lopez fired a bowl after only four hours. Rogers explained that a short drying time was possible because of the nature of the clay being used and the paddle and anvil technique, which forced water to the surface where it quickly evaporated. Placing an unfired pot near an open fire during humid weather hastened the process for some potters. On an unusually hot, dry day the pots were sometimes kept out of the sun to prevent checking. If checking occurred, the vessel was simply broken up and the clay reused.

Josefina Ochurte allowed for drying time as she worked. After smoothing a coil onto the vessel with a wet stone, but before paddling, she would often take a few minutes to work on a clay pipe. She began these pipes by rolling a single piece of clay in her palms to about an inch of thickness. She tapered one end into a stem and shaped the other with a conical wooden mold. Removing the mold, she enlarged the pipe bowl with her right index finger. She gave the stem a gentle arch and pushed a little pointed twig with the same arch into the stem to the bottom of the bowl. She smoothed the outside of the pipe with the help of a small smooth stone. The flat, triangular handle was attached last, after the bowl had been formed. The twig in the stem would be burned away during firing. Any residue could be pushed out with another small stick. The mouthpiece sometimes had to be opened by abrading it in a perpendicular fashion across a stone.

VIII. Decoration

Vessels generally received little if any decoration, although roughly painted bowls were commonplace among the Colorado River tribes. The Mohave were the most given to decorating their pots. As pigment, they used a yellow ochre (or limonite—hydrous ferric oxide) that turned red when fired. Their many design elements had meanings and names, each potter using a number of icons as her own. The Yuma painted designs on pieces not meant for cooking or hard usage, usually on water- or food-storage ollas. Large storage jars and cooking pots were not painted by the Kumeyaay but water jars and serving bowls often received designs. The decorations were irregular, inconsistent and without apparent plan. Incising was known by Yuman potters, but only painting had survived to Rogers' time and that was exclusively in red, applied in broad lines somewhat carelessly.

Rogers wrote that Kumeyaay design elements had no particular meaning and appeared to have derived from the Colorado River Yuman groups. A. Kroeber saw a similarity in some of these elements among the Mohave with tattoo marks, which seemed true of other groups as well. Some of the motifs are found in petroglyphs and pictographs and on the basketry of southern California.

Kumeyaay pigment or paint came from hematite or red ochre (anhydrous ferric oxide). Rosa Lopez obtained hers from the earth (a ledge in Carrizo Canyon near Jacumba), but a bacteria also deposited it as a scum in iron-bearing springs. The pigment was ground in a small pottery cup or a large concave potsherd then mixed with water that had been prepared by soaking an egg-sized piece of baked mescal *(Agave deserti)* in it for twenty-four hours. From time to time the sweet syrup from the baked mescal was squeezed out into the water. This sugary mixture set the pigment during firing.

Josephina's wooden mold used to make pottery pipe bowl.

The Story of the Pipe

That is no ordinary pipe, Benito Peralta was quick to point out as I purchased a small clay pipe made by his sister Josefina Ochurte. It has its mystery, its story, he told me; such pipes were smoked only once a year by one special man during a mourning ceremony which involved an eagle. Peralta, an elder of the Paipai, learned of its function in his youth from old people of his tribe who had learned the story in turn from those long before them. The pipe and the eagle were part of the same story.

Before the ceremony, which mourned those who had died the previous year, a specially designated man went out and captured an eaglet. He climbed a high cliff to the aerie, took the bird and descended. They held the eagle in a cage and raised him until he became a fully fledged adult. They treated the eagle well and respected him.

As the sun rose on that day of the mourning ceremony, the eagle was placed under a great ramada shade built especially for the occasion. He could be seen under the ramada weeping for the departed in the early morning light. He had known what was to befall him even before the dawn. It was then the man with the pipe approached the eagle and lit the tobacco—the coyote tobacco which grows around here—in the pipe. He drew the smoke into his mouth and blew it directly into the face of the eagle, usually only three or four times before the bird collapsed and died.

(It is interesting to note that Pedro Fages' eighteenth-century account of the Chumash, who are also of the Hokan linguistic stock, included mention of smoke from a pipe in a mortuary ceremony: At daybreak, the priest, smoking a large stone pipe, passed three times around the person's body and each time he stopped and blew three mouthfuls of smoke upon the departed's head.)

When we die, Peralta reflected, the eagle's spirit carries our soul to wherever it is we go. So, during the mourning ceremony, little bundles were made of the eagles' feathers and each bundle tied securely. Wherever anyone had passed away the previous year, there a bundle was laid. Then as a singer chanted the songs of the Paipai and the people danced in a long line, the eagle and bundles of feathers were brought together and burned, consumed in fire just as the deceased had been the year before.

The eagle is very special to us, said Peralta, we would never kill him for sport or for food though he might land right next to us. Neither do we smoke these clay pipes for mere pleasure.

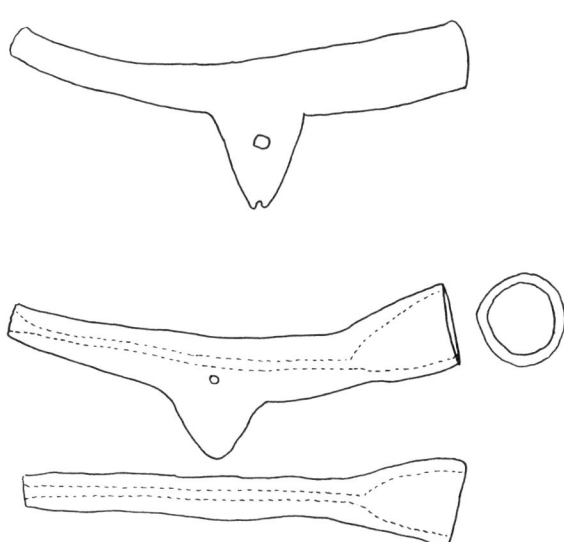

Above, old Southern Diegueño pipe (drawn from Rogers, 1936). Below, three views of a Paipai pipe (nearly 5-3/4" long), Santa Catarina, 1994.

129

Josefina Ochurte gives final polish to unfired plate and evens jar rim with a knife. Notice pottery anvils on ground beside her. Below: unfired water vessels to the rear of fired food bowl and canteen. She stands beside a seed olla, late fall 1997.

Above, cooking bowls of Paipai Josefina Ochurte, some with tab-like rim handles, flanked by food bowls and small canteen. Pipe and anvils to the front. Below, the cooking bowl resting on a Kumeyaay ring made of a hoop of split juncus strips wound with more split juncus. Mohave women used similar rings to carry large bowls on their heads.

The Kumeyaay vessel was held upright on the palm of the left hand while it was decorated with the right. The end of a 3-inch piece of agave-fiber cordage served as a brush. Milkweed fiber cordage was preferred in earlier days but they had stopped making this when Rogers observed Lopez in the late 1920s. The Yuma twisted two strands of the inner bark of willow into a 6-inch cord, doubled it over and twisted it into a 3-inch, four-ply cord and applied paint with the bent end. A thin red wash occasionally was coated over a Kumeyaay vessel with the palm and closed fingers or a broad design was painted with a single finger.

Manuela Aguiar, a Southern Diegueño or Kuatl potter in the Sierra Juárez of Baja, was making designs in red on some of her pots when I visited in the summer of 1994. Generally vessels from the Santa Catarina area were left undecorated.

IX. Preliminary Heating

The vessels were arranged 1 foot apart in a circle and at the margin of a brush pile on the surface of the ground. Once ignited, the brush burned away after fifteen minutes. If it was windy, soot might get on some vessels but the final firing would clean them. Rogers said that the potter explained this roasting as a test but the real function was to rid the vessels of all moisture before sudden exposure to the extreme heat of the kiln. Josefina Ochurte of Santa Catarina bypassed this stage. She allowed some drying time as she coiled the pots and the hot dry air of the Santa Catarina region likely made preliminary heating unnecessary.

X. Final Firing

To fire eight pieces of pottery, Rosa Lopez dug a pit 14 inches deep by 2 feet across and lined

Teresa Castro and trunks of Mohave yucca near pit oven in which pottery has been stacked and covered with yucca trunks, Santa Catarina 1997. Not until she had grown into womanhood did she know of modern pots and pans and glass dishes. Her Kuatl (Southern Diegueño) mother made everything of clay. Castro's Paipai father had taken his family to a remote valley 40 miles from Santa Catarina toward the Pacific Ocean near San Vicente, a valley rich in acorns and other gathering opportunities. Isolated in the valley called Dolores, they lived with only one other Paipai family for her childhood and youth. She recalled the day they discovered a cave full of wooden weapons and tools made by Indians long before. Her father said it was best to leave such things untouched and they did.

Where was Dolores Valley? I did not find it on the old maps or Baja guides, but I remembered an account of exploration in Lower California by Arthur North. In early 1906, he had taken a wrong direction as he headed south from Alamo into uncharted territory. A day of hacking through dense brush high in the Sierras, avoiding chollas and Spanish bayonets, brought him to an ancient trail worn deep into the granite of the mountain—at one point he measured its depth with a tape at 38" into the rock! Farther on the trail his party noted fresh mountain lion tracks mingled with those of barefooted Indians. The path descended into an arroyo and on a small sandy bench above the stream came abruptly upon an Indian village of some six huts. Men clad with knife belts, sandals and happy smiles met his party and gave him to know in broken Spanish they were Pai; naked children played, boys practicing with stout bows and reed arrows and girls carrying babies at their sides; on metate stones women crushed corn and a small black seed (like that "found in the crops of wild doves"). North described them as "a healthy, husky looking race of people." The Indians declared North and his party the first whites ever to come to the village known as Dolores.

North was not far from an agua caliente, or warm spring, he reached farther down the valley by nightfall, a perfect camping spot. This in turn was near the Mission of San Vicente. Both are found on modern maps. The village of Dolores and Teresa's valley of Dolores must have been one in the same and located upstream from Agua Caliente on Río San Vicente.

the bottom with small stones about 4 inches in diameter, spaced so that twigs could be placed between them to start the fire. Five pottery pieces were arranged upside down on the stones. Large slabs of dry bark from dead oak were set on edge between the pots and leaned against them on the outside, completely encircling them. A second tier of pots was stacked upside down over the first and even larger bark slabs were laid about and over the top of the entire pile. Unlike Pueblo firing, the fuel was in contact with the vessels.

The kiln had been dug on the lee side of a hill protected from the wind. A vertical draft was essential to distribute the heat evenly and prevent smudging. To avoid steam, dryness of the site was also important.

In the evening when the wind had subsided and the last bark slab arranged, the potter lit the twigs in the bottom of the kiln and walked away. It was bad luck to turn and watch or even approach the kiln until the fire had died out. They believed it would cause the pots to crack.

If the draft was strong, parts of the vessels would glow a dull red. Where the vessel was touched by fuel, a dark carbon patch would form that would burn away if enough fire remained. Highly carbonized cooking pots were often cleaned by placing them in the kiln with new vessels.

Rogers noted that the conditions of the kiln were not the same for all pots. For the first forty-five minutes, as the fuel was turning to coals, the temperature was fairly uniform. But for the next two hours the considerable heat of the coals mainly affected the lower tier. On the following morning the

Without preliminary firing but having only been dried in the hot sun, the clay pots were stacked in an open fashion, one on top of another, in the center of a shallow pit oven in the sandy soil. They were covered evenly with large pieces of dry trunks of Mohave yucca and some bark tinder. The fuel was set ablaze and allowed to burn to ashes, about one hour. Only toward the end did Castro rearrange some of the glowing embers to one side or the other to close up gaps in the fire.

pots were removed from the kiln and the ashes whisked from the vessels with a meal brush.

After the firing but while the vessels were still hot, the Yuma would flick a weak solution of mesquite gum in water over the entire outer surface of painted ware and on decorated water ollas to set the paint and waterproof them. The gum was found as globules on the trunks and branches of the old trees and dissolved in water by boiling.

Ken Hedges, in his studies of the Northern Diegueño at Santa Ysabel, specified that the coast live-oak bark was considered best for firing pottery, although they fueled the kiln with the bark of other oaks as well. In the desert foothill region of the eastern Southern Diegueño, dead leaves of the Mohave yucca *(Yucca schidigera)* replaced oak bark as the principal fuel. At Santa Catarina the dry trunks of the Mohave yucca commonly fueled the kiln. They were spaced to allow an even burn around the pots. Michelsen found that Petra Higuera's yucca fire lasted about one hour and saw that her ollas became a mottled cherry red at the fire's height.

With a long stick Castro carefully removed the hot, fired pots and clay canteens from the oven and placed them on the ground to quicken the cooling process. Half an hour later, the canteens were ready and strung with agave fiber string. Sections of the spongy white center of fresh Spanish bayonet (Yucca whipplei) flower stalk made perfect corks.

Rogers wrote that cattle dung was occasionally used by the Southern Diegueño, and it still is at Santa Catarina. The Yuma fired their pots with cottonwood, willow driftwood, mesquite branches or any other woody scrubs. The Kamia branch of the Southern Diegueño, living in the Colorado Desert, fired pots with the dead roots of the salt bush *(Atriplex lentiformis)*. Rogers felt that this plant's low resinous content helped prevent smudging and fire stains on Kamia pottery.

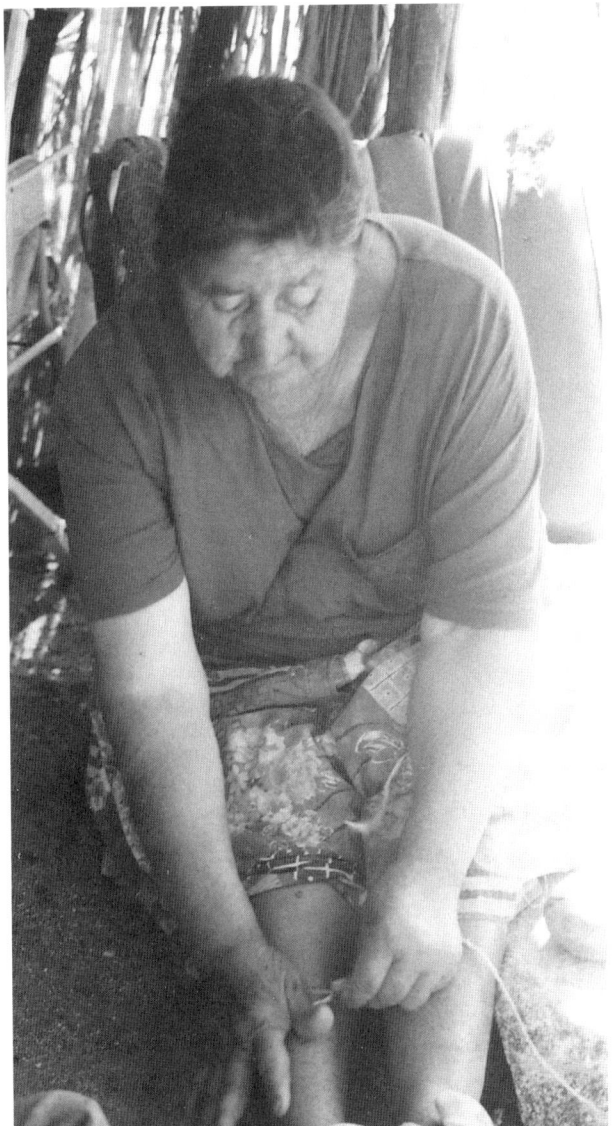

Teresa Castro had only short leftover scraps of agave fiber with which to make cords for her newly fired canteens. She had to splice in additional lengths with almost every roll of the palm but it did not seem to slow her down a whit. Like some cleverly designed machine, she rolled out long lengths of finished cordage from raw fiber in minutes. Where she held the finished cord separated from the two strands of yet untwisted fiber, she overlapped additional agave fiber about 1 inch onto the shorter, 1-inch strand; and pinching the splice between thumb and forefinger rolled the palm of the other hand away from her against her leg, twisting separately and at once both the spliced and unspliced strands. Releasing the grip, the two strands sprang naturally together for 2 or 3 inches. Often, when splicing like this, she did not reverse the rolling motion of the hand to tighten the two-ply twist but first twisted considerably more of the two strands on a second outward roll of the palm, firming up the splice. At the end of the outward roll, the back of the palm brought the nearer strand up and over the other, slightly winding them together, before reversing and twisting them firmly together in the opposite direction where tension on each strand naturally assisted. And so she continued making strong two-ply agave cordage.

Greens, Beans, Flowers and Other Vegetables

It staggers the mind to realize that diabetes currently afflicts 50 percent of Native Americans over the age of thirty-five in the Southwest, the highest rate in the world. Noting the rise of a host of diseases among Southwestern Indians since they dropped their native diet in favor of modern store-bought food, ethnobotanist Gary Paul Nabhan tried an experiment. At the National Institute of Fitness, he, six Tohono O'odham and a Hopi returned to traditional foods such as mesquite, cholla cactus buds, prickly pear fruit and stem, and chia seeds. These are foods known to slow the rate of sugar release into the bloodstream. They combined this diet with a level of activity precontact Indians would have experienced. In two weeks, a 1-1/2 percent loss of fat occurred on average. Especially important was a weekly 30- to 35-point drop in blood sugar and cholesterol. Admittedly, beyond junk food and sloth are features of modern life too wonderful to ignore, but the old ways have much to offer as well. Discipline and wisdom allow one to choose the best of both worlds.

The following is a limited, representative compendium of traditional California vegetable foods and methods of preparation. Not included are the cultural contexts in which the plants were gathered. The Kashaya Pomo, as described by Jennie Goodrich, Claudia Lawson and Vana Lawson, for example, still today explain to the Creator why they are taking plants and sing a special song to calm the Earth Spirit and ward off evil powers. They share the harvest with others, selfishness is bad luck the Pomo believe. Further, a menstruating woman and her spouse do not enter collecting areas or even touch plants. Respect for the world was general in Native California.

Seaweed *(Porphyra sp.)*: Of the Yurok, Powers observed: "They find on the coast a glutinous kind of algae, which they press into loaves when wet, then dry them in the sun, and eat them raw." Yurok elder Frank Gist recently told me that as a young man he would transport a group of older ladies up the coast from the mouth of the Klamath and drop them off for a few days so they could gather and process seaweed. On his return, their baskets were full. Goddard specified *P. perforata* as a seaweed used by the Hupa, obtained near the mouth of the Klamath, for the salt content which led to good health. A shaman was also said to eat it to intensify his thirst when refraining from water to improve his medicine in hunting. The Bear River people, as described by Gladys Nomland, gathered seaweed, dried it in the sun and packed it in baskets for the winter. It was not soaked for reconstitution but merely heated slowly near the fire to soften. V. K. Chesnut, in his inquiries among the Yuki and Pomo a hundred years ago, found that they made special trips to the coast for abalone, clams and especially a purple, gelatinous seaweed *(P. laciniata)*. They preferred to bake the salty plants but often chewed them raw—a prolonged process that made the seaweed mucilaginous and digestible. Goodrich found the Kashaya Pomo ate *P. perforata* and *lanceolata* fresh or baked. For storage it was formed in cakes a foot in diameter, 1/2 inch thick and dried in the sun and later baked for eating.

Bull kelp *(Nereocystis luetkeama)*: Gathered in the summer or fall, Kashaya Pomo cooked the thick part of the stalk in an oven or hot ashes until puffy. The stalk, cut into lengthwise strips, was also dried for the winter. (Partially dried until limp, slender pieces were employed as cordage or fish line.)

Sea palm *(Postelsia palmaeformis)*: Kashaya Pomo chewed fresh stems raw or baked them in an oven or hot ashes. Long strips of stem, laid in the sun or warm place in the house, were dried for the winter.

Sea lettuce *(Ulva lactuca linnacus)*: Light green lettuce-like seaweed had a peppery taste. The Kashaya Pomo ate it with other seaweed for flavoring.

Ice plant *(Mesembryanthemum chilense)*: The fruit of this plant of the coastal sand dunes was eaten raw by the Kashaya Pomo.

Bur reed *(Sparganium eurycarpum)*: The Modoc ate stems, shoots and roots.

Clover *(Trifolium sp.)*: California Indians relished fresh clover and none with more gusto than did the Pomo. They went to the clover fields in the spring and filled their stomachs as well as their burden baskets they carried back to the village. One variety of clover had large leaves with red and white flowers. Another was very small with almost no flowers. They would cut clover 6 inches in length in the harvest and, for eating, lay them together, a half dozen plants at a time with the flower heads aligned. They would break off an inch and a half of the heads, a mouthful, and throw away the rest as refuse, observed Barrett in 1904. Proceeding in this fashion, they ate so much that their stomachs would bloat. Pepperwood nuts, often made into small cakes, were consumed by some to counter the bloating.

The neighboring Yuki, who were recorded by Chesnut one hundred years ago, generally ate the fresh green part of the clover before it flowered but the flowers and seeds of some species were eaten as well. After flowering the leaves tended to be bitter and tough. Special clover dances marked the appearance of clover in the spring. Species mentioned by Chesnut included *T. bifidum decipiens* (eaten sparingly and only when young); *T. ciliolatum* (one woman ate the flowers); *T. dichotomum* (leaves eaten sparingly when young); *T. obtusiflorum* (one of the very best, a sticky exudation on flower and stems had strong acid taste, sometimes washed away, and dipping the plant in salt water added to its appeal); *T. variegatum*, or white-topped clover for the white tips of its red-purple flowers (much used as a green); *T. virescens* (all parts sweet and the favorite of them all, greens eaten even when clover in flower, flowers and seed pods eaten too—seeds not separated for pinole but eaten raw), and *T. wormskjoldii* (much gathered and eaten toward the last of June, flowers as well as leaves). This latter clover was also eaten by the Kawaiisu, preferably with salt, according to Zigmond. Goodrich mentioned that for the Kashaya Pomo, *T. fucatum's* raw leaves and flowers were eaten alone or with salt or pepper nut cakes.

The Yokuts enjoyed young and tender raw clover leaves alone or accompanied by acorn mush or manzanita cider. The Atsugewi ate clover tops raw and gathered the roots as well, which they cooked in an earth oven. The Miwok ate various species of clover including tomcat clover *(T. tridentatum)* whose leaves, stems and flower buds were eaten raw or steamed in an earth oven.

The Miwok earth oven, described by Barrett and Gifford, frequently baked and steamed greens. A pit was thoroughly heated and lined with a layer of hot stones, followed by a layer of green leaves. Gray mule ears *(Wyethia helenioides)* were best but wild grape leaves or green tule could also be used. On the leaves they placed a thin layer of food, more leaves and another layer of hot stones. Over these further layers of leaves, food and stones were piled until the pit was full. Over all was a layer of earth, often with a fire on top of the earth. Baking was overnight or sometimes for 24 hours. Food kept hot and delicious in the oven until it was desired. Water poured around the perimeter of the oven steamed the food. For preservation, the greens were dried in the sun on leaves of mule ears. To reconstitute for eating, they were soaked in water or boiled.

Tule *(Scirpus)* and cattail *(Typha)*: Pomo men of the lake region would swim out among the tules and cattail in late spring when the shoots were young and tender. They dove to the bottom for the very long rootstocks that they gently pulled and worked free from the deep mud. Sections sometimes 10 feet long were wrapped around their waists and when enough had been gathered, they floated them to shore where they peeled and ate the fresh young shoots as a green. The soft peeled skin was not discarded but saved and utilized as swaddling clothes or other soft padding. The roots were also peeled and eaten as a raw vegetable. Tule and cattail were important throughout the Californias. Farther south the Kawaiisu ate raw the tender lower tule stalk as well as the white base stem, the brown flowers and green seeds of the cattail. The Cahuilla ground tule roots into flour and ate tule seeds raw, or ground them and made mush. Cattail roots, gathered June through July, were also dried and ground into meal.

The Kamia, known through Gifford's early informants, gathered and ate the pollen of the tule, probably referring to cattail tule *(Typha)*, although the Cahuilla made cakes of tule *(Scirpus)* pollen as well as cakes and mush of cattail pollen. Kelly learned from Cocopa Jim Short and Sam Spa that cattail pollen heads were harvested in large quantities and brought to camp to dry before extracting the pollen, a tedious job. Once dry, the heads were struck against the rim of a clay bowl so that the yellow pollen would fall into the bowl. Or, in another method, they might be struck with a stick over the bowl. The pollen was sifted through a willow-twig strainer.

The prized substance sweetened many dishes such as mush made from unparched cornmeal or meal from unparched curlydock seeds or barnyard grass. Placed in a hollow pumpkin stem and baked in the coals for about ten minutes, it also made a kind of candy. A hollow stem of curlydock plugged at each end with twisted bark was used the same way.

They ate cattail pollen raw, boiled it into a thin gruel, shaped the pollen into flat cakes (which they baked overnight enclosed in a covered olla placed in the embers of a fire) and made it into a kind of cookie. To do this, according to Castetter and Bell, pollen was laid over a layer of moist silt on a bed of hot ashes. The cattail heads from which the pollen had been harvested were placed over the pollen with hot coals on top. The pollen cookie baked until it became hard. It was then broken into pieces and eaten or dried and stored in a clay pot.

Like the Pomo, the Cocopa ate raw the young cattail roots that grew in water. Roots were also dried in the sun, especially those from drier soil. They ground the desiccated roots on a grinding stone to extract a dry powdery starch, then added water and boiled it into mush.

Sedge *(Carex douglasii):* The Kawaiisu ate the enlarged base of the stem raw.

Umbrella plant *(Peltiphyllum peltatum):* The Karok ate the young shoots raw, according to Sarah Schenck and Gifford.

Pea *(Lathyrus graminifolius):* This was eaten by the Karok as a green in spring when tender.

California fuchsia *(Zauschneria latifolia):* The Karok sucked the nectar from the end of the blossom of this plant.

Poison sanicle *(Sanicula bipinnata):* The Karok ate the young greens.

Hawksbeard *(Crepis acuminata):* The Karok peeled and ate the stems raw.

Gumplant *(Grindelia robusta var. patens):* Greens were gathered by the Karok in the spring and eaten raw.

Narrowleaf mule ears *(Wyethia angustifolia):* The Hupa ate the fresh shoots raw of many plants including the narrowleaf mule ears.

Gray mule ears *(Wyethia helenioides):* The Miwok peeled young shoots and ate the sweet vegetable raw.

Leptotoenia *(Leptotoenia californica):* The fresh shoots were eaten raw by the Hupa, and the Karok ate the roots raw.

Cow parsnip *(Heracleum lanatum):* The Hupa ate the fresh shoots raw.

Shooting star or mosquito bill *(Dodecatheon hendersonii):* The Yuki ate the roots and leaves after roasting them in ashes.

Cream cups *(Platystemon californicus):* These were used for greens by the Yuki.

American vetch *(Vicia americana):* These were cooked as greens by the Yuki and the Pomo.

Foothill lomatium *(Lomatium utriculatum)* and pestle lomatium *(L. nudicaule):* Leaves were eaten raw by the Atsugewi, who also ate raw the tender stems of the pestle lomatium, observed T. Garth. The Kawaiisu boiled and ate the greens and flowers of the foothill lomatium, according to Zigmond. It could bloom as early as January. He found that they also ate raw the spring greens of hog fennel *(L. californicum).*

Redwood sorrel *(Oxalis oregana):* When in flower, leaves and stems were chewed for sourness by the Pomo. As the leaves get larger they taste tangy and can be eaten.

Sweet cicely *(Osmorhiza chilensis):* The Miwok ate the boiled leaves. The Karok ate leaves and stems in the spring.

Red maids *(Calandrinia ciliata):* When tender, this alien species was used as greens by the Luiseño, according to P. S. Sparkman.

Water dropwort *(Oenanthe sarmentosa):* The Miwok ate the raw stems.

Fiddleneck *(Amsinckia tessellata):* The Kawaiisu ate the fresh stems in the spring. They bruised the leaves by rubbing them between the hands and ate them with salt.

Wild rhubarb *(Rumex hymenosepelus):* Crisp and juicy stalks were eaten fresh by the Cahuilla. In the spring, these, along with stems of willow dock *(R. salicifolius),* the Kawaiisu boiled or roasted side by side in hot ashes. When ready, the ashes were removed with a stick, the pulp pushed out of the skin and eaten hot or cold like a banana. The Tubatulabal roasted the fleshy stalks of wild rhubarb (probably *R. hymenosepalus*) in hot ashes overnight and ate them the following morning, recorded Erminie Voegelin.

Wild celery *(Apiastrum angustifolium):* A small plant, unlike commercial celery, it was a source of some food in wet years for the Cahuilla, according to Bean, Saubel, and Bowers.

Wild parsley or Gray's lovage *(Ligusticum grayi):* The Atsugewi ate the tender leaves in the spring. They were soaked, then baked in an earth oven. After baking they could be stored or eaten with acorn mush as a meat substitute.

Indian or miner's lettuce *(Montia perfoliata):* This moisture-loving plant's stems, leaves and blossoms were eaten fresh by the Miwok, and fresh or boiled by the Cahuilla, Luiseño, and others. The Yuki cooked it with salt.

Thistle *(Cirsium drummondii):* The Atsugewi ate the young and tender stalks raw. The Cahuilla ate the bud at the base of the thistle in the center of the rosette. The Kawaiisu skinned the stems of the California thistle *(C. californicum)* in the spring and ate them raw. They did the same with the dwarf thistle *(C. congdonii)* and cobweb thistle *(C. occidentale).*

Purslane *(Portulaca oleracea):* This was used as a green by the Luiseño.

Monardella *(Monardella candicans):* The leaves and stalks were eaten by the Tubatulabal.

Live-forever *(Dudleya sp.):* The succulent leaves and flowering stems were eaten raw as a delicacy in the spring and early summer by the Cahuilla.

Angelica *(Angelica tomentosa):* The root was a well-known medicine and charm but the Karok, Pomo and Hupa also ate the young shoots as greens. The Yana after removing the outer rind ate the stem raw.

Wild carrot *(Lomatium macrocarpum):* The Kashaya Pomo ate the young leaves of this plant.

Soaproot *(Chlorogalum pomeridianum):* Shoots and pith of the soaproot stem were eaten as greens by the Pomo.

Wild onion *(Allium unifolium):* While the Pomo sometimes baked the wild onion in an earth oven, alone or as a seasoning for other bulbs, it was usually eaten raw. They were especially good when eaten both bulb and top like a salad. Consuming quantities in that fashion left the breath unbearable even at a distance, wrote Barrett. Leaves, stalks, and heads were eaten from the *A. peninsulare* and the *A. lacunosum* by the Tubatulabal. Leaves of the *A. campanulatum* were used as a relish by the Karok and the Northern Paiute. Seeds were also eaten. Many species of *Allium* were eaten by California Natives.

Wild cabbage *(Caulanthus coulteri):* The Kawaiisu boiled and ate leaves gathered in early spring before the plant would flower.

Desert candle *(Caulanthus inflatus):* The "candle" or soft upper section of the stem was roasted in a pit oven and eaten by the Kawaiisu.

Tickseed or Bigelow's coreopsis *(Coreopsis bigelovii):* This was an important food among the Kawaiisu. It was cut off at the base in the spring before blooming and eaten raw or boiled. The leaves could be rubbed and bruised between the hands and eaten with salt. The stems were chewed for the sweet juice after the flowers bloomed, the fibers spit out.

Common *phacelia (Phacelia distans)* and branching phacelia *(P. ramosissima):* The Kawaiisu gathered stems and leaves in the spring before flowers appeared. They laid them on a flat rock and placed hot rocks over them and then more stems and leaves. Water was sprinkled on the hot rocks to cook the plants. More hot rocks were placed on the pile as needed. Tickseed, foothill lomatium, and other spring greens were similarly prepared.

Milkweed *(Asclepias mexicana):* Though the plant was considered poisonous to sheep and cows, the Pomo occasionally ate the showy, purple, young blossoms as they did clover. Chesnut found them sweet, spicy and very pleasant. The Miwok boiled them and sometimes added the mass to manzanita cider for thickening.

Indian milkweed *(Asclepias eriocarpa):* The Karok broke this plant part way through in many places when the stem was very fresh, then in a leaf or mussel shell spoon, they collected the milk. Early morning was considered the best time. The liquid was stirred and slightly heated until it congealed. It made a chewing gum. Salmon fat or deer grease, if available, was added in chewing to help hold it together. Young and old enjoyed this gum, most commonly at World Renewal Festivals.

Desert milkweed *(Asclepias erosa):* From this milkweed the Tubatulabal made chewing gum. A cut was made on the stem near the top before it blossomed and the milky juice was collected in 4-inch tubular sections of long-stemmed eriogonum *(Eriogonum elongatum).* A joint on the eriogonum stopped the bottom end of each tube and the milkweed juice ran in through the open upper end. The filled stalk tubes were placed in hot ashes and roasted until the milkweed juice congealed. They were then cut open and the gum was taken out and chewed. "Better than store gum" Tubatulabal Estefana Miranda Salazar told Voegelin. The Kawaiisu boiled the juice drained from the split stalks until it thickened and chewed it as gum.

Agoseris *(Agoseris gracilens):* The Karok sucked the juice out of the root near the crown and chewed it like chewing gum. The Kawaiisu boiled and ate the leaves of the spear-leafed agoseris *(A. retrorsa)* in the spring.

Wire lettuce *(Stephanomeria pauciflora):* The Kawaiisu collected the thick exudation of this plant and chewed it as gum.

California poppy *(Eschscholzia californica):* Leaves were used as greens and flowers chewed with chewing gum by the Luiseño. The Yuki boiled the leaves as greens but were careful to throw away the water.

Columbine *(Aguilegia truncata):* This was boiled by the Miwok in the early spring.

Larkspur or delphinium *(Delphinium hesperium* and others): Leaves and flowers were boiled when young by the Miwok.

White watercress *(Rorippa nasturtium-aquaticum):* This was an alien plant used as greens by Luiseño. The Northern Diegueño boiled the leaves. The Kawaiisu boiled or ate them raw, usually with salt.

Horseweed *(Erigeron canadensis):* The Miwok pounded the leaves and new tops in a bedrock mortar and ate them uncooked. They tasted like onions.

Shining peppergrass *(Lepidium nitidum):* The leaves were eaten by the Luiseño.

Tibinagua *(Eriogonum nudum):* The Karok and Miwok ate this plant raw. The taste was sour. The Kawaiisu dried the flowers and ate them mixed with mentzelia seeds. The hollow stems served as drinking tubes or, filled with tobacco, as cigarettes.

Crevice *heuchera (Heuchera micrantha):* The Miwok ate these leaves first in the spring, after boiling or steaming in an earth oven. Steamed leaves could be dried and stored.

Pacific pea *(Lathyrus vestitus):* The Miwok ate these as greens.

Whitewhorl lupine *(Lupinus densiflorus):* In early spring the Miwok ran a hand along the stalk, stripping it of flowers and leaves that they steamed in the earth oven and ate with acorn soup.

Broadleaf lupine *(Lupinus latifolius):* The Miwok steamed the leaves and flowers in an earth oven. Many were dried and stored for winter. They were reconstituted by soaking in cold water for three or four hours to rid them of their bitterness. Then they were boiled and eaten or not boiled and enjoyed as relish with manzanita cider.

Miniature lupine *(Lupinus bicolor):* Galen Clark recorded the Miwok used this for greens. Young leaves of *L. affinis* were roasted and eaten as greens by the Yuki, according to Chesnut.

Green dock *(Rumex conglomeratus):* The Miwok cooked and ate leaves of this alien plant.

Sheep sorrel *(Rumex acetocella):* Sour leaves were pulverized, mixed with water and eaten with salt by the Miwok. This was an alien species.

Golden prince's plume *(Stanleya pinnata):* The Kawaiisu boiled the leaves and lower stems of this plant and squeezed them out in cold water to remove their bitterness.

Vinegarweed *(Trichostema lanceolatum):* An infusion was brewed hot by the Kawaiisu for relief of colds and stomach aches and likely for use as a beverage, according to Zigmond.

Musk monkey flower *(Mimulus moschatus):* The young plant was boiled and eaten by the Miwok.

Common monkey flower *(Mimulus guttatus):* The Miwok ate the boiled leaves and the Kawaiisu ate the tender raw stems.

Snouted monkey flower *(Mimulus nasutus* or *luteus):* Young spring plants were boiled and eaten by the Maidu, according to Powers.

Paintbrush *(Castilleja* sp.): The flower was pulled apart and the nectar sipped from the center by the Miwok.

Goosefoot *(Chenopodium fremontii* and others): Shoots and leaves were boiled and eaten by the Cahuilla, Mohave and Cocopa. The Miwok boiled the leaves of lamb's quarter *(C. album)* and sometimes dried and stored this alien. The Luiseño also utilized the leaves as a green. The Mohave boiled *C. murale.* Leftovers were later baked in ashes and eaten.

Desert primrose *(Oenothera clavaeformis):* This was used as a green by the Cahuilla. (White-lined sphinx moth caterpillar was also found on this plant.)

Chuparosa *(Beloperone californica):* The Diegueño sucked the scarlet flowers of this plant for the nectar.

Ocotillo *(Fourquieria splendens):* The sweet, red flowers, available from the beginning of spring until the middle of summer, were eaten fresh by Cahuilla or soaked in water for a refreshing drink.

Mustard *(Brassica geniculata):* Leaves of this European native, found growing even in the winter, were eaten fresh or boiled by the Cahuilla. Black mustard *(B. nigra)* was much used as a green by the Luiseño. Young leaves were boiled and eaten by the Northern Diegueño, according to K. Hedges and C. Beresford.

Tansy mustard *(Desurainia* sp.): Young plants were boiled and eaten by the Mohave and the Yuma.

London rocket *(Sisymbrium irio):* This nonnative mustard's immature leaves were boiled for food by the Cahuilla.

Locoweed or rattleweed *(Astragalus* sp.): Many species were poisonous but one described by Barrows for the Cahuilla was used as spice in beans and other foods. Celestino Tortes told him that in summer the dry yellow branches were covered with straw-colored pods, the size of the joint of a man's thumb, which rattled in the breeze. They were pounded to make the spice.

Matilija poppy *(Romneya coulteri):* The liquid of the stalk was drunk by the Cahuilla.

Dandelion *(Taraxacum californicum):* The stems and leaves were eaten by the Cahuilla in the spring and early summer.

Bladderpod *(Isomeris arborea):* Apparently a marginal food of spring found in the deserts and foothills, Barrows noted the Cahuilla gathered the plump capsules and cooked them in a small excavation with hot stones. The Kawaiisu ate the flowers boiled or placed them on hot rock, covered them with dirt and left them overnight. They turned red and were then ready to be eaten.

Tarweed *(Hemizonia fasciculata):* E. Palmer found this plant used by the southern California Indians in time of hunger. The plants were boiled down until the liquid became thick and tarry, then they were eaten. Bean and Saubel noted the entire plant was used by the Cahuilla, including its seeds.

Mariposa lily *(Calochortus catalinae, flexuosus, palmeri* and *concolor):* The Cahuilla gathered these bulbs from May through August and ate them raw or baked them for 12 to 24 hours in a stone-lined pit oven in which a fire had burned to ashes. Bulbs were placed on ashes and covered by a layer of leaves or brush and then dirt to lock in the heat. At times another fire was made on top.

Desert lily *(Hesperocallis undulata):* The spring bulbs were eaten raw or baked in an earth oven by the Cahuilla.

Golden stars *(Bloomeria crocea):* Corms were eaten raw at any time of year by the Cahuilla.

March pennywort *(Hydrocotyle* sp.): This was likely a plant used as a green by the Cahuilla. They described to Bean and Saubel a plant spread thick on top of water. Oscar Clarke advised them it was possibly a March pennywort species.

Seep weed *(Suaeda* sp.): The leaves were boiled and eaten by the Cahuilla.

Filaree *(Erodium cicutarium):* The Northern Diegueño picked leaves of this nonnative plant in early spring before flowering and cooked them as greens.

White sage *(Salvia apiana):* The young stalks of this plant were eaten raw by the Northern Diegueño.

Lemonadeberry *(Rhus integrifolia):* The Northern Diegueño kept a wad of its leaves in their mouth to lessen thirst on long foot journeys.

Pansy *(Viola pedunculata):* The Northern Diegueño picked this plant's leaves before flowers appeared in the spring, then boiled and ate them.

Wild peony *(Paeonia californica):* The Northern Diegueño picked the leaves in the spring before blossoms appeared and boiled them. After this they placed them in a weighted sack in the river overnight to leach them of bitterness or soaked them in changes of water or reboiled them. They were then ready to be cooked as greens, at times with onions, and eaten as an accompaniment to acorn mush.

Pinedrops *(Pterospora andromedea):* This saprophyte was sometimes eaten raw by the Kawaiisu but generally baked below a fire.

Pholisma (Pholisma arenarium): The Kawaiisu gathered the stem of this root parasite during February and March and ate it raw or baked it below a fire.

Broom rape *(Orobanche ludoviciana):* The succulent roots of this desert parasite with an asparagus-like stalk were dug by the Cahuilla while tender in the spring before the plant blossomed, then roasted in coals and eaten.

Bracken fern *(Pteridium aquilinum):* The leaves and tender stems were eaten raw by the Atsugewi. The Cahuilla scraped the asparagus-like shoots and boiled them. (The Kashaya Pomo used the juice of young fronds, still curled, as a body deodorant.)

Woodwardia (Woodwardia fimbriata): This large fern lined the top and bottom of the Kashaya Pomo's earth oven when they baked acorn bread and other food. Sword fern *(Polystichum munitum)* was used the same way and also to line the sand-leaching basin.

Lichen *(Alectoria fremonti):* This black, hair-like lichen that grows on pine or fir trees was used as a famine food by the Wailaki, observed Chesnut. Edith Murphey noted the northern California Natives dried, ground, and made it into a soup.

Moss: The Atsugewi gathered a form of moss from streams with their feet. After the bugs were shaken out, it was cooked and eaten.

Sierra puffball *(Lycoperdon sculptum):* The Miwok dried them in the sun for two or three days, after which they were pulverized in a mortar and stone-boiled. The result was eaten with acorn soup. The Pomo considered puffballs to be poisonous.

Tree fungus *(Polyporus* sp.): Esteemed by the Pomo, this red-edged yellow fungus also grew in the Miwok area on the sides of black and valley oaks. Raw, the shelf-like fungus was considered poisonous. The Miwok boiled, then squeezed and salted it to make it palatable and safe. The Pomo found it on the base of alder trees and logs. The inner, salmon-colored, layered portion was eaten after a thorough boiling. It was said to be soft and taste like salmon.

Other mushrooms and truffles were consumed by California Indians, but early anthropologists generally failed to precisely identify them. Goodrich, Lawson, and Lawson recently specified the following for the Kashaya Pomo. All were gathered after the rains in the fall and prepared by baking on hot stones.

Chantarelle *(Cantharellus cibarius)*

Coral mushroom *(Hericium coralloides)*

Deer or wood mushroom *(Agaricus silvicola):* Gathered in large quantity, only the tops were eaten from this mushroom of anise seed aroma.

Field mushroom *(Agaricus campestris)*

Hedgehog mushroom *(Dentinum repandum)*

Orange peel mushroom *(Peziza aurantia):* It was cooked on coals or eaten fresh.

Oyster mushroom *(Pleurotus ostreatus):* These were said to taste like meat.

Timber mushroom *(Boletus edulis)*

Black willow *(Salix nigra):* The Yuma pulled up the seedlings and worked the bark loose with two sticks (probably held together and the willow shoot run between them). They ate the bark raw or cooked it in hot ashes. Leaves and bark from the twigs were steeped for tea. The Mohave made tea from young willow shoots and the lower Colorado Indians in general were known to have made a drink from willow flowers. The Kawaiisu ate the sticky sweet substance found on some willows.

Curly dock *(Rumex crispus):* The Mohave boiled leaves in several changes of water and ate them as greens.

Spiny aster *(Aster spinosus)*, mustard *(Thelypodium* sp.) and mulefat *(Baccharis glutinosa):* The Mohave and Yuma ate these young shoots as famine foods after roasting them on hot ashes.

Carrizo cane *(Phragmites* sp.): The Koso pulverized the stems of this plant for meal.

Yucca or Spanish bayonet *(Yucca whipplei)* and nolina *(Nolina parryi):* In the spring, as the center stalks of the Spanish bayonet and Parry's nolina began to rise but before they had budded or bloomed, the Tubatulabal knocked them down at their base with a stave. With an obsidian knide they cut the tender young nolina stalks in half and laid the pieces on a fire made in a trench, covered them with dirt and left them overnight. The next morning they were uncovered, peeled and eaten. The Cahuilla were said to have done the same except in a stone-lined pit with a sand covering.

The stalks of the Spanish bayonet were laid directly on a blazing brush fire by the Tubatulabal. They were turned once, and when soft they were buried in dirt or sand and left to cool. This helped to make the peel slip off more easily. The Spanish bayonet stalks were harvested prior to blossoming in the spring by the Cahuilla, when full of rich sap. They were placed in a fire-heated rock-lined pit, covered with sand and baked overnight. Those not eaten the next day were dried and preserved, or ground, mixed with a little water and made into cakes. Fresh stalks were sometimes sliced up and parboiled like squash. Newly blossoming flowers too were parboiled and eaten or parboiled and dried in the sun and preserved. Older ones were boiled with salt as many as three times before eating. The Northern Diegueño of Santa Ysabel picked the blossoms before they opened and boiled them twice to rid them of bitterness. They were said to taste like cabbage. Because of the time it took for the stalks to grow and flowers to form and fall, and the later blooming times as one ascended in altitude, to 4,000 feet, the harvest of this important plant could last all spring.

Zigmond's (1981) account of the Kawaiisu's preparation of Spanish bayonet is especially detailed and indicates the season extended even further. In the very early spring, before the stalk began to rise, the Kawaiisu (with a long pole of dry California juniper or blue oak, a chisel or shovel-like cutting edge at one end) excised the apical merestem, the "heart" or cabbage of the yucca located at its center. The heart, from which would grow the stalk, was baked on a pit oven about 3 feet deep and 5 feet in diameter with a large stone in the center. Smaller stones radiated outward. First, a fire preferably made of blue oak burned in the pit for half a day. More stones and wood were added while the fire burned. When the stones became hot and the wood turned to coals, the pit was covered with sand or dirt to near-ground level. A small opening was left in the center through which flames would shoot out as the sand was tapped down. A layer of dry pine needles covered the top, and on this the skinned yucca hearts were laid. The position of each identified its owner; two or three families might share an oven. Another layer of dry pine needles mixed with California broom *(Lotus procumbens)* covered the heads. More sand and dirt was piled over it all and then patted down and smoothed with a basket tray. The mound, which may have reached 5 feet, settled as the baking progressed. The hearts of the yucca were roasted for two days. Sexual intercourse was prohibited "lest the hearts not cook." Finally, they were removed hot but allowed to cool before eating. Those left uneaten were stored by pulling them apart, lightly mashing them, and allowing them to dry. Stored hearts were later soaked and eaten.

  Later in the season when in blossom during May or June, the Kawaiisu prepared the Spanish bayonet in the following manner. The green, tender stalks were cut off about a foot above the base of the plant. Sections were covered by dirt in a trench and a fire made above them. Or, they were laid side by side on branches directly over a fire. In this latter case, they were turned when done on one side. Foxtail or grass protected the hand that removed and held the hot yucca as the other peeled the skin with a knife. Sections were split lengthwise and eaten cool, accompanied, if possible, with chia drink. Stalks became tougher later in the season; they would then chew a piece raw and spit out the fiber. Incidentally, small sections of the stalk also made stoppers for the basketry water bottle. The orange core of the root stocks was split and used as a pattern in coiled basketry. Green leaves were separated into three strands and tied end to end for cordage, binding the horizontal poles over the brush to the vertical poles in the construction of houses.

Mohave yucca *(Yucca schidigera):* This is a permanent plant with a tree-like trunk and no significant sap-rich flower stalks. The Mohave yucca produces large, 3- to 5-inch seed pods that were utilized as food for the Cahuilla. Gathered green early in the season (April to May) they were cooked in the coals of a fire. To Barrows they suggested the flavor of roasted green apples. When ripe and eaten raw they became sweet and slightly puckering. The Kiliwa stewed the Mohave yucca pods. The Paipai and Southern Diegueño treated them as a fruit. After removing the seeds, they made a deliciously sweet drink from them. The Cahuilla carried home clusters of yellow blossoms from the top of the Mohave yucca stocks. As with Spanish bayonet, they were boiled in an olla, dried for preservation and boiled anew when they were to be eaten.

Banana yucca *(Yucca baccata):* Palmer recorded that the flowers and pods of the banana yucca were prepared by the Indians of southern California in a manner similar to that described for the Cahuilla's use of the Spanish bayonet flower and Mohave yucca pod.

Joshua tree *(Yucca brevifolia):* The blossoms of the Joshua tree were used as food by the Cahuilla, who obtained them in trade from their neighbors, the Serrano of the Mojave Desert. Still farther north, the Tubatulabal knocked immature pods of the Joshua tree to the ground with sticks. (Joshua trees are still found extensively on the east slope of Walker Pass in the southern Sierras.) The green pods were then boiled like cabbage in a clay pot and eaten. The Kawaiisu prepared the pods as they did the hearts of yucca *(Y. whipplei).*

Desert agave *(Agave deserti):* The leaves, stalk and base of the flower stalk were baked for a day or more in a stone-lined earth oven by most southern California desert Indians. For preservation, the baked stalks and leaves were pounded and made into fibrous cakes that were dried in the sun. For the Cocopa, W. Kelly found young baked stalks could be molded into cakes without pounding. Farther south in the Sierra San Pedro Mártir of Lower California, the Kiliwa utilized both the desert agave and the larger coastal agave *(A. shawii).* Meigs described the baking of agave heads (base of the stalk) by the Kiliwa. After a fire had burned down, the heads, shorn of their leaves, were thrown on top of the hot stones in the pit. They covered the heads with the loose agave leaves and then agave fiber to keep the food clean. Dirt was spread over the pit and on this a fire was built. The agave was left to bake for three days and two nights. Heads which came out bitter were discarded. The sweet heads were cleaned and dried in the sun. These could be preserved but often lasted only a few weeks.

The Indians grew heavy eating this rich sweet food, "like fibrous candied fruit," recorded Meigs.

The flowers of the desert and coastal agave provided the Kiliwa with a rich nectar used for sweetening. Other groups also enjoyed the sweet liquid. One lazy afternoon in late spring at her remote ranchería, Southern Diegueño elder Manuela Aguiar recounted to me stories her grandmother had told of her great-great-grandmother so many years before. The older lady died in 1915, but as a girl in the first half of the nineteenth century, she collected the flowers of the desert agave. They were milked of their abundant nectar into a clay pot and the nectar drunk as a sweet beverage. But then one year near the middle of the century the flowers gave nectar no more. A new insect, they discovered, had sucked them dry. That was the first sign they had of the honeybee. And as the bee had stolen the flower's nectar from them, they began to take the honey from the bee and they still do to this day.

Red barrel cactus *(Ferocactus acanthodes)*: Cahuilla women gathered these flower buds throughout the spring and early summer. To protect themselves from the sharp spines of the plant, they plucked the buds with a pair of short sticks and dropped them in a gathering basket. The budding season lasted a long time for two reasons. Buds formed in concentric circles around the top of the cactus, beginning on the outermost circle and working inward as the season progressed. Thus, as Alice Kotzin pointed out to me, just one plant produced buds over an extended period. In addition, budding progressed from lower to higher desert areas. Bean and Saubel noted the entire season in the general Cahuilla territory could go from April to late July and collecting spots were visited repeatedly.

The fresh flower buds could be eaten raw but were somewhat bitter. Normally, the base of the bud was removed and they were parboiled several times and eaten or dried in the sun and stored. Stored buds were reconstituted by reboiling, often with salt to improve flavor. Fresh buds could also be steamed. First they burned a mesquite fire to coals in a pit. Next, rocks were placed in the bottom of the pit, and over the rocks were placed damp sand and leaves. Then the buds were spread on the leaves, covered with another layer of leaves and sand, and a fire was built on top of all this. After several hours the buds were ready to eat. Steamed buds were also dried in the sun and stored, often for years.

Barrel cactus buds were sometimes stewed and eaten with mountain sheep or jackrabbit meat by the Cahuilla. Kiliwa Indian Jose Ochurte told me that traditionally, the flower buds of *biznaga* (Barrel cactus, probably of various species) were boiled in a clay pot and eaten like *frijoles de la olla*—Mexican stewed beans in a pot.

As the flowers formed on the barrel cactus, though more bitter than the bud, they too were eaten. The Cahuilla prepared and preserved them the same way they had the buds. The Kiliwa also ate the seeds of *biznaga*.

Mohave mound cactus *(Echinocactus polycephalus)*: The buds of these were eaten by the Cahuilla.

Beavertail cactus *(Opuntia basilaris)*: The spiny flower buds of the beavertail and other *opuntia* cacti the Tubatulabal speared with a sharp stick and held them over a fire to burn away the spines. Then they spread them on a hot flat rock in a pit, covered them with another hot rock, and filled the pit with earth or hot ashes. After eight hours they took them out, peeled back the outer skin, and ate the inner part. The Koso or Panamint enjoyed this plant the same way. In March, the Kawaiisu took the buds with a flattened sharp stick. It was a favorite among the Cahuilla, who, after breaking the buds off with a stick, brushed the spines away with a bunch of grass or twigs, and, with hot stones, cooked or steamed them in a pit for twelve hours or more. The cooked buds could be dried for storage. The young, tender stems or joints of the beavertail cactus (and other opuntia or prickly-pear species) were cut up, boiled and mixed with other food or eaten as they were. The large seeds of the fruit were ground into mush.

Jumping cholla *(Opuntia bigelovii)*: Buds were gathered, prepared and preserved by the Cahuilla the same as those of the beavertail cactus.

Plains prickly pear *(Opuntia polyacantha)*: This plant was probably the opuntia described by Barrows, "with flat, ugly jointed stems, growing low and spreading over the ground in the most arid stretches of the valley." Buds the size of the last joint of a man's thumb were gathered in quantity, brushed clean, dried and stored. When needed they were boiled in water with a little salt.

Frequently, the cactus fruit ripened and was then gathered for its seeds. Dried, piled on a smooth, hard dirt floor, the fruit was flailed with the leaf stem of a desert palm by a woman seated next to them. Once the seeds had been threshed out, they were winnowed and stored for the winter. When needed, the Cahuilla pounded the seeds into meal and cooked the meal into mush. Barrows noted that some other species of cactus seeds were similarly used. The Kiliwa made and ate pinole from the seeds of a large cholla cactus.

Pencil cactus *(Opuntia ramosissima):* The Cahuilla removed the thorns of the stalk of this plant and boiled it into a soup or dried and preserved it.

Palo verde *(Cercidium floridum* and *microphyllum)* and *palo fierro (Olneya tesota):* In desert washes and foothills too dry for most other plants, often will be found the blue and yellow palo verde and palo fierro or ironwood trees. The Cocopa gathered the bean pods, which by October lay in piles beneath the trees. Unlike mesquite or screwbean pods, that were pounded in wooden mortars and the seeds discarded, beans of the palo verde and palo fierro were saved and the pod itself thrown out. The Cocopa roasted the seeds with coals in a pottery tray, ground them into meal on a grinding stone and boiled the meal into mush.

The Mohave and Yuma first thoroghly dried palo fierro pods, then trampled them to free the seeds. The seeds were parched, almost burned, and eaten in times of want, according to Castetter and Bell. Kelly found that after parching, the Mohave and Yuma ground the seeds lightly to break them in half and to rid them of their seed coat which was discarded. To remove the bitter taste, the seeds were next placed in a coarse basket and leached in the moving water of the river. They were roasted a second time and eaten or finely ground and eaten pinch by pinch as pinole. The meal could also be made into a flat thin cake and baked in hot ashes. The Kiliwa made pinole of the palo fierro seed and did the same with the seeds of the mesquite.

Amaranth *(Amaranthus palmeri* and others): Commonly called pigweed, or *quelite* in Baja, amaranth (in terms of sheer quantity and likely quality, since it is highly nutritious) was a tremendously important wild food of the Cocopa. It came up quickly in the fields after the Colorado River flood waters had subsided. When it reached about 8 to 12 inches in height, groups of older girls gathered it. This was one of their few regular food preparation responsibilities. They boiled the green leaves in water for about 30 minutes and poured them out into a basket to drain. They could be eaten as they were or with salt. Cooked greens that remained were squeezed into balls for use at a later time so long as they did not dry out.

Even more commonly the fresh green amaranth leaves were laid in a thick mat over a bed of hot coals. They were smashed down and packed further with the feet. Then they covered the leaves with amaranth plants. Over this layer, dry weeds and branches were placed and set on fire. After an hour or more the cake was lifted from the coals, the burned areas and ashes removed, and the loaf cut into pieces for the girls and their families to eat. The Mohave, Yuma, and others also ate amaranth greens.

Sugar and Salt

California Indians did not possess the commercial honeybee and they could not buy oversalted supermarket foods, but they knew the delights of sweet and salty. Flavorful substances were there for the taking in the natural world.

Honeydew Cane

Having left the Colorado River and Mohave Indians who provisioned them with corn and beans, Jedediah S. Smith and his party made their way across the desert toward Mission San Gabriel in November of 1826. During a hard week's travel, men accustomed to meat quickly exhausted the vegetables they had been given. When they reached the area known today as Afton Canyon, one of the Indian guides told Smith he knew where his people had cached some other food. The De Anza Expedition had traveled along the Mojave River in 1776 and Francisco Garcés had described the Vanyume Indians (related to the Serrano) living along the river not far from Afton Canyon. Two of Smith's guides were Vanyume, along with a Mohave. Likely it was a Vanyume who went off in the day and returned that night with a strange substance formed into bread-like loaves weighing eight or ten pounds each, "so hard that an ax was required to break it," wrote Smith, but in taste it resembled "sugar candy." On inquiry, he found that the strange sugary food came from cane grass that grew along the river, the same cane grass from which the Mohave Indians made arrows.

Lieutenant Robert S. Williamson (Brooks, 1977) reported cane growing in Afton Canyon in his surveying work for the railroad during November of 1853. He wrote that large quantities of it had been cut by the Indians and that it was like the cane found in Walker's Pass of the southern Sierras where the Indians collected it in August for a sugar-like substance on the leaves, an important food for the indigenous people. The cane was cut, spread in the sun to dry and threshed to separate the sugar from the leaf.

Other early authors noted this sweet among the Tubatulabal, Chemehuevi, Surprise Valley Paiute, Yavapai and Papago, who also obtained it from willow. The Owens Valley Paiute in addition to reed harvested it from juncus rush. Many insects remained in the sugar that the Paiute made into balls and later warmed and softened by the fire to eat like candy. Sometimes after winnowing, the loose sugar was stored in shallow tule baskets thought to preserve the sugar but not change its taste or color. With their hands the Panamint Shoshoni molded honeydew into balls that were later set near a fire to roast; the balls turned brown and swelled like taffy before they ate them. The Northern Paiute gathered honeydew from tule *(Scirpus)*. They made it into fist-sized balls that contained more insect than honey, according to one observer.

What exactly is honeydew? Mark Sutton explained that honeydew comes from insects of the *Homoptera* order. It is their crystallized excretion. Various plants are colonized and the dew is left on them. The mealy plum aphis prefers reeds *(Phragmites)* as a summer host, for instance, but will also deposit the sweet on the stems and leaves of cattails *(Typha)*.

Voegelin described the harvest and refinement of honeydew among the Tubatulabal of the Walker Pass region during her ethnographic work there in the early 1930s, almost one hundred years after its mention by Lieutenant Williamson. The sweet was produced by aphids in summer on the leaves and stalks of cane *(Phragmites communis)*. The Tubatulabal cut the cane in July or August, spread it to dry in the sun, then heaped it on a bearskin that was thick enough to take the vigorous blows of the hardwood stick beaters used for flaying the dried cane. The saccharine crystals that fell and clung to the bearskin were scraped off, winnowed on a flat tray and collected in a small cooking basket. Cold water was added and the mixture made into a stiff dough. They removed the mass from the basket by hand, spread it on a twined tule tray and folded the end of the tray over the dough. After putting this aside to dry for six or seven days, the food was ready.

Lumps broken off the hard brown loaf with a rock were eaten dry accompanied by chia gruel. Sometimes sections of the freshly cut cane were simply sucked untreated for their sweetness, according to Steban Miranda, a Tubatulabal Indian in his late eighties when Voegelin gathered her information. Tragically, cane *(Phragmites communis)*, known as *carrizo* by the Spaniards, and an extremely useful plant for the Indian (besides honeydew; arrows, darts, fibers, thatching, balsas, cigarettes, flutes, and who knows how many other useful items were made from it), has disappeared from many areas of California. I found healthy forests of carrizo cane on a small tributary of the sometimes flowing Amargoza River, on moist areas near the shore of dry Soda Lake, in parts of the Sacramento Delta, around the Pyramid Lake reservoir, and in canyons of the Anza Borrego desert. But in Afton Canyon, where Williamson found it harvested nearly 150 years ago, I could not find a trace. Bob Powers, a rancher and Kern County historian, believes the carrizo grass that was once common in Kern County, especially along Canebrake Creek near Walker's Pass, has been nearly exterminated due to overgrazing. Given the inaccessible corners where one still finds carrizo in California, I am sure he is right. Bob knows of only one stand—near Wofford Heights.

A Chimariko Treat

While blessed with an abundance of sweet berries during the summer months, Chimariko children, for a sugary taste, would peel and eat the inner bark of yellow pine in the spring. They would run a sharp stick up and under the outer bark and strip the bark away to reveal the sweet cambium beneath. "We children used to eat it much," Lucy Montgomery told J. P. Harrington.

Rock Salt and Salt Grass

The Tubatulabal made salt during the summer in much the same way as they did sugar. Saline crystals formed on salt grass *(Distichlis spicata)* during hot, dry weather in saline areas found on valley floors or at the base of the foothills. If it rained, Steban Miranda told Voegelin, they would have to wait for a month for the crystals to form again. But when they found the crystals the grass was cut, laid on mats to dry in the sun, and beaten on a bearskin, the same as with the cane for sugar. Unlike sugar, however, the collected salt crystals were formed into balls or flat cakes instead of being spread as a loaf on a tule tray.

The Tubatulabal did not use salt from salt grass to season meat or mushes; rather, chunks were broken from a ball (equal to two or three tablespoons), dissolved in a cup of water, and drunk for refreshment or taken as a laxative and a rinse for the stomach. A quicker manner of using fresh salt grass was to soak it in water and sprinkle the water over raw chopped clover. Or, a few sprigs of salt grass and clover were simply rolled between the hands and eaten. Children took willow switches and ran them through salt grass on a summer morning. When enough crystals had adhered to the sticks, they repaired to the shade to lick them.

Rock salt was gathered from a dry salt lake in Coso territory on the northern edge of the Mojave desert. For a man with a basketry water bottle it was a day's round trip. They brought back large lumps in deerskin sacks. Pounded on a mortar or pulverized on a slab, they sprinkled the salt sparingly on cooked meat or used it for drying meat and fish, but not to season any plant food such as acorn or piñon mush. Many California tribes obtained rock salt in trade and, because it was valued, they used it sparingly.

The Chukchansi Yokuts of the northern foothills in the western Sierra Nevada gave baskets and shell money for salt crystals (they were about 1/2 inch to 3/4 inch in diameter) that the Mono Lake Paiute had carried to them in burden baskets from the eastern side of the mountain. The Yokuts ground the rock salt into various degrees of fineness, recorded Gayton, and ate it with meat, nuts or seeds. For use with acorns the salt was covered with hot ashes then pounded in a mortar hole, mixed with a grass from the edge of the river, and everything mashed into 6-inch-diameter balls (with a little water, if necessary, to make it stick). Finally, three to five of these wrapped in a thick covering of grass were baked overnight in a hole with very hot ashes. In the morning the balls were dug out, the grass having burned away, and whisked hard with a soaproot brush. The dark balls were struck and broken into pieces.

Salt grass was pounded in a mortar and winnowed by the Chukchansi Yokuts. They dampened the crystals and pressed them into balls that were broken when needed for clover or sour berries.

The Southern Valley Yokuts, in a manner similar to that of the Tubatulabal, extracted much salt from various species of salt grass. The leaves seemed to exude salt as tiny globules which on a warm day dried and hardened by mid-afternoon. F. F. Latta described the late July or early August harvest. The process was precise and timing meant everything. Grass was first broken off close to the ground and laid in shallow wicker baskets. Next it was stacked carefully, stems on the ground and leaves upward, and exposed to the sun so that the salt would dry faster than the grass, which had to remain tough for the threshing. If not, the leaves would become brittle and pulverized during the threshing, mixing with the salt. On the other hand, if threshing was begun too early the salt would stick to the grass.

By two o'clock the salt was dry and easily dislodged and threshing began. Under the light flailing of peeled willow poles, which were wielded by three to four Indians sitting around a deer or elk skin on which a small amount of grass had been placed, the salt broke free. They took the grass in their hands and shook it thoroughly over the hide before discarding it. Bunch after bunch of grass was threshed this way until a layer of salt about an inch thick had accumulated on the hide. The salt was then poured into a basket and more grass threshed. Back at the ranchería they sifted and winnowed the salt. Many large sacks could be obtained by a single family. It was not used directly for cooking but a pinch might be placed in the mouth or under the tongue while eating or at any other time. Lumps of salt that were formed by wetting and drying were licked by the children. Latta described the flavor as sour and salty like dill pickles.

Gayton characterized the taste of a red salt, obtained from marsh grass by the Yokuts living in the Central Foothills, as mild vinegar. In 1925 Molly Lawrence, a seventy-year-old Wukchumni Yokuts, still possessed some of the prized grayish-pink substance that had the texture of course sugar. Years before, she had seen her Gawia Yokuts stepmother make it. Grass was dug up and put on the coals of a fire at sundown. Lawrence, who was a little girl at the time, was not allowed to look closely at the fire. After the grass burned to ashes her stepmother rested for a while. Then all the next day she gathered grass and continued the process. She ate nothing until sundown that day, and very little when she did finally eat. She did not drink, believing that if she ate much or drank, the undertaking would fail and she would find nothing in the fire when she finished. At last the ashes were brushed aside and, in the bottom of the fire, lumps of salt could be seen. She shook and cleaned them in an open-twined basket.

On the rocky coasts of northwest California, edible seaweed *(Porphyra perforata)* was gathered, dried and eaten as food, but it was also used for salt. Not dissolvable in the manner of seasoning, flakes of dried leaves were eaten with or between spoonfuls of acorn mush. Dried surf fish, presented on a small openwork tray laid across the top of an individual serving basket of mush, had a similar purpose.

Berries, Cherries and Other Wild Fruit

The Bear River women—described by Gladys Nomland—picked all kinds of berries over a special basket. They ate some raw with meat but most were sun-dried on large flat leaves or baskets. They stirred and turned them until evenly dried then packed them in deep baskets between layers of leaves. Each basket had a concave cover that fit the bottom of the basket preceding it. Thus, baskets were stacked one on the other with small even pieces of wood holding the lowest basket off the ground to prevent mold. They ate the dried berries with meat, cooked them in acorn cakes, or reconstituted them by soaking and eating them with acorn mush, tarweed seed or other foods. Warmed fat stored in whip-kelp containers was poured over dried berries to make them sweeter and tastier.

The Northern Maidu gathered various berries. If not dried whole for the winter, they were mashed, augmented with various seeds and pounded roots and made into little cakes. The cakes were dried or wrapped in leaves and baked, according to Roland Dixon. To reconstitute them, they were soaked and made into a soup.

California juniper berries *(Juniperus californica)*, oak gooseberries *(Ribes quercetorum)*, manzanita *(Arctostaphylos)* and boxthorn berries *(Lycium torreyi)* were knocked from the shrub with seed beaters by the Tubatulabal, according to Vogelin. Elderberries *(Sambucus)* they gathered by breaking off a stalk and shaking it over a basket. They boiled them in a clay pot with water and ate them. The ripe boxthorn berries were pounded in a pit mortar and, with a small amount of water, the meal was molded into small biscuits that were dried in the sun. They were stored in this form until needed and then broken up and soaked in water and eaten. Fresh juniper berries could be boiled for consumption. Juniper berries when dry and fully ripe were seeded by hand, the pulp pounded in a mortar and eaten raw. It was said to taste sweet.

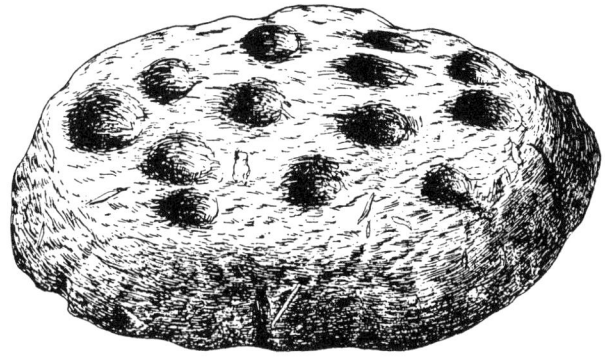

Maidu cake of berries, seeds and pounded roots, diameter, 15 cm. (Dixon, 1905).

Berries and fruit in various forms provided vitamins, minerals, carbohydrates and often a dessert-like sweetness, tartness, and refreshment to the Indian diet. Below are listed many of those known to representative Native California tribes along with their common, purely Indian, methods of preparation.

Manzanita berries *(Arctostaphylos sp.)*: Pomo children would suck or eat the globular waxy flowers of the common manzanita. The green berries came later and quenched thirst when eaten in small quantities. But if too many of these or even the ripe berries were consumed it could lead to death, noted V. K. Chesnut. Women went out with their babies to the dry hillsides in July or August and beat the ripe berries into great carrying baskets. The berries were transported home and eaten raw, stored for the winter, or made into a variety of foods. The Karok shook the bush so the berries would fall into an acorn basket and then spread them in a flat basket to dry in the sun. Later they were taken from a storage basket, pounded, mixed with salmon eggs, cooked in a basket with hot rocks, and eaten. The Karok, Hupa and Pomo utilized the common manzanita *(A. manzanita)*. The Karok also employed greenleaf manzanita *(A. patula)*, pinemat manzanita *(A. nevadensis)* and *A. canescens*. But the Pomo preferred the smaller berry of another manzanita, probably *A. tomentosa*, according to Barrett. The dried berries were ground into a very fine meal and stored. This the Pomo later dampened and molded into cakes 4 to 5 inches in diameter and about 1/4 inch in thickness that were dried in the sun. Some Pomo rock-boiled manzanita meal into mush. Still others baked bread from the meal in an underground oven. From parched manzanita berries the Central Pomo made a pinole (fine meal) that they mixed with water and drank as a beverage. E. M. Loeb recorded that the Pomo made manzanita cider from the berries. The Karok made cider by soaking the berries in water and straining the water through a basket plate or by running water through the berries. Manzanita cider was the universal California drink.

After the special dance and "big eat" which marked the ripening of the fruit, the Concow (Northwestern Maidu) carefully selected the manzanita berries, discarding those that were worm-eaten. The women scalded them for a few minutes until they were soft, then made a mash of the whole mixture. An equal amount of water was added and all of this at once passed through dried pine needles or straw resting in a shallow sieve basket over a watertight basket. Sometimes they allowed the mash to stand for an hour or so before straining. After cooling it was ready to drink.

The Yuki improved the quality of cider by sifting off the seeds and using the pulp alone. The dry berries were ground in a pounding basket and the seeds were removed by using a flat circular sifting basket about 1 foot in a diameter. In the same manner of sifting acorn flour, some of the meal was taken and thrown repeatedly in the air; the heavier seed parts were allowed to roll off the edge as the basket was held at an incline. The finer flour clung to the basket. The Yuki also employed the *A. manzanita* berry but preferred *tomentosa* for cider. Although the berry was smaller, the edible portion was greater in proportion to the seed content.

The Cahuilla preferred *A. glandulosa*, eastwood manzanita, and *A. pungens* or Mexican manzanita when fresh, finding *A. glauca*, the bigberry manzanita, too sticky. A very simple method they sometimes used to make a drink early in the season was to simply soak fresh, slightly red manzanita berries, uncrushed, in water. They also ate the ripe berries raw or dried them and pounded them into a flour that they mixed with water.

During July and August the Atsugewi knocked greenleaf manzanita *(A. patula)* berries from the bush with a stick into burden baskets. The berries were stored in pits. Later they were pounded and sifted. The fine flour was molded into small cakes that could be stored until eaten plain or stirred with water and drunk. Sometimes manzanita flour was mixed with wild plum flour and molded into cakes. Water added to pounded manzanita berries made a cider, which was brought to the mouth with a deer-tail sop. The Miwok used a short stick with small hawk tail feathers lashed to the end for the same purpose. When taken this way manzanita cider created appetite, they felt, and the hawk feathers cured stomach ailments.

The Miwok also dipped stems of bluegrass *(Poa pratensis)* and a species of sedge *(Carex)* as a sop in manzanita cider. The Miwok chewed raw manzanita berries for flavor but did not swallow them. For cider they preferred the whiteleaf manzanita *(A. viscida)*, *A. tomentosa* as well as the common manzanita. Greenleaf manzanita was for bears, they said, not people. The Miwok picked manzanita berries by hand into a burden basket or they simply shook a branch of manzanita over a flat sifting basket. Some fell on the ground, which had already been prepared by sweeping it clean with twigs and leaves of a wild buckwheat, naked *eriogonum (Eriogonum nudum)*. Later this was also used to sweep the berries together. They next winnowed the berries to eliminate leaves and dirt, often by simply tossing a handful in the air and blowing on them. Some berries were dried for the winter or the fresh berries were made into cider. For this they ground them into a coarse meal, occasionally boiling them briefly first, and placed the meal on a sifting basket set on top of a cooking basket. Water was dripped through the meal until all the flavor had leached out (tested by tasting the meal). Along with the cider, fine particles of manzanita meal collected in the cooking basket. After these settled, the pure, clear cider was decanted and drunk as a summer refreshment and at social gatherings. The drink kept for two to four days.

One of the Southern Maidu's favorite foods was bigberry manzanita *(A. glauca)*. They often ate the berries raw or pounded them into a flour, separating out the seeds. The flower was made into mush or stored for the winter. The Hupa and Nomlaki, it might be noted, ate manzanita flour directly as pinole. The preferred Northern Maidu drink was manzanita cider. The drink was greatly loved in the summer. Berries, dried or fresh, were crushed and the sweet meal mixed with water into a stiff dough. A small rough frame of willow covered the top of a soup basket; cross strands of bark had been twined about it to form a rude openwork tray. A few large leaves were placed on the tray, and on the leaves they placed the manzanita dough in the form of a truncated cone, 15 to 20 cm. in diameter and 10 to 15 cm. high. Into a depression in the top of the cone, water was made to trickle a little at a time. It percolated through the dough, leaching out the flavor and dripping as a clear amber liquid into the watertight basket below. Water was continually added until all the goodness had dissolved out of the heap of berry pulp. The cider was strong, sweet and refreshing. Slightly roasting the berries yeilded a darker liquid with a slightly altered flavor.

  The Yokuts, observed Gayton, poured the liquor through the mass of crushed manzanita fruit perhaps two or three times. Powers, in the 1870s, remarked on the great care they took removing the seeds from the flour and the high quality of the Yokuts' manzanita drink— "clear, cool and clean. . . ."

Oregon boxwood *(Pachystima myrsinites)*: The Karok ate the berries ripe but did not preserve them.

Wild grape *(Vitis californica)*: This fruit was eaten ripe by the Karok but not preserved. The Pomo, to a limited extent, ate the sour fruit of the wild grape. The Miwok mashed them with their hands in a basket. The Tubatulabal ate them raw or spread them in the sun and dried them into raisins for the winter. The Yokuts sometimes crushed them and made a red juice that they drank fresh. The Cahuilla ate wild grapes fresh, cooked them in stews or dried them and later reconstituted them by boiling. A mush was sometimes made from grapes.

Service berry *(Amelanchier alnifolia)*: This was eaten fresh by the Pomo. The Karok ate them fresh or dried them in the sun and stored them in big baskets. The Atsugewi mashed the ripe berries in a tule basket, adding water to form a paste which was eaten fresh. Service berries were also dried and stored. To reconstitute them, they were soaked in water. A service berry *(A. pallida)* was eaten fresh or dried, stored and eaten by the Cahuilla. The Kawaiisu ate the fresh berries sparingly.

Thorny gooseberry *(Ribes sp.)*: The Karok hit the branches with a stick, knocking the berries into a basket. In the basket they rubbed a basket cup over them to remove the prickles. A basket plate sifted out the rubbish. Put in a winnowing basket with hot hardwood coals, shaken back and forth, and parched to singe off prickles, the berries were ready to eat for the Pomo. These and other thorny berries were rolled between two rocks to remove the spines before being eaten fresh by the Atsugewi. The Yokuts of the Sierra foothills also ate thorny varieties of gooseberries. The Miwok first winnowed then pulverized them in a mortar to rid them of stickers. The Kawaiisu broke them open and ate the pulp.

Smooth gooseberry or currant *(Ribes sp.)*: The Miwok and Pomo ate these fruits fresh. Several species are in fruit during the spring and summer and were eaten by the Hupa. The same was true of the Cahuilla, who ate them fresh from April through August. They were eaten fresh by the Karok, Atsugewi, Kawaiisu and Yokuts. A large and juicy variety coming from higher in the mountains was eighty-year-old Jack Roan's

Kitanemuk Indian María Gamez beats bushes with a stick and collects the falling gooseberries in an openwork, twined winnowing basket. Photograph, J. P. Harrington, circa November 1916–September 1917 (Smithsonian Institution National Anthropological Archives).

Margaret Wheat described the great importance of these coarsely woven baskets among the Northern Paiute. In them not only did they gather berries and nuts but used as a sieve they separated seeds from mashed berries or, by tossing cracked nuts in the air, winnowed shells from their nutmeats; with coals continuously tossed in the basket, the nuts were parched. They could even be used for netting minnows from sloughs or as a serving tray for fish, fowl and meat or as a drying rack for curing meat. Finely woven versions were employed for gathering small seeds.

favorite berry, according to Gayton who interviewed the Chukchansi Yokuts and Southern Miwok man many decades ago. The Kawaiisu also dried them in the shade for a week or so and stored them, later soaking or boiling to reconstitute them.

Salmonberry *(Rubus spectabilis)*: This was eaten by the Pomo and Bear River People. Many northern groups ate them fresh from the bush.

Salal *(Gaultheria shallon)*: The Pomo and other northern groups, such as the Karok, picked and ate these berries fresh.

Wild strawberry *(Fragaria californica)*: This was eaten fresh by the Karok, Salinan, Cahuilla, Northern Diegueñ, Pomo, Yuki, and Bear River people.

Sand strawberry *(Fragaria chiloensis)*: These berries were eaten by the Kashaya Pomo, Wiyot and others.

Raspberry *(Rubus leucodermis)*: This was eaten fresh and dried for the winter by the Pomo as well as their neighbors and others such as the Cahuilla.

Thimbleberry *(Rubus parviflorus)*: These berries were eaten directly from the bush by the Karok, Cahuilla, Luiseño, Pomo, Bear River, Hupa and Yokuts who picked them into a seed beater they held in their hand.

California blackberry *(Rubus vitifolius)*: Karok, Hupa, Miwok, Salinan, Cahuilla, Luiseño and others used them in the same way as other Rubus species.

Blackberry *(Rubus ursinus)*: These were eaten fresh and dried for the winter by the Bear River, Pomo, Cahuilla and the Northern Diegueño. They were reconstituted by boiling them in a small amount of water. Half-ripe berries were sometimes soaked by the Cahuilla in water to make a refreshing drink.

Elderberry *(Sambucus sp.)*: The Pomo and Bear River people ate them fresh and dried them for the winter. The Pomo also made juice of the elderberry. The Atsugewi mashed the berries, mixed them with manzanita flour, and made cakes that they dried and stored. The Yokuts dried a large, sweet variety on rocks when they went higher into the mountains for pine nuts. During the winter they boiled and ate them about once a week; they never mashed them. The Miwok always cooked elderberries. They ate them at that time or dried them for the winter when they were eaten as they were or sometimes recooked. The Cahuilla ate them fresh or dried them in clusters on the drying floor, stored them in ollas and prepared them by boiling them into a rich sauce that needed no sweetening.

Black nightshade *(Solanum nodiflorum)*: The fully ripe berries were eaten by the Pomo and considered excellent.

Purple nightshade *(Solanum xantii)*: The Miwok ate these berries raw.

Red huckleberry *(Vaccinium parvifolium)*: The berries were eaten fresh in July or August by the Karok, Pomo, and Bear River people. The Karok waited until fall for the California huckleberry *(V. ovatum)*, preferably after the first frost, noted S. M. Schenck and Gifford, since this made them sweeter. They were stored in baskets.

Berry-picking basket made by Asunción Cervantes, Mutsun Costanoan Indian from San Juan Baustista. Construction appears obvious. The ends of the tules were looped over the withe hoop and twined with tule weft next to the hoop (and, for part of the course, over the hoop). The tule was twined again halfway down, and warps were tied together with tule at the bottom. Tule was wound with tule to make the handle. Such a simple basket suggests the quickly made fish-carrying basket of the Mohave described by Spier. Pencil-sized willow rods, bottom end up, were bound to a stout hoop and the thin ends bound to form the apex of a slightly rounded cone. The sides were not twined. It was held by a headband on the back below the shoulder blades to receive fish retrieved from a scoop. Berry-picking basket, circa 1929–1934 by unknown photographer in the J. P. Harrington collection (Smithsonian Institution National Anthropological Archives).

Pacific ninebark *(Physocarpus capitatus)*: The Miwok ate the berries raw. (The Karok did not but made stone-tipped arrows from the shoots.)

Yew *(Taxus brevifolia)*: The fruit was eaten by the Pomo.

Madrone or *madroña (Arbutus menziesii)*: The berries were roasted, parched and stored for the winter or eaten fresh by the Pomo, also the Bear River who sometimes roasted them like peppernuts. The Hupa shook them in a basket with hot rocks and ate them. The Miwok treated them as high-grade manzanita and made cider from them in the same way they did from manzanita berries. The Karok steamed and stored them. Hot rocks were added to a little water in an acorn cooking basket that was then filled with berries and covered with madroña leaves. After a thorough steaming, they were dried on basket platters and stored. They were soaked in warm water before eating and sometimes were eaten mixed with pounded manzanita berries.

Chokecherry *(Prunus virginiana or demissa)*: The Karok ate them fresh. The fruit was eaten fresh or dried by the Luiseño, Pomo and the Bear River people who considered them a delicacy and accompaniment to meat. Dried cherries were stored in layered baskets like berries. The Atsugewi mashed ripe chokecherries in a tule basket, added water and formed a paste that was eaten without further preparation. The Kawaiisu ate them fresh in August or September.

Toyon *(Heteromeles arbutifolia)*: This fruit was eaten raw but more commonly roasted over coals or parched in a basket by the Pomo. The Hupa thought of these as little madroña berries. The Karok put them in a basket plate before the fire and turned them until they wilted. The Chumash toasted them in a soapstone olla without water. The Cahuilla and Luiseño ate them cooked or raw. The Miwok first boiled then baked them in a deep narrow earth oven for two or three days. The heat was maintained with fire around but not directly over the oven. Another method they used was to store fresh berries in a basket for two months to soften them. After this they were parched with large coals to facilitate separation after they were cooked. The berries were eaten with pinole (seed meal). The Salinan people also ate these berries.

Sugar bush *(Rhus ovata)*: These berries were eaten fresh or dried or ground into flour for mush by the Cahuilla who also used white exudation on the fruit as a sweetener. They ate clusters of the small flowers after cooking them in water.

Lemonadeberry *(Rhus integrifolia)*: These acidic berries were soaked in water by the Cahuilla to make a tart drink.

Sourberry *(Rhus trilobata)*: Garth found that the Atsugewi gathered these berries in midsummer. They were washed, dried and stored. When needed, they pounded them into flour in a basket mortar, mixed the flour with manzanita flour and water and drank the preparation. The Cahuilla ate them fresh, soaked them in water for a drink, or dried and ground them into flour for a soup, according to Bean and Saubel.

Buckthorn berry or coffeeberry *(Rhamnus rubra, crocea, californica* and others): The Atsugewi, Kawaiisu, Cahuilla and others gathered and ate these berries fresh in the late summer and fall. The Kiliwa crushed and ate the fruit and seeds as pinole.

Wolfberry or boxthornberry *(Lycum fremontii* and *andersonii)*: Gathered by the Cahuilla between May and August, these berries were eaten fresh or dried. They were reconstituted by boiling them into mush or grinding them into flour and mixing them with water. The Kawaiisu ate them fresh or squeezed out the juice for a drink. They would also mash them in their hands, dry them for awhile, then soak them in warm water for an hour and eat them. Berries dried and stored were eaten as they were, or reconstituted by boiling. Edward Castetter and Willis Bell emphasized the importance of wolfberries (*L. fremontii* and *excertum*) among the Mohave and Yuma. These were more important than any of the greens, informants told them. They would go on expeditions and gather them in a basket. After washing, the berries were boiled and coarsely ground on the milling slab. The result was mixed with water and drunk. Fresh berries were also dried in the sun like raisins and stored in gourds or clay ollas. Drying them made them sweet and they were eaten as they were or pulverized and mixed with water for a beverage. The Mohave also crushed the berries of *L. andersonii* in water for a drink or dried and stored them. The Kiliwa ate wolfberry seeds that had been ground into pinole.

Barberry *(Berberis nervosa)*: The Yana of the northern foothills gathered and pounded the dry berries into flour for mush. Some California Indians made a drink of certain species of barberry.

Lotebush *(Condalia lycioides canescens)*: The Mohave gathered these berries in June and mashed them into a foam that they ate. Berries were also dried and stored, then reconstituted by soaking them in hot water.

Juniper berries *(Juniperus californica* and *occidentalis)*: This fruit was eaten by the Pomo.

The Atsugewi ate the berries fresh from western juniper and also dried and pounded juniper berries into flour for storage. The Cahuilla did the same and made the flour into mush or bread. The berries could be conveniently gathered during the piñon harvest since they were mature at the same time and grew in the same location. The Kiliwa ate juniper berries crushed and boiled. Maurice Zigmond observed the major importance of the California juniper berry among the Kawaiisu. Berries ripened in August and were knocked from the trees into a bucket or gathered from the ground. Some were boiled and eaten. Many were dried in the sun for about a week, then eaten as they were or stored. Others of the fresh berries had the large seed removed by hand or they were lightly pounded and the pulp was saved using a sifting tray. Some fresh pulp was eaten as it was or mixed with water and eaten. Much of the fresh pulp was pounded in a mortar and the meal was eaten or mixed with water and formed into a cake that dried hard, preferably on a base of Spanish clover *(Lotus purshianus)* for four or five days (said to improve the flavor), and was preserved for the winter. Most of the berries seem to have been consumed in this cake form.

Wild or Sierra plum *(Prunus subcordata)*: This fruit was eaten fresh by the Miwok and fresh or dried by

Manuela Aguiar opens and cleans seeds from opuntia cactus fruit. The opened, flattened fruit ready to dry in the sun.

the Pomo. The Atsugewi removed the seeds before drying the pulp that was then often pounded and made into small cakes and stored for the winter.

- *Crucillo* or wild plum *(Condalia parryi)*: Pulp of this red desert drupe was eaten fresh or dried and ground to flour for mush. The Cahuilla also ground the nut and leeched the flour before use.
- Wild rose *(Rosa californica)*: The Cahuilla picked the buds of this plant just before they blossomed and ate them. They soaked the flowers in water for a beverage. J. P. Harrington's notes indicate the fruit of the wild rose was eaten raw by the Chumash. I have found the rose hips growing along the upper reaches of Piru Creek in old Chumash territory to be extraordinarily delicious, not mealy but more like dried cherry pulp. The fresh fruit of the rose was eaten by the Panamint, Kitanemuk and Kawaiisu who reported them to be ripe and ready in August. Hips were eaten by the Pomo as well. This fruit, along with *R. gymnocarpa*—the wood rose—were eaten by the Kashaya Pomo. They were said to be sweetest after the first light frost or cold nights of fall.
- California and blue palm *(Washingtonia filifera* and *Erythea armata)*: Wild dates of the California palm were often gathered and eaten just as they were by the Cocopa when passing through a palm oasis. A long pole with a crossbar pulled the fruits from the tree. Juice could be squeezed from the fruits and added to water for a drink. Fruits were also dried. Fresh and dried fruit of the blue palm from Big Canyon in the Tantillas Mountains of Baja California were also consumed by the Cocopa.
- Juniper mistletoe *(Phoradendron ligatum)*: This is a parasitic plant of the juniper tree. The berries were sometimes eaten fresh but more often they were pounded into a powder and sprinkled on wounds to promote healing, according to Bean and Saubel who described their use among the Cahuilla.
- Desert mistletoe *(Phoradendron californicum)*: This parasite of the catclaw and mesquite trees produced berries that were ground up, mixed with a small quantity of ashes, boiled and eaten as a treat by the Cahuilla. Some experts consider the berries toxic.
- Ground cherry *(Physalis sp.)*: The ripe berries were eaten fresh by the Mohave and Yuma children.
- Crucifixion thorn *(Holocanthus emoryi)*: Yuman tribes of the lower Colorado ate these berries during their wanderings.
- Netleaf hackberry *(Celtis reticulata)*: These were eaten by lower Colorado Yuman.
- Mohave yucca *(Yucca schidigera)*: The fresh fruit was peeled and eaten by the Mohave. Teresa Castro, a Paipai and Southern Diegueño, told me that she still prepares ripe Mohave yucca pods for her family. She splits them lengthwise and removes the seeds, boils them for about half an hour, transfers them with a little water to a grinding stone, mashes them a bit and returns the liquidy pulp to the water in the pot. It makes a deliciously sweet drink.
- *Cardón (Pachycereus pringlei)*: This fruit was eaten raw by the Kiliwa.
- *Pitaya (Machaerocereus gummosus)*: The Kiliwa ate this fruit raw. There was no "second harvest" of the seeds as reported by early Spanish missionaries for groups farther south.
- Fishhook cactus *(Mammillaria dioica)*: The small red fruit was eaten raw by the Northern Diegueño.
- Buckhorn cholla *(Opuntia acanthocarpa)*: The Cahuilla gathered the tunas or fresh cactus fruit in the spring and ate them as they were or dried them for storage.
- Silver cholla *(Opuntia echinocarpa)*: The tunas were eaten by the Mohave and the Cocopa, as was the fruit of the *O. fulgila*.
- Pencil cactus *(Opuntia ramosissima)*: The fresh fruit was eaten or preserved in the same way as the buckhorn cholla by the Cahuilla. Barrows noted that fruit was the most commonly utilized product of cacti.
- Beavertail cactus *(Opuntia basilaris)*: The Northern Diegueño cleaned the thorns of the tuna on dry grass and dried the fruit before eating.
- Prickly pear *(Opuntia occidentalis)*: The Salinan people ate prickly-pear fruit. Many varieties of prickly-pear cacti were enjoyed by the Cahuilla, either fresh or preserved. Mohave and Cocopa ate the tunas of the *O. engelmannii*, according to Castetter and Bell. They rolled them on the ground to remove the spines. Barrows observed that an Opuntia cactus, called *na-u-tem* by the Cahuilla, possessed flat stems with exceptionally long spines, 2 to 3 inches in length. It yielded luscious fruit in large quantities. It was perhaps this cactus that Southern Diegueño Raúl Sandoval and his mother Manuela Aguiar picked for me late one year just outside the door of their home in the Sierra Juárez of Lower California. They called it *tapaha*. It may have been the Opuntia utilized by the Cocopa and the Mohave and

referred to in more modern terms as *O. phaeacantha major* (a variety of Engelmann's prickly pear). The Northern Diegueño of Santa Isabel ate the raw fruit of the *discata* variety of this cactus after removing the seeds.

In the remote Sierra Juarez Mountains, Raúl brushed off the spines and picked the tuna. He split one side lengthwise with his fingernail beginning at the far end. He emptied out the seeds. The pulp, held by the skin, was opened to the air, the fruit now somewhat flattened. It was left, pulp skyward and exposed to the sun, to dry for a few days and then stored until it was needed. It could be eaten like a large raisin. Dried cactus fruit was also ground with a little water on a milling stone, Manuela recounted. The resulting liquid was poured off and taken as a sweet refreshing drink. In fact, the fresh fruit cleaned of seeds can be mashed on the milling stone at once and the juice poured into a bowl and drunk. The seeds were not wasted but ground and used for mush.

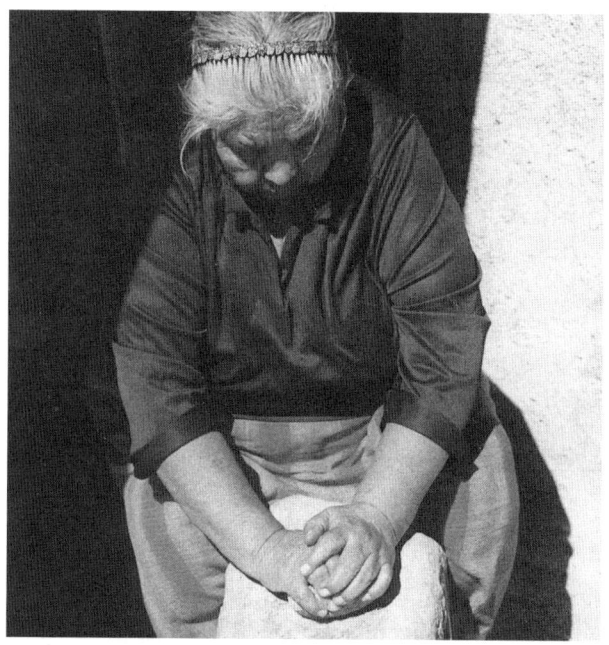
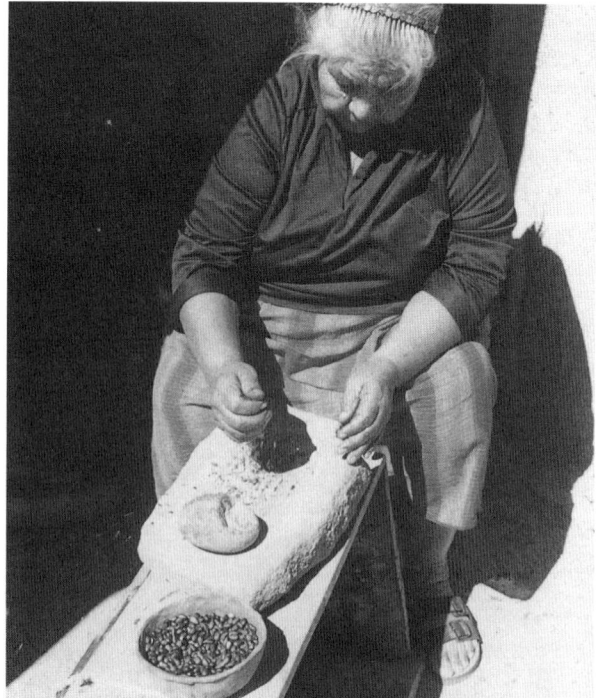

Manuela Aguiar hand winnows cracked shells from pine nuts. On the stone slab she grinds the pure nut meats into pinole.

Pine and Other Not-So-Bitter Nuts

Nuts in general are extraordinarily nutritious. The widespread gray pine nut of the interior California foothills, for example, is about 30 percent protein, 10 percent carbohydrate and 50 percent fat. The single leaf piñon, common in California, contains over 60 percent fat, 6 percent protein and nearly 30 percent carbohydrate (Zigmond, 1941). Piñon nuts sustained Indians near the foothills of the western margins of the southern deserts and the Great Basin. Nuts of one sort or another were enjoyed throughout California as much for their good flavor as food value.

Hazelnuts *(Corylus californica)*: The Karok ate these nuts in season or stored them in baskets like acorns. The Yuki and the Pomo gathered them by the sackful in autumn. A supply of stored hazelnuts was maintained through winter and spring. They were not ground.

Chinquapin nuts *(Castanopsis chrysophylla)*: These were cracked with the teeth and eaten when found or stored in big baskets by the Karok. They were collected by the Pomo and the Yuki and eaten without grinding. The Kashaya Pomo ate them raw or roasted, sometimes pounded into a meal; they stored them in the shell for winter. Kawaiisu hunters ate them raw.

Black walnut *(Juglans hindsii)*: The sweet nut meat was dried and stored by the Kashaya Pomo. If eaten fresh, the papery peeling was removed to prevent stomach upset. (Arrows, bows, mush stirrers and digging sticks were made from wood of the black walnut tree.)

Pepperwood nuts *(Umbellularia californica)*: Pepperwood, or California bay or laurel nuts, ripened in autumn and fell to the ground where the Pomo would harvest them. Shaking the tree speeded the process, noted S. A. Barrett. The unhusked nuts were gathered and dried in the sun until the thick outer covering loosened and split. At that point the husks were eaten raw, as they did not store well, and were considered an excellent food. (The Miwok roasted them in ashes before eating.) The nuts themselves, with their thin hard shells were stored away for the winter and, when needed, they were cracked open and the kernels roasted until they were dark brown and crisp. Or, the kernels were roasted at once, when gathered, and the meats ground into a very oily meal in a mortar. The meal easily held together when pressed and molded into flat cakes, 2 inches in diameter by 1 inch thick. They were set in the sun to dry and then stored for the winter. The cakes or roasted nuts (described by the Pomo as tasting like freshly roasted peanuts) were usually eaten as a condiment with clover or other greens, or with buckeye meal, acorn bread or mush. In western Pomo territory pepperwood nuts were eaten with seaweed. The Yuki would take a quantity of the nuts with them when forced to journey a long ways through the woods or go for a long time without food.

Gray pine nuts *(Pinus sabiniana)*: These were gathered twice each year. Miwok men climbed the trees in early spring and twisted off the green cones. They were beaten with a rock to split the covering that easily peeled away. Shells were still soft at this early time of the year and unshelled nuts were picked out of the cone and eaten whole. They saved the pith center of the green cone and roasted it in hot ashes for about 20 minutes. The result was a sweet, slightly syrupy food. The Tubatulabal, who harvested the green cones in May, sliced down the sides with an obsidian knife, picked the nuts out of the soft shells and ate them at once. The Kawaiisu removed the outer skin by tapping all around with a rock, then held the cone between their feet and struck it on top to split it open. They plucked out the seeds and ate them fresh.

Gray pine nuts mature in the fall. The Kawaiisu gathered the cones in October and roasted them like those of the piñones. The hard nut shells were removed and the seeds parched if not already sufficiently roasted by the brush firing. Shelled nuts were pounded and mixed with cold water or boiled. The Maidu made a pile of ten or twelve of the large, tough cones and set them ablaze to burn off the pitch and partially open them. Heavy stones were used to crush the cones completely open. The Miwok did much the same and ate the nut meats raw or parched them with coals on a flat parching or sifting basket. The Tubatulabal ate the nut meats as they were or boiled them like beans. The Karok picked gray pine nuts from the ground and abraded the ends, or an end and one side, on a rock to make holes for stringing them as beads on iris-fiber string to decorate dance dresses.

Sugar pine nuts *(Pinus lambertiana)*: The Pomo gathered and ate the nuts of both the gray pine and sugar pine in their territory. The Maidu of the mountains, on the other hand, traded sugar pine nuts to the Sacramento Valley people for the gray pine nuts of the foothills. Chukchansi Yokuts families of the foothills went up themselves into the Sierras around August to make camps for the harvesting of sugar pine nuts.

Hazelnuts, a high-quality elderberry and venison were further incentives. Men climbed the sugar pine trees and twisted off or knocked down the ripe sugar pine cones. Women gathered them into piles they surrounded with pine needles and set on fire. After the pitch had burned away and the cones cooled, they were set bottom end down on a rock and the tips struck with a heavy stone, splitting the cones open and freeing the nuts. Good ones were

Close-ups of pine-nut processing: nuts parching in a clay pot on a three-stone tripod hearth; eating bowl on pot-resting stone to the left; the darkened parched nuts on grinding slab, lightly pounding to crack the shells; and completed pinole with oily mano.

brown at one end, distinguishing them from the undesirable all-black nuts. They carried the pine nuts home in burden baskets. The Karok, at that point, would eat them without further processing or store them for the winter. The Yokuts, however, parched them with coals on a basket tray before eating them. They could be shelled and eaten directly or pounded in a mortar hole, and the fine greasy meal rolled into balls and enjoyed with acorn mush.

The Miwok had an interesting manner of gathering these cones, which were harvested after they had turned brown but before the nuts had fallen out. Men first swayed then twisted the limbs, causing the heavy cones to break off on their own. They did this with their hands or feet after climbing the tree. Small trees could be climbed without a ladder but larger trees with smooth trunks were scaled by means of a small dead tree laid against it or a special climbing pole. The Karok owner of a tree would invite relatives and friends to go and "bite" the nuts (gather the fall harvest). With hazel withes, they tied a stick at an acute angle on the end of a long fir pole. It was hooked over the first limb of the sugar pine tree for the climber, who was singing a charm to pull himself up. It was hooked over the next limb to go higher still. A smaller hooked stick grasped a branch near a cone and the climber shook the branch with the stick until the cone fell, as those on the ground sang, "Cut it off, Beaver, cut it off!" or they might sing, "Cut it off, Pitchy hands, cut it off!" referring to the gray squirrel.

Much like the Yokuts, the Miwok women spread dry sugar-pine needles over the many cones that had fallen. The cones were placed upside down, perhaps two tiers deep, and the needles ignited to burn off the pitch. Then the cones were struck with a stone on the tip to split them through the middle. Pressing them down on a rock, each projecting scale of the cone caused the nut to roll out. Many were shelled and eaten at once while still warm. Generally, among the Miwok, those who ate the first fruits of a season first had to have a shaman ritually press and blow upon them.

Nuts were winnowed in a basket by the wind. Some of these the Miwok pulverized in a mortar, soft shell included, until they turned into a kind of dark peanut butter that was especially esteemed at feasts. This was eaten with the fingers as an accompaniment to acorn soup or manzanita cider. The sugar of the sugar pine was saved as a delicacy. The Kawaiisu ate sugar pine nuts and collected the sugar sap, dry and powdery, after it had drained from a hole cut into the tree. They ate it without special preparation.

Ponderosa pine nuts *(Pinus ponderosa)*: Small nuts from green or ripe cones were infrequently eaten by the Miwok. Cones were dried in the sun to extract the nuts. The Kawaiisu gathered them from the ground in late October, cracked the shells in a bedrock mortar, and winnowed them in a basket tray. They ate the kernels raw.

White fir nuts *(Abies concolor)*: Generally considered inedible by the Kawaiisu, one informant told Zigmond, they were occasionally cracked open and eaten raw.

Deer nut, goat nut or jojoba *(Simmondsia chinensis)*: The Cahuilla ate these nuts raw or ground them into powder to make a coffee-like drink. The Kiliwa ate them as pinole. The lower Colorado Yuman tribes gathered the nuts as they traveled.

Piñon nuts *(Pinus monophylla* and *quadrifolia)*: The Tubatulabal knew that when the fruit of the California coffee berry *(Rhamnus californica cuspidata)* ripened in the foothills of the southern Sierras, the piñon nuts of the eastern side of the mountains were ready for gathering. Men scouted and found the best areas and the villagers followed. Piñon cones were gathered mature but before they opened (from mid-August in lower elevations to October higher up). Men and boys knocked them from the trees with staves (a straight stick 10 feet or longer) or pulled down branches with a crook staff (handle, 3 feet long; 5-inch crook at the end made by bending the green stick over the knee and tying it bent with outer bark of fremontia rope; left to dry in hot sun for three days and untied; crook remained). Men and women picked the cones from the tree and from the ground and placed them in conical lug baskets that were emptied into large conical burden baskets. A bed of sage *(Artemisia tridentata)* was prepared at camp and the cones dumped on it. They set it aflame and from time to time tested the cones to see if they had opened. If they had not, more sage was piled on and the roasting continued.

Zigmond observed a piñon harvest of the Kawaiisu, neighbors of the Tubatulabal, and gave much detail on this stage. The Kawaiisu believed a dark-skinned person should kindle the sage brush fire to make the piñons brown. Once lit, old people tended the fire, adding wood as needed. The cones were stirred to keep them from burning and blackened cones were pushed aside to concentrate the fire on cones that were still green. A finished batch was covered with dirt so that the steam might soften the cones and make it easier to extract the nuts. Cones were struck with a rock while still warm and the seeds removed with thumb and fingers. They put them in a winnowing basket held on their laps, with the basket pointing toward the fire and their feet away from it. This, they believed, would prevent their feet from aching. Empty cones were tossed backward over the shoulder. The names of animals that eat piñones could only be mentioned by circumlocution. A grizzly bear, for example, would be "pitch on the face." One must not leave for a drink or for other relief. Violators of the taboos became targets of tossed cones. Meaner individuals would throw the heavy green cones, informants told Zigmond.

After the opened cones had cooled, the Tubatulabal, as described by Voegelin, shook out the nuts or picked them out by hand or winnowed them from the ash and dirt. The nuts were spread on hides and dried for three to four days.

Most of the nuts were cached in pits 5 feet in diameter and 2-1/2 feet deep, dug with a stick in the floors of natural rock shelters near the piñon groves. Pits were lined with flat rocks or brush; the nuts were dumped in and covered with large flat rocks or grass and small stones. Men returned in the winter to carry the nuts home in skin sacks. Some of the roasted nuts were taken home at harvest time strung on long pieces of native cordage after piercing them with sharpened twigs from mountain lilac *(Ceanothus cuneatus)*. They hung them over the houses when they returned to the village and later ate them as delicacies. Nuts that fell naturally from cones that opened in the trees as the gathering season progressed were taken home unroasted.

The Tubatulabal heaped handfuls of the piñon nuts from their cache (nuts previously roasted in the cone) onto a grinding slab. This was a flat oval or roughly rectangular black slate or granite slab 14 to 20 inches long, 10 to 15 inches wide and 2 to 4 inches thick that was used on one side only, with the grinding surface flat or slightly concave. With a small oval rub stone, flat on the top and bottom and used in a rotary fashion, they gently crushed the shells. Since this was done outdoors, the wind blew some of the broken pieces away. A large basket tray winnowed the remaining shells from the nut meats that were then cooked like beans or ground into meal with a larger rub stone grasped in the right hand and drawn back and forth over the slab. The resulting meal was simply mixed with cold water for a white piñon mush, eaten by itself or sometimes with meat. Nuts that had been gathered from the ground made black piñon mush. They were cracked and winnowed as described but the meats were then parched with small coals on an oval tray and pounded into meal in a pit or portable stone mortar. Water was added to the meal to make a thin dark mush.

Among the Kawaiisu, piñon nuts were often eaten whole and unhulled as they were taken from the charred cones. Some nut meats were eaten after gently breaking the shells and winnowing. When stringing piñon nuts, the Kawaiisu used a stripped and sharpened rabbit brush twig *(Chrysothamnus nauseosus)*. They believed it improved the flavor. They recognized two piñon collecting seasons. The first was in August, after testing the cones for ripeness—they should be easy to open—and a less important season in September, after the cones had opened and the seeds had fallen to the ground. Those picked from the ground were hulled and parched black by being tossed with a live, gray, piñon-wood coal. They were then ground and mixed with water to make porridge that they enjoyed with chia drinks. Or the nuts were hulled and boiled like beans into a thick mush.

In September, Cocopa families from the Colorado River Delta journeyed for almost a week through the Cocopa Mountains and across the Laguna Salada Basin to the pine-nut forests of the Sierra Juárez. They joined mountain Southern Diegueños who had come for the same reasons, recorded William Kelly many years ago. Men and boys supplied the pine nut camp, traveling considerable distance for water with ollas carried on their backs (the tops of the ollas were covered with strips of cane held down by cords tied around the vessels' necks). They hunted deer with bows and arrows and by chasing them down. When men closed in on a wounded animal, they cut a leg tendon and then the throat. They also gathered wood.

Young women and girls climbed the trees and knocked down green cones. They placed them on a large brush fire. As the heat opened the cones, men and women drew them out with poles. Nuts were knocked from the cones with a stick or they were shaken out, then winnowed to clean them. In large deerskin bags, the men carried the nuts on the long return trip, going ahead one day with a load and backtracking the next to take a second load and their families. Sometimes they tarried at oases and prepared agave.

A pine nut could be eaten by simply breaking the shell between the teeth, but quantities were prepared by lightly grinding them in a mortar. Most of the broken shells the Cocopa plucked out by hand. The meat was ground and made into small cakes.

In 1996, Southern Diegueño Manuela Aguiar and her son Raúl Sandoval prepared pine nuts for me from these same forests, still remote and unconnected to modern roads, after journeying there as they do every year from their hidden mountain ranchería in the Sierra Juárez. They gathered cones by hand, Raúl emphasized. "Poles for us are a modern innovation only a few use." After freeing nuts from cones, they are stored in ceramic pots and prepared to eat as desired. Raúl builds a small fire of fast-burning twigs and sticks between three hearthstones. On top he rests a clay pot. The fire is fed with additional wood shoved between the slightly larger space left between two of the stones.

I watched small flames licking the brown, mica-flecked pot. After some minutes Manuela dropped in a few handfuls of raw piñon nuts. She stirred them from time to time to prevent burning. Eventually the soft popping of thin shells could be heard, a signal the nuts were almost ready. A moment or two passed and she removed them from the fire.

They could be shelled individually and eaten as snacks. I tried a few and they were delicious. They were also made into pinole. (Peveril Meigs recorded more than sixty years before that the Kiliwa of the San Pedro Mártir Mountains to the south made piñon-nut pinole.) Manuela began by placing a handful or two of the nuts on a milling stone. Using the flat bottom of an oval mano, she lightly and deftly pounded the brittle shells as they cracked and fell off with ease. They were winnowed by lifting them in her hand and dropping them back on the stone in the path of a soft wind or by blowing through the cascading mash. She winnowed them after this, in the wind or her breath, by tossing them in the air from a pottery bowl. The cleaned nut meats were returned to the milling stone about two handfuls at a time. With both hands, Manuela pushed the mano over the nuts farthest to the front, back and forth, and after a minute or two, finely ground meal began to form in front of the mano as whole nuts entered the process from the rear. The oily pinole was pressed into little marzipan-like globs and eaten, sometimes with salt. The piñon pinole was a much loved treat.

Seeds and Seed Beater

I was intrigued by a photo that Peveril Meigs had taken of Filipe Jat'am in the Southern Diegueño village of La Huerta in 1929. Dressed in ragged blue jeans with many patches and old cowhide sandals, the eighty-nine-year-old Indian was about to release an arrow from his bow. The pose belied his years—he stood tall, lean and strong. I wondered what had preserved him. Elderly Teodora Cuero, a girl at the time, still remembered Filipe when I visited La Huerta in 1995. Filipe lived to be over 100 years old, she said. His hair was black until the day he died. He attributed his health and longevity to the fact that for most of his life he ate only seeds. When the Mexican diet came into vogue, he also ate beans and rice but very little.

With the disappearance of the Pleistocene megafauna 11,000 years ago, the Paleo-Indian of the Americas, while still a hunter, more and more relied on foraging for food. The archaeological record is weak for this transitional period, perhaps because foraging artifacts such as digging sticks and baskets were perishable. But by 8,000 years ago milling stones became more common in the West. Along the southern California coast sites were characterized by deep stone mills and heavy hand stones, undoubtedly for grinding seeds. Similar stones were used this way into the twentieth century.

Small seeds of grasses, seeds of the sunflower family and other plants were beaten into a basket with a basketry paddle, wrote Goddard of the Hupa, although it was true of all of California. Through winnowing and handpicking they carefully cleaned the seeds. In a flatish basket they placed the seeds with coals of tanbark oak. Constant shaking and tossing prevented burning of the basket and charring of the seeds and left the seeds parched and ready for grinding. The Hupa crushed them the same way they pounded acorns but with a lighter weight pestle. They served the seed flour as pinole, dry meal, just as it was, on small saucer baskets. Of course, that was before weeds introduced by Europeans crowded out and mingled with the native plants. By the time Goddard wrote 100 years ago, the Hupa no longer gathered seeds.

Despite the great losses, one might still enjoy this highly nutritious food in many parts of California. In the spring, summer and fall, in the deserts, foothills and mountains, seeds ripen for the taking. How Native Californians harvested and prepared them has been preserved in the old ethnographies and memories of elders. The knowledge still exists.

Karok

The Karok ate the seeds of various grasses, such as *Bromus hordeaceus* and *rigidus*. Schenck and Gifford recorded that they gathered them in early July, striking the grass heads with a stick. The seeds would fall into a tightly woven burden basket held somewhat sidewise under the grass. They parched the grain in a tight winnowing basket shaken with coals of black oak bark. Chaff was winnowed and the basket was tipped slightly and struck on the bottom with a stick to rid it of remaining bits of burnt bark. The parched seeds were pounded in a hopper-topped mortar, mixed with water and eaten as cold gruel. The flour of western rye grass *(Elymus glaucus)* was mixed with water and eaten as a paste. Oats were also gathered and eaten, and the grass *Aira elongata* was harvested by cutting off the grain heads.

Maidu

The Maidu ate small seeds in quantity. Women struck the grass or plant heads with a basketry beater and caught the dislodged seeds in a tray held beneath the plant. They were transferred to a burden basket and carried on their backs to the village. The Northeastern Maidu ground them with water on a flat milling stone and made the dough into little cakes that were baked, or they mixed the flour with water and boiled it into a soup as they did acorn meal. Seeds of the sweet birch had to be thrashed to rid them of hulls. They did this when the seeds had dried. After winnowing, they were mixed

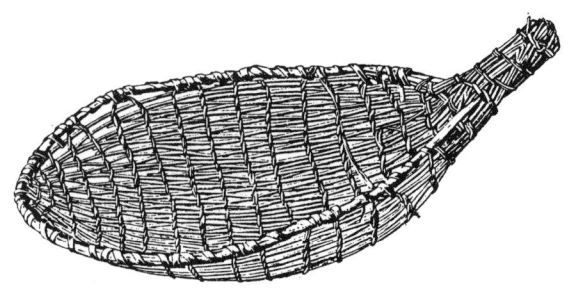

Northwestern Maidu seed-beater (Dixon, 1905).

with wild oats and parched on a basket tray with hot sand, coals, and ashes. They stirred the mixture to keep the basket from burning. Sand and ashes were winnowed away after they had cooled, and the seeds pounded into pinole and eaten dry.

Atsugewi

Garth identified three of the half-dozen or more sunflower seeds harvested by the Atsugewi, all balsam roots: arrow-leaved, Hooker's and deltoid (*Balsamorhiza sagittata, hookeri* and *deltoidea*). These, along with wild barley, mustard (*Sisymbrium pinnatum*), a fiddle neck (*Amsinkia parviflora*) and a *Chenopodium* species, were gathered in July with a basketry seed beater. They knocked them into a burden basket—a full one was a good day's work for a woman—and later parched them on a tray. The harvest took perhaps two weeks. In a shallow basket, the skins were removed by rubbing them against the sides of the basket with a rock. The seeds were winnowed and ground on the milling stone with a mano. The flour was eaten uncooked, either as dry meal pinole or molded into small cakes.

Pomo

The Pomo knocked the seeds with a handled seed beater into a tightly twined burden basket, often shelling the seeds by the force of the beater alone. To give them crispness and a nutty flavor, the seeds were placed with glowing coals in a tightly woven winnowing basket and, as Barrett described it, were alternately tossed with the coals in the air and shook vigorously to keep everything in constant motion. They were ground with a stone pestle and basketry hopper to make pinole. ("Pinole," by the way, is a Spanish word derived from the Aztec for dry finely ground cereal meal, eaten in that form or pressed into a small cake or ball.) The Pomo ate the meal dry or, if very oily, pressed it into little cakes, rarely over 2 inches in diameter by 1/2 inch thick, or into 1 inch balls sometimes reaching the size of a small pear. The same could be done with drier meal by adding a little water.

Pomo seed plants include:

Dense-flowered evening primrose (*Boisduvalia densiflora*).
Anise (*Carum kelloggii*): This was used to flavor meals made from other seeds. Most species of seeds were usually kept and processed separately but some complementary meals were mixed.
Tarweeds (*Hemizonia clevelandi* and *luzulaefolia*).
Madias or Tarweeds (*Madia capitata, elegans, sativa, densifolia* and *dissitiflora*).
Chia (*Salvia columbariae*).
Narrowleaf mule ears (*Wyethia angustifolia* and *longicaulis*).
Wild oat (*Avena fatua*).
Yellow pond lily (*Nymphaea polysepala*).
Wild rye (*Elymus sp.*).
Buttercup (*Ranunculus eisenii*): These were gathered in May for pinole by the Yuki, who lived near the Pomo.
Red maids (*Calandrinia elegans*): These were made into pinole by the Nomlaki, also neighbors of the Pomo.

Miwok

The Miwok, as others of Native California, harvested seeds, pulverized them in a mortar and ate the meal dry or mixed with water and cooked into mush or porridge. The following are species identified by Barrett and Gifford along with special considerations they noted:

Oats (*Avena barbata*): The seeds were pounded lightly in a mortar to loosen the hulls before winnowing, parching and pulverizing. They were stone boiled into soup or mush.
Arrow-leaved balsam root (*Balsamorhiza sagittata*).
Dense-flowered evening primrose (*Boisduvalia densiflora*): Seeds were stored unparched.
Upright evening primrose (*Boisduvalia stricta*): Meal was eaten dry.
"Rip gut" grass (*Bromus rigidus*).
Red maids (*Calandrinia caulescens*): The entire plant was pulled up at the end of May and spread out to dry on clean hard ground or on granite outcrop. Striking the dried plants sped the separation of seeds. Plants were finally picked up and shaken; seeds were swept together with a soap root brush, winnowed on a flat tightly coiled basket. The very rich, oily meal was pressed into balls and cakes for eating.
Painted cup (*Castilleia sp.*): Gathered in June, the seeds were stored for winter and eaten dry.
Fitch's spikeweed (*Centromadia fitchii*): This was eaten as mush.
Clarkia (*Clarkia elegans*): At times, the whole plant was dried before seeds were removed. Pinole was eaten with acorn mush.
Summers darling (*Godetia amoena*): The whole plant was pulled up as drying caused seeds to pop out. Pinole was eaten dry.

Farewell to spring *(Godetia biloba* and *viminea)*: Tops of the first plant were broken off and bundled using the stem of one. They were dried, then opened and spread, beat with sticks or treaded upon to loosen seeds. The whole plant of the second species was pulled up, soaked in water for two hours, then dried on a granite outcrop. Seeds were released naturally or by beating the plant with a stick. They were eaten as dry pinole.

Gum weed *(Madia dissitiflora)*: This is one of the seeds that was most valued. It was harvested in August and re-winnowed after parching. The oily meal was picked up in lumps.

Tarweed *(Madia elegans)*: It was struck with a basketry beater into a twined, soaproot-lined conical burden basket during a two-week period in midsummer. The seeds stored well, lasting until the next harvest. They were winnowed and sifted (after ground fine in a bedrock mortar) in the same circular basket plaque. Pinole was eaten dry.

Chile tarweed *(Madia sativa)*.

Buena mujer (Mentzelia sp.): This was eaten as pinole.

Skunkweed *(Navarretia sp.)*: Seeds were beaten from the plant in August, dried in sun and stored. They were eaten as pinole.

Valley tassels *(Orthocarpus attenuatus)*: These seeds were eaten dry as pinole.

California buttercup *(Ranunculus californicus)*: They beat the plant into a soaproot-lined burden basket in June. (Soaproot juice coated both the inside and outside of these baskets.)

Tubatulabal

The smaller seeds such as those from blazing star or chia they gathered with a seed beater. In contrast, bunch grass and beard grass were cut and the seeds dried in place on the severed stems. Wild heliotrope seeds they removed by hand and ate raw on the spot. Voegelin recorded the following species for the Tubatulabal:

Chia *(Salvia columbariae)*.
Thistle sage *(Salvia carduacea)*.
Bunch grass or wild rice *(Echinochola crusgalli)*.
Blazing star *(Mentzelia albicaulis* and *gracilenta)*.
Wild oats *(Avena)*.
Beard grass *(Polypogon monspeliensis)*.
Wild heliotrope *(Heliotropium curassavicum)*.
Many species of eriogonum *(Eriogonum sp.)*.

Kawaiisu

The Kawaiisu collected seeds in a twined basket sealed with the liquid from boiled soaproot *(Chlorogalum pomeridianum)* rubbed on a rock. The upper ends of the fibers of the plant were also dipped in the liquid, squeezed together and tied off to make the brush used to sweep fine seed meal from the sifting tray. As the brush wore down, it could be used as a hairbrush. When wet, it was a scrub brush. The Kawaiisu also obtained a starchy sealant from the corms of the golden star *(bloomeria crocea)* or wild hyacinth *(Dichelostemma pulchella)*: The fibrous skin was removed and the corms were rubbed on a grinding stone (the hyacinth corm was boiled first). The resulting substance was smeared over closely twined seed-gathering baskets to close the interstices. Zigmond was told that the translucent film hardened in one day. He obtained much information on the Kawaiisu's use of seeds:

Hairy-pod peppergrass *(Lepidium lasiocarpum)*: Seeds were gathered in June with a beater and basket. After pounding they were mixed with water and drunk.

Common sunflower *(Helianthus annuus)*: The whole head with ripened seeds was cut off and collected in a basket. Light pounding removed the seeds. They were winnowed, slightly roasted and lightly pounded once more to remove the outer membrane, then ground into pinole in a bedrock mortar and eaten dry.

Foxtail *(Hordeum jubatum)*: The bristly spikes were burned off, seeds winnowed and pounded, then eaten dry or mixed with blazing star seeds.

Buckwheats *(Eriogonum angulosum, baileyi, davidsonii, plumatella, pusillum, roseum* and *wrightii)*: Most of these were beaten into a gathering basket in August when they were ripe, pounded into pinole and eaten dry, or mixed with water and drunk. *Plumatella* was boiled into mush.

Wooly daisy *(Eriophllum ambiguum)*: These seeds were parched, pounded and eaten dry.

Sand cress *(Calyptridium monandrum)*: An edible seed.

Slender hair grass *(Deschampsia danthonioides)*: This was pounded and boiled into mush.

Tansy mustard *(Descurainia pinnata* and *sophia)*: Seeds were beaten out as the plant turned brown in June. They were parched on a flat tray, pounded, sifted, mixed with cold water and drunk. Seeds were stored as gathered or after pounding. Zigmond noted that this was an important food.

Docks *(Rumex crispus, hymenosepalus* and *salicifolius)*: Collected with a seed beater into a gathering basket; the seeds were parched, pounded in a mortar and boiled into a thick gravy.

Wild rye *(Elymus triticoides)*: The seeds were pounded and cooked into a thick mush.

Needle grass *(Stipa speciosa)*: Cut in bunches, spread and dried for half a day on flat rock, this grass was threshed by burning. If the fire burned too fast, green needle grass was added. As an alternative, the seeds were beaten out. They were winnowed by passing them from one basket to another. When boiled, the seeds swelled like rice. At times, they were pounded into meal and cooked.

Squirreltail *(Sitanion jubatum)*: This plant was cut into bunches, the seeds were threshed, parched, pounded and boiled into a thin mush.

Chia *(Salvia columbariae)*: The plant ripened by July. The seeds were beaten with a seed beater into a gathering basket, parched on a tray and pounded in a bedrock mortar. A beverage was made of the meal or a very thick mush. Often it was combined with other foods.

Indian rice grass *(Oryzopsis hymenoides)*: This was an important food seed.

Nama *(Nama demissum)*: The whole plant was spread to dry, the tiny seeds winnowed, pounded and boiled into mush.

Small-flowered melic or bunchgrass *(Melica imperfecta)*: This grass was gathered, bundled, spread on sand and beaten with a stick. Seeds were winnowed, pounded and boiled into mush.

Blazing stars *(Mentzelia affinis, albicaulis, congesta, dispersa* and *veatchiana)*: They were collected in June after their flowers had fallen. A seed beater knocked the pods into a gathering basket and winnowing separated the seeds which were used immediately or stored. Seeds were parched on a tray and ground on a grinding slab. They were very oily, like "peanut butter," and eaten as they were or made into a ball almost the size of two fists. It made one choke if too much was swallowed at once.

Cahuilla

Bean and Saubel (1972) identified and recorded many of the seed plants of the Cahuilla, their time of harvesting and their nutritional value.

White sage *(Salvia apiana)*: Seeds were available from July to September. Parched and ground to meal for mush, they were blended with other seeds because of their flavor. Seeds contained about 8 percent protein, 7 percent oil.

Thistle sage *(Salvia carduacea)*: This could be gathered from June to November. These seeds were also mixed with other seeds in mush.

Chia *(Salvia columbariae)*: Seeds were harvested from June to September. Stalks were bent over a basket and struck with a seed beater by women. Several quarts were gathered in a few hours. They were hulled on a grinding stone with a mano or by walking over them on a hard surface. They were then winnowed in baskets and parched with hot coals and pebbles either in a basket or ceramic tray. Unground seeds were stored in ollas. A beverage was sometimes made by soaking the unground seeds in water. Meal from ground seeds was made into cakes or mush. Seeds contained about 20 percent protein, 34 percent oil.

Black sage *(Salvia mellifera)*: Seeds were ground into meal. They were considered highly nutritious with a rich nutty flavor. Spring leaves and stalk were used for flavoring foods.

Tule *(Scirpus sp.)*: Seeds were eaten raw or ground for mush.

Panic grass *(Panicum urvilleanum* and *others)*: Seeds were singed to remove hair and boiled to make a gruel. One species analyzed was 15 percent protein, 6 percent oil with a trace of starch.

Sunflower *(Helianthus annus)*: Seeds were dried, ground and mixed with the flour of other seeds. They contained from 26 to 44 percent protein and 28 to 55 percent oil.

Buckwheat *(Eriogonum sp.)*: Seeds of various species were gathered from June until September.

Wooly flower *(Eriophyllum confertiflorum)*: Seeds were gathered from June to November, parched and ground into pinole.

Basin sagebrush *(Artemisia tridentata)*: Seeds were gathered by women from August through October in large quantities, parched, then ground into pinole for mush. The Kawaiisu told Zigmond that the people to the north of them would throw sagebrush seeds into a fire where they exploded like firecrackers.

Amaranth *(Amaranthus fimbriatus)*: Mush was made from seeds. The Indians gathered the plant's spikes in late summer and left them intact until needed. Then they were threshed, parched and ground to flour. Young leaves were boiled as greens or potherb.

Pin cushion *(Chaenactis glabriuscula)*: These strong-flavored seeds were gathered from June to August, parched, ground and mixed with other seeds in a mush.

Goosefoot *(Chenopodium californicum and fremontii)*: Seeds were parched and ground into flour. They contained 12 to 17 percent protein and 7 to 28 percent oil.

Mallow *(Malva sp.)*: These nonnative seeds were eaten fresh.

Blazing star *(Mentzelia sp.)*: There were many species, harvested as early as February all the way through October. Seeds were parched and ground to flour for mush.

Yuman-speaking Indians of the Lower Colorado River

As in the north, among the lower Colorado Yuman—the Mohave Yuma, Cocopa, Maricopa, and others—it was the women who gathered wild seeds. They knocked the kernels into baskets with a simple seed beater. The Maricopa were an exception. They always stripped seeds with their fingers and, at times, all groups were known to strip seeds by hand into a basket beneath the plant or into a basket hanging by a cord around their necks. They winnowed with a low pottery bowl, in some cases after lightly pounding the seeds in a wooden mortar to separate them from the hulls. Many seeds were parched in the shallow bowl or tray with hardwood coals, shaking them up and down, and twisting the winnowing bowl beneath them. They could be parched in the pottery pan alone, without coals, directly over the fire. Seeds were ground into meal with a mano on the milling stone. Edward Palmer, Castetter and Bell, and W. Kelly gathered detailed information regarding many of the wild seeds utilized by these groups:

Quail brush *(Atriplex lentiformis)*: The whole fruit was beat into a basket with a stick after the November frost turned it slightly red. Pounded and winnowed several times and then soaked, the seeds were baked two or three hours in a hot stone-lined pit covered by moist earth with a fire burning on top. Baked seeds were parched and ground on a milling stone. Meal was moistened and eaten or boiled into mush.

Desert saltbush *(Atriplex polycarpa)*: Gathered in November, the seeds were pounded in a wood mortar to free them from their hulls. They were then winnowed and used as any other seed.

Barnyard grass *(Echinochloa crusgalli)*: It was harvested in the late summer, pounded lightly in a mortar to free the seeds, winnowed, parched and ground. Pinches of the pinole were eaten with sips of water. The Cocopa stripped the seeds from the plant by hand and spread them on tamped ground. When dry, the seeds were rubbed lightly with a mano on a millstone to free them and winnowed. Then they were parched with embers in a tray and ground with a small amount of water. The meal was eaten in pinches. Seeds ground without parching they cooked into mush with fish.

Panic grass *(Panicum sp.)*: Seed heads were rubbed between the hands over a 2-foot-diameter pottery pan on the ground beneath them. Seeds were then parched in the pan, a few at a time, to free them from chaff, then winnowed once more in another pan and ground on a millstone.

Cupgrass *(Eriochloa aristata)*: The seeds were parched and ground, then eaten dry or boiled as mush.

Love grass *(Eragrostis mexicana)*: Treated the same as cupgrass.

Jungle rice *(Echinochloa colonum)*: This introduced species was treated the same as the two previous grasses.

Tansy mustard *(Descurainia obtusa and pinnata)*: The standard harvesting method was used with this plant and it was eaten as pinole. Young plants were boiled as greens.

Tansy mustard *(Descurainia sp.)*: This plant was not clearly identified. It would grow in the flood plain of the Colorado, reaching 18 inches while still in water, up to 3 feet when mature with white flowers and large leaves. The Cocopa stripped the heads into a pottery bowl and pounded them in a mortar with a wooden pestle. The seeds were then winnowed, parched and ground. They ate the meal as pinole.

Sprangle top *(Leptochloa viscida)*: With this plant the standard gathering and preparation methods were used.

Iodine bush *(Allenrolfea occidentalis)*: This was gathered in December after the frost and prepared in the standard manner.

Flat sedge, *chufa* or yellow nut grass *(Cyperus ferax)*: The standard gathering and preparation procedure was used.

"Wild rice" *(Uniola palmeri)*: Palmer, in 1885, described the 2- to 4-foot high plant growing on both sides of the Colorado River in stands 1 to

20 miles wide from the mouth upstream 12 to 15 miles. It grew in the tidewater and Indians came together in April to gather it between tides. They would sink to their knees in the muck. The brittle stems were broken or cut off with an old knife or flat, sharpened wood and thrown in a basket. The grain was still somewhat green—if dry, it would be easily lost. (At the edge of the land they gathered grain the tides had deposited in rows.) Palmer wrote that they made large fires and piled the heads close around them so they would dry quickly. They threshed them with a stick, breaking up the spikelets but not freeing the grain. For that, they placed them on tamped ground and tread and rubbed the grain with their feet. It was easier if the grain had been left in the sun for a while. The stiff chaff was painful to the feet. Kelly wrote that the Cocopa either walked through the fields to gather the rice or moved by raft. To dry it, they set it on fire (especially early in the harvest) and constantly stirred it, or they dried it in the sun for a day on hardened ground. Later in the season the women gathered the grain with a seed beater in the morning while it was still damp. The seeds which fell and were not caught, floated and were gathered after the tides had washed them into piles on the shore. Men, women and children transported the seeds home in carrying nets lined with straw. The seeds were ground and boiled as mush. This was the first important spring crop for the Cocopa. It was harvested before mesquite or screwbean. Wild rice was a high-quality, much-enjoyed food.

Ammannia (Ammannia coccinea): They prepared it in the usual way.

Evening primrose *(Oenothera brevipes)*: It was a Mohave food.

Chia *(Salvia columbariae)*: Ripe in July, the Mohave ground the seeds into pinole or mixed the ground seeds with water for a mucilaginous drink.

Sunflower *(Helianthus annuus)*: Ripe heads were broken off, dried and beaten with sticks. The released seeds were winnowed, parched, ground and eaten as pinole. Some seeds were stored in gourds or ollas. Parched seeds were occasionally eaten whole. The Mohave sometimes planted one or two rows of sunflowers at the edge of their fields (after the overflow of the Colorado) in small hills, like corn, 2 or 3 feet apart, with three or four seeds in each hill about 2 inches deep, according to Castetter and Bell.

Smartweed *(Polygonum argyrocoleon)*: This naturalized species was parched, ground and eaten by the Cocopa.

Curlydock *(Rumex crispus)*: Seeds were gathered from wild plants by the Cocopa. Other local tribes cultivated it to a limited extent.

Amaranth *(Amaranthus palmeri* and others*)*: This was a most important plant among all lower Colorado River Indians. Kelly obtained detailed information on the Cocopa. At full growth, later in the season, amaranth turned brown and the branches were covered with thorny pods holding tiny, black, lustrous seeds. The Cocopa harvested these after the domesticated corn and beans had been picked. Women in groups, often carrying their babies, did the work, although sometimes whole families went and camped at a good harvest area for a week. The seed heads were snapped off and carried in a basket or the crook of an arm to a collecting area where sticks and debris were separated out. Alternatively, they simply pulled the plant down over a basket and rubbed the seed pods off between their hands. They piled the harvest against an outside house wall—sometimes a pile 5 feet high—and for storage covered it with arrowweed or willow branches. Some Colorado River Indians left the seedheads to dry a few hours in the collecting area, sheltering them with a crude tepee of crossed willow poles, tied at the top and covered with arrowweed.

As needed, they threshed the pods by beating them with a stick and then pounding in a mud-lined mortar with a pestle, or they only used the mortar and pestle. They winnowed the seeds by pouring them into a blanket from a pottery pan or shallow basket, or by simply shaking and blowing them in the pottery pan alone. Winnowed seeds were kept in the house in either fired or mud-and-straw ollas.

Final preparation of the seeds always took place just prior to the meal at which they would be eaten, according to Kelly's Cocopa consultant Sam Spa. Seeds parched with coals in a pottery pan (they turned white from popping) were ground on a stone with a mano and the parched seed flour eaten as it was or made into a mush. It was usually not mixed with other grains. Unparched seeds were ground into flour on the grinding stone as well and made into a mush by adding bit by bit to a pot of boiling water constantly stirred to prevent lumping. Salt was added.

A mixture of corn, beans and raw amaranth flour was made into a mush. For a stew, fish were first boiled, the heads and bones removed, and raw amaranth flour added slowly to the liquid. When ready, small bowls of stew or mush were always sent to neighbors. The unparched flour could also be mixed with water, molded into a cake, 1 or 2 inches thick by 7 to 10 inches in diameter, and baked in hot ashes.

As a final note, it is important to point out that all seeds were not gathered from the bush itself. Seri women from Tiburón Island in the Gulf of California opened woodrat nests and caught not only the rat (which was commonly skinned and roasted beneath the coals of hearth or campfire) but pillaged the rat's caches of fruit and seeds as well.

Mats

Enough information has been preserved on aboriginal California mat-making to revive the tradition. In general, the variety and possibilities of the mat seem best represented by descriptions that have come down from the Chumash, while step-by-step details of manufacture and more subtle refinements of mat-making are the gift of the Yokuts.

Chumash Mat Technology

The Chumash made mats of tule but also of sea grass and, less commonly, juncus or cattail. They served as mattresses, pillows, partitions, doors, sitting mats, serving mats for guests, house coverings, coverings for stored dugout or board canoes, rolled storage containers and containers for ceremonial paraphernalia. People sat on Chumash mats during big feasts or when working (the mats had to be placed out of the wind). A rolled up mat served as a pillow. They were also rolled up and stood on end next to the inside wall of the house when not in use.

Mats could be of different colors, depending on how the tule was cured. They were twined with string or sewn with a wooden or deer-bone needle. These needles had a point at one end and an eye or a narrow section to hold the string at the other. Fernando Librado Kitsepawit told J. P. Harrington that his grandmother would pierce about ten tules with the needle, twist and pull the string through and draw the tules together. She squatted on the ground with her left knee and held the ten strung tules with her right foot as she added more tules. If the tules were drawn tight, the mat was for sleeping or sitting. If loose, it was a house covering put over the willow frame on the best Chumash houses before placing the thatching (the tule in a vertical position, the second tier outside of and overlapping the first about 1 foot). Hugo Reid, early Los Angeles settler, wrote that the Gabrielino, neighbors of the Chumash, covered their stick-frame houses with mats. The Chumash sometimes made the holes in the tule with an awl and could then substitute a juncus needle for one of wood or bone. Ordinarily, mats were rectangular in shape and not much longer than a person, but mats could be as long as 8 feet. They were wide enough for one or two people, Librado told Harrington. The tules ran lengthwise in the mats and, if they were not long enough, the first tule in a bunch would have its base at one end of the mat and the next tule would have its base toward the other end.

Rare fragments of Chumash mats, discovered in caves of the Sierra Madre north of the Sisquoc River, were described by Campbell Grant. Many were of California tule and Olney bulrush *(Scirpus californicus* and *olneyi)* twisted every 7 cm. with Indian hemp *(Apocynum cannabinum)*. On one, the tule fiber had been beaten and separated, making a very soft material, likely a cradle mattress. Some mats were twined every 8 cm. with tule itself. The sides of mats were reinforced with braided tule tied on with yucca cord. The most numerous mat fragments found were of common tule *(Scirpus acutus)*, stems flattened to 10 to 15 mm., twined with tule about every 20 cm. with sides of braided tule.

A variety of the first mat fragments combined twining for the outermost bindings with inner bindings threaded through the stems (flattened width, about 5 mm. each). These Chumash fragments recall tule mats described by Barrett for the Klamath Lake and Modoc who used tule for virtually everything from caps and quivers to warm winter moccasins, to mats to cover the house and to sit on. Warp and weft were often of tule in plain twining, though the best were said to have had a nettle-string weft. However, the outside mats of the three layers of mats that covered the willow-frame summer house had tules sewn or threaded together except along the two ends where ordinary twining was used to hold each mat together more securely and prevent the stitching from tearing out. The Indians explained that ordinary twining caused the mat to leak. Water running down the length of the tule would begin to soak in at the twining. In the sewed mat water followed the straight stem of the tule directly into the ground. Mats were placed with the stem up and down and were wide enough to cover the side of a small house. Two or more courses placed shingle-like might be necessary for a large house. Horizontal poles bound mats to the framework.

Various Yokuts Groups and Neighbors

Tule mats covered the outside thatch of the dome-shaped Tubatulabal dwellings in the southern Sierras. On the floors of houses mats were also spread. Mats served as beds with earth piled in a cylindrical heap under one end to make a pillow. Over these, they covered themselves with a deerskin, bearskin or rabbit-skin blanket. They slept with their feet toward the fire. Voegelin recorded that in the morning sleeping mats and bedding were rolled up and put to the side.

The early eyewitness accounts, the old histories and ethnographies document that tule mats were an inescapable part of the everyday life of most California Indians. One can imagine the comfort. Thomas Mayfield, who lived among the Choinumne Yokuts in the Sierra foothills as a boy in the 1850s, described the floors of their circular, willow-frame, tule-thatch houses as covered with several thicknesses of tule mats. Around the inside next to the walls, holes for beds were excavated a few inches deep and filled with loose tules. Over these, tule mats were piled several inches in depth for use as mattresses. Mayfield recalled that some of the old people were up most of a cold night rebuilding the fire in the center of the lodge. Others slept under grizzly bearskin blankets, fur outward with half the hide under the sleeper, or, if especially cold, with rabbit-skin blankets next to the sleeper within the bearskin—all on top of their tule mattresses. On the floor of the Great Central Valley, the Lake Tulare, or Tachi Yokuts, used tule mats alone to cover long A-frame houses. A wooden ridge held by crotched poles set in the ground provided the basic framework. The tule mats were laid on poles extending from the ridge. Shifting winds and changing water levels of the lake made these easily portable houses most advantageous. Mayfield saw the Indians simply roll up their light houses, load them on tule rafts and relocate in a few hours. Sometimes a tule mat was laid over a light frame of driftwood for a shade. Mats had unending functions.

Mayfield remembered something of the construction of the mats themselves. Tules were laid out on the ground parallel and close to each other and a milkweed string passed through them. Holes were punched in the tules with a bone awl. Other mats were made by tying the tules that had been laid out on the ground with other tules. A series of half hitches began every foot or so along the length of the stalks and went across the tules to bind them together.

Gayton recorded detailed techniques on making the tule mat from the central foothills Yokuts. They employed the huge triangular tule to make

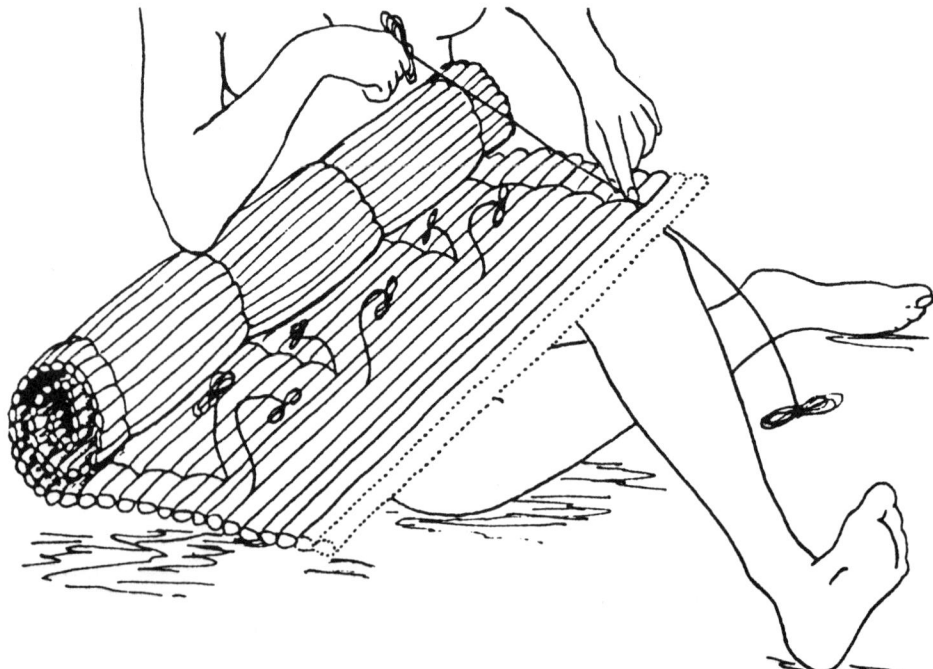

"Wukchumni method of twining small mats. Left hand about to press down on tightened wrapping, freeing right hand which will place next two tules (dotted in position) and pull under string up over them" (Gayton, 1948).

mats to cover their frame houses. The reeds were laid out side by side, the stem ends alternating, in the desired size and shape of the finished mat. Beginning at the left-hand corner nearest her, the mat-maker placed her right foot across the first few reeds. Kneeling on her left knee, she sewed through each stem with string of Indian hemp in a deer-bone needle. The needle was held more or less passively in the left hand as her right hand forced the tules onto it, according to seventy-year-old Mollie Lawrence, a Wukchumni Yokuts woman interviewed by Gayton fifty years ago. The sewer had to move out onto the mat itself as work progressed across it. She started back in the opposite direction at the next row, about 1 foot below the first.

Sleeping and floor mats as well as those for babies' mattresses, casings for feather ornaments or any household use (women invariably sat on them when working outdoors) were twined of the smaller round tules. Flat tules (cattails) were rarely used for mats.

Mollie Lawrence related that the mat-maker sat in the position favored by Yokuts women—the left leg forward with the knee slightly raised and the right leg doubled at the knee and under the left thigh. For a small mat two tules were tied together in four places, more or less in the center of four long strands of string. This formed the beginning of the warp and weft to which two tules at a time were added and the weft twined around them, beginning at the left and working away from the body, rolling the mat up in their lap as they progressed.

The string that passed under the next pair was twined, pulled back tight with the right hand, and held in place with the left index finger. At this point the right hand added another pair of tules. These were held in place by the second and third fingers of the left hand. The dangling lower string (beneath the added pair of tules) was now twined and brought up with the right hand and again held in place with pressure of the left index finger. Some six to ten tules were done in this way in the first row, at which point a single knot was tied to secure them. The procedure of the first row repeated in the three remaining rows, then returned to the first row and continued in that manner until the mat was completed.

Tachi Yokuts dancer and shaman Bob Bautista lived in a tule-mat house near the shores of Lake Tulare when J. P. Harrington befriended him in 1914. Bautista described and Harrington viewed the multifunctional tule mats still used by the Tachi. Tule, round or flat (cattail), was twined into various-size mats for the slanting walls of willow A-frame houses, for the floors of the houses, or for sleeping.

A sleeping mat was twined with string around pairs of round tule. (In another context, much later but with the same group of Yokuts, Harrington in his notes referred to a usual three or four tules per bundle for a mat.) It had seventeen rows of twining,

Close-up of Yokuts tule mat. Main section of mat twined from the braided piece to the other side; selvage likely twined from other side to the braided strip as shown. Ends of tules from each small bundle have been bent over diagonally and twined with the next group to give an even, closed finish to edge of mat. These bent-over ends are all found on the photographed face of the mat, presumably the underside; the opposite face would have been more presentable and most probably exposed in actual use (as displayed in the sleeping mat of the following photograph). Photographed by J.P. Harrington, circa November 1916–September 1917 (Smithsonian Institution National Anthropological Archives).

going from 6 inches apart at one end to 2 inches at the other. Apparently this was the end of greatest wear since it was specified that one end was for the head. The extremities of the tules themselves were simply cut, no special finishing mentioned. Both sides, however, were bordered by braided tules that were twined with the rest of the tule warps.

A three-ply braid of fine tules bordered the well-finished mat. The braids in effect became the first and last warps of tules. The loose ends could be finished by further twining as we see in an old Harrington photograph. In this detail of a Yokuts sleeping mat, a cord was twined as selvage along the edge; the last 1 or 2 inches of each small bundle of warp tules had been bent over diagonally and twined by the cord with the following group or warp. The ends of the doubled-over tules were laid on only one face of the mat (the back or bottom), leaving the opposite face more presentable. This was indeed the surface displayed, along with its maker, in another Harrington photograph.

Harrington described a sleeping mat of flat tules, or cattail, as 6-1/2 feet long by 4-1/2 feet broad with 16 rows of string, four tules twined in each bundle. A twined string row was 1 inch from one end. Tules at this end were merely cut with no further finishing. At the other end the tules were bent over about 1 inch at a diagonal, all on the same face of the mat, and twined with string about 1/4 of an inch from that end. Both side edges of this sleeping mat had three-ply-braided tule the whole length of the mat.

Some wall mats also had braided tule sides and others did not. They, too, could be of round or flat tules. The rows of twining were about 1 foot apart. A particular mat on Bautista's A-shaped pole-framed house had rows of twining 10 inches apart, three cattail leaves per twined bunch; it was 9 feet broad. Mats were always put on the wall frames vertically so that the tules were on end. Harrington noted that another mat, tied to the 11-foot ridge pole and hanging on the middle of the south side, was 8 feet square and twined with rows of tule 6 inches apart. In contrast, a floor mat of the house was a mere 4-1/2 feet by 3 feet.

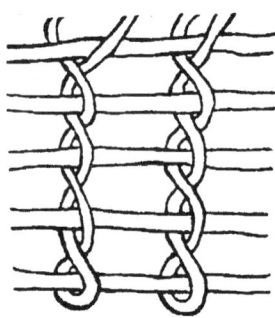

Sketch of twining for tule mat.

Yokuts lady in front of sleeping mat leaned against house. The principles described in Harrington's notes on the Tachi Yokuts of a few years earlier are here perfectly exemplified. Especially interesting is the ever-decreasing space between rows of twining from one end to the other (the top was presumably the head end of the mat). The fine finish of the uppermost ends of tule can also be seen, the last row of twining or selvage essentially reaching the top edge. Notice the braided sides of the mat. Photograph, J. P. Harrington, circa November 1916-September 1917 (Smithsonian Institution National Anthropological Archives).

Carrying Nets

From the Paipai of Baja to the Central Valley Yokuts, the carrying net was a basic survival tool of the Californias. The desert Koso and other Shoshonean bands of the Great Basin knew it as well. Described in A. Kroeber's handbook as a "small hammock of large mesh, gathered at the ends on loops which can be brought together by a heavy cord," the net functioned, in effect, as an extremely efficient backpack supported by a tumpline across the forehead. In a slightly different version, found farther north among the Pomo and Yuki, the ends of the netting itself continued into a headband, a feature that precluded adjustment to the load by means of end loops and cord as in the south.

Barrows found that the Cahuilla made carrying nets (called *to-ko*) for supporting burdens on the back from agave fiber or the bark of reed *(Phragmites communis)*. The stems of the reed were soaked in water and the bark easily removed—"a layer of soft, silky, yellowish brown fibers" that were twisted into a strong, beautiful cordage. An old woman could carry a stone mortar weighing 150 pounds in a carrying net, wrote Barrows. It was hung suspended from the forehead by a thick band. As a cradle or baby hammock the Cahuilla preferred a carrying net to a cradle board. The net and its baby within often swung from the corners of a ramada. Kroeber noted the meshes of the Cahuilla net measured from 3 to 5 inches.

Fragments of what may have been small Chumash carrying nets were recovered from caves of the Cuyama area and are now found in the Santa Barbara Museum of Natural History. They are of two-ply S-twist yucca *(Yucca whipplei)*. The strands of one measure about 1.5 mm. in diameter with meshes of 1.5 cm. Another has strands of 3 mm. and mesh spacing of 4 cm.

J. P. Harrington's Chumash informants said that a carrying net was of *tok* (Indian hemp) and looked like a miniature hammock. It was borne across the shoulders with a tumpline or tied around the waist. Many things could be carried in it: game, plant products, even a burden basket. When full, a slender stick a foot or less in length woven through the meshes of the two edges closed the net. A string was used the same way. In the early years of the twentieth century Fernando Librado Kitsepawit told Harrington that the loops or ears at either end permitted adjustment to suit the load while the length of the forehead band was not altered. The net was no trouble to carry empty yet convenient if one needed to transport something. The Tulareños (Yokuts) of the Great Central Valley brought trade products to the coastal Chumash using such nets just as the Eastern Mono of the Great Basin deserts used them to transport trade goods to the Western Mono and Yokuts over the Sierra Nevada Mountains. Father Geronimo Boscana (a Franciscan missionary serving the Juaneño, Luiseño and Gabrielino neophytes at San Juan Capistrano Mission from 1812 to 1826) wrote that old men spent a part of each day making nets of various sizes for heavy loads, utensils and babies.

Nets are neither stitched nor woven but are knotted, and Californians knew a number of netting knots. The most common may have been the sheet bend or mesh knot—a universally preferred manner of constructing nets. It was used by the northwestern California Indians in their iris-fiber fishing nets as well as by groups farther south. A fragment of a carrying net found in the 1940s on the Hummingbird Ranch in Ventura County, likely of Chumash origin, exhibits this knot as did the fragments from caves of the Cuyama area (Hudson and Blackburn, 1982). A complete Luiseño carrying net of large-

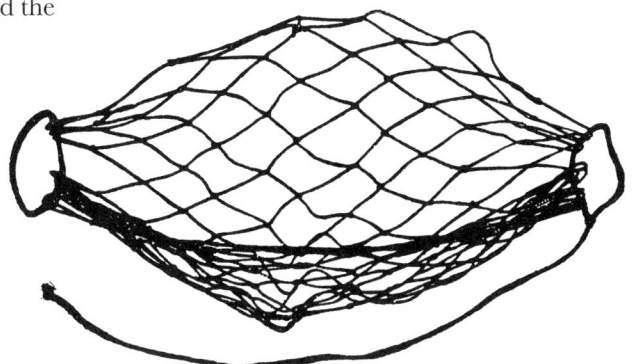

Cahuilla carrying net (Kroeber, 1925).

gauge meshes and constructed of sheet bend knots is on permanent display at the Southwest Museum in Los Angeles. The three explanations of California carrying net construction that follow (from the Southern Diegueño at Campo, California, the Kuatl lineage in Baja and the Central Valley Yokuts) reveal additional netting knots of Native California.

Construction of the Carrying Net at Campo, California

Old Jim McCarty, a Southern Diegueño Indian who lived in Campo during his last years, told Spier how to make a carrying net. The completed net of lozenge-shaped meshes was nearly 5 feet in length, at least as wide when stretched out, and fabricated from a single continuous cord of two-ply mescal *(Agave deserti)* around 28 yards long. The two braided end loops and tie string required an additional 20 yards or more of cordage. Spier believed that making the mescal cord alone took about a day (I would imagine longer). It required pounding the dry mescal leaves on a rock until the fibers were free of connective tissue, soaking to soften them and rolling small bundles of the clean fiber on the thigh where sticky mescal juice had been smeared to bind the cordage.

The first braided end loop was 6 inches in diameter and formed by doubling a cord of appropriate length back on itself six times and braiding the resulting strands in pairs. This should have left two loose ends to join the braided cord into a loop (refer to Spier's diagram, A). A completed tie string was 5 feet plus 20 inches. The approximately 20 inches, turned back and tied on itself, would become the second end loop. All of this had been braided in the same manner as the first loop (three pairs of strands) from the remainder of the 20-yard section.

The easy part was constructing the net. One end of the long cord was tied around the first braided loop in a slip knot (B in Spier's diagram). The cord returned to the loop, left to right, making more slip knots for a total of about nine. All of the meshes of the net, when fully extended, would be 7 inches long and created of 3-1/2-inch loops (meaning that each initial *loop* should be 3-1/2 inches in length, a doubled 7-inch piece). No gauge was used other than the estimate of the eye. (The Chumash measured them with the index finger or a stick of the desired length.)

At the end of nine, and for each succeeding row as well, the net was turned over (C) so that work would always proceed from left to right. The meshes were tied in a kind of crossover square knot resembling at once the sheet shank of groups to the north and the square knot typical for groups to the south. The cord passed first to the right (instead of the left as in the square knot) when entering the loop from the front, which had the effect of twisting (and thereby closing) the mesh. The long continuous cord ended on the same side it began (after about 18 rows) where it was tied in a secure square knot.

The braided tie string was threaded through the final row of meshes and tied in a loop similar to the first. Though Spier does not mention it, undoubt-

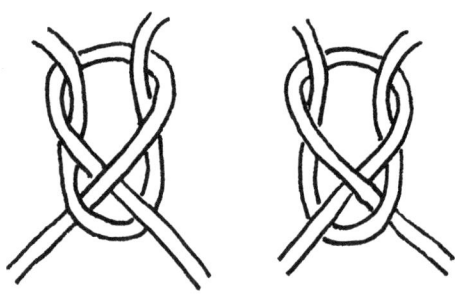

The sheet-bend knot—made from left to right. The knot on the right has been drawn from a northwest California iris-fiber net found in Kroeber and Barret 1960.

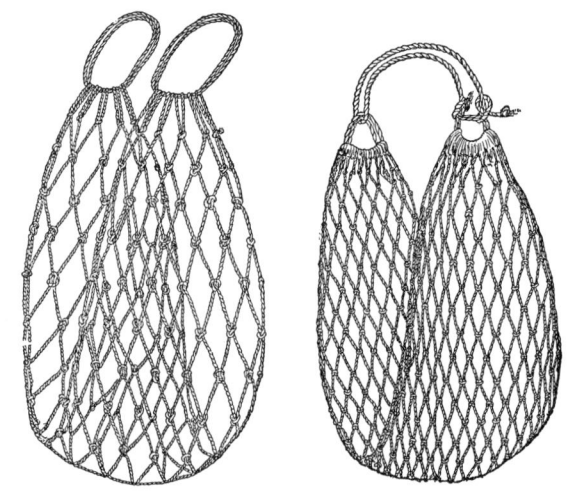

Carrying nets of southern California. First from Temecula of agave cord tied with mesh or sheet-bend knots. Second, said to have been used by the "Mission" Indians, is indistinguishable from net made by Manuela Aguiar in the Sierra Juárez mountains of Lower California in 1994 (James, 1909).

edly the first end loop was untied and removed. The slip knots of the first row of meshes were pulled out, and the end loop reinserted through these meshes and retied. This would allow the meshes to slip freely about the loop as on the opposite end.

In use they passed the tie string that dangled from the second end loop through the first loop and back to the second loop where it was tied. When toting a big load, the tie string often threaded through several meshes on both edges of the net to draw the edges together. Generally, the load rested on the small of the back and the tie string crossed the forepart of the top of the head, which they protected by wearing a basketry cap.

Construction of the Carrying Net—Rancho Escondido, Lower California

Manuela Aguiar learned how to make carrying nets as a girl from her grandmother who was of Kuatl lineage, the southernmost Southern Diegueño. She showed me how these versatile backpacks literally arose out of the desert floor as she gathered the short broad desert agave leaves *(Agave deserti)* found in abundance around her remote Baja ranchería. She baked and peeled them, pounded out the fiber with a stone mano, rolled cordage on her thigh, and wound the cordage into balls. From these she wove the net itself. In principle, it was the same as that described for Campo, California, farther north and 100 years earlier, but in detail there were differences.

Aguiar made a fairly heavy cordage (3/16 of an inch in diameter) but the meshes were small (2-

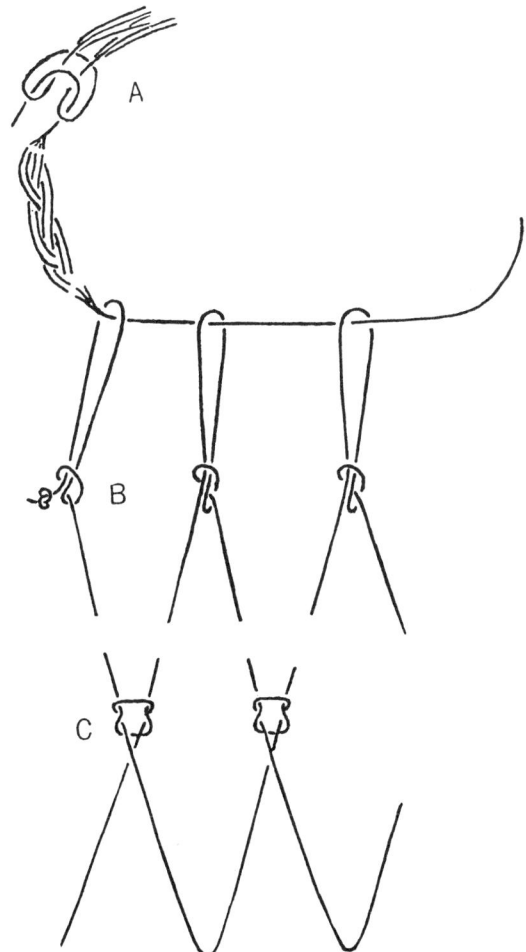

Diagrammatic sketch of carrying-net knots, Campo: A) knot of six-strand loop; B) knot of first row of meshes; C) knot of second and subsequent rows; second row has been reversed since loops are always made from left to right (Spier, 1923).

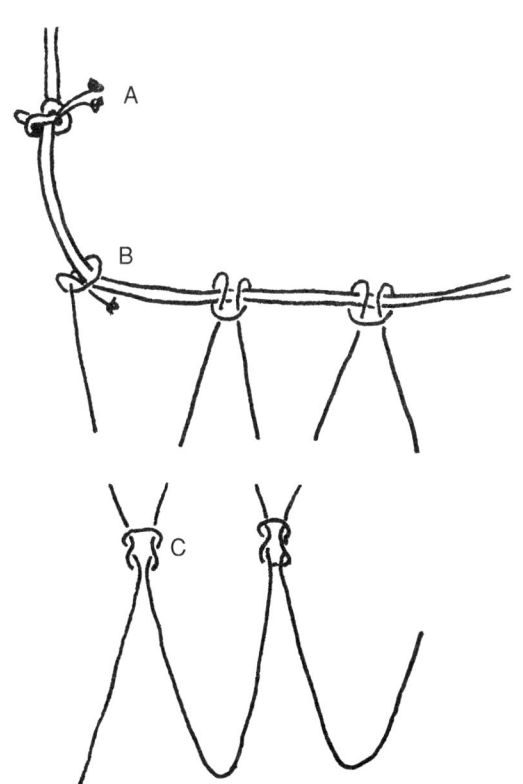

Diagrammatic sketch of carrying-net knots, Rancho Escondido: A) doubled cord joined into loop; B) beginning knot and temporary knots of first meshes; C) square knots used on second and all subsequent rows of loops; for the second row the net has been reversed since the loops are always done from left to right.

1/2 inches from end to end). The finished net measured approximately 3 feet in length, not including the two end loops, and almost 4 feet in width when fully extended. This was a perfect size for a modest load. With an extra cord woven in and out through the border meshes of one side (kept separated and across from the other), through an end loop and continued through the meshes of the opposite side and the second end loop, and back to its beginning where it was tied, she demonstrated how the net could be drawn tighter or constricted and adapted to small or large loads. The addition of a few zigzag weaves using still another cord from the border meshes of one side across to the other, secured even very large loads. It was a tough durable pack.

Here is how she made it. A two-ply cord tied in a circle and passed over any convenient pole, post or limb would be the temporary base loop of the net. A long cord with an overhand knot already at the end (and formed in a ball) was secured to the base loop with another simple overhand knot. Initial loops were tied left to right. These small loops were 1-1/4 inches long, one half the length of the desired size of the mesh, which, in this case, was 2-1/2 inches (note that the loops were 1-1/4 inches with the cord doubled and stretched taut). A lark's-head knot, a loop knot formed from two half hitches (see

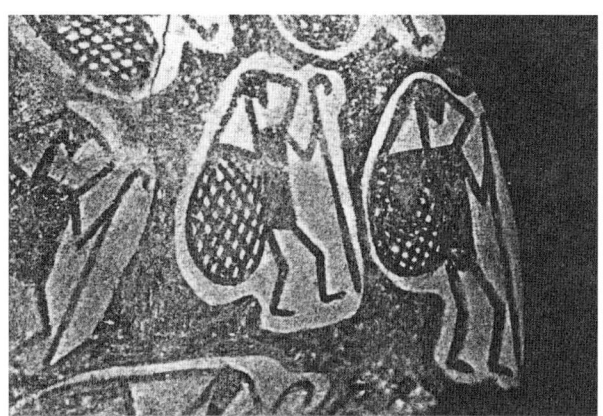

Detail from thousand-year-old Hohokam bowl, collection of Bruce Bryan (von Winning, 1974).

Manuela Aguiar and son Raúl with carrying net, 1994.

Above, Teresa Castro totes trunks of Mojave yucca to pottery kiln in large-mesh agave-cordage net, Santa Catarina, 1997. Notice that the net cradles the load not from side to side, the usual method, but from back to front, leaving the sides open. This is achieved by elongating each end loop into a tumpline; both are also widened where they rest on the front of the crown by two long braids of agave fiber; each cord simply passes back and forth through its separate braid every few inches. Such a net configuration is especially suited to the transport of long pieces of wood. Right, Manuela Aguiar makes a small net.

diagram), held them to the base loop for a total of twenty. Fingers of the left hand, palm up, were inserted into the loops as completed, the last two loops being held open and to size with the index and middle finger respectively while the ring finger provided a convenient post to guide the size of the loop under construction. This use of the fingers continued for all loops of the net.

After the first row was complete, the base loop was taken off and turned over on the post so that the making of the mesh always proceeded from left to right as in the Campo example. All subsequent mesh loops were tied with simple square knots (as shown), unlike the Campo reverse form that twisted the mesh. Once the left side of a knot had been adjusted to the proper mesh size, Manuela secured it between thumb and forefinger of her left hand, then finished and tightened the knot with her right hand.

When complete, Manuela's net measured twenty-seven rows of loops. The base loop was

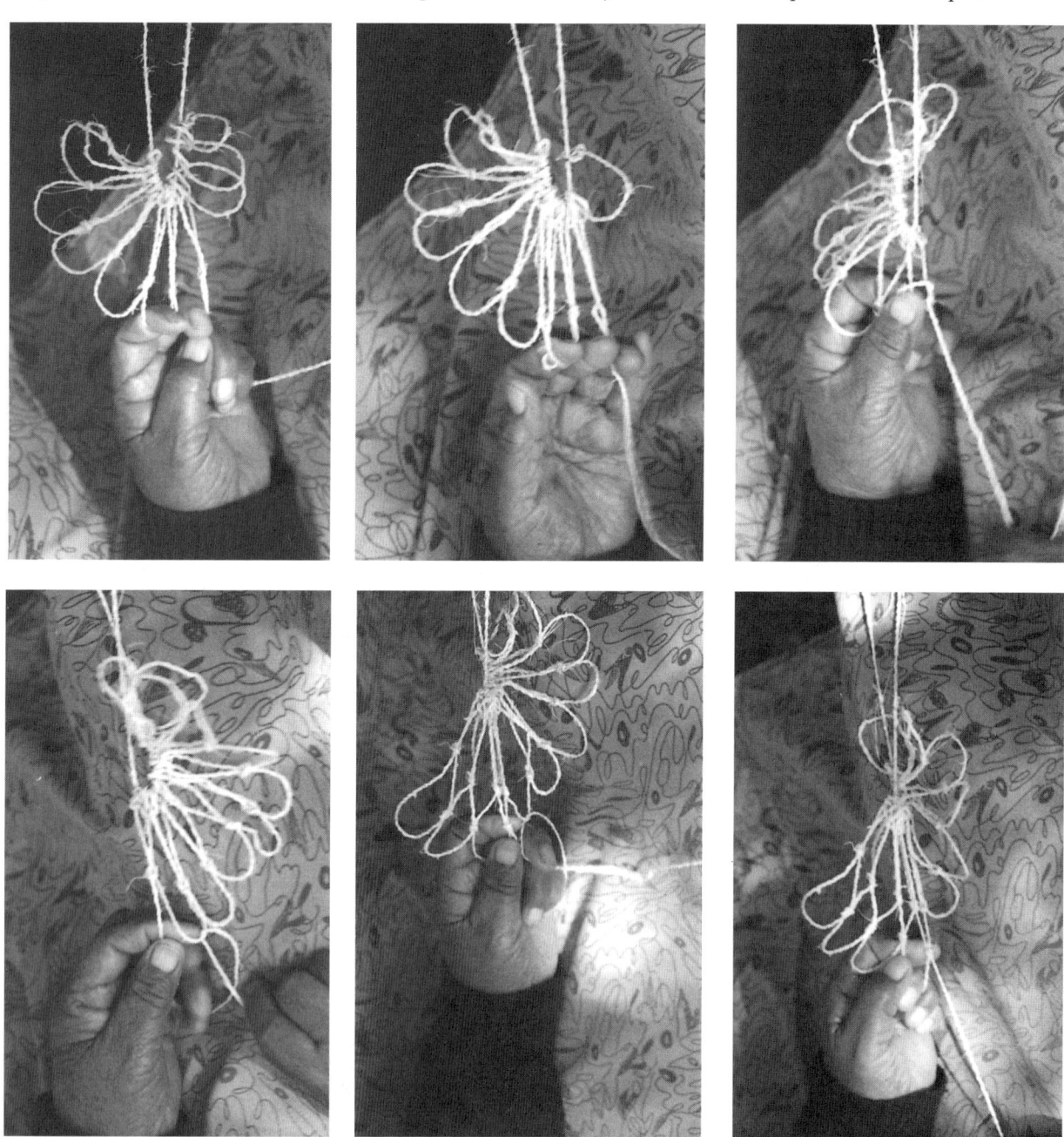

Manuela Aguiar knots a small net. Fingers of left hand gauge meshes as she ties square knots with her right from the long loose end of an agave-fiber cord. Notice that when she finishes last knot of last mesh in a row (photo upper right), the net is simply reversed (bottom left) to continue the same left-to-right pattern of knot tying.

removed, releasing the initial knots, which made the first row of meshes a little longer than the others. The base loop was doubled and reinserted in the now freed meshes and retied in a 2-inch-diameter double loop. Another doubled cord was circled through the last row of loops in the same way. Then the two free ends of a third doubled cord, almost 3-1/2 feet long when doubled, were passed through a base loop then back through itself (the loop formed by its other end) and drawn tight. The two free ends were tied as one to the other base or end loop. This doubled cord became the carrying strap. Manuela's son Raúl demonstrated the net in use, the strap slung just above the visor of a baseball-style cap, the load falling approximately in the small of the back.

Aguiar said nets of any size could be made in this way. Smaller nets with 3/32-inch-diameter cord, nineteen loops wide and ten loops, or five meshes long (each mesh about 3 inches, total length 16 inches) were formed into bags by inserting a single cord through the initial freed loops, drawing it closed, and tightly tying it off. It was then turned inside out.

Onto this cord another single cord was secured and spiraled once or twice around two loops, one from each open side of the net, bringing them together. It continued to spiral in the same way through the side loops to what had been the bottom of the net (while in construction) but was now the mouth of a net bag. (Note: for the first of these spirals the mesh from one side was actually lapped a little over the other, beginning with three meshes of lap, then two, then one, and then no lapping as they approached the mouth. This made the bag somewhat tighter at the bottom with the extra or overlapping meshes remaining on the inside of the bag.) The cord finally made a knot joining the loops from both sides of the mouth where the last knot of the mesh had been tied.

Just above this the ends of a doubled cord were inserted through both side loops, back through the loop of the doubled cord, and pulled tight. The two loose strands were carried together through two loops of the opposite side, turned back and secured on themselves with a couple of half hitches. (The ends of the cord had already been formed into little overhand knots to prevent slippage.) This made a sturdy handle that measured about 8 inches long between the knots at either end.

A single drawstring passing through all the loops of the mouth, with the two ends of the drawstring tied tightly together, would be pulled to close the bag when in use. One way they employed the bag was to clean the spines from prickly-pear-cactus fruit. Aguiar's brother, Celso, showed me how to pick the fruit safely with short tongs of a doubled section of yucca leaf. After a bunch had been collected in the agave bag, he closed the bag with the drawstring. The

Detail of lower, gathered edge of agave fiber net fragment found in burial cave by Dr. Edward Palmer at Bahía de Los Angeles, Lower California, 1887 (Massey and Osborne, 1961).

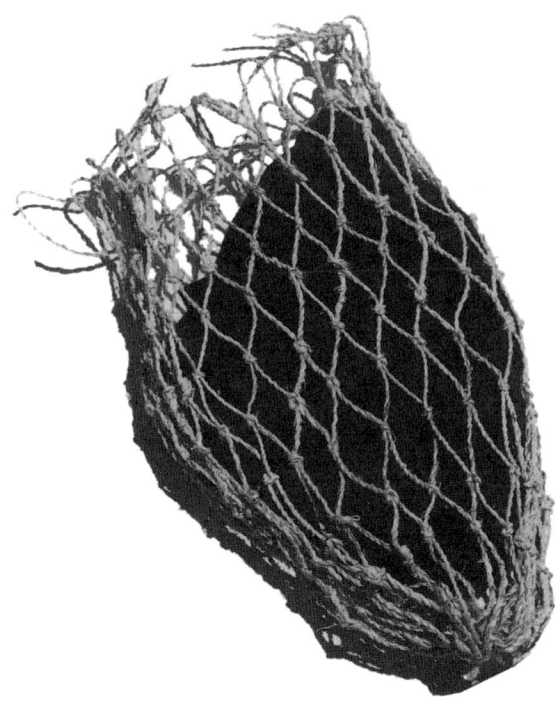

Manuela Aguiar's small agave-fiber net for cleaning cactus fruit, Rancho Escondido, Lower California, 1993.

ends of the bag were then held one in each hand and it was shaken parallel to the ground, toward one end of the bag then the other, back and forth, rapidly. The fruit emerged clean, the hundreds of fine, and not so fine, spines gone and no longer a danger.

Once grasped, the basic idea of netting finds many tasks. Vast nets for communal rabbit drives are well known but smaller nets also functioned as traps. The carrying net as a rabbit trap seems to be suggested by what the Diegueño Indians at La Huerta told Meigs in 1939. They described sack-size mescal nets for catching jackrabbits. Two sticks held the net up and made an opening in the front end. A little brush fence led up to it on both sides. The jackrabbit was driven in and a man next to the net killed it. Perhaps a specialized net was used but a carrying net would have worked.

The Diegueño of the Campo, California, region also employed nets the size of carrying nets to catch rabbits. They placed several over the runways. Cords passing through the meshes acted as drawstrings, the ends of which were entwined in bushes. If there were many hunters they drove the rabbits into these "purse nets." If only a few, they set fire to the brush to drive the rabbits into them.

The Yokuts Carrying Net

The Yokuts of the central foothills of the Sierra Nevada made strong carrying nets from Indian hemp or fine milkweed. They employed a simple overhand knot and a deft adjustment of size and number of meshes. The Waksachi Western Mono made them the same way. Mary Pohot, a Wukchumni Yokuts, demonstrated the manufacture of these nets to Gayton many years ago.

First, she wound a cord around her left hand four or five times and tied the ends together. This ring, about 4 inches in diameter, was fixed to any convenient spot, a ramada post or tree, at shoulder height.

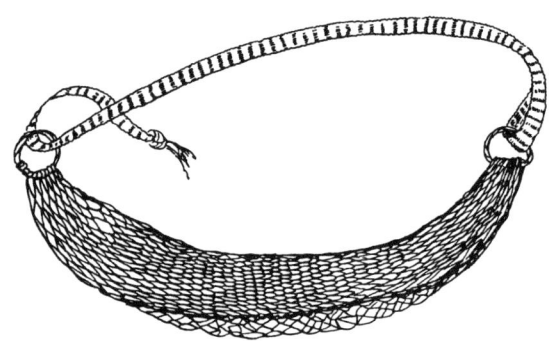

Carrying net and tumpline (Gayton, 1948).

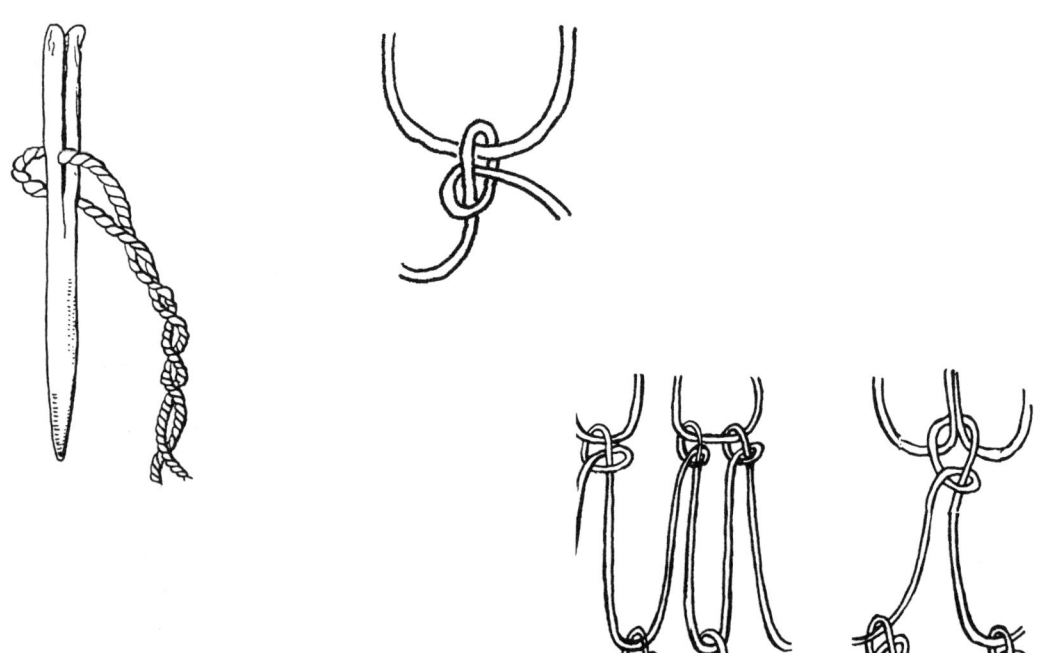

Split-end wooden needle (Gayton, 1948). Yokuts carrying-net knot. Increasing and decreasing the number of meshes (Gayton, 1948).

Twines of the netting itself were four-ply. The center of a length of two-ply string was wedged into the split end of a wooden needle and the two dangling ends rolled on her thigh into a single cord. The open end was secured to the ring with a few half hitches and the simple overhand knot of the netting begun (see illustration). Gayton found no particular rule regarding the direction in which the net-maker should start. The knot reversed, of course, from row to row. Some let the cord dangle as they worked, while some kept it coiled in the right hand. New cords were attached by knots.

Loops initially (and at the finish) were about 4 inches deep (8 inches between knottings). They quickly shortened toward the center of the net to about 1-1/2 inches deep. The only gauges were the fingers of the hand. As a knot was tightened, the fingers of the left hand spread along and adjusted the length of cord in the loop being formed.

Each knot was tied into the cord of the loop above. In order to compensate for the finer meshes after the initial long loops were made and to make the net capacious, two knots (an extra loop) were tied into some of the loops. Conversely, as the opposite end was reached, to offset the larger loops, occasionally one loop was tied into two of the preceding loops (this joined the loops).

The net made for Gayton had eighteen rows of loops and measured about 3 feet in length and 5 feet in width when pulled taut. A coil similar to that of the start was passed through the last row of loops and through the looped end of a tumpline.

Indian Tumpline

Yokuts women placed the tumpline across the upper forehead sometimes with a coiled cap for protection. (This was the only use of the coiled cap for Waksachi Western Mono women.) Yokuts men used the tumpline as a burden strap across the upper chest and deltoid muscles. It was they who generally made the strap and nets. (Both net and tumpline were made by women among the Waksachi Western Mono but were most used by the men.) The preferred material was Indian hemp or a fine grade of milkweed. They constructed the tumpline on the same principle as the Yokuts rabbit-skin blanket. Although it appeared woven or twined, the process was actually closer to sewing; a cord passed through parallel twists in a cordage warp.

Four two-ply cords, each approximately 12 to 15 feet long, were individually twisted and allowed to double on themselves into loosely twisted cords 6 feet long. The closed looped ends were wedged parallel to each other into the cleft of a split stick. Since each had been twisted with about the same tension, the sequential twists in the cords were more or less aligned.

The forefinger of the left hand poked through the loops and forced all of them open for about 4 inches below the stick. A cord attached to a split-stick needle was passed through the opening to its end and then returned by means of the needle through the first row of twists and back again through the next row, continuing in this fashion through adjacent turns in the cords as far as desired, generally about 3 feet. The weft, continually drawn tight, disappeared from view, except at the sides of the strap being formed.

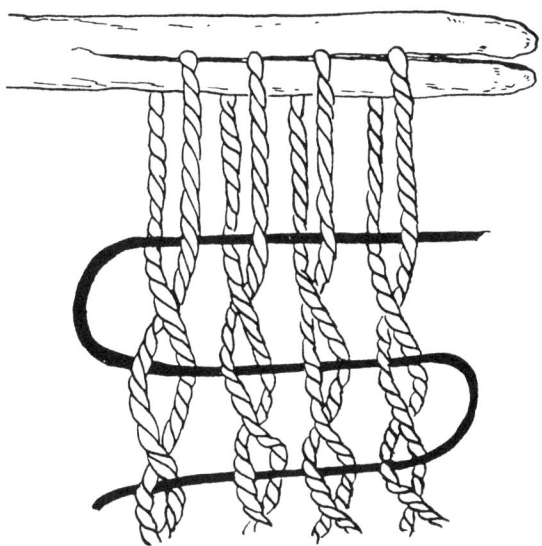

Tumpline beginning weave—enlarged and loosened to show technique (Gayton, 1948).

The 2 feet or so of warp cords that remained had been only loosely twisted and these were now separated out into eight two-ply strings. The weft was drawn through each of the original turns of these as it had been through the parallel twists of the four cords, making a finer continuation of the strap. After 6 or 8 inches, the weft cord was cut to the length of the remaining eight strings and drawn down alongside them to make nine strings. These were gathered in three bunches, braided into a single cord to the end, and tied off with a couple of knots.

At the other end of the strap a second weft cord was inserted through the parallel twists a few rows below the loops that had been formed with the forefinger, and worked back and forth until the loop cords themselves were reached. The weft, continuing on, then passed through the original parallel twists of the four two-ply loop cords (similar to the opposite end) until the loop had become solid and continuous with the strap. It would measure about 3/4 of an inch in width to the strap's 1-1/2 inch.

An end loop or ring of the carrying net passed through the strap loop while the other end of the strap passed through the other ring of the net where it was adjusted and tied. Though Gayton did not record it, the wider and finer section of the tumpline must have been sewn to coincide with a position on the upper forehead.

A belt that supported a breachclout for both men and women was essentially the same as the burden strap, except the initial loops were finally cut open and the cords grouped in threes and braided as at the opposite end. A fancy belt was of the finest milkweed cord and the weft carried a clamshell disk bead between each warp.

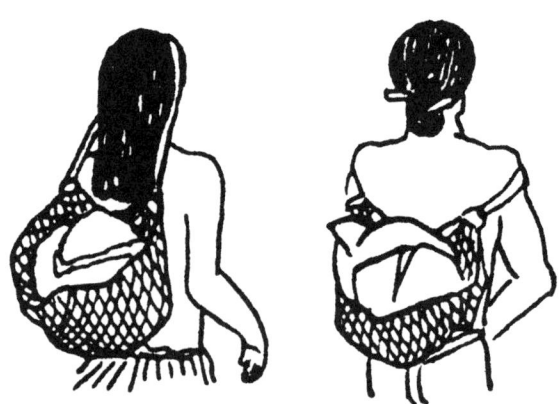

Uses of the tumpline (Gayton, 1948).

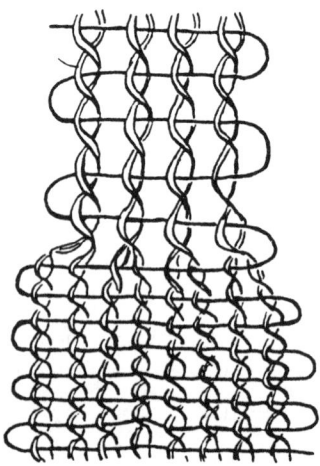

Change in weaving from four to eight parallel twists (Gayton, 1948).

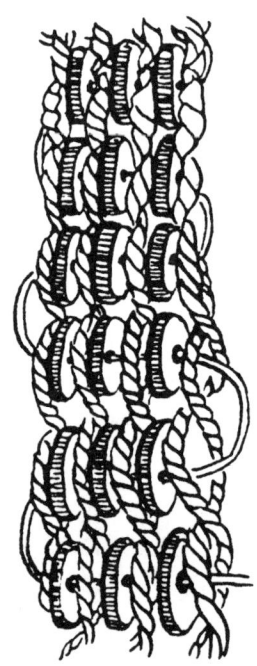

Manner of placing shell beads in fancy belt (Gayton, 1948).

California Survival Basket

This is a simple basket for gathering berries, cactus fruit, herbs, acorns, flowers or anything one might happen upon in the wild. Back at camp, it conveniently holds whatever goods have been collected. A large one can be twined in a few hours, a small one in minutes, and the basket can be fashioned any size or shape to suit the purpose. It comes from San José de la Zorra, a small Southern Diegueño ranchería scattered deep in the coastal range of northern Baja. Here, Celia Silva learned to make the basket from her grandmother, Petra Cuero Moreno, many years ago.

Celia's seven-month-old great granddaughter, nicknamed *Chaweé* (acorn mush), smiled and crawled for discarded basketry material as Celia selected eight long green stems of Mexican rush *(Juncus mexicanus)* she had gathered the day before. These were the same dried stems she employed for the foundation spiral of coiled baskets. Since she wanted to make a small twined basket, she cut the eight stems in half, stacked the sixteen pieces together in a bunch and placed the center of another single long juncus stem around its middle. "Any juncus green and flexible enough to twine could be used for this basket," said Celia, "even the thin withes of a flexible willow." Sometimes she split the juncus lengthwise but generally used it in whole sections.

She twisted two sides of the single encircling stem together 360 degrees, tightening it around the middle of the bundle. (Occasionally, instead of a single encircling wrap, the juncus weaver was circled twice around the bundle before twisting it 360 degrees.) Next she selected a warp stem to the right of the twist and bent it down between the two weavers, tight against the initial twist. She held the twist and bundle in her left hand and with her right she twisted the two loose weaver stems counterclockwise (looking to the right in the direction of the twining) 180 degrees around the first warp or spoke. She grasped this new twist with her left hand and pulled another spoke down between the weavers and tight against the twist. She brought the farthest weaver toward her enclosing the placed spoke. She pulled the weavers, and thus the twist, tight toward the center of the basket before completing the next twist. From this point on to produce each new twist, the weaver which was underneath or to the left was simply taken in the right hand, up over the other weaver and around the next spoke and back down toward the center of the basket where the two weavers were pulled tight. Both halves of all the stems of the bundle would become spokes of the basket for a total of thirty-two spokes. The twining (*shakwee*, sha•kweé) continued around the spokes in an expanding clockwise spiral. Care was always taken to encircle with the left weaver the next spoke and then pull the weavers and previous twist tightly toward the center of the basket before continuing the twining. This kept the spirals close.

As the twining weavers or weft ran out, and after a spoke had been placed and encircled, the leading ends of the old weavers were pulled to the center of the basket and left to be clipped off later. New weavers were added by inserting the sharp end of a juncus stem through the space beneath the previous spiral under the last completed twist. In other words, both the last completed twist and the previous spiral would be above the new weaver which was inserted and continued through the space to the center of the stem. This firmly anchored the new weaver. The two equal ends were then brought up and the twining proceeded over the last completed twist. (If weavers ran out before the first spiral had been completed, a new juncus stem was inserted in the space directly under the last twist of the first spiral.)

Additional spokes were not added as the twining spiral expanded. Instead, the space between them was simply allowed to increase. Beginning at about the seventh spiral, in place of a single twining twist between spokes, two twists were often made. However, sometimes just one long lazy twist would be used.

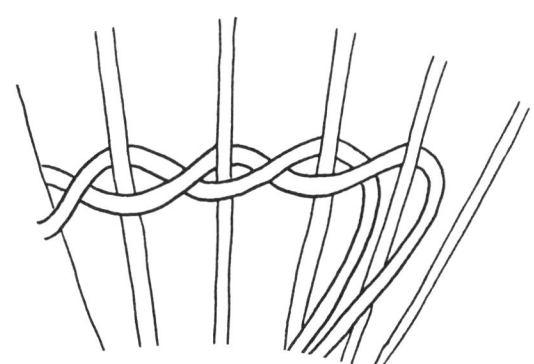

The twined stitch.

The sides of the basket were begun by a gradual bending inward of the spokes and tightening of the weave, work proceeding from the inside of the basket (spokes of larger baskets were bent outward and done from the outside). When the desired height had been reached, the twining simply ended and the spokes were clipped about 1/8 inch above the rim. The tail end of a length of juncus was tied in an overhand knot at some point around the top two rows or coils. With the sharp needle-like tip, a long clockwise spiral (which passed through the basket from the inside approximately every two spokes) was sewn in a clockwise direction around the top two rows of the rim. (In some larger baskets

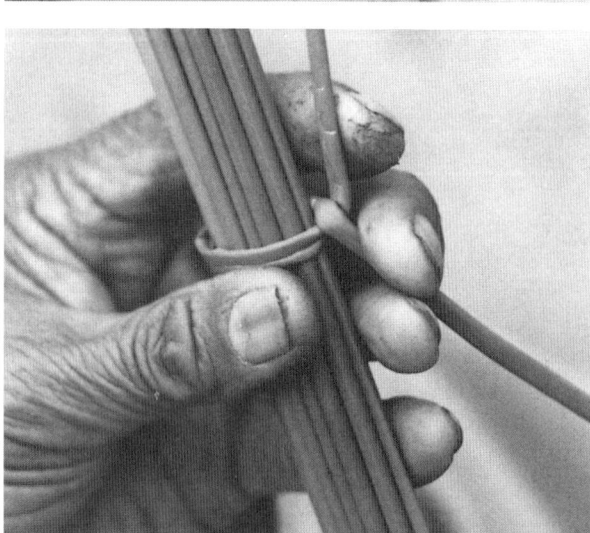

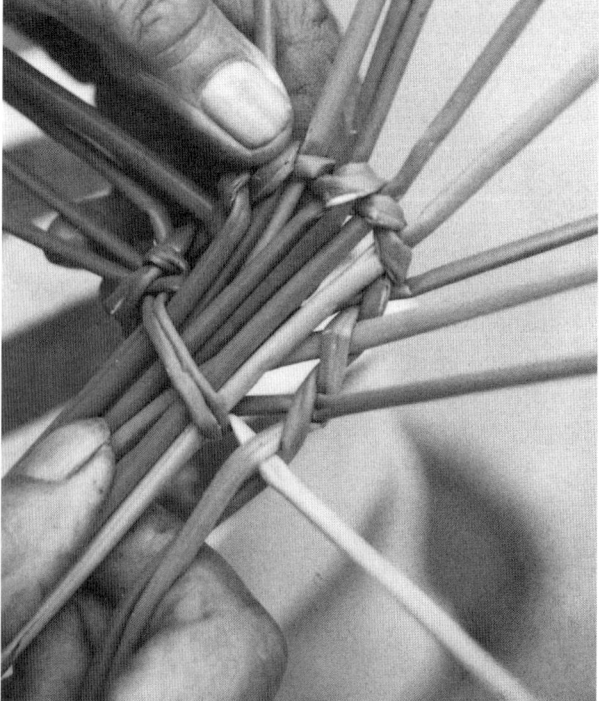

Celia Silva stands by green juncus gathered a day earlier. Beginning knot of the basket. Twining the first round.

Twining continues. A new weaver has been added (top left). Slight bending of the spokes inward, beginning the sides (top right). Inserting a new weaver (bottom left). Twining completed (bottom right).

Remainder of spokes have been clipped (top). Butt of juncus tied in overhand knot around two top coils. Needle tip of juncus spirals clockwise to secure rim.

the distance between spirals was a single spoke and the spiral enveloped the top three or even four rows.) This secured the rim.

At the point that the reinforcing rim coil had been tied, an optional handle was made by inserting a length of juncus beneath the second row from the top and doubling the juncus back on itself, then twisting it together and tying it over the last two or three rows on the opposite side and spiraling around the rim with any remainder.

Celia occasionally added a decorative rim to larger baskets. A weaver was anchored at its tail end: the tip was inserted from the outside between the fourth and fifth rows from the top, brought up, and the tail tied to itself around these rows in a single overhand knot. Working clockwise from the outside (counterclockwise when viewing into the basket) with the single long juncus stem, she entered the basket between every spoke, about three rows beneath the top coil. She made loops that extended over the rim almost 1/2 inch. Before proceeding on to each next loop, the juncus tip, penetrating from the outside through to the inside of the basket, went up in front of the loop just made, turned and entered the loop from the outside and, encircling the stem at that point, went on to form the next loop. To finish, the end of the juncus was simply stuck into the basket between the second and third rows from the top. There was probably no end to the permutations such a practical, adaptable basket might have undergone.

Above, decorative rim on one of Celia's baskets. Below, large twined basket, much used, made by Celia's mother, Vicenta Espinoza Cuero. Twenty-five or more juncus stems used in start. Note doubling and tripling of warps and doubling of finishing rim spiral for greater strength and stability.

Household Brushes

Along with tightly coiled sifting baskets, this simple, quickly made brush was still in use in early February of 1996 when I visited Celia Silva and her son Adolfo in the coastal mountain Kumeyaay (Southern Diegueño) settlement of San José de la Zorra. Adolfo showed me the stiff brush blackened at its tips from use around an old embellished cast iron stove purchased fifty years earlier from Russians who had settled in Valle de Guadalupe one hundred years ago. In the warmth the stove still provided, they demonstrated how the brush swept up particles of meal produced during the pounding and pulverizing of acorns in a mortar. The simple utilitarian brush could be used for almost anything.

Celia makes them from Mexican rush (*Juncus mexicanus*), the same dried juncus she uses in the spiral foundations of coiled baskets. I watched as she divided the juncus at one end with her fingernails and, placing one split side in her mouth, pulled the other section away with her left hand while grasping and guiding the main stem with her right. She completely split the stem lengthwise into two long halves. Each of these was again split and the quarter stems were grouped together. This bundle was then broken in two at the middle and combined into a thicker bundle half as high. She continued until she had a bunch which measured approximately 1 inch in diameter and 17 inches long. She next took a green juncus stem and wrapped it two or more times around the center of the bundle and tied it tightly with a square knot. She dampened the center of the bundle.

She now began to draw down the peripheral stems from one end, doubling them one or two at a time, over onto the other end. She began from the outside, working around the circumference and toward the center of the bundle. When all the stems had been folded back and pulled down snug, she

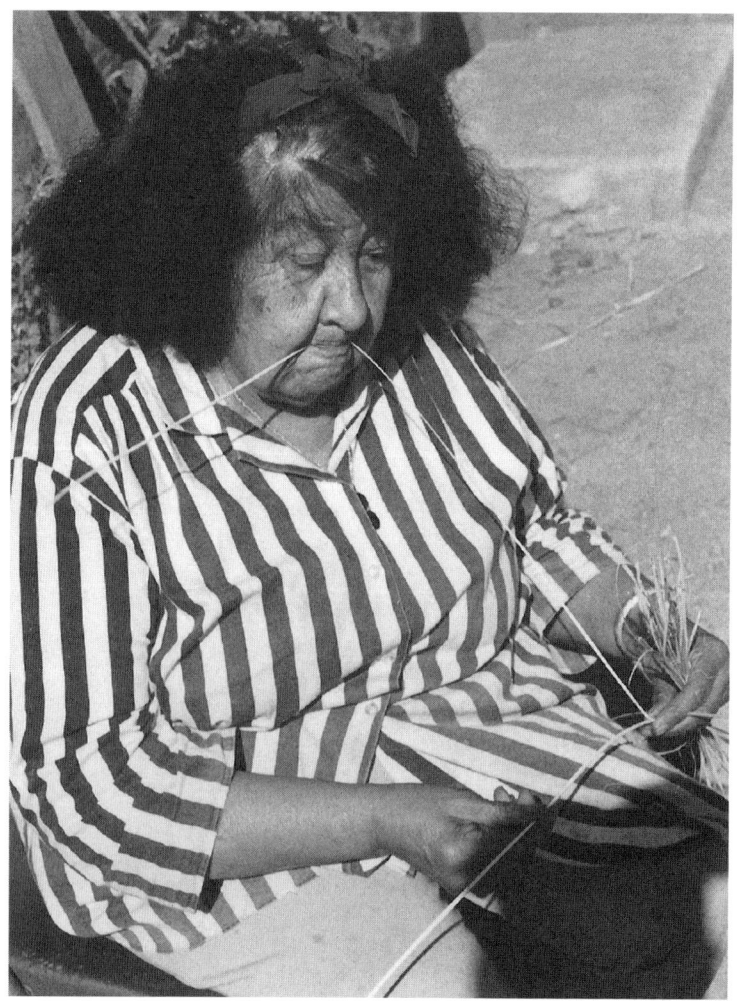

Celia Silva splits a juncus stem.

wrapped another green juncus stem, about 1-3/4 inches from the top, around the brush two to six times and tied it off with a square knot. She repeated this with another stem about 4 inches from the top. She snipped off dangling ends and trimmed the bristles even. It was ready for use. The Paipai make the same style brush of desert agave fiber.

The Northern Paiute made a similar brush of Great Basin wild rye roots that they gathered in winter when the plant was dormant. Long durable roots were selected from an overturned clump. They were cleaned and soaked in water for a few hours. This loosened the outer covering which they then scraped off with a knife or sharp stone. The roots were arranged in a bunch and tied in the middle with many windings of Indian hemp cord. The bundle was doubled over at the middle, altogether and at once, and the bristles were bound a few inches down with many windings of Indian hemp cord. Uneven ends of the brush were trimmed. It was now ready to clean pine nut meal from the grinding rocks, remove ashes from the cooking stones or comb the long black hair of Indian girls.

Paipai Cándido Cañedo made a cleaning brush (*cheeoot*) from the stem of an old Mohave yucca. A 6- or 7-inch longitudinal section of the fibrous inner trunk was cut—perhaps 1-1/2 inches across—and trimmed. The fibers at one end were then simply pulled open a bit or freed to make the brush. A flexible twig of *rama santa (Eriodictyon sp.)*, called *e'káy* in Paipai, was sharpened on either end and bent into a circle; the two points penetrated from opposite sides and overlapped within the top portion of the brush to form a handle (as one might find on a pail). By this they hung the brush when not in use.

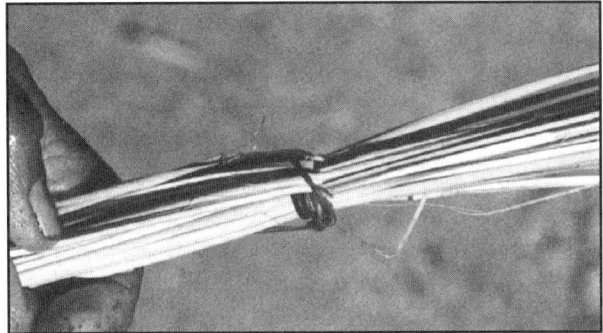

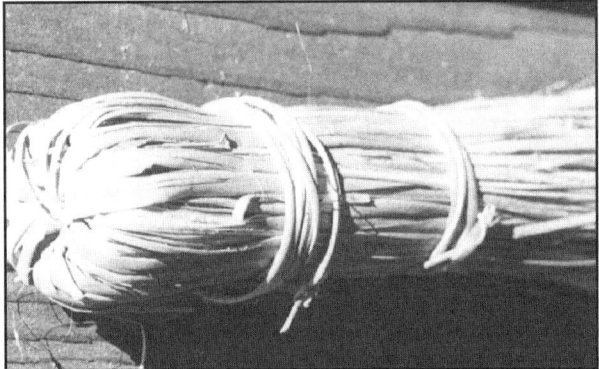

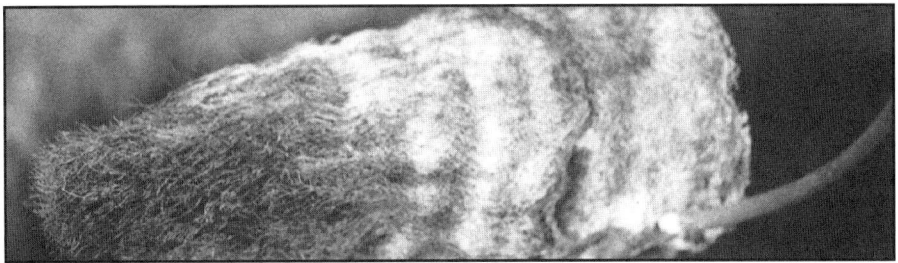

(From top) Silva bends split juncus stems over the center wrap to form the brush. Foreshortened view of brush. Split juncus brush, almost 8" long, 1-1/2" wide. Cándido Cañedo's brush from trunk of Mohave yucca.

A Strange Baja Basket

Otis Tufton Mason in his massive turn of the century study, *American Indian Basketry*, divided coiled baskets into ten structural types. The last, to which he devoted scarcely a page, was called *Fuegian*, characterized by a slight foundation of one or more rushes with the sewing in a buttonhole stitch, essentially a series of interlocking half hitches around a foundation coil. Striking resemblance to Asiatic examples on the Pacific was noted. Throughout the Americas interlocking stitches form carrying bags or nets but are generally without the foundation seen in a net of coiled work belonging to an Araucanian woman from South America (in Mason, from Simon de Schryver, 1887). At the very extremity of South America, however, where American Indian basketry reaches its southern limit, *baskets* in the buttonhole technique of coiled work with foundation are well known (thus the name of the type).

Araucanian carrying net and detail (Mason, 1904).

In leafing through Mason's tome I stopped at the page that depicted the Fugian coiled basket from the Strait of Magellan. I had seen that basket before but could not place it. Then I remembered. Manuela Aguiar had sold one to me a year earlier. Just another egg basket but with a sort of weird stitch, I had said to myself, not interested in the basket and preoccupied with agave-fiber sandals she was making at her remote ranchería in the Sierra Juárez mountains of Lower California. Of Kuatl (Southern Diegueño) descent, Manuela knows all of the old ways: this fascinating lady still makes arrow straighteners of soapstone which she learned from her grandfather 70 years ago. But I had returned to Los Angeles completely ignorant of how she might have come to craft a Fuegian coiled basket in the wilds of Baja. She had tried to show me, but as usual I had my own agenda and did not listen. I only knew it was made from palm and she had been speculating where she might obtain more palm leaves. "Go to the desert canyons," I had told her

Left: Yahgan tawe'la basket (Mason, 1904). Right: Manuela Aguiar's basket. Essentially the same as the Yahgan tawe'la basket except the material is palm and the coiling and weave are done right to left.

glibly. Now, I wanted to know more of this strange basket that appeared nearly identical to one from the bottom of the Americas.

The Yahgan Tawe'la Basket

Samuel Lothrop described the Yahgan as "the southernmost people in the world." Each family maintained itself moving about in a fragile bark canoe, finding shelter on favorable stretches of beach along the southern shores of Tierra del Fuego from Brecknock Peninsula to Cape Horn. They lived from the sea and the beaches and never camped where they knew someone had died. The most common basket of the Yahgan was of a native grass *(Juncus magellanicus)*, made in a half hitch or buttonhole stitch about a coiled foundation. They called it *Tawe'la*.

Three or four stems of grass bent into a small circle, 1/2 inch in diameter, started the basket. They were lashed in place by a series of half hitches that continued onto the projecting tangential stems in a spiraling circle. The second series of half hitches were inserted through the loops of the first row with help from an awl. The process continued as a circular base piece gave way to the curve of the sides. A spiral wrap finished the top edge.

Lothrop pointed out that coiled basketry is the most widely distributed and most ancient variety known in the New World. It occurred almost without break throughout western North and South America. The isolated, traditional Yahgan would be expected to retain a variety of such an ancient form. The Fuegian stitch itself, however, is not common elsewhere in the Americas. It is found among the Yahgan, Ona and Alacaluf and sometimes in the Amazon Valley and north. Lothrop mentions a Surinam hat in this weave.

"One of the most interesting specimens of basketry found in America," Mason called a coiled sifter uncovered among the relics of the ancient basketmakers in a southeastern Utah cave and described in a 1902 paper by George Pepper. The outer rows of coiling belonged to the single stick variety, but the openwork main portion, in which each stitch made a whole turn on itself, Mason felt was essentially the same in structure as the coiled basket from the Strait of Magellan.

We can only speculate how widespread the style might once have been or how many Fuegian coiled baskets have turned to dust along with their makers in a time when virtually everything was recyclable. What is surprising is that in a remote ranchería of the mountains of Baja the basket was still being made in 1994.

On a return visit to Manuela's home in Rancho Escondido, she was not to be found, but I did speak to her sister, Teresa Aguiar, who also makes

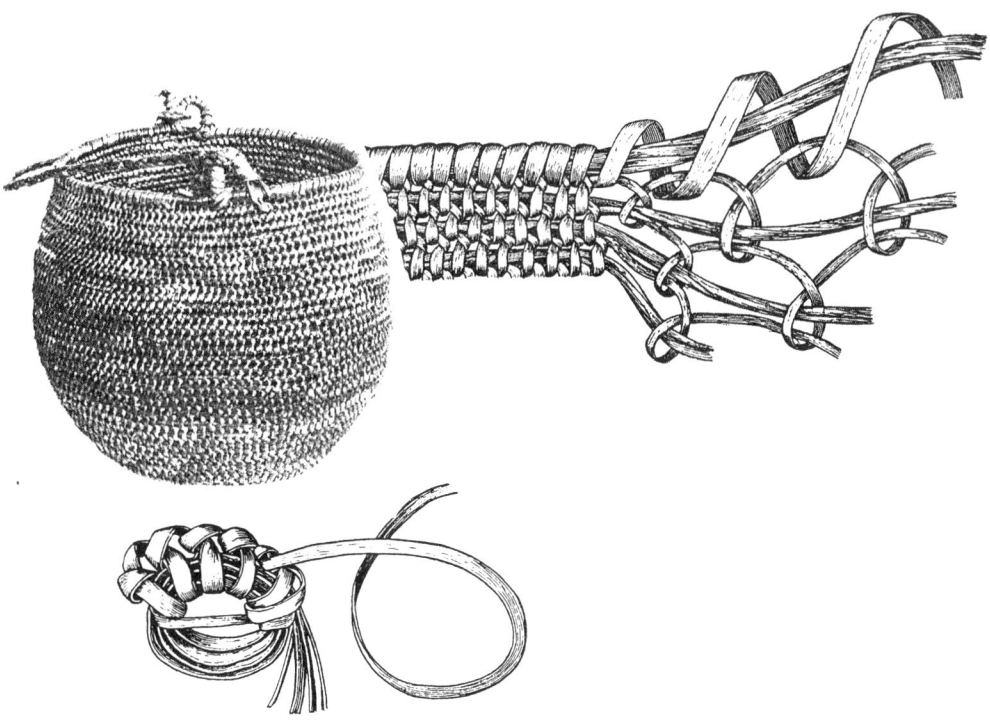

Yahgan tawe'la basket, detail of beginning, body and rim. Note that weave is left to right (Lothrop, 1928).

baskets in the Fuegian-style stitch, which she calls a *qua* stitch (apparently the same Kuatl word she uses for a small net). I asked where she learned to make such baskets and she said from her grandmother, Mariana Aguiar, many years ago. I asked where Mariana might have learned it and Teresa said the style stretches back through the generations for who knows how long.

Manuela Aguiar also learned from her grandmother to make these baskets. On a second return visit she showed me how.

Construction of the Baja Fuegian Basket

Materials

The only native palm of southern California Alta, the California fan palm *(Washingtonia filifera)*, grows in oases of desert canyons and extends south into the deep arroyos and washes of northern Baja California as well. Trails lead from Manuela's place at Rancho Escondido to the desert palm canyons on the east slope of the Sierra Juárez where in addition to the California fan palm, the blue fan palm *(Erythea armata)*, endemic to Baja, also grows. On the western slope of the Sierra Juarez, the California palm reaches even Valle de las Palmas. The closely related Mexican fan palm *(Washingtonia robusta)*, native to areas farther south in Baja, has been planted widely and hybridizes with the California species. Undoubtedly all were used traditionally and Manuela Aguiar employs whichever of these fan-palm leaves are available. She prefers the leaves green but soaking dry, brown leaves for a few minutes makes them almost as acceptable.

First, the thick spiny leaf stalk must be cut from the tree. Next, the lower shorter leaves and stalk itself are torn away and only the central fan of longer leaves transported home.

There, the leaves of a single fan are gripped a few at a time and pulled from the remaining stalk. Soon, a neat pile of leaves lays ready. One of these she takes and midway between either end makes a longitudinal tear about 1/8 to slightly over 1/4 of an inch from the margin; she strips in each direction along the natural fiber lines of the leaf. She does this quickly and without much precision for if a leaf is a bit too wide, it can easily be trimmed by additional splitting. Damaged ends may be cut and discarded. After one or two leaves have been torn into strips, she is ready to begin.

The baskets made of these leaves are not perfect gift-shop gewgaws but organic, working, hunter-gatherer tools. Fanciers of the flawless tourist piece should probably look elsewhere.

Starting Knot

Aguiar points out, and the baskets I see strewn about her home confirm, that depending on what and how much you want the basket to hold, the size and tightness of construction can vary widely. This is up to the individual weaver. Taking a bundle of about three to five strips and holding them across her knees (with the base ends of the leaves to the right), she twists together the right 6 inches or so, away from the body—or counterclockwise—with the left hand. In this twisted section with her right hand she winds a double overhand knot: a loop is formed and two turns of the right end spiral around and follow the circumference. The short right end completes the knot by passing behind the longer strips held to the left and back through the knot's loop.

Eventually, the loose shorter ends coming from the knot will be grouped with the longer ends and loosely twisted counterclockwise into the beginning of the coil. By pulling on the shorter group, which tends to dangle until it is absorbed by the weaving process, the basket base may be continually adjusted or tightened in the early stages of construction.

Manuela also makes a starting knot of a single overhand turn. This simpler knot is smaller and tighter but of less holding strength.

Starting Weave

The stiff base end of a leaf strip is cut to a point (if not naturally pointed). Manuela inserts this through the open knot away from herself; all but around 5 inches go through and these last inches are

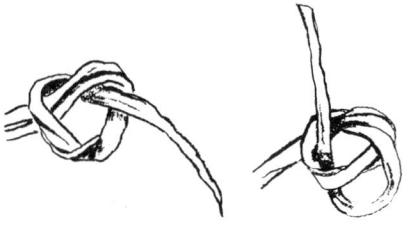  

grouped with the strands held in the left hand that will form the coil (the long loose ends of the knot). The weaver curves up and again enters the opening of the knot from the front and repeats this yet another time to form two tight overlapping coils on the circle of the starting knot. The pointed weaver next slips under the last overlapping coil (the one just formed), from the left to the right, and pulls through until only a small loop of it remains behind, slightly to the left. The weaver arches back through this loop, from front to back, and passes down and to the left and through the starting knot from back to front. This process forms another loop through which the end of the weaver passes (to make the first half hitch). The weaver is pulled down and to the left and again through the starting knot. It circles up through each new loop formed, working counterclockwise making these half hitches until the circle of the starting knot is full.

As the weave goes forward, the loose ends of the knot are simply incorporated in the circle of the knot. The remainder of these ends forms the coil around which subsequent rounds are stitched.

In an alternative start, the weaver may begin by circling over the loop of the knot and entering from the back. Winding twice in overlapping fashion around the starting loop, the weaver then slips under the last overlapping coil from left to right and bends back to the left and through the starting knot from the rear. This forms a loop through which the weaver passes and the forming of half hitches proceeds.

The Weave

The making of half hitches continues counterclockwise. For the second and subsequent rounds the weaver enters from behind not the circle of the knot but the opening between each of the half hitches of the previous row, passing around the twisted strips that form the coil in the process. The weaver passes back out through the loops formed and over the coil which gets a continuous loose twist with the left hand away from the body (counterclockwise facing toward the last knot) as the weaving proceeds. The openings between half hitches may be used more than once (more than one half hitch may be tied into it) to accommodate the expanding spiral. Openings too tight are widened with an awl. Occasionally, Manuela reverses the half hitch, enters the weaver from the front instead of behind, for what purposes save to relieve boredom she could not say.

When the base reaches a diameter of 1 to 2 inches, she puts it on a flat surface and gently pounds it with a flat-sided stone the size of a fist, apparently to bring the stitches in line and even the base. Bending and tightening a bit, controlling the material, produces the change from the base to the sides. This may be done either toward or away from the basketmaker and the work will thus continue from either the inside (usually open or smaller baskets) or the outside (more enclosed, higher baskets).

Splices

Everything begins and ends in the twisted coiling strips. When the weaver is nearly used up, a final half hitch is completed and the remaining 3 or 4 inches incorporated into the coil. The new weaver strip passes away from the basketmaker through the last completed half-hitch loop, leaving a few inches within the coiling strips to the left. It follows flush against the last half hitch at the end of the last weaver, often slipping under the last turn or hitch, and thus from the front or basketmaker's side becomes completely hidden. The weave appears to continue without interruption.

As the coil itself thins out, new strips are simply inserted in the coil and shoved back through it a few inches until they hold.

  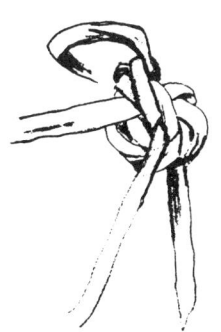 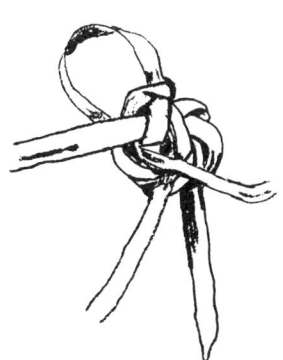

The Rim

When the basket reaches the desired height, the coil of twisted strips circles once around the circumference secured to the tops of the half hitches beneath with simple coiled wrappings of a palm leaf weaver. The old weaver may be buried in the coil and a new weaver run clockwise against the coil for a few inches then turned back on itself and secured with the rim wrappings that cover it in the counterclockwise direction. This corkscrew finishing wrap may reverse directions at the end for a turn or two and the tip of the weaver tucked back under the last wrap and pulled tight. Ideally, the twisted coil strips are completely covered by the wrapping.

The Ears or Handles

Handles may be anchored to the rim, to the coil beneath, around a half hitch that joins the rim and the coil beneath or combinations of these. A weaver strand goes around an anchor from the outside of the basket and circles back on itself; one end is just under the length of the handle, the other

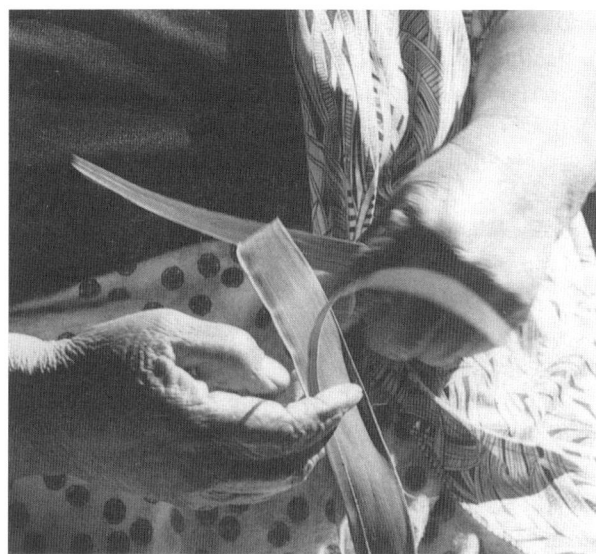

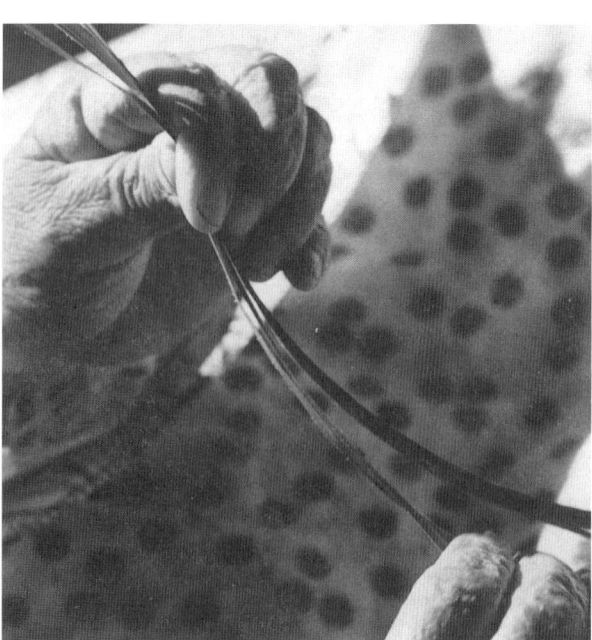

Materials and finished product.

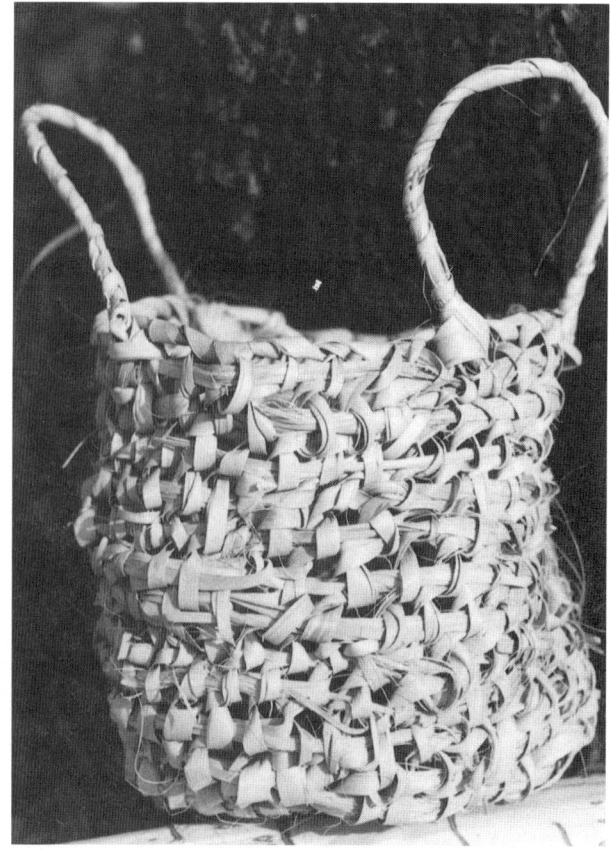

much longer. They are twisted together. Next, the longer end passes around a second anchoring point from the outside of the basket and then coils back, around and around the handle thus formed, returning to the first anchoring point which it circles (or seeks a second nearby anchoring point) and coils the handle again, back in the opposite direction. When it reaches the second point the second time, it anchors with a couple of turns or more, then secures itself by insertion beneath lower coils of the handle and through the weave of the basket (best of all the end simply passes under the last five or six coils of the handle). The same process repeats on the opposite side of the basket.

She had given me a theme and a hint of its variations. We must remember the basketmaker continually responds to uncertain material and accumulating error or miscalculation. The fast-moving adaptable stitch of the Fuegian-style basket quickly forgives mistakes and accommodates changing purposes.

Since basket-making is a nearly lost craft among the Southern Diegueño and Paipai of the southern Sierra Juárez, I thought with this I had seen it all. But as I rose to leave, the sun having already set, Manuela told me that in older days they made many kinds of baskets in this area, all from leaves of the palm. She said she alone still does. In the flickering light of her fire, she brought out a beautiful, very tightly woven basket and lit a kerosene lantern so I could see more clearly. It was southern California coiled stitching made with an awl, each stitch encircling the coil above and penetrating a bundle of fibers in the spiral foundation coil below. Had it been of juncus, it might not have been so unusual but it was completely of palm. The last basket she showed me was very large in a wonderful plaited style.

Detail of Kuatl basket in Fuegian coiled style. (From Manuela's basket.)

From Theresa's basket—note weave is opposite Manuela's but same as the Yahgan. (Coil is a single fine peeled willow.)

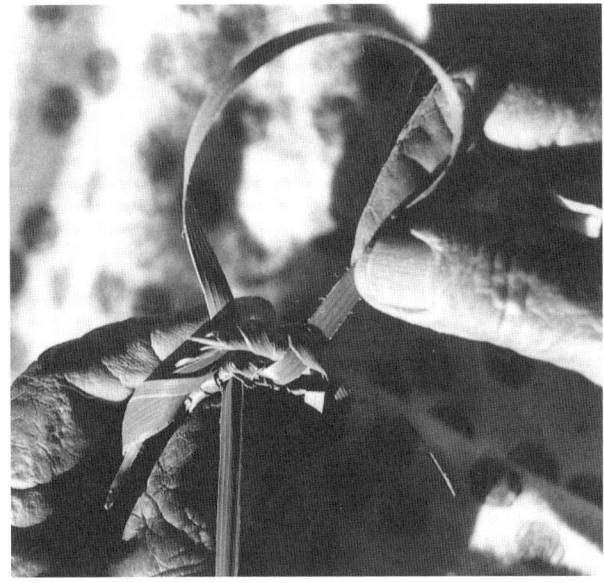

Manuela's hands weave a Fuegian coiled basket.

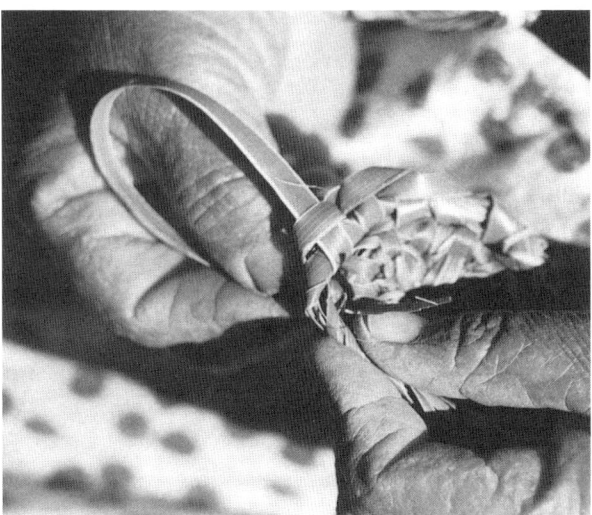

Wooden Bowls, Buckets and Vials

Some wooden containers were found and used almost in their natural state. Other vessels exhibited exquisite craftsmanship. They all went a long way toward turning wild California into home.

Wooden Bowls

Fragments of wooden bowl-making methods have been picked up here and there all across California. Around the turn of the century J.W. Hudson learned from a Gabrielino Indian at Tejón that to make wooden trenches or bowls of sycamore they burned the wood and scraped it with stone implements. The exact sequence of manufacture is unknown, but they likely repeatedly burned the cavity with live coals and scraped and chiseled it out in a manner similar to the making of a California dugout canoe. As a finish, the bowls were rubbed with sandstone, Hudson recorded. The Miwok employed a chisel and a pointed tool, both made from deer antler, to pick and dig out burls of the California black oak. These served as rough, unfinished bowls for cider. Barrett and Gifford suggested the Miwok probably learned the art from the neighboring Western Mono where oaken bowls were commonly made. Northwestern California Indians created simple, rectangular wooden platters for serving deer meat; large, thick-walled, wooden finger bowls for washing after a meal of meat; and huge, rectangular, wooden troughs for stone cooking quantities of food at feasts. These latter they excavated with an adze and fire. The Kawaiisu told Zigmond that Indians to the south hollowed out sections of California buckeye by burning, then carved them to the bowl shape desired. The Kawaiisu themselves carved a ladle about a foot long from the blue oak. A bulge in a branch was burned out to form the bowl, learned Zigmond. It was used to stir and dip food. They also made ladles of juniper. J. P. Harrington found from Chumash informants that after they boiled islay kernels and pounded them in a deep stone olla using a 9-inch-long masher of hollywood (toyon), ball-shaped on the end, they molded the mush into cakes, like small cheeses or breads, in a wooden ladle (those extant have very short handles). They pressed them by hand on the ladle, which was about 3 inches deep, placed them in a wooden bowl and served them on a coiled winnowing basket.

Wooden bowls and similar wooden containers were common household objects among the early Californians, but it was the Chumash who were the master craftsmen of wooden bowl manufacture. "Polished and perfectly formed as though turned on a lathe, beautiful and with inlay" is how Miguel Constansó described them in 1769. Two hundred years later, Travis Hudson brought together much historical and ethnographic information on these bowls, and with others he carefully analyzed one in the collection of the Santa Barbara Museum of Natural History. These efforts make possible the re-creation of the Chumash wooden bowl.

Chumash Wooden Bowl Materials

Hudson and fellow researchers concluded that the Santa Barbara example came from the burl of the California bay tree *(Umbellularia californica)*. They were even able to tell from its grain pattern that the burl had been mostly underground, that the part which would become the bottom of the bowl had been inward toward the tree and that it was worked while green (a slight surface wrinkling had occurred after the final polishing). Harrington's interviews with elderly Chumash over eighty years ago corroborate and extend these findings. Fernando Librado Kitsepawit emphasized that the wood was green and immediately worked, "for if they wait only two or three days, the wood will crack." The Chumash repeatedly referred to the working of green or fresh burls in making a wooden bowl which they called *hsh'o*. This was the same word used for the sycamore tree because it was from that tree, Simplicio Pico Pamaskumait declared, wooden bowls were made. Roots, burls, joints and elbows of sycamore were mentioned as well as the burls of small oaks in the mountains, whose wood is very hard. María Solares included the burls of willow and toyon. The grain of the wood was "mottled" or "all mixed up" on these bowls, informants pointed out. Hudson noted the desirable qualities of a burl are density, hardness and uniformity. Burls of oak and alder would lend themselves to smaller containers, with bay most suitable for larger.

Tools and Manufacture of the Chumash Bowl

They began on the inside and when this was done did the outside, recalled Librado. Their tool was a flint adze he thought. Most could not remember the earlier stages. Hudson found residual charcoal on the Santa Barbara Museum bowl, a sign that fire had been used as a tool to burn the wood into form. The Chumash hand adze used for boat-building usually had a wooden handle of manzanita and a blade of pismo clam shell. Hudson listed the Chumash woodworking tools: scrapers of red abalone shell or chert; "files of flint" (specifically mentioned for bowls), chert drills and knives, stone chisels and hammer stones, wedges and sandstone abraiders. Tiny drills (bladelets, one end sharpened to a point) were worked with the fingers, held in buckskin, or mounted on a wooden shaft and wrapped with Spanish bayonet string. Other small bowl-making tools were similarly mounted according to a Harrington informant. U-shaped scars on the Santa Barbara bowl led Hudson to conclude that very small stone flake tools, sharpened by pressure working, called burins, may have been used. These stone tools have been found along the Santa Barbara Channel. They have tips ranging from something similar to a screwdriver to V-shaped gouges.

Alternating burning with scraping and chopping the charcoal, in the same way they hollowed the dugout canoe, was likely the method the Chumash used. The Yokuts hollowed oak mortars in that way and even roughly shaped the exterior with fire. (The residual charcoal was found on the exterior of the Santa Barbara bowl.) Hammer stones, chisels and scrapers, knives, burins and file-like flints likely brought the Chumash bowl close to final form. Sandstone abraiders produced an even finer finish.

Faint, brush-like and U-shaped marks on the surface of the Santa Barbara Museum vessel suggested to Hudson that sharkskin had been used for polishing the bowl. Pieces of dried sharkskin were employed as a fine abrasive in Chumash boat-building. Scouring rush, or horsetail *(Equisetum)*, was used in boat-building for polishing shell. Luisa Ignacio Nut-u, a Chumash lady from the Santa Barbara region, recalled clearly the concluding steps of wooden bowl manufacture. She told Harrington as a last step they polished the bowl "well with dry *cañutillo*"—scouring rush, or horsetail. Perhaps the closely confined, parallel groups of about six grooves each, as though made from a "narrow-width abraiding tool" (Hudson found on close inspection of the Santa Barbara vessel), were left from the natural

Oak bowls collected from the Chumash of the Santa Ynez Valley by Léon de Cessac in 1878. Pairs of tiny, white, shell disc beads have been neatly inserted in exactly sized individually drilled holes to make inlay, held with asphaltum along rim of top bowl. A groove circumscribes the outer, flat rim edge. The bowl seems to have a red or dark mahogany stain and is finely polished. Largest diameter is 15 cm.; thickness of wall, 6 mm. Lower bowl has a diameter of 24 cm.; thickness, 9 to 10 mm. Both are similar in form to basketry containers and steatite and sandstone bowls found archaeologically in various sizes. Bowls are presently in Musée de l'Homme, Paris (drawn from photos in Grant, 1978; dimensions and details given in Hudson, 1977).

ridges on horsetail stalk. Ignacio described the final staining of the bowl. They mixed "squirrel oil" and red ochre. The thick, animal fat paste was smeared over the entire vessel, inside and outside. The bowl was then placed in the sun to cause the oil to penetrate. At the very last, it was polished again with dry scouring rush. The Santa Barbara bowl exhibits a beautiful red stain and polish.

Shell inlay on rims was also done toward the end of the process, as suggested by the Santa Barbara bowl where perforations for small shell beads cut through patterns of fine striations left by final polishing. These beads, likely of clam shell, white and uniform in size, were 1.9 mm. in diameter, 2 mm. thick, with a center hole of 1 mm. They were held by asphaltum in holes of the same size as the beads. Backs of cowrie shells, large brown and small pink types, were also inlaid on the rim according to Harrington's informants.

Decorative Bead Manufacture

Librado and other Chumash consultants of Harrington explained the process of making shell beads. The shell was first broken with a stone by direct or indirect percussion, then on a flat surface, an anvil of stone or wood, pecked or chipped roughly to the round shape of the bead. Cutting with flint (probably chert) and rasping were other shell-working techniques described by the Chumash.

The center perforation was drilled halfway from both sides, beginning with a sharp flint splinter lashed to an arrow-like reed or wood, some as long as 2 feet. Bits made of swordfish bones sharpened on a rock were for drilling holes in very long beads. Beads themselves were held in place by indentations in the anvil. After the center hole of the bead had been started with the flint drill, boring the bead gently at first and then spinning the tool rapidly between the palms as the hands moved down the drill shaft, it could be completed either with the flint or, as Librado described it, with a drill bit of sea lion whisker (likely with a fine abrasive). Sometimes beads were placed in hot water to soften them.

The center perforations complete, they were strung four fingerbreadths long on a strip of juncus that had been halved, the pith removed by running it between a finger and the edge of a shell, and sized to hold the beads snugly. The juncus rod was perhaps 12 inches long and thick enough to keep the beads from slipping or turning. A broad grindstone was placed over the thighs, and guiding the juncus to the left in a 1/4 inch opening formed by joining the left thumb and forefinger, the rod was rolled gently with the right palm over the stone until the beads were all equally smooth and round. In 1884 Henry Henshaw (recorded in Hudson and Blackburn) wrote that the

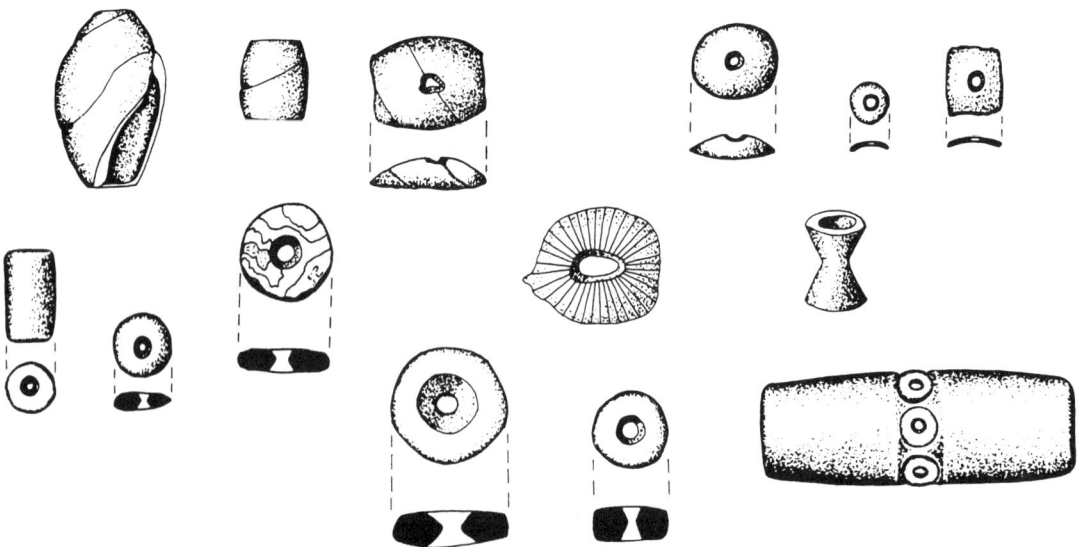

Beads of the late prehistoric peoples of the Santa Barbara coast and channel islands. Top row: lopped and perforated beads of Olivella shell. Second row: Tivela-shell tube bead; Mytilus-shell disk bead; Haliotis-shell disk bead; keyhole-limpet-shell bead; and bead from fish vertebra. Bottom row: disk bead of stone-ground serpentine; steatite disk bead; and steatite tube bead inlaid with clamshell disk beads held by asphaltum. All actual size (Chartkoff, 1984).

Chumash put a nicer polish on a bead by rubbing it over a piece of leather. Harrington's Chumash informants mentioned tossing beads with hot coals in a basket to whiten them.

Bowl Repairs

A technique found in the construction of the *tomol* (the Chumash sea-going boat) to sew planks together and in the repair of stone bowls was also exhibited in the Santa Barbara Museum wooden bowl. A natural 3 cm. rift extended down from the rim. In response, the Chumash artisan drilled two holes on either side of the split 8 mm. below the rim and 10 mm. apart.

The holes were linked by a 3 mm.-wide groove cut in both interior and exterior surfaces. Fiber twine, likely Indian hemp, passed about three times from hole to hole. The terminal knot in the Santa Barbara bowl was covered under tar (a similar three-wrap pattern on the tomol ended the tie in a half hitch). The crack was filled in and all exposed cordage covered by the asphaltum adhesive.

Variety and Uses of Chumash Bowls

Ignacio said bowls could be small—those of a foot or less were for chia seeds—or as big as 2-1/2 feet across. Some bowls were shallow, others deep. Candalaria Valenzuela, a full-blooded Chumash from Ventura, told Harrington that wooden bowls and trays were used extensively in preparing food. Wood jars could hold acorns, according to another Harrington consultant. Globular bowls or jars also likely held pinole or whole seeds. A circular redwood stopper, 8 cm. in diameter, whose core would have just entered into the mouth of such a bowl as the outer circumference rested on the upper mouth edge, was found on San Nicholas Island. A bowl with a wider more open mouth held pieces of prepared islay or acorn mush. Librado said they kept a *hsh'o* filled with cold acorn mush in the house. Loved by California Indians to this day, well-made acorn mush stiffens naturally into a cold pudding. Librado described how a man would stir his portion on one side of such a large bowl and eat it with two fingers. Or he would take his knife and slice crosshatching in his portion at the edge of the bowl and eat it cube by cube.

A Natural Bucket

For acorns, cactus fruit, piñon nuts or similar foods, Paipai Indian Andrés Albáñez made a very quick and easy gathering bucket from the base of the stem of the *Lechuguilla* or Spanish bayonet *(Yucca whipplei)*. The stem he chose was dead and dry, brown but not weathered gray or rotten. Albáñez cut it off just below its greatest point of constriction at the base above the roots and again almost 1-1/2 feet above this where the diameter would reach sometimes more than 7 inches. He pulled or hacked off the sharp leaves and with a convenient pointed instrument hollowed the fibrous interior to leave a bright and woody, capacious and elongate bucket. The exterior was sometimes polished. An inch below the rim on one side he drilled a hole with his knife and inserted a doubled rawhide thong for a hand carrying strap.

Cándido Cañedo, Paipai, hollowed out smaller buckets, taken from farther up the yucca stem, with a sharp, flat piece of stone, sometimes using an ancient stone knife or spear point he would find in his desert wanderings. To carry, a two-ply cord of yucca fiber was strung into a hole on one side, doubled and twisted into a four-ply handle, then joined to the opposite side. The bucket was ready to collect berries, piñon nuts, acorns or just about anything. A small one without a handle to carry honey was made on the spot when a hive was discovered, Cañedo told me. The bottom of the bowl I purchased from him had been carefully smoothed on the outside and rubbed and polished with beeswax.

Carrizo and Elderberry Vials

The Seri from Tiburón Island in the Gulf of California do not distinguish between native carrizo *(Phragmites communis)* and the introduced Mediterranean carrizo *(Arundo donax)*. The latter is larger, less elegant and possesses an enlarged base of the leaf blade but, in many respects, it is very similar. Artifacts made from either are virtually indistinguishable, according to Richard Felger and Mary Moser who spent many years among the Seri studying their ways. The Seri made a beautiful little container from carrizo. The hollow stem was cut just below a joint and at a point some ways above. Into the top end a wooden stopper was inserted as a cap. The container thus formed carried and preserved powdered or granular substances: cattail pollen for face paint,

Hupa elk-horn spoons, collected by P. H. Ray during the nineteenth century (Mason, 1889). Bowls of such spoons were about 2-7/8" long by 2-3/8" wide in measurements made by P. E. Goddard. Judging from museum examples they appear to have been very thin-walled. Handles could be scarcely longer than the bowl, or 4" or more, and were sometimes at nearly right angles to the bowl. Elderly Yurok Indian Frank Gist told me elk-horn spoons were made from the thick lower portion or butt of the elk antler. Isabel Kelly wrote that it was the thick cross section of the base that formed the bowl, and the handle was made from the vertical horn next to it, leading naturally to the 45-degree or more stem-bowl angle seen on these spoons. They were carved in geometric designs (the purpose seems to have been mere decoration) with projections near the bowl and a spoon-like termination. Smaller, less-elaborate spoons were made from the harder antler of deer. A. Kroeber recorded that traditionally northern California Indians rubbed designs into elk-horn spoons with sandstone. Yurok Indian Robert Johnson told Kroeber that in the old days the elk horn was soaked until soft, then rubbed to shape with sandstone to make a spoon. Northern California antler-working techniques included soaking in water for some time to make material more workable, rough shaping with coarse sandstone, cutting and carving with flint and obsidian, steaming to shape and final polishing with equisetum (horsetail). In a note left by J. P. Harrington, Karok Indian Phoebe Maddux 'Imkyanva'an told him that after the elk-horn spoon was finished, they soaked it in alder for a long time to give it a pretty red color. Chimariko informant Lucy Montgomery remembered they allowed elk-horn and manzanita spoons to dry for a while after they were finished and then briefly boiled them in water to make them hard. They should not be boiled too long, and they did not boil them before they were made or cut out of the elk antler, she said. Failure to boil the completed spoon meant it would break later in use. After boiling they painted them with some plant that grew in the mountains. Men used large spoons, children cute little ones, she told Harrington.

Men ate acorn mush with elk-horn or wooden spoons. They ate from small, tightly twined individual serving baskets. O. T. Mason noted that California Indian spoons were generally held near the mouth in the left hand while one alternately sipped from the rim and conveyed morsels from the spoon to the mouth. Harrington, in his notes, recorded a Karok name for the man's spoon, joramsikki, literally "corner spoon." It referred to the fact that a stranger, when invited into a house, was treated with respect and put in the best part of the house, which to them was the corner. So, in effect, the name signified "spoon for a stranger."

Women of northwestern California did not eat with decorated spoons but took their acorn mush, often from the pot where it cooked, with spoons of a valve of giant California mussel (Mytilus californianus). Although they appear to have been generally unworked, Montgomery recalled an Indian in the mountains who made and traded mussel-shell spoons "all rubbed down pretty and neat." He also traded boiling stones he had worked and made symmetrical. Montgomery had heard of, but had never seen, a deer-skull spoon.

Elizabeth Hickox, Karok, showed Harrington a deer-skull spoon, the natural fractures of the bone plainly visible. The top of the deer's skull had been sectioned in a plane straight across, making a spoon 3" long by 2" wide and 1-1/8" deep. A small bit of occipital remained, projecting 3/8" above the plane, and formed a kind of short handle. It was very reminiscent of many short-handled wooden, stone and ceramic ladles found elsewhere in California. Kelly called the deer-skull spoon a woman's spoon.

powdered ochre for painting various objects, and creosote bush lac. Lac was left by scale insects on the stems of the creosote bush. Plastic when heated, it would harden when cooled and formed a tough bonding agent used for hafting points to harpoons, stone heads to arrows and blades to knives, serving as well for sealing lids on storage vessels and for an all-purpose glue. Shamans put special sacred powder into small carrizo tubes and rented them to people for luck or to cure an illness. Carrizo containers were undoubtedly made in various sizes and for many purposes. They can be easily duplicated.

Harrington discovered in the early years of the twentieth century similar containers among the Ventureño Chumash. They removed the pith of a short elderwood stalk and plugged up both ends. The Chumash called it a *hap* and in this they carried the pounded and pulverized dried leaves of wild tobacco. (The leaves were picked in the spring. They were spread and dried on the ground or on a rock in the sunshine and turned from time to time so they would not get moldy.) The Kawaiisu also hollowed out a short section of elderberry wood to make a tobacco container. The Chumash carried the tobacco-filled tube over the ear. They smoked the tobacco from the *hap* in wooden elderberry or stone pipes, sometimes with a bird bone mouthpiece, tilting the large end or the bowl of the tubular pipe upward to pour in the tobacco from the *hap*, then touching the filled pipe to the fire or adding a fiery coal. They filled a carrizo cigarette from the *hap* the same way. The carrizo itself burned some and was discarded after the smoke.

As an aside, it might be noted that tobacco could be taken in many different ways. The plant minus the roots, for example, was boiled into a strong tea. The plant was then removed and the boiling continued until the liquid became thick as pitch. It was cooled in the pot, shaped into a stick with a hole in one end and worn on a necklace. The Ventureño Chumash wore it when climbing a mountain or when hunting bear. A touch of the tongue to the stick instilled bravery in the hunter, inspiring him to go forward.

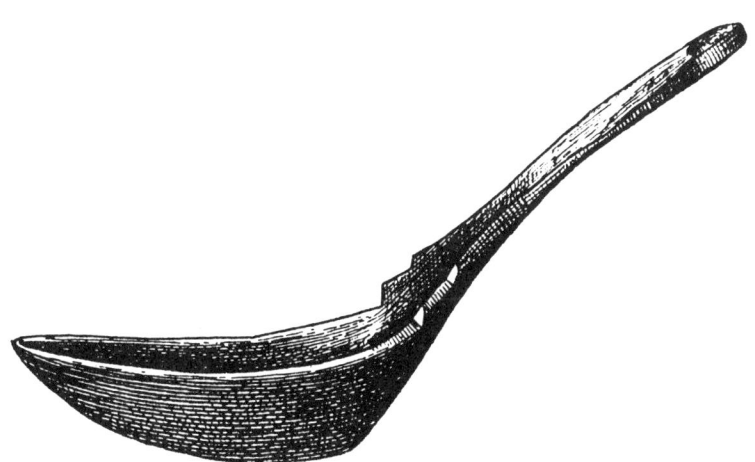

A Shasta wooden spoon, 7" in length (Dixon, 1907). They could also be made of elk horn and were similar to those of the Yurok, Hupa and Karok, though generally less decorated. Harrington's notes describe the making of a Karok spoon of Manzanita wood. He was told the Manzanita branch should be sawed off, not chopped, for that would crack it. The limb was split into two halves with an elk-horn wedge. To make the spoon the wood had to be dry. A rock, heated in the fire, was held on one of the halves to burn the shape of the spoon, including the bowl. (Harrington asked how the hot rock was held and his informant told him they tied an elk-horn handle on it.) Then, dried stalks of Indian sandpaper (equisetum) were rubbed on hard. The stalks, much more effective dry, were dehydrated for a month or even longer and were used for smoothing such things as arrows and arrow straighteners as well. The equisetum removed the burnt surfaces of the spoon and polished it. Finally, ornamental indentations were cut out with a sharp rock and smoothed with the equisetum sandpaper.

The Technology of Good Grooming

More than looking good, close attention to the superficial self, or good grooming, can mean the difference between life and death. Uncleanliness, poor skin care, improper hygienic practice—these are chinks that can eventually rend and destroy the whole body. Unprotected and unwashed, the small crack of a sunburned face can open the way to the infection which festers, spreads and kills. Grooming is a survival skill. In the California wilderness, Indians were the experts.

The Bath

Of the Wintun, Powers wrote:

They are as remarkable as all Californians for their fondness of being in, and their daily lavatory use of, cold water. They are almost amphibious, or were before they were pestered with clothing. Merely to get a drink they would wade in and dip and toss the water up with their hands.

Carl Meyer described a Yurok's bathing practice in the middle of the nineteenth century. He would arise at daybreak and wash himself all over at a nearby spring. He would dry by the rays of the rising sun. It was the father who went first from the hut for the bath after stirring the fire and allotting the daily chores to the rest of the family.

These northern California tribes may be seen in contrast to some of the Indians at the bottom of Lower California who were described disdainfully and with much prejudice by early priests as washing in their own urine when without a ready supply of water. Perhaps disgusting to those who have been pampered always with too much, it was likely an efficacious and antiseptic hygienic practice in a dry desert where meager fresh water would have gone toward the lifesaving slacking of thirst.

Both sexes among the Tubatulabal in the southern Sierras bathed frequently in springs or streams. Francisco Garcés noted two hundred years ago what fine fellows were the young men and described the women as "very comely and clean, bathing themselves every little while."

Soap, Shampoo and Scent

Ethnographer Erminie Voegelin recorded much later that Tubatulabal women brushed their hair every day with a soaproot brush and washed it with shampoo from the bulb of the soaproot, the wavy-leaf soap plant *(Chlorogalum pomeridianum)*. For the same purpose, they crushed the roots of the soap plant *(Chenopodium californicum)* by rubbing them on rock. Barrows reported that the Cahuilla also grated this long, hard carrot-like root on a rock for soap.

The Cahuilla made hairbrushes and soap from the soaproot plant as well. One hundred years ago Dixon found that Maidu men and women washed their heads frequently using soaproot. Barrett and Gifford recorded that the Miwok lathered their hair with soaproot every few days to bring luxuriant growth. Each washed his own, at a creek in warm weather and at home when it was cold. The Luiseño, as described by Sparkman, grated the roots of the soap plant or the root of the wavy-leaf soaproot plant for use as soap. When ripe, the fruit of the wild gourd, known too as the stinking gourd *(Cucurbita foetidissima)*, the Luiseño opened and rubbed the inside over articles they wished to clean. Benito Peralta of the Paipai in Lower California told me they would rub the large root of the wild gourd, called in Paipai *'caút*, on a rock and use the scrapings with water to produce a soapy lather to wash the body and face. Teresa Aguiar took me out and showed me this plant and its root that was larger than my fist. The Cahuilla cut both the root and squash into fine pieces for use as hand or laundry soap. The shell of the fruit was ground and used as a shampoo. Both squash and roots could be gathered in large quantities and stored. A dried gourd even became a syringe for feminine hygiene. Cahuilla Alice Lopez told Lowell Bean that mule-fat *(Baccharis viminea)* leaves and stems were boiled and the decoction used as a feminine hygienic wash.

The root of the Mohave yucca *(Yucca schidigera)* was grated by the Cahuilla and the scrapings used for soap. Manuela Aguiar, a Southern Diegueño of the Kuatl lineage whom John Peabody Harrington photographed in the Indian village of San Miguel of Lower California in 1926, told me that as a girl she knew no other soap. It left her hair clean, soft and lustrous. She still feels its sudsy lather is the best. Her son, Raúl Sandoval demonstrated the technology for me in the Sierra Juarez in early 1996. It was not the root per se, but the large globular base of the stalk just beneath the surface of the ground that was used. Less productive, but also yielding soap, was the entire stalk. Raúl and his wife Julia did not have to go far when I asked them for a demonstration. They already had some prepared since this is a soap they use regularly to this day. Raúl pointed to a long line of his daughter Yolanda's clean baby clothes washed in yucca suds. Raúl, Julia, Benito Peralta, Josefina Ochurte and others emphasized that yucca root was primarily for shampooing the hair, but Cándido Cañedo and his wife Teresa said it could be used for the whole body if rinsed off with pure water. Otherwise, the skin could become very itchy from the soap. Raúl dug out the large base of a Mohave yucca, opened the juicy fibrous ball and cut from it some cream-colored hunks about the size of his palm. In a tub of water he rubbed the pieces rapidly together quickly creating a frothy, bubbly white lather.

The Chumash made a shampoo of a fine, soft white clay. They beat it up a little with water in a bowl or basket and used the clean clay toward the top, the dirt settling to the bottom. They rubbed it into their hair and even their face making suds, then rinsed with water in the river. It could be used for clothes as well. Brown, yellow, red and violet clays could also be used. A violet clay made the hair grow and removed dandruff. Clay shampoo, in general, got rid of lice.

Every grooming problem had its remedy. The Tubatulabal used an alkali solution for lice, leaving the dried powder in the hair for several days. Cándido Cañedo mentioned that the Paipai would mix ashes with water and allow them to settle overnight; the clean water became a hair rinse to remove dandruff. The Cahuilla made an infusion of creosote bush *(Larrea divaricata)* for use as a hair wash to get rid of dandruff (once a week for two months). The infusion was also a disinfectant or body deodorizer. They mixed crushed leaves of white sage *(Salvia apiana)* with water for a hair shampoo and dye as well as a hair straightener. Crushed leaves of the white sage placed by the Cahuilla beneath the armpits upon retiring served as a deodorant. The Miwok put white fir leaves beneath the axillas to dispel bad odor from excessive perspiration.

The Paipai of Santa Catarina have told me they did not use underarm deodorants. They cleansed their persons and homes as they still do with the pungent, aromatic smoke of the white sage. The purpose was as much for spiritual cleansing as for air purifying. The tops of perhaps nine or ten sage plants were cut, around 7 inches long each, and tightly wrapped in a 1- to 1-1/2-inch-wide bundle with a string which spiraled from top to bottom. The bunch was set aside and allowed to dry for a couple of days and then burned like punk and taken throughout the house so its smoke would purify it. Smoke wafted over the body purified the person. With the smoke of the white sage, the Cahuilla purified things which had become contaminated. If a menstruating woman accidentally touched a man's hunting equipment, the deer or other game could catch the scent of contamination. Passing the weapon through the smoke of burning leaves of white sage cleansed it and restored the man's luck in hunting.

Raúl Sandoval makes suds from Mohave yucca. Cándido Cañedo points to wild gourd and root. Benito Peralta points to haplopappus plant.

The dried leaves and stems of Great Basin sagebrush *(Artemisia tridentata)* were burned as an air purifier in the homes of both the Cahuilla and those of Santa Catarina. The Cahuilla purified the air of sweat houses with it as well. In Santa Catarina the smoke cleanses a person after a death in the family and tranquilizes fear of the deceased's spirit.

Coiffure

The California Indian managed hair in a variety of ways. Despite countless styles, patterns emerge as we review Dixon's findings from the Maidu, Barrett and Gifford on the Miwok and some accounts of early explorers among the Chumash and others.

Maidu men of the Sacramento valley wore their hair long and loose like those of the northeastern Maidu territory or tucked under a netted cap or held away from the face by a band of fur. The southern Maidu tied it with a cord in a bunch at the back of the head. Maidu women generally kept the hair long and loose or tied with a band which passed over the top of the head and under the chin. The northwestern Maidu women cut their hair shorter. They cut the hair laid on a stick with a sharp flint or singed it off with a glowing ember. Tubatulabal women cut bangs in the front of their long hair by holding it out in a bunch and burning off the ends with a glowing stick of desert holly *(Atriplex canescens)*. Many California Indians shortened their hair in this manner.

Pine cones or pine needles in bunches served as Maidu combs. In the higher elevations of the Sierra a porcupine tail became a comb. Indians of the Modoc and Klamath Lake also made combs from the tail of a porcupine. In fact, this seems to have been general in northern California.

The Southern Diegueño, on the other hand, combed their hair with the hook spines on a nettle pod. Brushes of mescal fiber were also fashioned.

The Miwok wore their hair long, sometimes tied at the neck or on top of the head with a feather rope. They occasionally wore a headband of plucked beaver skin three fingers wide decorated with beads. Feathers or flowers were worn in the hair. Wreaths of tiger lily *(Lilium pardalinum)* or common monkey flower *(Mimulus guttatus)* sometimes graced the coiffure. Hair nets held the hair in dancing, gambling or dressing up.

Chumash children wore the hair uncut. This was probably generally true of most California Indians of all ages and both sexes. Father Boscana recorded that between Santa Barbara and San Lucas in Lower California, the Indians wore their hair long and cultivated length as a mark of beauty. Father

William Halsey, Achomawi, wearing a net cap with feathers. Photograph by J. P. Harrington in late spring 1922 (Smithsonian Institution National Anthropological Archives).

Pedro Font in 1776 wrote that Indians allowed their hair to fall loosely back over their shoulders or tied it behind their heads. Chumash women, he described, wore it long except in front which they cut in bangs. Much later Simplicio Pico told Harrington they trimmed their bangs with a hot coal which they drew along the hair steadily and slowly. Fernando Librado said it was a glowing live oak bark that singed the hair ends which projected from between the fingers where they were held. Ground charcoal was then rubbed in to cover the scent. The same charcoal treatment was accorded the hair when it was cut in mourning—the length of four fingerbreadths from the original length. An old widow would come and burn it off, then, in a big shell, she would grind charcoal, wet it sufficiently, and dip the hair on this to rid it of the burnt hair smell.

Pedro Fages wrote in 1769 that the Chumash tightly bound and gathered their hair at the back forming a short heavy queue. He noted they placed in their hair a coiffure of seashells. Font recorded that men tied a cord in the hair and in the cord put a stick or feather and especially a knife. Sometimes the hair was gathered or wound in a bunch on the crown of the head with the tail of the hair tucked under, and the bun fastened with skewers of wood or bone. Chumash men wore it this way slightly to the side or to the front. They used spatulate bone or wood hairpins, incised and inlaid. Some were of cane decorated with feathers. Women often gathered their hair in the back. Harrington's Chumash informants from the early years of the twentieth century said the hair was usually braided into a single queue tied at the lower end with buckskin or tied unbraided with a string at the neck into a ponytail.

The Chumash—mainly the women—combed their hair with a soaproot brush. The women, according to Harrington consultant Simplicio Pico, held their long hair out with one hand and brushed along it with the soaproot brush. Chumash men and women rubbed oil or marrow on their hair. Islanders, while eating whale or some other meat, would draw their fingers through their hair to oil it.

Beard

Some Miwok men of the central Sierras plucked their beard. Others let it grow. The generally scanty beard and mustache of the Maidu men of the northern Sierras was plucked with their fingernails or the nails and a piece of stick. The northeastern Maidu sometimes let their mustache grow, but not to the point of becoming thick or long.

Shaving Indian style might be accomplished as Fages described it for the Chumash of the eighteenth century. Most did not shave but the few who would endure the pain did so with the two shells of the clam or a large oyster. The natural hinged fastening of the bivalve allowed it to be used as tweezers. One at a time a hair would be clasped and pulled out by the root.

Teeth and Nails

Paipai Benito Peralta remembered that when he was young the old people generally had all their teeth. They were white and clean all the way across. They ate a traditional diet, he said, very low in sugar and no refined foods. They had no brushes for their teeth, they just left them alone. Now we buy food from outside and many of us have lost our teeth. Powers nineteenth-century observations of California Indians tend to confirm Peralta's memory: " . . . of the many hundreds I have seen there was not one who still observed the aboriginal mode of life that had not white teeth and a sweet breath." Peralta's fellow Paipai, Cándido Cañedo, agreed there was no aboriginal toothbrush, but he recalled that to clean the teeth they would sometimes take ashes from the hearth and with their fingers alone rub them over their teeth.

As for fingernails, the Tubatulabal allowed their nails to grow and break off naturally or they kept them short by filing them on a piece of rough rock.

Mirror, Mirror

To judge by appearance, modern professional Californians must dwell much of each day in front of mirrors to effect the "casual" California

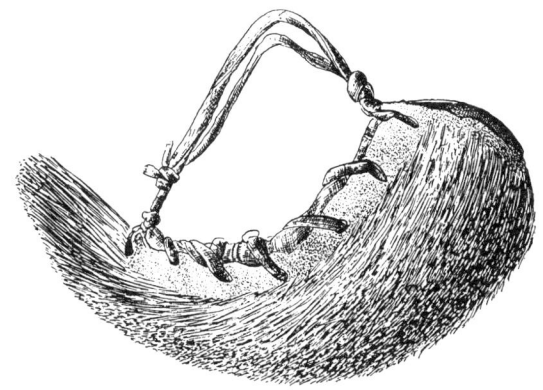

Maidu porcupine-tail comb, 24 cm. (Dixon 1905).

look. But how did Native Californians see themselves? Generally, they found their reflection in others and in this way developed an identity, but early Californians must have known their mirror image too. When applying face paint, the Seri of Tiburón Island in the gulf of California looked into a small bowl or shell filled with water placed in the shade as a mirror. Benito Peralta and Josefina Ochurte told me that if needed, the old ones among the Paipai also saw their reflection in water. Excessive vanity, however, was not likely a native California survival skill.

Skin Care

The sun burns even the darkest skin. True, those of fair complexion may be more prone to skin cancer from prolonged exposure, but dark color absorbs heat more readily than light and too high a body temperature causes heat stroke, a form of shock in a downward spiral that if unchecked results in death. Obviously, for everyone keeping the skin cool and out of the sun on a hot day is as important as staying warm and near the fire during a cold night.

Even a small rise in body temperature—to 107 degrees F—can kill, or cause convulsions and permanent brain damage. Anthropologist Dean Falk explained the evolution of the human brain's radiator. Finding its first indication in the gracile form of Australopithicus, subsequent development kept pace with an ever-enlarging brain to the time of the Neanderthals. A big brain accumulates dangerous levels of heat if not dissipated and significant size and intelligence would not have been possible without such an evolved cooling system. The evolutionary step consisted of a network of veins in the scalp and face connecting via emissary veins to veins in the brain case and surface of the brain itself. Thus sweat evaporating from a flushed face on a hot day and after exercise functions to cool the brain. Finding shade so that this mechanism would work was crucial in the harsh California environment.

There were times, however, when the Indian simply could not cross over the river and rest under the shade of a tree. The California desert sun beats relentlessly. The desert dwelling Seri of Tiburón Island in the Gulf of California, survivors of the relentless burning sun, ingeniously solved the problem by bringing the tree with them! They constructed and wore a coronet or wreath of vines and shrubs. In *Ethnobotony of the Seri*, Felger and Moser described a crown woven from leafy stems of such plants as balloon vine *(Cardiospermum)*, elephant tree *(Bursera microphylla)* and Mascagnia. Men and women wore it for protection from the summer sun and to keep their hair in place. Felger and Moser did not go into detail on the crown's manufacture, but evidently from the photo of a woman wearing one, elongate bunches of supple branches with leaves were encircled by a vine-like stem in a spiral enclosing the tube shape. The two ends were intermeshed and secured with a continuation of the spiral to form a cool sun-screening coronet whose outer circumference extended a few inches beyond the head on all sides in a thick leafy brim. Any flowers on the small branches used were left on by the Seri.

Boughs of grape, willow or the California bay *(Umbellularia californica)*, whose aromatic leaves the Yurok used to repel insects, or of the laurel sumac, which when crushed released a natural California mosquito dope, would work as well. We recall the Miwok of the Sierra Nevada Mountains made wreaths of such flowers as the tiger lily and common monkey flower. Tubatulabal women shaded their face from the hot sun when they pounded acorns by binding a string around their head and rolling up their hair to project over the string.

The Mohave, a desert dwelling group, directly protected the skin by means of paint. Given to tattoos and paint for adornment, the Mohave also applied red pigment in deer fat to the face and sometimes the arms, legs and body to protect the skin against both insect bites and sunburn. The red pigment may have been hematite since they said it was a clay, dried and ground into powder in a mortar. They kept it in a skin bag. When needed, it was mixed with deer fat from a small pot whose lid was sealed with greasewood wax. The deer fat was kneaded until soft in a pottery fragment, a little pigment was added and the mixture worked into a kind of dough. It was warmed slightly over a fire prior to application. This paste was also thought to improve the complexion and prevent rashes.

Black pigment from a shiny black rock, likely manganese, was pulverized and applied as a powder, without fat. It was sometimes applied with a small stick just below the eyes to reduce the glare of the sun.

The juice which exuded from a pumpkin burning in the fire was used by old Mohave women to prevent wrinkles and to protect against cold wind. They spread it over their face with shredded bark. After four or five days it peeled off. Peralta told me the Paipai would use the charred base of a desert agave (the mescal heart which had been cooked for some days in an earth oven for food) to remove blotches on the face caused by the sun and as protection from the sun. The reddish-colored material was ground into a powder, mixed with water and rubbed on the face where it was left for a few days.

To ward off fleas and flies which could bite and mar the skin, Indians of northwestern California kept the aromatic leaves of the California bay tree in their homes. The Northern Paiute drove mosquitoes away with smoky fires. When Meigs explored among the Lower California Kiliwa over sixty years ago, he found an old woman who kept a few sticks smoldering on the hearth of her hut even during the heat of the day in summer to keep away the flies.

Menstruation

A square piece of tan buckskin was folded and brought between the thighs as a breechclout for Tubatulabal men. It was held around the waist by a leather or braided milkweed fiber belt which had the tie in back. Women wore this in addition to their double-apron hide skirt when it was cold or when menstruating. It was said to be a protection too against coyote's raping her.

Paipai Josefina Ochurte said that in the old days a menstruating woman did not use a pad or any special device to catch blood. They simply decreased their activity and washed more frequently. To prevent cramps and excessive loss of blood, they took certain decoctions, however. One of these was *mia'jo* (mia'ho) or *romero* tea. This may have been the California sagebrush *(Artemisia californica)*, an important southern California medicinal plant. Saubel and Bean record its use in a boiled tea among the Cahuilla for comfortable childbirth and rapid postnatal recovery. Taken just prior to the onset of each period, and accompanied by dietary restrictions of no salt, grease or meat for several days thereafter, Cahuilla women also reported that excessive blood loss during menstruation was rare. Drinking the tea was said to lessen even menopausal trauma.

End Notes

For weeks I searched the library of the Southwest Museum bent over the old histories and early ethnographies but found no record of it. What could be more fundamental or what, if lacking, could more quickly lead to complete societal disintegration? And yet, nothing. Is this what happens when men accustomed to life in ivory towers make abstractions about real people in the natural world?

Modern survival books glibly specify some soft toilet-paper-like leaf which, even if recognizable, most would not likely locate in time. The 5,300-year-old Iceman whose freeze-dried body was found in the Alps in 1991 had with him a fair amount of a particular moss whose nearest source was a valley in Italy. From this scientists determined he had come from Italy. In Europe, mosses were used into historic times for wiping. But what of a real California Indian solution to the universal problem!

Paipai and Southern Diegueño Andres Albáñez made perfect sense when he responded to the question. He still remembered the old ways and often practiced them. He said they used whatever vegetation was available. The need was not perfectly predictable nor did every place have the same plants. It would have been foolish to be fixed on a special leaf for this.

Elderly Kiliwa chief Cruz Ochurte, who as a young man spent much time wandering the San Pedro Mártir Mountains unencumbered by toilet paper, recommended almost any plant could be plucked for this purpose. Chided by his wife that he could not possibly mean just any plant, he responded that any *soft young* plant would be a good choice. Pressed further, he said young *hierba del pasmo* would be best.

Reigning Paipai elder Benito Peralta of the Sierra Juárez laughed when I posed the question to him. As a boy he had heard the answer from the ancient ones themselves. Still curious, and with a ready laugh and strong sense of humor even while his eyes cloud over with age and his thin frame stiffens from arthritis, he took me out into the hills so I could see first hand. He had asked the question so many years before of those who had been born in the first half of the 1800s, and they all told him the same: *hierba del pasmo* it is called in Spanish, he said, and pointed to a haplopappus plant *(Haplopappus propinquus)* thick with small wispy dark green leaves. Smell it, he suggested, and that was the best part. It was aromatic like a pine—that's important, said Peralta. Be careful not to get any thick twigs or branches in the bunch you use, he chuckled. It should be soft and sweet smelling and the crowded leaves very small. Many plants are like that and work well. You use what you have where you are; the principal is what is important, Peralta emphasized. As we returned, he pointed to a low sagebrush *(Artemisia)* rich with soft, tiny, branching, gray-green finger-like leaves, strongly scented. It was another one good for the purpose, he said.

Native California Clothing—An Overview

Traveling up the Baja California Peninsula between Ensenada and Alta California in 1769, Father Junípero Serra entered an observation to his diary on the confident and peaceful manner in which the Indians approached him, and he noted their dress or lack of it: "All the males, adults and youths, go about naked," he wrote, while "the women and young girls, even female children at the breast, are decently clothed."

Other early observers seem in general agreement. Children and men are frequently described as without clothing. Men occasionally wore a hide loin covering (an animal skin about the hips or bark breechcloth) and women almost always wore an apron fore and a fuller skirt aft made of buckskin or the strips of the inner bark of cottonwood or willow, or some other dangling cords. For warmth, the fur or skin robe of bear, deer, mountain lion, wildcat, fox, rabbit, bird, land otter or the prized sea-otter was universal. The log of Juan Rodríguez Cabrillo makes mention in November of 1542 that the Indians in the region south of Cape Galera (Point Conception) wore furs from many kinds of animals. The entries in late August of 1542 record that at Posesión (San Quentin, about 100 miles south of Ensenada) Indians came covered with skins from deer which had been cured in the Central Mexican or Aztec fashion.

Northern California was rich in large fur-bearing animals that were combined and stitched together for cold weather. The thickly twined rabbitskin blanket used as a cape was the more usual wrap of the south, but it also kept nearly all of Native California warm. California Indians, however, are most noteworthy for what they did not wear. As we survey the tribes from the colder north to the warmer south over a thousand miles distant, and see some decreases in ornamentation and cold-weather wear along the way, the real story is how simple, similar and scant was the clothing over the entire region. The changing environments offered different materials but the basic spare wardrobe stayed much the same.

Young Yurok men of northern California, wrote A.L. Kroeber, folded a deerskin around their hips with the fur always left on. Women wore a foot-wide apron of deerskin, dressed or depilated and split into fringes wrapped with a braid of *xerophyllum* or strung with pine nuts. A considerably broader skirt, also fringed but with much unslit area as well, met the front piece at the waist from the rear and completed the dress. Women of means would ornament it heavily with haliotis and clam shells or a row of obsidian prisms which jangled from the ends of fringes as they walked. Adolescent girls, novitiate shamans and women who had fallen on hard times wore a skirt of fringed inner bark of the maple. Rabbits were scarce but single deer hides or furs of other animals sewn together were used to keep warm. Two deer hides formed a cape (a photograph from the Hupa shows them joined at the sides) that both men and women threw over their shoulders in cold weather. The cape was neither fitted nor squared and Kroeber recorded they seemed to value the natural dangling of legs and neck. Basketry caps were habitually worn by women.

For warmth Maidu men and women wore deer or mountain-lion-skin robes (the hair side next to the body), thick rabbitskin blankets, or a pair of

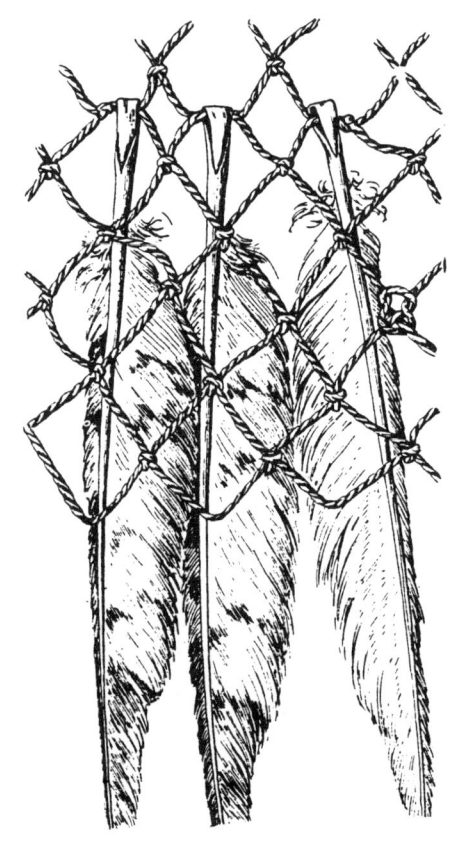

Detail of Maidu feather cloak worn in dances shows how feathers, usually of the hawk, were fixed to the net. They cut the quill base at a long slant, folded it over and inserted the quill in itself (Dixon, 1905).

large animal skins sewn together. Women and men went barefoot except in the mountains where both sexes wore similar single-piece moccasins, stuffed with grass for travel on snow. The calf could be protected with a deerskin legging, hair side inward, tied above the knee and wound with a thong down the lower leg. Older Maidu women, especially in the Sacramento Valley, sometimes went nude, but generally women wore two tassels of grass or bark of willow or maple attached to a belt of buckskin or a fiber cord. One tassel was in back, the other in front. Tassels measured about 40 cm. long and they would carefully tuck the front tassel between the legs when sitting. Maple bark was preferred. They peeled it in spring, then dried, rubbed and worked it into thin layers like birch bark. It was finally cut

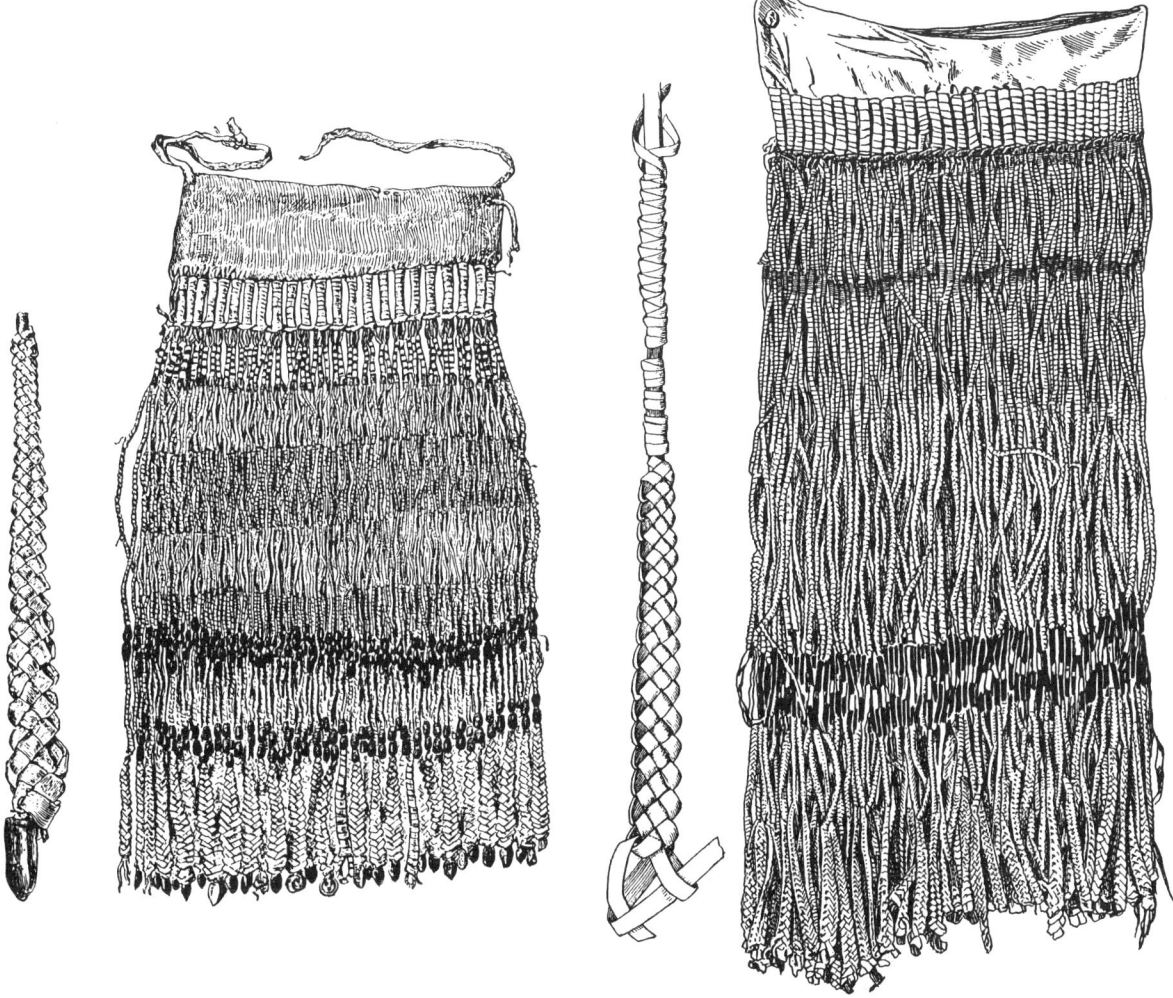

Shasta women wore various buckskin skirts. The simplest was a plain piece of buckskin wrapped from front to rear where it met, or nearly met, itself. Another, sometimes worn over this for special occasions, was a doubled or folded skirt that came from behind and met in the front, or nearly so. This second skirt was deeply fringed on both sides, braided with bear grass and strung with shell pendants, beads, pine nuts and other ornaments. Where this skirt came together in front, a third garment (an apron of long fringes) also braided with bear grass and strung with pine nuts and other seeds filled the gap. These latter skirts were sometimes double and worn one in front and another behind without other skirts. Such a Shasta garment appears to the right (length, 50 cm.) with a detail of the bear-grass wrapping that covered the buckskin fringe (Dixon, 1907). A detail of the Hupa wrapping and a similar Hupa skirt is on the left (Mason, 1889). Bear grass (Xerophyllum tenax) was gathered in June and July in mountain areas the Indians had burned over to bring new green leaves used both for dress ornaments and basket-making. Schenk and Gifford recorded how Karok Indian Mary Ike would split bear grass leaves to size. She held a hair from her head taut, inserted it in a split end of the leaf and pulled the leaf over the hair, severing a section of leaf along its full length.

into strips. These were bundled then doubled over and encircled many times with cordage at the folded, top end. Northeastern Maidu made similar long aprons of buckskin in addition to those of bark. They cut the skin into long narrow strips or cords and tied such things as pine nuts or deer hooves to the end. (The Achomawi filled the whole cord with pine nuts.) A basket cap of tule or reeds was worn by the northeastern Maidu women but apparently not others.

In the 1920s, Robert Lowie noted that the Paviotso or Northern Paiute covered themselves with rabbitskin blankets when sleeping and used the blanket as a cape for winter wear. Men wore a buckskin breechclout and fringed leggings held up by a buckskin cord. A boy's leggings were of deer and coyote hide. In even older days badgerskin caps had been worn by men. Babies were wrapped in a sagebrush bark blanket. Women dressed in an antelope skirt to just below the knees, without leggings, and wore a basket hat.

Wuzzie George, a Northern Paiute, told Margaret Wheat of sagebrush mats they used as clothing. The mats opened in the center for the head and hung down in front and back in the ancient Mexican style. They had no sleeves but were tied on the sides. She demonstrated the manufacture of the cloth. Strips of shaggy loose bark 2 or 3 feet long were pulled from the high sagebrush growing in river bottoms. She softened the bark by rubbing it between the knuckles of her clenched fists. Small bundles of the long fibers were twined together with Indian hemp string as one would a mat: the string was looped around the first bundle and twisted, another bundle was pressed against the first and the string twisted again and so on. Rows of twine were about 1 to 2 inches apart.

In a similar fashion, the Klamath made a blanket, worn as a cape, of sagebrush bark or shredded tule or both. Klamath mittens, made of coyote or other fur and worn in cold weather and for protection in war, were without fingers and of arm- or elbow-length.

Miwok men of the mountains wore a short hip skirt of skins and women a skirt from waist to knees of dressed deerskin fringed by means of slits at the bottom that were sometimes ornamented. Children went nude. Robes of wildcats, foxes, rabbits and hares, used as the top covering for sleeping, also functioned as wraps when traveling in cold weather, according to Galen Clark, a well-known early settler of the Yosemite and Wawona area. The skins were cut into narrow strips, twisted to bring the fur to the outside and used as weft on a warp made from the strong twine of the showy milkweed *(Asclepias speciosa)*.

Costanoans too had the usual rabbitskin blanket and women wore the common California short skirts of deerskin, tule or bark in front and behind. The men, as elsewhere, went naked, weather permitting. But Kroeber records that the men, in the morning before the sun shone warm, did something unusual. They coated themselves with mud, spreading it thick over themselves until the chill of the morning had passed.

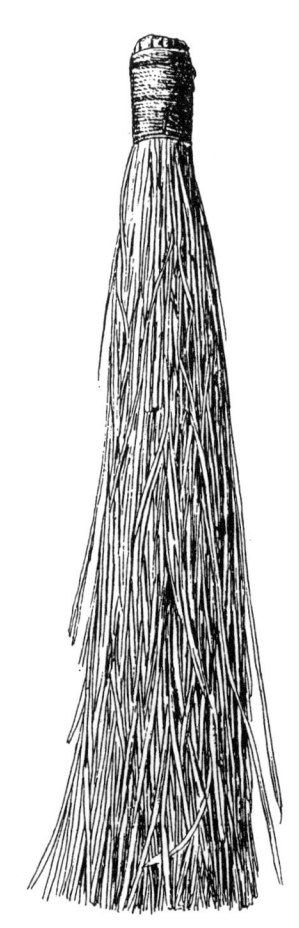

Maidu woman's apron of shredded bark. One worn in front, the other behind; they measured about 40 cm. (this one was 60 cm.) and were attached to a belt of buckskin or cord. They could be of grass or willow bark but maple bark was preferred. The bark was peeled in the spring and dried, then rubbed and worked until it separated into thin layers. The softened bark was cut into strips and bundled as shown. The front tassel was carefully tucked between the legs when sitting. The northwestern Maidu made similar aprons of bark and also buckskin. The ends of the buckskin cords were adorned with pine nuts and deer hooves (Dixon, 1905).

Tubatulabal men and women wore double-apron skirts that hung from 1 to 8 inches below the knee. They were deerskin according to Voegelin's informants in the 1930s, made of antelope in Francisco Garcés' 1776 account. Each piece, fore and aft, was rectangular, tanned and of the same size. Buckskin thongs laced them together at the sides. At both upper sides of each piece, thongs were fastened to tie in front for the back apron and in back for the front. Some skirts had a short fringe (1-1/2 inches) around the bottom. If they became wet in rainy weather, they dried stiff and had to be rubbed and pulled between the hands to soften them. In cold weather or during menstruation, women wore a tanned buckskin breechcloth with the skirt. It was worn regularly by the men and consisted of a square piece folded once and brought between the thighs and held up by a leather or braided milkweed belt. Women also put on round, coiled basketry caps that came down nearly to the eyes when they toted a load with a pack strap. Men did not wear hats. Children wore nothing at all except in cold weather when they also were dressed in a double-apron skirt. Babies were wrapped in tanned wildcat hides with the hair left on. For cold weather Tubatulabal men and women had a sleeveless coat or long shirt made in front and back sections of tanned buckskin. Similar to the skirt, it was laced on the sides below the armholes and on the shoulders. It had a 10- to 12-inch-laced slit below the throat. Rabbitskin blankets were draped over the shoulders and clasped with a hand at the chest.

Raised by the Choinumne Yokuts in the 1850s, Thomas Mayfield remembered how men made and used a breechclout. They cut a strip of deerskin about 10 inches wide from the neck to the tail, the longest piece in the hide. He did not describe the removal of hair nor the brain tanning which undoubtedly occurred, but he told how the long leather strip was draped over a string of buckskin and placed behind the wearer. The ends of the thong were then brought to the front and the ends of the breechcloth carried between the legs and to the front as well, and were held there under the chin against the heart while the string was tied. The ends of the breechcloth were dropped to hang loose in front. They wore it continuously, even to bed, removing it only to bathe, which they did before sunup, but not when they entered the water many times during the day. That was all men wore save in cold weather when they might tie a mountain lion skin about their shoulders. They used neither moccasin nor sandal and had feet as tough as shoes. Women wore a skirt of rabbitskins, woven as the blanket, with one piece in front and one behind that reached near the knee.

Generally, Mohave men and women went barefoot and bareheaded. Nearly naked, they usually wore only loin coverings made of the inner bark of willow. They stripped the bark from trees in September and October and left it weighted down to macerate for a month in backwater lakes of the Colorado River. Spier, who worked with the Mohave in 1931 and 1932, learned the willow bark strips were hung from waist cords of the fiber of the black-eyed pea. The pea fiber was obtained by soaking, drying and pounding the plant. Women wore a small, foot-long under apron of fine willow bark as a genital covering. Over this, a larger front apron of narrow bark strips was tied behind the back. The strips were thinly hung and came only to the knees. A thickly bunched rear apron of broad willow strips that reached the calves was tied with its own waist cord in the front. It lapped over the front apron at the hips but left the outside of the thighs slightly bare. Both aprons were made of bark strips draped over a waist cord and twined together, bunch by bunch, by two or three rows of cordage just below the waist thong. Men wore a breechclout. The ends hung in a short flap in front, a longer one reaching the knees or below in back. It was made from cloth of moderately broad willow strips in a checkerboard weave. In cold weather a wool blanket poncho obtained in trade from the Navaho, or a rabbitskin robe, a trade item from the Walapai, was worn by either sex.

Like the Mohave, the Luiseño women made a back skirt from the soft inner bark of cottonwood or willow. The small front piece sometimes came from the same bark but more generally was an apron of cords of the fiber they normally used for string: milkweed *(Asclepias eriocarpa)*, Indian hemp *(Apocynum cannabinum)* or stinging nettle *(Urtica holosericea)*. Coiled and twined caps of juncus were usually worn to carry loads with a tumpline. Long capes of rabbit furs, deerskins or the especially esteemed sea-otter furs protected them from the cold. Men generally went naked.

Diegueño men were similarly wont to wear nothing at all. Some donned a short narrow apron of white sage twigs hung from a milkweed cord. Women wore the aprons, fore and aft. A rabbitskin blanket was used in winter like a shirt, in poncho fashion with a slit for the neck. The sides were tied beneath the arms, like blanket shirts from the Indian civilizations of Central Mexico. Perhaps the idea came with the early Mexicans. They wore the basketry hat that was widespread in the South, coiled or twined (as seen among the Paipai), and used by women when toting loads with a tumpline from the crown of the head.

The Kiliwa men of Lower California generally wore nothing at all in warm weather. Women wore a small apron of deer hide, which had been soaked in water and worked until soft, along with a deer-hide skirt with the hair side out or scraped off, secured about the waist with a mescal cord. A rabbitskin blanket could be worn in very cold weather. At times, the Kiliwa wore sandals made from the fiber of mescal.

California Indians almost always went barefoot. They shod themselves only for long treks or for travel in the mountains or on a hunt traversing especially rough country. High-top single-piece leather moccasins were the standard of the north but found as far south as the Cahuilla where they overlapped with sandals of leather or fiber, the usual footwear of the south. The southern California fiber sandal had an antiquity of many thousands of years but then, so did the ubiquitous rabbitskin blanket. Much of the California wardrobe was ancient and tested by time.

The real lesson of native California for those of us who squander our lives getting dressed and worrying about being chilled is how little one truly needs. I remember Teodora Cuero, an elderly Southern Diegueño woman from La Huerta, describe Felipe Jat'am, who was over one hundred years old at the time he died when Teodora was a child. She only knew him with sandals on his feet, an old cast off shirt and patched-up pants. In the winter he went without a heavy jacket or blanket. He was quite a man, she said. He relied on fire to keep him warm. He built fires around himself and that is how he would sleep. Sometimes he would gather a special soft bush that grows around here to use as a bed. That's all he needed.

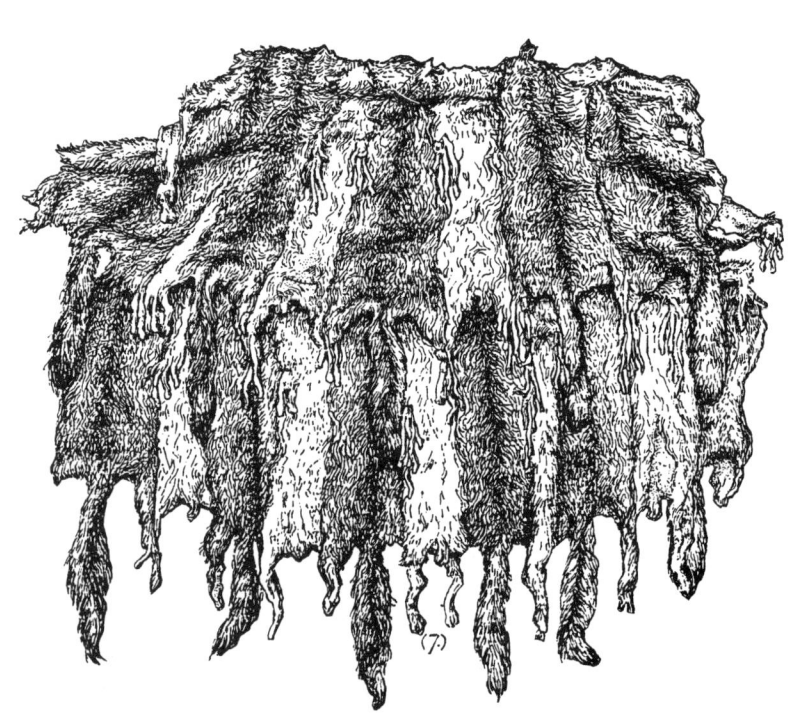

Hupa robe of various pelts sewed together for a man or woman. From the Lieutenant P. H. Ray Collection, Smithsonian Institution (Mason, 1889).

Rabbitskin Blanket

In 1579 Sir Francis Drake spent five weeks repairing his ship, the Golden Hind, along the coast of California. A narrative from the voyage described the Indians around a bay where the repairs were made. According to historians, it was Drakes Bay, a lagoon in Point Reyes north of San Francisco. The account reminded A.L. Kroeber of the nineteenth century Pomo and their neighbors. One of those groups, the Coast Miwok, inhabited the area of Drakes Bay. Men generally went naked, the ledger recorded, but "the Women combing out Bulrushes made them a loose Garment, which ty'd round their middle, hangs down about their Hipps: And hides what Nature would have concealed: They wear likewise about their Shoulders a Deer skin with the Hair thereon. . . ." And their leader had "on his shoulders a Coat of Rabbit Skins reaching to his Waste. . . ."

José Longinos Martínez observed blankets in northern Baja in 1792 of "twisted strips of rabbit, otter, or fox skin—this latter in the mountains . . . the corners tied together, the head and one arm thrust through the upper opening." Later ethnographers documented rabbitskin blankets for virtually the entire West and all of California with the exception of small areas in the north of the state.

Equally impressive is the rabbitskin blanket's depth in time. Remnants have been found in the lowest levels at caves such as Gypsum and Lovelock in southern and western Nevada, at Tularosa and Cordova in New Mexico, White Dog and Ventana in Arizona. Ken Hedges, of the Museum of Man, suggests that out of the early Desert Culture tradition, rabbit blankets, essentially unchanged in their method of manufacture, have been in continuous use in western North America for the last 10,000 years.

Gifford called them the warmest of all garments among the Southern Diegueño of Imperial Valley. The Northern Paiute wore the rabbitskin blanket as a cape tied with cordage around the neck; it would reach below the thighs and by squatting down, the blanket even enveloped and warmed the legs. Yet its primary use was as a cover at night. The Indians of California, Nevada, and Lower California, despite a generally mild climate of warm days, faced frigid winters of long cold nights and for that depended on the warmth of fire and the rabbitskin blanket.

Spencer Rogers extolled the inventiveness and dexterity of the blanket— that such a soft and pliable fabric could be created in an environment where most fibers were stiff and unyielding. The Paiute took prime pelts in November during large rabbit drives. Mountain tribes collected pelts as they

Mohave man wearing rabbitskin robe on the bank of the Colorado River early 1900s. Photograph by Edward S. Curtis (Southwest Museum).

were able, sometimes in group drives, sometimes individually with a rabbit stick or bow and arrow at any time of the year, until they had enough for a blanket. Twisted strips of untanned rabbit hides of all native species— jackrabbit, cottontails and brush rabbits—were twined with cords into small blankets for children or large all-purpose wraps for adults. As few as twelve to as many as 100 hides might be used for a blanket, which usually included more than one species of rabbit.

Brief descriptions of the manufacture of these rectangular blankets exist for nearly every native group, but Wheat's account of Paiute Jimmy George's way and Gayton's recording of techniques among the Yokuts seem most complete. Scattered details from other tribes on rabbitskin blankets as well as the closely related feather blankets bring the near forgotten images into even clearer focus.

Rabbit Blanket Technology of the Paiute and Others

To keep the whole pelt intact, Northern Paiute Jimmy George made incisions in the rear area and around the paws, then pulled the entire skin down and off the hind legs and over the head. Next, holding the knife in his teeth and beginning near an eyehole, he pulled the hide along the sharp blade with both hands and cut it into a long spiral strip, round and round, down the whole rabbitskin, like a spring. Each hide produced a fluffy ribbon 10 to 15 feet long. (Wheat did not record width but Voegelin's account of the Tubatulabal gives 1-1/2 inches). He linked these together one to the next by passing the tip of each ribbon through a small hole in the end of the last and then through its own eyehole at its opposite end, forming a large interlinked loop which he then pulled tight, ready for the next link. He did this until he had a chain 40 or more feet long.

With one end of this chain tied to a tree, he hooked the other end to a stick that was rolled on the thigh almost as though making cordage. The skin side of the pelt naturally folded in, creating a soft fur rope. This twisted rope was hung to dry and later the ears, which became brittle and would scratch, were snapped off.

He looped the fur rope around a crude loom of willows that Wheat did not describe further. Other groups, however, such as the Tubatulabal, Southern Diegueño and Kiliwa, made them of four wooden stakes or pegs in the ground at the points of a rectangle that represented the desired size of the blanket. The points were connected with native string. The long fur strips passed back and forth, over and around these strings to form the warps.

Jimmy George twined the warps together with cordage. The twining rows could be two, three, or four fingers apart, depending on the desired fineness of the finished blanket. The Tubatulabal, according to Voegelin, used milkweed fiber string for the warp and the twisted rabbitskin itself as the weft which they tied to the warp at one corner and twined over and under the warp.

Many groups reinforced the strips of rabbitskin by twisting them raw around string and letting them dry before weaving. The Kiliwa used mescal fiber string for this. The reinforced rabbit

Mohave Indian with rabbitskin blanket early 1900s. Photograph by George Wharton James (Southwest Museum).

fur wefts were then woven tightly through string warps using a bone awl. The Southern Diegueño wrapped the strips around milkweed or mescal fiber cord, overlapping the pelts on the cord. Drying tightened and held them in place. They made a continuous warp of these. A milkweed cord weft, tied to the warp at intervals, either wove or twined the fur strips together.

The Maricopa loom described by Spier was unusual in its simplicity. The weaver tied the end of a rolled willow bark cord to her toe and the other end around her waist. Strips of twisted rabbitskin were lapped a few inches each over the cord or doubled back over the cord if unusually long. She then wrapped a second cord close to the foundation cord, once around each strip and its short lapped end to hold the strips fast. To complete the robe she twined string through the rabbitskin warps at intervals of a hand's span and parallel to the foundation cord. (This method would have been difficult if commercially tanned rabbitskins were used, since any loose ends tend to unwind and lose their twist. Raw skins, twisted fresh and dried in the Indian way, hold their twist as they are made into a blanket.)

Yokuts Rabbit-fur Blankets

The Yokuts of the central Sierra foothills, recorded by Gayton, made what must have been a most luxuriantly thick rabbitskin blanket using a variety of looms and a clever technique of sewing through parallel twists of double-twisted ropes. This gave the appearance of twining to the fur strips but possessed the torque of twisted cordage. To begin, the rabbit was cut under the throat and around the

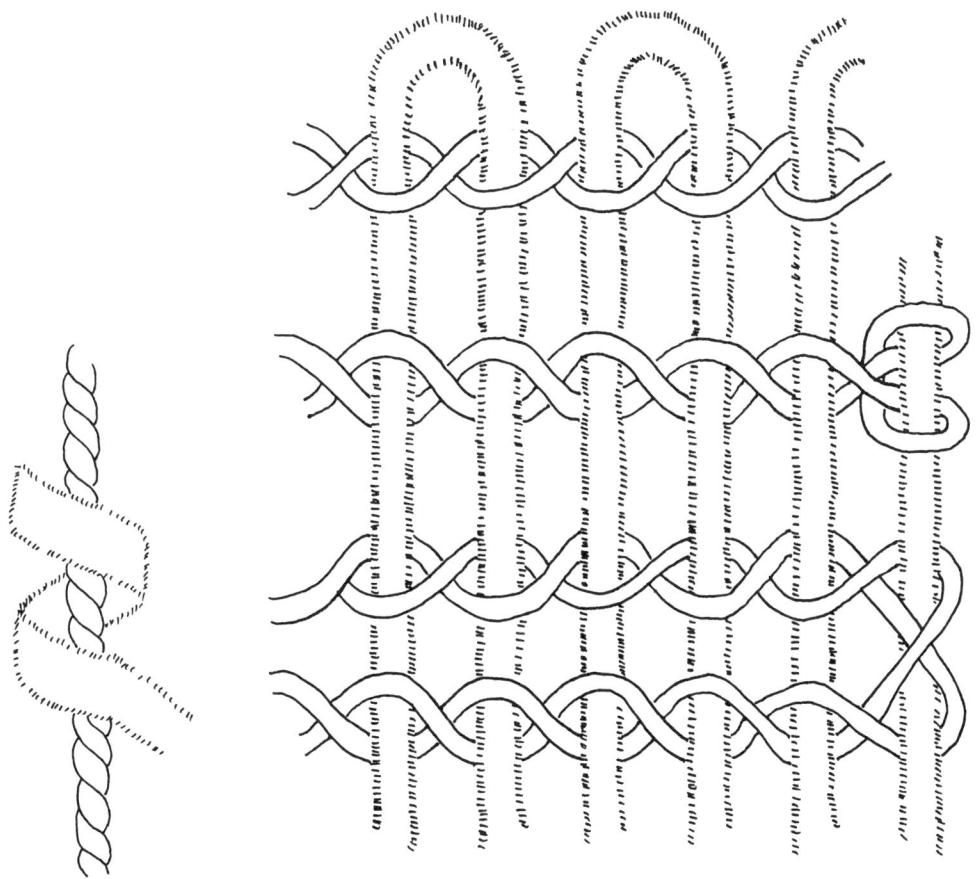

Diagrammatic sketch of continuous, back and forth (up and down) rabbitskin warp. Selvage twining at top—twining was generally of two-ply milkweed fiber cordage—also found at bottom in actual blanket. Beginning knot of twined milkweed cordage shown just below: the end loop of a doubled cord was taken around the first warp and the loose ends passed through the loop. Next, the manner of changing weft direction. Wefts were twined approximately every 4 cm. for length of robe. Enlarged sketch at left shows the rabbitskin warp made of fur strips twisted around two-ply agave cordage; the ends of the fur strips overlapped. Based on Southern Diegueño (Kumeyaay) rabbitskin robe in San Diego Museum of Man, made years ago by Josefa Tobac, Kumeyaay of Cuyapaipe, California (redrawn from Hedges, 1973).

head just in front of the ears. The paws were severed above the toe joints. Pulling on the ears, the skin peeled back over the shoulders and off the forelegs. After the skin slipped completely off, the ears were removed at the base, having served their purpose. The skin was dried inside out. A small rib bone scraped away adhering tissue (an obsidian knife was considered too sharp). Once dry, with an obsidian blade against a smooth flat stone, beginning at the neck, the blanket maker cut a strip by spiraling around and down the hide.

About four to six skin strips were tied end-to-end (and probably twisted), then doubled with the loose ends tied to something such as a ramada post. With a hooked stick through the loop end, the blanket maker twisted the stick and the two strands of rope until they twisted back again on each other when given slack, producing a four-ply rabbitskin rope.

Ropes twisted this way were simply laid out parallel on the ground in the form of the blanket to be made, usually 3 by 5 feet. One by one they were picked up, and through each parallel twist a slit wood needle was passed carrying a cord of milkweed. Continuing on in this fashion the blanket was completed.

One-hundred-year-old Yaudanchi Yokuts Mary Sanwihat, whose father had been a noted hunter of rabbits, saw them made a little differently. The strips of rabbit fur were rolled on the thigh with two strands of milkweed string. About 8 to 10 feet long, they were then twisted double, halving the length. The ropes were hung from a pole suspended between two forked sticks by passing the two loose ends of each rope through its looped opposite end and making a slip noose. The weft string, gathered in a hank of folds about 4 inches long, began at the top right and passed through the parallel twists as described. On reaching the bottom, the loose warp ends were tied. The loops at the top were slipped off the pole, twisted twice, and these parallel twists sewed through in the established pattern as selvage. Mary Sanwihat said only men made blankets in the old days.

Wukchumni Yokuts Mollie Lawrence described a third method. The double-twisted ropes were all tied together in one long continuous rope. This was wound vertically around a two-pole horizontal upright frame. The string weft went through parallel twists as in the other cases. Pegs holding the bottom horizontal pole were loosened as the weaving progressed and the blanket grew taut.

Blankets of Twisted Rabbit Fur, Birdskin and Other Materials

The Yokuts of the central foothills avoided combining the skins of jackrabbits and cottontails in a single blanket. Twisted ground squirrel and twisted duck skin blankets were sometimes made by these Indians. In the same fashion, they twisted quail skins into delicate blankets for babies.

Many years ago Frank Latta interviewed Yoimut whom he called the last of the Chunut (Yokuts from the northeast shore of Lake Tulare). Yoimut described blankets of mud hen skins made the same way as the rabbit-fur blankets. She recounted that for rabbit-fur blankets they took the animal's skin off and cut it around and around in a long strip which was twisted to bring all the fur to the outside. It was doubled (likely in a similar manner described above for the other Yokuts). String was sewn back and forth from one end to the other. It made a big blanket.

Kroeber recorded that the Maidu of the Sacramento Valley, where waterbirds were more numerous than rabbits, made most of their blankets from feathers. The only difference between the usual Maidu rabbitskin blanket and the feather blanket was that the more fragile birdskin with its feathers first had to be twisted with cordage to give it strength. The Maidu method for rabbitskin (and by extension birdskin) blankets was as follows. Skins were cut into strips, 1/2 inch or more wide. Uncured, they twisted on themselves as they dried, exposing the soft hair (or so they said). They were fastened end-to-end and this long rope wound between two upright stakes, forming a vertical plane of horizontal warps. The two ends of another skin rope were twined up and down the skin warps. On each turn, the twining cords were knitted to the outermost warp.

In turn-of-the-century investigations among the Maidu of the Sacramento Valley, Dixon discovered that the skins of crows were made into feather cloaks. The Maidu took crows in quantity with a collapsible net. Two light sticks from 2 to 3 meters long were tied loosely together at one end, opened like a V, and a net stretched between them. A hunter sat with this device on a platform or "nest" built high in a low bushy willow, reached by a simple ladder. He entered the nest at night and was concealed. Others went about scaring up sleeping crows, driving them toward the hunter who would raise his net as the birds passed overhead and collapse it on them like a fan, bringing the two sticks together when they entered.

Only fourteen California feather blankets are known to remain in existence. All were obtained indirectly and not from the tribes that made them. Sally McLendon found that for at least five of these blankets, which she analyzed, the makers selected only certain feathers from only three species: beige downy breast feathers of the Canada goose, contour feathers of the snow goose, and the dark iridescent speculum feathers (they have only eight per wing) of the mallard. In all of the fourteen blankets, noted McLendon, a warp of feathered cords was twined every inch or two by unfeathered weft cords. The blankets were made in contrasting bands of natural color. The fabric she described as thick, soft and downy, warm yet light and delicate. Wear patterns on the three blankets that show wear suggest that they were used as capes held by two corners and draped over the shoulders.

The Cocopa of the lower Colorado River extended rabbitskin blanket technology to willow bark. On the common horizontal loom of four corner stakes connected by string, long strips of rabbit fur (twisted around willow bark cordage) were run back and forth as warp. Strings of black-eyed pea fiber served as weft and were wrapped once around each warp at each crossing. That made a rabbitskin blanket. The willow bark blanket was the same except both warp and weft were solely of willow bark cordage (rolled two-ply by hand on the thigh). The blanket measured in excess of 5 by 8 feet and softened with use. Several children could sleep under one of these. Both rabbitskin and bark blankets were made by the men. In 1775 Pedro Font found the Yuma Indians, north of the Cocopa on the Colorado River, making capes of strips of rabbit or *beaver* skin woven with bark cordage.

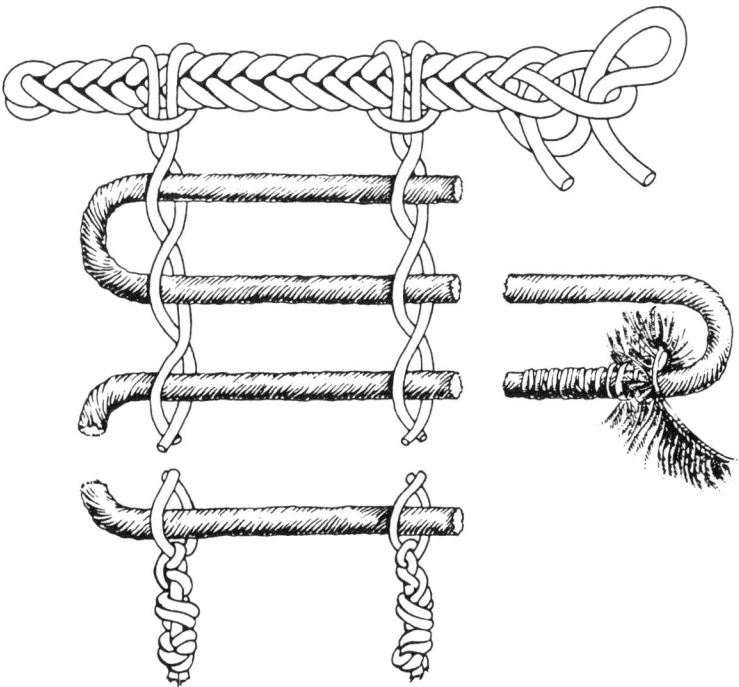

Early accounts record that feather blankets were made of twisted skins of birds, presumably the skin containing the small, soft, downy feathers. The above diagrammatic sketch of a feathered blanket, collected in 1841 and thought to be Maidu, shows the warp closely wrapped with laminae of split feather ribs, a technique seemingly most suited to somewhat larger feathers. Those on the blanket analyzed were of wood duck, mallard, and Canada goose. Cordage wefts had been attached to the upper chain-stitched cord with lark's-head knots and twined to hold the continuous feathered warp. Wefts were finished in columns of knotting at the bottom. Kroeber noted yet a third California method of making the feather blanket. Two cords were twisted on each other for a warp and at each turn a bit of feather inserted (sketch from Riddell, 1978).

Elderberry Bark Skirt

Before environmental degradation and overpopulation forced the drudgery of agriculture and slavery of civilization on nearly everyone, the land provided a bounty for the taking. Pushed into a small piece of their former vast territory, a few Paipai, Kiliwa and Southern Diegueño of the Santa Catarina region still on occasion go out into the wilderness and collect what they need. It is a storehouse they know well.

Raúl Sandoval, a Southern Diegueño, often descended to the dry arroyo where the old Mexican elderberry *(Sambucus mexicana)* trees grew to collect bark for the traditional skirt his mother Manuela Aguiar made. He would strip bark with his hands from trees so old that some parts of them had died, and the bark would come off easy in long strips and the light brown parchment-like inner bark would separate quickly from the rough flaky husk. On one side of the tree or another, he made cuts and pulled the heavy cortex from the plant, the dry inner bark streaming along with it. The strips, from 2 to 4 feet long, were bent every few inches toward the inner side, breaking the outer bark which he pulled off in chunks. This left the beige strips of paper-like inner bark ready for making skirts. They could be braided into cords for holding up a skirt or gathered into a breechclout or plaited into fabric for other uses as well.

Raúl Sandoval gathering the inner bark of an elderberry tree killed by fire.

But today he remembered a single tree killed by fire from a careless Indian cowboy or lightning years before. He went straight to that tree whose outer bark had burned black but whose inner bark was nearly white, startling for its purity. It fairly fell from the fire-blackened tree in long layered sheaths. In half an hour he had enough for an elderberry bark skirt.

Cottonwood was a tree they also sometimes used, said Raúl. Pedro Font found many dry cottonwoods and willow on the banks of the lower Colorado River in 1775. They died because the Yumas stripped the bark for women's skirts, he wrote.

Manuela Aguiar began a bark skirt by doubling back the ends of an 8-1/2 foot two-ply mescal fiber cord, tying the ends to each other and onto the center section of the cord itself so that a double cord "belt" 4-1/4 feet long was formed. Other strings were temporarily passed through the loops of both ends and fastened about 3 feet off the ground to a door pillar on one side and ramada post on the other, at a level convenient for Manuela, who was seated on a stool, to make the skirt.

She sprinkled water lightly over the dry elderberry bark with her hands, then began to drape the multilayered strips over the cord, starting at the right with longer bundles that were over twice the desired length of the skirt. When finally trimmed the skirt would be about 2 feet long. One size generally fit all, but length could be varied according to the person's desire and size. These longer bundles were hung one overlapping the next, each doubled over the cord. Shorter pieces, slightly longer than the intended skirt length, were used only if necessary and after the other lengths had been depleted. They were hung over the cord with about 5 inches of overlap and pushed together with the others.

Many bundles of bark had shredded naturally during the gathering. Combing the incipient skirt with her fingers, Manuela shredded others by splitting them lengthwise, beginning with a small vertical tear halfway down and pulling it open in both directions. Strips of a completed skirt ran about 5/8 of an inch in width although many much finer strips had formed.

With her fingers she sprinkled a little water over the bark at the area of the belt. She took a two-ply agave string of convenient length (about 3 feet) and at the far right passed one end around a group of strips, about 1 inch in width and 1 inch from the top, and drew the string firm around them, to about 1/2

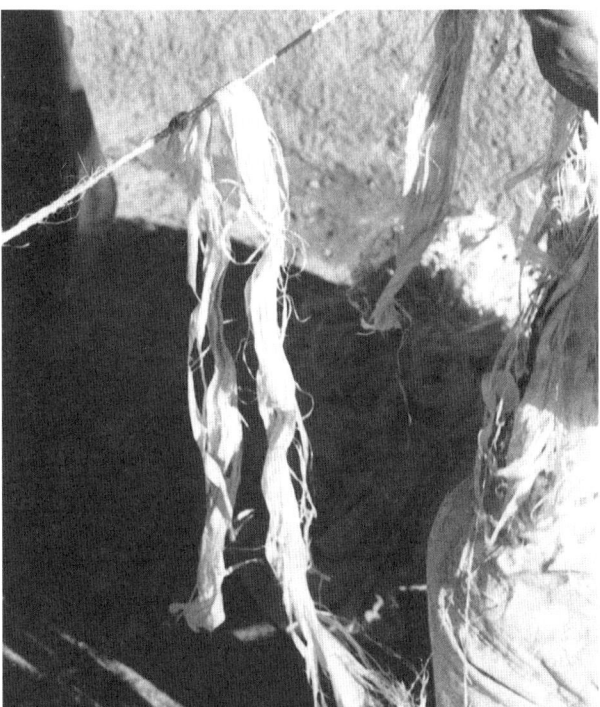

Manuela Aguiar dampens the bark strips and drapes them over the agave-fiber cord.

inch width, but not so tight as to crack the strips, securing the string loop with a square knot. She threaded a large 5-inch needle on the other end of the string. Traditionally, this would have been a sharpened wood stick, said Manuela. She poked the needle through the strips immediately to the left of the first encircled group. She extended it to the left along the back of the skirt for an inch, brought it out to the front and then to the right and again passed it to the back just to the left of the first encircled group and above the first string. She tightened the noose she had formed around the second group to around 1/2 inch across, again firmly but not so much that it would cut or crack the bark strips. She continued around the back roughly 1 inch past this second group, returned to the front and encircling this, the third group, passed the needle to the back immediately to the left of the second group, over the string, and pulled it snug. She continued circling groups of bark strips in this fashion.

For greater strength at a certain point, instead of continuing one inch beyond the last group, she brought the needle to the front immediately to the left of the last group and encircled the next group clockwise instead of counterclockwise. The next stitch could continue on one inch beyond this group at the front, doing now what had been done at the back, simply reversing the stitch. Or it could pass to the back, just to the left of the last group, to make an encircling counterclockwise stitch around the next group and continue on as in the beginning, according to convenience and desire.

If a cord ran out, it was simply tied off around the last bundle and a new cord begun. Reaching the last group at the left, she encircled it and tied off the cord in a square knot. She again moistened the top of the skirt and began a new cord as before at the right, this time *above* the first cord, halfway between the first cord and the double belt cord. The new row of loops divided the bundles that had been created by the cord below. That is, adjacent halves of two lower

Manuela splits the strips lengthwise. Beginning knot and encircling of the strips with the agave cord.

bundles were gathered as one in a bundle above, staggering the stitches of the two rows. This row ended on the left and was tied off.

She flicked water on the dress to moisten it slightly, combed it with her fingers and finished splitting strips of bark she found too wide, giving the dress a uniform appearance. Raúl, her son, clipped longer strips of the bottom to a roughly even length. The finished dress fluffed out half a foot thick. It was 39 inches wide. The inner bark, which had been laid to near the ends of the doubled belt cord, were gathered toward the center, giving the dress a fuller, thicker look and leaving enough cordage on either end to tie the dress off at the side of the wearer (where a woman might expose a little leg, Raúl suggested). The skirt was cut from the temporary strings that held it between post and pillar. Manuela demonstrated how the bark could be widened or narrowed on the belt to accommodate a heavier or thinner person. Either side of the dress could be worn outward.

This was the traditional garment of Indian women, but it is worn today only for ceremony and dance. Occasionally men also wear them for dancing. Aguiar said they could be made from the inner bark of willow or cottonwood or even from juniper bark but juniper and willow turn very brittle and the strips break off. Elderberry is the very best, she assured me (a fact personal experience strongly confirmed).

Gloria Castañeda, a Kumeyaay woman from San José de la Zorra and an expert in traditional ways, makes her skirt from willow (apparently black willow, *Salix nigra*) which she gathers green and then dries. She emphasized that long strips are taken only from part of each tree trunk in order not to kill the tree.

The Cocopa also made clothing from the inner bark of willow. Women wore a breechclout of loose willow bark and a skirt similar to that of the elderberry skirt described, except in two pieces: front and back, from hip to hip and from waist to halfway between knees and feet for both back and front pieces, observed Gifford. The back dress was put on first. Strips of inner bark were folded in half and placed over a girdle and tied down with two rows of

Second row of encircling stitches between first row and belt cord bisects bunches of bark strips created by first row. Raul Sandoval evens bottom of skirt. The completed elderberry bark skirt.

doubled two-ply willow bark cord. The woman moistened the bark with her fingers as she worked. Willow bark string sometimes took the place of the willow strips in the dress itself.

Cocopa men wore a breechclout, a foot wide and as long as the outstretched arms. It passed under a string girdle and hung below the knees behind, halfway to the knees in front. Bark breechclouts were said to be best in summer. Men made them by weaving a string in the manner described for Manuela's elderberry bark skirt, circling each warp strip, back and forth for the entire length of the breechclout and leaving no loose ends. While playing certain games the longer rear cloth was brought forward between the legs and tucked under the belt.

Bark for garments was cut by men, packed between four stakes and weighted down by green willow wood in a pond and left to soak for twelve to fourteen days. Women would remove the bark, peel off the outer bark and hang the inner bark, which had bleached white, on poles to dry until evening. It was then ready for use.

For women's skirts, the Cahuilla used red shank *(Adenostoma sparsifolium)* bark which was easily stripped from the tree.

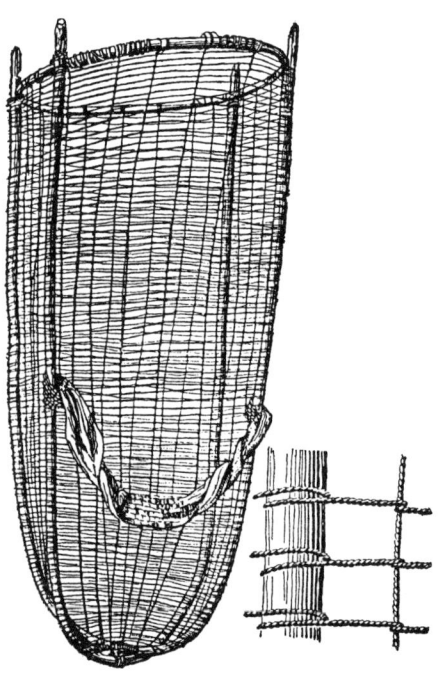

Sketch of Mohave carrying frame; example of wrapped weaving. Two bowed withes cross at right angles on the bottom and are securely lashed to a rigid hoop at the top. Warps of twine have been attached at top and bottom. A twine weft, tied to one of the frame pieces at the bottom, wraps once around each warp element, including the withes of the frame, as it coils to the top (Mason, 1904).

Yucca and Agave Fiber Sandals of Southern California

These most ancient sandals of the Southwest were of fiber and until this century the preferred footwear of southern California and northern Baja California Indians. The first yucca-fiber sandals I ever saw were Diegueño, collected from Mesa Grande in San Diego County, California, around 1900; of pristine condition, they were probably made for a collector. I later found examples of this thick protective sandal in many southern California museums but was unable to uncover the exact manner of manufacture: fiber wrapped around a twisted fiber loop tied at the toe, I speculated; others felt two additional heavy warps were used. Both ideas turned out to be wrong.

Normally, no foot covering at all was employed by southern California Indians who went about most daily tasks barefoot, reserving the use of sandals for special purposes. It must have felt like pure luxury, however, when they did put on their thickly wrapped fiber sandals.

Examples of the true southern California style extended from the Panamint Indians in the Great Basin, where they protected feet from mountain snow, through the Cahuilla east of Los Angeles, who called them *chawish* and where D. P. Barrows described them in constant use among the old people in 1900, to the Kiliwa of the northern Baja California San Pedro Mártir mountains where they functioned as expedition sandals when traversing rough ground. This was the same function described for yucca-fiber sandals of the Gabrielino of Los Angeles. In the scant account we have of them from the Chumash, Fernando Librado told J. P. Harrrington he wore them when the ground was hot so he would not blister his feet. Captain Newton H. Chittenden observed around 1901 that the Cocopa men of the Hardy and lower Colorado River wore rawhide sandals for ordinary service but made noiseless sandals of mescal (agave) fiber for deer hunting. Paipai elder Benito Peralta, when I asked of the southern California fiber sandal, quickly recalled that as a boy the old ones told him these sandals were for hunting because they made no noise.

The Shivwits of northwestern Arizona seem to have done it backwards. Made of the fibers of the yucca or Spanish bayonet, the two tie strings, which normally came off the heel, came off the toe, passing one to the left and the other to the right of the second toe, and pulled through a rear loop (the front loop in the standard southern California version) and back to the instep where they were tied. The heel rested against the rear loop as well as on the wrappings that normally formed the toe. Such sandals were worn on snow by men and women. In winter, bark was tied over the foot to the sandal by means of loops. If a man chased mountain sheep all day in the rocks, the sandals would be worn-out by nightfall. Otherwise, they lasted longer, it was said. These are modern ethnographic accounts, but the idea of the fiber sandal was very old.

Cahuilla sandal collected in 1875 (Bean 1978).

Antiquity of the Fiber Sandal

The southern California fiber sandal known historically was constructed from a two-warp base. The archaeological record of two-warp fiber sandals in the Southwest is fascinating in itself, but the variety of materials and variations on the basic theme uncovered in cave excavations also suggest ways we might reproduce these sandals today in a field or survival situation.

Mashed yucca sandals somewhat similar to those of southern California were described from Mogollon caves of west central New Mexico during 1952 excavations conducted by the Chicago Natural History Museum. In the four caves dug, two sandals of this type were uncovered, one of which was actually of grass. However, earlier excavations of Tularosa and Cordova caves, also Mogollon, had yielded other examples of these mashed yucca "two-warp wickerwork" sandals. In fact, at Tularosa Cave they came from all levels, down through the pre-pottery layer (probably before 200 A.D.). They were most common in the earlier strata. The warps were a loop of yucca leaf knotted at the heel and toe in square knots; according to excavators, those ends at the toe were then brought up to form toe ties. The ends of weft elements terminated on the undersole, frayed, and provided added cushioning (as in the museum Diegueño examples). The most common sandal at the Mogollon sites, however, was of *plaited* yucca leaf.

The Hohokam two-warp wickerwork sandals found by Emil Haury in Ventana Cave were also made of yucca leaves; they were the most prominent sandal at the site and are considered the norm for the Hohokam. For warp, leaves were bent at the toe and tied at the heel. Others of the long, narrow yucca leaves were woven back and forth, over and under the warp like a figure 8, and closely packed, the ends protruding on the underside. Most of the sandals used a whole-yucca-leaf weft, although some were of macerated yucca leaf, a few of shredded wood and even two of bark strips. Cordage warp was also found with mashed yucca weft (four examples) and one each of shredded wood, bark and gut weft. The evidence suggested that two-warp-style sandals were worn as early as San Pedro times (which has been estimated to have lasted from around 1500 to 200 B.C.).

Anasazi Pueblo III sites have yielded a few two-warp wickerwork sandals but of a more rigid appearance, with the ends of the weft elements extended over and frayed at the sides of the sandal.

Incidentally, Haury described two other very different styles of sandals from Ventana Cave. Fragments of a complex yucca sandal of rows or ovals of chain stitches, that looked superficially like braids, sewed to a matted fiber sole and reinforced with cords at right angles to the "braids," heel and toe rounded in the general shape of a foot, were unique in southwestern foot gear and apparently distinctive to the Hohokam. The other was as simple as this one seemed complex, being merely pads cut to the shape of a foot from the outer covering of the stem of the mature yucca. Yucca-leaf stitching helped overcome the tendency for the pads to pull apart into individual fibers or separate into layers. As ties for the foot, two shredded leaves of yucca were stitched through the pad, one through holes a few inches apart in the front and another in back. Haury observed that these, along with the other sandals, demonstrated the Hohokam "willingness to improvise and test any possible raw products."

From Newberry Cave in the California Mojave Desert, archaeologists in the 1950s excavated split twig figurines dating back 3,500 years. The twig models of deer or mountain sheep likely had been used in the magic of an old and far-flung hunter culture. Fragments of sandals of these hunters were found in the cave and were of the two-warp, figure-8-weft style. One was entirely of the slender willow (*Salix exigua*)—the warp, a split twig twisted into two-ply cordage .8 cm. in diameter and the weft, strips of bark .5 to 1.4 cm. in width. Two-ply yucca cordage (.4 to .6 cm. in diameter) formed the warp of other fragments with shredded juniper-bark (*Juniperus*) weft. Two-ply Indian-hemp cordage attached to one of the pieces probably served as binding to tie the sandal to the foot.

Fiber sandals of this sort were extremely ancient and widespread. At Etna Cave, Nevada, shredded yucca sandals of two-cord warp and figure-8 weft extended from the later Paiute occupation back to early Desert Archaic, a spread of some 11,000 years. Chris Moser, Riverside Municipal Museum archaeologist, described to me two-warp wickerwork sandals from caves of the Mixteca in Oaxaca, deep in Mexico where he has conducted excavations. The loop-sole frames were made of agave rope. He found that the remoter villages still manufactured such sandals. He also described the

Mixtec process of releasing the maguey fibers. They would soak the leaf for perhaps a month, allowing the pulp to rot away, then scrape the leaf with a "turtle-back" stone of the kind found in archaeological sites; the stone has a rounded upper surface, a natural handhold, and a sheared-off bottom, flat, like a plane, for scraping away the pulp. Afterwards, they returned the leaf to the water for another week or so to complete the rotting process until only clean white fibers remained.

Precise Methods of Manufacture of the Southern California Fiber Sandal

Information on the Cahuilla from the early years of this century in Harrington's notes indicate that the Mojave yucca *(Yucca schidigera)* was an ideal source of fiber for coiled-rope soles of sandals. Barrows found that leaves of this as well as desert agave *(Agave deserti)*, known as mescal, were soaked until the pulpy part and the outer sheath came off; the resulting fibers were buried in mud to whiten them and combed out ready for use. The best fiber came from young green leaves.

In 1908 Alfred Kroeber wrote of a field trip to the Cahuilla, Serrano and Gabrielino east of Los Angeles and described sandals of mescal still in use, especially on the desert. He was told they were worn mainly by men outdoors at night. He admitted he could not understand their construction, but by 1925 Kroeber, who found no clear report of indigenous sandals north of Tehachapi, summarized the southern California form of the Southwestern sandal as untwisted bundles of mescal fiber woven back and forth across a looped cord forming a pad nearly an inch thick. While clear and concise, this hardly comprised a step-by-step description. Other anthropologists gave even less. How exactly were the sandals made?

It was not until I turned to an ethnographic account compiled by Peveril Meigs in the 1930s on the remote Kiliwa Indians, who are related to the Diegueño, that I found something resembling a complete process—from fiber preparation to sandal manufacture. Meigs wrote:

The most important plant fiber was extracted from the leaves of the mescal. It was used for making nets, footwear, and cordage for miscellaneous purposes.

In the preparation of the fiber, a pit is dug and thoroughly heated by a fire built in it, the hot coals are raked out and green mescal leaves are placed among the ashes in the hot pit and covered with earth. After baking for two or three hours, the leaves are removed from the pit and the outer husk is taken off. The fiber is then scraped clean by being pulled between a wooden surface and a small rounded piece of wood (a spoon is now used) which is pressed down upon the fiber. After being cleaned, the fiber is allowed to soak overnight in water and is then ready for use. While a fiber article is being manufactured, the supply of fiber is kept on dampened ground with damp earth piled upon it, and is extracted from the pile as needed. The fibers are twisted into strands by being rubbed upon a piece of rawhide on the thigh of the operator. Two of these strands, still damp, are twisted together on the thigh to form a cord.

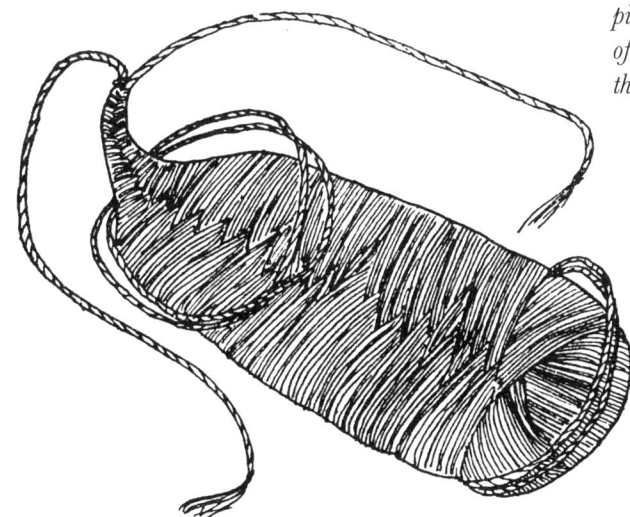

Meigs, 1939.

María, the old Japokelkawa mother of Emiliano, demonstrated the manufacture of mescal sandals. She showed great skill and produced an article of high workmanship. She first tied together the ends of a piece of two-strand cord, making a loop to serve as the framework of the sandal. Then, holding the loop taut with fingers and great toe (keeping the knot under the toe), she wrapped a mass of fiber around the end of the loop nearest her, making a bulky ridge as wide as the foot, to serve as the toe of the sandal. Into this ridge she also wound the end of a heavy strand of fibers from which to make the sole of the sandal. She passed this strand around the middle of the toe ridge and wove it back and forth from side to side around the framework cord, keeping the sides of the framework as far apart as the ball of the foot for which the sandal was intended. When the strand was woven as far as the base of the toes, she bound in a string loop, which would hold the toes of the wearer. When she had woven the strand as far as the beginning of the heel, she bound in a second double string loop. She then finished weaving the heel of the sole, making the heel part narrower than the ball part. The sole completed, she removed the cord from her toe, untied the knot, and with the two end pieces of cord took half-turns around the sides of the second string loop. To wear the sandals, the whole foot is thrust through the rear loop, and the three center toes are thrust through the front loop, leaving the outer toes outside of the front loop, the free ends of the framework cord are carried forward through the front loop, then brought back and tied together behind the ankle. The finished sandal is strong and symmetrical, with thick upturned end to protect the toes.

But even Meigs' wonderful description leaves questions unanswered. Leslie Spier's 1923 report on the Southern Diegueño, who made similar sandals, fills in most of the gaps. Spier learned from a very old man, Jim McCarty, living in Campo, California, near the Mexican border, that both men and women made agave sandals. They did not wear them around camp but for such things as collecting wood or embarking on journeys. Extra sandals were not taken when they traveled since they could make them quickly along the way—only about two hours for a pair.

Sandals (hamnyau') are of two types: woven, the most used, and rawhide. The woven sandal is made of the long dry leaves of mescal (ema'l), which are pounded and soaked in water to remove the connective tissue. The separated fibers are thoroughly dried on a rock. For use, they are dampened and gently pounded with the mano. For the needed foundation and tie cords, bundles of fibers are rolled on the thigh into loose strings (ikwi'p) about 45 cm. long and 1 cm. in diameter. To roll into a two-ply cord, two of these are placed side by side, the butt end of one opposite the tapering end of the other. Holding the two in the left hand, they are rolled separately on the right thigh by a single movement of the right palm; when the left hand is released, the torque in each springs to the left causing them to twine as a two-ply cord. Four loops of this cord, 40 cm. in circumference, and a fifth, 95 cm. in circumference, are tied with a square knot (these dimensions are for a child's sandal).

As the weaver sits on the ground, the large loop is stretched between foot and hand. The proximal end, destined for the toe of the sandal, is wrapped over a length of 8 cm. with bundles of loose fiber until it is 2 cm. in diameter (hutcuwa'wa, the beginning). The loose ends are

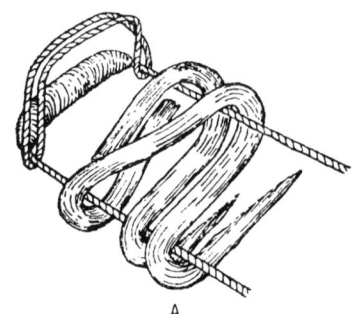
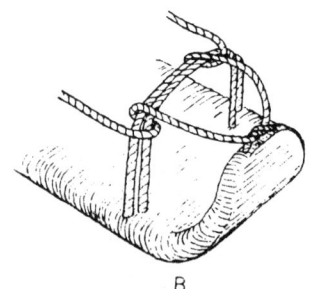
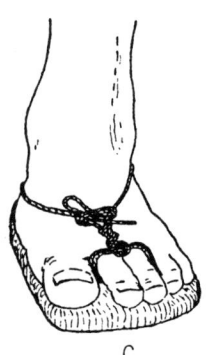

A B C

Diagrammatic sketches (Spier, 1923).

fastened by twisting together. At this stage the work may be temporarily held by slipping the loop over the knee or under the heel of the disengaged foot. One of the small loops, intended for the toes (mixanüke, foot loop, mi, foot), is passed over the foundation cord, as shown (fig. A). A loose bundle of fibers is placed against this loop, a second lapping it in the opposite direction; the two are woven together alternately over and under the foundation cord, and the whole pushed tightly against the toe portion. New bundles of fiber are added in pairs. The butt ends of the fibers are lapped; these ends protrude on the sole. The sandal is made the width of the palm. When the heel is neared a second small loop (miatiksaxanüke, heel loop) is introduced in the same way as the toe-loop. The weaving (we'kwil) is continued, but the sandal is made narrower, introducing but one bundle of fibers at a time. When the length is completed, the wefts are forced up on the foundation cord as tightly as possible. A sandal must not be too long, else it will slip and chafe. The ends of the foundation cord are then half-tied and carried through the heel loop, drawing the heel sharply upward (fig. B). To tie on the sandal, the ends of this tie-cord (miuso'la) are brought forward around the ankle, through the toe loop, wrapped twice about itself, and tied (fig. C).

Study of the Kiliwa and the Diegueño accounts reveals expected variations in fiber preparation, weaving, and tying the sandal to the foot, and yet they are essentially the same. Perhaps most amazing, Spier's informant told him that the agave sandal is reversible! In fact, it must be turned over frequently to prevent its wearing out. To accomplish this, the toe and heel loops are pulled through the sole and the tie cord retied to them on the opposite side.

These accounts together supply enough detail to allow us to actually duplicate the ancient fiber sandal of the Californias. From the Kiliwa comes the function and the construction of the toe, from the Southern Diegueño the importance of forcing the wefts up tightly on the foundation cord. Spier wrote that so tight were they woven that neither stick nor thorn could puncture them. We might add Kroeber's observation that Cahuilla toe strings passed either on the two sides of the second toe or to the sides of the second and third toes and that the sandal was tied to allow the foot to slide in without retying each time the sandal was worn.

Still, certain other details eluded me. For example, were each of the bundles of fibers used equivalent to a single agave leaf? Did the foundation cords taper to a slightly smaller diameter as they became tie cords? Museum examples look as though they do. The complete answer seemed so close and yet so far away. I should have been born one hundred years ago. Then a miracle happened. I found in the summer of 1993, near the Paipai village of Santa Catarina, a woman who still remembered the old ways. When I mentioned agave fiber sandals to Manuela Aguiar Carrillo, a Southern Diegueño, she effacingly tried to think if she knew anyone who could still make them. Eufemio Sandoval, elected chief of the Paipai, had overheard my question and said, "Why, you, Manuela know how." A little coaxing and she agreed to make a pair for me. These turned out to be very different indeed. They were made as the sewed sandals of Ventana Cave only appeared: a true braid of agave fiber was coiled and stitched together with agave cords into an oval sole. Very ingenious, and perhaps an important discovery. The Southern Paiute of the upper Colorado River, known for their love of distance travel for its own sake, made a bark or yucca sandal of a similar long braid looped in an oval spiral; the pad was held together with open twining.

A few weeks later I tried again. I found an ancient Diegueño woman in the mountains of Baja who still gathered acorns, ground them in bedrock mortars and sifted the flour in coiled juncus baskets she made herself, but when asked about fiber sandals, she could only reply, "They are all dead—those who knew how are all dead."

Yucca Slab Survival Sandals

These may be the simplest sandals of all. In an emergency or just to save energy, by minimally processing the soles and using raw yucca leaf strips for ties, an adequate pair could be completed in minutes.

Haury noted "a willingness to improvise" when he found these sandals among the Hohokam cultural remains at Ventana Cave, Arizona. S. M. Wheeler, in describing the fibrous yucca-stalk sole of a square-heeled, round-toed sandal from Etna Cave in southern Nevada, extolled the "ability of the Indian to adapt available materials to his everyday needs." The Hohokam of Ventana Cave cut from the mature yucca stele *(Yucca elata)* somewhat squarish pads about the size of the foot and around 3/8 of an inch thick. Yucca leaf fiber strips inserted through the pads formed the ties. Remarkably, sandals virtually identical are still made by Yuman-speaking Indians in the remote mountains of Lower California.

Manuela Aguiar learned how to craft them from her Southern Diegueño grandmother. That was a very long time ago and since then Aguiar has passed to her son Raúl Sandoval the ancient skill. In place of the quicker yucca leaf ties, they employ more serviceable two-ply agave fiber cordage. This takes more time to make, of course. Haury felt the agave pads were merely trimmed to shape, but Sandoval used a softening and straightening process. Working together as I watched, mother and son made me a pair in two and a half hours.

To begin Sandoval cut off a desert agave plant *(Agave deserti)* just below the heart; the rosette had been growing in the high Sonoran desert of the Sierra Juárez of Lower California only a few paces from his mother's home. He pulled the short, stiff, light green leaves with their broad white bases from the stalk. After allowing some wood chips to burn to coals in a shallow, quickly excavated earth oven, he placed the leaves in the coals, covered them with a thin layer of sandy soil and, over this, laid small random pieces of wood and a few dry sotol leaves taken from a roof he was replacing. He set ablaze the kindling atop the oven and returned in about one half hour.

Meanwhile, he threw water on an old dry inner trunk of Mohave yucca *(Yucca schidigera)*, the fibrous mass just under the bark. It happened to be laying about their remote ranchería where the plant commonly grows. After a few minutes to allow the fiber to soften, he cut from the hollow husk two rectangular pieces, larger by about 2 inches in all directions than the feet for which they were intended.

Next he pulled from the inner side of the husks bunches of loose fibers, working toward the more stable fibrous mass beneath, which would become the top of the sole, the cushion where the foot should rest. Some of the fibers he removed by gently sliding his knife beneath them and running the knife back and forth longitudinally.

He threw more water on the pieces, thoroughly soaking them. As the water took effect, he worked one, then the other, with both hands, carefully bending and limbering the husks. He often bent them back against the natural roll of the stalk which would otherwise curve up at the sides of the sandals. With an end in each hand, he repeatedly ran the sole lengthwise back and forth over a smooth horizontal bar on an old truck. Almost any tree limb would have done. One hand rose as the other fell. The bottom of the sole (or outer side of the husk) doubled back against itself during this operation. He continued to gently bend and soak the soles. He rolled them lengthwise tightly into little cylinders, again enclosing the underside of the sole, and he unrolled them. He continued to work against the natural curve. At times he stopped to strip fibers that had loosened from the top of the sole mats.

By now, the baking agave leaves had softened and Sandoval removed the sandy dirt and embers from the top of the earth oven and pulled from it softened, dark green leaves. At this point his mother stepped in with a knife, a small bucket of water, a large flat piece of wood and a smooth somewhat flattened round stone that comfortably fit her hand. She slipped the knife under the strong tough skin of the agave leaf and working it back and forth, easily freed large strips which she peeled off until she had finished about four leaves (all that were necessary for the sandals). Holding the peeled translucent mass by the spine at its tip, she laid the broad leaf on the board and gently pounded and mashed it with the rock to clean the fiber of pulp. A great amount of liquid ran from the pulp. It inflicts a disabling diarrhea, I was warned, to those who might drink it. The leaf became mushy. She pushed the pulp out with the rock toward the base end through the rich mass of fiber. She set each fiber bundle aside, still gathered at the spine and colored a weak green.

While she continued working, Raúl descended from the hot, dry bluff to a ravine below that I had completely overlooked until I followed him into it. Here, under three incredibly huge cottonwood trees on the banks of a steep arroyo, we drank from a cool spring-fed pool, the only source of water for this remnant band of Kuatl at Rancho Escondido.

When we returned, Manuela had finished pounding the leaves and had begun scraping them with the edge of a large old-fashioned metal cooking spoon. Formerly they used the edge of a seashell, said Manuela. Against the flat wood board she pushed the edge of the spoon's cup over the fibers and away from her (the concavity of the spoon facing her) toward the base end of the leaf. She

Raúl Sandoval makes sandals from a yucca trunk, Rancho Escondido, 1994.

grasped each bundle by the spine until at last she reversed the bundle and scraped even the spine away. Now she held only fibers in her hand and each bundle from each leaf was nearly white.

She placed them in the small bucket of water to soak as she took each in turn and worked it with her hands back and forth, one end of the bundle doubled back and against the other, squeezing and twisting until the bundle was perfectly white. She laid them in the sun to dry a little, then rolled the fibers on her thigh into the cordage that would be used for the ties of the sandals.

As Raúl resumed pulling off loose fiber, cutting, shaking and cleaning the sandal sole, bringing it into a closer approximation of the bottom of my foot, Manuela offered me a surprise: the dark brown base of an agave leaf which had been left three days in an earth oven. It was rich, sweet and caramel-like. I pulled the meat from the fibers with my teeth and sucked at its candy as one might a sugar cane. Raúl put the sandal pads in the sun to dry a little before attaching the tie strings.

I centered my foot on the sandal and he made a hole with an awl between my large and second toe. Through this, from the bottom of the sole, he inserted a small loop of Manuela's agave cordage and tied a knot on the underside, pulling it extremely tight to prevent it from slipping out. I replaced my foot and he inserted a string into the loop, one end of which he drew tightly back to the sole instep and the other to the outer side of the foot. He marked the points. They were across from each other and formed a line dividing the sole exactly in half. He made holes with the awl, inserted the cord, and on one underside, tied overhand knots, the second closer to the sole than the first, and pulled them very tightly together. Then with my foot again on the sole, he tightened and made his knot in the cord beneath the other side. About 1-1/2 inches back of these two holes, two more were custom-cut for a heel string which was similarly tied and tightened (around the back of the heel) with Manuela's agave cord.

Finally, the very square shape of the sole, which measured a good 1/2 inch thick, was trimmed closer to the shape of the foot. Raúl left the completed sandal to dry. Manuela estimated that in the Baja California wilderness they would last a week with constant wear. The convenient no-tie, slip-on yucca slab sandals lasted considerably longer in a pampered southern California backyard.

The completed sandals.

Moccasins

The California moccasin was an expedient wrapping of the foot, made from a single piece of buckskin sewed up the front and up the heel, generally unsoled and undecorated, with a high ankle extension which apparently was not turned down. It protected the foot while leaving the wearer in touch with the earth. This moccasin, typical of the Yurok, Hupa, Maidu and Miwok of northwestern and central California, varied, of course, and there were exceptions: The low cut Modoc three-piece moccasin had greater affinity with those of Eastern North America. The Lassik placed seams on the sides, and the ankle section rose so high it became a legging. The Cahuilla (near the southern limit of moccasins in California) had a high ankle but a hard sole which curled over the thick soft upper piece to which it was sewed from the inside, the stitch unseen from without. In typical California fashion they stitched it up the back but the divided front of the high ankle section was held around the calf by a thong which passed through the front edges once or twice like a modern boot. Kroeber found it of a Southwestern cast. In the far north of California and among the Clear Lake Pomo, moccasins and leggings of open twined tule were common.

Extra soles, insulation and leggings were added by some for colder, rougher conditions. The undecorated one-piece moccasin among the Wintu had an extra sole from the deer's neck sewed on, at least in historic times. Thongs were inserted at the ankle and the ankle wraps were especially long, one going much farther around the ankle than the other. Men and women wore them for travel or walking in snow, and grass could be stuffed into them for warmth and protection from the snow. Moccasins used for racing did not have the extra soles.

The Shasta buckskin moccasin, sewn with the common single front seam, had a heavy sole of elk or bearskin. In the winter the inner sole was cut out so the foot might rest directly on the fur of the bear hide. Some Shasta winter moccasins were made larger to allow the foot to be wrapped with squirrel or wildcat fur or to stuff them with long black moss they found hanging from the trees. Moccasin seams were often painted red. Above the moccasins, the Shasta wore separate buckskin leggings which reached from the ankles to the hip, often fringed and beaded, held by a belt passing through loops at the top and separated by a breechclout.

For dressing up, the Karok also wore buckskin leggings. They sometimes reached the ankles and were decorated with fringes. J. P. Harrington in his notes described them as pants-like chaps since they joined across the front covering the genitals and thighs, leaving the buttocks uncovered. "Arse absolutely bare" wrote Harrington. For rough travel, the Karok sewed elk hide soles on their moccasins.

Twined tule leggings from ankle to knee were part of the full or ceremonial dress among some northern tribes. Many groups, from Klamath to the Pomo, wore twined tule leggings for practical

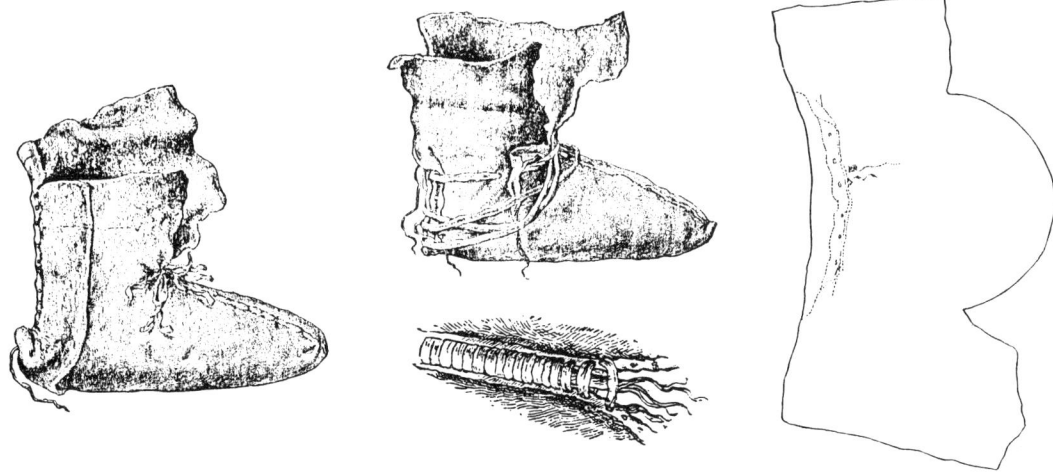

Hupa buckskin moccasins with pattern and blow-up of whipstitch used on front center seam. Items collected by Lieutenant P. H. Ray, nineteenth century (Mason, 1889).

reasons. The Achumawi and Atzugewi wore them in cold weather and especially when wading in icy water while fishing. Openwork twined tule moccasins were perhaps even more common. They were winter moccasins among the Klamath, Achumawi and Atzugewi who stuffed them with grass for even greater warmth. Spier described the Klamath tule moccasin as without a heel, the tules twined over the toe and the moccasin held to the foot by a cord laced through loops on the sides. For traveling they made them of swamp grass.

Most of the time most groups went barefoot—the Coast Miwok apparently all of the time—and put on moccasins only occasionally for journeys, hunting, war, gathering wood and special occasions. The southern valley Yokuts donned deer and elk-skin moccasins when traveling rocky, brushy country; the Cahuilla for traveling in the mountains; the Yurok for travel, collecting firewood, or as part of full dress. With the coming of the European-American, little-used California moccasins were soon forgotten, replaced with store-bought shoes, a symbol of civilization.

What survived of moccasin technology was scant and difficult to uncover. Voegelin persevered and discovered that the Tubatulabal (who had worn moccasins for hunting, gathering wood, harvesting piñon or traveling—but not during rainy weather) made them of tanned buckskin from the deer's neck where the hide is thick. They were sinew-stitched in holes punched with an awl made from the leg bone of a deer, about 4 inches long, topped with a lump of asphaltum. They worked the awl with a strip of buckskin wound around the palm of the right hand. Men made moccasins but both sexes wore them. Smearing the soles with melted gray-pine pitch made them wear longer, they told Voegelin.

Harrington observed that the Karok also employed thick tanned hide from the neck of the deer for moccasins, but preferred elk skin when available. They twisted sinew into a slender thread on the thigh as in making cordage and with this sewed the moccasin. They perforated the buckskin with an awl and poked the sinew thread through it, sewing in a very neat "over and over" stitch. No needle was used. A Chimariko lady, Lucy Montgomery, remembered her people making moccasins with bone awls. They did not use awls for sewing baskets, only their fingers for that, she told Harrington.

Maidu buckskin moccasin, 28 cm. (Dixon, 1905).

Some early ethnographers left drawings and descriptions of these early moccasins, perhaps detailed enough, supplemented by what we have reviewed, to re-create them and again softly tread the old trails.

Hupa

The Hupa made the classic California buckskin moccasin. It was rarely worn except for long journeys. If through brushy country or in the snow-covered mountains hunting deer, moccasins may have been accompanied by buckskin leggings over the thighs. Otis T. Mason analyzed the deer-hide moccasins collected among the Hupa by Lieutenant P. H. Ray over 100 years ago. Cut from a single piece of buckskin and made high "like gaiters," a curious seam followed the center of the instep. The edges of the two sides (formed from the semicircle of the pattern shown) had been slightly split. The two halves of the folded semicircle were then brought together and aligned, one over the other, like the edges of a carpet. Along the two inner margins of the split sides, a loose sinew cord was laid. A whipstitch of sinew thread next joined the two inner edges and enclosed at the same time the cord of sinew. It was all done inside out, on the inside of the moccasin. Turned right side out, the stitches were completely concealed. The back was stitched rather carelessly, wrote Mason, with a buckskin cord as in basting. It would have left the heel pointed like the toe. Thongs drawn around the moccasin, as seen in Mason's depiction, held the heel portion folded over to one side to fit the foot.

Obviously, the pattern shown is a guideline. Adjustment and trimming of the two halves of the semicircle before stitching, when fitting it to the foot, would be expected. A semicircle creates a slight puckering effect when stitched and worn. The Wintu apparently made the two sides of the center seam straight. As a general rule, the diameter of the semicircle should be approximately twice the width of the foot. Note that in the pattern and the moccasin at the top, only the lower part of the the heel was stitched along the back; the portion above was left open.

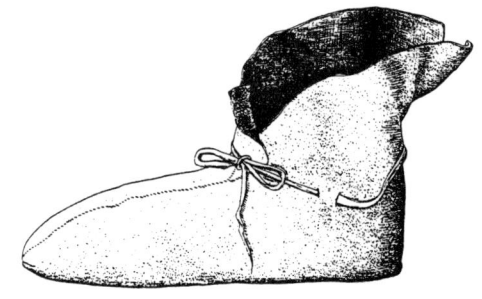

Maidu

The Maidu moccasin also exemplified the California type. It was made from a single piece of buckskin, unsoled, with seam up the front. A simple whipstitch appears to have been sewed from the inner side. The common winter footwear of the higher Sierra, Dixon recorded that the moccasin was stuffed with soft grass or sedge as insulation when walking through snow. A deerskin legging, tanned with the hair on and worn hair-side in gave further protection from the elements. The legging reached from the ankle to just above the knee where it was tied. A thong wound around and held it to the leg below.

Unlike the Hupa moccasin described by Mason from the Ray collection, the Maidu depiction in Dixon lacks the pointed toe and heel. This can be effected—the pointiness eliminated—by making a small perpendicular cut just above the natural pointed toe or heel. Bringing the flap which this creates on the sole inside (or trimming it off) and closing with a few stitches lowers and widens the moccasin at that point. The Wintu pattern inferred by Cora Du Bois suggests the toe was simply cut off perpendicular to the length of the foot and sewed. To work, this must be done from the side with the moccasin flattened from the top. The Klamath moccasin pattern that follows also illustrates a way of dulling the pointed toe.

Klamath

The Klamath Modoc men wore moccasins all the time. Moccasins generally were twined of tule or swamp grass. The buckskin moccasin was for the summer. The bottom of the buckskin moccasin was one-piece with a front seam in the California style. But it also had a tongue. This was a trait common elsewhere in North America but unique in California. Some of these moccasins had a third section, an ankle strip, sewed to the top edge of the bottom. It was worn turned up or down. A drawstring passed around the ankle and across in front of the tongue. Made of deer, elk, beaver or badger hide (deemed especially strong), the hair was left on and worn on the inside. They sewed the moccasin inside-out with the borders aligned, not lapped, generally in whip stitches using an awl splintered from the foreleg tibia of a deer and sinew from the backbone. They sewed the instep then across the toe; the two sides folded over to the sole, in effect, cutting off the tip of what would otherwise have been a pointed-toe moccasin. The same was accomplished by the cut A-A at the heel. The pattern shown in Spier's ethnography is not in perfect proportion; the length of the lines A-B should together equal A-A. They were sewn along the edge of this cut with the extra heel flap brought to the inside. After C-B had been stitched up and the tongue sewed in, the moccasin was turned right-side-out (the stitching had been done with the moccasin inside-out) and the cuts on lines D-D made. This left a decorative tab on the heel.

The Lassik

The Lassik made an unusual legging moccasin of a single, long buckskin strip. They cut the hide to an hourglass shape and folded it back over the instep. The instep was sewn along the inner side, inside-out, apparently in a whipstitch. The outside was laced as sketched. When worn, laced and sewn sides were brought up as flaps over the top of the foot. The buckskin back of the legging section was pulled up and the two lower sides of the back brought over the two flaps in front. The drawstring crossed over and held down the lower inside legging

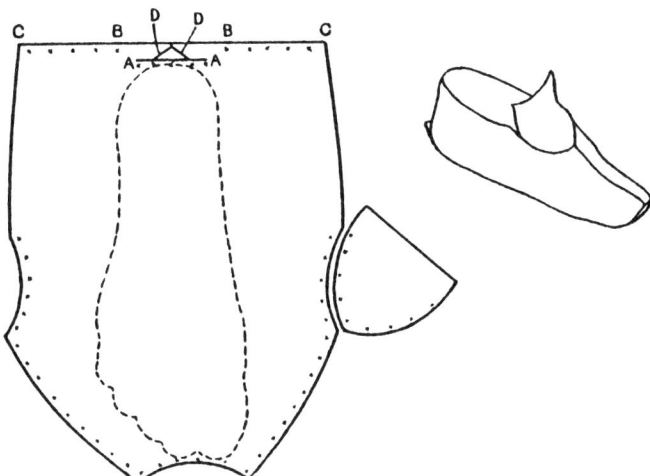

Klamath buckskin moccasin and pattern (Spier, 1930).

first, then in a continuing spiral caught and secured the lower outside legging. It wrapped many times around the calf to fasten the legging portion of the footwear. Buckskin was sometimes sewn along the back of the heel, and when the sole wore out, a new one was often sewn on. They wore the moccasin-legging on journeys in the summer as protection against rattlesnakes, they said. (The Pomo knee-high deerskin boot was said to provide protection from brush.) Water and mud made the footwear soggy and useless for winter travel.

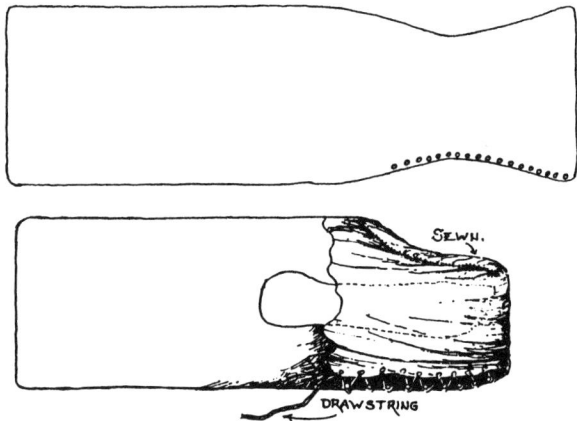

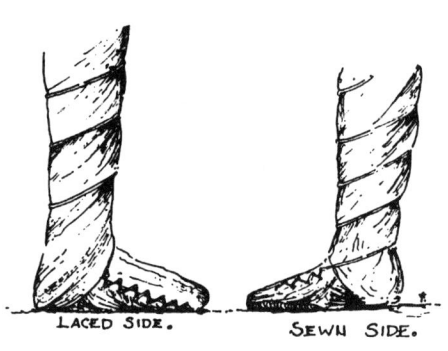

The Lassik legging moccasin (Essene, 1946).

Diegueño Rawhide Sandals

These are simplicity itself and very functional. Again the informant was old Jim McCarty, the Southern Diegueño Indian from Campo, who described them to Spier in the summer of 1920.

A piece in the shape of the sole was cut from any part of a raw deer hide. Two cuts were made on each side near the heel forming two tabs extending up both sides of the foot. Two long buckskin thongs were knotted beneath the sole at the base of the second and third toes and passed through the sole in small openings to the far sides of these toes. The thongs then crossed each other over the top of the foot and passed through holes in the tabs, continued behind the heel and forward under the string on the front of the tab on the opposite side and back behind the heel again and around to the front of the ankle. Spier's simple drawing is worth all the words.

McCarty cautioned that rawhide sandals may be slippery on wet ground and fiber sandals would be preferred in such a case and on snow.

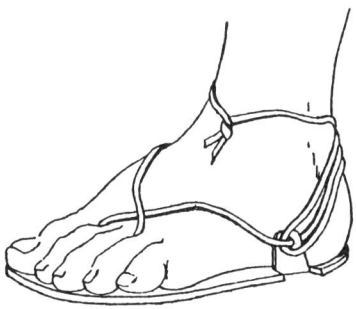

Sketch of Southern Diegueño rawhide sandal and method of tying it (Spier, 1923).

Plaited Yucca Sandals

A pair of plaited Mogollon sandals can be completed in a couple of hours. But it was their simple beauty that first caught my attention. The clean diagonal weave of a thousand-year-old sandal with frayed remnants of toe and heel tie hung in a dimly lit glass case of the basement of the Southwest Museum. My vague browsing stopped short, awed by the mind which saw in the leaf of the yucca this beautifully plaited sandal. The crafting in turn reflected the character of the plant whose long tough leaves grace many a mountainside of the Southwest. In the Spring thick stalks replete with cream-white blossoms grow from the yucca center and both stalk and flowers provided food for Indian groups from the Cahuilla to the Pueblo.

I studied the incased sandal for an hour or more until I captured its secret. Luckily, the yucca plant does not have to die so we might be shod. We need only two to four leaves per sole plus another for the ties. Yuccas are widespread throughout the American Southwest. The Mogollon used the banana yucca *(Yucca baccata)* common in southwestern New Mexico where many of these sandals have been uncovered in ancient caves. In Los Angeles I used the yucca common to the Los Angeles region, called simply "yucca" or Our Lord's Candle *(Yucca whipplei)*. The banana yucca leaf is thicker and softer but the Los Angeles yucca suffices. The Mohave yucca *(yucca schidigera)* is virtually identical to the banana yucca and I often go to the Mohave Desert to gather it for sandals.

Comfortable and durable sandals can be plaited from the unprocessed and green leaves of the whiplei yucca. However, as the leaves dry over the weeks, they shrink, and open spaces appear in the weave. This can be overcome by lightly pounding the leaves with a smooth stone against a log or also using two leaves paired for each plait, doubling the number of leaves. Archaeologists digging the Mogollon caves of west-central New Mexico felt most of the sandals they found were made from essentially whole, unprocessed leaves, but some seemed to have been made from leaves that had been pounded or crushed. They also found sandals where the leaves had been doubled.

My own observations and reproductions of Mogollon sandals indicated that leaves were halved for use as plaits, occasionally spliced. Banana yucca leaves (and the very similar Mohave yucca) are at once too wide and often too short. The leaf was first pulled apart (beginning with a small tear in the center) into two long sections and, when necessary, overlapped in a splice (a few yucca fibers can be stripped from the edges of a leaf to tie and temporarily hold the splice). In this manner one creates an appropriate, custom length (a little over three times that of the foot). Natural leaves this length are best of all of course. Cutting green fibrous leaves from a live yucca (especially the *yucca whipplei*) with a sharp stone or knife is trying work, and the razor-edged neighboring leaves can lacerate your hand in the process. Care should be exercised. Dead dry leaves, on the other hand, pull out easily. The ends of the yucca leaves, one too curved and too wide and the other too sharp, can be trimmed off by holding the leaf in both hands to either side of the spot to be cut and running the leaf over the sharp broken edge of a stationary stone. Dried leaves should be soaked for about twenty-four hours or more before you begin bending them to shape; otherwise, they crack. Fresh Mohave yucca and banana yucca leaves must be softened in the hot sun for a day or placed briefly near the coals of a fire. Heat turns their unworkable stiffness to rubber.

I have found seven simple steps to a completed sandal:

1) Bend a leaf, a half leaf (or a spliced set) approximately in the middle, perpendicularly, right over left, making a right angle open to the left. Now bend the left side—the base of the angle—under and parallel to the first bent half, leaving an approximately 1- to 2-inch perpendicular section between them as shown below.

2) Bend a second leaf once in the middle, right side over left, bringing the two halves side by side in a near parallel arrangement and overlapping the perpendicular section of the first leaf between the two parallel elements. Repeat steps one and two for a second set of leaves.

3) Face the two sets diagonally and begin to loosely plait them, using the left set as weft into the right warp. The pattern is first leaf (the right leaf of the left set) over, under, over, under. Next leaf (the second from the right) under two, over two. The next or third leaf is over two, under one: and finally the

last leaf goes under one, over two, which will be the pattern for all subsequent weaves.

    4) Tighten the completed plaiting as much as you can—this is most important. Then continue with your weave, pulling and tightening after each weaver has been passed through the warp, bent under one, over two, from the left and over one, under two, from the right, bending each leaf at a ninety-degree angle and pulling tight, until the leaves are used up. To keep them from unraveling tie a thin

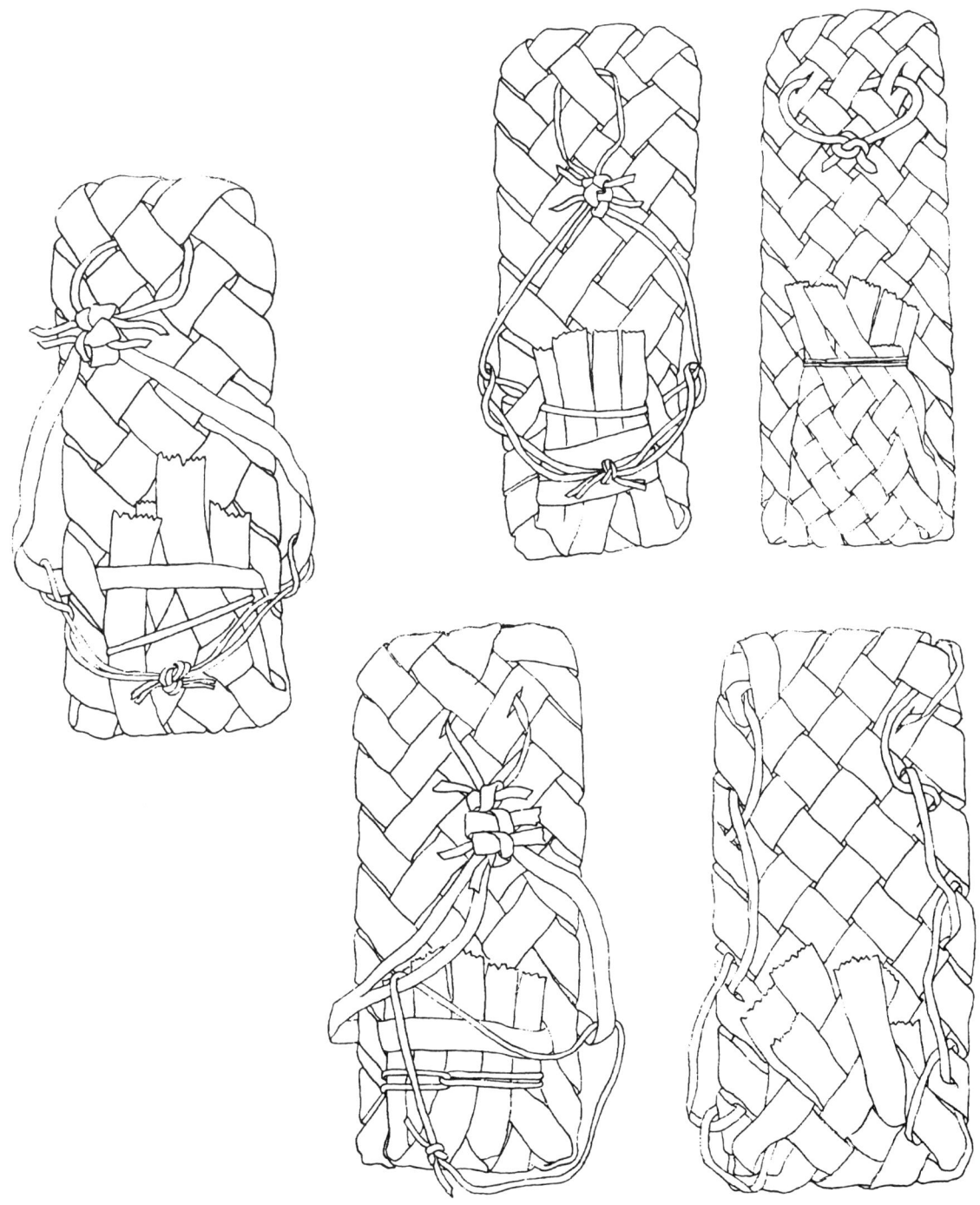

Mogollon Sandals. Plaited sandals from Tularosa and Cordova Caves: variations on a theme. Lower right example is likely a winter type; side loops may have held grass or bark insulation by means of cross ties (drawings by Gustaf Dalstrom in Martin, 1952).

strip of yucca around the completed end, as seen in the archeological examples.

5) Measure your foot to the piece and bend over excess at the loose end to form the heel. Mash the heel down forcefully and put something heavy to hold it that way while you cut a 1/4 inch to 1/2 inch-wide strap to pass through two side weaves about 2 inches from the back of the heel (see sketches of Mogollon sandals). This strap holds down the extra material that overlaps the heel and also forms an instep brace. Secure it in front of the foot with a square knot. Trim excess from the loose ends of the heel overlap.

6) Cut an approximately 1/8 inch wide piece for the toe strap and place it under the first long warp element in the center front, bringing it around the second and third toes and securing it to the instep brace with a square knot—adjusting to your foot all the while. Keep the ends of the strap wet to facilitate tying. The straps themselves dry fairly stiff; light pounding to mash and soften them is highly recommended.

7) Cut the final ankle tie about 1/8 inch wide. Soften it by wetting and holding the ends and running it a few times back and forth around a smooth surface, a sapling for example. Put the sandal on, adjust it; bring the softened thong from the heel and loop it around the instep brace on each side and tie it in back. For a custom fit, soak the sandal and wear it as much you can as it dries out over the next few days. Light pounding with a mano also gives it a custom feel.

The sandal described is the standard sandal found by archaeologists in Mogollon sites. Of twenty-seven sandals recovered from four Mogollon caves of west-central New Mexico during excavations by the Chicago Natural History Museum's 1952 expedition under Paul S. Martin, twenty-four were of plaited "whole" yucca leaves. Twice that number of whole-leaf plaited sandals had been found earlier by the museum in Tularosa and Cordova caves from the same west-central New Mexico region—all on tributaries of the Gila River. Generally archaeologists found no difference in the manufacture of left or right sandals, but some from Tularosa Cave were more rounded in front on one side or the other so that lefts could be distinguished from rights. A simpler version of these woven sandals with only three plaits or leaves was also found. Smaller, split-leaf varieties had apparently been worn by children.

Anasazi sandals, such as from Pueblo III sites of northeastern Arizona, are also plaited but of very narrow elements. However, the whole-leaf Mogollon style has been found in the southern Anasazi Pueblo IV sites of Camp Verde and Canyon Creek. Plaited sandals first appear among the Anasazi in Basketmaker III sites and are of the wider or whole-leaf elements. A Mogollon-style plaited-fiber sandal apparently of bark is in the possession of the Santa Barbara Museum of Natural History. Amazingly, the sandal is said to have been found in a dry cave on Anacapa Island. If true, this, the most common sandal of the ancient Mogollon of New Mexico, was probably worn by a Chumash Indian of southern California.

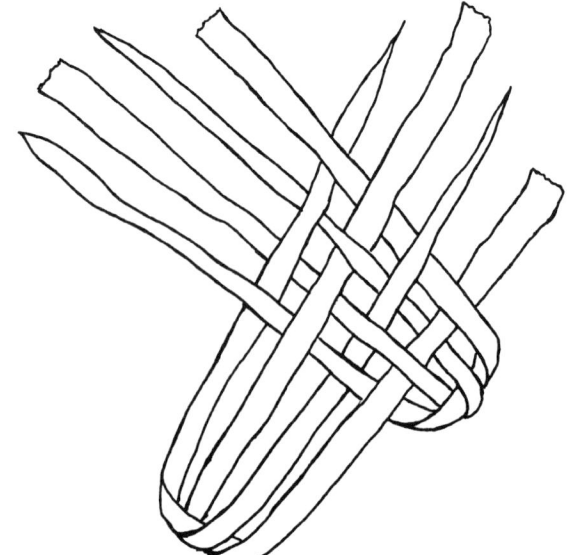

The simple secret of the plaited Mogollon sandal revealed. While there are variations or "mistakes," this seems to be the classic Mogollon weave. The pattern continues with loose weavers on the left bending under one, over two, and those from the right, over one, under two until completed.

California Elderwood Flute

Little clay balls in ceramic rattles, pebbles in shook cocoons, and palm seeds in gourds; deer hoof jinglers, bone whistles, clap sticks, foot drums, bull roarers, and rasps—none of these typical California accompaniments to ceremonies, chants and dances were instruments of melody. Save for the voice itself, and by extension, the musical bow (which was held in the teeth and tapped with a flat stick for personal amusement), the aboriginal Californians had only the flute to carry a tune. Only the flute was not purely rhythmic. However, flute music, irregular and untamed, was not suitable for the controlled atmosphere of ritual. The flute the Indian played for personal pleasure and for courting. These were survival skills too. The need to calm the panicked heart (or win one) can be more pressing than the craving for food itself.

Kroeber described the California Indian flute as "an open reedless tube, blown across the edge of one end. Almost always it has four holes, often more or less grouped in two pairs, and is innocent of any definite scale. It is played for self-recreation and courtship."

The Yurok made them of elderwood and a virtuoso was one who could not only play the flute by mouth but could sniff a melody into it with his nose. Besides being an instrument for a young man's courtship, the old people would play the flute before the sweat house as they sat in meditation. The Maidu also used the straight tube of elderwood with four holes as did the Yokuts, who grouped the four holes in pairs but without a rule as to relations of distance. They thought the flute invented by the falcon. The Cahuilla generally grouped the four holes in pairs by eye, producing, as the others, somewhat arbitrary intervals. The Yuki made an elderwood flute 10 inches long with four holes. Early Spanish priests at the Gabrielino and Chumash missions in the Los Angeles and Santa Barbara area mentioned elderwood flutes. J. P. Harrington found the four-hole flute among the Chumash. Those at Ventura also had the six-hole flute. Traditionally, the Chumash flute was played by young and old men—for pleasure and for making love, they told him.

How the Chumash Made the Flute From the Elderberry Bush

To make an elderwood flute they looked for a toyon tree *(Heteromeles arbutifolia)* because to extract the pith of an elderberry branch, a toyon rod of appropriate diameter was needed. But getting pith out of an elderberry branch is virtually impossible unless you know how. Almost one hundred years ago the elderly full-blooded Chumash Fernando Librado told Harrington exactly how. The end of the toyon rod was beveled on two sides in a gable shape. Between the two gables, a V-notch was made. (Rubbing it on any somewhat abrasive stone easily accomplishes both of these cuts.) The toyon rod was then rammed into the center of a prepared elder stick, and by twisting and frequently pulling it out, the pith was removed.

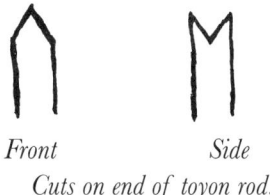

Front   Side
Cuts on end of toyon rod.

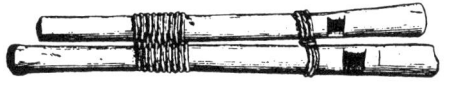

Top, Maidu elderwood flute, 45.5 cm. Love songs were played on this. Flutes were open-ended (Dixon, 1905).

Bottom, Maidu ceremonial bird-bone whistle. Eagle or goose bones were preferred, one longer than the other. The ends were stopped with pitch (Dixon, 1905).

An elderwood stick *(Sambucus sp.)* with joints not near together, green and flawless, was found and cut from the tree (when finished, according to Librado, it would be about 2 feet long, 1-1/2 inches in diameter). Placed in a pile of embers with a shovel full of sandy dirt at both ends to stop the respiration, the elder stick was left in the coals to sweat and harden. It was then they extracted the pith. If possible, they bored the hole even bigger than it naturally occurred. After two or three days of drying, the bark was removed and the outside scraped. That was the custom, although Librado did one piece right away.

Next, the stick was cut to the final desired length. The mouthpiece (one of the open ends) was sharpened (a knife or abrasive stone can be used to create this acute bevel around the mouthpiece). Four round holes were burned into the flute with a hot glowing stick of toyon, the last hole four finger breadths from the end opposite the mouthpiece. (T.T. Waterman wrote in 1908 that California Indians customarily measured the distance *between* holes by the length of the first joint of the performer's thumb—literally a rule of thumb.) S-shaped designs and Xs of inlaid carrizo and shell sometimes ornamented a finished flute. It was not recorded but asphaltum was probably the glue they used as with most other Chumash inlay. A man from Ventura had a flute, dark reddish in color, and on each side near the mouthpiece was an S-shape. Harrington's informants felt that some flutes in historic times were made of giant reed.

The Flute of Reed

A Cahuilla flute in the Fiske Museum of Musical Instruments at the Claremont Colleges, described simply as a pre-1940 courting flute, is made of nonindigenous giant reed or cane *(Arundo donax)*. It is a little over 1 inch thick and about 20 inches long with four finger holes. Looking down the flute from the mouthpiece, clockwise spirals approach from the far end. They were cut about 3/16 of an inch wide each, passing completely through the wood. They begin about 1/4 inch from the end of the flute into which thin cuts entered to begin the spirals. The spiraling continues to a point about 2 inches from the far end of the flute. The Cahuilla also made flutes from the indigenous common reed *(Phragmites communis)*.

A flute could be made quickly with only a knife and a section of the dry honey-colored giant reed now found almost anywhere in California, I thought. My first one looked very nice. But in trying to produce the dulcet notes I was sure it contained, I only wheezed, hyperventilated and saw stars. I finally freed from the tube a loud screechy cry, more a whistle of attack than a plaintive love call. I am not a musician let alone a musicologist, but through lengthy trial and error I did at last fashion a flute from reed and make sweet sounds. Here are some of the things I learned the hard way.

First of all, remember that it is a flute and not a whistle. The breath expended in blowing across the top should be light and natural. If made and blown correctly, the instrument will begin to resonate almost on its own. Experiment. The California flute did not rely on a complex mouthpiece for a no-brains operation; the sophistication was in the man. And the secret was the *embouchure*: the method of applying the lips to the instrument. I have found that occasionally, when the opening is large, the lower lip instead of merely resting on one side of the mouthpiece, might extend across and cover much of the opening as you turn the far side into the music-producing edge. Dixon wrote of the Northern Maidu "the flute is placed in the mouth, and blown partly across and partly into." A photo of a Pomo man playing a flute from the early years

Diegueño reed flute. Collected 1875. Incised, rubbed with brown pigment: 66.5 cm. (Luomala, 1978).

Pomo incised flute: 37.5 cm. (Wallace, 1978).

of the twentieth century shows him holding the flute horizontally, straight out to the front, while another of an elderly Maidu man from the middle years of the century has the flute down to the right with the right of the mouthpiece fully *in* the right side of his mouth. The opposite side of the mouthpiece would be open. Harrington recorded that Tintín, a Karok Indian, held the elderwood flute on the right side of his mouth, blew across the left edge and tongued a *tz* sound, vocal cords vibrating, along with the notes of the flute.

The tone from an open, end blown flute comes from directing the breath to the distal edge of the mouthpiece and the vibrating column of air which results. Clean the inside of the tube where this column works and the note sounds—a hot glowing stick works well—the inside joints should be smoothed down as much as possible. In fact, select the sections of reed which are long between joints, and make the mouthpiece at or just below the joint to avoid the stultifying effect of the joint on the sound. Heat treat the cane by placing it near the coals of a fire and let it dry thoroughly. It seems the more brittle it is, the better. The finger holes often work best placed near the far end.

How to Play— Chumash Style

To play the flute, the forefinger and middle finger of the right and left hands covered the holes.

Third Song, Deer Hunting Cycle

The musician held the flute half diagonal to the right side and put his lips to the thin mouthpiece to blow. There were special tunes for victory, a funeral or a man in danger. According to Harrington's notes from Librado, "the flute plays but the heart understands the words." It was possible to play but not

He holds the flute to the side of his mouth and "tongues the notes with a Tz sound, his vocal cords vibrating." It gives a "sweet and soft sound, with the whistling sound at times more prominent, at times almost absent," wrote J. P. Harrington of Tintín the Karok Indian shown above playing the flute. Photographed by Harrington circa May 13, 1926 (Smithsonian Institution National Anthropological Archives).

understand the mysterious meaning. When the shaman played, however, he knew what it meant. Chumash María Solares added that when the bear was a person, it took pleasure in playing the flute. It played every afternoon, alone, only the bear.

A Gabrielino Song

While the yearnings of the ancient California flute are lost and by the wind grieved, something of its faint echo might still be heard in a rare Gabrielino deer hunting song collected by Helen Roberts from an old Luiseño man, Celestino Awaíu, living at Pichanga in 1926. It is the third song in a cycle of five.

In the first, the hunter has started out to find the deer, walking, singing, becoming quiet. The second song occurs when the hunter spies the deer. It has been called down from the mountains. It falls when they shout. They cut its throat and have plenty of meat.

In the third they have killed a deer. A green fly has found it dead and with a motion or sign hints at the deer's location. The hunter follows the fly and finds the deer. The word "*sari'wut*" means "green fly" (the Gabrielinos used "r" where the Luiseños employed "l") and *nomi'wut*, "following." Remember, the flute plays but the heart understands the words. This implies that the flute substituted for the voice and that it could legitimately play a song which normally would have been sung. Indeed, of the elderwood flute with four holes William Joseph, a Southern Maidu, told Paul-Louis Faye at Berkeley in 1919: "They imitate a song with it." Librado recalled: "When a man was in practice he could play any Indian song on a flute."

The hunter honors the green fly in the fourth song by calling him great-grandfather fly and asks assistance. The last song has to do with a time when there was no water. The old people would travel and not find water and would sing this song. A whirlwind would form and go over a place of water and the people would go there and drink.

Mohave man plays flute to the girls. Photographed by J. P. Harrington and Michael Tsosi 1911 (Smithsonian Institution National Anthropological Archives).

Filtered Cigarette

We had finished gathering the inner bark of elderberry along a dry wash a few miles from Rancho Escondido in the Sierra Juárez Mountains when we happened upon some coyote tobacco *(Nicotiana attenuata)* growing nearby: long, thin white trumpets in perfect harmony with bright green lance-shaped leaves. Southern Diegueño Indian Raúl Sandoval said his wife's grandfather, Kiliwa Indian Rufino Ochurte, had shown him many years before how to make a cigarette with this tobacco. Such cigarettes were often smoked by the older people. They made them from a hollowed elderberry twig. Raúl said any small branch with a pith channel could be used. Meigs recorded 60 years ago that the Kiliwa smoked coyote tobacco in a "reed tube." They called tobacco *ijíp miltí* and said smoking it was very good for a cough. "A smaller branch was sharpened and used to ream out the pith channel," Raúl continued. Tobacco leaves were plucked and placed on a rock to dry in the sun. They were then rolled in the palms into a cylindrical shape and stuffed into the tube. But that was not all. Clean agave fiber *(Agave deserti)* was rammed into the opposite end for perhaps 1/2 inch or so to function as a filter. This was thought to keep the flame from reaching and burning the mouth. It also kept the tobacco in place.

One day, more than a year later, while sitting with Raúl and Sam Ochurte, who is Raúl's father-in-law and Rufino's son, I asked if they might make me a native cigarette. It was the worst possible time of year, the first day of spring, and new tobacco plants had not begun to sprout. The old ones were mere skeletons, dry and windblown when you could find them. Raúl and Sam, however, recognize a plant at any stage and in half an hour had located remnants enfolded by larger protective vegetation and collected a handful of the wispy dry tobacco leaves.

Raúl cut approximately 5 inches long by almost 1/2 inch diameter sections of green elderberry. He scraped the bark from them by running his knife back and forth edgewise until he had two perfect white cylinders. With a sharpened twig he quickly reamed out the pith channel. Lacking prepared agave fiber, Sam picked a bit of exposed fiber from the trunk of a Mohave yucca growing about 20 paces from the elderberry tree. This he stuffed into one end of the hollowed elderberry tube. He tested the draw of the cylinder at this stage to ensure that air could pass through the filter.

With a small twig, the other end was rammed full of dry tobacco leaves. "Too dry," said Sam, who capped the tobacco with another small wad of fiber to ensure the tobacco held. It also seemed to help ignite the tobacco, although the cigarette Raúl made for me had no second fiber plug and it lit and smoked without a problem. Sam drew deeply. Slowly, he smoked his cigarette down to a butt. He said the smoke was strong but good for a cough. Indian cigarettes were not consumed in chain fashion as people smoke commercial cigarettes today. They were occasional pleasures and medicinal. Sam told me that the tubes were often made of greater diameter and then would not burn down so readily with the tobacco. A thick tube could be used more than once.

The Southern Diegueño of Campo, California made a *mentholated* filtered cigarette. Spier found they too fashioned cigarettes from short lengths of elder with the pith removed and plugged the end with fiber (of the milkweed for those of Campo) and filled it with coyote tobacco by fillliping the side with the fingernail. But they also smoked in these a tobacco of *salva real (Salvia clevelandii)*, an aromatic sage. Smoking a cigarette was appreciated any time of day and was done to cure a cold or cough. By the time the following accompanying song had been sung four times, the symptoms should have ended:

Ko sa mi xa no
(I am sick with a cold)
Artc mi yai
(Groan)
Artc mi 'kwilp.
(Tossing with malaise.)

Thomas Jefferson Mayfield, who was raised by the Choinumne Yokuts in the Sierra foothills in the 1850s, emphasized how the Indians smoked sparingly. A 4- to 6-inch section of carrizo, having a diameter of a pencil, was filled with tobacco seed that had been ground in a mortar. The hollow tobacco-filled reed burned like the wrapper of a cigarette. Women did not smoke. Older men carried one of these cigarettes behind their ears. From time to time they would take it out, light it, take a puff and pass it around. The smoke was powerful and they took only a single puff. When they inhaled the smoke from the cigarette, they held the cigarette perpendicular so that the lit tobacco would not fall out. They inhaled deeply and made a blowing sound in the throat as they exhaled. Mayfield believed they did not take more than one or two puffs in three or four days.

Over eighty years ago, Tachi Yokuts Bob Bautista spoke to Harrington about the carrizo cigarettes they smoked in the Great Central Valley of California. Bautista had holes in the lobes of his ears; he said the old men would carry the carrizo cigarettes in such perforations. He recalled he once stole Indian tobacco from his father and went outdoors to smoke it. He put some in a piece of carrizo, lit the cigarette and took a gulp of the smoke. It was so strong it made him momentarily drunk. His father never found out, he confided.

Sam Ochurte smokes filtered elderberry cigarette and stuffs a hollowed elderberry branch with coyote tobacco.

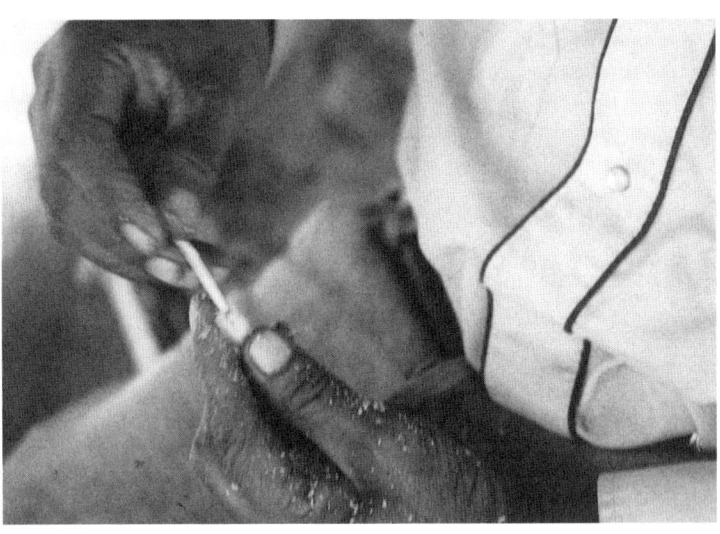

Sam Ochurte prepares a native cigarette.

Indian Stick Game

California's first ethnographer, Stephen Powers, on finding men drowsing for hours in earth-covered assembly houses, dubbed the daily life of the Maidu "vacuous." He waxed even more extreme when summing the lassitude of the California Indian in general:

Of all droning and dreary lives that ever the mind of man conceived this is the chief. To pass long hours in silence, so saturated with sleep that one can sleep no more, sitting and brushing off the flies! . . . Kindly nature, what beneficence thou hast displayed in endowing the savage with the illimitable power of doing nothing, and of being happy in doing it!

Early explorers often interpreted the leisure of California Indians as a form of laziness. But explanations are never so simple. The nineteenth-century California natives Powers encountered were survivors of the genocide perpetrated by the gold-seeking 49-ers and hordes of white settlers from the east, many of whom hunted Indians for sport and collected scalps as they collected pelts of animals. Indians who survived could be made virtual slaves. Little wonder then that native Californians might lose their zest for life and fall into depression. On the other hand, in part, doing nothing was an Indian survival strategy.

Thomas J. Elpel noted that studies of nomadic hunter-gatherers indicate they generally work but two or three hours a day to live. In contrast, those who try and live like them end up working nearly 24 hours a day in a frenetic attempt to produce as many "primitive" objects as possible. We forget we have become slaves to civilization: things. The Indian knew how with less and accumulation of things only slowed him down. Elpel calls this freedom from encumbrance the art of nothing.

The do-nothing method, for example, would find a natural shelter and improve upon it if necessary, not build a house, particularly if rain was unlikely and the need temporary. This was the California Indian way. In the wild a deadfall trap could be constructed from whatever was at hand, without so much as a knife. "When we reach the point of needing nothing," writes Elpel, "we can choose to do nothing or even to go do something."

One of the things California Indians did in the freedom of their leisure was play games and one of these in various forms was a game widespread in Indian America, often referred to as shinny, stick game or field hockey. It was a rough sport that pitted village against village and tribe against tribe and directed built-up and potentially dangerous energy into exuberant recreation.

Piác: A Paipai Ball Game

They did not have a written language but the Paipai knew their history, their legends, their myths and stories. Libraries resided in the minds of the people, in particular in those with great curiosity, intelligence and memory. Not very long ago near Santa Catarina, the highway was paved, one family bought a satellite dish, the cash economy began its ugly work in earnest. Benito Peralta may be the last embodiment of Paipai history, the last great oral historian of the Paipai. His uncle, Cosmé Gonzales, who was old when Peralta was a boy, told everything he remembered to Peralta who in turn retains and tells it to others. One day Peralta described to me *piác* (pee**ak**), a game the Indians would play when they gathered together in large numbers. Cosmé had been told of this game by old ones before him and had never played or seen the game himself though he was sure it had been played.

Two goal lines were drawn, perhaps a few yards long, on either end of a large field or flat open space. In the center of this field, within a circle about 4 to 5 feet in diameter which was marked in the sand, a wooden ball perhaps 4 inches in diameter or less was secretly buried, fairly close to the surface. Two opposing teams consisting of four to six members each then came onto the field and surrounded the circle. Each player carried a stick the end of which had been formed into a small loop or circular hook. With this, they would strike the ball and move it toward the opposing goal line. The hook was smaller than the ball and had no mesh or reinforcement.

On a signal the game began. The teams dug furiously with their sticks in the sand for the ball. Only the stick could be used to move the ball. Once found, the ball entered and remained in play until one team or the other was able to hit it across the goal line drawn in the sand of the other team. There were no points or scores kept. When a ball crossed a team's line, the opposing team won and that was the end of the game. However, the teams could choose to abide by rules that required a team to not only cross the opponents' goal but bring the ball back out of the end zone of the opposing team and return it to their own end zone to score a point and win the game. They always used the sticks to move the ball, but in this special form of the game the players could use their sticks to trip their opponents as they attempted to move the ball across the field. They could poke the stick between the running legs of an opponent to make him fall.

Mohave boys and young men played a game similar to *piác* which remained popular at least into the 1920s, according to George Devereus. The ball which they buried in the middle of the field was usually made of the stem of a gourd. They also used sticks with a curve at the end. His informants declared that enthusiasm ran high but physical clashes or quarrels were rare. Adults bet on the outcome. Girls sometimes played.

Pi k'o: A Pomo Ball Game

Pomo consultants told E. M. Loeb in the 1920s that they formed teams based on positions in the sweat house, east or west, and any number of men could play. The Lake Pomo called the game *pi k'o* (perhaps a cognate of the Paipai "piác," the two groups were distantly related) and used a straight stick, 4 feet in length by 1-1/2 inches in diameter, although in more recent times they employed one with a crook, like a golf club. Those from the coast used two attached hazel sticks with a net on the end which allowed them to drag the ball along.

For a ball, the knob that forms under the bark on exposed roots of California laurel was cut out and hardened in hot ashes for a week or more. If one of these could not be found, the knee bone of an elk or the knob from the pelvic bone (which they burned off) served the purpose.

Goal lines were from 1/4 to 1/2 mile apart. An arch of two vertical saplings 6 to 8 feet from each other with their tops inward and lashed together formed a goal on each line. Driving the ball through the oppositions' goal but once constituted a game—as with the Paipai there was no need to keep score. In the crowded struggle to reach the opponents' goal the players generally batted the ball along the ground, but if there was opportunity, a player might pick it up and hit it like a baseball toward the goal. It was largely a game of endurance. Complete exhaustion and fainting from overexertion were common. When the game ended the players jumped into a lake or creek to revive.

Kato Hardball

In northern California the Kato Wailaki made a tennis-sized ball of an oak knot. A doubled, long slender stick bound along its length, opened and bent into a circular hoop at its far end and covered there with a string mesh, served as a racket for thrusting the ball along the ground. They formed themselves into two groups and put up things of value for wager. A center line divided the field. The women threw the ball on this line between a representative from each team facing the opponents' baseline to put the ball in play. The ball fell and the two struck at it. As one or the other gained the advantage, both teams immediately entered the fray. Old and young, men and women, all at once participated in the attempt to propel the ball across the enemy's baseline. Stephen Powers wrote:

> *They enjoy this sport immensely, laugh and vociferate until they are 'out of all whooping'; some tumble down and get their heads batted, and much diversion is created, they are very good-natured and free from jangling in their amusements. One party must drive the ball a certain number of times over the others' base-line before the game is concluded, and this not unfrequently occupies them a half-day or more. . . .*

The Northwest Stick Game

Here the sport became intense and athletes trained. Yurok elders recounted to anthropologist Thomas Buckley in the 1970s the traditional physical training of young men: They would run, wrestle, lift river rocks, and take strenuous swims. On stormy nights fathers would make their boys pull the heavy redwood dugout canoes at a fast pace up the shore to condition them for the stick game.

Passing along the Trinity River one bright July morning in 1998, I encountered seventy-nine-year-old Hupa elder Jimmy Jackson, still spry as a youngster. He endured my prolonged inquiries into iris fiber cordage and net making as long as he could and then he made a suggestion. Just down the river, where the Trinity joined the Klamath and Hupa territory met Yurok, there was a stick game between Hupa and Yurok at that moment. I could go and watch. The teams had already entered the fray. Jackson warned me I would see some ferocious fights but that I should not be afraid: when it's over, it's over and they are friends again and no ill will is kept.

Without the warning, I would have turned and come back up that hill at Weitchpec because a few minutes later below me on a flat field on a bank of the Klamath, three pairs of tough, sweaty, soot covered and even bloody young men grappled as if in some ancient arena. Thuds of body slams blended with spectator exhortations.

"An exceedingly rough athletic contest, especially as played in former times, is kittékich, colloquially known as the stick game," recorded Edward S. Curtis during his visit among the Athapaskan-speaking Hupa in 1916. "Originally almost any tactics short of murderous assault were permitted, and even now the players wrestle desperately."

Pliny Earle Goddard succinctly described the Hupa version of the game 100 years ago.

Village is pitted against village, or tribe against tribe. The shinny stick, called milkitukutc is about 3 feet long, or more exactly, the length of the leg of the player. It has a natural turn at the end. Two round sticks about 5 inches long tied together with a piece of buckskin are used for a ball. They are called yademil. A straight course is laid out with a stake at each end. At least six players take their places in pairs, two at the middle and two at the points halfway between the middle and the stakes. The pair at the middle has the balls. Those at the other points stand facing each other with interlocked sticks. They are said 'to tie' each other. One of the two at the middle of the course takes the two balls in this teeth. Suddenly he drops them and tries to drive them toward his goal by catching the buckskin loop on the end of his stick. If he succeeds he runs after the balls and tries to strike them again before he is overtaken. If he is overtaken the next pair of players releases one another and starts after the balls while the first couple wrestle. The third pair takes up the game if the second couple become involved in a wrestling match. The side which succeeds in getting the balls to the stake wins.

Slight variations and additional detail come from Curtis' observations among the Wiyot, of the Algonquian stock like the Yurok and close neighbors of the Yurok.

Ráqhlaiyúwuk, the so called stick game, was played between representatives of different villages. On each side were three players armed with sticks (ráqhlaiyúwuhl, thrower) with a crooked end. Two pieces of heavy wood about 3 inches long were tied together near one end with a short piece of deer skin thong. In the middle of a 200 yard course two opposing players stood with their sticks. One held the missile (rakíhl) between his teeth. At the word of the umpire (luwúisihl) he dropped it, and each tried to toss it toward his opponents' goal. The other players stood in opposing pairs about half-way from the middle point to the goals, and each grasped the wrist of his opponent and held his stick between his teeth. As soon as the missile was dropped, and tossed, the pair in the center began to wrestle, and each man of the other two pairs grasped his stick in both hands, placed it behind his opponent's back, and endeavored to bend him backward to the ground so that he himself might escape and throw the missile toward the opposite goal. Any hold was allowed, but the stick could not be grasped by an opponent. When at last someone broke away from his antagonist and raced toward the missile and hurled it, his opponent leaped up and pursued him, and, if he succeeded in catching him, seized him by the waist or the leg or the neck and hurled him to the ground with all possible violence. Heavy wagers were laid.

In the 1920s J. P. Harrington took notes among the Karok (who spoke a language of the Hokan stock). Ben Donohue explained the stick game (*imtháva*) to him. The field was about 200 yards long, each end a goal. There were six players, three on a side, paired man-for-man. A line was scratched across the center and on this two men faced each other, crossways in the field. Toward each goal, pairs grasped hands, one hand each as though shaking hands, with the other clasped on the opponent's wrist while the sticks were held in the mouth, near one end of the stick but not so close to endanger the eyes.

Sticks were preferably of wild plum but those with natural bends that began about 2 inches from the extremity were difficult to find. Service berry sticks with this bend were more common. The stick was about a yard long by 7/8 of an inch in diameter at the lower thicker end. Except for the bend, they were straight as possible. The tossel (the two pieces of wood joined by a thong) dangled from the mouth of one of the center pair, an end of the tossel in his teeth. Sylvester Donohue cut tossel sticks for Harrington from a hazel branch but they could be of wild plum, service berry or almost any hard wood, even green manzanita. Each of the tubular tossel sticks was about 4-1/8 inches long by 1-1/4

Scratchers face each other in center field, other players hold sticks in mouth as game begins; opponents grapple for advantage; runner brakes away and races to throw tossel over goal. Hupa vs. Yurok, Weitchpec, July 1998.

inches in diameter; 3/8 of an inch from one end a groove 1/4 inch wide by 1/8 to 1/4 inch deep held a buckskin thong 3/8 to 1/2 inch wide which joined the two sticks with a distance between them of 4-3/4 inches. The tossel was hooked with the bent thicker end of the shinny stick and thrown through the air. Unlike a ball it stayed where it was thrown and would not roll. In many ways this was an advantage, especially in somewhat rough or sloping terrain.

The two center players scratched stick against stick. The player with the tossel in his mouth might hold it a long time, waiting for an advantage before he let it drop into play. One player would grab and throw the other to keep him from the tossel and then he would race toward it. Any of the opposing players could trip him on the way. They might wrestle for hours, the tossel moving back and forth only every now and then. One could not hit other players with sticks or fists but head butting was usually permitted. Fritz Hanson told Harrington it was not permissible for a player to jab backward with the upper pointed end of the stick at someone overtaking him from behind. Sylvester Donohue had said this was in fact done. Hanson and Ben Donohue affirmed, however, that when one player ran ahead of another player, the player behind, grasping the pointed end of the stick, could thrust the unpointed end between the legs of the man in front to trip him. (He would use the curved, dull end in order not to wound the other player.)

Two umpires kept order. Each team had eight or ten "coaches" or rooters. The Karok word was literally "hollerer." There were two men, one at either end of the field but sometimes together, who straightened the tossel whenever it was cast. They would run to the spot and lay it out transverse to the field so that it could be easily caught on the end of a stick and thrown.

Ben Donohue told Harrington that one of the worst beatings he ever got was in a stick game at Katimin ("upper falls") above the mouth of the Salmon River. He was only sixteen and his much older opponent had Ben on his back beating him against the ground for ten minutes. He could hardly bear it but would not give up. It was the last time he played the stick game.

It was a rough game, played by the Hupa, Yurok, Wiyot and Karok. Together they represent three of the great linguistic stocks of North America. Some days later, I happened upon Yurok elder Frank Gist standing on a cliff at the mouth of the Klamath looking over fishnets in the river below and at migrating gray whales in the ocean beyond. Later, he displayed for me old dentalium, an iris fiber and feather headdress and a huge obsidian blade that had passed down through countless generations. It was still used in traditional dances. He revealed for me too the scars on his back received as a young man from an opponent's stick in the stick game.

The Yurok called the game *hurhlpúr*. I had become intrigued but did not fully understand it. Yurok Glenn Moore II explained to me the finer points. He was instructed in the sport by his grandfather Glenn Moore I who had participated in the ritual as a boy. It meant serious business in those days, emphasized Moore. There were ceremonies and prayers, not something anyone took lightly. This he would like to revive among the Yurok today.

Fist fights might have erupted over an infraction, though his grandfather always tried to avoid real fights. Respect for your opponent was and is fundamental. While it is a nearly no-holds-barred contest, one never hits below the waist or strikes an opponent with a fist or stick. The director, or head referee, can stop a game and start it over or deduct a point from a side which breaks the rules. He can eject a player for unsportsmanlike conduct, leaving a team a man short. Usually, he just lets the play continue and counsels the players after the game. There are no time outs or game stoppages for injury unless the wound is life-threatening.

The director, usually an elder, passes a hat among the spectators before each game. They contribute money which is awarded to the winning team. Sometimes, depending on prior agreement, instead of winner-take-all, it might be divided proportionately according to the day's score. Scores are achieved by picking up and throwing the tossel or "double ball," by means of the stick across the opponent's goal. That comprises a game but games are played in units of three, five or seven and the winner of the day is the side that wins the best of three, five or seven games, the number again depending on agreement before the contest begins.

A goal of two willow stakes marks either end of a field from 250 to 350 feet long. The tossel consists of two sticks of hard wood, yew or hazel, 3 to 4 inches long each and one inch in diameter, joined by a cord of buckskin or sinew tied in a groove on the end of each stick, leaving about 3 to 4 inches between the two. Each side has three players: a scratcher, an anchor and a runner. All players hold sticks of hard wood usually made of yew, hazel or juneberry. The sticks have a slight bend at one end, found naturally, or, if of yew, they may have been cut that way since only the heart of yew is used. Or a stick may be bent after warming in a fire. The tossel can only be forwarded with the stick but it can be done by any player at any time. The usual throw is underhand but if one has time, longer overhand throws are attempted.

The two scratchers face each other in the center of the field. The man from the home team holds the tossel in his teeth. Both scratch the ground with their sticks, meeting each other's stick in the center of the ground between them. They scratch in the direction of the other fellow's village, one upriver, the other downriver, meeting in the center. (Karok literally means "up river" in the Karok language and Yurok, "down river," referring to their location on the Klamath.) The home team scratcher drops the tossel at will and the game begins in earnest.

One of the scratchers might throw the tossel with his stick and move after it or the two might lock up, wrestling until one or the other frees himself and can go after the tossel. Meanwhile, halfway to each goal, the other two from each team begin by a face-off with their opponents. They grasp each other's wrist, stick held in the mouth. Closest to the goal one will attempt to cross is the team anchor, a man selected for strength and size. His job, once the tossel is dropped and play begins, is to try and hold his opponent who is selected for quickness and speed and who tries to break free, run to the tossel, hook his stick under it and toss it toward the opposite goal. The anchor himself may also throw the tossel; all have sticks and anyone can hook and throw the tossel for a goal. The team's own runner at the opposite end tries to break free, cross the field and score.

It becomes one of the primary objectives of the game for the players to free themselves from these lockups which might last for hours, said Moore. Every man is entitled to have his personal coach with him on the field. The coach instructs and encourages the player to hold or break free from his opponent and the coach carries an extra stick should the player drop or lose one. Referees, also on the field, are basically tossel straighteners. As the players wrestle, a referee finds the tossel and straightens and lengthens it out crosswise on the field so a freed player can easily catch the bent end of his stick under it and give it a toss. Players sometimes pass the tossel to one another but often throw it down field and race after it for follow-up tosses until it crosses the goal.

There are no age limits, but attempt is made to evenly match players and teams. Among the Yurok only men play the stick game with wooden sticks as tossel. Curtis observed among the Tolowa, neighbors just to the north, only women played a tossel stick game (as elsewhere in California and the continent); Tolowa men used a 5-inch-diameter wooden ball.

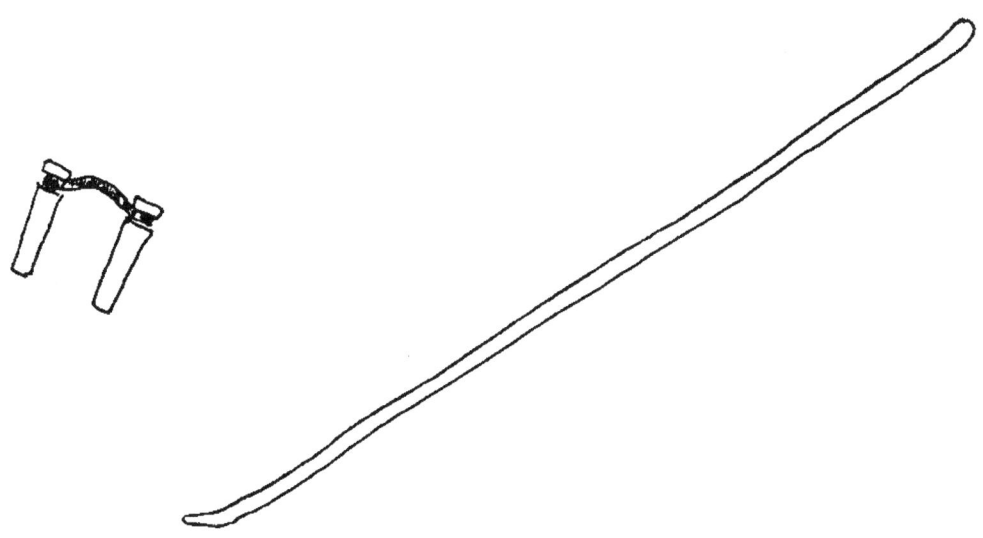

Karok playing stick and tossel, drawn from photos in J. P. Harrington collection of the Smithsonian Institution.

Part Two
Hunting and Fishing

California Indian Bows

Native California bows run the gamut. Colorful, sinew-backed yew masterpieces of northern California shade into the more modest cedar bows of the Sierra Nevada mountains in the central part of the state. These in turn gradually give way to humble willow staves of southern and Lower California. The continuum appears to be of declining technological sophistication. Since the northern reflex bow is flashier and more complex, closer to a modern machine-made lamination, we tend to assume it is best. We might even begin to imagine ways advanced tools and technologies could improve it. We view this world in the spirit of our own civilization that, alas, fishes by sonar and shoots wolves from planes.

An interest in primitive technology, on the other hand, implies support for the natural world. Our inclination as moderns is reversed and we find value in simple, recyclable, low-impact technology. Northern California reflex bows are undoubtedly wonderful survival tools. (It is interesting, however, that Kroeber found the northwesterners may have taken deer more often in snares than with their wonderful bow.) Those unique recurved bows from the center of the state have great merit as well. But we must not disparage the simpler bow of the more practical south solely because it is simpler.

The Yuman-speaking people of the harsh southern environment were never without this bow. They used it continuously for hunting and war. Anybody could make one on the spot from mesquite or black willow (while northern sinew-backed bows were made by specialists), and they compensated for lack of fine wood or sinew by increasing the length of the bow and rolling cordage of mescal for the string. It was a simple bow but perfectly suited to a life of great distances and individual self-reliance. Moisture would not ruin it (as it might sinew) yet it was easily discarded in an emergency to travel unencumbered and remade when needed. In its context, it was as useful as the often more powerful, but more difficult, bows of the north.

The Northern California Wide-Limbed, Flat Sinew-Backed Bow

The distinctive northern California sinew-backed bow of the Yurok, Karok, Modok, Shasta, Hupa, and others had a constricted grip, wide limbs, nocks carved into the wood at the end of the bow and often the back painted in geometric design. Kroeber, based on his fieldwork during the first years of this century, described the exaggerated Yurok style.

The bow was of yew, short, broad, and so thin that only the sinew backing kept it from breaking at the first pull. The grip is somewhat thicker, pinched in, and wrapped with a thong. The string is sinew. Only that side of the tree which faces away from the river was used for bow wood. The sinew backing is often painted with red and blue triangles . . . the usual length was 3 to 3-1/2 feet, the breadth 1-1/2 to 2 inches, and the thickness 1/2 inch, of which a considerable fraction was sinew, whose pull gave the unstrung bow a strong reverse curve . . . extreme flatness is a characteristic of the Northwestern tribes, who often shave the sides of these bows to a knife-edge. Elsewhere even the most elaborate pieces become somewhat longer, narrower and thicker.

The design of the bow was not arbitrary. A short stave could be carried freely through the dense northern forests and brush, but needed wide limbs for enough power to take down deer. Thickness could have added power but in short limbs it would have stopped their bending, stiffened them, and slowed the cast. Every inch of the short bow had to function all the way. Thickness was reserved for the narrow grip where too much width would deflect an arrow beyond the point it could self-correct. The tips of the bow were narrow in order to minimize weight where it most slowed an arrow. Superior wood allowed the bow to be reflexed when sinew-backed, adding power in the early draw (since the braced bow would be under considerable tension) without loss of energy storage in the full draw. Early ethnographic records reveal secrets of the bow's manufacture.

The Hupa Bow

Hupa Bows were made by specialists but all men used them. Pliny Earle Goddard, who lived among the Hupa at the end of the nineteenth century, wrote: "The bow and a quiver of well-made arrows were the essentials of every man's well-being." Bows were generally short and wide. One, he measured, was 3 feet 3 inches long (3 feet along the string from nock to nock). Unstrung, it had a reverse curve of 5 inches. The grip was 1-3/4 inches wide; at mid limb, 2-1/4 inches, and 5/8 of an inch at the nocks which were an inch long and bent back at an angle of 45 degrees. The grip was wrapped in buckskin for 3-1/2 inches; the sinew string, 1/8-inch thick. Triangles often decorated the back of Hupa bows, noted Goddard.

Lieutenant P. H. Ray of the U.S. Army briefly described the manufacture of Hupa bows in a Smithsonian Report in 1886. The wood was of yew *(Taxus brevifolia)*, a sapling about 2-1/2 to 3 inches in diameter. It was hewed to shape, the heart inward, the back carefully smoothed to the form of the finished bow.

Dried sinew taken from the back and the hind leg of the deer was soaked until pliable and stripped into fine shreds for both string and bow. The Hupa laid the sinew over the still green wood, according to Ray, beginning from each end and terminating at the center of the bow. The sinew was slightly twisted and dried before being placed. Glue to hold the sinew had been made by boiling the gland of the lower jaw and nose of the sturgeon, then drying the sticky substance in balls for future use. They applied the glue by simply dipping one of these balls in warm water and rubbing it on the wood. A twine wrapping held the sinew in place on the bow until everything dried.

To dry and thoroughly season, the bow was hung in the sweat house. It would develop a reverse curve of about 3 inches. The proper tension of the sinew backing was crucial: if it was too tight, the wood crimped or splintered when the bow was strung; too little tension left a weak and worthless bow. It was finished, strung, and sometimes the back was painted. Lieutenant Ray gave this assessment of its range: "The bows made by these people are effective for game up to fifty or seventy-five yards, and would inflict a serious wound at 100 yards. At fifty yards the arrows will penetrate a deer 5 or 10 inches."

The Yurok Bow

Elderly Yurok Homer Cooper learned how to make a wide-limbed bow from the old ones before the end of the nineteenth century. A 1961 University of California documentary film captured his technology. With two elk-horn wedges driven by a stone maul Cooper split the end of a small yew log. It came from a tree felled by fire in a sheltered valley where it had grown straight, even-grained and nearly free of knots. Cooper moved the wedges to the side of the log as the splitting progressed. Using a hand adze he roughed out a stave from one of the pieces and left it to season in a cool shady place to prevent checking and warping. Then he patiently rasped it into final form with the abrasive quartz-crystal surface of a hand-held fractured rock. The flat bow was smoothed with Indian sandpaper, or equisetum, strung in a reverse curve and left that way to season for a second time.

Cooper chewed the air bladder of a sturgeon and spit it into a steatite bowl to make glue. The masticated substance kept well and was heated just before he spread it with a small flat stick over the recurved back of the bow, beginning in the center and applying it little by little. Sinew from the back of a deer was pounded between stones and rubbed between palms to loosen the fibers until completely shredded. The fibers were straightened and pressed a few at a time lengthwise into the glue on the back of the bow, care being taken to keep them parallel and not criss-crossed. They were spread from the center of the bow to the tips. One layer dried before another was glued on. The process took several days. Long strands of sinew overlapped the fairly wide squared tips of the bow and came down onto the belly. About 1 inch below the tip a small bunch of sinew fiber dipped in glue was wrapped a few turns to create a ring just below the slight inward-slanting indentations of a pin-style nock. This would keep the nocks from splitting and the bowstring from slipping. The long fibers that overlapped the end were trimmed just below the ring on the belly side of the bow. As a final touch, ground mineral pigments were mixed in warm glue which Cooper applied with a small stick to the back in simple geometric designs. He shot the completed wide-limbed bow horizontally using a pinch grip.

Ishi's Yahi Bow

Saxton Pope's 1913 fieldwork with Ishi, a Yahi Indian of northern California, preserved essential detail on the sinew bow technology of the northern California type. The bow was Ishi's glory and delight—he loved it like nothing else, Pope recorded. In form it fell between the extremes of the Hupa and Yurok bows and those farther south. The back was only occasionally painted (in green or red, with transverse stripes or long snaky lines). The best, or preferred, were of mountain juniper (Western or "Sierra" juniper, *Juniperus occidentalis*). Ishi was aware of yew bows but the wood was not available in his area. Pope guessed that another suitable wood Ishi described was incense cedar *(Libocedrus decurrens)*.

A limb of suitable size was simply broken from the tree. It did not matter the time of year. With deer-antler wedges, the Yahi split the rough bow into staves. Ishi would then hold an end of one

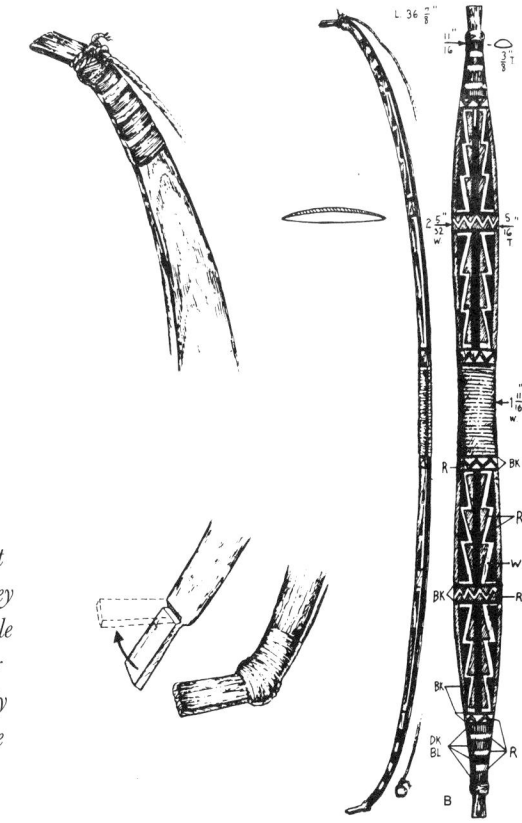

The Yuki bow

A classic Hupa bow drawn by Steve Allely, whose examinations of Indian bows uncovered many insights. These included how the Hupa bent the nock to keep the string from slipping off a short bow at full draw. They cut a V-groove on the back between the nock grooves and bent it at the angle shown (likely after being heated or steamed) and tied it in place. The later sinew backing and wrapping at that point gave it sufficient strength. Allely did not take all the credit for the revelation. A mouse had eaten away some of the sinew on an old bow and exposed the process (Allely, 1992).

of these at his right hip with his right hand and extend the stave across his chest to his left hand which had been extended straight out to the side at a 45-degree angle. This gave the proper length of a bow that, for Ishi, was about 50 inches. For a hunting bow, the width at the middle of each limb was three fingers; a war bow was measured at four fingers. The grip was less. After splitting or roughing out the wood from a limb, it was laid horizontal in a protected place and seasoned for an indefinite period.

Exhibiting infinite patience and care, Ishi then scraped the bow into form with flint or obsidian and finished it with sandstone. He worked toward a flat stave, limbs wider at their center than at the handle whose cross section was oval. Sapwood formed the back of the bow but was often scraped away to the extent that only a thin stratum of white could be seen at the edges. The bow tapered to small short nocks at the ends.

The last 6 inches were occasionally recurved by holding the back of the bow on a hot rock and applying pressure near the end, working it back and forth until the curve held. As the wood cooled, Ishi kept it pressed against his knee protected by a buckskin pad.

The recurving of the ends of a sinew-backed bow maximized arrow-throwing power. In a simple wooden bow such recurves, when at full draw, would likely be bent to the point of breakage—their unfolding would simply be too much for wood alone. In fact, for that reason the ends of plain bows of weaker wood were usually curved *inward* so that the brace plus the bowman's draw would bend them very slightly. They acted mainly as a catapult or extension of the center of the bow. In the recurved sinew-backed ends, however, full potential unfolded. As the bow was drawn back, the ends did not only leverage the center most effectively but were themselves bent back or unfolded under pressure and they recoiled tremendously. It was like having the power of two small additional bows at either end of the main bow.

The back side of the bow Ishi left somewhat rough to help hold the sinew cut from either the back *(dorsal fascia)* or the long tendons of the hind legs of the deer. The strips, from 8 to 14 inches long, dried to the thickness of parchment. They had to be soaked in warm water for several hours before using them.

Meanwhile, the back received a heavy coating of glue that was made by boiling salmon skin and macerating it while hot. After the glue dried, Ishi chewed the wet sinew until it softened, then laid it in overlapping parallel strips down the back and folded over the nocks. A lot of sinew and tremendous patience were required. He held the applied sinew in place with spirals of maple bark wrapped around the bow. These bindings were removed the following day. The drying sinew contracted and drew the bow back in a reverse curve. At this time Ishi applied more glue over the surface of the sinew.

He waited several days to allow the backing to thoroughly dry and harden, then scraped and ground it smooth, bringing the overlapping margins even with the edges of the bow. After this he wound strips of tendon around the bow from the nocks down an inch or so. Finally he let the bow season, exposing it to sunlight for anywhere from a few days to a few weeks.

The bow string was of sinew—a finer quality than for the back of the bow— taken from the outer more slender tendons of the deer's shank. With his teeth he cut these free far up into the muscle and, if fresh, chewed them apart into fine threads. If they were dry, they first had to be soaked in warm water.

Attaching one end of a bundle to a fixed point, he spun single-strand string by rolling the fibers in a single direction in his fingers, adding fibers as he went, making a very tight string 1/8 of an inch thick. He twisted the end after it reached about 5 feet and tied it off taut between two points. Finally, with saliva, he rubbed and smoothed it and left it to dry (the diameter shrinking to about 3/32 of an inch).

For use, he formed a loop at one end, tapering the end by scraping it. Doubling it back, he wrapped about 2 inches of the overlap with sinew,

Karok Indian Fritz Hanson demonstrates wide-limbed bow. Photographed by J. P. Harrington, 1926 (Smithsonian Institution National Anthropological Archives).

leaving a loop about 1 inch in length. (If it came apart, which it often did for Ishi, he would tie a regular loop knot in disgust.) Ishi furnished the loop with a small cord to the nock which kept the bow string more or less in place while unstrung. Pope noted that he never kept the bow braced for too long.

When it came time to brace it, the loop was placed over the end of the bow stave which had grown uppermost in the tree. Failure to shoot a bow with this end up would throw the arrow from the mark, he believed. He sat on the ground, placed the *top* of the bow behind his left heel, belly facing him with the handle against his right knee and the lower portion of the bow held upward in his left hand. He bent the bow and secured the string about the other nock by winding twice around the nock, under the bow string and back in the opposite direction a few laps, fixing it with two slip knots.

Subsequent bracings had the *lower* end of the bow on his partially flexed left thigh. Holding it with his left hand in the center, back of the bow down, he grasped the string between the forefinger and thumb of his right hand and with his other fingers he held the bow near the upper nock. He depressed the handle, bent the bow and slipped the loop over the nock. If it was too long, he unstrung the bow and twisted the string until it shortened to a proper fit. The desired distance between the string and the bow grip was about 4-1/2 inches. A good bow would sing or make a high musical note when the string was tapped with an arrow or flicked with a finger. On cold days he warmed it over a fire before bracing it.

A finished bow should form a perfect arc, a crescent at full draw (25 inches for a 45-inch bow). Where too strong he filed or scraped on the belly gradually forming an even bend. Ishi's bow pulled between 35 and 50 pounds. A 1/2-inch-wide piece of buckskin was spiraled around the handle for 5 or 6 inches; it did not overlap and was secured at the ends with a final wrapping of buckskin or sinew. A bow left upright was thought to continue to work, to sweat and become weak. It was always unstrung as soon as possible, kept in a leather quiver or, best of all, in the tail of a mountain lion and laid horizontally.

Jack Harding, a Montgomery Creek Yana Indian draws the wide-limbed bow. Photographed by H. W. Williams, 1902. From the Harrington Collection (Smithsonian Institution National Anthropological Archives).

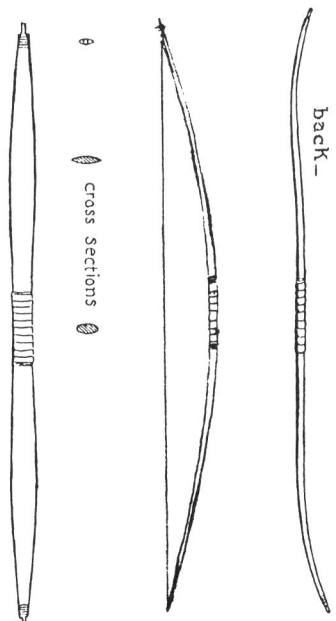

Ishi's short bow. Length, 44". Handle diameter, 5/8" thick by 1-1/2" wide. Midlimb, 9/16" by 1-7/8". Limb at nock, 5/16" by 3/4". This bow pulled 40 pounds. Another pulled 45: was 54-1/2" long; handle diameter, 3/4" by 1-5/8"; midlimb, 1/2" by 1-3/4"; limb at nock, 1/4" by 1/2" (Pope, 1918).

The California Sierra Nevada Hook-Ended Sinew-Backed Bow

These unique, reflexed mountain bows were in great demand. Their recurved ends did not bend toward or follow the bowstring as curved or straight staves tended to do, decreasing the effective length of a bow's limbs and increasing weight on the ends. Rather, they stood up to provide maximum leverage during the draw and high speed on release. Sinew reinforced the vulnerable back of the bow. This allowed longer pull without breakage of the wood and added recoil potential, greater elasticity, as sinew would stretch farther over wood than the wood itself during the pull. The sinew terminated in extremely thin, light hooks or nocks at the very tips of the bow, which increased recoil speed even more. The manufacture, variety, and extent of these bows emerge from old accounts and preserved specimens.

Tubatulabal Sinew-Backed Bows

For war and large game the Tubatulabal of the Kern River in the southern Sierras made a sinew-backed bow of juniper (*Juniperus californica*) or occasionally of tamarack (perhaps "tamarack pine," a name for lodgepole, *Pinus contorta*). Sinew-backed bows were more powerful than the simple wooden or self bows they also made. After selecting and obtaining the bough, they immediately peeled off the bark and shaved it to shape with a flint knife. Erminie Vogelin, who obtained information from older tribal members in the 1930s, recorded that the length would be about 48 inches. At the grip it was 2 inches wide by 1/2 to 3/4 of an inch thick; it tapered to the ends that were about 1 inch wide by 1/4 inch thick. Both back and underside were shaved flat with the edges rounded. After achieving this shape, they warmed the bow in hot ashes or over a fire and bent the ends back over the knee. A cord tied taut between the extremities kept it in an arc opposite from how it would be when strung and in use. This compressed the back of the bow and increased the amount of bend needed to bring it to full draw, adding tension and power. It remained in this position for six to eight days to season, after which the string was removed and sinew applied.

Taken from the backbone of a deer, sinew was softened in water and glued in a 2-1/2-inch wide strip to the back of the bow with the overlapping sinew at the edges glued to the sides. Glue was made from deer antler boiled in a small amount of water. At each end of the bow the sinew was wrapped around the wood several times forming knobs to prevent the bow string from slipping. This eliminated the need for notches. They wrapped a strip of buckskin around the grip after the sinew had dried (it would keep moisture of the hand from loosening the sinew). A three-ply bowstring of sinew, rolled on the knee, completed the apparatus.

Western Mono Bows

Similar bows were widespread throughout the central California Sierra region. The Waksachi, Michahai and Wobonuch bands of Western Mono, like the Tubatulabal, made them of juniper. After the ends had been recurved, the Wobonuch applied the sinew with the bow resting back upward on two forked sticks. According to records of A. H. Gayton, glue from bits of deer antler and sinew boiled together were first smeared on the back of the bow. They next pounded sinew lightly into place with a rock, wrapped the bow completely in milkweed cord, and left it to dry in the sun for a day. After removal of the cord, an obsidian blade smoothed down any adhering fuzz or roughness of the sinew.

Gayton interviewed noted hunter Bob Osborne, a seventy-five-year-old Western Mono who knew the old ways. The plain bow was the first bow for boys, Osborne told him. It was made of pepperwood (California laurel or bay, *Umbellularia californica*), in the same proportions and curvature as the sinew-backed bow and with a two-ply sinew string. Every man knew and used the plain bow.

Not every man, however, could make a sinew-backed bow. These special bows were of juniper and measured 3 or 4 feet, from sternum to finger for a shorter bow, from shoulder to opposite fingertips for a longer one. After heating over coals, each end was recurved by putting it into some crevice and bending it by leverage from the center of the bow. It had to be done repeatedly and was a slow process.

Deer-leg sinew was soaked in water and beaten between two flat stones. A heavy glue of boiled antlers (which were obtained in spring when they were soft) was spread over the back of the bow and the sinew placed over this extending about 1 inch beyond the bow at either end. These extensions curled back when dry (they were probably molded with the fingers to curve back when somewhat dry before they were completely dry and hard). They formed hooks for better attachment of the bowstring, Osborne told Gayton. Leather glued around the unconstricted grip sometimes had small feathers inserted about its edges.

A bowstring of two-ply sinew was strung on the bow with the looped end first and the other pulled to the desired tautness and tied off permanently. To unstring the bow (its normal state) the tied-off end was placed against the right instep and, with the left hand on the upper end, the bow was bent inward and downward and the string slipped off with the right hand. Osborne, a Waksachi, said the Wobonuch Western Mono made the best bows because their glue was clear. The Waksachi glue was murky.

The Miwok Bow

Most accounts of the reflexed bow's technology, however, come from the Miwok of the central Sierra Nevada whose bow was generally more oval in cross section and shorter than that of the Tubatulabal in the southern Sierras. Miwok sinew-backed bows were made of incense cedar *(Libocedrus decurrens)* although "spruce" (perhaps "Douglas" spruce, *Pseudotsuga menziesii*) and Oregon ash *(Fraxinus latifolia)* were also used, according to S. A. Barrett and E. W. Gifford. They obtained their data around 1906 directly from the Miwok, but only after this group had ceased making bows.

The Central Miwok mountaineers hacked a cedar bough from the tree and roughly trimmed it down with a sharp-edged stone. The stave was further worked with a flake of black obsidian or a split deer-leg bone. For a finish, they rubbed it with an emery-like rock, perhaps a fine sandstone, and a scouring rush, or horsetail *(Equisetum arvense)*. With the same abrasive stone, they worked down the nock ends of

Sinew nock of an old, hook-ended sinew-backed bow (Dixon, 1907).

the bow. The completed wood stave was about 3 feet in length and 2 inches in width at the widest part.

While still green they bent the bow to shape—a gradual recurve toward the ends—after warming over fire. They seasoned it four or five days and applied chewed sinew heavily to the back using soaproot juice *(Chlorogalum pomeridianum)* as glue. (If left without sinew, it became a bow for killing birds.) The recurved tips of the nocks were of sinew *only* (an example referred to by Barrett and Gifford). They were hard enough to resist the pull of the string. The sinew passed over the ends to the belly side. Nowhere on the back of the bow was a loose end of sinew visible. A small soaproot, roasted and dipped in water, was rubbed on each layer of the dried sinew to give the sinew backing a watertight seal.

Three-ply sinew cord or twisted milkweed fiber *(Asclepias cordifolia*, also *giffordi* and *speciosa)* served as bow string. To deaden the twang of the string, a 1/2-inch strip of beaver, otter or some other skin, hair side out, was wrapped 6 inches from the top for 2 inches (or perhaps even more than 2 inches, as suggested by very early photos and depictions). A 1/2-inch strip of otter fur, again hair side out, lashed with sinew to the center of the string, provided a secure hold for the nock of the arrow and may have cushioned the wrist against the snap of the string as the arrow left the bow. A narrow strip of buckskin was wrapped around the bow 30 times at the grip. Barrett and Gifford record what we might expect of so complex a tool. While normally every man owned a bow, not every man made his own. A specialist made both bows and arrows.

J. W. Hudson's description of the bows of the Southern Miwok of Yosemite Valley, obtained around the turned of the century and reprinted by Bates from an unpublished manuscript, elucidates best of all (save for a failure to describe the recurved limbs) most elements of manufacture of this style bow:

> *War bows are made from a large cedar limb, cut high in the tree because having more life or spring. This limb is cut off, split in the center, and trimmed to a rough shape from the inside. The bark peeled off and enough sap wood left to shape the*

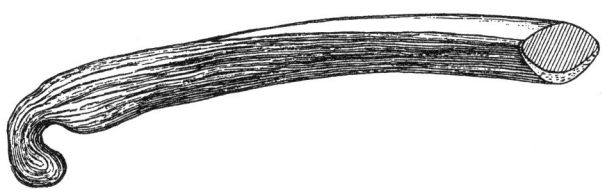

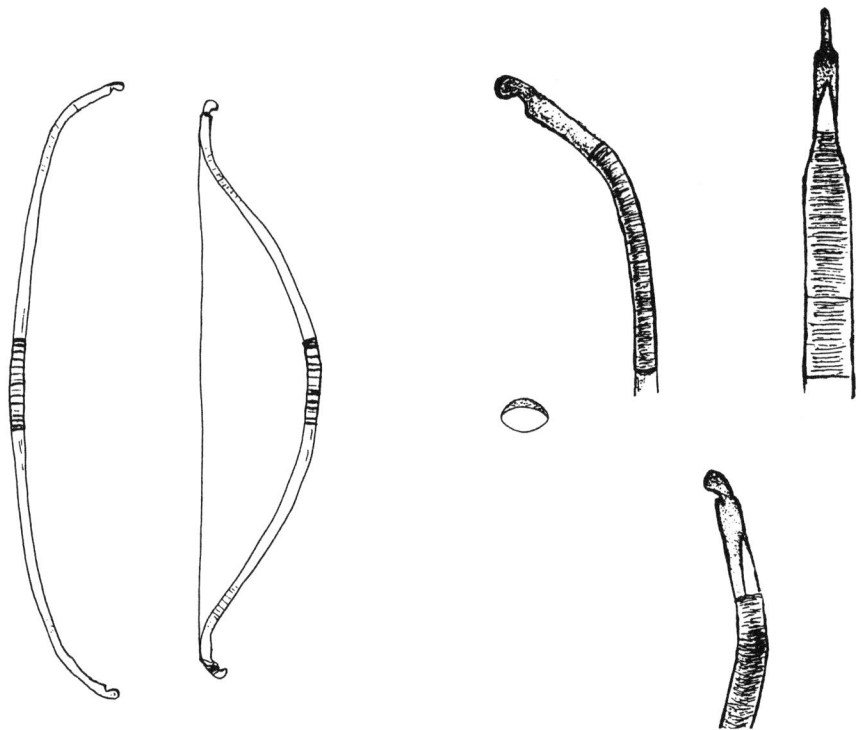

Miwok bow from Yosemite area in San Diego Museum of Man, probably collected around 1900. Entry reads: "Made before the Indians ever saw a white man. The finest workmanship in North America Indian Bow craft. Made of sinew and incense cedar. . . ." Stippled areas indicate sinew backing that has been brought around on belly side of the bow at the nock end. On the remainder of the bow, the sinew only very slightly overlaps the sides. Long, tendril-like sinew, thickly coated in light brown glue, can be seen in the actual example. Barrett and Gifford wrote the overall appearance of the sinew back was "of the bark of a tree or shrub"—apt for the bow depicted here whose back is furrowed with strips of sinew. Bates gives the length of this bow at 97 cm. (about 38") which must have been measured in a direct line, unstrung, from tip to tip, for following the arc, the entire bow measured 112 cm. (44"). The wood was regular and finely polished (my rough sketches do not capture its symmetry and elegance). Other measurements I took were center of the handle, 31 mm. wide by 21 mm. thick (including sinew and thin buckskin band); midlimb, 30 mm. by 17 mm.; 5" from end of nock, 25 mm. by 15 mm.; 2" from end of nock (near peak formed on belly by overlapping sinew), 15 mm. by 15 mm.; sinew hook at end of nock, 7.5 mm. by 16 mm.. This particular bow also has fine, red-colored thread wrapped around it, generally without overlapping, near either end (held by glue that can also be seen to exude from a margin). The grip of this and other Miwok bows is wrapped with a narrow strip of buckskin for 10 to 15 cm.

Craig Bates, in his study of Sierra Miwok reflexed sinew-backed bows, noted that they averaged 95 cm. in length (likely direct line from nock to nock), were under 5 cm. wide and had a bi-convex cross section. At each end the sinew backing was brought around on the belly of the bow—for the last 2.5 cm. the bow was covered with it. Layers of sinew then extended beyond the wood and were folded back to the wood to make small hooks that were another 2.5 cm. in length. These hooks, hard and rigid like wood but more resilient, served as nocks. Upon examining the Yosemite Miwok bow I have depicted, it appeared that after the sinew had been layered on and before it had dried, the ends were temporarily tied off just beyond the tip, constricting the sinew at the end of the wood. With the fingers, the small bundles of concentric fibers remaining at the very end were then molded and bent back to form the hook. (Drawn from photographs in Bates 1978—except belly view and cross section sketched from original bow that the San Diego Museum of Man allowed me to examine.)

back. In many cases the red color shows slightly on the inside at middle where it is thickest. The wooden frame of the bow is always thin and weak before sinewing, but exceedingly quick and springy. Seasoning for a day or two is ample before sinewing as the wood must never be perfectly dry or seasoned and must retain part of its sap. The final process before sinewing is rubbing the back of the bow across a grooved stone, granite, to insure cleanliness from grease, and so roughened for adhesion of the sinew. The sinew strips come from both deer's neck and hing [sic] legs. These dried strings are to be found in every aboriginal cabin in early times. They are laid upon a smooth stone and anvil and with stone hammer are shredded until frayed out. They are then stripped between the fingers and a stick, or hackled until broken into a fine thread, then placed in water ready for use.

The Chlorogallum [sic] roots are roasted in hot ashes for three hours and when cold are chewed and sucked to extract the paste which is taken from the mouth as needed, and smeared over the entire back of the bow and its tips. The sinew is also slightly chewed and passed frequently through the mouth glue pot until thoroughly incorporated with the glue. These glue-filled bunches or strings of sinew are laid to one side ready to be pasted on the bow. One sinew bunch is laid along the center of the back of the bow and the others following it are slightly overlapped or laid beside, lower at ends, until each tip is reached. Then the terminals are carried over the bow tip and lapped and tied at the notches. When the back is being covered glue is freely added and rubbed in. When the back is being completely covered with sinew, the bow is finally wrapped closely end to end with a string to keep tight the sinew while drying. Then, when dry, is bent and strung backward and laid out in the sun until perfectly dry. This backward bending prevents the sinew from slipping longitudinally. The equisetum sand paper was used freely in finishing.

In the earliest (1880) account of Miwok bow construction found by Bates, Lafayette Bunnell gave the bow wood as cedar and California nutmeg. In a book published in 1904, Galen Clark, who homesteaded Wawona in 1856, confirmed the use of incense cedar *(Libocedrus decurrens)* and California nutmeg *(Tumion californicum)* as the two woods used for bows of the Miwok. Clark's words also extend our understanding of sinew application and the affect it had on the bow which was flat on the outer side (before applying sinew) and rounded smooth on the inner or belly side.

The flat, outer side was covered with sinew, usually that from the leg of a deer, steeped in hot water until it became soft and glutinous, and then laid evenly and smoothly over the wood, and so shaped at the ends as to hold the string in place. When thoroughly dried, the sinew contracted, so that the bow when not strung was concave on the outer side.

When not in use the bow was always left unstrung. To string it for use, it was necessary in cold weather to warm it, thus making it more elastic and easily bent.

Wood Treatment

Bows in southern California were not oiled and there is scant record of the practice farther north. Ishi, the Yahi, did not oil his bows. In his travels among the tribes of California in the early 1870s, Stephen Powers found that the Indians of the Central Valley plains, to which the Sierra Nevada descends in the west, did not make bows but purchased them from the mountaineers. The reason, he wrote, was the lack of cedar (in early usage "cedar" often referred to juniper) from which the bows were made. One magnificent and powerful bow he saw in the hands of an aged Yokuts chief was about 5 feet long and so carefully kept (normally in the fur of the tail of some animal) that when it became even a little soiled, its owner would scrape it lightly with a flint and rub it with marrow. Cedar is extremely brittle when dry, Powers explained, and the poorest wood for a bow, but by applying deer marrow every day while drying the Indian made it the best.

The bow referred to was likely of the sinew-backed knob or hook-ended tradition of the Sierras. Powers pointed out that the cedar bow, such as owned by the Yokuts chief, came from the sapwood; the outside of the tree became the outside of the bow. Great effort went into scraping and polishing and insuring that it bent evenly. The ends recurved slightly. It was sinew-backed making the flat outside of the bow semicylindrical. The sinew was lapped around the end of the bow and doubled back a little. Glue made from boiled joints of various animals and combined with pitch held the sinew to the bow, according to Powers. It must have been after all of this, after the bow was essentially complete, that the marrow treatment began. If done before, the glued sinew would likely have come unstuck. So loved was the bow by the old chief that while not in use a section of fur about 4 inches long was slipped over one end. The reason for the fur, wrote Powers, was to carefully protect both string and bow when the string was wrapped around the unstrung bow.

The hook or knob-ended sinew-backed bow seems to have been in great demand and traded even into the San Francisco Bay region where the early expeditions of Vancouver (1793) and Kotzebue (1816) admired and collected it. Scattered, partial but overlapping accounts of manufacture endured. They give an idea of the bow's variety and at the same time, when taken together, preserve a complete process. The old hook-ended sinew-backed bow could be crafted today in the Sierras of California.

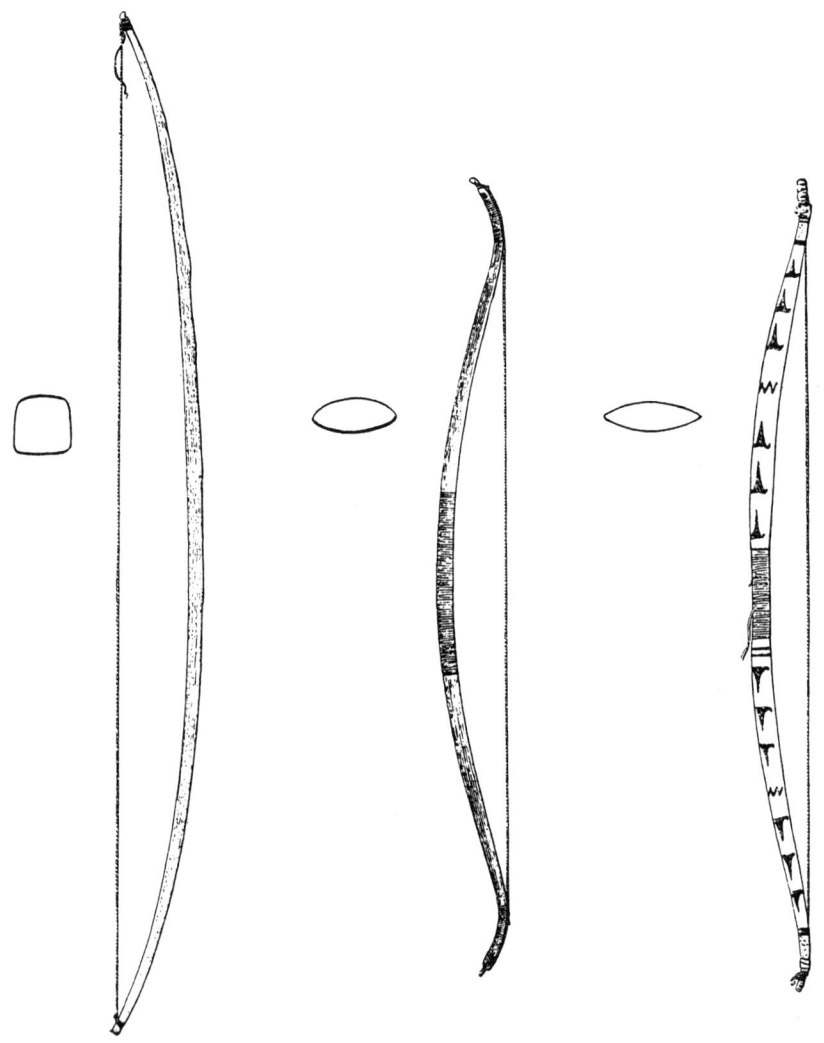

Bows of California. Left: Southern California Diegueño bow collected by Edward Palmer, nineteenth century. Bark and knots remain on back. Length of bow is 4', 6". Middle: sinew-backed bow from Tejón at the southern end of the Great Central Valley, collected by John Xanthus in the nineteenth century. Sinew has been wrapped around the horns of the bow and molded to form nocks. Grip and horns are wrapped in buckskin string. The bowstring is of three-ply sinew cord. The length of the bow is 3', 5". Right: broad flat sinew-backed bow of yew, decorated in green, of the Achomawi, northern California. Grip somewhat narrowed and bound with buckskin string. Buckskin glued around horns and wrapped with bands of sinew. Tufts of fur adorn nocks. Sinew bowstring. The bow is 3', 8" in length (Mason 1894).

The Southern California Plain Wood Bow

In 1827, Kentucky trapper James Ohio Pattie and his party left the friendly Cocopa, a Yuman-speaking tribe, to continue their float down the lower Colorado, catching a few beaver along the way. The Cocopa had warned them of another Yuman group to the south called "Pipi," likely the present day Paipai, who soon met Pattie with a shower of arrows from the bank of the river. After routing the attackers with guns, Pattie examined twenty-three bows dropped by fleeing Indians. The bows were 6 feet in length, made from a tough elastic wood: "Tarnio." This was Pattie's rendering of the Spanish *tornillo* or "screwbean mesquite" *(Prosopis pubescens)*. Pattie recorded that "they polished them down by rubbing them on a rough rock."

Over 150 years ago the Cocopa, Paipai, Southern Diegueño, Mohave, Yuma, Kiliwa, and other Yuman-speaking tribes of the extreme Southwest, southern California, and upper Lower California made long simple bows of mesquite, ash, and willow for hunting and war. They had been making bows for a thousand years before that. Amazingly, some of these remote Yuman groups still make these bows today.

I flicked the remote control to the morning news on my state-of-the-art, flat-screen television, the automatic percolator brewing coffee from beans I had freshly ground in the electric grinder; I buttered toast from a preset toaster, and warmed cereal in the microwave oven. I pushed a button, my garage opened. I turned the key of my Jeep and minutes later passed over an eight-lane freeway through the busy megalopolis of Los Angeles en route to Baja California. After six hours, having crossed deserts and mountains, and followed dirt roads that narrowed to nothing in the distance, reappearing as horse trails through narrow canyons and treacherous arroyos, I entered Rancho Escondido. This region is the home of mixed Southern Diegueño (Kuatl) mountaineers and Paipai desert wanderers who still make the ancient coiled pottery of the mountains, tie the mescal carrying nets of the desert, gather pine nuts in the old way and make authentic Yuman bows. My Jeep was the only vehicle in sight as it stood next to untethered horses under the shade of desert scrubs, atop a promontory overlooking a small spring—their only source of water.

The bows I saw that day could almost have been those found by Pattie over 150 years ago. There were strong similarities to bows of the Southern Diegueño of Campo described to Spier in the 1920s, or to those of the Mohave, Cahuilla, Tubatulabal, or Chumash as recorded by Harrington in the early years of the twentieth century and even in certain ways to those of Ishi as described by Pope around the same time. I recalled Pattie and his party and those long-dead "Pipi" when some of the men told me of bows of mesquite they had made. Kiliwa elder and traditional singer Trinidad Ochurte, who lived farther to the south in the San Pedro Mártir Mountains and regularly made long bows of mesquite *(Prosopis glandulosa)*, once told me that ironwood *(Olneya tesota)* also makes a good bow. His brother José Ochurte preferred arroyo willow *(Salix lasiolepis)*. The Paipai generally use black willow *(Salix nigra)*. Screwbean mesquite does not grow near present-day Paipai villages and traversing the low deserts to the east is now a rarity.

The Yuman-style bow I saw among the Kiliwa of Arroyo Leon, the Paipai and Kuatl of the Santa Catarina area and the Southern Diegueño of Nejí and Ha'a, was not distinctive for its refinement. It was a simple curved bow of wood, not the vulnerable, delicately preserved sinew-backed masterpieces made by specialists of more northern tribes, though Yuman-speaking people were aware of sinew backing and the Maricopa occasionally made a sinew-backed bow. (Instead of gluing the sinew, however, they merely tied it on with another piece of sinew.) Even the wood commonly available to these southern groups was relatively weak and brittle. They compensated with bow design. A recurved or straight stave, when braced, expended energy storage capacity for the sake of power in the early draw. In contrast, the southern bow generally had the limbs curved toward the belly in a kind of permanent brace, and very little bending was needed to fix the string. The limited capacity of the wood was conserved for the draw. Strings were often of fiber which did not stretch so much as sinew (nor absorb the snap of the limbs) but put the full force of the bow to the arrow. In addition, the central section of most of these bows was thick and long and did not bend easily. It did not set or stop during the draw but continuously stored energy. Long tapered limbs acted as efficient levers on the center during the draw and effective catapults in the recoil.

Economy was the beauty of the Yuman bow along with quickness and ease of manufacture—the perfect survival tool of the far-ranging nomadic hunter-gatherer. Living in small bands, they would often set out alone. Survival depended on every individual possessing all the skills. Everyone knew how to make a bow.

Many Indian groups in California, when exigencies demanded or boys were old enough, made plain wooden bows. But among the Yuman speakers, and in southern California in general, the simple unbacked bow predominated. Unfortunately the details of manufacture are scant for most groups but, beginning with the Shoshonean-speaking Tubatulabal of the southern Sierras and ending with Yuman groups in southernmost California and northern Baja California where more complete information is still available, the fading memories and ignored record of the plain wooden bow can be brought back to life. This wonderful tool can put meat on the coals of a campfire again.

The Tubatulabal Self Bow

The Tubatulabal of the Kern River made a plain bow of either willow *(Salix)* or juniper *(Juniperus californica)* with a milkweed fiber string. One informant told Vogelin in the early 1930s that it was shaped with a flint knife, had rounded edges and was generally 45 inches long and 2 inches wide at the grip. One specimen she obtained was 50 inches long. Another seen by her was 68 inches in length, the grip 1-3/4 inches in width and the tips, 3/4 of an inch. Though one informant denied the Tubatulabal had formerly bowed in the grip, this most unusual bow made from green willow had first been shaped with a knife then bowed in at the grip by placing it across two flat rocks 16 inches apart with weight placed in the center of the wood. Furthermore, the ends were re-bowed by placing flat rocks under and on top of each tip to hold them in place and then suspending rocks underneath 8 inches from each end. In this way it was left to dry for eight days. Great length made such a construction viable. A shorter bow of willow with this curvature would snap in a normal draw.

The Plain Wooden Bows of the Chumash and Their Neighbors

Fernando Librado, an elderly full-blooded Chumash, recalled to Harrington what the old Indians used to say. A man who has a bow is the defender of the world. The Chumash speak a Hokan language, a large family of Indian languages that includes the Yuman groups. They made both a simple self bow and the sinew-backed bow, although most of the sinew-backed bows, of toyon, elder and piñon, seemed to have come in trade from the Yokuts. Despite the many statements from his Chumash informants on the plain bow, Harrington's notes from the early years of the twentieth century provide scant information and much repetition. Worse, little was recorded before Harrington. The following summarizes what Harrington heard.

A plain bow without sinew backing could be less than 3-1/2 feet long or as long as 4-1/2 feet. (Sinew-backed bows were about 3 feet long.) At times they used a limb of juniper, creek dogwood or a young sprout of a live oak. But by far the most desired wood for the self bow was elderberry *(Sambucus mexicana* or *cerulea)*. A branch of elderberry 1-1/2 inches or so in diameter, straight and free from knots was cut green and made into a bow. If the elder wood split when drying, it was because the branch had been cut when it contained too much sap—during the full moon, which made the sap swell, according to Simplicio Pico, a Ventureño Chumash.

Chumash bows were strung with the belly of the bow behind the left knee, the bow passing up in front of the right knee and the top end fastened. But Librado said hunters of small game preferred the elderberry bow because it could be strung on the run with arrows under one armpit. The end was simply placed on the ground in front of you with the belly facing away and strung. They always kept the bow unstrung until ready to shoot. Bowstrings were of sinew or Indian hemp *(Apocynum cannabinum)* twisted into a double cord. The Indian hemp or *tok* bowstring had an additional bit of string at the end formed into a loop to slip over the nock when not in use.

While the shorter sinew-backed bows pulled more powerfully and were used to take down a deer, the small-game Chumash self bow was sometimes employed for larger game too. Carrizo cane *(Phragmites communis)* arrows with foreshaft-like wooden points of California sagebrush *(Artemisia californica)*, carried in a quiver at the waist, complemented the Chumash self bow. Because of the leverage effect, weight, as it moved toward the end of a bow, increased geometrically its drag on the bow's cast. A long bow, therefore, was extremely sensitive to any increase in weight at the tips and that included weight of the string as well as of the arrow. It was probably no coincidence that the southern California arrow, par excellence, was of carrizo, an extremely light durable grass stalk. Even today the Indians of Lower California prefer the very lightest of woods for arrow shafts.

The Kitanemuk, Shoshonean-speaking neighbors to the east of the Chumash, made simple self bows of "button willow" *(Cephalanthux occidentalis)*. J. W. Hudson collected four of these in 1901 that are now at the Field Museum. The bow strings on all four are of fiber. One examined by Hudson and Blackburn had a square-cornered pin-style nock, the stave was curved or bent inward toward the belly only at the grip; the length was 1.32 m. and the width, 3.1 cm. J. W. Hudson learned from a Gabrielino consultant (southern neighbors of the Chumash from what is now Los Angeles) that the Gabrielino used bows of buckeye *(Aesculus californica)* for small game.

Like the Chumash, the Yokuts to the northeast, also of the Hokan family of languages, made bows of elder. Sam Garfield, a Wukchumni and Yaudanchi Yokuts, told Gayton that few could make a sinew-backed bow but any man could make a plain bow. The plain bow was of elderwood, apparently very crudely made. Unusually the bark was left on the *inside*, extant examples show little or no recurving of the ends. Thus, Kroeber wrote that the Yokuts bow for small game was little more than a shaped stick. The string for a plain bow came from Indian hemp.

Most interesting, however, is how the stave was split for the bows described by Garfield. After the limb had been selected, cut and peeled, it was set with one end in the crotch of a tree and the other pulled until the stick split down its entire length. I imagine—though it was not recorded—that the end set in the crotch must have been cut at an angle in order to apply pressure differentially to the two sides of the stave. Once the splitting began, the stick must have been pushed farther into the crotch as the sideways pulling on it continued to effect the complete split. Garfield said if it split right, a bow could be made from each half.

According to P. S. Sparkman's turn-of-the-century information, the Luiseño, Shoshonean-speaking southern neighbors of the Gabrielino, made bows most commonly of willow but also of elder and ash. They were about 5 feet long, strung with two-ply string of Indian hemp (occasionally of milkweed or stinging nettle) or three-ply sinew thread. They could cast an arrow about 100 yards but were only effective for up to 50.

The Southern Diegueño Bow

In the early 1920s, Leslie Spier obtained a description of the manufacture of bows among the Yuman-speaking Southern Diegueño at Campo, California. Old Jim McCarty, a true cultural relic who knew all the ancient ways, was the informant. "Mountain" ash, likely "foothill" or two-petal ash *(Fraxinus dipetala)*, made the best bow, he felt, followed by screwbean mesquite, common mesquite *(Prosopis glandulosa)* and a "course" willow, likely black willow *(Salix nigra)* or perhaps desert-willow *(Chilopsis linearis)*, not a true willow but in the same family as catalpa. Both were used by the Cahuilla for similar bows.

After obtaining a green branch, it was allowed to dry until worked. Then it was buried in wet ground for softening and warmed at a fire. The back of the bow was left uncut, the original surface of the bough, a feature modern bowyers have shown makes a simple wooden bow less likely to break. When drawn, ruptures often begin with an opening or cracking of the back of the bow. Traditional English archery also acknowledges the importance of using the heartwood for the belly of the bow and the outer sapwood for the back. The heartwood has great compressive strength and the sapwood, recoil. The Diegueño tapered the bow on the sides and on the inside toward the ends (heavy extremities would only slow it down). The width at the grip was that of the stick itself and the thickness half of that. (Greater width adds power. Thickness adds more power, but if it is too thick the draw becomes difficult and the bow easily breaks.) Notches were cut within 2 cm. of the ends but these dimensions were not fixed. While still warm, the ends of the bow were bent in and held that way by being lightly strung. The bow was roughly in the shape of an arc but with more of the curvature in the limbs. The middle portion was somewhat straight.

After remaining lightly strung for a day, the Southern Diegueño bow was trimmed to its final form. Undoubtedly this came through testing the pull of the bow and trimming the inner surface of the lower or upper limb, whichever of these was not forming an even arc or not bending as much as the other, in order to achieve some kind of symmetry. They were careful both in manufacture and in use, to keep the butt of the bough as the lower end of the bow. The upper nock was shallower in comparison to the lower. The inner face of the finished bow was flat.

Around the turn of the last century, Captain Newton H. Chittenden described Cocopa bows of willow. When dry they were less elastic and more liable to break, thus old ones were seldom seen, he wrote. For hunting deer, bows were 6 to 8 feet long. Arrows were of cane with a foreshaft of hardwood secured with sinew. Hunting parties he met invariably had them.

The strength of such a bow, not of superior wood nor sinew-backed, came largely from its length. Spier's Southern Diegueño bow maker told him it should be two arm lengths (from the tip of the middle finger to the head of the humerus) with the lower or butt half a little longer than the upper. The Maricopa said they measured out a bow from the ground to the maker's forehead and that the Yuma bows were the full height of a man. This would have meant bows were around 6 feet in length. Explorers and ethnographers alike indicate 6 feet of stature was common among Yuman-speaking men. Their long bows were used for large game or war and the length of these bows allowed a full draw even when they were made from somewhat brittle wood.

Shorter bows, often used by boys, were generally for hunting small game. Spier described a Maricopa hunting bow he obtained that was 50 inches long, 1-1/2 by 1/2 an inch at the grip and 6 inches from string to belly. A Maricopa boy's bow of mesquite was 51 inches long and 6 inches deep with a grip of 1 inch by 3/4 of an inch. The Maricopa said their bows would penetrate a deer only 1/2 an inch at a hundred feet.

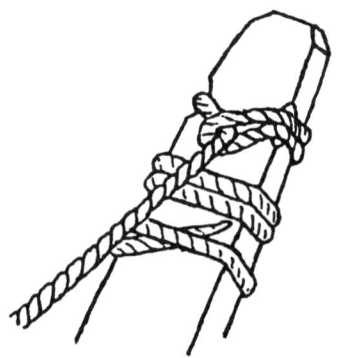

Southern Diegueño method of fastening bowstring (diagrammatic sketch, Spier, 1923).

The Southern Diegueño made bowstrings of milkweed fiber. They scraped off and discarded the outer layers of the stalk, then mashed the center of the stalk to work out unwanted connective tissue. Finally, only the fiber remained. The Southern Diegueño tied the string to both ends of the bow in the very efficient manner shown.

The screwbean-mesquite bow was stored unstrung by the Southern Diegueño. Dampness could pull it into too great an arc. The common mesquite bow was kept strung but only slightly flexed and the willow bow, more so. In general, bows were kept loosely strung, a fillip of the string would slap the bow. For hunting jackrabbits it was tightened until it rang.

The Mohave Willow Bow

The Yuman-speaking Mohave along the Colorado River distinguished between hunting bows and war bows, although both were simple self bows without sinew backing (a few war bows had sinew tied on the back of the bow at the grip). Hunting bows averaged 3-1/2 to 4 feet in length. War bows were longer with the ideal length from the ground to the chin. Both averaged 6 inches from string to belly and took the form of a simple curve. The grip was 1-1/2 inches wide by 1 inch deep. The wood was willow (desert or *Salix*), even though they believed mesquite superior and sometimes used it for war bows.

Bowstrings, which were four-ply, might be of fiber on a hunting bow but never on a war bow whose string was of sinew. Although not specified for the Mohave, Barrows wrote that the Cahuilla, also desert dwelling and western neighbors of the Mohave, made bowstrings from the Mohave yucca (*Yucca schidigera*) which would last for years. Almost all southern California groups also used sinew bowstrings. Sinew strings and sinew-backed bows, however, were prone to water damage where the simple self bow and fiber string held up better in wet conditions.

The tips of the Mohave war bow at times were wrapped in sinew. The war bow was painted black on each end and red in the middle. The hunting bow was left unpainted. Fifty years ago Kenneth Stewart recorded how these bows were constructed.

Each man was responsible for making his own. A green willow bough was cut and dried in the sun. It was then split lengthwise and worked to shape with stone knives. Next, willow bark soaked in water was wrapped around half the bow and this end was pushed into a damp pile of earth over which a fire was burned. They left it that way for about thirty minutes and repeated the process with the other half of the bow. It was then taken out, bent back and forth over the knee to even the leverage and give it flexibility. The ends of the bow were curved during this process and the bow was immediately strung.

Generally bows were unstrung when not in use. Warriors waited until nearing the country of the enemy to string their bows. Maximum flight of a Mohave arrow was said to be 200 yards.

Paipai and Kuatl Bows

The willow bough was cut and left in the sun for about a week, according to Paipai Benito Peralta who as an old man still made hunting bows in the way he had learned from his grandfather in his youth. While accounts of other groups rarely give the species of willow, Peralta was emphatic that it could be only one—black willow *(Salix nigra)*. After curing, he trimmed it to the shape he desired: about 52 inches long, 1 inch thick; slightly tapered to the ends; vaguely lenticular in cross section but more circular; often with even the bark of the tree left on the back of the bow, and little alteration to the rest.

He then slid the bow under the coals of a fire to warm and soften it for bending. After a week of curing the bow should still have been somewhat green; but if the wood was too dry, before warming it in the fire it was soaked in water until less brittle. He curved the bow with his hands or by placing one end in a hole in a board or some other place that might hold it. He levered the stave into a curve that began in earnest at points about a third of the way from each end. The middle portion was left nearly straight as among the Southern Diegueño described by Spier.

Peralta boasted that a well made black-willow bow, such as his, lasts indefinitely. Boughs of black willows from the hot arroyos of the Sierra Juárez exhibit tensile strength, springiness and durability even while still alive on the tree.

The string for such a bow was two-ply desert-agave *(Agave deserti)* fiber, almost 3/16 of an inch in diameter. Peralta gave the best reason for an agave-fiber string as opposed to one of sinew or twisted rawhide—

Mohave Indian Clinton Fisk (Tusk) shoots the plain wood bow. Photographed by J. P. Harrington 1911 (Smithsonian Institution National Anthropological Archives).

rats—they will gnaw the sinew or rawhide string to pieces but leave the agave string alone.

His bows were lightly strung until ready for use, the nocks were cut in 1/8 to 3/16 of an inch at a 45-degree angle about 1/2 inch from the end. The string at the nonadjusting end was wrapped around the nock with a clove hitch—an overhand knot at the end prevented it slipping through. The other adjustable end went around the back of the nock, returned to the bowstring, passed over it and reversed direction under it to return to the back of the bow, around and to the bowstring again where a double half hitch secured it.

Benito Peralta is the acknowledged historian and repository of tribal oral tradition. He is the grand teller of coyote stories and general wise man of the Paipai. I asked him how it is that the Paipai still make bows and arrows in the waning years of the twentieth century. Every man knows how. Not far from Santa Catarina a paved road opened 20 years ago and now and then a tourist seeks out a Paipai for a bow. A government agency also sometimes buys a few for sale in Ensenada. But supplies seem far greater than the meager demand. Making bows is a skill passed from father to son. I thought perhaps tradition kept the bow and arrow alive, but resting

under a ramada, Peralta told me the reason. "We still *use* them," he said. A man sitting across from Peralta agreed. "We own rifles, but bullets are expensive and not always available. We can always make a bow and some of us still hunt rabbits with the bow and arrow. In the old days, they were very patient and took pains making a hunting bow. It had to be perfect. Survival depended on it. We have other sources of food now and the bow no longer has to be perfect."

Peralta recounted his childhood and how, at the age of nine or ten, a boy was given a bow *(j'pu k'rok)* and taught how to shoot. Any branch or bit of brush would be set as a target perhaps 20 feet away. He practiced and practiced. Finally, one day he was allowed to go on a hunt for rabbits. A boy's first kill was special. It was supremely important that he not eat it himself. He had to divide it among those who lived around him and Peralta remembers doing this and later being cleansed in the smoke of the fire that was necessary after the first kill. All of his body had to be "washed" in the smoke. He demonstrated, holding his arms and legs over an imaginary campfire, even his hair, and he ran his fingers back and forth through his hair, rinsing with the imaginary smoke as they had done to him so many years before. Failure to follow these steps after a first kill would result in tremor, he said. One would feel a chill when confronted with the chase and lose all desire to hunt. But if one followed these simple steps all would go well as it did for him.

Raúl Sandoval, of Kuatl (Southern Diegueño) heritage, learned how to make bows from a great uncle now dead. Raúl terminated his bows in a gable-like point, and every 6 inches or so burned an approximately 3/4-inch line around them with an ember of willow. This burn was a very superficial charring, meant only to create a design. The nocks in some cases were 4 inches below the ends. The middle third or half became heavier somewhat abruptly (when viewed from the side); the curve of the ends also seemed to begin in earnest somewhere around this point. Raúl explained that the bending was done when the stick was green. It was warmed in a fire and bent by placing one end in the fork of a tree. The arms of Raúl's bow had a much sharper bend and were less curved than others. It was strung to hold it in position and allowed to cure for a few days.

The string of the bow I purchased from Celso Ayares, Sandoval's uncle in Rancho Escondido, was extremely well made with single-ply tightly twisted agave fiber only 1/16 of an inch in diameter. It had been rolled by his sister Manuela Aguiar on her thigh. It was tied off tightly at one end

Fernando Librado Kitsepawit, Chumash, shows how to carry bow and arrows. Photographed by J. P. Harrington, August 1913 (Smithsonian Institution National Anthropological Archives).

of the bow and wrapped at the other for easy adjustment like Peralta's. It was taut, always in a state of readiness, and I have used it many times.

Ayares' bow was of black willow, a very springy 52 inches long and about 5 inches from bowstring to bow at the grip. The center of the bow was about 1-1/4 inches wide, a little less in depth. Almost circular in cross section, the grip, or center of the bow, extended about 10 inches in a slight reflex. It began to thin on the belly side to the arms, which were flat with rounded edges and went from about 5/8 of an inch to less than 1/2 inch thick at the end. The back of the bow was curved in cross section and the belly was flat. The width decreased little until the very end where the sides curved together and terminated in an arrow-point shape. The nocks were 3/16-inch perpendicular cuts on the sides met by 45-degree cuts below. These side-cut nocks effectively formed arrow-point shapes a little over 1 inch long at the ends of the bow. The bow was carefully rasped and without knots. It pulled easily and sent an arrow smartly to the mark at the range one might encounter a black-tailed jackrabbit or wood rat in the brushy, high Sonoran desert chaparral. Another of Ayares' bows measured 57 inches long and was 8 inches from bowstring to grip when braced.

Andres Albáñez of Santa Catarina explained that bows as long as a man were needed to kill a deer. His bows are not so long and are for small game. Albáñez makes stout black willow bows, like those described for the Southern Diegueño—round on the back, flatter on the belly—they are about 4 feet or more in length and about 6 inches from the wood to the twisted rawhide string where it is drawn. The nocks are a sudden tapering of the bow at the end, the tension on the wood from the string forming trace indentations. The limbs taper only slightly in thickness, much more in width. The center is only very slightly curved with most of the bend in the limbs. His bows appear very clean and free of knots. The wood is well chosen. Because his bows are fairly thick, some do not draw easily and quickly reach a point too stiff to continue the draw. They are virtually indestructible, however, never a hint of a crack. The craftsmanship of his bows sets them apart. It was not surprising to learn from an elder of the tribe he still uses the bow to hunt.

Celso Ayares bow. Black willow, 132 cm. (52") in length. Center of bow, 28 mm. thick, 30 mm. wide. Midlimb, 16 mm. by 29 mm. Just before nock, 11 mm. by 27 mm.

I *was* surprised when Albáñez himself told me the black-willow hunting bow could be completed within a day if circumstances demanded. Having selected a perfectly straight limb, he simply cut and carved it. Then warming it in the embers, he bent it to shape and strung it. It could be used the same day, he averred.

The string he tied on most of his bows came from the back of a deer. A strip less than 1/4 inch wide was cut the entire length of the back. Several could be taken from a single hide in this way. He split the strip from 2 inches to 1/2 inch from one end, forming a loop. The strip was then twisted. Unlike rabbit fur for a blanket, the *hair* side of rawhide folded in, creating a neat tubular cord 1/8 inch thick. It was tied loosely between two points and allowed to dry. Then the opposite end was passed through the loop and the resulting loop was hooked over the nock at one end of the bow. The other end was passed tightly around the bow at the other nock, returned to the belly, under the bowstring and up and over to return the same way it had come to the back again (as in the Campo Diegueño diagram), overlapping the first turn, then around to the taut bowstring, over it and completed in a double half hitch. Any extra string at this end would be tied in a loop for hanging the bow.

Albáñez learned his craft from his father Eugenio Albáñez, a famous Southern Diegueño (Kuatl) ceremonial singer who lived into his eighties. His mother was Paipai and when his father married her, he left his village of La Huerta to live in Santa

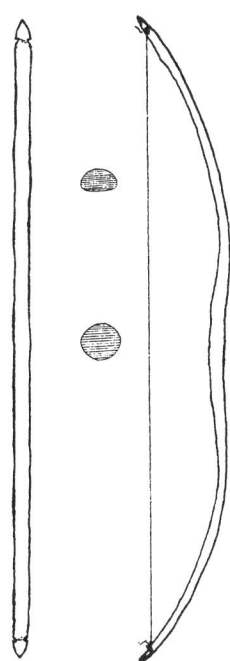

Catarina. Andres remembered well hearing of the longer bows the old men would sometimes make for hunting deer with stone-tipped arrows. They were the same bows and arrows used in war and the old men would recount how they were once used against other Indians in disputes over territory.

How to Make the One-day Bow

It was a particularly hot high noon in late July of 1994 when I challenged Albáñez to make his one-day bow. He had seen me wading the arroyo and coming up the hill toward his house built into the side of a huge boulder but he did not say a word. I had not seen him slouched back in the shade of a ramada. After a few minutes grandchildren exposed his resting spot to the importuning stranger. With the graciousness I depended on, he agreed to the undertaking.

The very blackness of the black-willow trunk catches the eye. The tree grows tall, huge and fantastically shaped along the arroyo and we walked under its graceful white leaves for about a quarter mile until Albáñez spotted a straight clean limb about 1-3/4 inches in diameter rising straight up off of a thick horizontal trunk, perhaps bent that way in the torrents of many winters. With his machete Albáñez cleaned a few twigs from the sides of the limb. A stone or obsidian knife would have worked almost as well. Then, with a couple of whacks, he separated the limb from the tree. Stone tools would have taken longer. Sitting under the brush-covered ramada shade, Albáñez dug his fingernails under the bark at one end and began pulling out long strips, exposing the shiny white cambium and wood, cool and wet to the touch. Willow bark can be used for binding so he carefully set each piece aside. He sighted down the length as he slowly rolled the clean branch in his fingers. Only in this way could he find the slight curve of the stick. The concave side would become the back of the bow and except to remove bumps where the twigs had grown and to polish and lightly rasp, the back would remain uncut.

Using a knife and machete he carved and hacked at the belly until the stick was reduced to nearly half. Except for trimming on the sides at either end, narrowing and evening, all the wood removed was from the belly of the bow. He wielded the machete in hacking downward strokes. He pulled the knife toward him for finer carving. Sharp-edged rocks and carefully knapped stone knives could have done the same but taken longer. At the end of this stage the belly was flat, the back still rounded. What remained was an approximately half section of the original limb with a bit cut from either end; the two ends tapered at the sides and belly and had been made uniform to each other; the edges where the belly met the back had become sharp.

From a pile of dry shavings and wood scraps, Albáñez started a small fire on the open ground, feeding it the tinder piece by piece until it took blaze. He let it burn for about ten minutes, then, while still aflame, he slid one half of the bow into and under the fire, which was as wide as the length of the limb. He generally kept the bow beneath the flames. As the wood darkened and yellowed, he moved it about to warm the half stave evenly and keep it from charring.

In less than ten minutes in the slow flames (on a very hot day) the limb became flexible enough for Albáñez to bend, slowly and tentatively at first, back and forth, levered in the branches of an old tree. After a few minutes of this he began bending it one way only, against the natural curve, making the concavity on the flat belly side of the bow. He used at least three different positions in the tree to bend the end of the limb. He focused the bend near the tip of the bow, a little farther up and almost a third

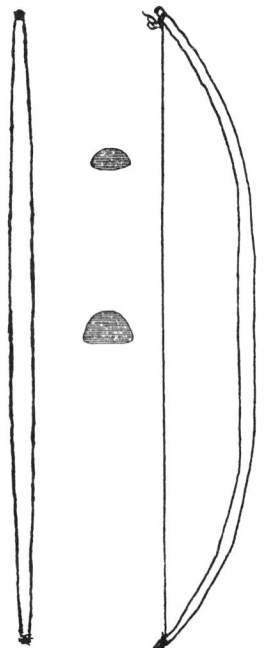

Andres Albáñez bow. Black willow, 132 cm. (52") in length. Center of bow, 26 mm. (1") thick, 39 mm. (1-1/2") wide. Midlimb, 21 mm. (13/16") by 35 mm. (1-3/8"). Just before nock, 15 mm. (9/16") by 23 mm. (15/16").

of the way from the tip. He bent the limb again and again, holding it in position for a few moments each time. Then he returned the stave to the fire and treated the other half in the same manner.

While the wood was still warm he strung the bow. He deftly formed the two circles of a clove hitch, looped the combination over one tip of the bow and pulled it snug. (To hold it, an overhand knot

Andres Albáñez takes the measure of a black-willow bough he has just cut and trimmed (upper left). After stripping it of bark, limb is halved lengthwise with machete and sighted for proper shape and uniformity. A knife drawn toward him in the old Indian manner tapers the ends and finishes the initial roughing out stage. Back of bow remains untouched.

The stave is warmed one end at a time in a small fire and bent into a curve in a dead tree stump. Following this, the bow is immediately strung and belly selectively thinned to achieve desired symmetrical form.

had been tied in the end of the fiber string.) Then, placing that tip on the ground with his knee on the belly, he pushed it into an arc with one hand near the top. With the other hand he wrapped the string around the back of the bow at the nock, returned to the belly and over the bowstring, down and reversing directions to the back again, around to the belly once more where he pulled it taut and secured it with two half hitches on the bowstring itself. The gap between bow and string at the grip was 5-1/4 inches.

He next used his knife to shave wood from the belly of whichever half of the stave was stiff and not bent equally to the other limb. Then he unstrung the bow—it retained only a slight curve—and worked the wood with a course file, the modern equivalent of the rough rock described by Pattie so long ago. He smoothed the sharp edges and brought the bow closer to its final form. He carefully rasped the raised areas on the back where twigs had grown. He smoothed and shaved the wood of the bow with a knife at about a 30-degree angle, working it back and forth where more wood needed to come off the sides of the limbs and belly. He carved and cut the ends, not indenting nocks

Sharp edges are rasped smooth and the ends cut narrow for nocks. The knife blade planes the bow and finally polishes it. Albáñez strings the completed weapon.

Justin Farmer holds a bow from his collection. It was discovered in a cave along Malibu Canyon, southeastern limit of historic Chumash territory bordering the Gabrielino. Some of bottom tip appears missing. Like the bow made by Andres Albáñez, stave is semicircular in cross section: the wood has been removed from the belly, which is flat with the back of the bow essentially untouched. Also, the nock is simply a narrowed end. Unlike Albáñez's bow, the curve occurs in the body and the extremities are slightly recurved. Remaining length of the bow is 56-5/8"; the width at the grip, 2-1/16"; thickness, 1". At 18" from the end, the bow narrows slightly to 2" wide, 15/16" thick. By 4" before the tip the width is 1-1/4", the thickness 7/16". At the tip the thickness is 1/4".

but depending on a final sharp taper alone, beginning about 1-1/4 inches from the tip of the bow, to hold the string. Sometimes he even returned to the machete, interchanging techniques to solve the immediate problem of removing wood. He polished the bow by rapidly rubbing the sharp edge of the knife held vertically against it.

The hot day and fire treatment had dried the wood but because it had not cured completely the polishing left the surface smooth but slightly soft and fuzzy to the touch. Normally, the process of finishing and polishing occurred during the next fifteen days when the wood had cured more completely, Albáñez explained. He cured bows in his home away from the wind that could quickly warp a new bow.

He strung the bow as before, prepared some arrows and declared it ready. The length measured 52 inches, the width for about 1-1/2 feet of the center of the bow was 1-1/2 inches. The thickness of the same portion was 1 inch. The very end of the limbs (or nock) averaged about 5/8 of an inch wide, the thickness a little over 3/8 of an inch. The cast was around 100 yards. It was effective at shorter ranges and already had power and spring enough to take down a rabbit. The bow had taken barely three hours to make though the concentrated effort Albáñez had expended seemed that of a complete day. It was not as thick as an earlier bow I had received from Albáñez (which had warped slightly) and for that reason superior. Thickness beyond a certain point makes a bow stiff and slow. If too thin, there is no power. This one was just right and a joy to use. Despite the lack of prolonged curing it did not warp over the next year. The one-day bow proved an ingenious survival tool from the traditions of Andres Albáñez's hunter-gatherer forebears.

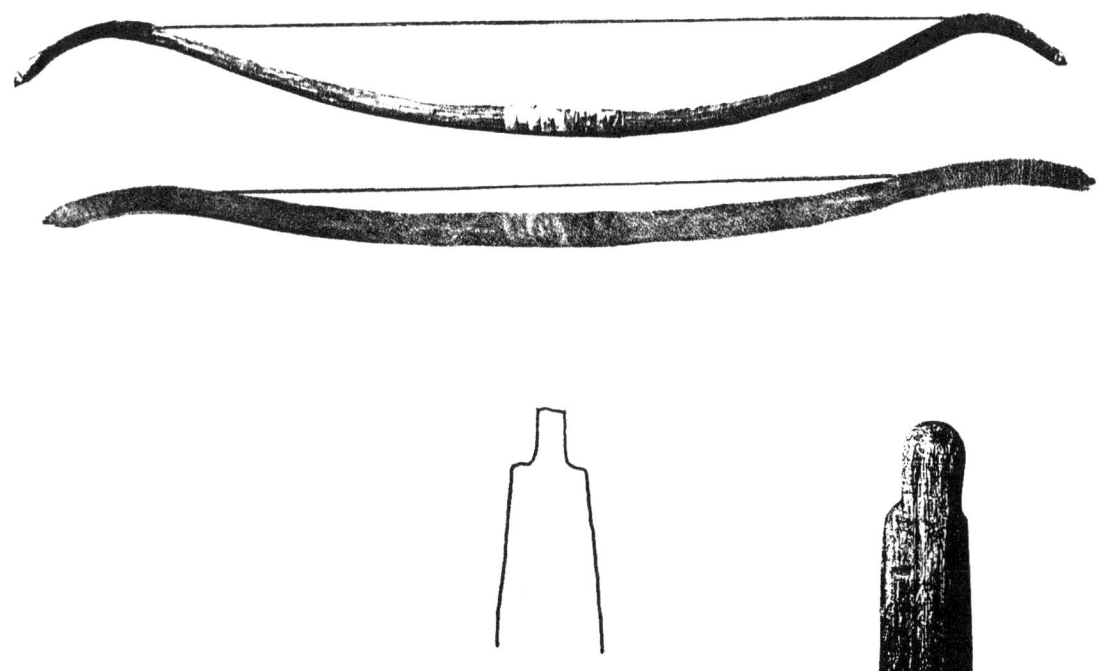

Diagrammatic sketch of pin nock used on some California bows. The Kitanemuk fashioned self bows with this nock. The Chumash also had pin nocks on their short (1 m.) reflexed, sinew-backed bows, which were recurved at the ends—the best, after warming in hot water. (The width at the handle of these tapered Chumash bows was about 3.5 cm., the thickness, 1.8 cm.; they were lenticular in cross section; fine strands of sinew applied with pine pitch covered the pin nocks and came down for about 2 cm. on the inside of the bows; a wrapping of leather strips just below the nock and at the handle completed them.) Strung, sinew-backed "Chumash" bow from collection of Jerry Gaither shown. Top: viewed from side but at an angle slightly toward the back. Just below: pin nocks of bow seen at slight angle. Bottom right: pin nock on curved willow bow thought to be from San Diego Mission, Justin Farmer collection. Bark on back of this 43-1/2" bow had not been removed. (Most of the nearly round center section is 1" wide by 15/16" thick, tapers to 1" by 5/8" at 12" from the end. The stave is 15/16" wide and 1/2" thick 6" from the end and 5/8" wide by 7/16" thick just before the nock.) Northern California wide-limbed bows often employed the pin-style nock as well.

And Arrows

Nothing so improves the quality of hunting as its simplification. The exhilaration of stalking a watchful buck in a deep forest, getting close enough to draw back the bow you have cut from the forest and silently releasing an arrow fletched from the wing of the hawk who soars over that forest—there is simply no experience like it. The culminating vision of the arrow in flight is as perfect as our adventure will ever get (the antipode from the rifleman who murders cougars in trees).

The Indians of the Californias crafted a variety of arrows for the hunt. Since every early account of them is necessarily abstract and limited—no one ethnographer ever sees the whole, let alone records it—and because floral and faunal conditions vary greatly even within a single region, the approach will be to search out natural materials and arrow technology from a number of representative tribes and bands. From each, something special and useful got written down. A lost piece from one may be found with another, perhaps the very detail needed to complete a particular arrow. The whole becomes greater than the sum of its parts.

We begin in the northwest with the Hupa and to the east and south, with Ishi, the Yahi whose 1913 description by Pope is by far the most complete. We follow with the mountain Miwok, the Western Mono and the valley Yokuts. In the south we find the Kern River Tubatulabal, who stand at the confluence of five of the great ecoregions of California; the desert Maricopa, Mohave, and Yuma, the coastal Chumash and the Luiseño. We end at the bottom of California with the Southern Diegueño whose territory includes the deserts and mountains of northern Baja California where some isolated members of this group as well as the Paipai make traditional California arrows to this day.

Albáñez draws an arrow in his one-day bow.

Northern California Arrows

Seemingly an arrow for every occasion and from every terrain, as we go from north to south, syringa *(Philadelphus lewisii)* generally gives way to reed *(Phragmites communis)* as a preferred mainshaft. Heavier, wooden arrows, which were more common in the north, are slower but have more stopping power than the lighter, faster cane or reed arrows. They are most suited to the stronger sinew-backed bow and for larger game.

Hupa

Goddard knew the Hupa in the late-nineteenth century and recorded how they made arrows. A professional fletcher made them, many at a time, keeping them all at the same stage of production until he had finished. Then he sorted them to size and painted the shaft and sometimes the foreshaft of each bunch with distinctive rings of blue, black or red. This was to allow the purchaser to prove it was his arrow in a slain deer or man.

The war and hunting arrow measured about 32 inches from nock to point. The mainshaft was a straight shoot of syringa *(Philadelphus lewisii)* with pith removed to receive a 4-inch foreshaft of Juneberry *(Amelanchier alnifolia)*. The nock was usually cylindrical in form. The distal end of the mainshaft was wrapped with sinew to prevent splitting. Three halved hawk feathers were attached with sinew. With a little help from sturgeon glue, sinew held a point of obsidian or flint to the foreshaft by passing through the notches on either side of the stone. (It should be noted that Yurok Homer Cooper split a syringa shoot lengthwise into four parts and rasped each section with stone and smoothed it with Indian sandpaper, or equisetum, to make an arrow, stone-tipped but without foreshaft.)

Hupa hunting arrows for small game and practice were without stone points but retained the foreshaft. If broken, the foreshaft could be quickly replaced. Boys used arrows of huckleberry *(Vaccinium ovatum)* with two *unsplit* feathers from the wing of a yellow-hammer (probably red-shafted flicker, *Colaptes auratus*).

The Yahi Arrow (sawa)

Ishi gathered tall, straight shoots of hazel *(Corylus cornuta)*, each a yard in length and just over 3/8 of an inch at the greatest diameter. With his thumbnail he stripped them of bark, bound the best sticks together (he always made arrows in groups of five) and laid them in a horizontal position to season. He used them anywhere from a week to a year later. Other woods preferred by Ishi for arrows included reed, dogwood, mountain mahogany, "arrow bush" (western peony, *Paeonia brownii*) and *bakanyau'an* (syringa or mock orange, *Philadelphus lewisii*).

To begin the manufacture he passed the wood back and forth close to a small pile of embers or hot stone while straightening the shafts by applying pressure with his thumbs over the convex side of any bend. In this way, it took less than a minute to straighten a crook in the shaft and it remained straight after cooling. It was bad form to cause a burn to the wood and the test of straightness was simply to sight down its length.

Ishi's hunting arrows were obsidian pointed or blunt, the former used for deer, bear and large predators and the latter for birds, rabbits and similar small game. A 6- to 8-inch foreshaft, of wood heavier

Northern California arrow. Mainshaft of "rhus," (Mason notes wild currant and willow also used) striped black, brown and red. Feathers held by sinew only. Hardwood foreshaft painted red, sharpened and inserted in mainshaft, bound with sinew. Obsidian point, side-notched, held with diagonally lashed sinew. Total length, 30" (Mason, 1894).

Hupa arrow. Red painted sinew and glue hold feathers to shaft striped with narrow bands of blue, red and natural wood. Shallow cylindrical nock. Hardwood foreshaft polished with naturally ridged equisetum to appear bound with fine thread, painted blue, inserted in mainshaft, held with red painted sinew. Side-notched triangular jasper head secured with diagonal lashed, red painted sinew. Total length is 30" (Mason, 1894).

than the mainshaft (such as hazel, buckeye or wild currant), was sometimes added. With cane arrows its use was invariable. A typical arrow including foreshaft measured 29 inches with a diameter at the middle of 11/32 of an inch. Three plumes from a buzzard started 3/4 of an inch from the nock and ran 4-3/4 inches long. They began at 3/8 of an inch wide and were trimmed straight to the forward end whose width was 1/8 inch. At both ends the feathers were secured with wrappings of deer sinew. Pope recorded Ishi's arrow shafts were particularly smooth. Ishi accomplished this by scraping and rubbing them between two pieces of sandstone. For finishing, he turned the shaft on a "hand lathe": while rolling the dowel back and forth on his thigh with his right hand, he rubbed a piece of sandstone over it with his left.

A flake of obsidian cut the notch for the bowstring. On a typical main shaft of 21 inches (where a foreshaft would be added) he cut the nock 5/32 of an inch wide and 3/16 of an inch deep. It was cut 1/2 of an inch deep for a larger arrow. Nocks were at the smaller end of the stick.

At the larger end he drilled an opening for the foreshaft by placing a sharpened bone upright in the ground, steadying it with his feet and twirling the shaft upon it while bearing down just as in making fire with sticks. The opening went to about an inch in depth, 1/4 inch in diameter, and ran to a point. To prevent splitting, the end was firmly bound with sinew or cedar cord before drilling. The foreshaft was sharpened to fit the socket leaving a slight shoulder where it met the main shaft. Salmon glue or pine resin secured the two pieces and the joint was wrapped with sinew for an inch or more.

After bringing five arrows to this stage Ishi painted them to make them fly straight. He preferred green and red. (When others excelled him in marksmanship, he switched colors to blue and red.) The design, which covered only the area to be fletched, was usually alternating 1/4-inch rings of blue and red, three of these near the nock, followed by a space sometimes filled with dots or snaky lines lengthwise and a group of ten more rings of blue and red at the lower end. He used a little stick of wood as brush. He held the shaft between his left arm and chest and while rotating it with his left hand, applied paint with his right arm steadied on his knee. For serpentine lines he had a pattern of wood or deer hide and passed his brush along it. There was no symbolic significance to the pattern, or at least Ishi did not reveal any. When the paint dried, broad bands of glue were applied, above and below, where the ends of the feather ribs would lie; and these areas were allowed to dry.

Ishi preferred hard-to-obtain eagle feathers but would use many others including hawk, owl, buzzard, wild goose, heron, quail, pigeon, flicker, turkey and bluejay. Three feathers from the same wing went on each arrow. Though wing feathers were preferred, tail feathers sufficed.

He held the bottom of the feather between his two palms and separated the fine filaments at the tip to pull the feather perfectly into two parts, splitting the quill down its length. Only the larger posterior half was used. Holding one end under his toe against a rock and the other pulled taut in his left hand, he shaved and scraped the rib with a chip of obsidian to a translucent thinness, leaving no pith. Three of these, chosen for similarity of form and color, were tied with a thread and set aside until used.

For the actual fletching they were soaked in warm water until soft, shaken dry, separated and tested for strength by pulling at the ends. He then bent down 1/2 an inch or so of laminae (feather filaments) against the tip of the feather rib and

Achomawi arrow. Mainshaft striped green. Feathers held with sinew. Head, gray chert, side-notched, sinew-bound. Total length, 34" (Mason, 1894).

Klamath arrow. Mainshaft of spruce. Hardwood point bound with sinew (Mason, 1894).

Arrow made by Ishi while still in the "wild." Mainshaft of hazel; buzzard feathers; deer sinew; shaftment painted in rings of red and blue. Foreshaft of hardwood to which a chipped glass head has been bound with sinew (Pope, 1918).

ruffled the rest of the laminae backward for space to apply the sinew which he had made ready.

Very delicate tendons, split and soaked in water, he chewed to a stringy pulp and drew them from his mouth in thin ribbons about 1 foot long. He held the arrow between his chest and left arm and attached one end of the sinew to the arrow by a couple of overlapping turns near the nock. The nock he twirled in his left hand, holding the other end of the sinew in his teeth. He then placed the three feathers as described, with the laminae against the feather rib, one by one, parallel on the arrow shaft, making sure the first was perpendicular to the plane of the nock and that there were equidistant spaces between all of them. He rotated the shaft, binding the 1/2 inch of laminae and rib of each feather to it with an accumulating spiral of sinew now held between right thumb and forefinger. He smoothed the sinew with his thumbnail. He completed the process for five arrows.

At the lower, larger end of each feather he stripped away the laminae completely where the sinew would be wound. He held the top feather against the shaft with his left thumb, and the other two with his second and third fingers. Again he drew sinew from his mouth and wound a few turns around the ribs and shaft. He now released the hold on the feathers and made final adjustments, offsetting the base of each feather vane about 1/16 of an inch from the parallel, toward the concave side of the feather. He pulled them taut and cut the bare rib 1/2 inch long. On this he completed winding the sinew by rotation as with the upper end and smoothed it with his thumbnail the same way.

In all of the wrappings Ishi made a close spiral, not overlapping the sinew except at the beginning and for the last few turns.

After some hours in the sun to dry, Ishi would take an arrow and strike it gently against his palm to return the laminae he had ruffled to their natural direction. He fluffed and stroked the feathers,

Fritz Hanson, Karok Indian, straightens an arrow. Photographed by J. P. Harrington, 1926 (Smithsonian Institution National Anthropological Archives).

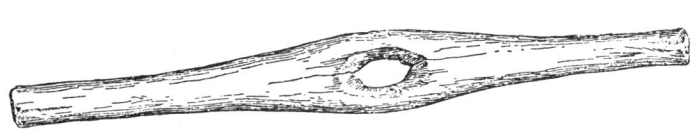 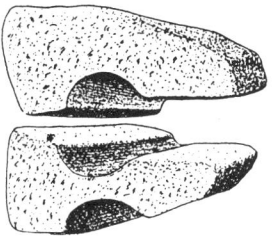

Hupa arrow straightener made from yew, 10" long. Arrow shaft inserted and pressure applied to ends of tool (Mason, 1894). Northern Maidu sandstone arrow straightener, 2" long. The arrow was run back and forth between two pieces of convenient size with a groove having been worked in them. In straightening arrows the Maidu also used their teeth a great deal (Dixon, 1905).

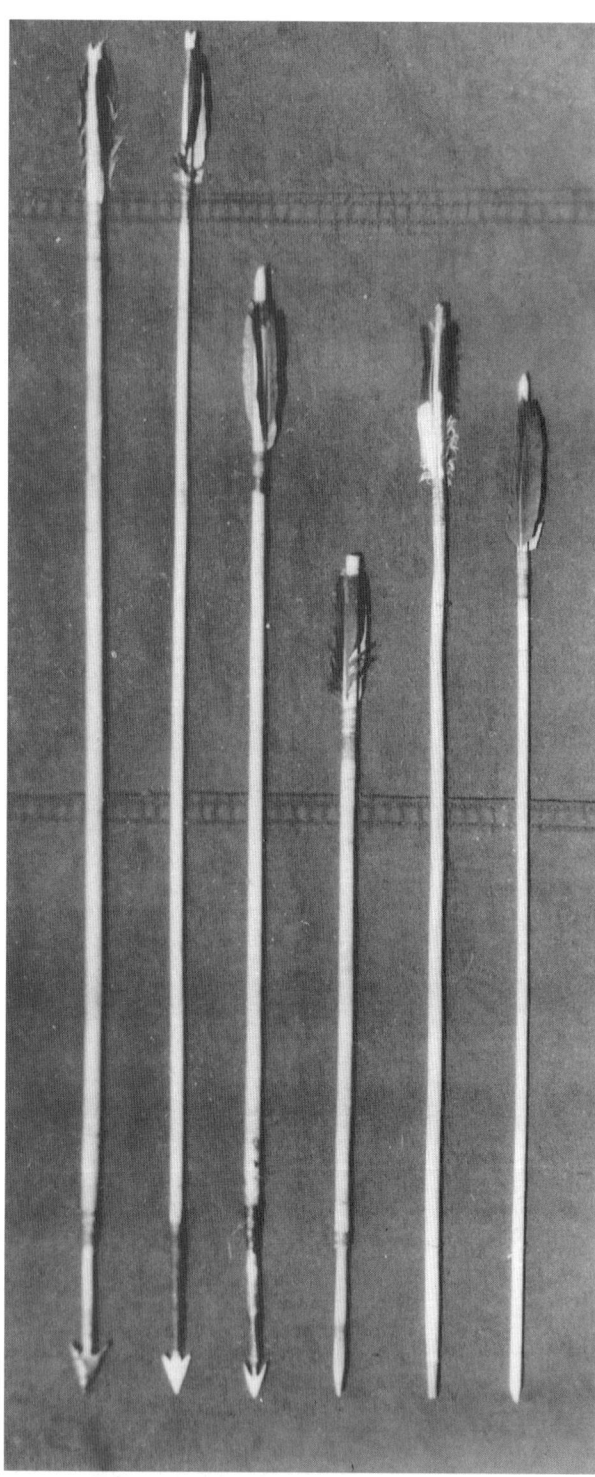

Karok arrows: first, flint-pointed; next two, bone-pointed; fourth, foreshaft only, no stone point; fifth, no foreshaft, end-wrapped with sinew; last, simple pointed arrow, no foreshaft—whole, unsplit, tangential feathers. Photographed by J. P. Harrington, 1925 (Smithsonian Institution National Anthropological Archives).

then trimmed them with a sharp obsidian flake as they lay on a flat piece of wood, using the edge of a straight stick as a guide. Pope recorded that Ishi's feathers usually were given a straight edge with a width 1/8 of an inch at the forward end, 3/8 or 1/2 inch at the rear. At times, though, the edge was slightly concave. Normally, no trimming was done near the nock, leaving the natural and graceful curve of the feather tip. Some of Ishi's arrow feathers were barely 3 inches long, others on those used for war or exhibition nearly 1 foot—the natural length of a hawk pinion. Interestingly, the vanes did not stand perfectly perpendicular to the shaft but were set at an angle and after much use and time in the quiver tended to fall or lie closer to the arrow.

He now took the final measurement of the arrow by holding the nock in his sternal notch and extending his left arm almost in shooting position along the shaft to the end of his left forefinger where he would make the cut. He used an obsidian knife in a filing motion. Then he slightly rounded the point and bound it with sinew if the arrow was intended for small game. If for large, a notch similar to the nock was cut for a stone head. He placed it perpendicular to the arrowstring notch since he shot his bow in a near horizontal position and desired the head to be vertical in flight; this, he thought, facilitated penetration of the ribs of an animal (not realizing the arrow revolved in flight). Pope observed that Old English archers had the same mistaken notion: since they held their bows in a near vertical position, they placed their broadheads in the same plane as the arrowstring notch.

To fix the head to the arrow, Ishi heated pine resin, applied it to the notched end of the arrow and set in an obsidian point. He molded the resin about the base of the arrowhead and, when firm, bound it with sinew—three wraps about each side notch and around the arrow shaft for 1/2 an inch below the head. When dry, a little polishing with sandstone gave a fine finish to the binding.

Miwok Arrows

Galen Clark who settled in Miwok territory at Wawona around the middle of the nineteenth century, wrote that the Miwok made arrows of reeds and various kinds of woods such as the syringa or mock orange *(Philadelphus lewisii)* and a shrub or a tree called *le-ham-i-tee,* "arrowwood." It grew plentifully in Indian Canyon near Yosemite Falls. For small game the hard wooden arrow was simply sharpened to a point, but for large game or battle obsidian was obtained from the area around Mono Lake. The old men worked the volcanic glass into fine heads for these arrows.

Barrett and Gifford found that for ordinary hunting the Miwok used a simple wooden shaft with an obsidian or flint arrowhead, pine-pitched and sinew-lashed. The war and big-game arrow included a foreshaft. Mainshafts were made from the young shoots of a tree (*gilme*) closely resembling the willow (growing commonly where willow grows and superficially looking like willow), young spice bush shoots *(Calycanthus occidentalis)* or elder *(Sambucus glauca)*. They stripped the bark and scraped and trimmed the shaft to an even size, straightened it through heating and bending, and finally smoothed and polished the result with scouring rush *(Equisetum arvense)*. The foreshaft was of white oak *(Quercus lobata)* or greasewood *(chamise)* with a stone arrowhead.

The top of the stick was notched for the string and said to have been painted red. They attached split feathers, usually of western red-tailed hawk, but especially esteemed were those of the roadrunner, which they believed to be unfailing in killing deer. The half feathers were lashed toward the point first, each arrow in a group of ten or so, before completing the lashing of the first feather at the nock end. The arrowmaker, holding the chewed sinew in his mouth and with the arrow nearby, began the winding with his fingers, then simply revolved the shaft in front of his face as he fed fibers from his mouth onto the arrow.

Some museum Miwok arrows show sinew-lashing reinforcement at the end of the mainshaft where the foreshaft begins. Others reveal small encircling grooves for the full length of the hawk fletching. This would have increased the holding power of the sinew.

Western Mono

The Waksachi Western Mono made arrows from a single shaft of cane for hunting large game and for war. After being pulled back and forth through the stone groove of a heated arrow straightener and sighted down the length for straightness, the cane arrow for large animals, such as deer, was cut off square just before a joint and wrapped six turns with a fine sinew thread about 3 inches above this. They then opened the partition of the joint by turning it on a sharp wooden point. A flint head, round in cross section with a cylindrical stem, or a wooden point was wedged in place. Such points detached and remained in the wound.

War arrows were the same but shorter, and the obsidian head was flat with a flanged butt. The opened partition of the front of the arrow was split to receive the head, which was lashed with fine sinew and smeared with glue.

A compound arrow of cane, like that for the deer but with a foreshaft of a white oak shoot or spicewood and occasionally tipped with obsidian, was used to take small game. The foreshaft remained in the wound.

Ishi hunting arrow. 8"-long turkey feathers bound with sinew, not glued. Obsidian head set in notch with resin, sinew-bound. Length, 30"; width, 5/16" (Pope 1923).

Arrow made by Ishi at museum (Pope, 1918).

Yurok arrow. Sinew wrapped. Just below sinew at nock end is a thick black band followed by very thin bands of blue. Foreshaft of barbed bone (each barb 3/4" long) to which is fastened with diagonal lashings of sinew a red jasper blade. This style arrow insures recovery of fish and small game. Total length, 30" (Mason, 1894).

Winton foreshafted arrow (Mason, 1894).

A single shaft of alder wood made an arrow for birds. It was scraped smooth with an obsidian blade, heated over coals and straightened with the hands and over the knees. The point was ground on stone and fire-hardened. Three split hawk wing feathers could be attached to such an arrow or, if for birds only, none at all. In this case, four small crosspieces were tied perpendicular to the point.

Noting the tendency for sinew-wrapped feathers on deer arrows to bow up and slip from the binding at each end, Western Mono or Monache Indians added a small daub of pitch to the center of each feather rib to insure its adherence to the shaft. (Ishi followed a similar practice, gluing his feathers to the shaft, only after he entered civilization.) The Western Mono also understood to lay the feathers of deer arrows perfectly straight or parallel. This produced a silent arrow, which did not alarm the deer and permitted more than one shot. Slightly spiraled fletching (a common Indian feature as with Ishi) created a slight warning whir. It made a more accurate arrow, however.

Yokuts

The Yokuts of the Great Central Valley of California used cane arrows with an oak sprout as a foreshaft. The cane stele with the foreshaft removed was grasped at each end and drawn across the hot groove of an arrow straightener before and after each use. It was pushed through the straightener in a rolling motion. The joints were warmed in the polished transverse groove of the rectangular block of stone and bent by hand or on the ridge of the stone. The groove would also smooth the shaft. If the foreshaft itself was made the point, it was ground on a rock and hardened over coals.

The Yaudanchi Yokuts notched the long wooden points of war arrows and measured the arrow from finger tip nearly to the opposite shoulder. Ordinary hunting arrows had long sharpened foreshafts. Deer arrows were set with a flint head in the foreshaft and the foreshaft was socketed without glue so it might disengage from the mainshaft after penetrating its target.

The Yokuts sometimes made arrows from buttonwillow *(Cephalanthus occidentalis)* which were straightened by the same method as the cane. Early ethnographer Stephen Powers included arrows of the straight shoots of buckeye *(Aesculus californica)* pointed with flint among those made by the Yokuts.

Modoc and Klamath Lake carrizo cane arrows with points of mountain mahogany (88 to 96 cm.). Feathered are regular hunting arrows. Unfeathered have a small ring of sinew and pitch (sometimes carved out of the foreshaft itself) near the point; this deflects the arrow upward when it strikes the surface of water, causing it to skip along into a flock of birds. A regular arrow shot across the surface would submerge at the angle it strikes the water (in Barrett 1910).

Yokuts of Tule River arrow. Carrizo reed mainshaft painted white. Feathers, 4-3/4" long, bound with sinew. Obsidian head in end of hardwood foreshaft fastened with gum molded to the lines of the arrowhead. Total length, 33" (Mason, 1894).

Southern California Arrows

The typical southern California arrow mainshaft used by virtually all groups was cane, or reed (the culm of *Phragmites communis*). It combined with a hardwood foreshaft, usually chamise (*Adenostoma fasciculatum*). The cane arrow was light, fast and perfectly suited to the generally simpler, less powerful bows of this region of California. As elsewhere, there were many variations on the theme and other light, often reed-like, shafts were used. In the desert areas of southern California arrowweed, without foreshaft, made a popular arrow.

Tubatulabal Cane Arrows

Tubatulabal war arrows had cane mainshafts (sometimes of wood) 34 to 36 inches long with a hardwood foreshaft 8 inches in length, split at the end for an arrowhead. Asphaltum alone secured the head to the foreshaft. Feathers of eagles, crows, owls and three varieties of hawk, with two or three vanes, square-trimmed and 1 inch wide were attached spirally with sinew at each end. Hunting arrows for large game were the same but 48 inches long with a 9-inch foreshaft and a smaller black obsidian point inserted loosely so that it might remain in the animal when the arrow fell away. These arrows accompanied the sinew-backed bow.

The willow bow used cane arrows 40 inches long, tipped only with a wooden foreshaft whose point had been sharpened by rubbing it on rough rock. These were for rabbits and other small game. For birds, still shorter cane arrows were used with the pointed wooden foreshaft. Waterfowl arrows had sinew wrapped thickly around the joint where the foreshaft entered the mainshaft. This bulge made the arrow skip over the water in flight, likely in much the same way as the Modoc and Klamath Lake waterfowl arrow.

Chumash Arrows

The Chumash fashioned plain wooden arrows of toyon (*Heteromeles arbutifolia*) about 1/4 of an inch in diameter for deer, coyote and birds, such as ducks. The point was hardened while still green by placing it in hot ashes. One informant told John P. Harrington the feathers were fastened with sinew from the long tail of a *yu'm* (perhaps a mountain lion) and a bit of asphaltum. Sometimes these arrows had obsidian arrow points. They also used toyon as well as coastal sagebrush (*Artemisia californica*) as foreshafts on cane arrows.

Simplicio Pico, a Ventureño Chumash Indian, described for Harrington some elements of the manufacture of the cane, or *carrizo* (*Phragmites communis*) arrow. A hardwood point was hardened in fire, stuck into the cane shaft with a little tar and wrapped firm with sinew. Feathers from various species of hawk were split down the middle and trimmed with a hot coal for fletching.

Fernando Librado told Harrington they allowed the carrizo cane to dry for two days, then they used a grooved arrow-shaft straightener stone quite hot for hardening and straightening the shaft. They kept turning the shaft until the cane looked

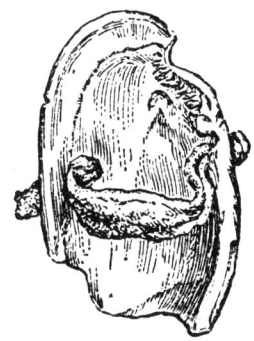

Northern California mussel-shell device worn as artificial nail on finger or thumb and used to smooth down glue and sinew on bows or arrows (Mason, 1894).

Shasta blunt-headed arrow. Crossed pieces made of bone or hardwood (mountain mahogany preferred). Ordinary shaft length used for small land animals; a longer arrow for trout from quiet reaches of mountain streams in water up to 18" deep. Head of arrow placed below the surface and aimed at the head of the fish (Kroeber and Barrett, 1960).

smooth as porcelain. With a knife they smoothed the joints. Cane joints were frequently crooked and needed straightening to produce perfect arrows. Set in the groove of a heated stone straightener (of steatite, which expanded little when heated and was unlikely to fracture) the joint relaxed and the shaft could be straightened by applying pressure to the ends of the cane. The bottom end of the cane was toward the point end of the arrow.

The hardwood point, 6 to 9 inches long, was made with minute notches to hold it in the flesh. Sometimes they had a noticeable barb at the tip, fashioned from a natural branching of the twig. Other foreshafts held stone points. Longer cane arrows were for war and the joints of the cane were left rough to prevent the arrow's removal from the wound. Wooden nocks, 7 to 10 inches long, for insertion into the *proximal* end of cane arrows have been found in some Chumash archaeological sites. Likely this allowed arrows to be used with stronger sinew-backed bows, eliminating breakage of fragile cane nocks.

Most cane arrows, judging from those found in a cache in Peachtree Canyon and now in the Santa Barbara Museum of Natural History, had mainshafts around 60 cm. in length with hardwood foreshafts around 16 cm. The bowstring notch was U-shaped and a stone point of the desert-side-notch style was inserted in a notch of the foreshaft and tied crisscrossed with very fine sinew. Librado said a mixture of tar and pine pitch helped secure such points. The foreshafts of the Peachtree Canyon cache had been painted red. The nocks were also painted and the shafts decorated in ribbons of red, green and black. Sinew bound halves of two hawk feathers and an eagle feather to each arrow and reinforced the end of the mainshaft just before the foreshaft.

Harrington also noted the cane arrow with hardwood point among the Kitanemuk and Gabrielino neighbors of the Chumash. Three Kitanemuk examples in the Field Museum (shown in Hudson and Blackburn, 1982) were between 1 and 1.22 m. long. Foreshafts were 20 to 28 cm. The arrows had hawk and crow fletching.

Luiseño Arrows

According to P. S. Sparkman's early studies, Luiseño arrow mainshafts were generally of "cane" *(Elymus condensatus*—rye grass or giant wild rye), about 2 feet 3 inches in length, with a 9-inch foreshaft of greasewood (chamise: *Adenostoma fasciculatum)* generally fire-hardened. It was glued in the hollow end of the cane with pitch or asphaltum and bound with sinew. Smaller arrows, with foreshafts, were made from the plants *Artemisia heterophylla* and telegraph weed (*Heterotheca grandifolia*). Arrowweed *(Pluchea)* was also used. Arrows were straightened using a grooved stone.

Some arrows had stone points inserted in a notch at the end of the foreshaft, tied with sinew and held with asphaltum or gum—especially from greasewood. A scale insect deposited this most esteemed gum. Three trimmed hawk feathers from various species, twisted slightly to rifle the arrow in flight, were wrapped on the arrow with sinew and held in place with a little asphaltum.

Maricopa Arrows

The Yuman-speaking Maricopa, Chalhidhoma, Mohave and Yuma as well as other desert groups such as the Cahuilla made arrows of arrowweed *(Pluchea)*. The Cahuilla used an arrowweed mainshaft with a foreshaft of chamise. The Maricopa arrow, on the other hand, was simply a stele of arrowweed measured from the fingertips to the armpit and the diameter was simply that of the peeled wood, around 3/8 of an inch. They ran the shaft through ashes to soften the bark and make it easier to peel. With a fragment of stone they scraped it smooth. Any heated stone served to straighten the arrow and they bent it with the aid of their teeth. The butt end of the stick became the forward end of the arrow.

War arrows occasionally had stone heads set into the split end of the shaft, sinew-wrapped and glued with the same gum that exuded from the arrowweed itself. Other arrows were merely sharpened at the tip and hardened, likely through briefly heating the point near a coal. Any stiff wing feather served as fletching: hawk, buzzard, crow or eagle (if purified by a shaman—otherwise it was believed to

Cocopa arrow. Carrizo or reed shaft has two bands of red connected by longitudinal stripes. The sides of the notch have been made parallel by cutting out a little piece. Sinew-bound at either end of feathers and just before foreshaft. The hardwood foreshaft point is 12" long; mainshaft, 25-3/4" (Mason, 1894).

be too dangerous to touch). The split quill was carefully scraped to an even width and thickness so that it would lie close to the shaft. Halves of a single feather were not used on the same arrow. The vanes were placed just short of the nock (leaving a meager grip), parallel to the axis of the shaft and bound at the ends only with sinew. Three vanes were used for war arrows and two for hunting arrows, which included an additional wrapping of sinew at the midpoint of the feathers. The fletching was trimmed parallel to the shaft. The nock half of the arrow was usually painted red.

Mohave Arrows

Mohave arrows described by Kenneth Stewart were also of arrowweed, like those of their enemy the Maricopa, and also without foreshaft but untipped with stone. They measured 3/8 of an inch in diameter by nearly 3 feet long. Children's arrows had two feathers; war arrows, three; and hunting arrows, four. They could be of any large bird except eagle or buzzard. Hawk and crane feathers were the most common.

Arrows were made less with quality than quantity in mind. The Mohave were known to be a warlike people who had need of a great number of arrows. Green arrowweeds were pulled up by the roots and left in the sun to dry. Afterwards, the incipient shaft was heated, the bark scraped off with a stone knife and the end carved to a sharp point. This point was moistened and placed in hot ashes to harden. Then they heated the shaft over the fire to make it limber and straightened it with their hands and teeth alone, sighting along its length.

Feathers were split down the rib with the teeth and the halves used *on the same arrow.* They trimmed the outer edges. Only sinew, wrapped around the top of the feathers and brought down to the bottom and tied, held them to the shaft. For identification as Mohave, they painted the shaft between the feathers black on one side, red on the other. On the shaft of war arrows, boys would sometimes twine the bark of green arrowweeds and light it; where the bark burned away a black spiral design remained.

It is interesting to note that the arrows described in the diary of Jedediah Strong Smith, who stayed among the Mohave in 1826, were not exactly the same as those described by Stewart over a hundred years later. Smith wrote that "the arrows were very long and made of cane grass with a wooden splice 6 inches long for a head." While cane arrows may not have predominated in Stewart's research, he did acknowledge them and noted they were sometimes straightened on a plain heated stone. Smith would know their sting during a return trip in August of 1827 when the Mohave attacked his party and killed ten men.

The Mohave had a warrior class made up of boys selected for their spartan endurance. They received their calling and instruction in dreams. The entire occupation of these *Kwanami* was the contemplation and practice of war. James Ohio Pattie's group clashed with Mohave allies, the Yumas, only a few months after Smith's encounter. And shortly after that they did battle farther south with the "Pipi" whose arrows Pattie described as of reed grass "with a foot of hardwood stuck in the end of the cavity of the reed, and a flint spike fitted on the end of it." He

Mohave arrow. Mainshaft of carrizo reed; shaft has band of red and spiral band of black. Feathers are sinew-wrapped (below, a shorter style of Mohave fletching). Also sinew-wrapped just before hardwood foreshaft. Triangular head of chalcedony set in notch and held by mesquite gum, smoothed to form an unbroken surface between head and foreshaft. Total length, 37" (Mason, 1894).

Yuma arrow. Shaft has bands of red paint. Foreshaft of hardwood is very short, neatly inserted into mainshaft and daubed with brown paint. Head of bottle glass inserted in the end and held with diagonal sinew lashings. Total length, 34-1/2" (Mason, 1894).

wrote that they were the same length as the bows which were 6 feet long.

Yuma Arrows (i pa')

These arrows were much the same as Mohave arrows but the Yuma apparently did not distinguish between war and other arrows, or perhaps they had simply forgotten by the time C. Daryle Ford spoke with them in the 1920s.

The arrowweed arrow was without foreshaft and more common than the foreshafted arrow of cane *(Phragmites communis)*. Since many arrows were lost in war and reference to warriors with arrows "sticking out all over them" were frequent, it seems likely the arrowweed was in fact the preferred Yuma war arrow. Many arrows were carried and shot in battle, probably to intimidate and demoralize more than to kill (an act that was left to the wooden club).

Cane arrows, with a fire-hardened point of arrowweed or mesquite, 6 inches long and wedged into the cane, were especially esteemed for hunting game. Faster and lighter, they carried farther and were more accurate. Prior to use, the archer chewed the joint between the tip and the shaft so that it might dislodge on impact.

Both arrows (likely only the mainshaft of the cane arrow) were measured along the arm from the tip of the index finger to the near nipple, about 30 inches for the Yuma. Rarely, a triangular, chipped-stone arrowhead was lashed with sinew to the arrowweed arrow. Fletching consisted of two or three 6-inch crow or goose plumes attached with mesquite gum and sinew-wrapped. Arrows used for fishing were unfeathered. To indicate ownership an archer usually painted red and black markings on the feathered end of the arrow. Shafts were straightened after wrapping in damp bark and heating in a fire.

Southern Diegueño Arrows of Campo, California

Cane or "reed" arrows with chamise foreshafts as well as arrows completely of wood were made by the Southern Diegueño. The length of the reed arrow mainshaft the Diegueño from Campo, California, as recorded by Spier from Jim McCarty, was measured from the tip of the middle finger to the head of the humerus (half the length of their bow). The chamise foreshaft protruded about 15 cm. Reed arrows measured with the elbow slightly bent were 6 cm. shorter but had longer pointed foreshafts and were used for rats, rabbits, squirrels and quail. Generally, the arrow was straightened on a heated soapstone with grooves of graded sizes. They also made arrow straighteners of clay that included a hole to assist in bending the arrow. The straightener should not have been so hot that it burned the arrow, which they moved back and forth and turned in the groove while bending it straight by sighting down the shaft.

After straightening, they cut a nock in the smaller end and cut the forward end square. The best feathers, they felt, were from brown chicken hawks or, somewhat less preferred, "black" hawks. They went so far as to raise these birds in large domed structures to have a constant supply of feathers available. They split the quill carefully in two but did not use the two halves on the same arrow; the rear end of the arrow would rotate out of the axis of flight if both halves were used. The three vanes faced the same way; this gave the arrow a slight spin. They cut square the top of each half feather and left a few feather filaments for attachment to the arrow. Down was left on the lower end. The feather was buried in damp earth and straightened prior to burning the side obliquely to the shaft, leaving it wider at the nock end.

They chewed sinew and wrapped the three vanes near the nock first, then the forward ends. They also sinew-wrapped any place on the shaft where it looked as though it might split. They bit the sinew ends off close and did not tie them.

They warmed and straightened the green chamise foreshaft and whittled it to size, notching it to hold a stone arrowhead if it was for big game. The arrowhead was 2.5 cm. long or smaller, in the form of a triangle, notched at the base or preferably the sides and tied in place, not glued. For smaller

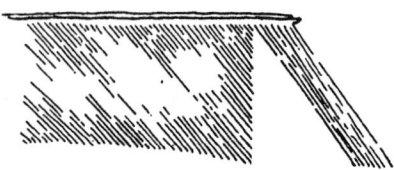

Southern Diegueño method of trimming arrow vane (Spier, 1923).

game, the Diegueño foreshafts were simply whittled to a point. Such a pointed foreshaft, however, could serve even for deer. The opposite end of both styles of foreshaft they sharpened and inserted in the pith opening of the reed to the first joint and glued it with piñon gum.

Santa Catarina Arrows of Lower California

The Paipai and Kuatl (Southern Diegueño) of Santa Catarina made arrows of carrizo into the 1990s. (As with the Cahuilla, Seri, Kiliwa, and undoubtedly many other groups, historical Paipai and Kuatl did not distinguish between the native *Phragmites communis* and the introduced *Arundo donax*.) Benito Peralta, who remembered when Indian women tattooed their faces, told me he gathered carrizo reed for an arrow (*pa'*) when the cane was dry but still standing. Fellow villager Andres Albáñez made beautiful cane arrows from carrizo perfectly straight with a diameter about 5/16 of an inch. He cut off any buds or branches and smoothed the joints of the light, cream-colored stele with a back and forth movement of a perpendicular knife edge. He cut square the slightly larger lower end about 1-1/2 inches below a joint and carefully wound wet sinew thread at the cut for 1/2 inch.

Into this natural hollow he eventually inserted (usually as the last step) a peeled and squared-off chamise (*Adenostoma fasciculatum*) foreshaft. (In contrast, for placement into mainshafts of mule fat, where the pith must be reamed out, the chamise end of insertion was sharpened.) He screwed in the foreshaft (*pambal*) gently, sighting down (or up) the shaft until he reached the point of the twist where the foreshaft was straight. The two pieces became one perfectly aligned arrow. No glue was used. He was not aware of any special reason for this. (The Yaudanchi Yokuts left the flint-tipped deer arrow unglued so the foreshaft would disengage after penetrating its target.) The distal end of the 6-inch foreshaft came gradually to a point around 5 inches from the 25-inch mainshaft.

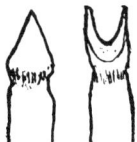

Two quick slashes just before a joint forms a sturdy nock.

Just above a joint at the other end of the cane he made the nock. A single quick slash to one side and another to the opposite side formed two steep gables between which a U-shaped notch naturally appeared—the result of sectioning the hollow cane at an angle. A joint just below would reduce likelihood of the shaft splitting from the force of the bowstring. Sinew wrapping would make it even more secure.

Immediately below and in line with the open nock, split hawk feathers, dark brown and banded, the larger halves from two separate feathers, were sinew-wrapped for 1/4 inch to either side of the arrow. The quill ends, 3-1/2 inches or more below this, were attached for 1/2 inch with additional binding. Only the tops of the feathers had been cut, in a graceful rounded fashion. Nearly straight sides with a width slightly over 1/2 inch had a gentle, natural, convex curve. The arrow was one of a set of three, a customary practice.

Arrows seen by Meigs in the nearby Diegueño village of La Huerta in 1929 were about 3 feet in length for a 4-foot plain hunting bow. A long wood point was inserted in a shaft of carrizo reed or *mirasol* ("sunflower," still used for arrows in Rancho Escondido and Santa Catarina). Sinew-wrapped hawk fletching completed the arrow. Meigs noted pine gum was sometimes used on the sinew to prevent it from coming unwound. Albáñez told me they also occasionally employed pine pitch to help secure the feathers to the arrow.

Carrizo and mirasol were not the only mainshaft materials. A 2-foot-long Paipai arrow made in 1993 by Benito Peralta, had a 20-inch mainshaft of 3/8-inch-diameter *guatamote* ("mule fat": *Baccharis glutinosa*). It was surprisingly light, very slightly burnt in one spot attesting to the fire straightening process, smooth but still recognizable as mule fat. The three hawk feathers cut square at the top tapered for 4 inches in a straight line to about 1/4-inch width at the bottom. Vanes of feathers on the arrows could be two, three, or four depending purely on taste, according to Peralta. Sometimes they were placed on the shaft in a slight spiral, causing the arrow to spin in flight. The split-feather spines were sinew-wrapped top and bottom. Glue also bound some of the feathers in the middle. Sinew reinforced the shaft where it was cut square to hold a 4-inch hardwood chamise foreshaft 5/16 of an inch in diameter, the tip whittled sharp. The other more acutely sharpened end (which created a slight shoulder) was inserted and glued in the pith channel of the mainshaft. A chamise foreshaft required no fire-hardening, according to Peralta. But the best foreshafts by far, he felt, were made of fire-hardened jojoba *(Simmondsia chinensis)*. He placed the jojoba stick in the coals with the bark still on and fire-hardened it that way before carving it into a foreshaft. The notch of a Peralta arrow was U- to square-shaped with the front and back cut off to an inverted V-shape when viewed from the side. Like the Maricopa arrows, the vanes were just short of the nock, leaving a meager grip for drawing and releasing.

The proximal sinew wrapping on the Paipai or Kuatl mainshaft had a dual function. It secured the arrow feathers and by beginning immediately below the nock reinforced the wood of the shaft at that crucial point. Without it, the arrow would eventually split under the exploding force of a taut string suddenly released. At first I wondered why these Indians so carefully and delicately gripped the arrow just at the nock between thumb and forefinger. Impatiently and clumsily I would squeeze much of the end of the arrow and sometimes after the release the sinew binding from the arrow would be left in my sweaty fingers. I thought lowering the binding would be an improvement but when I did, the arrow split. So I learned to grip lightly the old fashioned way.

Albáñez made arrows with extremely straight, well polished mainshafts of guatamote (over 24 inches long). He was especially fussy about selecting the wood, preferring a ready-cured dead branch but not one that had become overdry or weathered. I have been with him in extensive thickets of guatamote where not one branch met his standards. He felt carrizo arrows were too light and preferred guatamote for the mainshaft. When necessary, Albáñez straightened his shafts by warming them over the coals, sighting down their lengths and bending out the curves with his fingers until they were true. Sometimes the process had to be repeated: they would warp slightly out of line. Shafts meant for arrows with three feathers had a diameter of 3/8 of an inch. Those for two feathers were 5/16 of an inch in diameter. The only tool Albáñez needed was a knife. He cleaned and polished the shaft with the blade held vertical, rubbing it back and forth. The smaller end of the stele was beveled sharp into a gable and notches were U-shaped.

The arrows were carefully and tightly sinew-wrapped, spiral fashion, with overlap only at the beginning and termination of the windings that bound the feathers or reinforced the distal end. The width of the sinew of the reinforcement band at the distal end was 7/8 of an inch; at the base of the feather, 5/8 of an inch; at the nock, 1/4 inch. The sinew always came from the deer's leg. His fletching was trimmed in a curve taking it naturally into the arrow shaft at the top. Some were a little less than 1 inch wide, on other arrows they were a little more. The feathers extended for about 4 inches along the shaft.

Beautifully carved foreshafts of chamise had a slightly longer, narrower point on one end for insertion into the stele. They were held unglued by the tight squeeze of the distal opening of the mainshaft and could even be reversed or easily replaced. As

Carrizo arrows and yucca-stalk quiver made by Andres Albáñez.

often as not they remained stuck in the target after the arrow's mainshaft was pulled free. Albáñez kept the foreshafts separate until the arrows were used but did not carry extras. They measured about 6 inches before insertion and about 5-3/8 inches after. They were 5/16 of an inch in diameter. The hole to receive them was made with the point of a scissors twisted in the pith channel of the shaft as a sharp bone must have been formerly. The sinew reinforcement kept the shaft from splitting during this operation.

The difference between a well made and poorly made arrow became apparent when in use. Poorly made arrows would not fly to the mark nor for any distance and rough sinew wrapping would take the flesh from the hand that guided it. Albáñez's arrows, over 2 feet long in total length, were shot with ease and flew to the mark. They were perfectly straight.

Manuela Aguiar, of Kuatl parentage, who lived near her brothers Celso and Tomás in Rancho Escondido, had often astonished me. But I was not prepared for what she drew from her bag of tricks when I showed up one day in the fall of 1994. It was a stone arrow straightener complete with central groove and three decorative incised lines enclosing Xs on either side, common in archaeological examples from southern California. I wondered aloud where she night have found it, and she told me she made this one herself. As a little girl she had watched her grandfather make and use them. He died a long time ago, she was ten and could not remember his name; she only knew him as grandfather. But he was never without an arrow straightener. Bow, arrow, and straightener—they were of a piece. He did not warm the straightener or the arrow in the fire as she recalled but rubbed the arrow back and forth in the groove, over and over. He made the straightener from a special soft stone, abrading it with a piece of metal. They probably used an abrasive stone in the old days, she thought. She herself made them until the only quarry she had ever known was closed off to her by a rancher. He told her to keep out, the land is private property.

The Kiliwa, another Yuman-language group to the south in the San Pedro Mártir mountains, no longer made arrow straighteners when Meigs visited them 70 years ago. But they remembered how they were used. The arrow shaft was rubbed back and forth on it, they told him. And how they were made. The leg bone of a deer rubbed on the stone created the groove.

Peralta used guatamote for arrow mainshafts but even better, when he could get it, was a similar looking but much lighter, more segmented wood he called *jatbil* (hotbeel). Tomás Ayares and Raúl Sandoval used jatbil exclusively for arrow mainshafts. Tomás Ayares' jatbil mainshaft measured 30 inches with 2 additional inches of slightly shouldered foreshaft point. Bare ribs of three feathers were sinew-wrapped at the distal end, followed by 3 inches of fletching cut as a long curve, 7/16 of an inch at the widest, with bent down laminae and ribs together sinew-wrapped at the proximal end. But to all my questions of what "jatbil" was, they would only point to the far side of a distant mountain.

How to Make an Arrow from Jatbil

After many months of familiarity with arrows of the dark, ruddy brown jatbil stalk, I finally saw the plant itself. Raúl Sandoval had described bunches of beautiful yellow blossoms, each about the

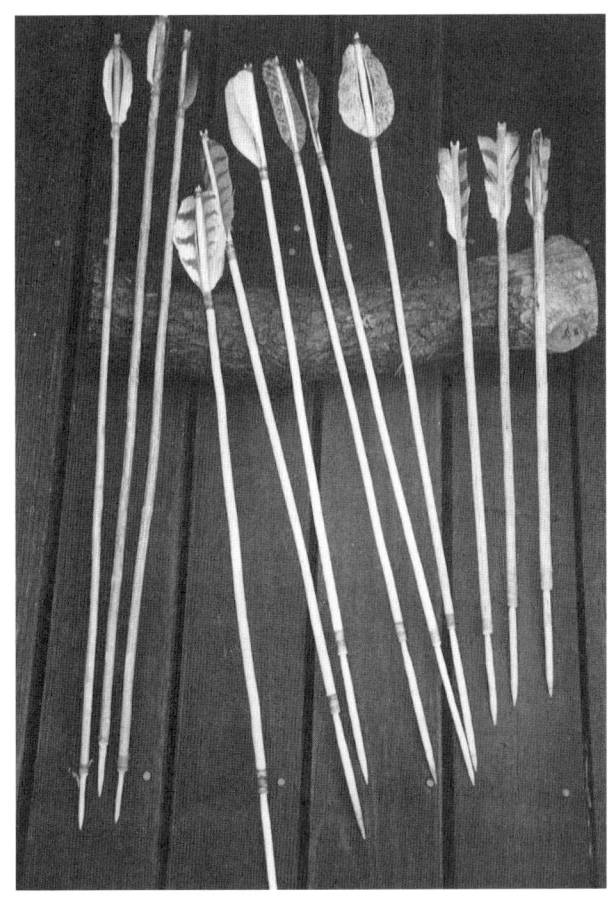

Arrows: first three of jatbil made by Tomás Ayares; next six of guatamote by Andres Albáñez; last three also of guatamote by Benito Peralta.

size of a dollar, atop the stalks. He led me one day high into the mountains, through piñon-pine forests, among the ponderosa, down a far escarpment and along a narrow dry arroyo that pointed toward the low desert. We were flanked by small emory oak trees, which produce acorns with little bitterness. They were greatly loved by Raúl. We could see wild horses pasturing in the mountains above us. Finally, at the confluence of two creeks, I beheld a thicket of tall dry stalks of jatbil, higher than a man. They stood near the edges of the little streams and horsetail *(Equisetum)* grew among them. I gathered stems and dry leaves, since new plants had not yet sprouted that early in the year, and Raúl tore out a rhizome, suggesting I grow one at my home in Los Angeles. I did, and eight months later in October of 1995, after it had grown over 8 feet tall, I was able to identify it as *Helianthus californicus*—California sunflower. The bright yellow flowers, as Raúl had described them, possessed wide folded back phyllaries or bracts that allowed me to distinguish the plant from the very similar Nuttall's sunflower.

Andres Albáñez learned the arrow-making craft from his Southern Diegueño father, Eugenio, born in La Huerta where arrows of sunflower were still being made in the 1920s. Andres showed me how to make such an arrow in December of 1994 in the village of Santa Catarina where he lived.

Albáñez selected extremely straight shoots of jatbil for the mainshaft. Jatbil is very light in weight with a pithy core and slight nodules every 4 inches or so. These nodules were lightly smoothed by scraping with a perpendicular blade. Generally, but not always, he left the thin bark of jatbil in place, explaining that it kept the fragile wood beneath from breaking so easily. He selected shafts already dry but not weathered. If the stele warped or if only a curved piece was available, he wet it and waited a few minutes then warmed it over the coals of a fire. Sighting down the length, he bent the shaft with his fingers until it remained perfectly straight.

The base of the jatbil stalk was cut square. Albáñez then took a 5-inch strip of ivory-colored sinew that he had been soaking, and gripping it from the sides with each hand, pulled a little opening or tear into it and split it longitudinally into two string-like fibers. If too thick, these in turn were split until he had strips 1/16 of an inch wide (when pressed flat against the arrow shaft) and extremely thin. If the sinew began to dry out, he held it with his fingers in his mouth to wet it. He wound a sinew thread around the stele base: he began about 1/16 of an inch from the bottom, made a turn which he overlapped at its start and then proceeded, generally without overlapping, for about 5/8 of an inch up the shaft and overlapped again the last turn. He began by winding with the sinew-holding hand, but after the first round and a half or so seemed secure, he rolled the arrow in one hand while guiding the sinew over the top of the roll and onto the arrow with the other. Frequently the strip of sinew would not reach the full 5/8 of an inch and a second was begun and

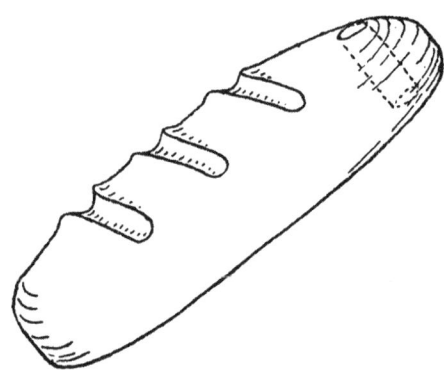

Arrow-shaft straightener: Southern Diegueño of clay from Campo area (Spier 1923).

Steatite arrow straightener found by Paipai near Santa Catarina: 1 7/8" by 1 5/16" by 1/2"; groove, 3/16 to 1/4" deep. Kumeyaay Teodora Cuero of nearby La Huerta told me they called it j'-pechul. The Tubatulabal cut arrow-straightener grooves and made decorative incisions in them with a stone knife. In central and southern California joints of phragmites cane arrows were warmed in the groove of the heated stone and bent on the edge of the stone. The groove also smoothed the shaft. The Yokuts realigned arrows before and after using them. With the foreshaft removed and grasping the mainshaft at each end, they pushed the cane through the hot groove in a rolling motion. Anna Gayton noted they straightened willow arrows the same way.

ended as the first, next to the first. He smoothed the sinew wrap slightly with his fingers and set it aside for a few minutes to dry.

The chamise foreshaft had been seasoned for some days. He carved it round in cross section and gradually curved along its length culminating in sharp points at either end. He planed it smooth with to and fro motions of his knife held at a near perpendicular angle. Finished, the pointed foreshaft measured 1/4 inch in diameter by 6 inches in length. With the reinforcing sinew already dry and dark brown, he reamed the base of the jatbil stalk with a scissor point and fit the foreshaft to it, twisting it into the stele approximately 1 inch.

The length of the mainshaft, already generally determined, was now made final with a single approximately 1/2-inch bevel cut to either side the proximal end of the arrow creating an acute gable. The natural circular nock that this formed between the bevels because of the pith channel was enlarged slightly with the edge of the knife. The completed mainshaft averaged 5/16 of an inch in diameter and was 24 inches long.

From his basket of feathers, mostly of hawk, he selected two opposite, mirror-image wing feathers, similar in size and shape and with the same beautiful brown stripe. Those of most any bird of prey would do. Domestic turkey feathers were also a favorite. He pulled from the quills the bottom 1 inch or more of filaments. Then he laid a feather flat on a board and pounded the spine gently with the end of his knife handle, slightly compressing and flattening it. Leaving the feather on the board's surface, he inserted the end of his knife into the quill and ran it

Raúl Sandoval in patch of dried stalks of jatbil, Sierra Juárez, February 1995.

up and down lengthwise to split it in half. He discarded the thinner fore edge of the wing feather and taking the fuller rear edge in his fingers, he placed the knife nearly flat against the cut side of the quill and deftly scraped it, drawing the sharp blade toward him, at times running it gently in the opposite direction as well. When the quill had been thinned (but not so much as to weaken it), he repeated the process with the second feather and cut both quills off about 3/8 to 1/2 inch below the lower vanes.

He prepared sinew as before. Seated, he held the arrow in his right hand, the point of the arrow to the right across his right thigh (Albáñez was generally, but not exclusively, left handed). He placed

The completed jatbil arrow.

the two feathers in line with the nock to either side of the shaft, and held them in place with the thumb and forefinger of his right hand at the bottom of the bare quills. He adjusted the feathers so that the bottom of the quills were 4 inches below the bottom or "saddle" of the nock. (He did this with his eye but the three in the set were within 1/8 of an inch of this mark.) With his free hand, he wrapped a thread of wet sinew once around the shaft and quills (the wrap went over the arrow, toward the body and down) exactly at the point where the plumage ended, the same on both sides, overlapping itself (the end of the sinew was sometimes held by a fingertip). He gave the thread another turn or two spiraling toward the bottom of the quills. At that point the quills were released and the forefinger was used to guide and smooth the sinew onto the shaft as the middle finger and thumb turned the shaft and the left hand fed the sinew onto it. The sinew spiraled down until the bottoms of the quills were covered. The sinew

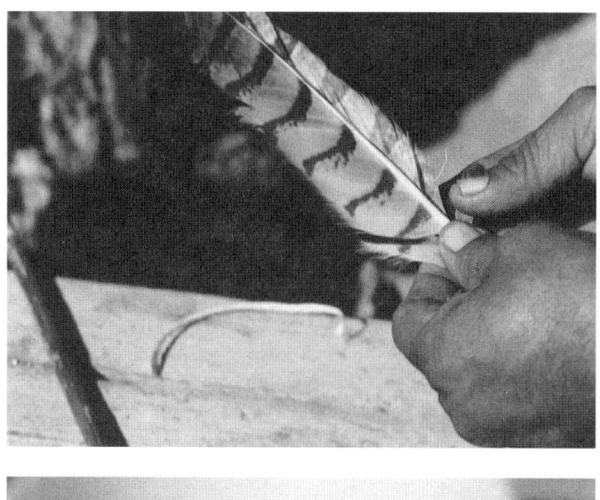

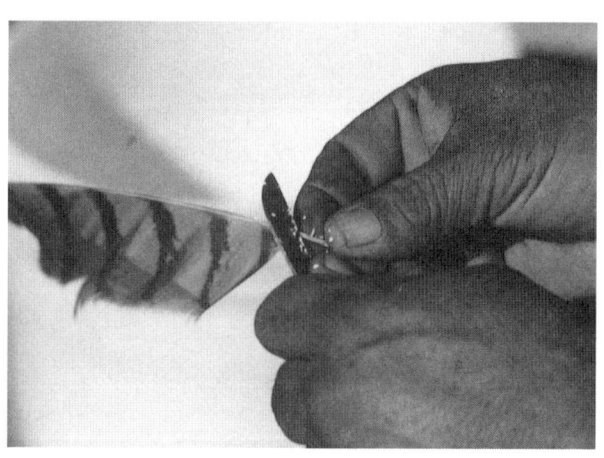
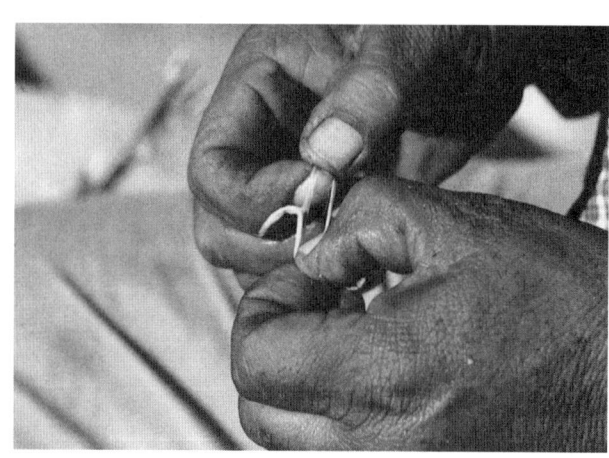
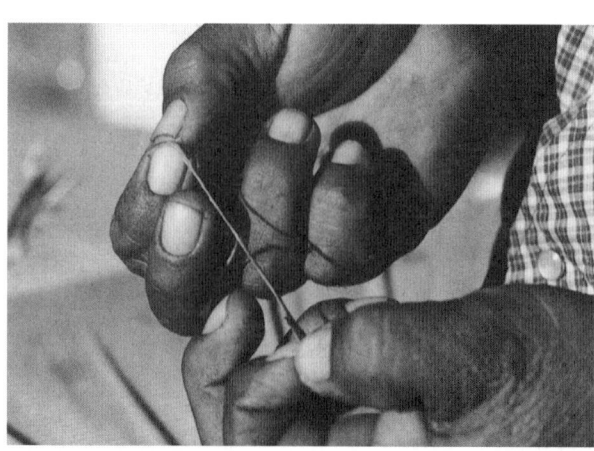
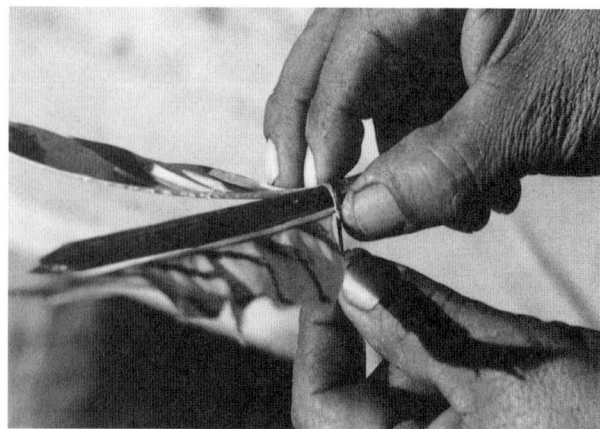

Andres Albáñez fletches the arrow of jatbil.

usually overlapped at the end. If another piece was needed, it too overlapped at beginning and end. He smoothed the wrap with his fingers and set the arrow aside for a few minutes for the sinew to dry.

With the point of the arrow now to the left and the arrow held in the left hand, plumage was snipped away from the top of the feather spines to a point 5/8 of an inch from the nock end (about 5/16 of an inch below the bottom of the bevel cut). These bare spines were grasped, as before, with the thumb

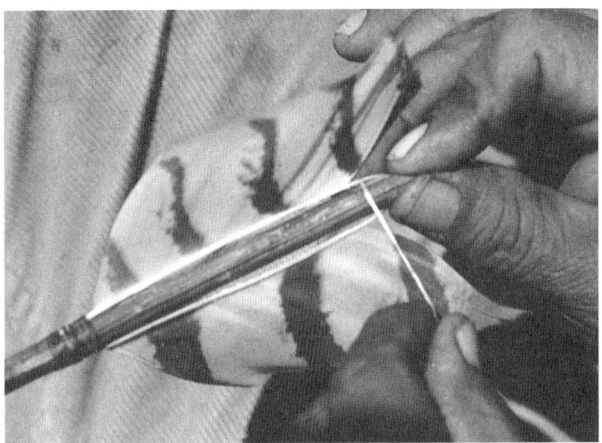

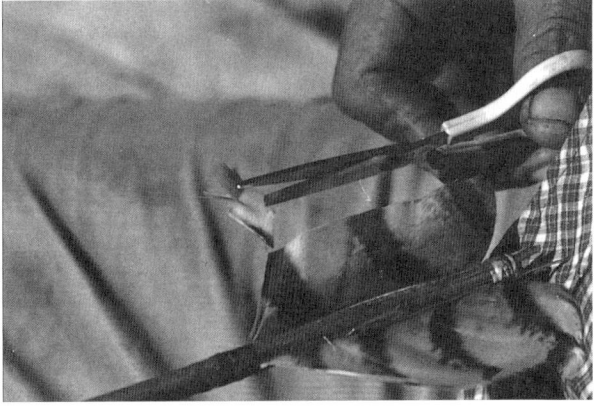

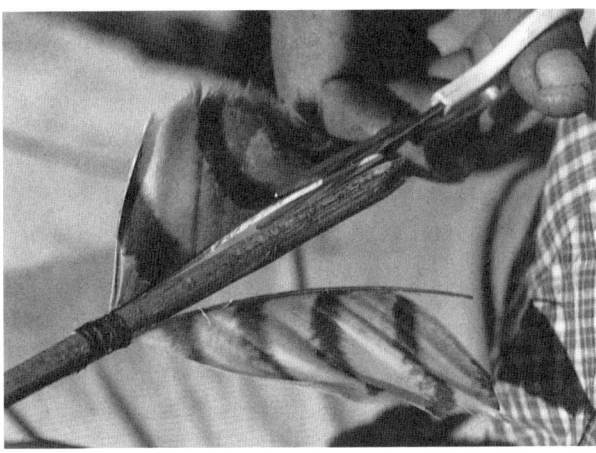

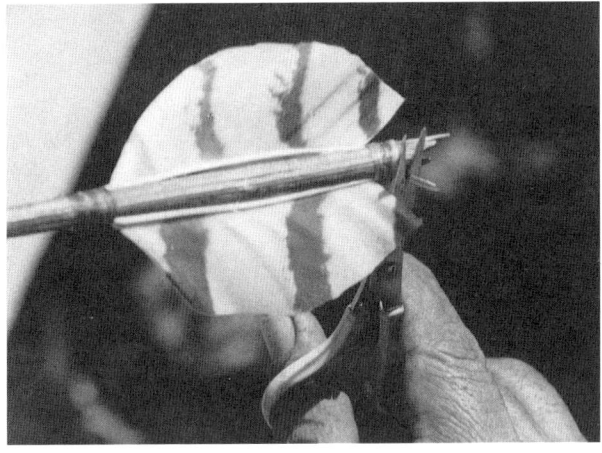

Andres Albáñez fletches the arrow of jatbil.

and forefinger of his right hand and held tight to the shaft, pulling slightly to keep the vanes flush against the shaft. The winding of sinew began next to the plumage, again with Albáñez's left hand. A length of sinew, the end held against the far side of the arrow's shaft with the middle finger, was wound over (toward the body) then under the stele and overlapped. The sinew was then taken up in the right hand, the arrow's stele in the left and revolved away from the body as the right hand fed the sinew. In a turn or two it reached the lower edge of the nock bevel then spiraled slowly back to the beginning of the plumage where it was overlapped and smoothed. Additional lengths of sinew were added if needed.

Albáñez clipped the side of the vanes in a curve, about an inch from the shaft at the widest. He cut any quills protruding from the sinew at the nock. The arrow finished, he slid it with the others into his yucca-stalk quiver.

A Quick Cahuilla Survival Bow and Arrow

The best Cahuilla bows were made from a seasoned limb of screwbean mesquite, but a bow suitable for small game was fashioned from black willow *(Salix nigra)*. Rolled sinew made a bowstring but a twisted cord of agave fiber was also used. Andres Albáñez turned out a black willow bow in a few hours, cutting it to size green, warming it at a fire and bending it to shape. The very simple black willow bow that Barrows found among the Cahuilla in the 1890s must have been much the same.

Cahuilla arrows of reed *(Phragmites communis)* or arrowweed had a foreshaft of mesquite or greasewood (red shank: *Adenostoma sparsifolium*), the point hardened in fire and the other end inserted in the natural or improved hollow of the shaft, secured with glue and sometimes sinew-wrapped. This arrow had two feathers. Again, Albáñez made similar arrows. The Modoc are known to have used foreshafted cane arrows *without fletching* when hunting birds. The light cane naturally followed the heavier pointed foreshaft. I have made such arrows in minutes while in the field.

But for sheer simplicity as a complement to the willow bow with fiber string, the Cahuilla made *unfeathered arrows* from the shoots of sagebrush *(Artemesia ludoviciana)*. They simply peeled, notched and pointed them. They were straightened with their teeth, presumably after being warmed near the fire.

Andres Albáñez draws a carrizo arrow in his black willow bow. Yucca-stalk quiver holds two additional carrizo arrows.

Quivers

Quivers seem to have been much alike among the Indians of California. They were made of animal skin, hair side in or out, tanned or untanned, always with the tail left as a pendant ornament. The Yana preferred the fox; the Central Miwok, the skin of the black fox or otter; the Tubatulabal valued the whole untanned antelope, coyote, or wildcat skin (since the fur was on the inside of the Tubatulabal quiver of wildcat skin, it doubled as a muff: men on winter hunts kept their fingers warm and limber by putting them inside the furry quiver slung across the chest); the Chumash made quivers from deer, young bear, mountain lion or sea otter. The Northern Paiute employed the whole skin of the coyote, desert fox, or bobcat, or they might have used a section of a hide of deer, mountain lion, antelope or bear. In addition to arrows, a bow and fire-making kit (of cane drill, sagebrush hearth and fibrous tinder rolled into a cord-like length) were carried in the quiver.

The Yurok made a quiver from the skin of a raccoon or martin. Powers described the process in 1877. The hunter turned the skin inside out, sewed up the head and placed moss therein to act as a cushion for the arrowheads. A string passing over one shoulder and under the other held the quiver on his back. The striped tail was left on to flutter in the air at the archer's shoulder.

The Mohave quiver was the whole skin of a fox, hair to the outside and tail streamer at the top. They made quivers too from coyote, wildcat and deerskin. The quiver measured about 3 feet long and 3 to 4 inches across and was reinforced along its length with an arrowweed rod. To each end of the rod a sinew cord was attached for slinging the quiver over the back. During battle, removal of arrows was facilitated by holding the quiver under the arm while a willow-bark cloth wrapped around the torso helped secure it in place. The quiver carried 15 to 20 arrows.

The Southern Diegueño near Campo, California also apparently made quivers from coyote, fox and mountain lion hides, but the quiver old Jim McCarty described to Spier in the early 1920s was made from tanned de-haired buckskin. A rectangular piece, which included the tail, was folded lengthwise while a strip, similarly folded, was inserted with the open edge to the outside a short ways into the open edge of the first piece. The four layers were then sewed together with a running stitch. The flap that extended out from the first piece was repeatedly cut across in a perpendicular fashion to form fringes. (It would seem, though Spier does not tell us, that the first rectangular piece should be cut with the tail at a top side edge, not in the middle top, so that it would lay directly over and in a sense begin the fringe down the back of the quiver.) A straight stick was fastened in the fold (opposite the fringe) of the first piece. The lower end was sewed shut to form the bag or quiver. Loose arrowheads were carried in the bottom of the quiver. A mescal-fiber string threaded around the mouth enabled the archer to tie the quiver around his waist, where it hung obliquely at the back with the opening to the right. Others hung it at their right hip.

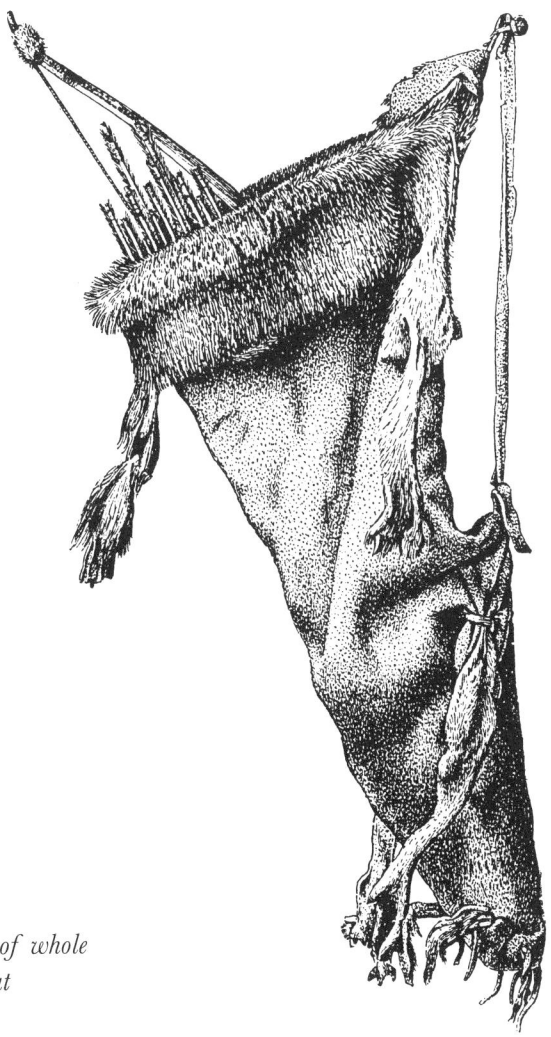

Large Wintun quiver (40") from the McCloud River made of whole deerskin with hair inward. Legs are pendants, mouth sewed shut (Mason, 1894).

Paipai and Southern Diegueño in the Sierra Juárez still make deerskin quivers. I purchased one of these from Raúl Sandoval in Rancho Escondido. He had made the small quiver from the rawhide of a deer. It had been sewn up the side, dried to shape and a thong attached to top and bottom. The hair was on the outside.

Perhaps the most ingenious and at the same time simplest quivers were the ones Paipai and Southern Diegueño Andres Albáñez made for me at Santa Catarina. Capacious and exotically beautiful, Albáñez believed they had been used even before hide quivers were in vogue. An approximately 2-foot section of the stem of the *lechuguilla* or Spanish bayonet *(Yucca whipplei)* had been cut square then hollowed from the top by pulling and scraping out the fibrous inner layers with a metal rod. (I made them in the canyons above Los Angeles by using toyon or live oak sticks with the end carved into a gable, like a ridged roof, then cut crosswise with a perpendicular V through the center of the ridge, making two sharp points on the end of the stick. The Chumash used a smaller version of this to hollow an elderberry branch to make a flute. A thrusting, twisting motion did the job.) The length had a slight arch, and at either end of this concavity a hole was drilled (and another small hole on the bottom) to accept a rawhide carrying strap. The bottom had a corky feel and protected the hardwood tips of the carrizo arrows (which came with the quiver) while the thin sides seemed to be made from a very light but durable wood. Good for the field, the pattern of discontinuous, alternating, brown horizontal lines suggesting brick work (where the stem scales had been) against a beige background made it an attractive and functional storage container for arrows around the home as well. He called the quiver *shqua pa'*.

Ishi's Yahi quiver was made from the skin of an otter, removed by means of a cut over the buttocks. Head end down and mouth sewn shut with a tendon, the split tail became a carrying strap. The hind legs, also split, dangled as ornamentation while the forelegs were inverted into the quiver which had the hair side out. At the opening to the quiver, a strip of buckskin was stitched and, inside two-thirds of the

Ishi's otter-skin quiver (Pope, 1918).

Modoc and Klamath Lake quiver of plain-twined tule, 81 cm. in length (Barrett, 1910).

way down, the strip was again stitched; it likely functioned as another carrying strap. The completed quiver measured 34 inches in length, 8 inches wide at the opening and 4 inches at the bottom. It generally held about 20 arrows as well as a bow and was slung over the left shoulder.

On a prolonged hunt Ishi took as many as 60 arrows. Those not in the quiver he covered with skin, which he tied with buckskin thongs and slung over his shoulder. Because extraction of arrows from the quiver was somewhat slow, he carried a few arrows in his hand. When shooting, these were laid on the ground or held under his right arm, which did not interfere with drawing the bow, according to Pope, because of his unusual style of shooting.

My favorite quiver has to be the Northern Diegueño full coyote pelt quiver. The Northern Diegueño tanned a whole coyote skin and sewed up the belly from the nose almost to the tail. It was hung on the back, the hind legs looped together to fit over the archer's neck and the forelegs tied around his waist, like a knapsack. The coyote tail hung down the quiver back. In the bottom of the quiver they placed a conical clay cup in which to rest the arrow tips. In time of war the cup also held rattlesnake or gila monster venom.

Gifford recorded how the Cocopa made the coyote skin quiver. They killed the animal in the winter. They did not cut him down the belly but cut the mouth wide so that the whole skin could be peeled off. Once the fat and flesh were removed from the hide, they dried the skin wrong side out. Then they turned it back and stuffed it with grass. After more time, they again turned it wrong side out and rubbed it with greasy, parched pumpkin seeds that had been mashed in a cottonwood mortar with a wooden pestle. Again, the skin was stuffed with grass for final drying and shaping with the hair side out. The head formed the bottom of the bag (and must have been sewn closed) and the tail hung down from the top. The posterior portion of the skin had been cut for the mouth of the quiver.

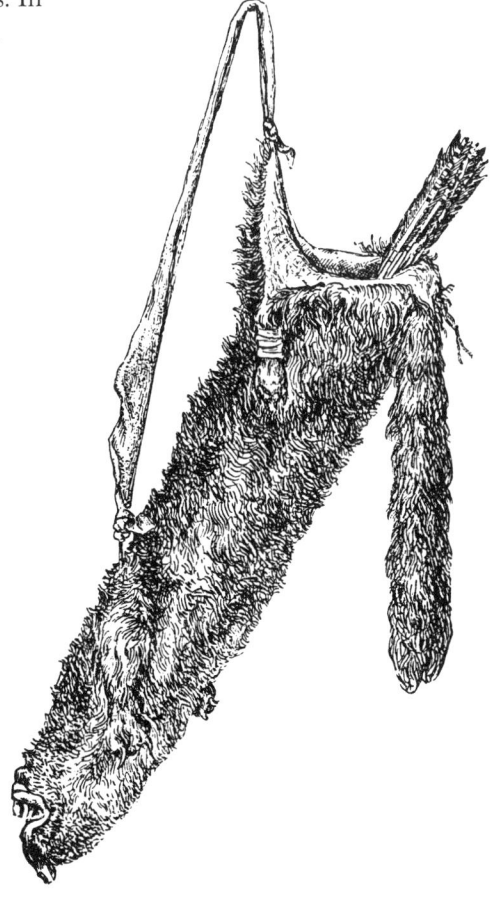

Hupa coyote-skin quiver for bow and arrows (Mason, 1894).

How to Shoot an Indian Bow

There were probably as many ways to shoot an Indian bow in California as there were Indians. Except for the Yahi, who employed an unusual Mongolian-like style, and the single, isolated occurrence of the Mediterranean release among the Luiseño, who at the time of its recording by Sparkman had been under "Mediterranean" influence in the form of Spanish and European-Americans for a hundred years, almost all California techniques involved pinching the arrow tip between thumb and forefinger and drawing it back. But this weak grip alone severely limited the length of draw. The arrow would easily and too quickly slide through finger and thumb and release. More powerful shots generally required that in addition to the pinch-grip, which was maintained, the string itself be grasped by some combination of fingers.

Arrows rested to the left of the bow, sometimes to the right. The bow could be held vertical, diagonal or horizontal, the archer standing or kneeling. With the archer seated on the ground, the bow could be placed across the soles of the feet and shot. Extant accounts and surviving Indians merely hint at the variety of technique early California must have known.

Techniques of Yuman Speakers

Grasp the bow just below the middle and hold it vertically almost at arm's length. Nock the arrow to the left of the bow, holding the vanes between right thumb and second joint of the forefinger with the tips of the forefinger and middle finger on the string. The left forefinger guides the arrow on the bow. Pull the arrow back to the right shoulder and release. Do not throw the bow forward with the shot.

Spier recorded the above technique among the Southern Diegueño of Campo, California in the early years of the twentieth century. Jim McCarty was an old man when he demonstrated for Spier his rapidly disappearing world. Around the same time Gifford found that the Cocopa archers on the lower Colorado also grasped the arrow between the thumb and forefinger and in pulling, the tips of the forefinger and middle finger rested against the string in the same manner as the Diegueño of Campo.

At La Huerta in Lower California, eighty-nine-year-old Felipe Jat'am demonstrated for Peveril Meigs III in 1929 another Diegueño technique. With the bow held vertically, arrow to the left of the bow, he raised his elbow and gripped the arrow between his thumb and the middle of his forefinger, *the middle finger alone* on the bow string. A photograph shows his right elbow slightly above the plane of the shoulder.

Yuma Indians shot from a crouching position with the bow held horizontally. The left forefinger guided the arrow and pointed at the target. When C. Daryll Ford gathered his information around 1930, archery had been abandoned by the Yumas for many years and memories bore the haze of time. One man described the Mediterranean release, but another claimed the arrow traditionally had been gripped between the tip of the thumb and knuckle of the index finger. In confirmation of the latter method, Forde saw arrows held this way by scouts in mimic warfare at a Yuma Keruc ceremony. Not long after this, Kenneth Stewart discovered neighboring Mohave men who still remembered how to shoot a bow. Like the Yumas, they customarily pinched the arrow between the thumb and near the second joint of the forefinger. But sometimes the *middle and ring finger* pulled the string as well. Mohave warriors generally shot standing, the bow held vertically and grasped in the middle. Hunters sometimes held it horizontally.

Spier's Maricopa informants told him they held the nearly vertical bow exactly in the middle, the arrow to the left guided by the left forefinger, and the nock of the arrow grasped between right thumb and forefinger. In that way alone they drew back the arrow. They failed to mention, but Spier could see, when the technique was demonstrated by two old men, that *in practice the middle and ring fingertips pulled on the string*. This and other wide ranging studies led him to conclude that all such Indian arrow releases were simply variations on the single theme of pinching the arrow during the draw with or without the aid of fingers on the string. In other words, division of these differences into formal categories is somewhat artificial, a scholarly pursuit, not an Indian one.

Paipai elder Benito Peralta, whose rich memory of tribal lore and history makes vivid the context of Indian archery, kept a black willow bow lightly strung when not in use but tightened so it rang when he was going to shoot. He strung it at the top with the belly toward him and the bottom near or against his left instep. At times, he simply wrapped the bow string at the nock, overlapping it once or twice and securing it with a half hitch on the taut string. But he more often brought the bow string around the back of the bow to the belly, over the string, then immediately reversing it under the string to the back of the bow a second time, overlapping the first turn as he tightened the string and continued around to the bow string again where he secured it with two half hitches.

Peralta held the bow in the middle with his left hand, gripping at the same time a few extra

Clockwise from upper left: Benito Peralta pinches an arrow lightly between his index finger and thumb while the index and tip of his middle finger pull the bowstring. Raúl Sandoval uses a simple pinch grip on an arrow nock. Tomás Ayares releases an arrow using a pinch grip with the tip of his index finger on the string. Seated is his sister, Manuela Aguiar.

arrows, feathered end up, along the back of the bow, available for a quick second or third or even fourth shot. He emphasized that this was an integral part of shooting a bow, not a mere flourish. His left extended forefinger rested lightly over and along a nocked arrow in order to keep it aligned against the bow which was perpendicular; otherwise the arrow would dangle to the left. The forefinger remained lightly over the arrow to guide it even as it was released. It was almost like pointing a pistol to the mark. He seemed to site along the arrow.

The right thumb and the area just before the second joint of the forefinger softly pinched the stele at the end of the nock. The tip of the forefinger to the first joint paralleled the bowstring and along with the tip of the middle finger pulled the string back. The emphasis was on pulling the string with the free portion of the index finger, not on pinching the arrow or using the arrow to pull the string. The release was quick and came as a surprise.

He seemed to draw the string of the bow and let the arrow fly in a continuous pulling motion

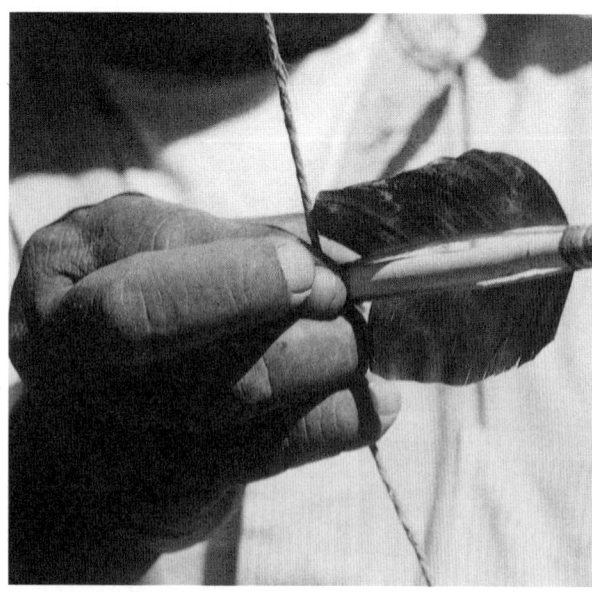
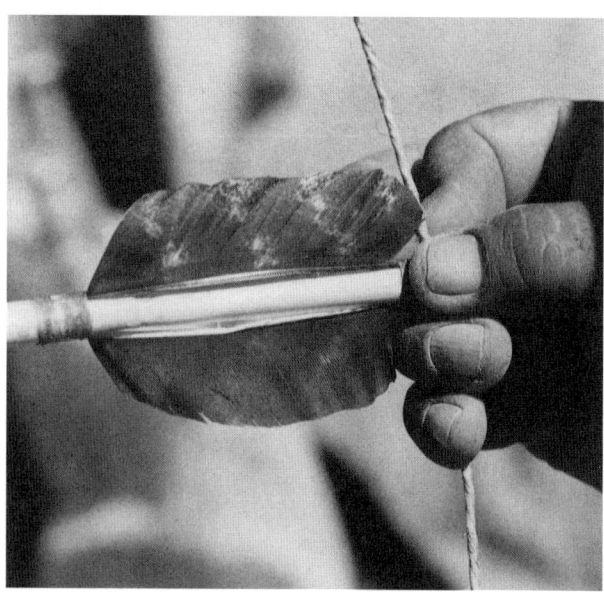

Andres Albáñez demonstrates a pinch grip aided by his middle finger over his index finger and ring and little finger gripping the bowstring.

with no fixed hesitation at release. United States Marine Corps marksmanship instructions exhort "hold and squeeze," which means to hold your aim on target and squeeze the trigger in a slow steady manner, stopping only if the site wanders from the target and resuming the slow pull on the trigger when the target is again in the site. The exact moment of release should be a surprise. The technique avoids the common anticipatory jerk and the inevitable missed shot.

Peralta's right arm drew the bowstring back evenly until it simply slipped from his fingers by the increasing tension of the string. Though the right hand moved away from the bow and against the direction of flight of the arrow, the impression was almost of throwing the arrow in the natural follow through of the right hand as it continued away from the bow even as the arrow soared in flight.

I saw, too, a subtle pushing away of the bow itself as the arrow was drawn back and shot. Tomás Ayares a Southern Diegueño of Kuatl lineage in Rancho Escondido very clearly pushed the bow away toward the target as he shot using a pinch grip with the tip of his index finger on the string. I took a sequence of photographs of him to prove this to myself. The arrow was to that extent literally thrown at the target.

Peralta's was a light hunting or rabbit bow. A larger bow—wider or longer—would propel the arrow farther, of course, but deer were taken even with small bows and with arrows having only sharpened wooden foreshafts, Peralta told me. Getting close and deft shooting might land an arrow from a light bow in a nerve of the back of the neck or at the joint of a leg and this would kill the deer in the first case and slow it in the second. Thus wounded, a deer can be run down and dispatched, said Peralta.

Indian archery was close range archery and relied on the outdoor skills of the archer and less on the machine. Those dependent on fiberglass and pulleys, peep sites and arrow glides might prefer a good gun to an Indian bow.

Justin Farmer, of Ipai or Northern Diegueño descent, first suggested to me something certain southern California Indians had told him: bows were not drawn all the way to the chin as the European longbow. Demonstrations by Benito Peralta, Raúl Sandoval and Andres Albáñez proved him to be at least in part correct. With medium-sized rabbit bows (around 4 feet in length) the men often pulled only a short way toward the head or shoulder, sited down the arrow and let fly. I found some of these bows fairly stiff and the pinch grip sometimes automatically led to an early release. Also short-range targets (wood rats were shot within a yard or two) often did not require the full potential of the bow. In Peralta's case, age and stiff joints could have been a factor. Finally, war and big game longbows, which invited a long pull, had generally fallen out of use.

Raúl Sandoval placed the arrow to the left or right of the bow. When at the right, his raised and arched left thumb held it in position next to the bow. He gripped his arrow with his thumb and the area roughly between the first and second joints of the first finger of his right hand and pulled back the string with the nock of the arrow. This necessarily led to release before the arrow was pulled very far. Such a pull, as Kroeber writes, "depends wholly on friction." A similar pinching release was recorded in the early years of the twentieth century among the Luiseño of southern California. They used it when shooting simple arrows of arrowweed. Pope, whose archery studies were also conducted in the early years of the twentieth century, found that the pinch grip was the weakest and allowed him to pull a mere 25 pounds on the bowstring. With a thickened arrow butt, using the same grip, he was able to increase this to 35 pounds of pull. Separate nock shafts (for insertion into the proximal end of the mainshaft) with the butt thickened into a knob are known archaeologically for the Chumash area of southern California and short knob-ended separate nock shafts are still made by the Kumeyaay of San José de la Zorra in Lower California. Arturo Torres of San José told me these hardwood nocks resisted the air to stabilize long flights and incidentally provided a solid slot for the string. He denied that they were employed to improve the grip.

Andres Albáñez, a Southern Diegueño and Paipai of Santa Catarina whose rabbit bow was fairly thick and stiff, held his bow almost vertically in a standing position. He gripped the very end of the arrow between his thumb and near the first joint of his index finger and pulled the string with his fourth and fifth fingers. The middle finger was placed on top of and reinforced the index finger pinching the arrow tip. The arrow ran to the left of the bow. It was held by his left index finger which rested lightly over the arrow and pointed in the general direction of the target. He aimed along the arrow toward an imaginary object nearby on the ground, the most likely location of a quarry—rat, rabbit or ground squirrel. The arrow would fly straight and direct. The left index finger was not removed when the arrow was released but continued to guide it. The remaining three fingers at the back of the bow often held, at the ready, extra arrows with their feathered ends upward. Despite the effective grip, because his bow was so strong and the quarry he feigned to shoot so close, he did not pull all the way back to the chin. His left arm was also particularly rigid during the draw.

In contrast to the pinch-grip style alone which would lead to an early release and a short pull, Pope, using his middle and ring fingers along with the pinch grip was able to pull 40 pounds on the bowstring. He exerted a significant 60 pounds of pull when using his fingers in the style described for McCarty of the Kumeyaay of Campo. In this approach, the forefinger, in addition to pinching on the arrow's end, pulled, along with the middle finger, on the string. McCarty, wrote Spier, would have the bowstring pull all the way to the right shoulder—even beyond the chin! Yuman bows for war and deer hunting were generally close to the height of a man. It does not seem surprising an effective grip on one of these approached the chin or shoulder.

In this connection we might consider what Spier wrote about the Diegueño archer when shooting for distance. He would sit on the ground and place the bow horizontally across the soles of his feet, like the Mohave, and let fly the arrow. This technique would not significantly improve the range of the small plain Yuman hunting or rabbit bow, around 4 feet in length, whose maximum pull even with the best of grips might not easily or often reach the chin. It would, however, maximize the effect of the long Yuman bow used for big game or war. I recently saw a pair of these bows, which were found in a Baja cave, on display at the Ensenada Museum of History in the Riviera del Pacífico Cultural Center. Although somewhat square in cross section, they were shaped much as Spier described Jim McCarty's bow and as Andres Albáñez made them: straight in the center with most of the curvature in

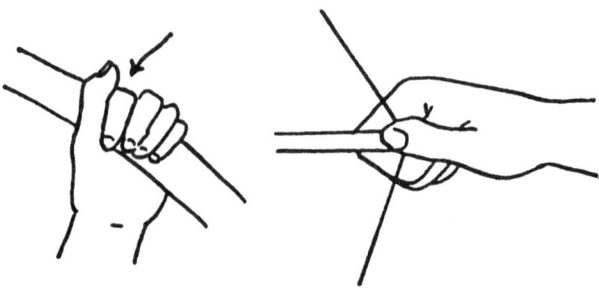

Position of bow hand and arrow release in Waksachi Western Mono archery (Gayton, 1948).

the ends. They measured over 6 feet in length. Even a long pull on one of these to the chin or shoulder would fail to fully exploit its potential. With long limbs the angle of leverage on the center of the bow would be slight during such a draw and the style of release using one hand alone would perhaps not be so important. But using the feet and both hands would change everything. Gripping the arrow, which must have approached 6 feet in length (making those 6-foot carrizo arrows described by Pattie for the "Pipi" in 1827 not unreasonable), and the bowstring with *both* hands, the bow across the soles of the feet, we can imagine a very full draw and an arrow like a spear sailing fairly out of sight.

Chumash Style

Harrington's notes from the Chumash show that sinew-backed bows were often shot vertically and the longer plain bows of elder, horizontally. An arrow might be positioned to the left or right of the bow. If right, it was guided between the index and middle fingers of the left hand gripping the bow. If left, the upright or vertical bow actually slanted toward the right shoulder to hold the arrow into the bow and prevent it from going crooked.

They drew back the arrow with the right hand in hesitational increments of about 2 inches each while the left hand gripped the bow and moved away from the body (more than the right hand moved). In aiming and releasing, the fingers were held lightly on the bowstring, often with only the nail of the middle finger.

Fernando Librado Kitsepawit told Harrington that after a shot, the bow and arrows were carried side by side in the hand with the bowstring up.

Notes From the Sierras

Steban Miranda told Erminie Voegelin the Tubatulabal drew back the bowstring between the thumb and forefinger. When standing they held the bow vertically; but if kneeling with weight on the left knee, they held the bow horizontally.

Bob Osborne of the Waksachi Western Mono held the bow in his left hand with the left end of the bow thirty degrees above horizontal, the arrow to the right side of the bow. This was the manner for all types of shooting. To guide the arrow the middle finger of the left hand raised slightly from its grip to form a groove over the index finger and between the middle finger and thumb. According to Osborne, they grasped the arrow one way only:

between the thumb and main joint of the index finger of the right hand. None of the fingers pulled on the bowstring itself.

As recorded by Barrett and Gifford, the Miwok, makers of the sinew-backed hook-ended bow of the Sierra Nevada Mountains, held the bow vertically and drew the string back between the thumb and forefinger. That is all that is written. Undoubtedly, there is a range and variety we will never know for the Miwok and many others.

A Yahi Technique

Arrows in general were likely released in the north much as in the Sierras and south. Dixon found, for example, that the Maidu, whose bow was similar to that of the Yurok and other northern wide-limbed bows, held the bow nearly horizontally with the index finger of the left hand crooking over the arrow; the thumb and index finger of the right hand gripped or pinched the arrow's nock. The Yurok Indian Homer Cooper was taught as a boy to shoot the wide-limbed Yurok bow horizontally grasped in the left hand, palm upward. A wide bow, even if slightly narrowed at the grip, threw the arrow to the side of the bow and off the mark. Held horizontally this dynamic of the wide bow would result in a slightly increased angle of trajectory and range. Gravity would continually adjust the arrow back toward the center. When such a bow was shot vertically, however, distance only made greater the effect of an angle of error. Cooper used a simple pinch grip.

Ishi, the last Yahi or southern-most Yana in northern California, was aware that neighboring tribes used this pinching technique. However, Ishi's Yahi release, as recorded by Pope, was of a most distinctive Mongolian style. He drew with his right thumb bent beneath the string and his middle finger on the thumbnail reinforcing the grip (the true Mongolian style would have the index finger on the thumbnail). The flexed right index finger held the arrow to the string and against the lower half of the thumb. To avoid ruffling, the ends of the feathers near the nock were carefully folded on the shaft under the gripping fingers.

The bow itself was held diagonally across his body, upper end to the left. Four or five arrows were held under his right arm, points to the front. Another arrow in his right hand he placed on the right side of the bow. The first and second fingers of his left hand received it but held it away from the bow to protect the feathers which were longer than the distance from string to bow. The bow was held lightly in the notch between the thumb and fingers of the left hand. He slid the arrow forward gently and nocked it at the center of the string. He hooked his thumb under the string, flexed his forefinger against the arrow and placed the middle finger on the thumbnail. He drew by extending his left arm, which was almost in front of him, at the same time pulling his right hand toward him to the top of his breastbone. When drawn, the arrow rested on the bow and the left thumb and middle fingertip steadied it. He sited along the arrow shaft with both eyes open and estimated the elevation according to the distance of the shot. On release the bow revolved in his hand which only retained it by a light grip of the fingers. It turned over completely and ended with the back of the bow toward him. Pope recorded that his release was firm and he held his position until the arrow struck.

Ishi was very careful about all aspects of shooting. A missed shot could mean a shattered arrowhead. He preferred to kneel or squat when shooting. He believed these were the most favorable positions for hitting game. He shot at close range,

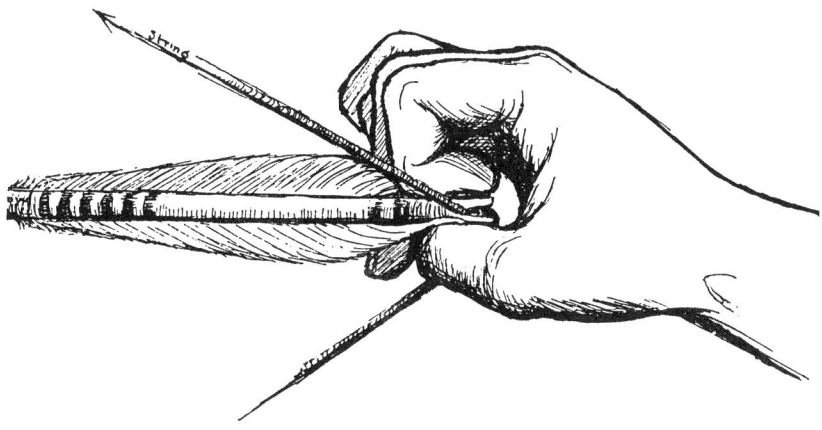

Ishi's release (Pope, 1918).

from 10 to 50 yards. Beyond this distance, he held his shot and attempted to stalk his quarry more closely. "Like all other archers, if Ishi missed a shot he always had a good excuse," wrote Pope. "There was too much wind or the arrow was crooked, or the bow had lost its cast, or, as a last resource, the coyote doctor bewitched him. . . ."

Perhaps most important was the fact that he practiced. Before entering civilization Ishi shot at little oak balls or bundles of grass tied to suggest rabbits or at small hoops of willow that were rolled on the ground. Whatever the style of shooting, only practice produced quick and accurate archery. At the other end of the Californias, Johann Jakob Baegert's recording of Guaicura custom in the middle of the eighteenth century illustrates the point. The Guaicura shot 6-foot willow bows and cane arrows with hardwood foreshafts. Baegert wrote that these Indians practiced with bow and arrow from early childhood. As a result many good marksmen were found among them.

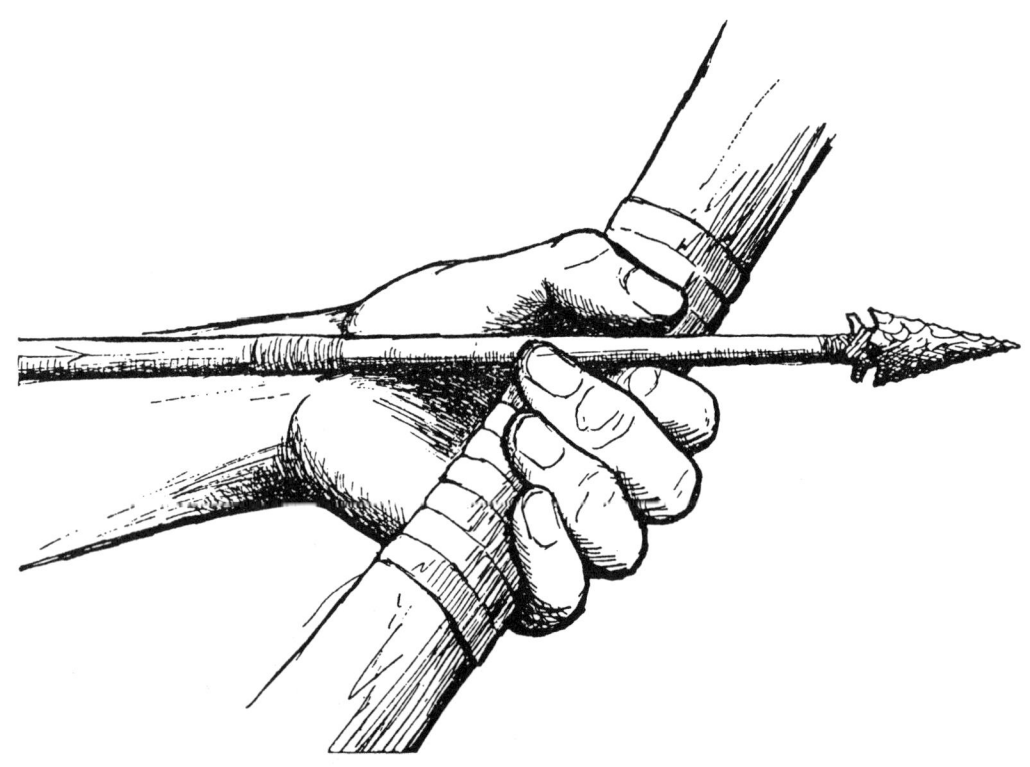

Ishi's bow hand (Pope, 1918).

Bowguard

When you shoot a bow often or use any powerful bow, you need a bowguard, Paipai Benito Peralta told me. His old uncle Cosme González taught Peralta as a boy how to make them. They protected the forearm of the bow hand from the snap of the bowstring. In Paipai the guard was called *Sshátelumu*.

Stewart found that Mohave hunters made and wore disposable bark bowguards braided and tied at each end. Warriors used a bowguard of deer hide on the wrist of the bow hand. The guard sometimes reached halfway up the arm and it was split on the ends and tied.

The Paipai guard was made completely from the hide of a deer pulled carefully from a carcass that had been split down the belly; if done correctly, the hide came off clean. After it dried, a rectangle about 9 by 11 inches was cut from any part. The piece could be slightly rhomboid, about 10 inches on the end opposite the 11-inch side, to accommodate the smaller wrist end of the forearm when completed. The hair was left on except for the borders where the edge of a knife scraped the hair away 1 inch on all sides. It was an easy job when the hide was dry.

Small cuts were made just over 1/8 inch each along and just into the hair of the two longer depilated edges, about 1 inch apart. These two edges were then dampened to soften them and folded over toward the hair side for 1/2 an inch and pressed tight. A thin, 1/8-inch-wide strip of rawhide was inserted through the cut at one end and wrapped corkscrew-fashion through the rest of the cuts on that edge to finish and secure the fold. The ends of the rawhide strip were tucked under windings at beginning and end. The opposite side was completed in the same fashion.

Five holes were next punched down the center of each of the two remaining dehaired strips on the now 8-inch sides. Holes were about 1 inch from the top and bottom edges and 1 inch from one hole to the next. The piece was then turned into a cylinder hair side out, and the ends of the rawhide thong inserted from the skin side of the piece through the two opposite holes nearest the wrist end of the guard. They were crossed over above and reinserted down into the next two holes. The thongs crossed over underneath as on top and reemerged from the third hole on each side. They again crossed, entered, crossed and emerged as before. Finally, the bow arm was inserted and the two loose ends of the rawhide thong were tightened and tied to hold the guard to the arm. Like early Mohave deerskin guards, it covered much of the forearm.

Peralta told me that hide guards protected the archer not only from the slap of the bowstring but from the cold as well. On a winter's day two of these were sometimes worn, one on each forearm, and they kept the man warm. He added that for battle with other Indians large pieces of deer hide were occasionally fashioned into protective vests, covering the front and back of the warrior with armor against enemy arrows.

Benito Peralta models a deerhide bowguard.

Clockwise from upper left: Closeup of Benito Peralta's bowguard. Back of bowguard. Alternate style made by Peralta.

The California Atlatl

The atlatl slew the megafauna of the European Paleolithic. It endured in North America well into the twentieth century. Knowledge of the weapon is still vivid among the Yupik of Alaska who used the spear thrower against seals at the mouth of the Yukon River and among Tarascan Indians of Mexico who took wild fowl with it on Lake Patzcuaro. Less known perhaps is the fact that an ancient relic form of this longest-used weapon in the western hemisphere lasted even to historic times in an isolated corner of the Californias.

In a sense, the atlatl, or spearthrower, represented an evolutionary advance over the handheld spear. It artificially extended the arm, increasing the speed at the end of the arc of the toss, and utilized fully the power of the man. But to be effective it demanded that the whole body perfectly execute the release. In the centuries around the birth of Christ, the bow largely supplanted the atlatl in North America, spreading from the northern hunters south. The newly introduced bow was easier to shoot and even a novice could hit a close and fair-sized target. With a bow a hunter could release arrows stealthfully from cover without alarming the prey.

Notwithstanding the bow's superiority in some aspects, the atlatl had endured for good reasons. A missile flung from an atlatl was often more powerful than an arrow and the atlatl itself, simpler and generally more quickly made than most bows. The atlatl was a useful survival weapon. It was also perfectly suited to situations where one arm must be free to guide a dugout or kayak into striking position. Not surprisingly, some few groups retained the old alongside the new, recognizing the utility of the older simpler technologies. The mighty Aztec of Central Mexico, even after the Spanish decimated them with smallpox and incited the Indian subjects of their empire to revolt, held off a combined Spanish and Indian siege of their capital Tenochtitlan for three months. Against European cannons and steel, cavalry and massed Indian assaults, the Aztec defended their island home with rocks and slings, spears and obsidian-edged clubs, bows and arrows and *darts hurled from atlatls*. Indeed the word *atlatl* is Aztec. Spaniards during the seventeenth century found atlatls still being used in California.

The End of the Earth

They found atlatls at the tip of Lower California in the physical and cultural cul-de-sac of North America. An extremely arid climate, difficult terrain and remote geographic position slowed infiltration of ideas from the north and across the Sea of Cortez. Old primitive ways of life got stuck here and once established seemed to change not at all. While the conqueror of Mexico, Hernán Cortés, had landed at the Bay of La Paz in 1535, Jacob Baegert, a German Jesuit missionary who served 17 years at the nearby San Luis Gonzaga Mission, could write in the later eighteenth century that the Indians of southern Baja California were still extremely isolated, even from their brethren to the north. Baegert was amazed by the simplicity of their ways: they spend their whole life in the open air, he wrote. "In lieu of knives and scissors they use sharp flints for cutting almost everything—cane, wood, agave, and even hair—and for disemboweling and skinning animals. . . . Of a division of labor not a trace is to be found among them; even the cooking is done by all without distinction of sex or age, everyone providing for himself. . . ." He goes on to say that the only craft known to the men was the manufacture of bows and arrows, and to the women the making of reed skirts.

The Guaicurian-speaking people of whom Baegert wrote were semi-nomadic hunter-gatherers and their material culture was necessarily simple to accommodate a very mobile way of life. Because the resources were scarce, division into small isolated roving bands maximized chances for finding something to eat. It also meant everyone had to know and be able to do everything since individuals were frequently separated from the group. That the inventory of tools was meager should not imply, however, the people were of inferior intelligence or somehow lacking in culture. These were expert survivalists and their very lack of material resources and tools meant they had to be doubly clever in how they exacted a living from their hostile environment. It is fitting the atlatl, a weapon requiring more skill in its use than in its manufacture, should have survived so long among them.

William Massey reviewed Spanish documents of the seventeenth century and found clear record of the use of the dart thrower by Indians of the Baja Cape region and offshore Gulf islands. He cites Nicolás de Cardona who explored the pearl fisheries of the area in 1615 and 1616. "Their weapons are bows and arrows and dart-throwers . . . ," Cardona stated of the Indians of the Bay of La Paz.

References to darts are found even earlier for Cabo San Lucas. Both areas are in the southeastern tip of Baja and were inhabited at the time by Guaicurian-speaking Pericú Indians.

A Complete Atlatl Discovery

Massey, whose intensive search of the historical documents turned up no further mention of dart throwers after 1642, found the throwers themselves in the spring in 1947. He discovered four of them tied together in a burial enclosed by a sewn palm-fiber mat in the deepest section of a burial cave on Cerro Cuevoso at the very end of the Baja peninsula.

One of the throwers was completely intact. Comparable to the others, the slender, long, tubular shaft measured 82 cm. in length and from 1.1 to 1.3 cm. in diameter. A highly polished, rounded, tapered hook with slightly projecting spur, rose near the distal end, carved of the same piece of hardwood. A sinew wrapping strengthened the base just below this. On the opposite end sinew wrapping secured a single bark loop, set at a right angle to the plane of the hook, on the right side of the shaft. The sinew was stained red. No weights were used.

Fifteen years later and twenty miles north of La Paz on the Pacific side of the peninsula, two more atlatls came to light when they washed from a shallow shelter near Buena Vista. Lee Massey saw and described one of these (the other, a "left-handed" thrower, apparently went to "scientists from Carnegie"). Except for a decorative strip (19.5 cm. by 1 cm., consisting of fifty-six pairs of tiny incised squares extending on the shaft from about 3 cm. in front of the hook) the atlatl from Buena Vista was similar to those found at Cerro Cuevoso. It measured 81.5 cm. long with a fairly regular circumference of 4 cm. The hook was 4.5 cm. in overall length, projecting 2.2 cm. beyond the shaft; and the hook and the shaft were of a single piece of wood. The tapering 8 cm. shaft beyond the hook was tightly wrapped with fiber (probably palm). A bark loop, 14.2 cm. in overall length, began on the left side of the shaft about 9 cm. from the end. Its original position on the shaft showed clearly though the binding had disappeared.

William Massey related the male, or projecting-spur, style dart thrower to the oldest and most widespread of the known types, originating in the Upper Paleolithic of Western Europe. For more recent times, male throwers have been found throughout the world but always in extremely marginal locations. In the Americas they were supplanted by the mixed type of atlatl (female groove terminating in a male spur) typical of Mexico and the southwest. Types somewhat intermediate between the Cerro Cuevoso male thrower and the southwestern type were found at Roaring Springs Cave in southern Oregon and Lovelock Cave, Nevada. These have raised hooks carved from the same piece of wood as the shaft but the shaft is a flat board like the southwestern mixed types, and the Lovelock Cave specimens even have a groove near the hook. Massey speculated that the round staves with a male hook, either carved from the shaft or lashed to it, found historically in the Andean regions of Columbia, Ecuador and Peru and the lowlands of Columbia, the Greater Antilles and coastal Peru were survivors of an older archaic tradition. The rounded shaft, male hook and single loop grip placed to one side of the throwers of the Tainan peoples of the Caribbean and extreme northwestern regions of Columbia matched the dart throwers found in southern Baja California and were likely far flung relics of the very same extremely old atlatl tradition.

Cerro Cuevoso atlatl with detail of hook and grip (W. Massey, 1955). Thin spur tapers to the tip and is carved from the same piece of wood as the shaft. Palm-bark loop is bound to shaft with sinew.

Alta California

Single-loop finger-grip atlatls with a projecting engaging spur are depicted clearly and commonly in the ancient rock drawings of the Coso Range a few hours drive from Los Angeles in Alta California. However, the only complete California atlatl itself (or nearly complete atlatl for the spur is missing but can be inferred from the cups of the dart fragments found in the cache with it) comes from the northern California site of Potter Creek Cave in Shasta County. The board-style atlatl, excavated by Louis Payen in the summer of 1965, is similar to those from the Southwest and Great Basin, especially the intermediate type from Lovelock Cave with the groove near the hook. The remaining length is 35.3 cm. and, like the Roaring Springs Cave atlatls, only finger notches form the grip with no evidence of Southwestern basketmaker style double cord loops. Associated darts were radiocarbon dated at around A.D. 50.

Though the wood of the atlatls themselves has been lost and dates are few, engaging hooks, attached separately and of less perishable stone or bone, as well as so-called boat stones or weights, are especially common in central California. As Payen points out, they appear adapted to a rod-shaped shaft —Massey's early form of atlatl. (In the Southeastern United States carved antler "male" hooks along with weights called banner stones or bird stones give evidence of the same rod-shaped male atlatl.) An engaging hook found in a deeply buried cultural deposit on the shores of Buena Vista Lake in the southern San Joaquin Valley of California came from a horizon radiocarbon dated at around 6000 B.C. In western Nevada at the southern end of Lake Winnemucca a rod-shaped atlatl with weight and engaging hook still attached was discovered around 1961. The hook had been carved of bone or antler and the weight fashioned from a grayish slate-like stone. Sinew still held them to an approximately 23-inch shaft. Traces of red ochre suggested the distal portion had once been stained red and in fact red still stained the sinew binding the hook. A dark blackish substance stained the proximal handle end of the piece including the stone, but not the sinew holding the stone (perhaps explained by old lash marks on the wood which implied new sinew had replaced the old). Steve Allely found paint worn away to the bare wood at the very location on the handle where the thumb of a right-handed thrower would have rubbed while carrying the atlatl before use. This remarkable weapon had been buried under nearly 16 feet of fill in a vertical shaft cave of a tufa formation. Unfortunately, its excavation was uncontrolled, but twined baskets found in a cache just above it were radiocarbon dated to around 6000 B.C. The probable age and style of the atlatl tend to confirm once again Massey's idea of the antiquity of such throwers and that the southern tip of Baja California was a time warp and the rod-shaped male thrower of Cerro Cuevoso a relic of an ancient form.

Atlatl Manufacture

The spring of a good atlatl was probably not unlike that of a good bow. While a rigid thrower works, recoil from a springy atlatl can give extra speed. Extra energy is stored in the piece and released in a burst at the very end of the throw when the cocked stick recoils. This also utilizes to the full the natural flex of the dart. Both atlatl and dart should recoil simultaneously against each other at

Buena Vista rock shelter atlatl with detail of hook and decorative pattern (Grant, 1979).

the very end of the throw for maximum effect. Without flex in the atlatl, the dart simply uncoils against thin air, wasting potential energy.

It may be no coincidence that bows from southern and Baja California were generally long and somewhat circular in cross section—like the Cerro Cuevoso atlatl—and bows from northern California short, broad and board-shaped—like the Potter Creek atlatl from Shasta County. Archaeological atlatls look like the bows which supplanted them. It would seem reasonable, therefore, that the historic processes used for bow making among California Indians might be extrapolated back in some measure to the manufacture of the pre-historic atlatl.

The stick must be broken from the tree, cut to rough shape with a sharp fractured stone, adze or knife, in some cases cured, warmed in the fire and bent to shape, then rasped with rough rock into final form and smoothed with an obsidian chip, abrasive stone or horsetail (scouring rush) stalk. Yuman-speakers of southern California and northern Baja, except for light smoothing, would leave the back of the bow untouched. Modern bowyers know the principal is sound: cracks begin in exposed grain.

Avoiding such cuts was not possible, of course, in the flat bows of yew hardwood of northern California, but they sinew-backed the bow for the same protection (a practice not found in atlatls). The dowel form of the Cerro Cuevoso thrower is amenable to natural protection if a single, long hardwood branch (of scrub oak perhaps) with a regular diameter is chosen. Some of Benito Peralta's willow bows, circular to lenticular in cross section, are close to the form of the Baja thrower.

A heavier main limb from which the shaft branch is cut could be retained in part and fashioned into a dart spur continuous with the shaft. The spur must be dull, like archaeological examples, to allow the cup of the dart to rotate in ball-and-socket fashion as the angle of the dart of the atlatl increases or opens during the throw. It seems fairly simple. Such a stick for an atlatl could be found, carved, straightened (if of the Baja style) or slightly bent (many atlatls not warped out of alignment have a slight recurve toward the spur side) and the finger loop made in minimum time. How long it might take to bring the thrower into perfect harmony with a dart, of course, is another story.

Nicolarson Tufa Cave atlatl. Bone hook lashed to thrower with sinew (Allely, 1992).

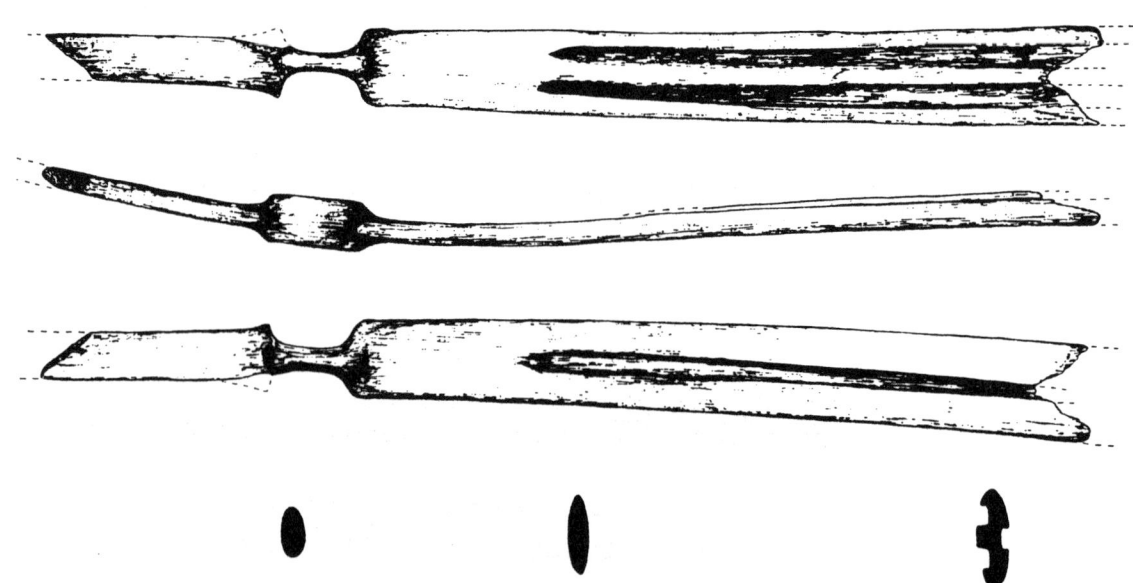

Potter Creek Cave atlatl (Payen, 1970).

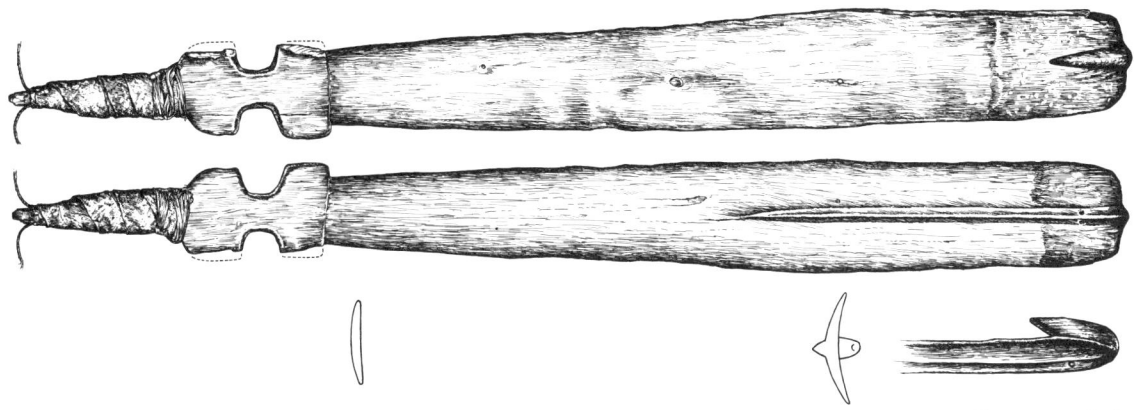

A Roaring Springs atlatl (23-9/16" long). Made of mountain mahogany, covered in red ochre. Small remnant dogbane (Indian hemp) strings at handle had feathers tied to them when first found. Male spur made of same piece of wood as atlatl board (Allely, 1992).

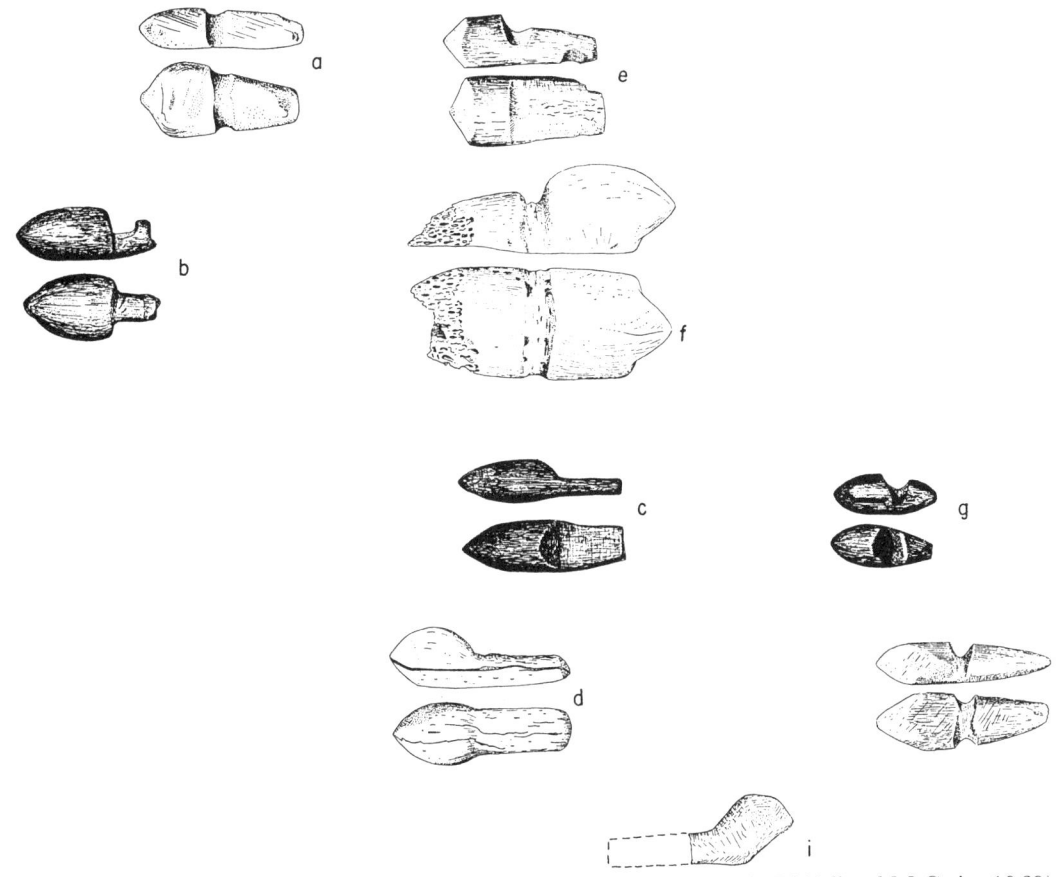

California atlatl spurs, about 63 percent actual size (drawn by Donald McGeein in Riddell and McGeein, 1969). Note grooves or platforms for lashing them to the atlatls. Figure F from the southern San Joaquin Valley and H from the San Francisco Bay region still have adhering traces of asphaltum. With the exceptions of A and I, all depicted are of bone. A is of shale, found on Santa Rosa Island. (B and G come from the Sacramento area, C from San Nicolas Island, and D and E from Santa Cruz Island.) I is of steatite and found in the Sierras. Similar stone spurs in this region are associated with periods as old as 4,000 years, but the oldest of the stone "snake head" style that could be dated comes from the shores of Lake Buena Vista in the southern San Joaquin Valley and has an antiquity of 8,000 years. Riddell and McGeein suggest snake-head spurs tend to be found in the same cultural deposits as atlatl weights, while the other so-called acorn-style spurs shown above lack this connection. Acorn-style spurs are generally more recent than the snake-head, although a fragmentary atlatl spur of antler likely in the acorn style from the Little Sycamore site in southern California may have an antiquity of between 5,000 and 7,000 years.

The Atlatl Dart

The dart is the key to the atlatl system. They are not all alike. At the same speed, a heavy stone-pointed dart will have more stopping power and go farther, for example, than a light dart. But obviously getting the heavy dart to that speed requires more energy or strength. With an equal effort, the lighter dart goes faster and farther, but if too light, will not penetrate or bring down the quarry and becomes a mere toy. An ideal weight for the dart depends in part on the intended object of the hunt.

Length and flexibility are crucial considerations. Generally, if the faster recoil speed of a lighter thinner dart is to match the recoil of a slower heavier atlatl, the dart must be made considerably longer than the atlatl. The additional weight of longer ends increases the flexing and slows the straightening of the shaft to equal that of the thrower. Conversely, the dart thrower might be shortened and lightened.

If the main shaft is long enough and thin enough, its own weight at the tip is usually sufficient to cause it to flex, always depending on the material from which it is made of course. Shorter, thicker, less flexible darts require heavy points to cause them to flex. In many cases, weight in the form of a hardwood foreshaft and stone point is required to cause the dart to coil in the initial stages of the throw. A dart coils or bends under the inertia of front loaded mass. Weights attached to atlatls probably functioned to stabilize the throw and to create a resisting mass causing the spear thrower to flex or bend (when too short or stiff to do this naturally) and store energy for the launch. Similarly, the dart head of stone was at once a sharp and deadly stabilizing missile *and* a resisting mass causing the dart to flex and store energy. William Perkins described the effects of stone points in the atlatl-dart system: the point mass of the head resists the acceleration of the dart pushed by the atlatl spur; this bends and compresses the dart and stores spring energy released in the launch.

Length and flexibility of the dart and mass of the projectile point can be brought into optimum relation with each other and to the atlatl. Deviation from optimum point mass for any dart-atlatl system once determined, lessens the efficiency of the system. Experiments by Perkins revealed that in lighter faster systems, less deviation is tolerated. For example, if a 4-gram stone point functions optimally in a light system, and the point is altered by even one gram, distance the dart travels significantly falls. A 12-gram stone point system, however, can vary either way by as much as 2 grams without loss of efficiency. Examples of local consistency of this sort, especially of the dart head weights, can be seen in the archaeological record.

Perkins suggests that any deviation in the sensitive atlatl-dart system (dart length and flexibility, atlatl length and flexibility, point mass, atlatl weight mass, materials) once the hunter achieved an optimum, appreciably changed the entire feel and performance of the system. That is why foreshafts were used. It was likely that the stone or haft of a well launched dart would break on impact. A repaired but shortened dart or dart head of less weight would significantly alter the hunter's throw and the dart's point of strike. Foreshafts allowed repair of the dart by replacement of the foreshaft without destroying the specifications, the consistency, of the dart. They gave new life to the mainshaft and fletching.

As with arrows, feathers stabilized the flight and brought the missile more surely to the mark. While there was much congruency between California arrows of historic times and archaeological California darts, the darts seemed to exhibit more variety of styles, especially in the feathering.

A Lower California Dart

Unfortunately, no darts accompanied the perfect dart thrower found in the cave at Cerro Cuevoso at the bottom of Baja. Farther up the coast at Bahía de Los Angeles, Dr. Edward Palmer excavated a small cave in 1887 and found one. William Massey and Caroline Osborne analyzed the cane projectile, which had been broken but was obviously of a piece, 92.5 cm. long without foreshaft, tipped with a stingray spine set directly into the split end of the cane and apparently bound with a two-ply agave cord. The cane had been split to a node. The 2 mm. diameter cord ended at that point caught under three wrappings. The other end extended up through the split and again wrapped three times around the end of the cane—here it had broken but likely it had been drawn under the wrappings to secure it as in other examples from Bahía de Los Angeles.

This whip-finish knot was the perfect cordage shaft reinforcement. I almost figured it out on my own but primitive technology expert Scott

Jones, who ties this knot on darts, clarified my understanding. The lead end of the knot was drawn down alongside the tail end forming a loop along the dart shaft. The lead end coiled around the shaft over the tail end and at an upward angle over itself. It coiled toward the ever diminishing loop. To finish, the lead end was simply put through the loop and the tail end pulled, constricting the loop and forcing it and the lead end under the coils. Twisting the coils and pulling at both ends of the cord hardened and secured the spiral wrappings to such a degree that non-sinew cordage became a viable seizing material. In one instance at Bahía de Los Angeles the end of a cordage binding had been pulled under a series of twelve wrappings.

The butt had a cup-like depression. There was no indication of fletching. Massey and Osborne also noted a possible wooden foreshaft 38 cm. long in the Palmer Cave collection.

Leonard Rockshelter

Robert Heizer described in the 1930s a most complete and unusual compound cane atlatl dart. It came from the lower levels of the Leonard Rockshelter in western Nevada and measured 129.5 cm. Foreshafts from the stratum were radiocarbon dated at around 5000 B.C. In the same bat guano layer were found olivella shell beads that could only have come from the California coast, 250 air miles across the Sierra Nevada Mountains.

The mainshaft of the Leonard Rockshelter dart was made from cane *(Phragmites communis)*, 45 cm. in length and 9 mm. in diameter. The unusually long foreshaft point of greasewood *(Sarcobatus vermiculatus)* measured 57 cm. and telescoped 10.5 cm. into the mainshaft in a fine cylindrical taper. The foreshaft had been scraped and polished to a uniform diameter of 7 mm.

The backshaft, also of cane, measured 38 cm. with a diameter of 12 mm., and the mainshaft telescoped into it. Red-stained sinew was wrapped 10 mm. wide at both ends to prevent splitting. A decorative red-stained flat sinew wrap 4 mm. wide began 41 mm. from the cup, or proximal, end and spiraled 24 revolutions down the butt for 26.5 cm. Over this, two whole eagle tail feathers 23.5 cm. long laid flat, or tangential, on opposite sides and along the shaft. They were wrapped with sinew 30 mm. from the distal end of the backshaft around the beveled quills; slender sinew seizings bound the feathers to the shaft at four other places along the feather midribs. Tufts of four decorative bluebird feathers 45 mm. long were held between the two eagle plumes by the lower sinew binding alone. The butt end of the cane was open to engage the atlatl spur.

Potter Creek

In California many dart fragments have been uncovered in caves. Louis Payen felt those from the Potter Creek cache he unearthed in 1965 in northern California came from compound darts with a butt or backshaft, mainshaft, and foreshaft, sometimes pointed, sometimes notched and tipped with a stone point. A complete pointed hardwood foreshaft measured around 19 cm.; another, deeply notched with an obsidian point attached with pitch and sinew, measured 19.5 cm., 17 cm. without the point, and had a maximum diameter of .9 cm. Foreshafts at Potter Creek were radiocarbon dated at around 50 A.D. Payen noted that the obsidian dart points at Potter Creek Cave were relatively small.

He found no complete backshafts at Potter Creek Cave but the longest hardwood fragment measured 32.5 cm.; diameters ranged between .7 to .9 cm. Shallow conical cups were present. Sinew wrapping 4 cm. below the butt on one measured 1 cm. wide and held the distal ends of two feathers; another example had seizing 1.6 cm. wide and held

Details of Bahía de Los Angeles dart. Stingray-spine point, cuplike butt, cane shaft (W. Massey and Osborne, 1961).

Restored Leonard Rockshelter compound cane dart with long, hardwood foreshaft (Heizer, 1938).

the base ends of several clearly unsplit feathers. This suggested that feathering of the darts may have been tangential as at Leonard Rockshelter, Lovelock Cave and Gypsum Cave—all just across the California border in Nevada.

Mainshafts had suffered at Potter Creek Cave but Payen was able to see they were from a light strong wood with a pith center and had been carefully smoothed and in some cases stained a reddish brown. The longest fragmentary sections reached 45 cm. Diameters of the Potter Creek mainshafts were from .9 to 1.5 cm., most around 1.0 to 1.2 cm. (At Leonard Rockshelter they ranged from .8 to 1.17 cm. and at Lovelock Cave, .85 to 1.43 cm.)

Newberry Cave

Found amid the magical paraphernalia of a hunter society that was carbon dated to around 1500 B.C., mainshaft fragments from Newberry Cave in the California Mohave Desert measured from .7 cm to 1.6 cm. in diameter. The longest fragment was 57.2 cm. Some were socketed for foreshafts or backshafts. Most mainshaft fragments were of slender willow *(Salix exigua)* followed by common reed *(Phragmites)* and elderberry *(Sambucus mexicana)*. Some of the drilled or reamed-out sockets had been reinforced with sinew wrappings. Mainshaft wood fragments had been carefully smoothed by scraping or abrading. Some even had a dull polish. Cane shafts, stripped of branches, appeared otherwise unmodified. Pieces with nocks were of slender willow or elderberry and measured .6 cm. to 1.2 cm. in diameter. The cupped depressions in the end were somewhat V-shaped and, according to Alan Davis and Gerald Smith, who analyzed the artifacts from Newberry Cave, they appear to have been drilled. One of the thin-walled

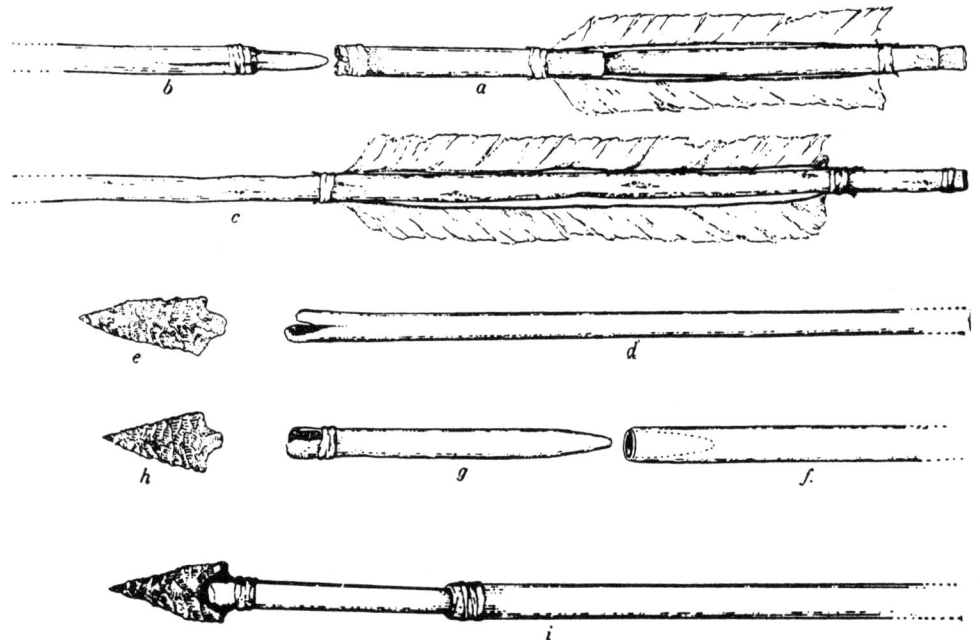

Gypsum Cave darts restored, showing construction: a) Separate cane backshaft 10-1/4" in length, butt 3/8" diameter, at socket 7/16" diameter. Reamed-out cup kept from splitting by natural joint 1/2" below the butt. Near joint, roughening suggests sinew binding may once have been present. b) Mainshaft joint—note distinct shoulder where it meets backshaft. c) Simple shaft, probably elder, peeled and trimmed, from 5/16" diameter at butt to 3/8" where it had been broken 13-1/8" farther down; remnants and sinew mark position of 3 feathers 8-1/2" long, uncertain in this case if whole or split—some loose, split feather fragments found were trimmed to about 1/2" wide; cup 3/16" diameter, 1/8" deep. d) Another simple shaft, distal end, wood near slot roughened to hold sinew band. e) Gypsum point. f) Arrowweed mainshaft with conical socket; 1/2" diameter at this end, which was generally roughened with gritty stone or scored transversely to make a seat for sinew binding. g) Foreshaft—note lack of shoulder where it meets the mainshaft—the drawing is based on a perfectly preserved specimen nearly 5-1/2" long, just under 1/2" at maximum diameter, perhaps of mesquite. The surface shows the marks of a grinding stone. The slot, which still retains traces of pitch and sinew seizing, is 1/2" deep, U-shaped, 1/8" wide at the bottom, 1/4" at the end. h) Gypsum point. i) Complete compound attachment. (Drawings by C. P. Baldwin, in M. Harrington, 1933.)

cupped ends was reinforced with sinew. No feathers were found but a single nock had sinew wrapping 1.6 cm. from the proximal end probably to bind fletching.

Fragmentary notched foreshafts, all of slender willow, ranged from .9 cm. to 1 cm. in diameter with the notches themselves, .6 to 1 cm. deep. The foreshafts had been smoothed by scraping or abrading. An unidentified black adhesive remained on most notches and impressions left by tightly wrapped sinew confirmed its use to bind the dart heads. Many Elko and Gypsum type points were found unattached. Fragmentary pointed shafts that were found may have functioned as simple pointed foreshafts; others somewhat duller may have been proximal ends of foreshafts—in fact, one was still tightly inserted into a mainshaft socket. Still visible on some shaft pieces were painted decorations (solids, stripes, bands, spiraling bands) in black, red and green.

Gypsum Cave

Mark Raymond Harrington brought to light in 1930 a style of dart from Gypsum Cave near Las Vegas which had extensive and complex painted decorations in black, brown, red, gray-green, dark-green and blue. The patterns were in bands sometimes bordered with fine lines and included zigzags, spirals, cross-hatches formed by intersecting spirals and squares containing dots, all in fine lines. The reconstructed darts seemed somewhat crudely made of elder, peeled and smoothed, thin and light, about 5/16 of an inch in diameter at the butt which contained a small drilled cup to engage the spur. The cup was reinforced with sinew binding and 2 inches below the butt sinew seizing held three feathers, in at least some cases not split, 6 to 8 inches long where more seizing held them to the shaft. A drilled socket at the distal end received the foreshaft and was reinforced with a sinew band. The foreshaft itself was of harder, heavier wood, creosote brush or mesquite, and about 4 1/2 inches long, tapered to fit the mainshaft socket. The other end was slotted about 7/16 of an inch deep, U-shaped, 3/16 of an inch wide in order to receive a Gypsum Cave style point that was secured with pitch and sinew.

A second type of dart uncovered at Gypsum Cave was, in contrast, very well made, of arrowbrush (*Pluchea sericea*). It tapered from 3/8 of an inch in diameter near the shoulder for the backshaft to 7/16 or 1/2 inch before the foreshaft. It was peeled and smoothed, and over 5 feet long. Foreshafts were estimated to have been slightly heavier than the first type. There was little or no decoration on the darts. However, some had a separate butt-piece of decorated cane, 10 inches long, with three apparently split feathers. Others, without backshafts, had evidence of sinew seizing 1-1/8 inches from the butt and 6-1/4 inches farther down. Cane "couplings" that were found suggested a use to extend or repair the mainshafts. In two darts the stone point had been set directly in the mainshaft. One of these was arrowbrush with a 7/16 of an inch diameter at the base of the V-shaped slot. One quarter to 3/8-inch-wide bindings of sinew were wound on mainshafts where splitting or cracking had already begun. Coils made of flat strips of sinew were found without shafts—all that remained—and one coil of a flat strip of inner bark (light-colored, perhaps a willow or elderberry binding) may have been used in place of sinew on a shaft. Three bunts, or blunt wooden points, of Basketmaker style, one seemingly painted white, were excavated. The bulb on one was 1-1/2 inches long by 1-3/16 inches in diameter and its 1-1/2-inch stem tapered from 7/16 of an inch to 1/4 of an inch. Foreshafts at Gypsum Cave were radiocarbon dated at about 1000 B.C. (Basketmaker atlatls generally date between 100 B.C. and 400 A.D.)

Pisgah Crater

In the fall of 1988 a badly broken but fairly complete atlatl dart was discovered in a lava tube cave of the Pisgah Crater lava field on the California Mohave Desert. The approximately 4-1/2- to 6-foot-long dart may have been left in the cave by a hunter who had entered the tube after crossing two

Exact size dart butt, apparently of elder, shows cup which engaged spur of atlatl. The stick had been trimmed and scraped. Coarse sinew seizing holds remaining tips of 3 whole, unsplit brown feathers. Found during excavations of Gypsum Cave in southern Nevada cica 1930 (drawing by C. P. Baldwin, in M. Harrington 1933).

miles of barren and extremely hostile sharp volcanic rock terrain around 4,800 years ago (dated by both radio-carbon and mass-spectroscopy methods). These are the tentative conclusions of Philip Wilke who kindly allowed me to see the dart at the University of California at Riverside.

The mainshaft had a diameter reaching nearly 3/4 of an inch and an elderberry-like pith core. The ends were tapered, socketed and sinew-wrapped. The complete foreshaft looked like catclaw and contained a white side-notched chert point, the very tip of which was drawn out and particularly sharp. It was held with sinew but no glue. Together point and foreshaft measured 8 inches long. The fit of the tapered end of the foreshaft with the mainshaft was so perfect Wilke suggested some abrasive material, fine sand for example, may have been used between them while they were rubbed and fitted together. Abrasive marks on other archaeological dart foreshafts have suggested this technique.

The long backshaft, made perhaps from willow, had possibly two whole feathers attached at the quill or front end in a most unusual manner. To help bind them to the shaft a thin thread of sinew had been sewn at least twice through each quill. The holes were minute and their placement would have meant that the feathers at the proximal quill end were attached to the shaft radially, the feather filaments of one side of each feather sticking straight out. Wilke suggested they could then have been drawn down alongside the shaft and attached tangentially at the distal end of the feathers.

A small piece of the backshaft had broken off and remained inserted in the mainshaft. It had little shoulders cut in from both sides just behind the point and was reminiscent of the piece that results from the production of foreshaft slots by a sudden sidewise break of a stick. Harrington's reconstruction of this technique at Gypsum Cave is described in the following section.

Dart Manufacture

The principle of transference of materials and technique is strikingly apparent when we compare archaeological atlatl darts to the arrows used after the introduction of the bow. Both were plain wood or composite missiles with light mainshafts and hardwood foreshafts, the wood carved to a point or stone tipped. Some had separate butts or backshafts (much more common in the atlatl). Both darts and arrows had glue and sinew bindings and unfletched or feathered vanes (often whole feathers for the atlatl, split for the arrow, but occasionally vice versa).

We can easily extrapolate back historically known processes used by California Indians for arrows to reinvent the atlatl dart. Undoubtedly the wood was cured and heat straightened with fire or a stone heated in the fire. Besides replacing the bowstring nock with an atlatl spur cup, the only real difference was greater size for the dart, and even in this there was considerable overlap. Size almost seems to fail as a distinguishing criterion when we look at the reed shaft. Compound reed, or cane, arrows usually with hardwood chemise foreshafts seem to have been universal in the Californias but probably were nowhere so great in length as those described by James Ohio Pattie in his 1827 hostile encounter with the "Pipi" on the lower Colorado River. They were as long as their bows, he wrote, and the bows he estimated at 6 feet—longer than the reed dart from the Leonard Rockshelter. Not surprisingly, fragments of arrows (cane shafts and chemise foreshafts) were found in the upper (and most recent) levels of the Leonard Rockshelter. The Maricopa arrowbrush (arrowweed) arrow with the point set directly in the mainshaft echoed arrowbrush darts found at Gypsum Cave but measured only from the fingertips to the armpit (compared to over 5 feet at Gypsum) and 3/8 of an inch in diameter (compared to 7/16 of an inch at Gypsum).

Atlatl dart fore shafts from Gypsum Cave. First was likely broken from a stick in such a way as to create slot for stone head. Second (6-7/8" long) is pointed and acts as a dart point itself, similar to later California arrow foreshaft points; no pitch was used to hold foreshafts in the mainshafts. (Drawing by C. P. Baldwin in M. Harrington, 1933.)

Techniques of manufacture can be read on the piece itself although sometimes it takes a Mark Harrington to decipher them. His interpretation of the clues left on a dart foreshaft found in Gypsum Cave reveals a clever manner of breaking a foreshaft from a longer stick and at the same time creating a slot for the spearhead. Harrington must have noticed the little shoulders cut in from both sides about 1/4 of an inch from the point meant for insertion into the mainshaft (see illustration). The little tongue left by the side cuts suggests in a positive form the space created for a spearhead on the part which would have remained below. Harrington surmised that two cuts had been made directly across from each other on a live growing stick, each cut about one-third through the stick. Then, on the two remaining sides, opposite each other and about 3/8 of an inch below, two more, much shallower cuts were made. A sudden sidewise pull broke the top of the stick away leaving a slot in the bottom portion which with minimal finishing was made ready for a stone point and would become a dart foreshaft.

Harrington also noticed the short transverse incised lines over the fine finish near the tapered end that would prevent the foreshaft from slipping from its socket, and the four parallel incised lines encircling the shaft near the darthead slot to hold secure the sinew binding for the stone head.

Top row: archaic coastal southern California atlatl dart or spear points drawn slightly less than 3/4 scale, 6000–2000 B.C. Second row: coastal southern California and offshore island dart or spear points and finger-held drill. From the so-called Campbell tradition, about 2000 B.C. through A.D. 500. Note small retouch marks on edges of some pieces, made by holding pressure flaker more perpendicular to the plane of the dart head. (All of these and many other stone artifacts are found in Joseph and Kerry Chartkoff's The Archaeology of California, *1984.)*

Throwing the Atlatl Dart

In the rock drawings of the Coso Range shadow hunters of early California can be seen hurling the atlatl with an overhand swing. We know that in at least some instances the throw was for 50 to 75 feet, the approximate distance from rock blinds discovered in the Cosos to canyon floors below where Campbell Grant and others believed that game must have been driven in archaic times. Sadly, that is all that is left of the archaic style.

In general, we depend on modern students of the atlatl to teach us precisely how to hold it and the finer points of throwing the dart. This is what I believed at any rate until I encountered on the streets of Los Angeles a bonafide Yupik Eskimo who grew up using a spear thrower at the mouth of the Yukon River! Wanderlust took him from home as a young man and as H. L. Mencken once remarked, there is a tilt to the North American continent and sooner or later everything loose in the land rolls into southern California.

Vitus Jack learned from his father how to hunt seals from a boat with an atlatl. There were a lot of seals and a lot of hunters and a rifle would have ricocheted across the water and hurt someone, he related. So, they continued to use the atlatl. You could guide a boat with one hand and fling your spear with the other. Or if someone else was propelling the boat, you might stand, Jack demonstrated, and point at your target with your left hand as you cocked the right hand behind your head for the overhand throw. It had to be quick, though the hurl might be for 30 or 40 yards, for the seal would not be still. You aimed just below the head where you had a larger target.

Because sometimes more than one hunter claimed the same kill, every family painted their spears a special color—Jack's family color was green. The meat they could share but the hide and blubber were most prized and they went to the one whose spear was most responsible for the kill—often a matter for discussion. Usually the seal did not die with a single spear in its flesh. For that reason, the barbed head was attached by a line to various points along the wooden spear shaft which separated from the head and floated on the surface of the sea to mark the seal's location for final deadly thrusts of a spear or a shot to the head with a rifle.

Spear throwers themselves, of the female or mixed type (recessed groove and spur), were about 18 inches long, shorter for shorter range work, longer for distance he told me. It depended on the hunter. They gripped the spear thrower with the last three fingers of the right hand and held the spear between the thumb and forefinger.

Modern students also affirm that the atlatl can be gripped with the last three fingers while the thumb and index finger pass from the back to either side (through loops if provided) and hold the dart in front. Or the atlatl may be gripped by only the last two fingers with the middle finger and index finger passing to either side of the thrower to clasp and guide the dart between them in front with help from the thumb. With the index and middle fingers passing through loops on either side of the atlatl (or with a loop on one side only), the dart may be held in place between the tips of the thumb and third finger. In all cases, David Wescott advises that the dart be gripped as far forward as possible in order to create back pressure against the spur and reduce the chance of slippage during the throw.

For the throw itself, he uses the analogy of the baseball pitcher whose slow wind-up and last-second snap of the wrist maximizes speed. The throw is smooth, beginning with the throwing arm cocked behind the shoulder, force slowly increasing until the final wrist snap which, if the target is near, must perfectly control the dart's flight. For distance, the release is at a higher angle and the approach like that of the javelin thrower. A subtle lunge of the body during the throw adds force and lowers the body as the throwing arm rises, thus keeping the rotation of the dart over the spur on an even plain

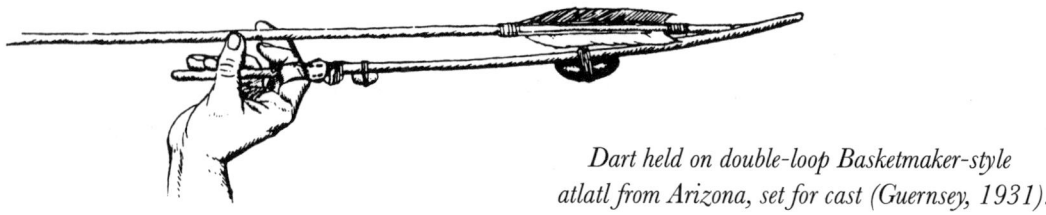

Dart held on double-loop Basketmaker-style atlatl from Arizona, set for cast (Guernsey, 1931).

and avoiding slippage. It allows controlled follow through and greater accuracy.

Having achieved basic competency, the problem of the stone weights found attached to some atlatls might be approached in earnest. As interpreted by Perkins, they acted as a timing device to adjust the spring of the atlatl to the spring of the dart, to bring them into phase and release all the energy at the final moment. The amount of weight and its position could vary on the atlatl arm to achieve this.

Perkins explained that because of the heavily forested environments of the eastern United States, quarry were taken at close range, and for this shorter atlatls worked best. Eastern atlatls were shorter than those recovered in the west, where land was open and targets often longer range. But shorter atlatls required more weight to force them to flex and store energy for the release and to be in phase with the dart. That is why eastern weights that have been recovered archaeologically, are heavier. Western-style atlatls generally required less weight because of the mechanical advantage of their greater length. In many cases no additional weight was used. The weight of the atlatl combined with that of the dart was sufficient. The front loaded weight of the dart could also be varied to achieve the perfect recoil match. This sometimes entailed a stone point.

Petroglyphs of the Coso Range, California (Grant, Baird and Pringle, 1969).

California Knapping

Eleven thousand years ago Clovis mammoth hunters ranged over North America and left a record of the knapper's art in beautifully fluted spearheads, no two exactly the same. What followed Clovis and the later bison hunting Folsom tradition was much cruder, yet even these points were often well crafted and certainly functional and a pleasure to view. After the passing of the big game and the Paleo-Indian, distinctive regional cultures took form. In California it was the San Dieguito.

Malcolm Rogers made endless treks into the California deserts in search of the remains of these ancient people and discovered what was left after perhaps ten thousand years of exposure to sun, wind and rain—rocks. Most of the material culture had long since vanished. But the rocks told a story. The earliest San Dieguito preferred andesite as their medium, a volcanic rock less smooth in texture than obsidian or even flint. From this they made not mold-perfect points but crudely chipped choppers and spearheads, rough knives and percussion cracked tools whose flat surfaces resembled planes for cutting, shaving or smoothing wood or scraping hides or freeing the fiber from agave. The San Dieguito percussion-flaked stone stands in sharp contrast to the painstaking regularity of much pressure-flaked work which, though technically of the highest caliber and virtuosity, too often looks almost factory plastic and lacks the character of the ancient artifacts. It may have something to do with respect for the stone itself. The earliest San Dieguito did not use the refined pressure flaking technique at all, apparently, but simply banged stone against stone and thereby produced useful tools for millennia. Naturally fractured rock, direct and indirect percussion, pressure flaking and heat treatment—Native Californians would in later times exploit all the wisdom of the flint knapper's art.

Unworked Rock

Rock can be surprisingly useful and beautiful just as it is. For the Miwok of the Sierra Nevada, a naturally fractured rock became a simple knife. Barrett and Gifford recorded they employed these unworked pieces to hack off hazel branches and cut maple shoots or roughly trim down a cedar bough for a bow. A simple unworked flake struck from a flint core served to scrape split maple withes for basketry or to finish the smoothing of the bow.

Indirect percussion as practiced by the Wintuns, from firsthand account of Redding (Holmes, 1891).

Percussion Technology

By the time ethnographers began asking questions, the art of flint knapping had pretty much been lost. With the great influx of Europeans and European-style goods to California in the middle of the last century, the Indian quickly replaced his stone knife with a steel blade. The accounts of flint knapping are few. Fortunately, Saxton Pope obtained some information in the early years of this century from Ishi, last of the Yahi, on the old stone-working technique.

For arrow points the Yahi used bone, flint, or obsidian, especially the latter, which was widely traded among the Indians of California. As a first step the obsidian boulder was simply shattered by throwing another rock against it. Ishi next selected one of the pieces and from it broke off large flakes in the following fashion: holding a short segment of antler or bone at a slight angle from the perpendicular against a projecting surface, he struck the top of the antler smartly with another stone and a flake would dislodge.

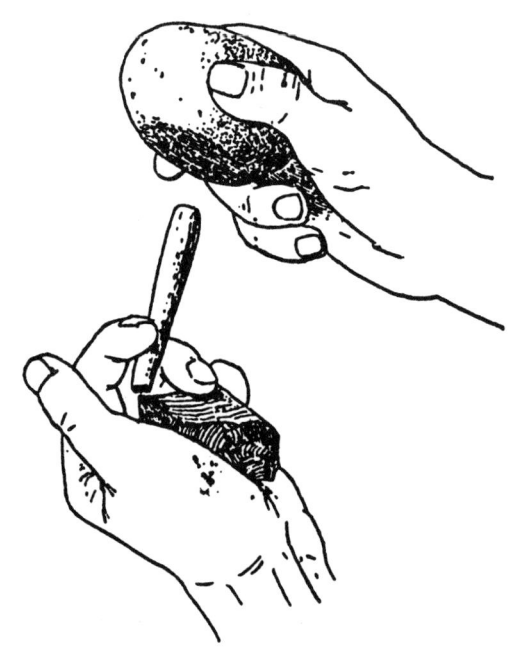

Flint knappers know that some stones break more evenly than others. Stones such as flint and obsidian are among the best. Modern knappers know this is true because of the nature of the crystalline structure. Obsidian has no crystal structure. Like a fluid, applied force spreads equally in all directions, radiating like a cone with the apex at the point of impact. Rippling down and outward, the ripples actually can be seen on pieces struck from obsidian—waves of compression in the cone of force rending the rock. Flint, on the other hand, has a cryptocrystalline structure but it is so small and fine it behaves almost like obsidian when struck with an object. Lack of large crystallized structure means that when the stone is fractured, the form of the fracture depends more on how it is struck (giving the craftsman the control) than on inherent but unpredictable structure in the stone. Both flint and obsidian and other good flint knapping materials, such as chalcedony, chert, andesite and jasper, have this vitreous (glass-like) quality and, like glass, are rich in silica. For knapping, materials must also be elastic and homogeneous. They must have the ability to snap back and be free of impurities.

Good stone breaks like glass: a direct perpendicular hit to a flat surface creates a cone of force spreading out in obtuse angles from the line of force, causing a small conical pyramid to break away, as when a bullet strikes a window. All flint knappers, ancient and modern, know instinctively from endless trial and error how fine stone breaks. The basic theory holds true for direct percussion (stone against stone), indirect (bone or other object held against stone and then struck) and pressure flaking. In order to take a thin and useful flake from a projecting surface, or platform, the blunt tip of a section of antler must be held against its edge at an angle tilting away from the vertical cliff wall beneath (which hopefully will break away and become the flake). The antler tine tilts so an edge of its imagined cone of force passes just under the vertical face of the cliff below. The antler punch is also positioned in line with a ridge on the cliff wall to make a long flake. A rounded stone about the size of a fist strikes the antler smartly. A tentative weak hit will only crumble the rock or cause a step fracture (terminating the flake too soon with a right angle break) and will not produce a long sheer flake. Too hard and the rock shatters. Step fractures can also result from too straight an angle of force, not following ridges (on the cliff wall) or improper preparation of the striking platform (it may need grinding with sandstone). Hinge fractures, a blade with a premature rounded blunt break, occur when the platform forms an angle greater than 90 degrees with its cliff wall.

The Chumash, recorded Henry Henshaw in the last century, placed the flint in the cleft of a large stone to steady it while a very hard obtusely pointed pebble of agate was held against it and struck a quick tap with a quartz rock. In this way they made knives and arrowheads.

Direct percussion requires greater skill than indirect. A deft blow with the hammerstone or a baton of thick antler is struck directly against the edge of another stone held in the hand or on the leg. It is not as accurate or reliable and the flakes produced tend to be less straight or uniform. However, direct percussion requires fewer parts, and in that sense is simpler. It was probably the only method used by the San Dieguito. Through direct percussion large broken pieces could quickly be roughed into bifaces with the shape of a crude hand ax and they could be used as such. They were convenient forms to transport and from the two roughly chipped sides useful smaller flakes could be struck as needed. Direct percussion with a hammerstone could also rough out platform cores, spearheads, knives, and arrow points. In the early 1870s Stephen Powers observed the Wiyot shaping an arrowhead in this way.

Many hammerstones used in direct percussion have been found in California archaeological contexts. They tend to be about the size of a fist,

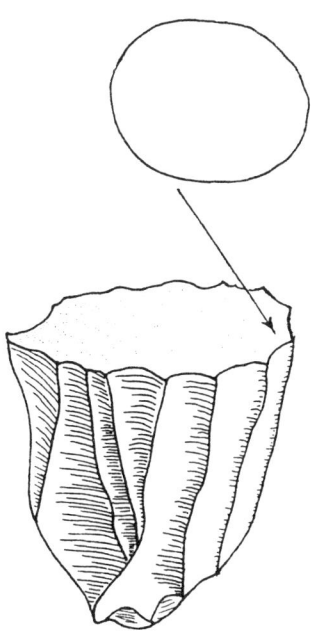

Direct percussion angle for a desirable shear "feather flake."

hard and compact, with wear marks indicating their use as hammerstones. Theodora Kroeber writes that for a hammerstone, Ishi was accustomed to using a water-worn boulder of heavy stone. The size and shape fit his hand well. He used it for indirect percussion against a blunt-ended piece of strong bone to remove flake after flake from an obsidian core—long flakes for large spear points or knife blades. The core itself could be fashioned into a tool. But the hammerstone brought directly against the obsidian mass—direct percussion—produced smaller flakes from which Ishi made arrow points.

One hundred years ago Cephas Bard wrote of the Chumash: "Within the recollection of early American settlers now living, these natives have been known to flake off a piece of obsidian with an indescribable motion of their hands, and to dexterously sharpen its edge so that it would almost cut a hair" (Hudson and Blackburn, 1987). Undoubtedly, Bard referred to direct percussion, breaking a flake from a chunk of obsidian with a hammerstone, and refining it through the technique known as pressure flaking.

Pressure Flaking

Powers quoted E.G. Waite's description of pressure flaking as he witnessed it during an even earlier day among the Klamath River Indians and the Indians of Central California.

The palm of the left hand is covered with buckskin held in place by the thumb being thrust through a hole in it. The inchoate arrow-head is laid on this pad along the thick of the thumb, the points of the fingers pressing it firmly down. The instrument used to shape the stone is the end of a deer's antler, from 4 to 6 inches in length, held in the right hand. The small round point of this is judiciously pressed upon the edge of the stone, cleaving it away underward in small scales. The buckskin, of course, is to prevent the flesh from being wounded by the sharp scales. The arrow-head is frequently turned around and over to cleave away as much from one side as the other, and to give it the desired size and shape. It is a work of no little care and skill to make even so rude an instrument as an arrow-head seems to be, only the most expert being very successful at this business. Old men are usually seen at this employment.

The shaping and sharpening of the edge of a struck flake normally involved the technique of pressure flaking. Pope recorded that Ishi selected one of the pieces of obsidian he had struck to pressure flake into an arrowhead. It would be about 3 inches long, 1-1/2 inches wide, 1/2 inch thick and of appropriate shape and grain. Larger pieces were desirable for a gift or war arrow, a knife or spear; smaller and flatter for the oval heads he used for bear.

Ishi placed the obsidian in the palm of his left hand which he had protected with a pad of buckskin. He rested his left elbow on his left knee and with his left fingers held the flake securely against his palm. He gripped a large flaking tool near the tip in his right hand as the wooden stick handle rested beneath his forearm, the butt against his ribs, for steadiness and for leverage. The left hand, protected by a double piece of buckskin, held the obsidian with all four fingers against the lower fleshy part of the palm, the edge of the flake parallel to the lines of his wrist, the thumb straight and parallel to his fingers. He engaged the sharp edge of the obsidian with the antler point, pressed forcefully upon the lower edge increasing the pressure downward and outward and clicked off a flake.

From personal experience I have found that the pressure often begins directly into the edge of the blank arrowhead but ends with a slow shift downward. The desired flake will detach when the edge of the cone of force begins to reach the lower surface of the blank, as the force shifts and increases in that direction. Continued direct pressure into the edge only crumbles it. Perpendicular force alone merely nicks it. Trying to remove too large a flake from the side or excessive force to an end

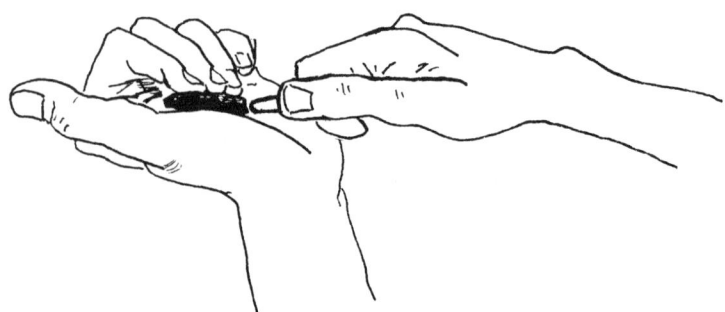

Pressure flaking with antler tine.

without supporting the whole piece will break the stone in half. Grinding the edges slightly with a piece of sandstone and leaving the grit helps the antler grip the edge. Incidentally, careful creation or preparation of platforms for the antler tine or striking stone by grinding in this way is a hallmark of modern flint knapping and was practiced by ancient masters as well.

In forming the arrow point Ishi took advantage of the natural outline of the stone. His first flakes from it were large, becoming smaller towards the end of his work. He turned the head over and over until the desired triangular shape had been formed. So as not to break the stem, a finer bone tool finished and notched the arrow point. Ishi wore a buckskin thumbpiece, and with his left index finger he held the arrowhead on this while with an awl-sized bone flaking tool he pressed out little notches against his thumb. Then he went back along the edge of the blade over and over again, flaking from point to base, producing fine, very sharp serration. A finished point was generally 2 inches in length by 7/8 of an inch in width and 1/8 of an inch in thickness. It was larger for a war arrowhead.

Ishi was a Yahi Indian from the foothills of the California Cascades. The Hupa of northwestern California used a flaking instrument similar to that described for Ishi and in essentially the same way. Goddard knew the last Hupa flint knapper. Old Roger worked the stone on a piece of buckskin held with his fingers on his left palm. The flaking tool held in his right was a piece of antler perhaps 7 inches long lashed for around 5-1/2 inches of its length to the side of a 15-inch stick handle. The handle would pass through the hand and along the forearm, enabling the knapper to develop considerable leverage, wrote Goddard.

Paul Schumacher's 1877 description of stone flaking from the "last arrow maker" of the Klamath River Yurok, whom he observed on the right bank near the mouth of the river, suggests there were alternatives in the precise positioning of the flake being worked (the edge perpendicular to the lines of the wrist rather than parallel as in the case of Ishi) as well as in flaking tools.

To work the flakes into the desired forms, certain tools are required, one of which is presented (A) in the figure opposite. It consists of a stick, which is in the form and thickness not unlike an arrow-shaft and about 1 foot in length, to one end of which a point is fastened, of some tough material, as the tooth of the sea-lion or the horn of

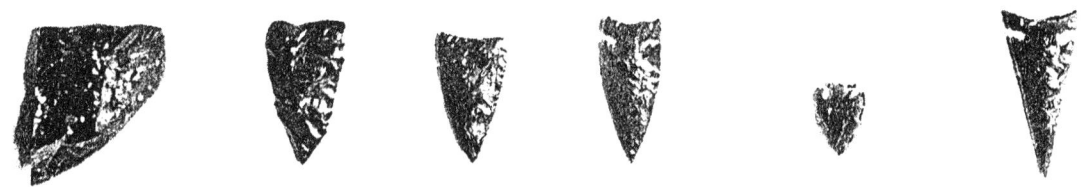

Examples from Ishi's knapping process. 1) Detached obsidian flake; 2) Arrow point initial stage; 3) Nearing completion; 4) Completed arrow point; 5) Small broad arrowhead of obsidian, 1" long, 11/16" wide, 1/8" thick; 6) Obsidian arrowhead, 2" long, 15/16" wide, 1/4" thick (Pope, 1918).

Aboriginal California bone-pointed pressure flakers: top, from the Yurok, 17-3/8" long (University of California collection, pictured in Pope, 1918); below, Northern Maidu, 11-1/2" long (drawn in Dixon, 1905). Simpler flakers, not fixed to a wooden handle, were also used. Those found by M. Léon De Cessac on San Nicolas and San Miguel islands during the nineteenth century were of a heavy mammal bone, a rib and split rib, and a sea mammal penis bone. Short sections of deer antler were often employed as flakers in California.

elk, and even iron among the present Klamaths, although the rock does not work as well, and brittles where the edge ought to be sharp. The point (B of the figure) is represented in natural size to better illustrate its beveled curve, which form admits a gradual pressure to a limited space of the edge of the sherd. During the operation, the rock is partly inwrapped in a piece of buckskin for better manipulation, its flat side resting against the fleshy part of the thumb of the left hand, only the edge to be worked (C) being left exposed. The tool is worked with the right hand, while the lower part of the handle, usually ornamented, is held between the arm and the body so as to guide the instrument with a steady hand. The main movements are shown in figure (D). With the first movement as illustrated, larger flakes are detached, and the rock is roughly shaped into the desired form; while with the second movement long flakes are broken, which frequently reach the middle of the sherd, producing the ridge of the points or knives; finally with the third movement the smaller chips of the cutting edge are worked. The work proceeds from the point, the more fragile part of the weapon toward the stronger end, as illustrated by the unfinished bore, the form of which, as frequently found, is shown by dotted lines. To work out the barbs and projections of the arrow or spear points (E,F), a bone needle (G) is used, as pictured in natural size in the figure, about 4 to 5 inches long, without a shaft.

Gayton wrote the Western Mono held the obsidian in the left hand beneath the straightened thumb and bent index finger and braced by the middle finger. The buckskin guard was not always used. They detached flakes with the little bone of the deer's dew toe. The antler tine in a pressure-flaking kit from the Tejón Pass area, probably Kitanemuk (collected in 1901 by J. W. Hudson and found today in the Field Museum), is bluntly pointed, nearly an inch thick and almost 6 inches long. Ishi used a piece of antler, neither too sharp nor too blunt, bound to a stick about a foot long (actually the length of the distance from the elbow to his extended middle finger), but he employed a much smaller tool for the finer work of arrowhead notches. His flaking tools were pointed almost like a screwdriver, according to Pope, only rounded instead of square at the tip, filed quite sharp.

The Yurok method of making stone weapons (Schumacher, 1877).

Ishi kept completed heads in a small skin bag. Often these heads were not attached until a few hours before the hunt. Heated pine resin was applied to the notched end of the arrow, the head was set in and the resin molded around the base. When it cooled, three wraps of sinew were made criss-cross, up and about each notch and around the shaft, then continued around the arrow for half an inch just below the arrowhead. Once dry, the binding was polished lightly with sandstone.

Ishi told Pope that men made arrowheads in a secluded spot away from camp. They daubed their faces with black mud and did not talk. When a flint fragment flew in his eye, Ishi pulled down his lower lid with his left forefinger—he did not blink or rub the lid—he bent over, looked at the ground and gave himself a forceful thump on the crown with his right hand to dislodge the sliver of stone. Modern knappers wear safety glasses.

Heat Treatment— An Old Indian Trick

Powers described how the Wiyot of northwestern California made long delicate arrowheads used in war:

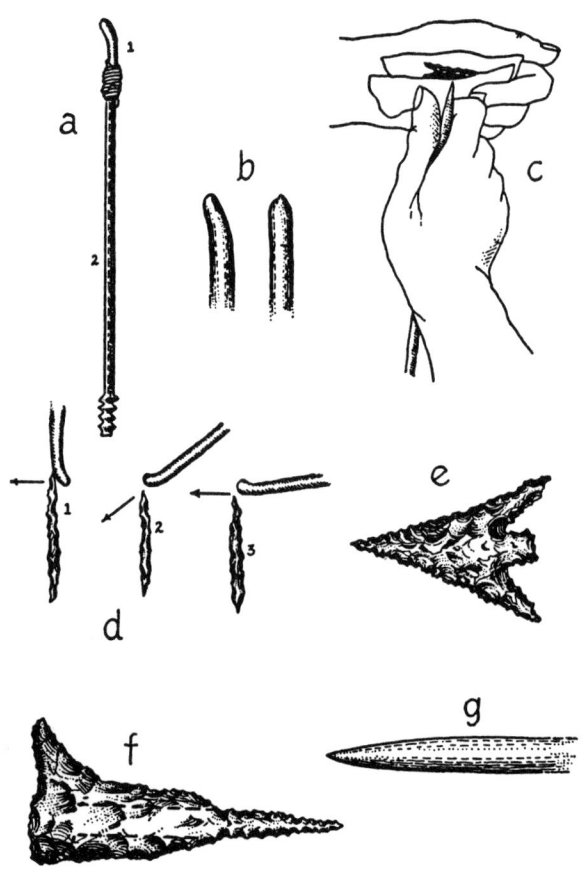

Taking a piece of jasper, chert, obsidian, or common flint, which breaks sharp-cornered and with a conchoidal fracture, they heat it in the fire and then cool it slowly, which splits it in flakes. The arrow-maker then takes the flake and gives it an approximate rough shape by striking it with a kind of hammer. He then slips over his left hand a piece of buckskin, with a hole to fit over the thumb (this buckskin is to prevent the hand from being wounded), and in his right hand he takes a pair of buck-horn pincers, tied together at the point with a thong. Holding the piece of flint in his left hand he breaks off from the edge of it a tiny fragment with the pincers by a twisting or wrenching motion. The piece is often reversed in the hand, so that it may be worked away symmetrically. Arrowhead manufacture is a specialty, just as arrow-making, medicine, and other arts.

Detailed descriptions of Native California flint knapping are rare and the preceding by Powers, who traveled among the Wiyot in the 1870s, is interesting on three counts. First, it records the trimming of a flake by direct percussion; second, it is apparently a unique method of pressure flaking and third, it gives what may be in part a confused observation of fire cracking and fire treatment of cryptocrystalline rock (such as jasper or flint).

It is known that the flaking characteristics of such stones improve after they are heated. They become more vitreous and easier to flake, perhaps through the breakdown of the crystal structure. Ideally, a temperature around 500 degrees F (260 degrees C) must be reached and maintained for ten to twelve hours and both the increase and decrease in temperature must be very gradual to avoid breakage. Indian earth ovens would work well. Knapper Paul Hellweg suggests a bed of hot coals covered with a 2 to 3 inch layer of sand, followed by flakes and prepared blanks, a second layer of sand and a second fire that should burn down to a bed of coals before it too is capped with more sand and left for 24 hours. The sand insures a slow buildup of heat and gradual cooling. The stones should not be removed until completely cooled.

The process does not need to be so elaborate or so long, however, if both heat treatment *and* fracturing are desired. A quicker rise and fall of temperature would work. It may be that the Wiyot did not cool the stone so very slowly, or perhaps the stone was heated somewhat rapidly, for the breakage mentioned by Powers was clearly purposeful and occurred in the fire.

Much clearer is Schumacher's 1877 description of heat treatment and heat fracturing by the Yurok.

The rock is first exposed to fire, and, after a thorough heating, rapidly cooled off, when it flakes readily into sherds of different sizes under well directed blows at its cleavage. The fragments are assorted according to shape and size best corresponding to the weapons desired; the small ones best fit in shape and thickness, are used for arrowheads; similar sherds, but larger in size, for spear points; the long narrow pieces for borers, and so on.

In an article on the heat treatment of lithic materials in aboriginal northwestern California, R. A. Gould made no mention of Powers' or Schumacher's early observations but based solely on archaeological

Sinew-secured stone arrowhead (Mason, 1894).

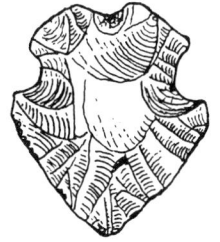 

Pressure flaked obsidian heads found by Paipai near Santa Catarina: first, likely for atlatl dart; second, for arrow—both are actual size.

evidence came to the same conclusion: Indians of northwestern California fire-fractured raw lithic material for stone tools. He found the quality of the material also altered by the fire. The site was Point St. George, California, and prehistorically stone chipping there was a major activity.

Gould found evidence for heat treatment of common beach cobbles of agate and red or green jasper. Discoidal cortex flakes, known as "pot lid" flakes, are frequently associated with archaeological hearths and artifacts of the Point St. George region, beneath the ground and on surface sites. "A planoconvex flake leaving a concave scar" was how Don E. Crabtree, flint knapping expert who accompanied Gould on a survey of the area in 1972, described them. They lacked bulbs of percussion and the compression rings of force lines left by hammerstone technology. The differential expansion and contraction which breaks off "pot lids" was caused by heat. When these pieces (from 2.1 cm. to 8.89 cm.) were tested by chipping, they also showed definite signs of heat alteration. Many of the sites contained large amounts of crazed and shattered agate and jasper, further evidence of a rapid elevation in temperature. Finally, the finished arrowheads, harpoon tips and other implements themselves exhibited signs of having been altered or "improved" by heat. Clearly, heat treatment was part of the pressure-flaked stone technology in aboriginal northwestern California, particularly along the coast.

Gould speculated that as well as rendering tough materials such as agate and jasper more susceptible to pressure-flaking through heat treatment, cobbles of agate and jasper may also have been placed in fires for lithic reduction. Most of the usable beach agate and jasper had the form of hard rounded water-worn cobbles and were very difficult to break open by direct percussion with a hammer stone. Repeated efforts by Gould found it almost impossible to form a striking platform (required for

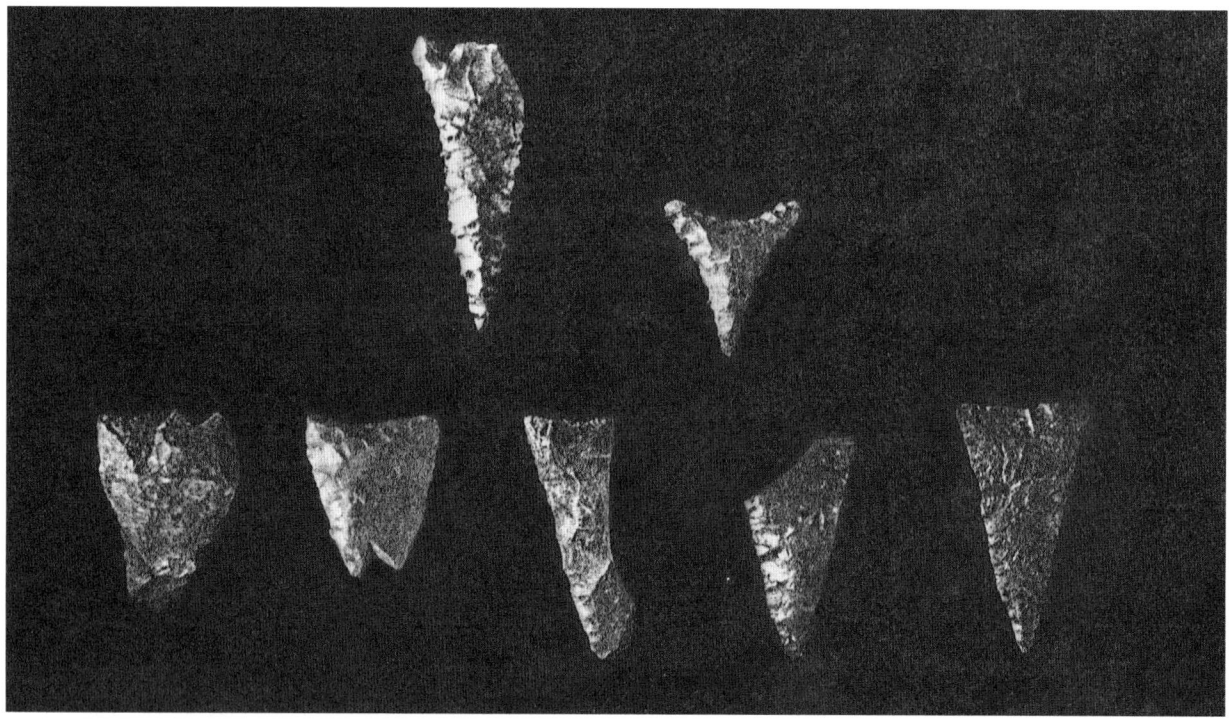

Hypothetical manufacturing sequence for Cottonwood triangular projectile point from initial blank (on far left), which had been chipped from a core, to completed point (on far right). These examples are taken from actual lost or discarded points (probably because of undesirable shape or breakage—note missing corners or tips) from an archaeological workshop site in Afton Canyon, California (Schneider 1989). The Cottonwood style of very simple arrowhead began around A.D. 1000 and continued in use to historic times. Most of those found at Afton Canyon were of local jasper or chalcedony. The Eastgate example (with broken barb, above left), according to some researchers, preceded Cottonwood points in the archaeological record (A.D. 700-1300). "Cottonwood point" may even have been a stage in the production of Eastgate until, through simplification, they gradually became the end product itself. The small point above right is probably a rejuvenated Cottonwood point that had been broken during use. All points above are actual size.

orderly flake removal) by knocking off an end of one of the cobbles. But in fire without a careful effort to control the rate of heating of the cobbles, they shatter (often into useless fragments frequently found in the Point St. George hearths) in some cases into a pot lid flake and its negative, a core with the bulb scar whose angular facet provided the needed striking platform. From these cores, flakes could be struck while the pot lids themselves were left where they fell, unused or retouched, thus perhaps explaining their prevalence at Point St. George. Such a method would have economically produced needed platforms from which heat-treated and therefore superior flakes might have been obtained.

There is some evidence of heat treatment from the other end of California. While no detailed analysis was performed, archaeologist Joan Schneider concluded through visual inspection that chert and jasper artifacts found at an Afton Canyon site in the Mojave Desert had been heat treated. Such treatment produces a change in color and a waxy luster.

The Afton Canyon lithic workshop overlooks the generally dry Mojave River at a point where the river has come from beneath the desert floor and flows year round. Good quarries for chert, jasper and chalcedony are found in the mountains nearby. Thanks to rugged and fairly remote terrain, even today when walking this area, I see raw material and old Indian camps and workshops everywhere.

B.B. Redding's Account

A nineteenth-century description by B.B. Redding preserves in simple words and rich circumstantiality the process of flintknapping. Step by step we experience a California Wintun Indian flaking an arrowhead.

Hupa pressure flaker, antler lashed to crooked handle, collected by Lieutenant P. H. Ray during the 1880s. This was used to make arrowheads from flint or obsidian for war or big game. The ball of the handle would rest in the right palm as the antler pressed on flint held in the palm of the left hand protected by a buckskin pad. According to Ray, the flakes were first knocked from a larger piece with a section of deer antler (piece pictured to the left longitudinally and in cross section). The hard antler was used between the hammer and core as a kind of cold chisel. It detached high quality flakes (Mason, 1894).

He brought, tied up in a deer skin, a piece of obsidian weighing about a pound, a fragment of a deer horn split from a prong lengthwise, about 4 inches in length and 1/2 an inch in diameter, and ground off squarely at the ends—this left each end a semicircle, besides two deer prongs (Cariacus columbianus) with the points ground down into the shape of a square sharp-pointed file, one of these being much smaller than the other. He had also some pieces of iron wire tied to wooden handles and ground into the same shapes. These, he explained, he used in preference to the deer prongs, since white men came to the country, because they were harder and did not require sharpening so frequently. . . . Holding the piece of obsidian in the hollow of the left hand, he placed between the first and second fingers of the same hand the split piece of deer horn first described, the straight edge of the split deer horn resting against about one-fourth of an inch of the edge of the obsidian—this being about the thickness of the flake he desired to split off: then with a small round water-worn stone which he had selected, weighing perhaps a pound, he with his right hand struck the other end of the split deer

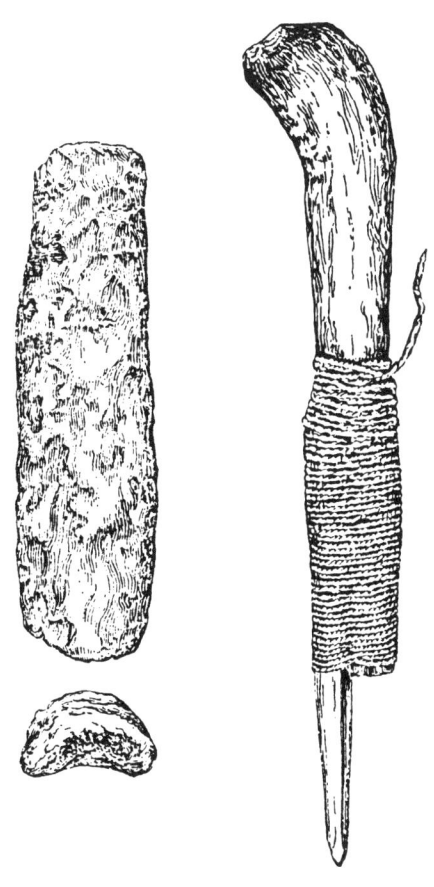

horn a sharp blow. The first attempt resulted in failure. A flake was split off but the blow also shattered the flake at the same time into small fragments. He then repeated the operation, apparently holding the split deer horn more carefully and firmly against the edge of the large piece of obsidian. The next blow was successful. A perfect flake was obtained showing the conchoidal fracture peculiar to obsidian. . . . The shape naturally taken by the obsidian when split off in this manner is that of a spearhead, and it could be put to use, for this purpose, with but slight alteration. The thickness of the flake to be split off depends upon the nearness or distance from the edge of the obsidian on which the straight edge of the split deer horn is held at the time the blow is struck.

    He now squatted on the ground, sitting on his left foot, his right leg extended in a position often assumed by tailors at work. He then placed in the palm of his left hand a piece of thick well-tanned buckskin, evidently made from the skin of the neck of a deer. It was thick but soft and pliable. On this he laid the flake of obsidian, which he held firmly in its place by the first three fingers of the same hand. He then rested the elbow on the left knee, which gave the left arm and hand holding the flake, firm and steady support. He then took in his right hand the larger of the two deer prongs, which, as has been stated, had its point sharpened in the form of a square file, and holding it as an engraver of wood holds his cutting instrument, he commenced reducing one edge of the circular form of the flake to a straight line. With the thumb of the right hand resting on the edge of the left palm as a fulcrum, the point of the deer prong would be made to rest on about 1/8 of an inch or less of the edge of the flake, then with a firm downward pressure of the point, a conchoidal fragment would be broken out almost always of the size desired. The point of the deer prong would then be advanced a short distance and the same

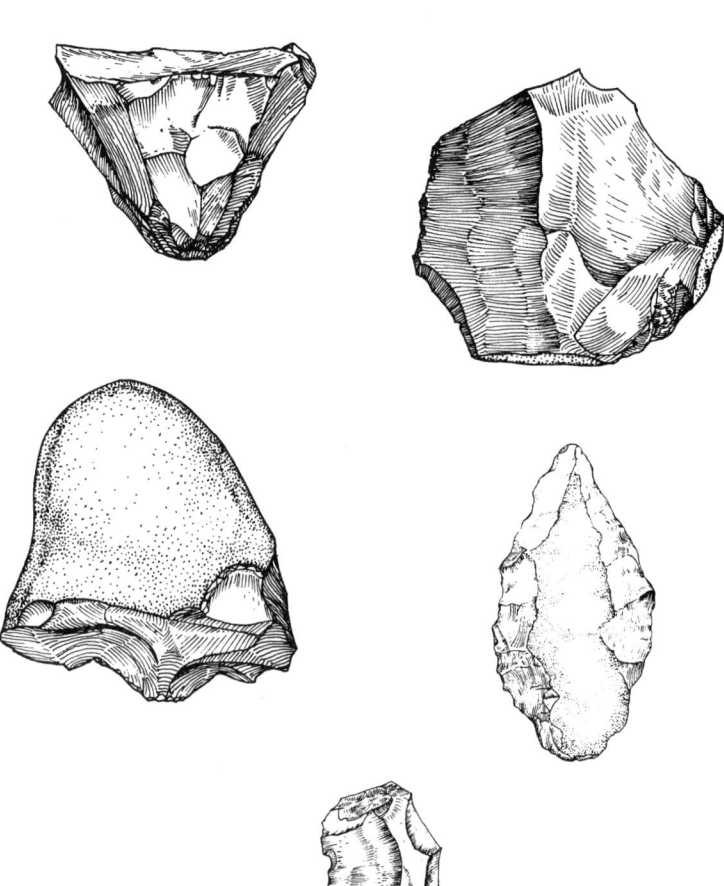

Early San Dieguito artifacts (from left to right and down): crude prepared platform core, cutting flake, chopper, biface "knife" and blade. Size reduced almost 1/2 to 2/3 (Rogers, 1966).

operation repeated, until in a few minutes the flake was reduced to a straight line on one edge. As this operation broke all the chips from the under side of the flake, if left in this condition the arrowhead would be unequally proportioned, that is, the two cutting edges would not be in the center. He therefore with the side of the deer horn firmly rubbed back and forth the straight edge he had made on the flake until the sharp edge had been broken and worn down. The flake was now turned end for end in the palm of his hand and the chipping renewed. When completed an equal amount was taken from each side of the edge of the flake and the cutting edge was left in the center. It was now plain that the straight edge thus made was to be one side of the long isosceles triangle, the form of the arrowheads which is used by his tribe.

With the flake of obsidian firmly held in the cushion of the left palm and the point of deer horn strongly pressed on the edge of the flake, the effect was the same as the blow which split the flake from the larger piece. While, however, he was not always sure of the effect of the blow in splitting off the large flakes out of which to make the arrowheads, he in no instance appeared to fail in breaking out with the point of deer-prong the exact piece desired. The soft thick pliable piece of tanned deer skin on which the flake in his left palm was held, may have added to the cushion, but seemed to serve no other purpose than to save his hand from being cut by the countless sharp chips as they were broken off. One of the long sides of the arrowhead having been thus formed, the flake was turned over and the other side formed in the same manner. As, however, very much more of the obsidian had to be chipped away, he brought more pressure upon the point and broke out larger chips until the flake began to assume the shape desired, when the same care was exercised as when the first straight edge was made. In breaking out large or small chips the process was always the same. The pressure of the point of deer horn on the upper edge of the flake never

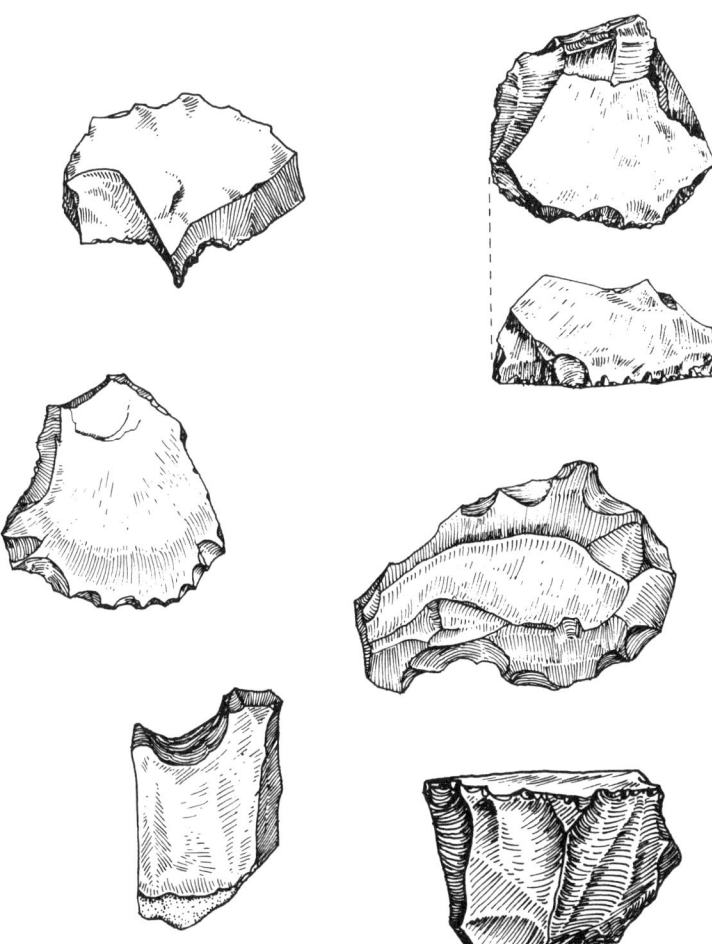

More early San Dieguito artifacts: graver, pulping plane, convex scraper, concave scraper and combination scraper. Last is a rare prepared platform core, 2/3 actual size, from later San Dieguito phases when andesite and to a lesser extent, quartzite continued in use, but basalt, jasper and chalcedony also came to be employed. (Additional early and later examples of San Dieguito stone artifacts can be found in Malcolm J. Rogers' Ancient Hunters of the Far West, *1966.)*

appeared to break out a piece, which, on the upper side, reached beyond where the point rested, while on the under side the chip broken out might leave a space of twice the distance. Invariably when a line of these chips had been broken out the sharp edge was rubbed down, the flake turned end for end and the chipping renewed on the other side. By this process the cutting edges of the arrowhead were kept in the same line. The base was formed in the same manner. . . .

The chipping out of . . . (the side notches) . . . was the last operation to be performed. It seemed to me more difficult than any other part of the work, and I thought that in this would be the danger of the loss of all the patient labor that had been expended. In practical operation it was the simplest, safest and most rapid of all his work. He now held the point of the well-shaped arrowhead between the thumb and first finger of his left hand with the edge of the arrowhead upwards, the base resting edgewise on the deer-skin cushion in the palm. He then used the smaller deer prong, which had been sharpened in the same form as the larger one, but all its proportions, in every respect, were very much smaller; its point could not have been larger than one sixteenth of an inch square. He rested this point on the edge of the arrowhead where he desired to make the slot, and commenced sawing back and forth with a rocking motion, the fine chips flew from each side, the point of the deer horn descended, and in less than a minute the slot was cut. The arrowhead was turned over and the same operation repeated on the other edge. It seemed that by this process, if he desired, the arrowhead could have been cut in two in a very few minutes. He now examined his work in the strong sunlight and, being satisfied, handed me the completed arrowhead. It had taken him forty minutes to split the two flakes from the large piece of obsidian and chip one of them into the arrowhead. A younger man, equally expert, would probably have done the work in half an hour.

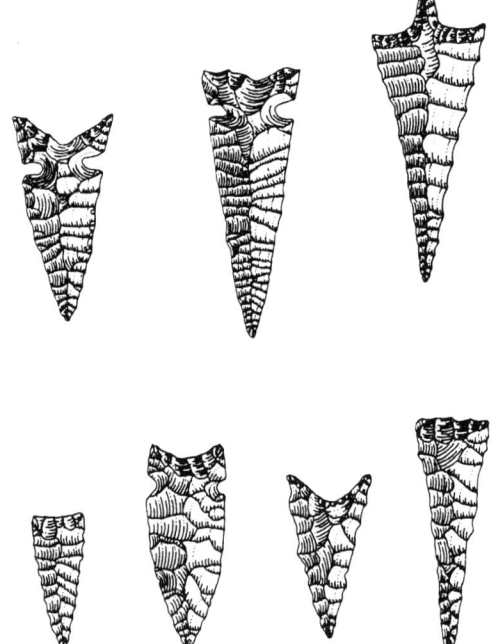

California arrowheads. Top row: from foothills of southern Cascades near Oroville (including Yahi territory), about 3/4 scale, before A.D. 1000. Point on left is desert side-notched style. Bottom row: arrow points from coastal southern California and offshore islands, about 3/4 scale, from A.D. 500 until European contact. (All of these and many other stone artifacts are found in Joseph and Kerry Chartkoff's The Archaeology of California, *1984.)*

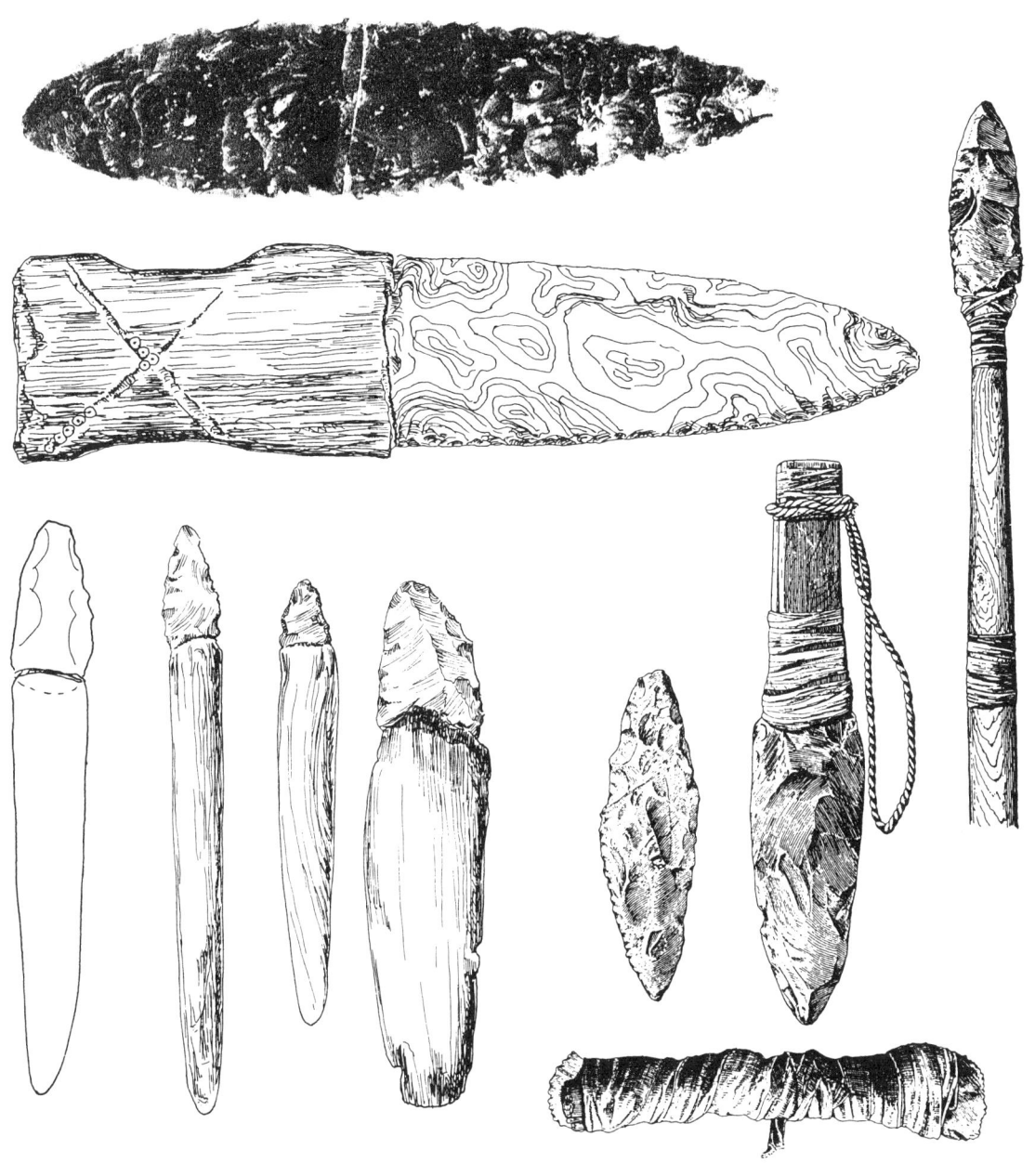

Knives, spears and scrapers. Top: archaic coastal southern California stone knife with serrated edges from Topanga Canyon, about 3/5 scale (in Treganza, 1958). Below: blade of chert hafted with asphaltum, handle decorated in shell bead inlay; found on beach in Long Beach area, possibly washed ashore in 1934; 26 cm. in length (sketched by Georgia Lee; Hudson, 1987). Left: Chumash knife from San Nicolas Island, around 7" in length, redwood handle, gray flinty shale blade attached with asphaltum (collected by De Cessac, sketched by Georgia Lee; Hudson 1987). Next three: Chumash knives found on Santa Barbara and Santa Cruz islands in the 1870s (collected by Schumacher, sketched by Lee; Hudson, 1987). Maidu knives and spear of black basalt; knife points, 11 cm. and 17 cm.; spear point, 16 cm. Knife handle is made from two pieces of wood, lashed and pitched. Spear point inserted in shaft, wrapped with sinew and heavily pitched (Dixon, 1905). Bottom: serrated stone scrapers hafted at either end of wooden handle. In use, they were drawn toward the body; Maidu (Dixon, 1905).

Glue

Native Californians tied their world together, then for additional reliability they glued it as well. Glues of representative tribes are surveyed in the following sample.

Karok Glue

Schenck and Gifford described the Karok glues used to hold sinew to the wide-limbed northern bow. The back of the bow was first dressed with the gum of the chokecherry. Then salmonskin glue and the first layer of sinew were applied. In making the salmonskin adhesive, the first step was to take a descaled, dried skin of salmon (one informant suggested only a Chinook salmon, another the skin of sturgeon—this would have had to have been the inner side of the skin because of the large plates outside) and scrape it fine. Thus prepared, it was chewed for a long time and then spit into a small "cup" made from a single madrone leaf (maple leaves were used in a fable recorded by Kroeber). A glandular substance from the throat of the sturgeon was chewed and added to the chewed skin. (J. P. Harrington found the gums of the fir and "wild plum" substituted for the chewed sturgeon throat gland in Karok glue.) The cup was placed among young protective leaves of a madrone branch and the branch placed in the warm ashes of a fire—not the hot coals—to cure into glue. Special care had to be exercised to keep ashes out of the glue or it would fail to stick. Old glue could be softened with water.

The Pomo made a variation of this sort of glue by mixing pulverized fish skin with juice from the bulb of the soaproot (and presumably heating the mixture) to secure sinew to the back of a bow and to add red-headed woodpecker scalp decorations. The Miwok roasted the soaproot bulb, and sucking the juice from it, employed this alone as a glue for sinew backing of a bow. Harrington learned that the Chimariko would sometimes pound Indian potato with soaproot and dried salmon skin, soak the mixture in warm water, add raw pitch from any tree, then boil all four ingredients together to make glue. To back the bow they soaked sinew from any part of the deer and shredded it; pieces as small as 2 inches long could be used. They dipped the shreds in the glue and applied them to the back of the bow. When the layer of sinew was thick, they finished the backing with a coat of salmonskin glue sopped on with a little grass found growing in wet areas. Strips of a "money" snake skin were sometimes dipped in the glue and applied as decorative rings around the bow, as human blood sometimes banded their arrows. Bands of the glued snake skin also went around the recurved tips of the bow.

Western chokecherry gum was further utilized by the Karok to hold 4-inch western serviceberry *(Amelanchier alnifolia)* points in the ends of syringa arrow shafts. The joint was bound with sinew and smeared with chokecherry gum. In addition the gum served as a base for applying larkspur *(Delphinium decorum)* paint to bows and arrows. Schenck and Gifford recorded they made the gum into a ball, stuck it on the end of a stick, heated it a little in a fire and rubbed it on the parts of the bow or arrow to be painted. The blue-purple flowers of the larkspur had been pounded in a small stone mortar or small round hole in a boulder and mixed with salmon glue and fresh mountain grape *(Berberis aquifolium)* berries. The result was painted on the arrows or bows in various designs.

Besides these, the Karok applied the pitch of the sugar pine *(Pinus lambertiana)* as an adhesive, the same sap, noted Schenck and Gifford, that when coagulated in a hollow tree was eaten without preparation or mixing with other foods as "sugar." Kroeber recorded their neighbors the Yurok plugged knotholes of dugouts with pine pitch and cracks were calked and pitched, and if serious, also held together with lashings. Farther south, the Kashaya Pomo used the pitch of the Douglas fir *(Pseudotsuga menziesii)* as glue, Goodrich observed.

Paiute Pine Pitch

Margaret Wheat witnessed Johnny Dunn, scion of a much noted Paiute family of Pyramid Lake fishermen, make a harpoon. Part of the process entailed the melting of pine pitch for glue. He built a tiny fire of chips and twigs and held a small amount of pitch on a stick near the fire. When the pitch melted, he added bits of charcoal to it and ground the mixture together between two rocks. The charcoal increased the hardness of the pitch. For use the pitch was reheated and daubed on with a small stick. It kept a string from sliding off the bone point to which it had been tied. As the pitch cooled he smoothed out any roughness with his fingers.

Chumash Asphaltum

The Chumash reversed the process. They added pitch to a carbonaceous substance, to asphaltum, naturally occurring tar which oozes from the ground even to this day in many areas of the old Chumash country. They called it *woqo*, which meant "hard tar," and this was the form they sought. Soft tar, or *malak*, was not used as glue.

Fernando Librado, the Chumash elder who remembered so well the old ways when Harrington interviewed him in the early years of the twentieth century, told how they formed woqo into cakes with their hands. They would trade these cakes with islanders for steatite from which cooking pots, trinket bowls or arrow straighteners could be made. For use, tarring a *tomol* (plank canoe) for example, they pounded the hard tar and mashed it well removing all the stone debris that otherwise would prevent its sticking. The crushed tar they boiled in an olla. Then finely powdered pitch was added. They had collected the pitch in the mountains to the north when they went for piñon nuts. Any pitch they saw, hard lumps and doughy lumps, they would gather in carrying sacks of Indian hemp. They used it for anything of wood that required an adhesive. Librado said Palatino added "two double handfuls" of pitch to a large olla after a half-full measure of woqo had melted. He stirred it briskly as one would acorn mush until it all dissolved. Felipe, Librado continued, used no pitch in the tar for his canoe, but he boiled the woqo for a long time to thicken it enough to hold the boards. Librado recounted that in general they always used more woqo than pitch in the mixture they called *yop*. Sometimes crushed woqo and crushed pitch were mixed before boiling to make yop.

Usually yop was used as it was but Librado saw Palatino add red ochre to a caulking tar for a finished canoe. Librado said they also added red ochre to yop to make paint for the tomol and some of its accessories. In the 1770s Pedro Font had recorded all tomols were painted red with hematite.

Tubatulabal Glue, Pitch and Asphaltum

The Tubatulabal visited the Chumash to obtain asphaltum and the Chumash from Ventura brought lumps of asphalt when they came up to trade with the Tubatulabal for piñon nuts. The Tubatulabal, recorded Voegelin, melted it and applied it with a small stick to attach prongs to harpoon shafts, bone points to fishhook shafts, foreshafts to cane arrows, arrowheads into foreshafts, knife blades to handles and basket hoppers to mortars. They smeared it over fish lines and from asphaltum they made knob handles for bone or cactus spine awls.

Gray pine pitch *(Pinus sabiniana)* the Tubatulabal smeared over the soles of moccasins so they would wear longer. Jeffrey pine pitch *(Pinus jeffreyi)* was put on torches for quail hunting. A lump of piñon pine pitch *(Pinus monophylla)* together with a handful of red earth and a quantity of heated rocks, each the size of a thumb, were shaken vigorously in a basketry water bottle for five to ten minutes to coat and waterproof the inside. The red earth was said to make the water taste sweet; pitch alone made it bitter. Over the outside they daubed hot pitch with a small stick. After it had cooled slightly red earth mixed with a little water was rubbed into the pitch.

Gum from greasewood *(Adenostoma fasciculatum)* filled the walnut-shell dice.

Glue to fasten sinew to the back of bows was made by boiling deer antlers in a small quantity of water. The Wobonuch Western Mono recipe for this included sinew with the bits of deer antler; the two were boiled together. It made an especially clear glue.

A Kawaiisu Sealant and Adhesive

Only the pitch from the single leaf piñon *(Pinus monophylla)* could waterproof a basketry water bottle, thought the Kawaiisu. Any other would crack away. They applied it hot inside and outside. A red powdered paint was applied by hand to the bottle.

Hupa glue stick: wood stick with daub of glue at one end. Tool of the arrow maker. Collected by P. H. Ray over 100 years ago (Mason, 1889).

Similar to a substance left on creosote bush, insects deposit a tar-like lac on sagebrush *(Artemisia tridentata)* which, according to Zigmond, the Kawaiisu formed into a ball and softened at the fire. It could be molded into an awl or knife handle. The awl needle, used for making coiled basketry, was made from the spine of a Mojave mound cactus *(Echinocactus polycephalus)*. Others found that the sagebrush lac had held knives set in wooden handles or bone awls in their handles.

Cahuilla Gums and Adhesives

The Cahuilla collected the gum of a scale insect from chamise, or greasewood *(Adenostoma fasciculatum)*, to fix arrow points to shafts, baskets to mortars and for other binding needs, reported Bean and Saubel. Sparkman had found it used as well by the Luiseño. The creosote bush *(Larrea divaricata)* yielded lac, a dark amber-colored gum deposited on the branches by a small scale insect. It also served the Cahuilla as glue, Barrows observed.

Bean and Saubel identified a species of milkweed *(Asclepias syriaca)* as a Cahuilla adhesive. Barrows noted they collected the white sap of the narrow leaved milkweed *(Asclepias fascicularis)* for the same purpose.

The branches of honey mesquite *(Prosopis glandulosa)* exude a gum also utilized by the Cahuilla. Its adhesive qualities held a fire-hardened foreshaft of mesquite in the socket of a cane mainshaft for example. The pitch of the single leaf piñon was used as well. The Cahuilla also applied asphaltum as pitch or for caulking.

Stalking

Stalking was not so much a skill as an unfolding of character. It began with organization, cooperation and respect—respect born of a sense of closeness, an identity with the animal. Nearly eighty years ago Paul-Louis Faye related of the Southern Maidu:

When the people went out hunting for rabbit they selected one of their number as head hunter. He was responsible for the conduct of operations and they obeyed him. They also took one with them who acted as a luck-bringer. . . . The head hunter and the other hunters planned the hunt. It was necessary for them to speak in a whisper lest the rabbits hear them. When the first rabbit was killed the head hunter picked it up, and, pressing it tenderly against his chest, petted it and spoke soft words to it. All the hunters sighed while he was going through this performance. . . . No food should be carried on a hunting expedition. The meat, however little was caught, was divided equally among all the hunters.

Sam Garfield, of the Wukchumni and the Yaudanchi Yokuts, told Gayton of the great respect shown deer when they were killed. A hunter would tell the deer he wanted him to rise in three days. An ordinary man (without special dream power) would just say he was sorry he had killed the deer. Jim Britches, a Wukchumni, spoke of his Patwisha father-in-law, Ha'nyash, whose dream helper was deer. Ha'nyash supplied deer meat to large gatherings. He was a fine hunter. He too ate the meat of deer but abstained from it for three days after killing one. He spoke to the animal he was about to kill: "I am going to kill you. These people are going to eat you. I kill you every year."

In the first world, the Yokuts believed, Deer had been a quiet man who neither talked nor traveled. But when the time came for his transformation into an animal, Eagle warned, "All your body will be worth something although it isn't everybody who will be able to kill you." The next morning, Deer ran from his home and made a big cave to live in. The day following, thousands of deer joined him. On the third day three hunters—Cougar, Elk and Spotted Cat—came to kill Deer. Coyote interfered and caught a deer himself. The other deer became angry and ran but Cougar, the best hunter, was able to kill some of them. Deer himself still lives back in this cave. When a deer is killed it goes there. Big Deer has put an arrow up in the cave. When the right sort of person kills a deer respectfully, the arrow holds fast. But a careless hunter can expect the arrow to fall and kill him within a month.

Disguised in the skin and head of a deer, a cluster of pine stems for antlers, on all fours and head sidewise like a buck, the Miwok hunter sometimes lured a real enraged buck so close he could stab it with a sharpened staff of mountain mahogany. The Wukchumni Yokuts removed the deerskin whole for the deer disguise. They cut the legs lengthwise on the inside and made a ventral cut from the crotch to the chin. As the skin was worked off, it temporarily turned inside out. The antlers came with the skin for the disguise. To make the disguise, the cut under the throat was sewn back up and the head and neck stuffed with shredded tule. The head rested on the hunter's head and the skin was draped over his back. Bow and arrows were secured to the body with a belt pushing the skin up at the back to make a more deer-like appearance. The hunter held and leaned on two short sticks as he imitated the walk of the deer. From time to time he would crack them together making the sound of antlers in combat. The Yokuts estimated the disguise could generally bring a hunter to within 20 feet of grazing deer.

Petroglyph from Renegade Canyon, Coso Range, California

Aside from supplying needed protein, fat and a useful hide, stalking a wild creature thrills like nothing else. I felt I touched the Mountain Sheep Spirit herself the first time high in a remote region of the San Gabriels I crept within yards of a family of mountain sheep watering at a small pool. My boot dislodged some pebbles. They turned as one, saw me, then bolted into the chaparral. Moments later they picked their way up a secret sinuous cliff trail. Many animals in Nature, particularly animals hunted for food, have evolved acute senses of smell, hearing and sight. The stalking Indian countered this hypersensitivity by becoming odorless, soundless and invisible. He exhibited great patience, knowledge of animal ways and, perhaps most important, respect for the animal as an equal, as something akin to himself. At times he even pretended to be the animal he hunted or to become its prey, drawing the animal to him for an easy silent shot with bow and arrow.

Indian archery was close-range and depended on approaching the quarry unseen or on tricking or driving the animal within the killing field of the bow. Clavigero in his history of California published in 1789 extolled the perspicacity of the Californians in scanning and following the tracks of animals. (He further admired their infallibility in identifying the tracks made by barefooted fellow tribesmen.) Michelsen found tracking to be a highly developed skill among the Kiliwa. Two or more men tracked deer. They broke off the chase as they approached the daytime bedding area. One or two hid beside the trail while another circled above or beyond the deer. Then by shouting or setting fire to the brush the hunter frightened the deer in the direction of the trail sitters, who hearing the commotion got ready to ambush the startled deer, escaping back down the trail at close and lethal range.

Many of these skills can be taught. I have scoured the early records for Indian techniques. The Monache or Western Mono, for example, knew brown bear were difficult to approach as they ate; they were suspicious. Grizzlies, on the other hand, paid attention only to eating, but the hunter still had to be aware of the wind. They also knew that for a lone tracker to take a bear, the bear must be hit behind the shoulder on the first shot or the bear would attack and kill the hunter. But there was much more, and Indian knowledge of specific animals has been largely lost. We might compensate by gaining familiarity with modern studies of wildlife through universities or in societies such as the Audubon or Wilderness or by joining the Sierra Club. We might go to the woods alone to be with the animals and learn their behavior, tracks and signs. Combined with the values described and techniques that follow, we might approach the hunter ideal. But there were qualities of character not so easily gained.

To strengthen the hunter and increase his courage before a hunt, the Yahi drew blood with small flakes of obsidian; they cut the flexor side of forearm and calf. I suppose this might have served to desensitize the squeamish. Approaching, killing and flaying a large buck in the wild is not for the faint of heart. Courageous must be the stalker of wild beasts.

Finally, all of the values, the character traits, the bits and pieces of knowledge, were integrated into a whole hunter. The Diegueño hunter tested his grandson with bow and arrow on rats before teaching him about rabbits and only the boy of exceptional promise would become a hunter of large game. He would learn not only practical skills and animal habits but star lore, rituals, calendrics, mythology, songs and appropriate hunter behavior toward people and animals. Sharing game was important: the ideal hunter looked on proudly as others ate his kill. Hunters became either trackers or trail-sitters. In their mythology the three stars of Orion represented Mountain Sheep which were trailed by the hunter, a bright star to the east. Two other stars were the trail sitters. Before the hunt, the Diegueño hunter fasted, taking only a thin gruel, contemplated his dreams and, as with all Indians, avoided women. He was focused. He was ready.

Becoming Invisible

He must not be odoriferous. To cleanse the sweat glands and eliminate human odor, the Cahuilla hunter of southern California crushed fresh leaves of the white sage and put them in his armpits before retiring. Game could not catch his scent the next day. Similarly, when the Chimariko hunter of northern California laid in ambush near a salt lick or spring, he smeared his bow and arrows with *yerba buena* (mint) to mask the human odor from the deer. Ishi, the last of the wilderness-bound Yahi, would not eat fish the day before since deer could detect the odor. He also avoided tobacco smoke and on the morning of the hunt, he bathed from head to toe, washed his mouth and ate no food. (It is interesting to note that the Salinans of the coast chewed tobacco on approaching game in the belief this would stupefy it.)

Ishi always approached game downwind. Pope, who frequently observed him on the hunt, described the rule as almost an obsession. Ishi would skirt an entire mountain to avoid approaching an animal on the wind side. By wetting his little finger (likely the least callused) he found the direction of the wind. The Salinans followed the same rule, approaching deer on the leeward side, and dropped a little dirt to tell which way the wind blew.

Equal concern was accorded sound and sight. Ishi dressed only in a long shirt or breechclout. Pope recorded the reason:

Any covering on the legs made a noise while in the brush, and a sensitive skin rather favored cautious walking. While Ishi was proud of his shoes acquired in civilization, he said they made a noise like a horse, and he immediately discarded them when any real work in the field was encountered. In climbing cliffs, or crossing streams or trunks of trees, he first removed his shoes. So in hunting he preferred to go barefoot, and the strength of his perfectly shaped feet gave him a very definite advantage over his civilized companions.

For small game, such as quail, squirrels and rabbits, Ishi's "method was that of still hunting: walking over the ground very quiet and alert, always paying particular attention to wind, noise and cover."

In hunting deer Ishi employed the ambush, hiding behind rocks or bushes near deer trails while others beat the brush from a mile or so away to drive the deer to him. He showed Pope ancient piles of rocks the Indians had constructed on old deer trails, just large enough to hide a crouching hunter. The Miwok hunter sometimes concealed himself in a pit beside a deer trail. He hid under boughs and when deer passed to the watering hole at night, he rose up and with his bow shot the animal. Another Miwok means of becoming invisible to deer or antelope was to completely cover the body with the vine of the wild cucumber.

Ishi stalked tirelessly and rarely left a spot where he suspected game until everything had been tried. He was always alert and the first to sight the quarry. He would occasionally shoot arrows into rabbits which were on the run but he shot most game standing still, generally at 10 to 20 yards.

Tom Brown, Jr. has written of the Indian method of silent walking. His mentor was Stalking Wolf, an old Apache scout. The stalker, writes Brown, only moves when the air or an animal moves or bird song can be heard. When there is silence or the animal such as a grazing buck lifts its head to look, the stalker freezes and holds his breath. As the animal lowers its head to graze again, the hunter again approaches, having positioned himself so his shadow falls behind him. He lifts his knees high and places each footfall carefully, the outer edge of the ball lightly touching the ground to find the stone or twig before the full weight descends. Should the foot sense an obstruction, the stalker compensates with a shift of foot or weight. Otherwise, his step proceeds and weight rolls slowly forward and toward the arch.

What if a stalked deer or jackrabbit suddenly saw the hunter? The Seri Indian of Tiburón Island in the Gulf of California would distract or lull it into resuming to feed by twisting or rotating his bow back and forth before him, hypnotically like a wand.

The Miwok hunter was a trail sitter at night when deer become active and are on the move. Conversely, we should understand not to be a trail sitter during the middle portion of the day when deer rest in a thicket or bed of grass or browse nearby. At such times it would generally make more sense for the tracker to be on the move. Benito Peralta (a Paipai whose memory stretches back to a time when old women exhibited facial tattoos and boys became men when the septums of their noses were pierced for shell pendants) tracks deer over light snow. He follows the tracks and when he sees they are fresh, goes very slowly, quietly. If he reaches a hill which a deer has ascended, he does not follow in the deer's tracks but goes up by another route. Deer expect to be followed and will stop and look where they have gone. He continues to go slowly, noticing areas below the rocks, under branches, where the deer might have stopped or be lying. Deer have extremely sensitive hearing so you cannot touch even a twig. When the ears and tail stop moving it means they have heard you.

As Peralta and a few Paipai men recounted stories of deer hunting, I realized how keenly they appreciated the habits and cleverness of deer. They would sometimes follow deer tracks only to realize the deer had circled back and was watching them follow him. The deer constantly turns to look for anyone in pursuit. Sometimes the trail would end in an area of cover and they knew the deer must be nearby. If the air was still and the deer could not smell them and they kept quiet, they had a chance. A raspy unvoiced snort between constricted tongue, pallet and lips might bring him out for a look and give the hunter a shot. Or a rock cast beyond where they suspected the deer to be hiding might fool the deer to come toward the hunter.

Calling the Animal

Ishi called game to him. Hiding behind a bush in country suitable to rabbits, Ishi pressed two fingers against his lips and made a kissing sound, shrill and plaintive, like a rabbit in distress, repeatedly. He told Pope that jackrabbits, wildcats, coyotes and bears would respond; the rabbit to protect young, the others to eat. Pope had to see for himself:

Upon one afternoon's hunt, to test the truth of his assertions, I had Ishi repeat this call twelve times. From these dozen calls came five rabbits, and one wildcat emerged from the brush and approached us. Some rabbits came from a distance of 150 yards, and approached within 10 yards. The wildcat came within 50 yards, and permitted me to discharge five arrows at him before a glancing hit sent him into the forest.

As the game drew near, Ishi kept up a sucking sort of kiss with his lips while he adjusted an arrow on the bow. When the game was within a dozen yards, he shot.

For calling doe with fawns, a new, tender madrone leaf folded lengthwise was placed between his lips. He then sucked vigorously to render the bleat of a fawn. The Seri blew through the leaf of the ashy limber bush for the same effect. To attract deer the Western Mono hunter hit the antlers of his disguise with a stick. Likely, this would have simulated a dual over females and attracted bucks to the imagined fray.

Chasing the Quarry

There were other less subtle, less invisible methods. The Miwok occasionally drove deer over cliffs or ran them down. A large buck might be followed all day. After a night's sleep the tracker would likely overtake his quarry by that afternoon. Good runners could run down a deer in a single day. Western Mono explained that a pursued deer gets hot and his fat melts and chokes him. Deer do not have the endurance of a well-conditioned hunter.

The Seri would try and locate deer as they rested during the heat of a summertime day for an easy shot with an arrow or catch them swimming near shore and club them from a boat. The spread hooves of pregnant doe the Seri hunter recognized and tracked until the doe tired and could be dispatched at close range.

Contrary to the usual rule of not exerting oneself in the heat of a hot day, the advice of Paiyo'n, the oldest Diegueño at Campo in 1923, held that this was the best time to chase a wounded buck because it would become exhausted more quickly. He also suggested shooting a buck with spreading antlers, not straight, because the brush would slow its flight. In the Sierra San Pedro Mártir the Kiliwa ran down deer and slayed them with war clubs. They chased down old bucks late in the summer when the animals had become fat. According to Michelsen, this was the only time they attempted to run down deer, and then only during the middle of the day when the heat was intense—only then did a man have more stamina than the deer.

The Whole Hunter

Lonnie Bill's words on the stalking of deer as recorded by Bev Ortiz in 1992 bring the ancient pursuit into modern American terms.

I use the number one rule. I just walk really slow once I get to know where they're at. And it's like all my senses—my smelling, my hearing, my sight—just jump up another notch. It gets to where I can smell them. . . . Once in a while you catch just the slightest smell, and you know he's there somewhere. So you kick back and wait, and see where the wind goes. . . . If the wind's blowing down hill, I'll work my way up to him. . . . If it's blowing up, I'll try to keep low or rub some of this [wormwood] on me, or bay leaf. Whatever is close by. I'll just rub it on me and kill the scent. . . . And if he doesn't catch me, I'll catch him.

Lonnie Bill, a modern Mono Indian, learned the old ways while watching his grandfather feather arrows and flake arrowheads. He learned that if you shoot something, you track it down, even if it is only a leg wound and takes two days—that's the law. His grandmother taught him that what you shoot, you eat. By killing an animal, you take away his purpose in life and must give him a new purpose: to feed or clothe man. Parts not used are given to brother coyote who needs to eat too and may one day return the favor by flushing rabbits for the hunter.

In the end, of course, stalking was not entirely a practical matter. Tubatulabal hunters usually went to the mountains in groups of three or four because of fear of White Coyote. A single hunter alone at night in the mountains did not even dare build a fire lest White Coyote find and kill him. Before the hunt an old man who knew the songs sang all night for the hunters. They left about two or three in the morning. And when they got up in the mountains they sat down, probably with a good vantage, and looked for deer. After a short while, if none were seen, a little spot was cleaned and smoothed, and tobacco, beads, and eagle down were presented there to the mountains. Then they saw deer right away, Steban Miranda told Voegelin when he was interviewed on the South Fork of the Kern in the 1930s.

Nearly ninety at the time, he added that sometimes they just offered eagle down. Not many today carry beads and eagle down, but a little tobacco might work: a small gift to the mountains for the bounty they give.

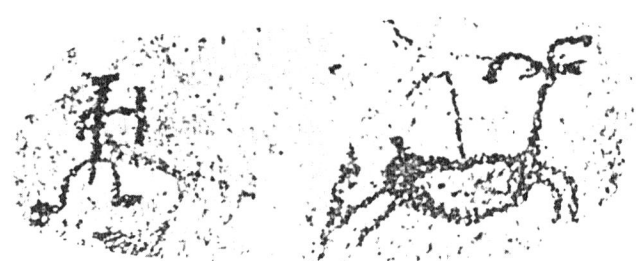

How To Stalk, Kill and Eat a White-throated Woodrat

I suppose the gap between the lean self-reliant hunter-gatherer and the rest of us has been widening since the beginning of the Neolithic. But never had the chasm seemed more profoundly unbridgeable to me than after a trek into the high desert of the Sierra Juárez with Kiliwa Indian Sam Ochurte in late 1995. In a single day Ochurte redefined forever my idea of a true man. Ochurte would have been standard in the Californias of two hundred years ago. Before pudgy, silk-suited money-changers, before the white man's museum boutique Indian, in short, before the fall of the California paradise, men were men and Ochurte had learned well from his father Rufino what that meant.

He rose at sunrise on remote Rancho Agua Colorada where he lives with his sons, daughters and grandchildren. The pleasing acridity of hearth fires spiced the cold clear morning air. Only the ululation of coyotes had broken the silence of a perfect night's sleep. He readied the necessary weapons: bow and arrows and a sharp pointed mesquite pole about 4 feet long with a diameter of around one 1-1/4 inches. Near the unpointed end of the pole which had been "split" with a small V carved into it, he had also carved, about 8 inches apart, two encircling grooves each perhaps 1/8 of an inch across by another 1/8 inch deep. These he explained as improving the grip, but another two grooves a few inches apart near the point, similar to the first, he admitted were purely for decoration. He sharpened the hardwood points of his arrows, pulling the knife toward him in slow even strokes.

The Hunt

We set out from the rancho with his son Catarino Ochurte Espinoza, who carried the bow and arrows, and a grandson who would learn much that day from his grandfather. We followed old trails into the desert chaparral, through chamise, mesquite, nopal, scrub oak, manzanita, cholla and juniper. No one carried water or other provisions. Sam Ochurte, around seventy years old, thin and wiry, walked with the agility, alertness and endurance of a man much younger. When he thirsted, he stopped for a moment and knocked a nopal fruit to the ground. He brushed it with a small, low-growing broom-like bush, plucked nearby, until the fruit was free of spines. Some spines were large and many nearly invisible. All were bothersome if not removed. Beginning at the narrow end opposite from which it grew, he then safely peeled the thin skin away with his fingers revealing the bright succulent red pulp beneath. The flavor was like a sweet, rich watermelon. He spit out the hard seeds in a single exhalation and continued the march. Other sources of water and food were pointed out as we went along.

The white-throated woodrat (*Neotoma albigula*) and related species build dome houses of sticks, cacti and anything else available—including horse dung—under a large shrub or beneath a prickly-pear cactus plant, which also forms a large part of its diet. Sometimes an underground chamber is built. Only one adult resides in each house, usually in a nest in the center on the ground where it passes the daylight hours. These desert woodrats weigh from five to ten ounces.

The party spread out in a search for nests. It was early November, the Mexican Day of the Dead. Ochurte said it was a good time to hunt; spring would not have been good for woodrat mothers were with young at that time and to kill them would affect the entire local population of woodrats. It was important to think of such things said Ochurte.

We soon found a nest. Ochurte approached slowly and quietly though the others continued to talk. He told them where the entrances or runs into the nest were located. These were where the rat would likely exit when disturbed. His son positioned himself near the runs with bow and arrow at the ready. Sometimes a shot would be possible as the rat poked out its head. His grandson and I took up positions on the other sides of the nest. Ochurte from the side opposite the entrance began his probe with the long pointed mesquite stick. He stabbed it in firmly, through all the branches and debris to the bottom of the nest. As in everything he was unhurried and methodical covering all parts of the nest repeatedly. He whispered a soft "ooosh" in an attempt to stir the rat.

This woodrat nest, as many that day, proved to be empty. Ochurte declared it old, noting the signs and the lack of fresh nibble marks on the prickly-pear cactus that surrounded it together with the failure to find fresh cactus fruit in the entry ways. In other cases where a rat could not be roused, Ochurte explained the rat had probably built an underground chamber where he was hiding.

Southern Diegueño Andres Albáñez and his family of Santa Catarina told me how to catch a woodrat. Two people would go to the nest, one armed with a special forked pole, the other with bow and arrow. The one with the pole would probe the wooden pile nest. The fork on the end might locate the rat and with a few hard twists would bind the rat to the pole with its own fur—at least that was how

Setting out, prodding with the rat pole, stalking with bow and arrow, the animal corralled in clump of cactus.

the pole was used for rabbits in their burrows. More likely the pole would simply dislodge the woodrat and the archer would then shoot it as the rat emerged from its pile of sticks.

Wheat found that the Northern Paiute used a rat or a rodent stick to thrust into burrows and if they struck the quarry, they twisted it into the fur and pulled the critter from the hole. If the animal bit at the stick, they impaled it. A desirable husband was one who returned at night with a dozen or more rodents hanging from the thong around his waist.

Michelsen spent many hours with Sam Ochurte and his father Rufino wandering the Baja wilderness thirty years ago. Michelsen told me just before his death in 1996 that woodrat hunting among the Kiliwa was often an informal undertaking, a quick survival method he had seen many times while on the move through the desert. In such a case any makeshift stick served as a rat stick and once the rat was on the run, feet and stones substituted for the bow and arrow of more formal hunts.

From one nest a rat was finally set running—a small streak of white and gray easily missed by the unwatchful eye. It took momentary refuge under a nearby bush that we surrounded in an attempt to corral the little animal. It had gone past Catarino before he had a chance to shoot. Catarino now approached with a nocked arrow increasing tension on his bowstring. This was a most delicate stage. Those participating in the corral had to be hypervigilant and keep the rat within the circle of hunters. One had to quickly scurry faster than the rat to get in front of it and block it should a run be attempted and they often were. Then those reforming the circle around the rat had to come in slow and just close enough to keep the rat frozen in position but not so close as to set him off again. Any quick movement would also incite the animal to run. The rat's strategy was to streak to the nearest clump of bushes or cacti and freeze, hoping to remain unseen. As Catarino drew back his arrow, he continued to approach the rat—to within a yard—too close for this rat who took off again in a mad dash, hunters in pursuit. After two or three such stops and starts the rat had come full circle and was back in his nest. When further probes failed to dislodge him, Sam Ochurte set the nest ablaze, hoping the smoke and heat would drive him out. It did not and we went on to another nest, the tip of Ochurte's rat stick red with the juices of the rat's cactus fruit hoard.

The Kiliwa, Paipai, Paiute and Southern Diegueño were not alone in their appreciation of woodrat. Barrett tells us that among the Pomo they were eaten by the old people regularly and by others in times of scarcity. One method of catching them was to jump repeatedly on their dome-shaped houses. When the rat ran out and took refuge in near-by trees, it was shot with a bow and arrow. Gifford and Kroeber included the firing of their stick and leaf house to get them out or probing the nest with a straight stick. Rats were shot with an arrow as they emerged. The Mohave trapped them in snares or deadfalls or drove them from the brush house with a sharpened straight stick or a stick with a hook at the end and killed them with sticks or a bow and arrow.

Hunting success. Rat at end of Catarino's arrow and under Sam's belt; Sam holds rat pole.

Sam's hunting strategy finally worked. A rat had fled to a nearby clump of cactus and was attempting to hide under a stem. Catarino drew back the arrow, which he gripped between thumb and the second joint of his forefinger, and let fly. The arrow passed through the rat impaling it on the chamise foreshaft point. The rat struggled for a moment and died. Catarino held it up on his arrow for all to see. His father slid it off. Cradling it almost tenderly in his hands, he stroked its fur and said it was of average size. He slid it under his belt on his right, the head above the belt which held the carcass to his waist by the neck. A few drops of red blood colored Ochurte's faded jeans. A belt or thong around the waist was often the only item of clothing worn by a hunter two hundred years ago, from here to the Paiute a thousand miles north, and it was used in exactly this way to hold the game. I had become a time traveler but I did not realize at that moment how vivid and complete my experience was to be.

Soon we had another, fatter than the first, shot in the same manner at extremely close range, a yard or two distant. Ochurte said in the old days about a dozen would be taken in this way and cooked together for all of us. However, for him today two sufficed.

Sam Ochurte making kindling of juniper, which he is laying over juniper-bark tinder. Savoring singed skin. Roasted, skinned rat ready to be pulverized with stone mano.

Cooking and Eating Woodrat

Traditional Indians, in my experience, never build a fire larger than necessary and this one was exceedingly small, just enough to accommodate two rats. We had returned to the side of a large boulder near Sam Ochurte's thatch home. On the way he instructed his son to gather up boughs of dead mesquite while he picked small dry branches and twigs of juniper. He stripped bark from the juniper for tinder and covered the shredded bark with the juniper twigs and branches for kindling. It quickly took flame and burned fast and hot. As it did, he broke the longer boughs of mesquite over his lower leg and knee, pulling the ends back with his hands, and put the resulting pieces, less than a foot in length, on top of the fire. In fifteen or twenty minutes they turned into a bed of slow burning embers. These would broil the rat's meat. He placed a few new sticks of mesquite on the coals and, as they burst into the flames that would singe the rat's hair, he laid the two whole rats side by side on the fire.

He turned the rats once or twice with his fingers and after a few minutes when they had blackened, removed each in turn. With a small handy piece of extra kindling he quickly rubbed the hide removing the singed hair. He returned the rats to the coals which had burned down flat and hard and acted as a grill.

After a few more minutes and turns on the coals, he removed a rat and with his fingers rubbed the skin to clean it. Then he began peeling off pieces of skin from the shoulders toward the tail. He produced a pouch of salt, placed a pinch in the center of each small blackened strip of skin as it was removed and popped it into his mouth. He ate with gusto and agreed with my suggestion that its flavor was similar to bacon. (This is where I failed as a true outdoorsman. I could not bring myself to eat the skin.) We could afford to waste nothing, he said; only the tail, which he pulled off as he spoke, was discarded. The intestines he removed by inserting his fingers near the anus and pulling them out. He threw them to his hungry dogs.

The liver and other organs remained in the light pink-brown carcasses that he now returned to the coals to roast thoroughly. From time to time he turned them. Meanwhile he positioned nearby a large stone with a flat upper surface about the size of a small dinner plate. He cleaned the stone with his palm. He sent his son for a smooth, flatish hand-sized rounded rock he would use to pound the meat. Either a whole or a half carcass was taken from the dwindling embers and placed in the center of the anvil stone. He held the smooth rounded rock in his hand and with its narrow side began to pound the flesh and bones with teeth and all. The blows were firm and methodical, not hard enough to splatter the meat or even harm an inadvertent, interposing finger. The bones disintegrated under the soft hammering and the tenderized meat spread out like a tortilla. This flat cake was folded in half and the pounding process continued. The pounding and folding repeated for some time. When the bones were completely crushed—unbroken specks were

Small fire of mesquite coals, new sticks just added for flame. Note size of fire in relation to size of rats that cover the coals.

Pounding roasted rat with smooth handheld stone on flat stone surface.

picked out and discarded—and the meat shredded, Ochurte broke off pieces, added salt and ate. One small morsel remained slightly pink and this he discarded. It was clear he felt the meat should be thoroughly cooked.

My prejudices against eating rat were extreme, I was at the limit of my ability to play Indian. This was real, no phony fry bread, this. Courageously, however, to salvage something of my image as intrepid adventurer, I pushed forward and ate rat. It looked and tasted almost like dry pork, not bad. It was a fairly common item on the Indian menu of two hundred years ago and undoubtedly for thousands of years before that. Many older Indians remember it. Manuela Aguiar of Southern Diegueño descent told me later they also placed rats whole into pots of boiling water. Once cooked they removed the rat, skinned it and pounded up the rest, all of which was eaten. Not even the insides were removed. This pounding process extended to rabbits, hares, ground squirrels and other small animals, she said.

The Bear River people of northern California threw rats and field mice whole into the fire to singe the hair; the animal was then cleaned, washed, wrapped in leaves and cooked in ashes.

Sparkman observed that the Luiseño Indians were especially fond of woodrats which they occasionally caught in deadfalls. To roust them for a hunt they would often set fire to their stick nests, found in brush, undergrowth, cactus or sometimes even in trees. One woodrat (rarely two) occupied a nest. The most common Luiseño manner of hunting woodrat was to overturn the nest and kill the fleeing rat with bow and arrows or sticks. Sometimes a flood in undergrowth along a river drove woodrats out of their nests and many could be killed. Woodrats, along with mice, quails, squirrels and other animals, were cooked by broiling on coals. Sparkman did not record further preparation for the woodrat but did note that rabbits and jackrabbits, which also were generally broiled on coals, sometimes were cooked in earth ovens and in such cases their flesh together with their bones were occasionally pounded in a mortar and the mashed meat and bones either eaten at that time or stored.

Grinding, or pulverizing, especially for storage as Kroeber pointed out, was a widespread and established California food process. Seeds, dried salmon, vertebrae, berries, fruit and whole small rodents were prepared in this way. The nutritional value of even one complete rodent must have been considerable. The Maidu crushed deer vertebrae in mortars and made a cake of the meal which they set before the fire. Pounded salmon backbones they ate raw. Salmon that had been split, lightly smoked and dried the Shasta kept in thin slabs or pulverized and stored in large tule sacks. Crushed salmon bones and crushed deer bones were stored in tule sacks as well and made into soup in the winter. They ate the dry powdered salmon mixed with sugar pine nuts that had been steamed in an earth oven, dried, stored and later retrieved and ground.

Sam Ochurte finished eating the pulverized rats. He left nothing. The rocks were returned to where they had been found. Ashes of the fire had almost disappeared and those remaining he covered with sand.

Eating mashed meat and pulverized bone.

California Hunting Magic: Split-Twig Figurines

Discovered in a cave amid atlatl darts, mysterious crystals (from wands, the pitch and green pigment still adhering), pictographs of bighorn sheep, sinew-wrapped sheep dung and a feather bundle—these ingenious split-twig figurines were no mere toys. Most of the artifacts from the cave known as Newberry gave a radiocarbon age around 1500 B.C. and suggested the magic paraphernalia of a hunter society widespread in the Southwest and Great Basin at that time.

One of the figurines (somewhat atypical in that sticks were *inserted* for the legs and head) had stuffed within its body cavity dry grasses in which a small, retouched chalcedony flake had been placed. Newberry Cave is located near the Mohave River of southern California in an area that historically abounded in bighorn sheep. Artifacts associated with day-to-day living and food preparation were notably lacking in this cave of hunting magic.

Split-twig figurines seem first to appear in the Grand Canyon region perhaps as early as 2000 B.C. at Stanton's Cave. There, two figurines containing deer droppings in the body cavity suggested again the magical function of these objects. Sir James Frazer spoke of two varieties of sympathetic magic: homeopathic, such as the representation of the animal in a cave painting or stick figure; and contagious, control over an actual part or dropping of the animal.

Lost forever are the exact hunting rituals the Archaic Californians might have followed but their split-twig figurines of sheep or deer can be re-created with ease. According to Alan Davis and Gerald Smith (from whose study much of this chapter was drawn) the Newberry Cave hunters used slender willow *(Salix exigua)* to make their figurines. Long, slender withes are common on these trees and I broke one from a shrub on a stream in the northern San Gabriel Mountains of Los Angeles. I began

Remnant of a split-twig figurine from Newberry Cave. It has a doubled rear leg. The solid front leg has been lost (Davis and Smith, 1981).

splitting it from the narrow end, a little ways down, where it became thick enough to divide with a knife or fingernail. I slowly pulled it into two parts as I had seen basketmaker Justin Farmer, a Northern Diegueño, or Ipai, do with sumac or juncus (which he splits from the thick end into three parts). The unsplit thicker end I held taut between my knees, and the two split portions, arching outward in opposite directions, I pulled gently to the sides, one in each hand. Pressure had to be equal in all directions to split the twig into equal parts. If the spline on the right, for example, was allowed to go a bit limp and vertical, it would become too thick, and the other too thin would simply be stripped off. I had to let up pressure on the thin side immediately, making that length more vertical, while applying increased pressure to the thicker segment. They would even up almost at once. I split the stick to within a few inches of the end, which would become the front foot. (In some examples, especially from the Grand Canyon area, it represented the rear foot.)

I held the stick vertical before me, the splines leaning to the left and right. I bent the right half twig to the right, 90 degrees at the split, continued to the animal's pelvis and bent it down, again at a right angle (see diagram). I doubled it back at the foot, bark side out, and followed up the leg and a 90 degree turn to the left over the haunches and back to the chest. The split twig had been folded onto itself the entire route and gave the illusion now of a *whole* twig rear leg and body.

The half twig continued around the chest, back to the haunches and again back to the chest in repeated horizontal wraps until near the end of the spline. Then as it left the chest it was wrapped vertically five or six times tightly around the ribs and secured under itself. The bark side was always out.

Next, I bent the left spline to the left in a slightly obtuse angle at the split. A little ways above this it was again bent in an obtuse angle outward to form the snout at the end of which it abruptly turned back over itself and followed the snout and neck back to the front ribs, again giving the effect of a single whole twig. However, the snout could be opened a bit at the rear for a more realistic look.

The half twig continued down around the front ribs, looping under the body and back up the neck and over the top of the head and back down in vertical wraps until near the end. At that point, the spline came from under the body just behind the front leg and wrapped horizontally around the neck five or six times with the tip of the twig finally tucked in under a previous wrap. The reddish brown to yellow bark side of the twig was always kept facing out. Was it a mountain sheep or a deer? I let the spirits judge.

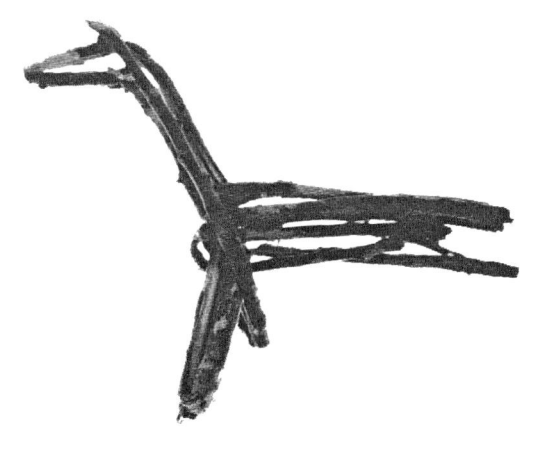

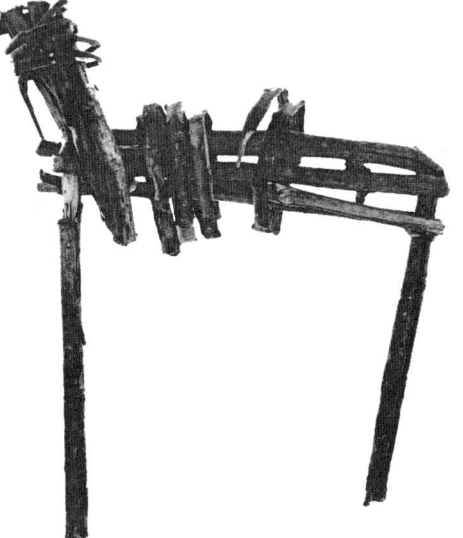

Remnants of split-twig figurines from Newberry Cave. Lower figurine has solid front leg, doubled rear leg. Height of this figure is 21.6 cm. Small figurine above has doubled front leg such as those from Grand Canyon sites (Davis and Smith, 1981). Split-twig figurines have been found in nearly 20 rock shelters and caves of southern California, southern Nevada, northern Arizona and central Utah. D. D. Fowler and D. B. Madsen point out that they usually measure 10 to 11 cm. tall and 13 to 16 cm. long.

Diagrammatic sequence of manufacture of California-style split-twig figurine made in minutes in a first time effort. These are not difficult with the correct willow (Salix exigua).

California Rabbit Sticks

There is something alluring about a weapon that seems so simple and yet, in experienced hands, comes to be preferred above all others. The quest for knowledge of the California rabbit stick took me from cloistered archives to distant mountains where Indians still make and use it. The beginnings are obscure. The historical accounts are few. But by bringing them together with the handful of Indians who still know how, we are able to step back in time to a better place.

The southern California rabbit stick was the culmination of a long history in the Southwest. Robert Heizer suggested the Southwestern stick evolved from a light grooved throwing stick or club carried 2000 years ago as an adjunct to the atlatl. The shapes were similar and when the stick's use for parrying oncoming atlatl darts or dispatching wounded enemy or animals waned with the advent of the lighter, faster, more accurate arrow shot from a bow, the stick continued, finely adapted now to throwing. It was hurled effectively against man and beast and complemented the newly introduced bow and arrow.

The Luiseño hunter of southern California carried a rabbit stick in addition to bow and arrows. Philip Stedman Sparkman recorded one hundred years ago that the Luiseño took ducks as well as rabbits and jackrabbits with the flat curved stick they called a *wakut*. At a running quarry, the hunter threw the stick. If stopped and standing, he drew an arrow and shot at it with the bow. The whirling stick cut a wide swath a few feet above the ground greatly increasing the odds of hitting a moving target, especially one running *away* from the hunter; while the arrow, relatively silent and unseen, could often give him more than one shot at an animal frozen in protective camouflage.

Perhaps earliest mention of the California rabbit stick comes from the diary of Sebastián Vizcaíno at Bahía de San Quentín, south of Ensenada, Lower California in 1602. The ancient Southwestern connection with combat suggested by Heizer apparently persisted as a hundred Indian warriors met the Spanish landing party with insolence, bows and arrows and "clubs for throwing." The function of the stick for war endured into later historic times among the Gabrielino of the Los Angeles basin. Pedro Fages, one of those in the first expedition of Spaniards to Monterey, California in 1769, wrote that the Gabrielino make " . . . a kind of war club of tough wood in the shape of a well balanced cutlass, which they use in war and in hunting conies, hares, deer, coyotes and antelope, throwing it so far and with such certain aim, that they rarely fail to break the bones of such of these animals as come within range." Even in the early years of the twentieth century one of John Peabody Harrington's Gabrielino consultants, José de los Santos Juncos, recalled that the *wákat*, or throwing stick for killing rabbits, was used once by an Indian at Tejón to kill an American soldier.

The throwing stick extended from southern California deep into Baja California. In the northern part of its range, an early account by Father Pedro Font described the Cahuilla stick as " . . . made of hard wood, thin, about 3 inches wide, shaped like a crescent or sickle and about 2 feet long. With this stick they hunt hares and rabbits, throwing it in a certain way and breaking the animals legs." The Cahuilla in more recent times often fashioned such sticks from red shank *(Adenostoma sparsifolium)* branches or ironwood *(Olneya tesota)*.

In the southern part of its range, beginning at about the San Pedro Mártir Mountains in Lower California, the California rabbit stick becomes more circular or oval in form. During the middle of the eighteenth century, Reverend Ferdinand Konšcak on a journey of exploration through mountains between the 28th and 29th parallels described the stick:

> . . . *a piece of wood in the shape of an imperfect ellipse, not closed like the letter O, but open on one side almost like the letter C or G, with the point turned slightly in. Its largest circumference is perhaps three spans and a half; the wood is hard, it is not round but flat and when they seize it with the hand in order to throw it, it represents an inverted C. They use this arm when they hunt hares and rabbits, throwing it low, so that it grazes the ground, and if it does not kill them it knocks them down and wounds them. They use the same arm when they first get angry and in sudden attacks as the preamble of the fight that they later engage in with arrows.*

Among the Kiliwa of Arroyo Leon in the San Pedro Mártir Mountains of Baja, this southern style throwing stick was called *japí*. Vicente Espinosa was seventy-two years old when sixty years ago he made one of live oak for Peveril Meigs III. (Espinosa was a traditionalist: he would not go near an automobile, scorned horses and always walked.) He cut a branch about 1-1/2 inches in diameter, 4 feet long and free of large knots. The butt end he heated for about a foot over a fire and began to bend it in the crotch of a tree. Alternating heatings and bendings, he gradually worked up the stick to form a semicircle of the butt end about 14 inches in diameter. The curve was tied into place with willow to dry in that shape. The smaller end he left straight.

After it had dried, the wood was whittled flat, only 1/3 of an inch thick with edges so sharp they could "cut like a knife," according to Vicente. Meigs pointed out that in carving the stick Vicente whittled toward himself like a shoemaker. The finished stick was about 3-1/2 feet long. Another, described by Emiliano Uchurte, took the form of a question mark, the bend going for nearly two-thirds of the circle instead of only half.

Explaining a crack in the stick he had made, Vicente said it was caused by the new moon. The "moon"—or circle—of the throwing stick could be made more successfully if the moon above was full.

Better than a bow and arrow for killing rabbits, they claimed, the stick was thrown held at the straight end, the opening curving forward, in sidearm fashion. It whirled just above the ground.

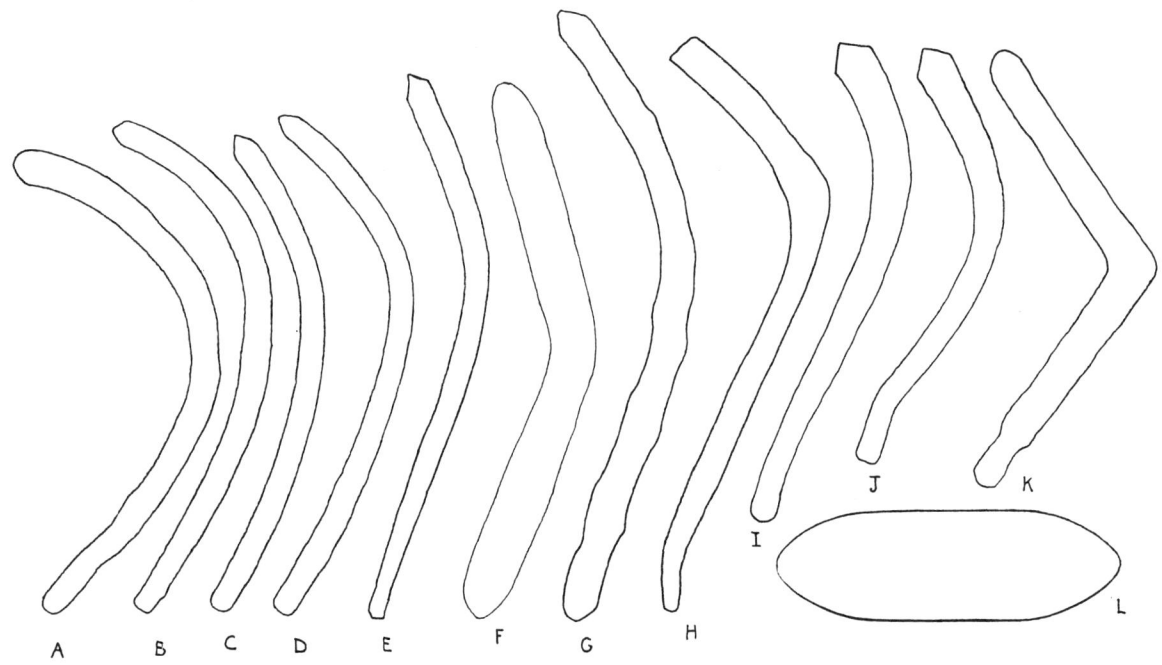

California rabbit stick, northern range. From around the Los Angeles basin south through the Sierra Juárez of northern Baja, the rabbit stick varied as shown above. Its less severe or more open bend distinguished it from sticks farther south. A. Mohave (length—outside arc—31-1/2"; width 1-1/2"; thickness 1/2"). (This, next three examples, as well as "G," were drawn in Heizer, 1942. The sticks themselves are found in the University of California Museum of Anthropology.) B. Luiseño (length 31-1/2"; width 1-5/8"; thickness 1/2"). C. Cupeño (length 27"; width 2"; thickness 5/8"). D. Luiseño (length 30"; width 1-3/4"; thickness 5/8"). E. Southern Diegueño from La Huerta. Antonio Vaquero's last stick (length 30"; width 1-3/8"; thickness 1/2"). F. Southern Diegueño from La Huerta, drawing from Meigs, 1972 (length 30"; width 3"; thickness, Meigs wrote "lenticular and thin in cross section"). G. Also Huerteño (length 33-1/2"; width 2"; thickness 5/8"). H. Southern Diegueño, outside La Huerta, one of Gerardo Aldama's sticks (length 34"; width 1-5/8"; thickness 5/8"). I. Gabrielino, obtained in 1872 in Santiago Canyon, Orange County, now in University of California Museum of Anthropology. Drawn from photo in Hudson and Blackburn, 1982. (Length 26.5"; width around 2"; thickness Heizer records as flat. J. Diegueño, located in Southwest Museum, Los Angeles. Decorated with transverse red bands. (Length 23"; width 1-3/4"; thickness around 3/8", flat ellipse, soft-edged). K. Gabrielino. From University of California Museum of Anthropology. Drawn from photo in Hudson and Blackburn, 1982. G. Davidson recorded in 1873 that it was "procured from the natives by Mr. Samuel Shrewsbury, of Santiago Cañon, 25 miles from Anaheim." They could throw it 100 yards or more skimming the surface of the ground. The elbow was formed by a natural bend in the wood. Transverse grooves on handle improved grip. (Length, according to Heizer, 24"; width 2"; thickness 5/8"). Cross section shown in "L" (from Davidson, 1873).

Kiliwa elder Cruz Ochurte told me in 1995 that in the course of his life he had killed rabbits a lot of different ways: with a rabbit stick, a bow and arrow, even stones. Rabbit sticks, made of jojoba *(Simmondsia chinensis)*, were thrown from horseback in his time, he said.

Rabbit Sticks of the Mountaineers of Santa Catarina

Surprisingly in remote mountains of Lower California, Indians still manufactured the rabbit stick when I visited not long ago. Many of these sticks the mountaineers make in a kind of modified northern style. It was a heavier stick meant to cripple or kill the quarry at very close range. Though appropriate for the rugged, broken terrain of Santa Catarina in the Sierra Juárez, the sticks were marginal to those sleeker sticks found farther north.

In the same measure he had been so particular about the exact species of wood to be used for a bow, Paipai Benito Peralta of Santa Catarina emphasized almost any tree could be fashioned into a throwing stick, or *peruay (pear-ū-ā)*. Fellow villager Andres Albáñez used a thick branch of willow bent into a curve. The 4-inch-long handle was nearly round in cross-section, the rest flattened into a more lenticular shape and from above and below brought to a sharp edge the length of the inner side. Altogether it was 3 feet along the curve, 2 inches across, 1-5/8 inches thick at the handle and 1-3/4 inches for the blade which thinned to 1-1/4 inches at the far end. Flatter sticks were for distance, said Albáñez, as he threw this one sidearm, the concavity forward, spinning into some nearby bushes to demonstrate its deadly, crushing effect. Atanasio Castro of Santa Catarina made them of catclaw *(Acacia greggii)* bent abruptly 125 degrees in the middle, a natural crook, and again with the cylindrical Paipai handle. The blade portion was wider and fine edged on the inside. In total length his sticks measured around 27 inches; the tubular handle end alone was 1 foot long by nearly 1-1/2 inches in diameter. The blade section went from 1-1/2 inches wide on some to 2 inches on others and came to a sharp tip. In thickness blades were from 1 inch to 1-1/4 inches, rounded on the back and tapering from top and bottom to a sharp inner edge. Castro's sticks felt deadly, like throwing a scythe, a piece of sharpened steel. The catclaw wood was heavy and hard.

It may be that flexibility in selection of woods came from the need for expediency. Finding oneself without a weapon in the rapidly changing vegetation zones of the mountains, the wood at hand was fashioned into a hunting stick. Peralta said he preferred *ycasél* (laurel sumac, *Rhus laurina*) for his throwing stick; oak was too heavy he felt.

Like the Kiliwa of sixty-five years ago Peralta tried to cut the wood during the time the moon was full—otherwise the sap would all be in the ground— and not too early in the morning for the same reason, or too late because then there would be too much sap; midmorning would be just right he

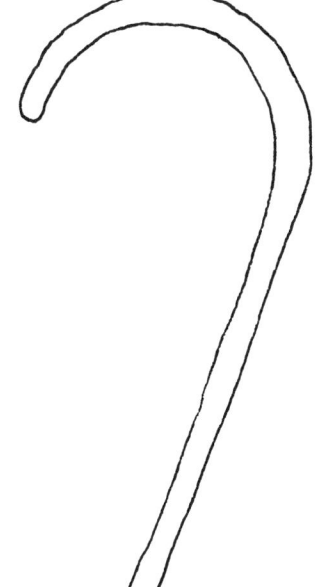
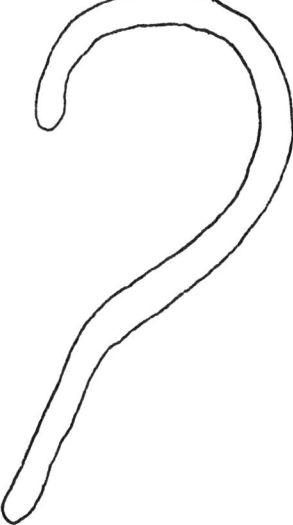

California rabbit stick, southern range. Beginning around the San Pedro Mártir mountains south through the remaining Baja peninsula, the rabbit stick seems to have been less open and in the form of a semi-complete oval or circle. These were redrawn from a study of Meigs. Both are Kiliwa, the one on the left from Vicente Espinosa, on the right, Emiliano Uchurte. The semicircle at the butt end of Espinosa's measured about 14" in diameter.

said. A slight natural curve was sought to avoid heat bending. The scrub oak stick he made for me was simply cut and carved and put in the shade without any special curing. It did not split like the one made for Meigs, cut during that new moon long past. The completed stick measured 28 inches in length with a rounded handle about 1-1/4 inches in diameter. The approximately 22-inch blade was like a crude saber in cross section, 1-1/4 inches wide by 3/4 inches thick, coming to a sharp edge on the inside. The end thinned to 1/4 inch and was beveled to a point from the back of its arc.

It was designed principally for hares and rabbits, but woodrats, birds or almost anything could become a quarry. "Always throw it sidearm," Peralta advised, "and give it lots of spin—that's what will take down the rabbit." The opening of the arc faced forward. Benito Peralta swinging his arm to the side and close to the ground gave a flick of his wrist and laughed: "It will take the head off a rabbit . . . or sever its legs. Very effective." He had learned from his elders. Now in the spring of 1994 Peralta himself was an elder of the Paipai.

Peralta said we remember how to make a hunting stick but have not used one in years. The last man he knew who used it in earnest was an old uncle who died in the 1920s. He would go out with his stick in the afternoon and return at dusk with three or four rabbits—Peralta could still see him coming back with the rabbits, holding the stick.

La Huerta: The Northern Tradition Continues

During the course of two years I searched for some lost remnant band who might still remember a more spectacular throwing stick, flat and aerodynamic, spinning a path of death only a few feet above the ground, the long range stick that grew out of the basins and valleys of a southern California which had existed pure and pristine two centuries ago. At last I did find the people who remembered.

Miguel Costansó, engineer to the Gaspar de Portolá expedition of 1769, had written of the Southern Diegueño around San Diego Bay: " . . . they use a sort of throwing-stick of very hard wood, similar in form to a curved saber which they throw edgewise, cutting the air with great force. They throw it farther than a stone, and never go into the surrounding country without it." This hunting or throwing stick was still in use among the Southern Diegueño when Peveril Meigs and his brother Stewart visited the village of La Huerta in northern Lower California in June of 1929. The village was made up primarily of the Jat'am lineage with Kuatl and Kwaljh also represented. Meigs wrote that they called the stick *pel-wí*. Guillermo Jat'am told him that it was easier to hit a rabbit with a throwing stick than with an arrow. The stick, whirled along the ground, could kill a running rabbit at one hundred yards. Meigs recorded in very brief notes that the rabbit sticks he saw in the village were made from oak, about 2-1/2 feet long and 3 inches wide with a single bend, lenticular and thin in cross section and tapered to a sharp edge.

I visited La Huerta in late 1995, over sixty-five years after Meigs and his brother. I found the rabbit stick tradition alive and if not perfectly well, certainly on the road to recovery. The last great practitioner of the skill, Antonio Vaquero Aldama, had died a scant three years earlier, his cousin Teodora Cuero informed me. She still had his last rabbit stick or *piruiy* (peeruee) and pointed out targets one hundred yards distant he could have hit with ease. Approaching eighty, Doña Teodora, who had six daughters and five sons, all living, and who also happened to be the chief of La Huerta, seemed surprisingly fit as she displayed Antonio's stick and demonstrated his style of throwing. Made of scrub oak, it was a long, narrow and aerodynamically thin curved stick, like those historic sticks farther north from the coastal valleys, inland canyons, desert plains and Los Angeles basin.

Hunting sticks from the Santa Catarina area were much heavier and rounder in cross section, perhaps because those groups were peripheral to the northern rabbit stick tradition, perhaps because they lived in a hillier, more mountainous region where shorter crushing throws would be more advantageous. The Southern Diegueño, or Kumeyaay, of La Huerta have also been pushed into a redoubt of the Sierra Juárez Mountains but at the mouth of a canyon near the edge of a great plain they once knew well: the vast San Rafael Valley. This is perfect long-range rabbit-stick country.

Vaquero would go for the legs of the animal. He preferred the piruiy to a bow, a rifle or any other weapon. He killed rabbits, hares, squirrels, quail, fox, coyote—almost anything with that stick. Doña Teodora permitted me to examine and take measure of her cousin Antonio Vaquero's last rabbit stick. Though fairly smooth and even, well made and somewhat polished; the heirloom had the look of

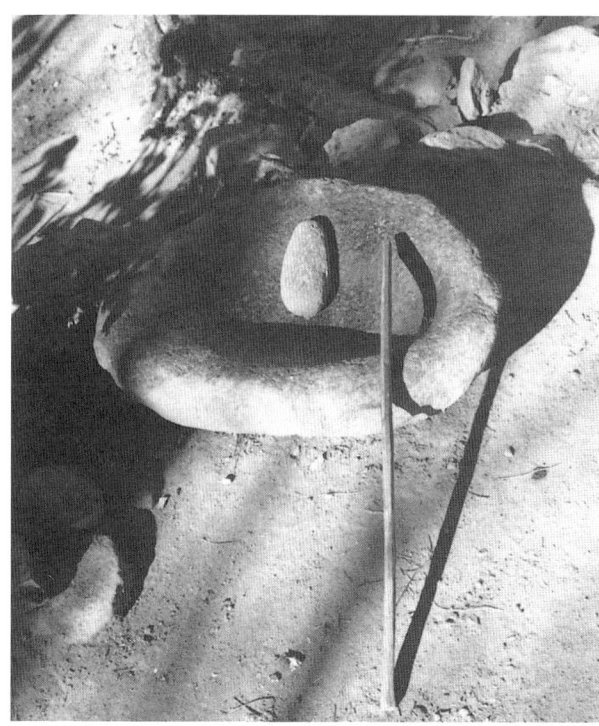

Antonio Vaquero's last stick. Eugenio Aldama demonstrates how Vaquero rasped the stick thin on a rough granite boulder the ancient way. Cousin Teodora Cuero displays it. Below, the stick itself, edgewise and side view. La Huerta 1995–1996.

reality: organic, darkened and dented from much handling and use. Made of *juap* (pronounced whawp) which is dunn oak *(Quercus dunnii)*, a scrub-like oak that is hard, tough and dense and the very best wood for the piruiy, Vaquero's stick measured 2-1/2 feet in length. Teodora's son, Eugenio Aldama took me out into the mountains to find a tree from which such a weapon had been cut.

Dunn oak is a short, gnarly, jerky, many branched tree. Straight, even sections are few. But Eugenio found one, thick, free of knots and long enough for a hunting stick. A straight section was always cut around the time of the full moon as the moon would be on this evening. The full moon brought up and held the sap in the wood. If not done at this time, the stick would bleed when cut, it

Captain Adolfo at La Huerta demonstrates how to throw the rabbit stick. Photographs by J. P. Harrington circa 1925–1926 (Smithsonian Institution National Anthropological Archives).

would dry and easily break. The principle applied to any wood, said Eugenio. To prove the point his father once made him cut a few branches during a full moon and a few more, closer to the new moon. They placed all of the branches a few inches into the ground with the limbs sticking straight up. He watched the sticks for a long time. The wood cut during the full moon still stood after the others had broken and fallen away.

Teodora said that if the stick became somewhat dry and inflexible even though taken during a full moon, or simply to be safe, it was often soaked in water for a day or two. After that it was warmed in fire until it could be bent on the knee with both hands pulling the ends back. They did this until it held. It was a lot of work and Teodora emphasized it had to be done slowly, carefully. Vaquero's piruiy measured about 10-1/2 inches from the point of the stick to the center of the curve and 19-1/2 inches from the handle to the center. One of Teodora's older sons, Benito Aldama, remembered that sometimes they would place the bent stick among large boulders, one end in a crack and the other held in place under tension with a heavy rock to fix the curve in the stick. The curve was gentle, as shown, and around 140 degrees.

With that accomplished the tedious work began of rubbing the stick into final form. They did not always have machetes and metal rasps. Benito remembered old Antonio Vaquero rubbing the stick on a rough granite boulder hour after hour in the ancient way. Eugenio demonstrated, sitting on a large granite rock. He held one end of a stick he was making in his right hand while with his left palm he applied pressure to the other end that had been placed against the flat incline of the rock beneath him. In this way he pulled the stick back and forth rasping it into shape.

Vaquero's stick went from 9/16 of an inch in thickness at the handle to 1/2 inch near the point. In width it was 1-1/8 inch at the handle and 1-3/8 inch before the point. It was lenticular in cross section tapering to 1/4 inch vertical edge around the circumference. The handle was somewhat rounded, the other end was cut near the termination straight to a point, slightly acute (as seen from the width).

Eugenio said Vaquero had to adjust his sticks. Sometimes they did not fly in a plane to the mark but rose up over the target. In that case he lengthened the curve of the underside of the stick (as seen in cross-section) by taking wood off the underside along the edges. If the stick dipped in flight, he did the same to the top side. As in the wing of an airplane, greater, more circular distance over which air passes lessens air pressure on that surface and creates lift. Sometimes a limb of the piruiy would warp and no longer be in a perfect plane with the rest, and it would have to be warmed over the coals and bent by hand back into position. That was a lot of work, Teodora sighed.

Rabbit Sticks Forever

One day as I left the Aldama household, Benito Aldama remarked matter-of-factly that he had an elderly uncle who lived deep in the mountains and still used the piruiy. It would be much to speak of the discovery of a California Shangri-La, but when I returned two months later, trekked into the mountains and discovered Benito's uncle and his beautiful family on a great long bank of the Arroyo Barbón, in an open park of giant live oak beyond all civilization, I thought I had. Three generations of Aldamas were living in a simple adobe within this wonderful hidden valley whose flat extent Los Angeles boosters would probably envision leveled of trees for another development and the creeks and springs channelized and covered in concrete. The surrounding red shank forest had burned within the last year, but already green sprouted from the base of the twisted blackened forms. The fire had swept around and over and left the huge oaks and little Indian ranchería untouched.

Gerardo Aldama walked into an area larger than a football field only a few paces from his doorway to demonstrate the piruiy. He agreed to do this for me on condition I had brought no one else—he had never sold a piruiy or taught outsiders. He carried two of the rabbit sticks with him. This was the custom, he said, you should have at least one in reserve. He used them for rabbits at rest or on the run. He threw them gripping the stick by its rounded handle in his right hand, the point of the curve forward. He reached way back, his weight on his right foot to the rear. The stick almost touched his left shoulder, the curve opening to the sky. In an easy, smooth, sidearm motion that reached far forward and transferred weight to the left foot, he uncocked his arm, snapped his wrist and sent the stick sailing.

I could see at once this was not just a curved club meant to bludgeon a beast at a range of only a few paces. The piruiy seemed to float along the ground down the field, not losing altitude, its flat

Gerardo Aldama throws the piruiy.

propeller blade whirring parallel to the earth. But this was no mere Frisbee or delicate spinning toy either. It had unusual weight for its size and though it appeared to have been used hundreds of times, had never splintered or cracked. A solid whirling buzzsaw, the stick would have been deadly to anything in its path.

You can make them of live oak if you have to, Gerardo and his son, also named Gerardo, told me; but the old people from whom the elder Gerardo had learned would not have been content with this. Live oak will eventually check and crack they said. Other woods are too light. What they sought was the scrub oak of the chaparral and in this area that meant dunn oak.

In form the stick was similar to Vaquero's: a flat lenticular handle of rounded edges (this one had a slight reverse bend beginning 4-1/2 inches from the termination) with the main curve about a third of the way from the point. From the tip to the center of the curve measured 10-3/4 inches and from that spot to the end of the handle was another

Top left: dunn oak foliage. Right: Gerardo Aldama places a limb in the fire. Bottom left: the fire heats the limb.

23-1/4 inches. The curve opened about 125 degrees. The bottom of the stick was flat and the top surface convex, rising to a ridge along its center, in cross section like a low gable. The sides were square to rounded, generally about 1/4 inch thick with the inner side sharper near the point like a knife. Measured along the ridge it was 1/2 inch thick at the point, 11/16 of an inch at the handle and from 5/8 to 3/4 of an inch in the center section. Width near the point was 1-5/8 inches, the same in the middle and 1-1/4 inches at the handle. (His second stick was similar but nearly 1 inch thick and 2 inches wide.)

It seemed best at about 50 to 60 yards, although could go much farther, and the heavy dents left in an empty oil can used as a target at this range were not reflected on the seemingly indestructible stick itself. I believe the significant lift the plano-convex shape gave the throwing stick compensated for its weight. If thrown even and parallel to the ground, it stayed that way in a straight line to the target. It covered a wide swath, and while a thinner lighter stick might have gone farther, I wonder how it could have been deadlier. The purpose of the stick, after all, was not to win a distance contest but to stun, cripple or kill a rabbit.

Manufacture of the Piruiy

It was near the day of a full moon when after much persuasion the elder Gerardo agreed to demonstrate the manufacture of the piruiy. He would like to have gone still deeper into the mountains in search of a perfect dunn oak limb, straight and completely free of knots; this is how the old ones would have wanted it. But I had limited time. After an hour or so he and his son found a suitable dunn oak branch not far from his home. It had only a few small knots and soft bends. It was cut green from the tree, over a yard long (longer than the envisioned piruiy it would become) and nearly 2 inches wide. It felt heavy, solid, almost like a piece of steel.

Gerardo the younger gathered kindling and sticks of dry red shank and started a fire about 2 feet in diameter. Once it was fully ablaze Gerardo the elder laid the scrub oak stick across it directly in the flames, not beneath the flames or among the few small coals that had formed. Over the next fifteen minutes to half an hour he moved it about to heat it evenly, above, at and below where the bend would be made. Finally for the last ten minutes or so he placed the area of the proposed curve, which was closer to the butt end, directly in the hottest flames. The thick dunn oak bark had been left on and was allowed to char black but not ignite. The stick was often turned so the bark would not burst into flames.

Meanwhile, they positioned small boulders in the hollow of an old oak tree, making a fulcrum on the ground at its mouth and wedging a stone above and to the rear to catch the end of the stick. They then removed the smoking branch of scrub oak from the fire and inserted the butt beneath the stone wedged in the rear of the hollow and levered slowly, tentatively the far handle end toward the ground with the center of the expected curve on the fulcrum of stacked rocks. The hot steamy limb, though solid and thick, bent easily to shape. The handle touched the ground and over the handle they set two large stones to hold it in place. Ideally they would leave it in this form for a day. To hurry the process the younger Gerardo poured cold water over the curve.

After two or three hours they removed it from the stone form. The elder Aldama hacked the permanently curved stick into a roughly flat shape with a machete, working both top and bottom sides. He cut the point and removed excess length from the handle. He then used a farrier's rasp to effect the flat bottom and convex low gable-shaped top and to soften some sharp edges, particularly those of the handle. This work would have been done with stones originally. The rasp would have been a boulder of rough granite.

Aldama bends it over rock fulcrum in hollow of oak tree.

Gerardo Aldama and son place rocks on the end of the bent stick to hold it in place.

Top: Aldama hacks the curved stick into roughly flat shape with a machete. Bottom left: a rasp gives it flat underside, low gable-shaped top. Bottom right: a flake of glass smoothes and polishes the stick.

Gerardo Aldama demonstrates how to throw the rabbit stick.

Finally to smooth the stick he broke a bottle, and taking a sharp flake of glass, he held a fine edge perpendicular to the surface of the wood and rapidly rubbed it sidewise back and forth. It was easy to see in this the substitute for the obsidian glass chip that his forefathers must have used though the memory of it had been lost.

He tested the piruiy and found it too thick. He returned to the rasp and thinned the stick its entire length. He again finished it with a glass chip. After this effort it felt right. Over time the piruiy would dry and lighten.

The very outside edges or margin of the stick averaged about 3/16 to 1/4 inch thick and had been little touched during the manufacturing process. In fact on this as on older sticks, such as Vaquero's, slight charring often can be seen here and there along the encircling rim. In many Indian manufactures the economic use of the original shape suggests respect for the natural object itself. Additionally, like the southern California plain wood bow where the back was left untouched, preserving the integrity of the surface may have lessened likelihood of breakage from bending since the edge bore the brunt of impact. I have made sticks this way: thick end of the branch toward the point, thin end as handle, edges untouched except for removal of bark. They require minimum effort and result in the very profile of the old museum pieces.

Aldama displays rabbit sticks he has made.

Sling

It has been questioned whether Californians possessed the sling before European contact. Powers, however, reported it among the remote Mountain Winton during his travels in the early 1870s and wrote that miners of the area knew its sting from these Indians before that. It was reputed more deadly than an arrow and its missile said to have gone farther. The Western Mono mountaineers employed the sling for war. Among the Yokuts, boys hurled the sling. Gerardo Aldama and his son Gerardo, Kumeyaay of La Huerta in the Sierra Juárez of northern Lower California recently told me they have made and used the sling which they always considered Indian, not Spanish. They twirled it against small game and birds. They felt it had more stopping power than an arrow. An arrow often only wounds or passes through a bird while a stone from a sling stuns or kills it. Of the Indians of Lower California in general the explorer José Longinos Martínez wrote in 1792, that they were very expert with the arrow, a curved club for rabbits and the sling. The sling was old and widespread and likely an original California weapon.

The Pomo made a sling for hunting or war. Loeb described the technology. A strip of deerhide about 4-1/2 inches long and between 2 and 2-1/2 inches wide formed the pocket. At either end they attached sinew or nettle fiber strings, each approximately 2-1/2 feet long. A knot was tied at the far end of one string and the end of the other had a loop for the middle finger.

A ball or stone was placed in the pocket and the pocket then folded over it. With the middle finger inserted in the loop, the thumb and forefinger of the same hand grasped the knot at the end of the other string and the hunter or warrior twirled the sling twice around his head and released the knot. Thus the missile was hurled.

Sling throwers stood a little to the rear of the front battle line. Boys brought them stones in baskets. For geese, hunters hurled a round stone 1-1/2 to 2 inches in diameter. But for ducks or mud hens balls of clay 1-1/2 to 1-3/4 inches in diameter were used. The clay or adobe had been rolled in the hands while moist, then dried over a fire or in the sun. Clay balls were preferred to stones for ducks or mud hens because their lighter weight allowed them to skip along the water, sometimes taking more than one mud hen at a shot.

Fernando Librado Kitsepawit, Harrington's famous Chumash informant, gave important detail on the manufacture of the sling. The center strap or pocket to hold the stone was cut from elkskin. He trimmed the corners and made it broad in the center and narrow at the ends (he doubled it transversely and trimmed the entire edge). Then he made a hole in each end for the string. (He also spoke of a strap with a 3 inch slit in the center to grasp the stone though he had never seen one of these.)

He made two *tok* (Indian hemp) strings, each about 33 inches long. He opened or untwisted one closed end of a string enough to insert an end of the elkskin strap. This done, the other end of the string he inserted and pulled it through the hole in the end of the strap, firmly fixing it to the strap. Librado said that it would weave or tie itself (see diagram). He did the same with the other string on the other side.

He also made the finger loop "without tying." About 3 inches from the end, he untwisted a small opening in the string. He put the end of the string through the opening. Then he untwisted the string just below the tip and inserted the other end of the string all the way through this second opening

Fernando Librado Kitsepawit method for making a finger loop and attaching strings to pocket of sling—without tying a knot.

(see diagram). He pulled snug the finger loop this procedure created.

As an alternative and to the same effect, instead of the other end of the string, the loop itself was inserted through the opening just below the tip after the tip had passed through the first opening about 3 inches beneath it.

A knot was tied in the end of the other string, even with the loop of the first string. Some string beyond the knot was left dangling. A completed sling measured about 3 feet. You swung the sling three times around, then let go of the knot and the stone would fly, said Librado.

There were other Chumash ways and sometimes well worked bark of the "curly" willow was made into a sling pocket. Indian hemp string also could be woven into a pocket. There were many Indian ways of making the sling.

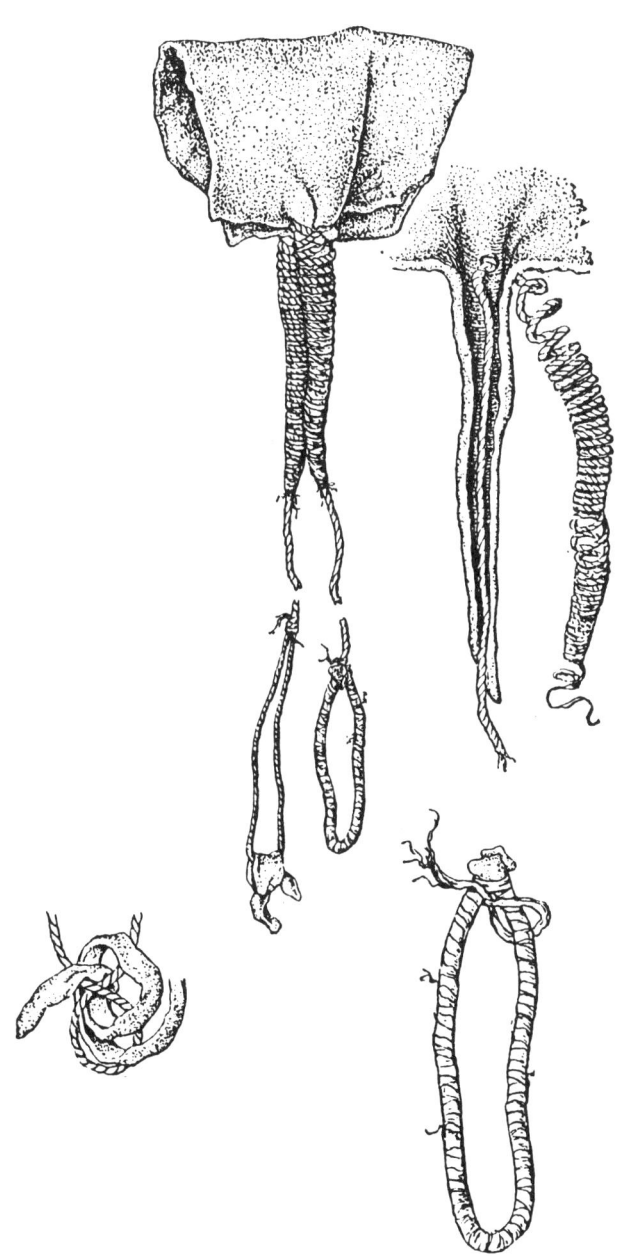

More complex Hupa sling: buckskin pouch, sinew or fiber strings, knot on left, sinew-wound buckskin loop on right. Blowups in this sketch make construction clear. String passes through the hole on the long tab at the side of the pouch and wraps about itself. It was probably secured with one or two half hitches. Collected by Lieutenant P. H. Ray, nineteenth century (Mason, 1889).

Snowshoes

The California snowshoe was a small oval hoop with thongs tied across. The Yurok employed two-ply or four-ply grapevine cross ties on snowshoes they wore along with moccasins and knee-length buckskin leggings when they trekked up into the hills for a winter hunt. Snowshoes allowed Indians to follow game in deep snow and greatly extended hunting range and advantage. On snowshoes Indians could run down jackrabbits and deer. Northwestern California groups from Karok to Lassik commonly made them of hazelwood hoops with iris fiber cord netting and buckskin ties. The Shasta in extreme northern California wound them with thongs of deer hide, the hair left on. Roland Dixon noted the Shasta wore snowshoes extensively in the winter. During 1926 John Peabody Harrington spent a day with the knowledgeable Karok Indians Fritz Hanson (Tia:Kitcha'an) and Ben Donohue. He photographed them warming a raw stick of hazelwood over a fire and bending it to the desired hoop shape. He recorded exactly how they made a snowshoe. From the dusty boxes of scribbled notes Harrington left behind on these two men, secrets of making the deceptively simple California snowshoe emerged.

A Day with the Karok

"A man will spend one day making snowshoes and the next day go out hunting with them," the Karok told Harrington. They were for snow 8 feet deep, when you go hunting in the mountains, "way up." Fritz Hanson and Ben Donohue made the hoops and webbing out of hazel branches, finishing them with buckskin ties.

The best hazel boughs came from where there had been a fire. New growth (lighter, more yellowish in color) was preferred over older second year shoots. When cut, one should not at once remove the twigs and twiglets from the branch, for the stick will weep and become brittle by the time it arrives home and is ready to be used, they told him.

For the hoops, branches selected were about 6 feet long by 3/8 to 3/4 of an inch or more in diameter at the butt. They could be bent raw into an oval but likely would break. Warming over a fire made them flexible. They should not be charred, however, for this would shorten their longevity. They were warmed just enough to allow them to be bent into a hoop.

The branch was bent with the bark unpeeled. Hanson held the butt end to the ground with his foot and bent the stick with his hands. Both ends were brought around and held. They were considerably overlapped with much extra length. The thicker less flexible butt would give the shoe its traditional elongated or ovular shape. During this process the bark often naturally fell away and what remained was plucked off. Finally, excess length was trimmed.

Thinner hazel withes were warmed at the fire. Hanson took one and began twisting it to loosen the fibers. He began at the thin end, a short ways down, bending the stick into a crank that he turned in a circle, round and round while the stick farther down was held firm. This had the effect of twisting the withe along its length. The bark naturally fell away and what did not was pulled off. He judged the withe too big and so split it lengthwise. It would be used to bind the overlapping ends of the hoop. To make the lashings lie tight on the rim, he lightly pounded the split withe with a rock as it rested on a small boulder.

He laid a short section of the tip of the prepared withe along one of the hoop ends and with three or four wraps, coming back to the withe tip, bound it under securely and continued binding the overlapping ends of the hoop. Hanson wrapped it

Sketch of split end tie. Redrawn from J. P. Harrington notes held by Smithsonian Institution.

neatly, the rounds side by side, and remarked that a good-looking lashing was like a thousand-legged worm, a millipede. It should look like the segments of the worm. Donohue explained they wrapped it ten times or so and then stuck the tip in the crack between the two overlapping ends of the snowshoe rim. A little whittled stick of pine was driven in alongside to wedge it securely. Such a tie never comes loose he said.

The other end of the hoop rim was lashed the same way. A considerable overlap of the two ends of the rim on the side of the hoop apparently helped preserve its elliptical shape.

More hazel withes were warmed at the fire and twisted as before. These would become the snowshoe webbing. If a butt were stiff and not twisting, Hanson laid it on the ground and pounded it with the first rock he picked up, then twisted it. (Donohue said grapevine was treated the same way.) After twisting, the hazel sticks were split. If used whole and untwisted, they would be at first too soft then too brittle when dry. The split sticks were twisted again when strung about the rim of the shoe and that gave them the appearance of a whole withe. A twisted split stick was much stronger than a whole stick of equal diameter. Hanson spit on his hands from time to time while twisting. He threw one after another on the ground until he had about ten. Basted and twisted hazel withes could be coiled and kept six months or more; a soaking in cold water for 12 hours or longer made them ready for use.

Next he tied the webbing of the snowshoe. He began with the cross thongs. Taking a prepared split hazel withe he laid a short length of either the

Karok Indians Fritz Hanson and Ben Donohue demonstrate method of making snowshoes: heating a hazel stick over the fire and bending it into a hoop. Photograph by J. P. Harrington, April 29, 1926 (Smithsonian Institution National Anthropological Archives).

butt or thin end on the snowshoe rim and with the continuation of the withe wrapped three or four rounds over it. Such a tie does not pull loose, at least after it dries, he noted. Carefully twisting the remainder of the thong he brought this across (over the top of the shoe) and wrapped it several times around the opposite side of the rim. This end he split for a few inches (if he had not done so already) and with the two sides of the new split tied a special knot, the same knot employed to make scaffolding on the river and to bind almost everything they made. Both Hanson and Donohue knew the knot. The split side closest to the last round of the wrappings was passed under the last wrapping from the side against the previous round; it passed under and out and then over the other split side and back the

Achomawi William Halsey demonstrates the wearing of snowshoes. Note position of his feet on the shoe. Photograph by J. P. Harrington, May or June 1922 (Smithsonian Institution National Anthropological Archives).

way it had come. It pulled the other side under the wrapping while that other side was given a tug to make the wrappings tight. Pounding such a tie with a rock allowed one to make the knot even tighter. The ends were trimmed.

The second and third cross thongs were tied on in the same way. Then two longitudinal thongs were tied, crossing the transverse thongs with half-hitches. The fourth cross thong, nearest where the toe would go, was tied last, crossing the two longitudinal thongs with half-hitches.

Hanson set his foot on the snowshoe and tied two buckskin foot straps. Indians, he said, wore moccasins when on snowshoes; they did not go barefoot.

Donohue wrapped some of the extra split hazel withes around the original ties on the rim to make them stronger. Ideally, Hanson would have preferred buckskin to lash over the original hazel ties—in order to keep them from wearing through, he said. The best snowshoes also had two extra twisted buckskin thongs, one up against each of the two center hazel cross thongs and tied securely to either side. The function was to relieve the strain on the hazel crosspieces and make them last.

Incidentally, that same day Hanson demonstrated another binding with hazel shoots, one used for larger constructions. He put a withe around a plum tree and twisted the ends together, about three revolutions. Then he passed the ends back around the tree and twisted them even more, finally tucking them under the binding that encircled the tree. It had been a special day for the demonstration of Karok technology and Harrington had captured it all.

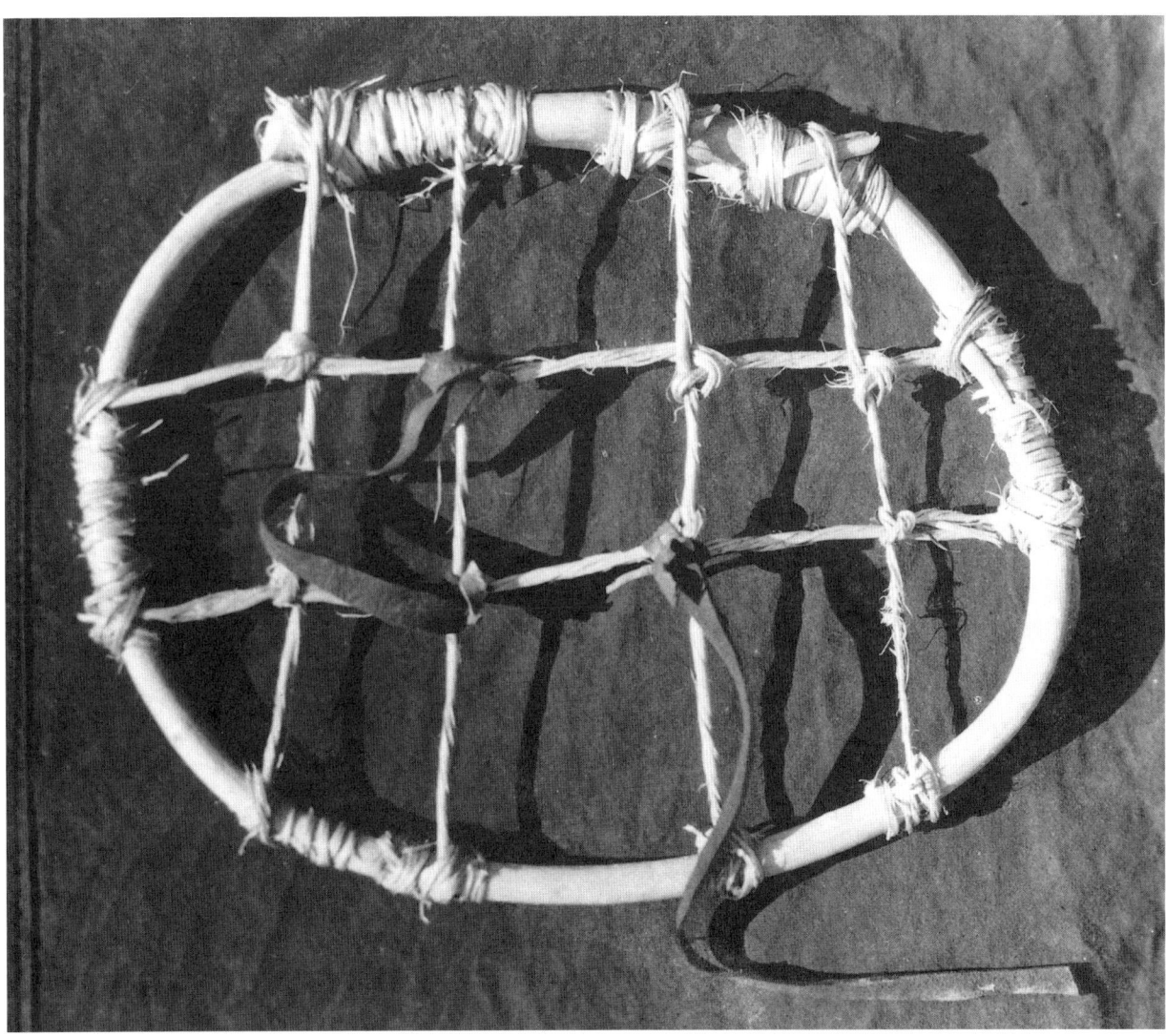

The finished Karok snowshoe, twisted, split hazel thongs, buckskin ties. Photograph by J. P. Harrington, April 29, 1926 (Smithsonian Institution National Anthropological Archives).

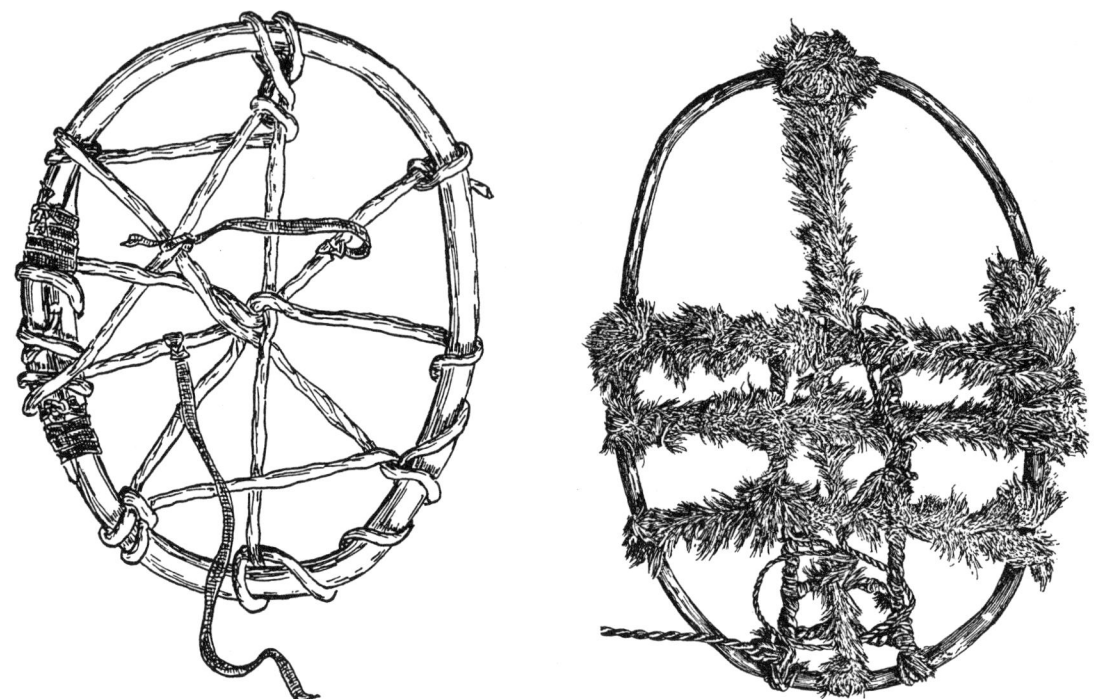

On left, Wintu snowshoe. Frame of hazel, cross laced with grapevine (Wintu also used deer hide with hair left on). Loose heel strap would pass around heel and through toe loop. Greatest diameter, 18". (In Du Bois 1935) Shasta snowshoe on right. Thongs of deer hide with hair left on. Longest diameter, almost 19"; shortest, almost 14" (Dixon, 1907).

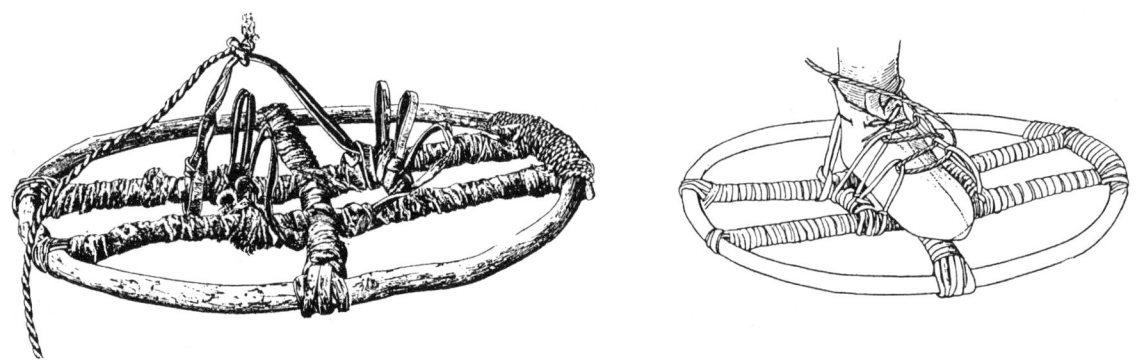

Northern Maidu snowshoe. Cord leaves heel strap, passes back and forth between 3 loops on outer side of foot and 2 on inner side and back to heel strap. Ties solidly fixed shoe to foot without heel-play. Used in heavy snow in the mountains. Deer could be run down in them. Greatest diameter, 17 1/2" (Dixon, 1905). Elderly Maidu Indian Bryan Beavers, raised in the Indian camp of Happy Hollow, made a similar snowshoe or "tromper" at his log cabin in a 1969 PBS documentary. The Creator showed them how to make the first snowshoes he recounted as he took a green hazel stick about one inch thick, peeled and put it over the fire. He bent it and passed it through the fire again, bent it again and kept this up until he had made a complete loop. Both ends were "whittled off" or tapered to lap smoothly. They were lashed neatly together with sinew or buckskin. Two buckskin thongs next were tied on longitudinally, about 2" to either side of center and two more transversally, each a little more than 2" from center. Around these and around the entire hoop he wound an approximately 1 1/2" buckskin strip; it slightly overlapped itself on each round as it spiraled over the webbing and circumference of the shoe. He had made the strips by pulling a large piece of buckskin against a knife stuck in the flat wood surface on which he worked; an indentation cut on the bottom of a log to one side of the knife measured the proper width as he pulled it along. At last, he melted a large pot of pine pitch and beeswax over a fire and with the forked end of a stick daubed the buckskin with the cooling pitch mixture until the entire shoe had been covered. It soaked in and kept moisture from the buckskin and wood when they tromped through the snow.

Brain Tanning

"Tanned and dressed better than is done in Castile" was Sebastián Viscaíno's 1602 description of the skin of sea lions worn by the Natives of the California coast. Three hundred years later, the elderly full-blooded Chumash Fernando Librado gave Harrington some idea of how it was done, at least for buckskin on the southern California coast. He suggested that one should begin with the skin of a *fat* deer since it makes the best buckskin.

Goddard found the Hupa of the northwest coast of California during the last years of the nineteenth century using buckskin as we today might use cloth, paper and string. Buckskin was in great demand for bedding and clothing, for wrapping, covering, and tying various articles. A white or almost entirely black deerskin was tanned with the hair on and used in the White Deer Skin Dance. A fine and spotted fawn skin might serve for the dance too or be turned into a quiver. The otter, fisher or fox might also become quivers. A panther hide was worn by a man as a robe. A little mole pelt became an infant's toy. In short, California Indians treated the hides of many creatures for many purposes.

For breechclouts and aprons the Wukchumni Yokuts of the central foothills tanned deer and wildcat skin with the fur removed. They left the fur on cougar and bear hides which served as bed covers, or, folded, as seats for important men. Only a great hunter dared kill a cougar, according to Gayton. (For many expert hunters, cougar was a supernatural dream helper and they would not kill them even if given a chance.)

The making of Native California tanned hide—a far softer, more functional material than raw skin—generally involved seven steps. With the expected variety of technique and the failure of any one chronicler to capture all the nuances of a process at once extremely complex and physically exhausting, a survey of methods of various representative California tribes best imparts an understanding of this important craft.

1. First, the animal had to be skinned. This was begun for large game with an obsidian knife, hafted or unhafted. The Tubatulabal and Chumash set the blade in a wooden handle with asphaltum only and without the sinew lashings common among some groups. The Hupa had flint knives hafted to short wooden handles, often unlashed, and with these blades, which Goddard described as almost 3-1/2 inches long, 2 inches wide and quite thin, they carefully removed the hide.

The Tubatulabal skinned deer and other large game warm, where they killed it, on the ground. A stone knife made the incisions but the skin was separated from the meat with the knuckles of a closed hand. There was "not much fat left on a hide when it was skinned this way," eighty-six-year-old Tubatulabal elder Steban Miranda told Voegelin 60 years ago. In the old days the Yokuts would lay a deer on a pile of brush while skinning it. When removing the deer skin whole the Wukchumni Yokuts cut the legs lengthwise on the inside and made a ventral cut from the crotch to the chin. As the skin was worked off, they turned it inside out.

The key in all of the above may be in the words "worked off" because, as buckskin expert Matt Richards advises, after the initial knife cut the skin should be pulled off and separated from the meat with the hands and fist alone. Slicing it off with a knife would inevitably score and damage the hide as well as violate the protective membranes that encase the meat, opening it to flies and deer hair. An intact skin is much easier to tan than one that has been damaged by the slip of a sharp knife.

2. The Tubatulabal threw the fresh hide over a line, flesh side out, to dry for six to eight days. If not tanned at that point, it was folded and stored in the house. The Miwok staked the hide out on the ground to dry; it was said to take about three or four days. The Yokuts pegged the hide out on sand, flesh side up, for about a week. After this they folded it by stepping on it and put the hide in storage unless they wanted to tan it at once. Surprisingly, drying and storing a hide for only a short time makes it more difficult to remove the grain (step 4). But storage for more than a year—the longer the better—breaks down the mucus, according to Richards, and makes graining, braining and softening easy. Minimal soaking in plain water for a day or two during step 3 readies such a skin for the remaining stages. Librado did not include drying at all for the Chumash but went directly to the next stage, soaking.

Hides such as wildcat skins, which the Tubatulabal tanned with the hair on, were scraped clean on the flesh side. (Richards emphasizes hide scrapers must have a distinct but not sharp edge and they should be very straight and free of nicks that might cut the underlying skin.) Goddard recorded that the Hupa scraped these skins with the ribs of a deer and with stone scrapers. In most cases such skins then went directly to the braining stage. The Yokuts men normally did the tanning but women made wildcat skin cradle blankets. They pegged the pelt fur side down on dry ground or sand, positioned so that dry air played over it but not in direct sunshine (except in winter). A dull obsidian scraper took off all adhering tissue. The pegs were then loosened to prevent tearing of the delicate skin as it shrank while drying, which would be complete from 24 to 48 hours later. It was then ready for the braining stage (see step 5).

The Miwok did not tan bear hide but staked it out hair side down and covered it with rotten wood from a hollow tree. This was to absorb the fat and the bits of wood were stirred frequently. They alternated this with a scraping of the hide with a long-grained fine-edged piece of wood. The entire procedure lasted four or five days. The hide eventually became stiff and was used as a seat or bed by only the chief.

3. Tubatulabal informant Miranda told Voegelin that hides to be depilated were next soaked in cold water for three days. Mike Miranda, his son, thought it was as long as a week. From time to time the hides were removed and as much hair as possible pulled out with the fingers. The Miwok soaked the hide in a creek for two days. Similarly, the Hupa buried the hide in wet sand for several days. The Chumash too soaked the skin for several days.

Extremely important is information from Harrington's Chumash informants that wood ashes were used in the tanning process. Richards has found this true for many Indian groups, and while specific ethnographic information is scant, he emphasizes its great utility from practical experience. Soaking a hide in a wood ash solution (which makes the water alkali) for from two to four days (shorter time for a thin hide in hot weather) makes the grain much easier to see and remove in the following stage. It also prevents bacterial build up, rank smell, hide deterioration and infection; and, by ridding the hide of protective mucus, it allows the braining solution to penetrate completely in one application (stage 5) which leads to a softer hide in much shorter time. Richards recommends at least two gallons of hardwood or three gallons of softwood ash for the first hide and one and one half gallons for each additional hide. It is the white ash not the charcoal that is used. A softwood ash solution should be about as thick as a milkshake. Water is slowly added until the ash is completely wet but not watery. The hardwood ash solution is weaker, about two parts ash and one part water. Unlike the softwood solution, care must be taken to not make it too strong and thereby weaken the hide. Skins should be completely coated with the alkali water. It would not be harmful to oversoak them. They are ready when the grain is swollen everywhere and hair falls out easily. At this point the hide should be rinsed of all superficial ashes that otherwise might stain the skin. After scraping (stage 4) such alkali-soaked hides should be rinsed thoroughly to leach away the mucus and alkali—overnight in naturally moving water is best. The hide is ready for braining when swelling is gone, the mucus is gone and the hide stretches. It has a dry feel and air passes through from the flesh to the hair side. It is thoroughly wrung out and left damp for the braining solution to penetrate.

The Yokuts combined a "soaking" or depilation stage with the fifth stage. They pegged the hide fur side up over damp sand or earth and worked a *strong* solution of deer brains (which had been soaking over night) into the fur. They left it for a day or day and a half, moistening any spot that dried out. Then it was ready for the next (fourth) stage. Soaking in brains to prepare the skin for graining seems also to have been a Chimariko method. After fleshing the hide on a slanting log, they put a prepared brain cake in warm water and spread the mixture all over the skin. They folded the skin up, weighted it with a stick and left it for around three days. If not enough after that, they did another brain treatment.

Hides tanned with hair left on were not soaked. The Hupa and others simply bypassed soaking for such pelts. The Chumash, on the other hand, treated fox pelts wrong side out, washing them with amole (soaproot) to cut the grease and soften them. When covered with soaproot suds, they turned the skin right side out and worked it with the hands so it would dry in a proper shape. They rubbed the flesh side with a stone. When done, they spread it to dry and that was all, according to Librado. There were no further steps.

4. After the complete soaking, any hair and fat that remained was scraped off with a deer-bone scraper. The entire lower leg bone of the deer was used by the Tubatulabal. The Shasta employed a

Hupa cape of two deer hides sewed together and painted. Necks extended around shoulders and fastened in front. The Chimariko told J.P. Harrington they put two buckskins side by side and trimmed the limbs off (where the blanket would be sewed together). They kept the hair of the hides on the inside against the Indian's bare skin for warmth. Buckskin was sewed by the neighboring Karok with sinew, buckskin thongs and Indian hemp, Harrington recorded in his notes. No needle was used. Holes were made with a bone awl and the thread poked through. To stiffen the tip of the thong or string so that it would pass through, it was moistened with mucous—taken from the nostrils with the fingers—and allowed to dry (Kroeber, 1925).

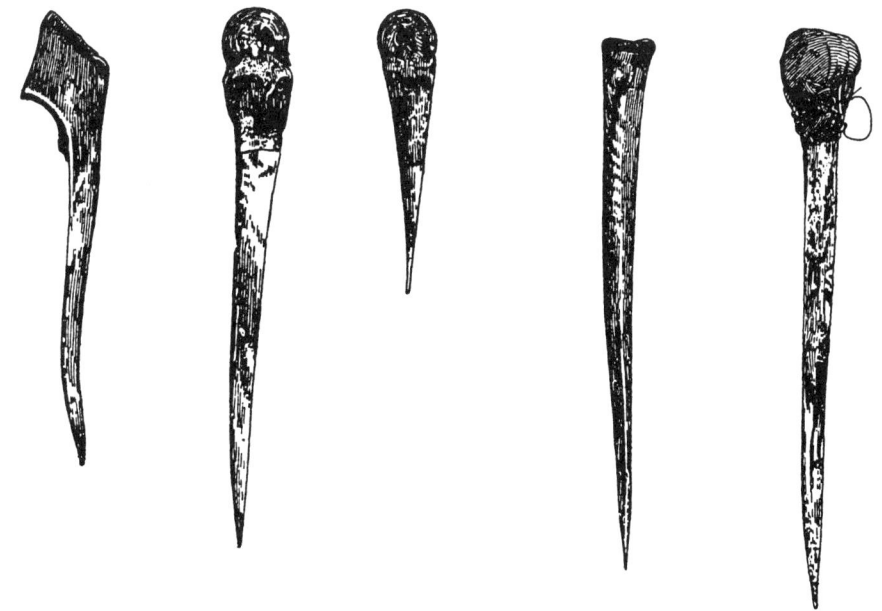

Bone Awls: from left to right; Maidu; next two, Yokuts; last two, Miwok. With awls, they made holes to stitch hides into clothes and moccasins and opened spaces to coil baskets. They could be used as fighting daggers among the Wintu (Kroeber, 1925).

deer ulna or elk rib or even a stone scraper with the hide on a slanting post set in the ground. A fine edged tibia from the deer, unworked with the flesh removed, served the Miwok in removing hair from a hide. The hide was draped over a small stump or post and the scraper drawn down. While it may be inferred from many of these early accounts that graining of the hide (that is, removal of not just the hair but the grain or papillary layer beneath) was the object at this stage, it is not often explicit. Graining is necessary to produce a fine buckskin, otherwise a stiffer, less adaptable grain leather results. The grain layer is under the epidermis and requires much scraping with a dull-edged tool in order to separate it from the resilient fiber core, the basis of buckskin. Harrington, in his extensive field notes, did specify very clearly that the Karok used an elk rib as a draw knife for "graining" hides. He also recorded from his Karok consultant Fritz Hanson that they would stretch a hide on a frame and with a hard wood chisel, 4 feet long by 1 inch wide, "grain" the buckskin. More likely this latter description represented the stretching and softening of a hide pulled out on a frame at the end of the tanning process.

The Chumash erected a forked upright post, leaned another into the fork and used the incline for dressing hides. If they did not have the rib of an animal, they used a piece of toyon or other hard wood, curved and with an edge like a rib. With this they removed the flesh and hair from the skin. The hide was next hung in a tree to dry and they would rub it with a stone. Any hair, flesh or defects remaining were rubbed off.

The strong deer brain solution of the Yokuts having soaked into the hide, they now cleaned it of fur with a deer rib scraper. Remaining hair was plucked with the fingers. A dull obsidian blade scraped adhering tissue from the flesh side. (Richards points out that during these scraping procedures it is important in making buckskin that not only the grain layer be removed from beneath the hair, but that the membrane or hypodermis be scraped away on the flesh side.) The skin, already brained, was ready for step 6.

The Hupa and others also scraped the hair from the hide at this point. If the hair was to be left on, however, they had skipped soaking, depilation and graining, and went on to the next step.

5. The Tubatulabal put the hide in a warm water and deer-brain solution and soaked it overnight. The following morning it was dried and returned to the water and brain solution for a 24-hour soaking period. The Miwok soaked their grained hides overnight in a basket of pulverized boiled deer brains. Librado told Harrington they put raw brains in water "hotter than tepid" and worked them until all the fiber was out. With their hands they then worked the brain water into the hide, rubbing the skin between their hands. When the brain water cooled, they threw it out and began with fresh warm brain water. They held fistfuls of skin and rubbed it, working from one end of the skin to the other, rubbing one surface of the hide against another until it was softened.

Deer brains soaked in a small quantity of water were rubbed directly with the hands into the hide on which hair had been allowed to remain by the Tubatulabal (likely on the flesh side only). Brains were worked in with a scraper on bear hides. The Hupa applied a mixture of deer brains and water to the flesh surface of furs and worked it with the hands until the skin was soft and pliable. It must have taken some time but that was apparently the end of the process for the Hupa. The Yokuts women rubbed deer brains that had been soaked in water over the wildcat skin destined for a cradle blanket. Once the hide was completely wet, the brains were worked into the skin with their hands. Only a bland brain solution was used in order not to weaken the hair on the reverse side. The skin was again loosely pegged out and left.

Fresh deer brains could be used to treat a hide but dried brains were more common. Voegelin described the process. With a rock the deer skull was cracked open and the brain scooped out. It was smeared on both sides of a circular mat 3 inches wide and 1-1/2 inches thick, made of shredded Indian hemp twine. The mat was hung in a tree to dry then stored. To use, it was soaked in warm water and broken up into pieces; the shredded twine rose to the surface and was skimmed with the hands and discarded; the brains sank to the bottom. The mixture was stirred and the hide put in. The Chimariko combined brains and moss. They worked it with their hands and flattened it out like a pancake to dry. The Miwok mixed fresh brains with a long water grass which was then made into a discoidal cake and dried. For use, it was boiled about an hour and cooled to lukewarm. Cooked deer brains were kept by the Miwok in a small bag of a buck's scrotum tied at the top with a string. The Southern Diegueño mixed brains with mescal fiber and dried it until needed. The brain mixture was rubbed over the inside of the dehaired hide. The hide was allowed to stand, then rinsed and rubbed over a post.

6. The treated hide was rinsed in clear water and thoroughly wrung out by being looped around a post and twisted with a short stick as a lever. The Tubatulabal left it tightly twisted by inserting the end of the stick between the pole the hide had been looped around and another pole about 1 foot away. It remained this way for about thirty minutes. Then the hide was removed and flattened out, stretched, and rolled and rubbed between the hands. Thus, only partly softened, it was flung over a horizontal bar (which had been set in the forks of two posts 3 feet high) and pulled back and forth over the bar off and on for two to three days.

The brain-soaked, depilated Yokuts deerhide was thoroughly rinsed. By looping a deer hide around a ramada post or sapling and twisting the ends, or with one man holding the two ends as the other turned a stick in the loop, they wrung it of as much water as possible. It was then pulled, stretched and rubbed, being careful to keep it clean by working on tule mats or grassy ground. To complete the drying it was hung lengthwise over a horizontal pole out of the sun. Later, for softening, it was twice folded and pounded gently with a mano, then pulled and rubbed until soft.

The Miwok, after removing the hide from the brain solution in the morning, wrung it out then pulled, rubbed and worked it until it was dry (stopping only for meals). The Chumash, similar to the Tubatulabal, twisted and wrung out the skin by securing one end to a fixed point and, through a hole at the back of the neck, inserting a stick which they revolved over and over. As it began to dry they rubbed and worked it over the pole and forked stick on which they had first scraped it. Present-day brain-tan experts know too well that this stage of manipulation and softening the hide into buckskin is very hard work and can last hours. The hide must be continually worked, pulled and stretched until dry to prevent the fibers from locking up, and both surfaces must be buffed to avoid a crusty stiffness. The magic of damp hide turning to soft buckskin in your hands makes it worth all the effort.

Furs that had not been soaked but that had brain solution rubbed into the flesh side were dried and worked with the hands, pulled and rubbed between the hands until they became soft, according to Voegelin's Tubatulabal account. The Yokuts wildcat blanket which had been pegged to the ground was taken up after a day or two, rinsed in water and cleaned of any remaining tissue. They wrung it lightly with their hands, rubbed it until soft and hung it to dry on a pole in the shade. Finally, it was pulled, rubbed and stretched to soften the skin, then shaken to fluff the fur. Mollie Lawrence was seventy years old and blind when she told Gayton how to tan a wildcat skin blanket.

7. Some groups smoked the hide. It altered the hide fibers and made permanent the softening treatment. Even after being washed or soaked in water, smoked buckskin dried soft. It was more stable when exposed to various natural chemicals and bacteria. Smoking also darkened the color of buckskin. The Kawaiisu told Zigmond that buckskin turned from white to yellow when smoked with burning alder wood bark *(Alnus rhombifolia)*. Spier gave some detail on the Klamath smoking process: "The skin is stretched over a teepee-like frame of little willows set over a hole as deep as one's forearm. The fire is made of rotten wood." For the Shasta, hides were "well smoked" according to Dixon, but they were then sunned and whitened by rubbing them with white clay.

Many California groups were not recorded as having smoked buckskin. It would seem not to have been done regularly among the Chumash as evidenced by Librado's statement that in the old days buckskin when it got wet, shriveled up. Tubatulabal consultants specifically stated they did not smoke hides. They did, however, sometimes whiten them by rubbing clay into them. Richards points out that clay powder was used by some people to clean buckskin. Oil and grime is absorbed by the powder and can be shaken out with it. There were probably many manners of finishing or coloring buckskin in Native California. To smooth or "polish" buckskin, the Karok would peel off the white underside of the shelf fungus *(Fomis pinicola)* found growing on fir logs and rub it on the buckskin. Schenck and Gifford recorded in their field work among the Karok that a smaller tree fungus *(Trametes subrosea)* carried the same Karok name and was used in the same way as the shelf fungus.

Meat Preparation

Cahuilla elder Alvino Siva, erect and proud though of advancing age when I spoke with him in 1996, said that as a boy he did not sit in front of the television and grow obese on foods laden with fat. He and the other boys played in the mountains all day. Every day they would venture a little farther. They hunted small game and their mothers would cook it. A boy could not eat his own kill. That was for others. The meat was very lean and they had little of it. Sometimes the men caught a deer. Siva's mother prepared the fatty meat of the loins as a special treat for his father. Boys should not eat fat she told him. He remembered other old people bemoaning the fatty foods the youth were beginning to eat. When he was a boy, all the traditional elders were lean and walked straight and lived a long time. Now people are fat, bent over and get sick easily. Even before modern medicine traditional Cahuilla knew that too much fat was not good, said Siva.

Certainly modern assembly line meat can be dangerous to one's health. That it is cheap and thrust upon us at every turn only makes it worse. But there was a time when meat was a precious component of the Indian diet: protein, fat, carbohydrate, vitamins and minerals—a complete food and a spiritual one as well.

Religious custom enveloped the hunt, the butchering and the preparation of meat. Before and after a successful drive, the Mountain Maidu made offerings of beads and food to the mountain spirits and to the deer. Only then was the animal butchered, the antlers and jaw-bones hung from a bush or small tree where the animal had died, and the meat divided equally among the hunt's participants. They had abstained from their wives, they had been careful not to allow deer bones to be thrown away or burned or eaten by a dog, and only the liver had been consumed during the hunt. Now they could eat the rest of the animal. During the hunt, the leg bones of the deer had been cut off and placed on a platform in the branches of a tree near where they made offerings and prayed to the deer. Now these were taken down and divided for the marrow.

Goddard observed of the Hupa:

None of the animal was wasted save from religious scruples. The blood was drunk at once. The stomach in which other parts were put was buried in the ashes until cooked and then eaten. The ears were a delicacy to be roasted in the campfire and eaten after the hunt. The bone of the leg was saved with its marrow, which was of service in mixing paint. The sinews were saved for bow strings. The brain was removed and dried that it might be used in dressing the hide. The meat which was not needed for immediate consumption was cut into strips by the women and cured over a fire.

Meat was roasted on the coals or large pieces were placed before the fire and turned until cooked. The basket pot was used for boiling, the heat being applied by dropping in hot stones. The meat was cut in flat pieces called kiniltats, or in strings, lolkyuwiltowen, before it was put in to boil. The basket was kept only for this purpose. The meat was served in wooden trays called kisintokiwat. For religious reasons these were never washed. After the meal a wooden bowl was passed for each to wash his hands. The water was carried away from the house and thrown out. This was done to prevent the least particle of the animal remaining in the house.

Sharing of large game varied. Among the Western Mono of the Sierra Nevada only skilled hunters who had dream power from Deer divided their kill with fellow villagers. The doctors or shamans got the biggest pieces, the chief did not care whether he received any at all. Some felt the ham was best, but others did not have a preference. Among the Bear River people of the northwest coast of California if two men shot the same deer, the one whose arrow had found a vital spot owned the kill but he had to give pieces to all participants. He kept for himself the ears and tongue, considered delicacies, as well as antlers, hooves, brains, hide and some meat.

When the Bear River men were successful snaring a deer or elk, they immediately slit its throat and cut it down. Then it was skinned and gutted. The heart, liver and stomach were tied with a thong for hand transport back to camp along with the carcass if it was not too large. The hind quarters were cut off larger animals and slung over their shoulders with a thong while the front quarters were hung in a tree with a rope to keep them from scavengers or covered with leaves and grass in the shade to protect them from flies until the hunters could return. At camp they butchered and divided the meat. One's share was cut up outside the house. The tongue and eyes were roasted and consumed with some of the meat. Brains were saved for tanning, antlers for knives and fishhooks. The rest of the meat was cut into strips and dried for the winter. Gladys Nomland specified that the pieces of meat were 1 inch by 3 inches by 6 to 8 inches in length. These along with the tongue and ears, if not already roasted and eaten, were strung on a long slender stick of pepperwood placed in the forks of two sticks over a fire of young willow. The meat was smoked in this way for about two days then stored as berries were stored in conical baskets stacked two deep. The upper basket had a lid tied down with rawhide thongs and, over this, a large piece of deerskin covered the basket and was tied on tight.

Women could cook meat after it had been smoked and dried but not the raw meat; only men cut up and cooked fresh meat. They made cooking pits similar to those for vegetables. As some hunters butchered the carcass, others were already preparing the pit. They covered the meat with young alder leaves, placed hot rocks over the leaves and over everything sand. They left it all day undisturbed. When done, they scraped off the sand, hot rocks and top layer of leaves and with hazel tongs removed the meat to curved fir-bark platters. It was eaten from individual basketry plates. When desired for consumption, dried meat, which had been stored, was stone boiled in baskets.

Smaller animals such as fawns, squirrels (not ground squirrels, they were not eaten since they lived with rattlesnakes), cottontails and birds were skinned, slit open and cleaned. They were roasted over the fire, held by the pointed ends of young willow and pepperwood sticks stuck fan-wise into the ground. The ends pierced the meat at various points to spread the meat well and keep it directly over the fire so it would cook evenly.

Black bear were skinned and cleaned as deer and elk, but the flesh was cut up and the pieces cooked as the whole of smaller animals. The end of the meat was positioned over the fire at such an angle that the fat would run down and drip into a large clam or abalone shell beneath it. The warm fat was poured into a dried whip-kelp three feet long, tied at the bottom with a buckskin thong, and when full, tied at the top as well. Stored until winter, it was reheated and poured over vegetable foods or dried berries to make them sweeter and tastier.

Rats, field mice and gophers were singed in the fire whole, cleaned, washed and wrapped in leaves and roasted in the hot ashes. Gophers were for the sick and convalescing, obtained for them by relatives or friends.

According to Clark, the Miwok generally cooked fresh meat by broiling it on hot coals or roasting it before the fire or in embers. Sometimes, they used an earth oven lined with stones. They built a fire in the earth oven, then removed the fire and placed meat wrapped in herbage within, covered it with other hot rocks and earth and left it until ready. Surplus fresh meat was hung in the sun to dry. To prepare for eating, it was later roasted in hot embers then beaten to tenderize it.

The Salinan people to the west prepared meat in much the same way and J. Alden Mason explained the purposes. Meat roasted in the flames or coals of the fire was for immediate consumption. If they meant to eat it gradually, perhaps during the next week or more, they baked it overnight in the earth oven and it would then keep for that time. For longer preservation the meat was "jerked," dried in the open air. They rarely boiled meat in cooking baskets.

The only mammal the Salinan did not eat was the skunk. (Whether they ate dogs is not known; some groups did and the Yokuts even ate the skunk.) Old bears were not especially enjoyed but cubs were a delicacy. All birds, including owls, hawks, condors and buzzards (which were excluded by many groups such as the Yokuts) were eaten by the Salinan, and their eggs were boiled and eaten. Unlike the southern Yokuts and Tubatulabal but in line with the northern Yokuts and Miwok, northern Salinan groups enjoyed the flesh of snakes and most other reptiles although frogs were disliked by some. The Salinan people broiled reptiles in the ashes of the fire.

Gayton discovered in her inquiries among the Yokuts of the central foothills of the Sierra Nevada Mountains that some ate bear and cougar, if they were under no totemic taboo, but generally bear was not a good animal to eat. The Chukchansi Yokuts from the northern foothills believed bear was too human because he lies down like a man when dead, has breath like a man and may even have eaten a man. Chiefs never ate cougar; he had been a chief before there were men. Especially appreciated by the central foothills Yokuts were wildcats and raccoons, squirrels, woodrats, quails, doves and pigeons. The tails of rodents, such as ground squirrels, were broken off and discarded and the hair singed on coals before they were roasted in a hole maintained for this purpose under the fireplace. Venison was cut up with an obsidian blade and the pieces boiled in a clay pot, sometimes with salt although not in older times when salt generally was eaten with greens and other vegetables and only in tiny pinches. Most commonly deer meat was roasted and the men were the ones who roasted it. Jerked meat was cut in lateral strips from the initial cut down the backbone to remove the sinew (the back sinew was considered best). The strips of meat were rubbed with rock salt solution or pulverized rock salt and hung over branches where they would not receive too hot a sun. They turned the jerky daily until it dried.

In the southern Sierras Voegelin observed that the Tubatulabal's utilization of deer was complete and explained some of the processes. Meat and innards were laid directly on live coals to broil. They preferred the meat only half done but not raw. Bones too were roasted then cracked and the marrow removed. The liver was pounded in a mortar or on a flat rock and eaten by the elderly who had lost most of their teeth. Other large game was broiled in the coals like the deer or stewed in clay pots. The head of the deer with antlers removed was baked unwrapped in a pit oven. The sides and bottom of the pit were lined with flat rocks that had been heated on an open fire. The head was put in and covered with another flat hot stone and the pit sealed with sand or soil. Baked for 12 to 14 hours, it was usually put in around sundown and eaten the following morning.

Birds were gutted, or not, and plucked then roasted in ashes or stuck on a stick and roasted over the fire. Rabbits were skinned and gutted and broiled on coals or in the ashes or stewed. Raccoons, squirrels and woodrats were gutted, hair singed off and roasted in hot ashes. All this small game was removed from the ashes with any available stick.

Margaret Wheat described the Northern Paiute's roasting of ground squirrels. The scorched hair was removed with a grass brush. The intestines were stripped of their contents, tucked back and pinned into the body cavity, and the squirrel was then roasted, head and all. Sometimes they were cooked whole without any cleaning. Children loved to thrust inside to the warm juices and then lick the juice from their fingers or suck the brains from the skull as one would marrow from a bone.

The Owens Valley Paiute, after removing entrails and pinning the body cavity with a stick, roasted small mammals buried in coals. Steward described mice, gophers, chipmunks, woodrats, ground squirrels, large mountain groundhogs, porcupines, badgers and possibly even wildcats prepared this way. Waterfowl, on the other hand, such as geese, mallard, canvasback, brown head, pintail, spoonbill, teal and other ducks, were boiled in pots. Quail could be boiled or broiled on coals. Sage hens, grouse and blue jays were also eaten. The Paiute ate snakes and lizards, and possibly chuckwallas since the Panamint Shoshoni ate them. Intestines of large animals the Owens Valley Paiute split open and cleaned, hung them until dry then boiled them for consumption.

While most California groups butchered larger animals with stone knives (wide across but pointed, keen edged, sharp and very thin in cross section), Hugo Reid noted in his letters of 1852 that the Gabrielino invariably cut meat with a knife of cane. Chumash Indian María Solares told Harrington that in addition to knives of flint they made knives of carrizo to cut meat and fish and to cut an animal. She said they selected the thickest carrizo and split it down the middle in two, then scraped it to a fine edge and made a point on it. Harrington found bone saws and flint knives were for butchering and split cobbles for general cutting but his Chumash consultants, as Hudson and Blackburn emphasized in their analysis of Harrington's field notes, specifically linked the carrizo knife to the cutting of meat.

Sparkman recorded the ways of the Luiseño, people south of the Gabrielino. Often before a hunt, they stood around a fire of white sage and in the smoke cleansed themselves of any social breach they might have committed. It would help their luck in the hunt. They killed quail with bow and arrow; or, at night, they set fire to dry cholla cactus and when the quail flew toward the light, bashed them with sticks; during prolonged cold rainy weather, boys would run them down. These along with woodrats, mice, and ground squirrels were broiled on coals. The eggs of quail as well as ducks were also eaten. Rabbits and jackrabbits, taken with bow or rabbit stick, were broiled on hot coals or baked in the earth oven. When baked, they might be pounded in a mortar along with their bones and eaten or stored for the future.

Much farther south, Michelsen observed Kiliwa Indian Rufino Ochurte grind the cooked spine of a jackrabbit in a shallow mortar. After removing the ribs, he would pound the spine with a small pestle into a thick paste, adding quantities of salt as he pulverized the bones. Something like liverwurst if not for the chips of bone, Michelsen concluded. He was told an old Indian woman of the region would spend an entire day grinding deer bone to a fine paste in a mortar.

The Southern Deigueño, Spier discovered, roasted game on coals or in ashes and ground some of the bones into meal for gruel. Manuela Aguiar of the Santa Catarina region told me they often boiled small animals whole and ground flesh and bones together. Sinew might be taken from a rabbit along with the skin before cooking. The sinew was used for cordage or to secure feathers to an arrow. Small rabbits were often roasted in the fire. Raúl Sandoval stressed that the smaller brush or cottontail rabbit was more tender than jackrabbit, which was first boiled to tenderize it then roasted in the fire.

Kelly observed among the Cocopa, women generally cooked in clay pots over the campfire, baking or boiling the food, but a man would cook directly on the coals. A fish or duck was placed on the coals and sticks set ablaze and stuck in the ground so that they angled over the food to broil it evenly.

Kiliwa Indian Jose Ochurte, with a rabbit carcass hanging from a tree next to his home deep in the mountains of the San Pedro Mártir, described to me two ways rabbits were prepared in the old days, boiled and broiled. In both cases, they were first skinned. The rabbit was cut in pieces and thrown in a clay pot of water to boil. The pot rested on a tripod of stones over a small fire. If broiled or roasted, the intestines were removed and the animal laid directly in the coals of a fire to cook. In the old days they seasoned the meat with salt sparingly or not at all, he said.

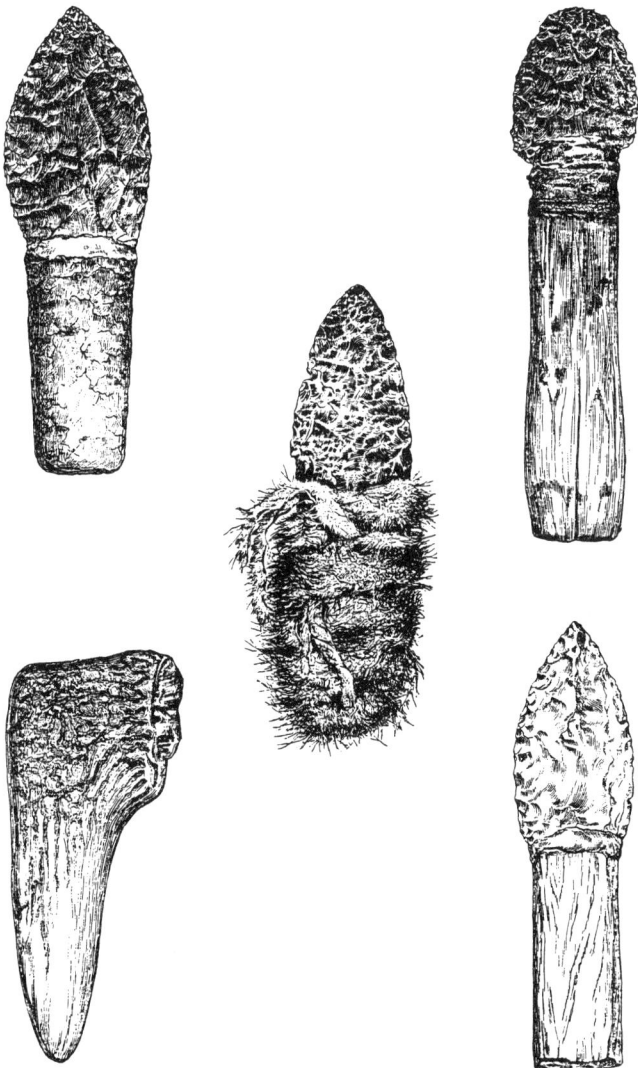

Hupa stone knives to cut the hide for removal and to butcher meat. From the Lieutenant P. H. Ray collection (Mason, 1889). P. E. Goddard described such Hupa stone blades as about 3-1/2" long by 2" wide and quite thin.

Twined Bags and Hide Sacks

Some collapsible and adaptable storage and carrying containers from native California were quite elaborate in design. In contrast, those convenient forms which follow are remarkable for their sheer simplicity.

An Easy Twined Bag

A small twined bag of seagrass *(Phyllospadix torreyi* and *scouleri)*, found today in the Antelope Valley Indian Museum, was collected over 70 years ago from San Nicholas Island, 70 miles off the southern California coast. Judging from similar seagrass fabrics found on the island, the bag may be over 2,000 years old. People of Uto-Aztecan stock (San Nicholeños) occupied the island at the time of European contact. Many hundreds of miles to the north in the Great Basin, bags of essentially the same construction made from tule *(Scirpus)* were found by the dozens in excavations at Lovelock Cave. Northern Paiute Indians, also of Uto-Aztecan stock, occupied this region historically. Wuzzie George, a Northern Paiute who learned to make these bags from her grandmother at the end of the nineteenth century, demonstrated their manufacture for Margaret Wheat around 1949.

The San Nicholas Island bag, about 3 inches wide by 6 inches high, made from tightly twined bunches of seagrass warps, had about 3/4 of an inch between the twining rows, also of seagrass bunches. The bulkiness of the multiple strand warps made the bag tight, without holes and capable of holding fairly small objects. In fact, a 1,400-year-old seagrass pouch found on San Clemente Island off the California coast contained a multitude of fishing tools such as circular shell and composite fishhooks, drills, abrading stones, scaling scrapers, knives, asphalt in mussel shell containers, and small weights. Charles Rozaire, who analyzed the San Nicholas Island material at the Antelope Valley Museum, found that Indians had preferred the leaves of the *P. torreyi* seagrass species in their manufactures. The leaves were narrower, thicker, more wiry, and meters longer than the other seagrasses. The Nicholeños tended to use younger leaves. They may have harvested them directly but seagrass commonly washes up on the island beaches.

The Northern Paiute bag of single tule warps and wefts could be made tight, if the purpose warranted, by leaving very little space between the rows of twining. The size of these bags also varied greatly. Men made them large enough for a catch of fish or ducks. Wuzzie made one, perhaps 10 or more inches high by 6 inches across, for gathering about three or four dozen duck eggs. The bottom rows of twining were tight together with increasing distance between rows until the vertical open space reached around 2 inches near the top. The bag was made from green tules and intended to be used only once.

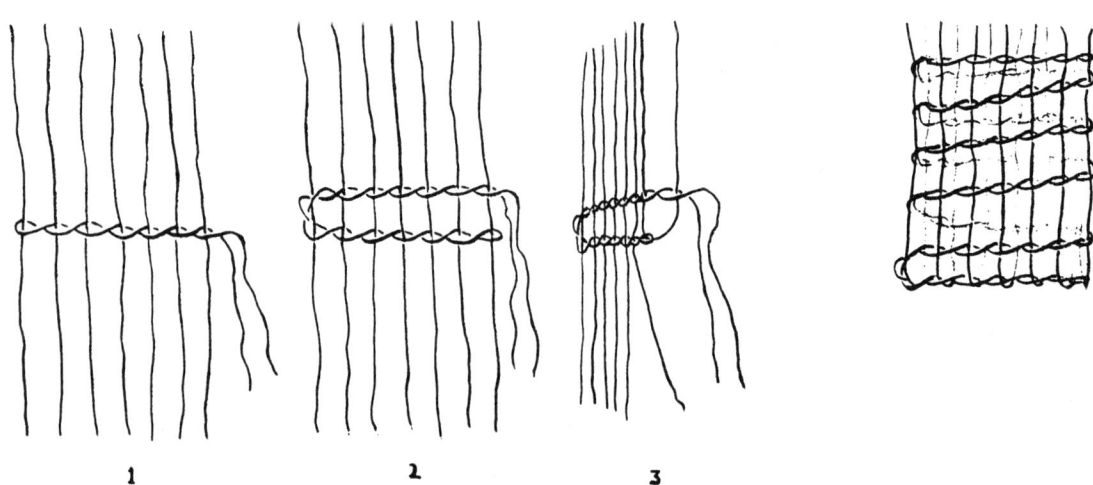

Diagrammatic sketch of basic steps in the manufacture of San Nicholas Island-Great Basin twined bag. Easy as one, two, three. Many variations possible.

Both the island seagrass and the Great Basin tule bag (which Wuzzie mentioned could also be twined of sagebrush bark) had upward slanting twining (counterclockwise twist in the direction of the twining) and proceeded in a left to right clockwise spiral to the top.

Construction was simple. After Wuzzie had pulled out by the roots approximately two dozen long tules, she flattened the longest one between her thumbs and fingers and twined it once over the middle of a second tule. She continued twining over the center of tules until she had about 17, the desired width of the particular bag. These were bent up, making 34 warps and the sides of the bag, as she continued twining around them and upward in a spiral.

Warps could easily be spliced in if they became too short. Not apparent was how a new weft was added. It may have been centered, as in the beginning, a column before and just beneath where the old ran out. Then, in a manner similar to that of the simple survival basket of the Kumeyaay, twined over the last twist of the previous twining weavers to secure them and continued on.

Often such bags were simply ended near the top and the loose warps gripped as a handle. Wuzzie showed how three of the longest loose warps which stuck out from the top of the bag might also be braided into a handle. Splicing in others, if needed, she tied the braid to the opposite side of the bag. As a finish to the rim she bent the loose tules over and with a new tule spiraling over them bound them to the last row of twining.

Sacks

The Tubatulabal made convenient sacks from whole untanned skins. Deer, antelope, coyote or wildcat skins were peeled whole from the carcass after cutting around the neck, lower legs and anus. They were then turned hair side out (except those for quivers) and the anal and leg openings closed by sewing with Indian hemp and a bone awl. Set on end, dirt was poured in through the neck opening and they were left this way to dry for two to three days. Once dry, they emptied the dirt out and the sack was ready. It served to carry acorns, piñons and arrows or for storing food, shell money or other household goods.

The Shasta made a receptacle in the general shape of the conical carrying basket from rawhide which had been lapped and sewed over a wooden rim. Packed on the back, it became a gathering and carrying basket.

Fritz Hanson, a Karok Indian, described to Harrington a hide sack or "pail" they used before the coming of the white man. When they killed a deer in the mountains and were some distance from water, they would skin the deer and place the fresh hide on a large wooden hoop. (They were never made with tanned hides.) With this they would go off and get water. Since the Indians were wont to drink the blood of a freshly killed deer anyway, the fact the water in such a container was bloody did not cause a care, Hanson added.

The Chumash made small bags from buckskin or, as Longinos Martínez observed around 1792, from the skins of smaller animals, leaving the pelt whole with head and feet and a single opening between the thighs. These bags held tobacco or whatever pleased them and were worn in the hair, he recorded. As in the small-mesh net bags made by the Chumash in all sizes and for all variety of purposes, the hide bags probably had a drawstring at the top, at least in some cases (Chumash net bags often had drawstrings at both top and bottom). Fernando Librado described hide bags to Harrington in the early years of the twentieth century as 8 inches long by 5 inches wide, semicircular on the bottom, straight above and sewed with Indian hemp or buckskin string from the outside. Perforations were made on one side or small loops attached so the bag could be carried on the string belt of the Indian. It was worn on the left side. Some had a small flap hanging over the opening from the inside near the belt to the outside of the bag or purse. They carried such things as string, noted Librado. Simplicio Pico Pamashkemait remembered tiny bags were for red ochre.

Dixon found that the Shasta kept dentalia in a finely made cylindrical basket with a cover fitted inside the rim; the basket in turn was enclosed in a small buckskin bag.

The Western Mono made a miniature sack of hard leather, from a piece of deer neck for example, and filled it with a single round stone. The sack was tied to a long cord of braided deerskin and swung around and thrown as a bola. It was used against small game and worked especially well for birds or squirrels in the treetops where arrows often were deflected by twigs. Gayton discovered that young boys used the bola more commonly than men and frequently fought mock battles with them.

The Miwok stored and carried tobacco (*Nicotiana attenuata* and *bigelovii*) in a little sack or skin pouch. Whole tobacco plants were gathered around the time of the ripening of seeds when leaves were still green then dried in the shade and the leaves broken into fine bits. When taken from the pouch for smoking in a tubular pipe (often of elderberry), the bits of leaves were placed between the palms and with a rotating motion ground up even finer. A lesser grade tobacco came from the small tobacco stems and refuse.

Harrington recorded in his notes of interviews with the Karok of northern California that they too had a small hide bag for tobacco. They made it from the scrotum of the elk. They tied a buckskin thong around its mouth to complete it.

The neighboring Chimariko made a small sack to hold the male parts, in effect an athletic supporter. Lucy Montgomery recounted to Harrington that some Indians had trouble getting a deer for the buckskin breechclout they wore long before the whites came. Naked, one could get hurt. Playing and running around, the parts could become scratched. So they made a small pointed bag from any small skin, especially mink, and it was attached to a string around the waist. To take the parts out they had to undo the string, Lucy told him.

Wooden War Club

Carved from a single chunk of wood, it crushed the heads of enemy in battle but could bring down a deer as well. Historically, the wooden potato-masher style war club extended from the Pueblos of the Southwest to the westernmost band of Uto-Aztecan speakers on San Nicolas Island in the Pacific. It was used by the original inhabitants of Los Angeles, the Gabrielinos. In 1540 Hernando de Alarcón found that the weapons of the Indians of the lower Colorado River consisted of "Bows and arrows . . . and two or three kinds of maces of charred wood." Later references to wooden war clubs of Indians of southern California, in particular among Yuman-speakers of the lower Colorado River, were many. Surprisingly, Yuman-speaking survivors, Kiliwa, Kuatl (Southern Diegueño) and Paipai, in the remoteness of Lower California, but not far from the mouth of the Colorado and only half a day's drive from Los Angeles, still make these fearsome thick-headed clubs.

The clubs are widespread among the Yuman-speaking Indians of Baja. The line to the past is not so distant as one might think. Sixty years ago, Meigs was able to locate a great grandson of Jatñil who could still describe the great war leader of the Southern Diegueños. Jatñil ("Black" or "Dark Brown Dog") had led thousands of Diegueños on the side of the San Diego Mission against threatening Yumas of the lower Colorado. But then about 1840 he turned and took Guadalupe Mission in Lower California, retaliating against the padres who had forced baptism and servitude on the Indians of Nejí. Large and imposing like his great grandfather who lived until ninety, Juan Cuñúrr as a young man attended a *Wakurrók* fiesta given by Jatñil at El Alamo (*Ha'a*). He said Jatñil had fought the Yumas and killed many. He used arrows and a club of mesquite. The head of the club was 3 or 4 inches in diameter, Cuñúrr told Meigs, and the handle about a foot in length with a fiber thong that held the club to the wrist.

Kiliwa Jose Ochurte made large, rough, ball-headed war clubs by hacking them from a mesquite tree with a machete. He pointed out to me the natural swelling or knot in a live mesquite limb where it spread into many branchlets. The branch and burl were easily envisioned as a club. Before finishing the work, he let the wood dry.

Kuatl Raúl Sandoval's war club was something to behold. The roughly spherical burl of an oak about 4-1/2 inches across comprised the hammer end. A branch coming off the top of this at a right angle about 1-1/2 inches thick and tapering to a horizontal wedge formed the 8-inch handle. A cord of untreated deer hide passed back and forth through a hole in the end of the handle and made a wrist loop to secure the club to the hand when in use. Sandoval indicated this club was for war or protection of the home and was a smaller version of a maul that might dispatch a deer. His grand uncle knew them well and taught him how to make them a long time ago. Just a touch of the central mass of this weapon to one's head convinces of its instant lethality.

Kroeber summarized the southern California war club as a Pueblo type, "a rather short, stout stick, expanded into a longitudinal mallet head . . . meant for thrusting into an opponent's face rather than downright clubbing." The Mohave club of the last century epitomized the description. Stewart's investigations among this most warlike tribe of California found a club carved from a single chunk of green mesquite or screwbean mesquite. It measured about a foot over all; the handle was 7 or 8 inches in length and 2 inches in diameter; the cylindrical head was 4 or 5 inches in length with a diameter of 4 inches. Stronger warriors carried clubs larger and heavier. Occasionally the Mohave burned a slight hollow in the upper surface (the circular working end of the club) which created sharp edges they carved even sharper. They painted this part red and the rest of the club black. A buckskin or willow-bark fiber wrist loop attached to a hole 3/8 of an inch from the tip of the handle. Unlike Yuma and Cocopa clubs, the handle was not sharpened or used for stabbing.

Special Mohave warriors carried this "potato-masher" club or *halyawhai* in combat. They preceded the archers and bearers of the *tokyeta*, a 2-foot-long, 2-inch-thick heavy, straight club of mesquite used for cracking skulls. The halyawhai, however, was the most lethal weapon in the Mohave arsenal. It was grasped near the cylinder head, not at the end of the handle. It could be brought downward on the enemy's temple but the usual Mohave manner was to smash upward into the chin or face. Much feared, Mohave warriors were known as "the clubbers."

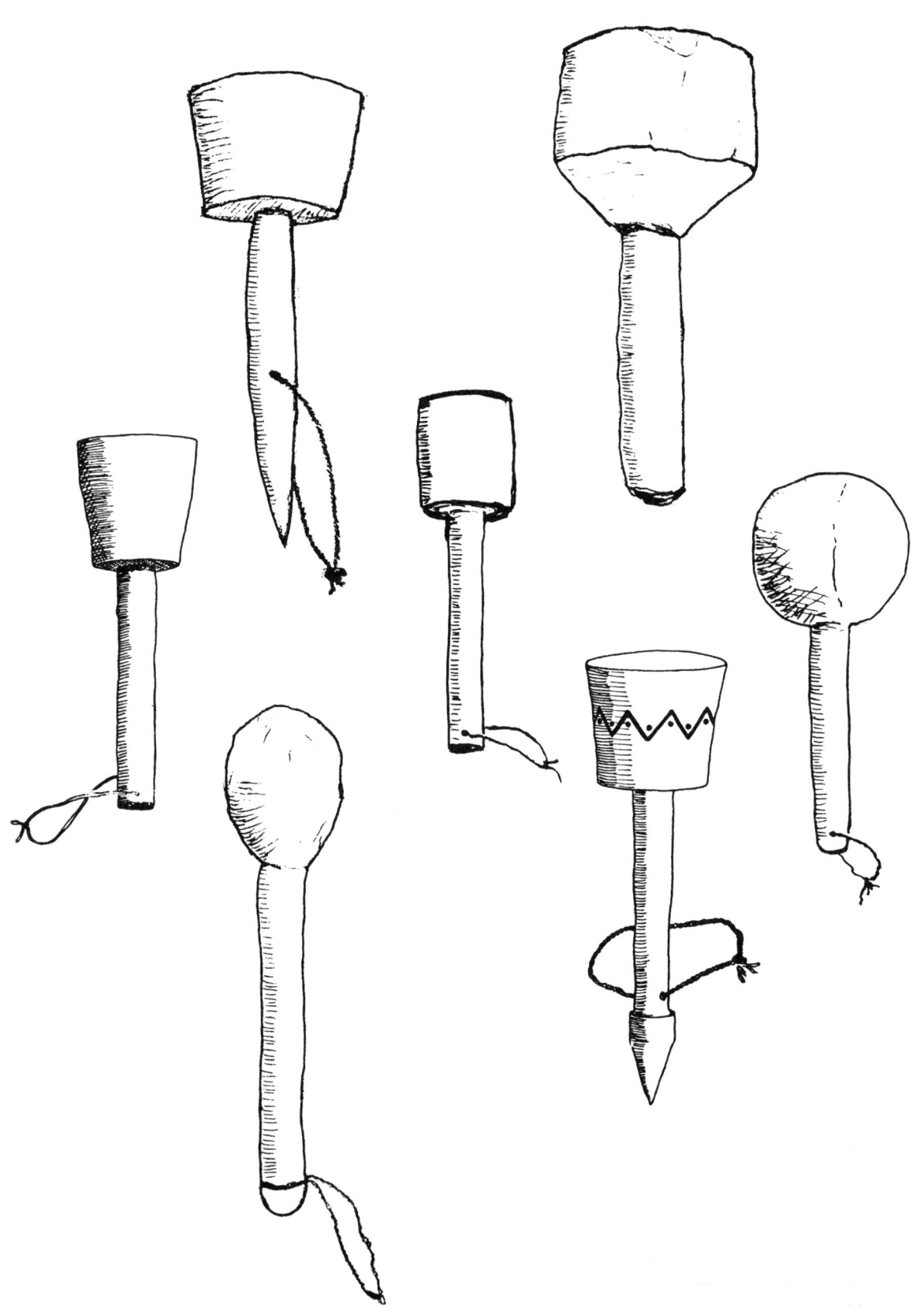

Early ethnographic examples of war clubs of the Colorado River Yuman-speaking tribes: top, Cocopa (first, drawn from Gifford, 1933; second, from Williams, 1975); middle, Mohave (first, in Forde, 1931; second and third from Smith, 1977); bottom, Halchidhoma (from Spier, 1933) and Yuma (in Ford, 1931).

The Cocopa club or *shyawhai*, discussed by Gifford, was also of mesquite or screwbean. The cylindrical head was about 4 inches in diameter and 4 inches in length with a foot-long handle which was pointed for stabbing, especially the abdomen. A turn of the wrist could bring either the point or the head into play since it was grasped just below the head. The example Gifford saw weighed 3 pounds, 4 ounces and was for a warrior of exceptional strength. They carried it along with a shield and used it in surprise attacks. The enemy would double over from a stab to the stomach. Then, grabbing the enemy's hair in the left hand and pulling his head over, the warrior would smash his face with the edge of the club's mass. An undercut to the chin or temple with the edge was the correct manner. Blows from above or the side were believed to be easily dodged.

Gifford learned that they carved the club with a stone adze and knife and finished the piece by rubbing it on stone. Red hematite and black manganese dioxide (with some limonite admixture) colored it. A bit of moistened willow-bark fiber dipped in a pouch of pigment was used to apply the paint.

The Maricopa would seize the enemy by the hair but would smash his temple always with the downward stroke. Their club was of mesquite or ironwood. It measured 18 inches long altogether and had a straight handle with a wrist loop and a cylindrical head like the Mohave, Cocopa, and Pima but without the sharp contours.

With the head a near perfect cylinder made from a thick branch or trunk of mesquite, Paipai Odelón Cañedo's war club was very close to the Mohave clubs in use a hundred years ago. The one I purchased from him near Rancho Escondido measured 13 inches long overall. The handle was 7 inches long and 1 by 1-1/2 inches in width. The head measured 3-1/2 inches in diameter. Natural white wood on the sides of the head contrasted with the dark reddish brown heartwood of the top end and handle. The ends of a thick two-ply cord of black horse hair passed each way through a hole in the base of the handle and were each tied in a knot

Paipai and Kuatl war clubs made around 1994: left, two views of Tomás Ayares' club; right, two views of Odelón Cañedo's; bottom, Raúl Sandoval's club.

to prevent slipping back. The heavy hard wood made this a formidable weapon.

Tomás Ayares of Rancho Escondido and of Kuatl descent, carved his huge, heavy, truly awesome, potato-masher style fighting club from a laurel sumac *(Rhus laurina)* knot—the thick heavy base from which branches spread. The central branch formed the handle, naturally colored by the strong orange glow of the laurel sumac wood. Weathered grays of the trunk, charcoal blacks where branches once began and the whiteness of freshly cut sapwood spangled the head. The overall length was 17-1/2 inches, the handle alone 10 by 2-1/2 inches, the final 4 inches gradually flattened and brought to an edge and a point. A braided loop of agave fiber passed through a hole burned in the wood 2 inches from the butt. The ends went in opposite directions and each was knotted to keep it from slipping back. The loop secured the club to the hand while in use. Without it, the grip was weak. The mallet head itself measured 7-1/2 inches long by about 5-3/4 inches wide in a roughly cylindrical shape, rapidly contracting at the base into the tubular handle. Instead of being concave as in the typical Mohave style, the top of the club was crudely convex like that of the Maricopa. It weighed over three pounds. But pretty colors and Goliath-like dimensions alone do not capture the thunder—one must touch and wield such a cudgel to know its primitive power.

Paipai elder Benito Peralta described how to use the club (which he called *chacúa*) as though he returned only yesterday from battle. In fact, he learned of it as a boy from elderly men during the early years of this century and though he never carried one in combat, they had obviously impressed him. It was a real weapon employed in conflicts with neighboring groups of Indians, Peralta told me. It hung from a waist band. They brought it out after their arrows were gone and they were closing with the enemy in hand to hand fighting. The club was not raised over the head and swung down—that would have been cumbersome and easily blocked—but brought smartly up and thrust into the opponent's face, solar plexus or chest, knocking him off balance and perhaps breaking a rib or two in the process. Once the enemy had fallen, he could be finished by the swinging crushing blow to the head. Peralta, wielding his own club, demonstrated with unnerving gusto.

Paipai elder Benito Peralta demonstrates how to thrust the war club, Santa Catarina, 1994.

Insects: Small Quarry, Big Protein

The disgust expressed in early immigrant records of the California Indian utilization of insects as food makes clear such repugnance is not uniquely modern. Early settlers did not and modern California farmers do not like bugs. The millions of gallons of poison farmers pour on California crops every year to kill "pests" staggers the imagination even as it destroys the health of exposed workers. But few insects themselves are naturally poisonous and most all of them are highly nutritious.

I conquered my prejudice against insects twenty years ago while passing through an Indian market south of Mexico City. A man was standing by a pot crawling with hundreds of six-legged little creatures he called *humiles*. A woman stopped and encouraged me to try one. She said they mashed them in a mortar to add flavor for salsa. As a further persuasion, she then and there devoured a couple of live *humiles*. By that time a crowd had gathered around the fastidious gringo, so I placed one of the bugs in my mouth and as he marched bravely back toward my throat, squashed him dead between tongue and pallet. Rather spicy and good.

There may be 28,000 species of insects in California alone, more than any other division of animals. Unfortunately, though Indians used many, we have accounts of only a few and many of those do not distinguish species. Pioneers had their own ideas about how to tell a locust from a grasshopper, and they often called cicadas "locusts," and crickets "grasshoppers," further confusing the picture. The European antagonism toward eating bugs probably inhibited and in many cases put an early end to the Indian practice as well. (Crane fly parts, for example, are known archaeologically in California from a human coprolite but not from the ethnographic record.)

It may be that exact identification of species was not always especially important. Mark Sutton brought together information on insects as food for the Great Basin which includes much of eastern California. He showed that grasshoppers (*Melanoplus* and *Schistocerca*), dried, had a protein content from 51% to 77% and one *(Melanoplus)* tested 10-20% fat; crickets *(Anabrus simplex)* were 56-60% protein, 13-19% fat; cicadas *(Proanna* and *Okanogodes bella)* from 46% to 72% protein; adult shore flies *(Hydropyrus hians)*, 60% protein and their larvae, 36%; the white-lined sphinx moth *(Hyles lineata)*, 36% protein; the pandora moth *(Coloradia pandora)*, 12% protein and 11% fat; bee larvae around 15% protein and 4% fat; and june beetles 20% protein and 5% fat. In other words, insects generally, regardless of species, are rich in food value. Sutton concluded they were often a critical resource, more than just an occasional addition to the diet.

We know California Indians caught a variety of insects by many ingenious methods and rendered them palatable in the same ways they did other foods: roasting, boiling, baking, parching, pulverizing and drying.

A Stone Fly

The California adult male salmon fly *(Pteronarcys california),* a kind of stone fly, measures 3.3 to 4 cm. in length and females are even larger, 4.1 to 4.6 cm. The salmon fly is widely distributed in Western North America. The larvae crawl out of fresh water streams and emerge as adults in the spring. They are poor flyers and easy to catch. Sutton felt they must have been a good food source given the size and ease of procurement. Indeed, Cora Dubois found salmon flies swarmed on the river's edge for a few days every April and were a great delicacy among the Wintu of northern California. They were gathered early morning, before their wings had strengthened to fly, and boiled or, if many, dried for the winter.

Ants

Ants were widely consumed in the Great Basin according to Sutton's research. He noted, however, the kind was usually not specified in the early accounts. A common ant of the area was the red harvester, but other ants available were the red ant, carpenter ant and American black ant. A variety of red harvester ant *(Pogonomyrmex occidentalis)* is quite large, about 1 cm. long, and a carpenter ant *(Camponotus maculatus)* averages .6 to 1 cm. in length. This may have been the "large black ant" the Western Shoshone dug from its nest in the early morning while the insects were still stiff from the cold. They were winnowed from the soil with a basket, parched in a tray with coals and ground to flour. The flour was boiled with water into mush. Other Shoshone would place a chunk of fresh hide or bark on an ant hill, wait until it was covered with ants then brush them into a bag. Once dead, they dried and stored them until needed.

Northern Paiute preferred ants over locusts because of high oil or fat content. The Cahuilla dug up ant hills for ants and larvae. They pushed the swarm into a pit where hot rocks roasted them at once, or they boiled or parched them. The Mono Lake Paiute also ate the larvae of ants.

Ants emit an acidic, trail marking substance and this characteristic was exploited to flavor salad by the Nishinam or Southern Maidu in the foothills of the Sierra Nevada near Auburn. Powers recorded the unusual process. In the spring the Indians would gather the tender fleshy slightly succulent wild lettuce (specified by Powers as *Claytonia perfoliata*—also called miner's lettuce, a very common plant and high in vitamin C) as a green. They would lay quantities of it near the nests of certain large red ants which built conical heaps over their holes. These may have been red mound ants *(Formica)* known for their mounds of sticks and detritus and their swarming behavior when disturbed. After the ants had circulated through the lettuce the Indians would shake them off and eat the lettuce with zest. "They say the ants, in running over it, impart a sour taste to it, and make it as good as if it had vinegar on it. I never witnessed this done, but I have been told of it, at different times by different Indians whom I have never known to deceive me," wrote Powers.

June Bugs

The common june beetle *(Phyllophaga fusca)* emerges in the spring and mates in trees. Nocturnal, it lives for a year. Nomland in her 1938 ethnography of the Bear River people, an Athabaskan group of northwestern California, mentions june bugs as part of their diet. They would throw them into the fire to roast and eat them at once. They did the same with black caterpillars which were also used for making a thin soup (to which angleworms were sometimes added). Sutton recorded the Owens Valley and Mono Lake Paiute roasted june beetles as recently as 1981.

Crickets

Powers discovered in the early 1870s the Nishinam roasted crickets for food. He wrote that even earlier they had burned wooded areas to roast large numbers of them. The Washo, Shoshoni and Southern Paiute ate crickets according to some reports. Bean learned the Cahuilla gathered quantities of the nymphs of a cricket in the family *Gryllidae*. They were roasted, dried and stored.

Cicadas

Sometime in early summer the cicada nymph crawls out of the ground where it has passed one or more years, depending on species, and moults to the adult, becoming a large flying insect of the order *Homoptera*. It takes about a day for the adult to be fully ready to fly. The Cahuilla gathered them from the salt bush *(Atriplex)*, roasted and ate them, or roasted, dried and stored them to be later eaten without special preparation, often as an accompaniment to acorn mush or other foods.

The Washo, Owens Valley Paiute and Panamint Shoshoni also ate cicadas, according to Sutton's ethnographic sources. The Western Shoshoni gathered them in conical baskets from bushes in the early morning while the weather was cold and the insect slow. Parching on hot coals burned off the legs and wings before they were dried and ground on a metate and stored. The Northern Paiute gathered them in the evening as well as the early morning, cooked them in a small pit, which also burned off the wings and legs, and stored the body whole for the winter. It was said they tasted like cooked oysters. They kept indefinitely.

Grasshoppers

Grasshoppers were eaten wherever available, wrote E. O. Essig, especially in the large interior valleys and along the foothills of the Sierra. The Cahuilla went after the swarms which were common in the spring. They dug long trenches, noted Bean, placed heated rocks and sand in them and scooped and pushed the grasshoppers in to cook. They ate them at once or stored them. Small net bags at times were used for this.

The Southern Paiute too roasted grasshoppers in pits, according to Sutton's sources, or on the fire, after which they ground them into flour and stored them in bags. Additionally, they gathered grasshoppers by hand, sometimes even eating them raw. The Washo gathered locusts in baskets or set brush and grass on fire and drove them into a ditch. They cooked the locusts in the ground or roasted them in the coals of a campfire then dried and ground them into flour which they stored and later mixed with other foods.

The Miwok gathered grasshoppers in the same manner they gathered seeds: they beat the bushes with seed beaters. In the cool early morning air while the grasshoppers were still slow, they beat the bushes where they had come together. Below the bushes they held burden baskets to catch the falling insects.

But more important were the grasshopper drives the Miwok held in June. One or more villages assembled in open grassy areas teeming with the insects, recorded Barrett and Gifford. Each family dug at least one hole, 1 foot in diameter and 3 feet deep. Among the holes they spread dry grass. Pine branches were set in the same area to give the bugs a landing roost. Men, women and children then formed as large a circle as possible around the holes and with bunches of grass swinging back and forth began driving the grasshoppers toward the pits. Because the pits were narrow, once a grasshopper jumped in, it had a difficult time jumping back out. With the insects corralled in the area of the pits, the dry grass was lit and acted as a smudge, smothering the insects and singeing the wings of those that might attempt to fly.

They next parched the grasshoppers in an open-work basket or baked them in an earth oven. The circular ovens, excavated by the women or old men, were 6 feet in diameter and 12 to 18 inches deep. The women put in a layer of hot stones followed by a layer of green tule. On the tule they placed the grasshoppers and then, in reverse, a layer of tule and more hot stones. Several families baked in a single oven and kept their food separate with layers or partitions of tule. They baked the grasshoppers for half a day. "Everyone eat and have a good time," the chief would finally say. Some of the cooked grasshoppers were dried for the winter.

Shore Fly Pupae

Shore flies *(Hydropyrus hians)* by the billions bred in fishless salt lakes of the Great Basin. Adult flies laid their eggs around April. The eggs settled to the bottom and hatched. The larvae clung to rocks when they were not returning to the surface to breathe. Later the pupae (each about 12 mm. in length) moved toward the shore and were washed up with the winds. Early accounts, brought together by Sutton, described huge numbers of the insects around August and September on the California lakes of Mono and Owens. One observer on Mono described the deposits as 2 feet high by 3 or 4 in thickness in a vast rim around the lake. Sutton surmised that *kutsavi*, as the Mono Paiute called the mass of insect matter, was a "conglomeration composed mainly of pupae, a few larvae, some adults, and discarded pupal cases."

It looked like a coarse black pepper, according to an early writer, and the taste was described as similar to shrimp flavored with epsom salts. Women would gather the kutsavi into baskets of willow branches and would dry them in the sun. Threshing and winnowing followed, after which they could be eaten like popcorn or stored for winter in skin bags. The pupae were at times mixed with acorns, pine nuts, stews and soups. Combined with berries and grass seeds or acorns and other mountain products, they became *cuchaba*, a Mono Paiute food. Ground and mixed with water, they were boiled into a soup or mush. The ground meal could be mixed with another flour to make bread. Kutsavi along with seeds and rabbits sustained the Mono and Owens Valley Indians through the winter.

The Panamint Shoshoni, Washo and Southern Paiute also collected the shore fly pupae. The Mono Lake Paiute traded kutsavi to the Tubatulabal, Washo, Monache and Miwok. In the late nineteenth century John Muir writing of the Sierra Nevada mountains noted: "The Indians of the western slope venture cautiously over the passes in settled weather to attend dances, and obtain loads of pine nuts and the larvae of a small fly that breeds in Mono and Owen's Lakes, which, when dried, forms an important article of food. . . ." Sutton found the shore fly pupae being collected from Mono Lake into the late 1970s.

Yellow Jacket Larvae

Anyone who has wandered the chaparral, stepped on a yellow jacket nest and been stung repeatedly by a swarm of these aggressive wasps, as I have, might like this one: revenge food. The Chemehuevi and Cahuilla ate yellow jacket larvae. The Mono Lake Paiute ate the larvae of wasps (yellow jackets are a kind of wasp) and bees (the Washo too ate bee larvae and honey). The larvae of the yellow jacket were a favorite accompaniment to manzanita berries among the Yokuts. The Yokuts observed the entrance hall of a nest at sundown. They watched for yellow jackets returning to the nest because that could lead to the discovery of three or four other nests nearby.

The Miwok also enjoyed eating yellow jacket larvae. Barrett and Gifford recorded their method for locating nests. They put out a grasshopper leg as bait. To the leg they had attached a dry pod *(Holcus lanatus)*. When the wasp flew off with the grasshopper leg bait, they followed the very visible pod to the nest.

Gayton learned that after discovery, early the following morning before light had warmed and aroused the yellow jackets, the Yokuts built a fire over the nest and beat the smoke into the entrance with a fire fan. When the yellow jackets became stupefied, they dug out the entire nest (two or three thousand larvae or pupae) and carefully placed it on a bed of coals. Once dry the larvae were shaken onto a tray and washed. The Yokuts next put them in a basket to boil and finally drained them. The boiled larvae were eaten with acorn gruel or mixed with whole manzanita berries.

A Special Moth Larva

While information on most California insect foods is scant, a number of rich accounts of the Cahuilla *piyatem*, larvae of the abundant white-lined sphinx moth *(Hyles lineata)*, were brought together by Gerrit Fenenga and Eric Fisher. Philip Wilke of the University of California, Riverside, collected specimens, later confirmed by Cahuilla consultant Ruby Modesto as the Cahuilla piyatem.

In 1884 William Greenwood Wright had made the identification and described the vast armies of caterpillars as "huge worms three and four inches long," and a small army of Indians, "gathering them as though they were huckleberries. . . . Seizing a fat worm, they pull off its head, and by a dexterous jerk the viscera are ejected, and the wriggling carcass is put into a small basket or bag, or strung upon strings and hung upon the arm or about the neck. . . ." Later they were transferred into a large gathering basket. At night at home they parched them and feasted. People came from long distances. Larvae not quickly consumed were put on ground that had been heated by a fire. They were thoroughly dried and stored whole or pulverized into meal. Modesto told of still another way to eat them. After pulling off the head, they were skewered on an arrowweed branch and roasted over the live coals and fire.

Modesto noted that piyatem outbreaks occurred in years when the spring flower bloom was especially rich. Many years before, K.J. Grant had found a similar correlation with rainfall: they would come in huge numbers during a spring that followed a wet winter preceded by a dry year.

The larvae feed on a variety of plants, but the explosion of their population happens only in desert areas. Wright's account described them consuming the desert sand-verbena. Bean noted that the Cahuilla celebrated a first-fruit ritual on the arrival of the piyatem.

Far to the north Powers found the Nishinam ate the larvae of a sphinx moth. They called it *kût*, which means "buck," on account of the horn on the black worm.

Pandora Moth, Caterpillar and Chrysalid

Rich in protein, carbohydrate and fat, the larvae of the pandora moth *(Coloradia pandora)* feed on the needles of the Ponderosa and yellow pines common in the Sierra Nevada and the mountains of southern California. Essig described a full fed caterpillar as almost as large as an index finger, from 2 to 2-1/2 inches long after a year of feeding on pine needles. High in the trees, they would finally descend during the spring and summer to enter the pupal stage in the ground. Indians awaited their natural coming, wrote Essig, or built a fire under an infested tree to make a smudge, stupefying the caterpillars that would then fall like rain. More recent ethnographic accounts collected by Sutton showed the Owens Valley Paiute, a group that continued the practice at least into the 1980s, would trap the larvae in a trench dug around the tree after the area had been cleaned of debris and smoothed. From these trenches the caterpillars were collected and stored in open-twined globular baskets or earth pits before processing.

Some were skewered on willow sticks, roasted and eaten at once. However, most were roasted in the heated earth, coals and ashes of a sandy 1-meter pit for thirty minutes to an hour. Traditionally, an open-twined parching basket or cone-shaped sifter would next be used to remove and screen them. They were then washed and any "flat" caterpillars discarded. Those destined for consumption at that time were boiled with or without salt for about an hour. The heads were removed as the food was plucked out and eaten with the fingers. Bread from pine nuts and sunflower seeds accompanied them.

Caterpillars destined for storage—literally tons in a good year—were not boiled but air-dried for two days to two weeks after the initial roasting. The Mono Lake Paiute used sheds constructed of strips of bark for drying or placed them in the shade. Some elders claimed that drying directly in the sun would make them rancid in a short time. Dried caterpillars were stored in the shed or other cool place, sometimes near where they had been harvested. Preservation was difficult but with luck they could last until the following summer.

Other groups such as the Monache, Klamath and Modoc gathered caterpillars and pupae of the pandora moth. Kawaiisu ate the caterpillars. The Miwok gathered and parched the chrysalids which they found high in the mountains. The Monache parched the chrysalids with coals in a winnowing basket; they could then eat them at once or store them for long periods. The Klamath and Modoc roasted the chrysalids. The Mono Lake traded both chrysalid and caterpillar to the Central Miwok, the Tubatulabal and Monache.

Army Worm Hunt

When Samuel A. Barrett happened by the Pomo ranchería of Yokaia on the morning of May 15, 1904, he was surprised to find the entire village nearly deserted. Only two old men remained. One of these, too frail to walk, accompanied Barrett in his buggy to a grove of ash on the east bank of the Russian River. There, for the first time since 1898, hoards of army worms had descended and the villagers were busy collecting them.

Army worms belong to the family *Noctuidae*, the most numerous group of the order *Lepidoptera*, moths and butterflies. There may be more than a thousand species of *Noctuidae* in California alone. While Barrett did not identify the scientific name of the caterpillars he saw that day, he did describe them: almost hairless, about 2 inches in length, brownish with Indian red stripes along the sides. The male, according to the Pomo, had a pinkish white belly and the female yellow. They come, the Indians told him, in early summer for only a few days and only in years of much fog. They belong to thunder and travel on the fog from the west. They eat only the leaves of the ash tree.

As the tree becomes denuded, the army worms let go and drop, apparently without harm, a veritable rain of caterpillars, experienced by Barrett. It was then on to the next tree. To block and trap them the Pomo surrounded a tree with a series of small vertical-walled pits, circular, square or rectangular, each about 6 inches wide and up to 2 feet, sometimes even 3 feet long, always from 4 to 6 inches deep, with not more than an inch separating one pit from the next in the moat around the tree. Barrett also observed pits made in lines to block the route to the next tree in the grove. Fine dry sand was placed ingeniously along the edges of the tops of the pits so that an escaping caterpillar crawling up the side of the pit would lose its foothold in the dry shifting sand and tumble back into the pit. Fresh sand was added from time to time and the pits emptied of caterpillars before they filled with worms. New trees in the line of march of escaping army worms were girdled with collars of ash leaves and the arrested worms collected from these by hand. Worms were also handpicked from saplings.

Everyone talked in hushed tones and no unnecessary noise was made; loud sounds alarmed the worms and caused them to leave. One who spoke crossly to another while collecting worms would be bitten by a rattlesnake, they believed.

Gathered worms were placed in a vessel of cold water where they drowned. From there they went into a tightly woven basket with hot coals and hot ashes to parch and roast. It turned them a reddish color and imparted an excellent sweet flavor. They were separated from the ashes by means of an open-work sifting basket. Some were not parched but boiled. Everyone ate to surfeit. Cooked worms that remained were spread in the sun to dry for the winter. Perhaps several hundred pounds of dried army worms came from this small village alone, estimated Barrett.

Material on other caterpillars eaten by California Indians contains few details. An army worm moth *(Homoncocnemis fortis)* was apparently a food source for some Indians. Powers bequeathed the knowledge that the Southern Maidu ate the caterpillar of the ceanothus silk moth, a worm reaching 10 cm. in length, as well as the caterpillars of two species of tiger moths whose hairy larvae are known as "woolly bears." All three species they dubbed *shek*. The Monache ate a hairy caterpillar, species unknown. And the Miwok collected cocoons of a hairy caterpillar. They called *"lul"* which caused the cocoons to shake on the bushes from which they hung; brown in color, the little sacks otherwise could be difficult to see. They were boiled or steamed in the earth oven and eaten with salt. Extras were sundried, stored in twined storage baskets, reconstituted by soaking in hot water for 2 to 3 minutes and eaten with acorn mush.

How California Indians Made Tule Balsas

Cattails, sedges, an armful of tules, a piece of driftwood, a log—all served the Indian as floats for crossing a river, even one as grand as the Colorado. Tied together and made larger, these brush piles became rafts that could carry people and goods. In small basketry or pottery oracles infants or freight were ferried over streams. Fire-sculpted dugout canoes glided along rivers of northern coasts carrying hunters, fishermen and gatherers. More complex craft of fitted pieces of plank tied with Indian hemp and glued with asphaltum transported Chumash and Gabrielino trade goods as well as fishermen on southern coasts. Simpler tule balsas California Indians poled through shallow inland waters as whole families hunted and gathered from them; propelled by double-bladed paddles, tule craft plied the deep waters of the coast and connected one village to another. In short, many were the modes of water transportation in aboriginal California.

The theme of the widespread tule boat varied considerably from one place to the next. Unfortunately the details have often been scattered and lost. These were quickly built vessels usually meant to last only a season though the tradition was extensive both in time and space.

Tule balsas reached from northernmost Alta California to southernmost Lower California and the Sea of Cortez with few interruptions along the way. Such boats were mostly inland toward the north where they were propelled by a pole and coastal toward the south from Bodega Bay to the tip of Baja; the double-bladed paddle was the consistent maritime means of locomotion. Because the balsa and double-bladed paddle complex was so pervasive along the coast, Robert Heizer surmised it was likely the oldest seagoing boat and paddle combination of California.

Poled tule boats, on the other hand, became integral to the way of life which evolved in the Great Central Valley. John Barker, Kern River pioneer of the early 1850s, described the lakes of Kern, Buena Vista and Tulare and the tule balsas of the Yokuts (in a statement written about 1904 found in John Peabody Harrington's notes). The lakes were:

. . . all the time full of water, and extended for a distance of more than one hundred miles north and south in the lowest depression of the Valley, and were abundantly stocked with excellent fish, not to mention the myriads of water fowl that congregated here during the fall and winter season.

The shallow shores, when you could wade into the lake for a mile or more, were literally paved with the fresh water clams, and the fringe of flag that grew around the shallow shores produced a root that yielded a starch that was as bountiful as it was nutritious.

In order to facilitate the removal of their camps from point to point, as well as to cross the lake when necessary, they had to have boats or canoes, and as there was no timber suitable for such, they found a ready substitute in the Tule stalk, which grew in the greatest profusion everywhere. . . .

In this great valley around the shores of Tulare Lake lived people who in the early years of the twentieth century could still craft tule boats. Of one we have a record. Tachi Yokuts Indian Bob Bautista was living in a tule-mat house seven miles south of Lemoore when Harrington found him in September of 1914. A dancing or medicine man, according to Harrington's notes, Bautista kept a full weasel-skin charm with him all the time. Harrington once saw him rise at dawn, face and talk to the sun. He spoke earnestly and vigorously and followed with an "impressive silence" while he ran a smooth *'unuk'* (plummet-shaped stone) over the body of a sick friend who stood next to him. He then made motions with his right hand as though to cleanse from the stone the sickness it had gathered and continued to address the sun. Bautista, whose Indian name was Trehlawat, bemoaned to Harrington the loss of the delicious shellfish from Tulare Lake which for so long had sustained the Tachi, a lake the Americans now dredged and shrank. At times, the Indians had set fire to the tule around the lake close to where Bautista lived—it pruned the wild blackberry and everything would come up afresh—and when the tule had burned off they could get raccoons, he told Harrington. Lately the Indians had taken to eating dog and dead animals as the people were driven from place to place.

In October of 1923 Bautista accompanied Harrington to the Ventura County Fair and built at that exposition a tule balsa. From the notes Harrington left on Bautista and other Tachi, and filling in the blanks and providing confirmation and context with additional ethnographic material, the old Lake Tulare tule balsa-boat technology can be restored. Hopefully, one day the lake itself will come back.

Gathering and Preparing the Tule

"They sent the women in with knives and cut the longest tules they could find," wrote Barker of the Yokuts. Tules or bulrushes up to 9 feet in height grew in tremendous profusion along the sloughs, ponds, lakes, rivers and marshes. Specific scientific names were rarely if ever given in the old accounts but the best tules for boat building and most widespread in California were the California tule *(Scirpus californicus)* and the common tule *(Scirpus acutus)*. In the late 1940s Margaret Wheat interviewed and observed Northern Paiute who made tule boats on marshes of the Carson Sink; she specified *Scirpus acutus* as the tule used. At that time Paiute Jimmy George cut the tall round rushes with a modern knife, but in years past "sickles" made from the shoulder blade of a deer or a thin sheet of slate with fluted edges would have been employed, according to Wheat. From her account and pictures it appears the boat was constructed in a single day with the tules still green, without curing or further

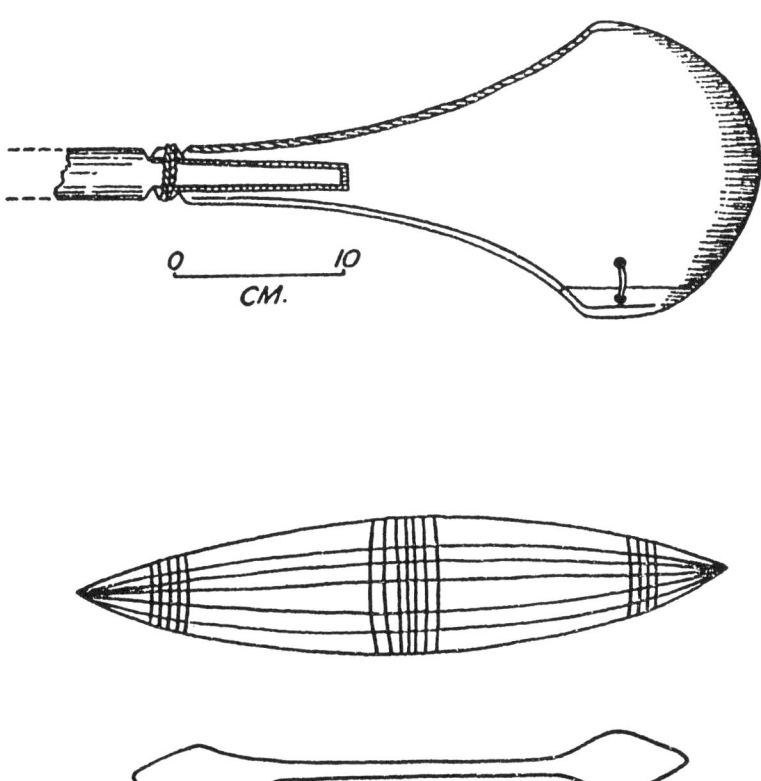

California seagoing balsa and double-bladed paddles. Father of the California missions Junípero Serra had written of "fish which they catch from rafts made of tules and formed like canoes, with which they venture far out to sea." Chumash paddle blade above, collected by Captain George Vancouver Expedition at Santa Barbara 1793, hafted to shaft by means of groove and asphaltum. Fernando Librado, J.P. Harrington consultant, said Catalina ironwood, which had been dried then straightened in the fire, was customarily used for shafts, redwood for blades. Below, sketch of a coast Miwok balsa and paddle from Bodega Bay, 1791, by Colnett, who wrote that 3 bundles made the bottom, plus 2 more, one on each side. The paddle was held in the middle and used alternately, one end, then the other. Five-bundle tule boats as well as 3-bundle boats were put to sea by the Chumash. The tules were cut green, dried in the sun for 2 days and on the third day the boat built, Librado told Harrington. The bundle for the bottom was thicker and longer than the other two. All three tapered to a point and in each an inserted willow pole stiffened and strengthened it. Indian hemp held the bundles together and to each other. The prow and stern were raised, the bottom coated with asphaltum, then powdered with fine dry clay to remove the stickiness. Sizes varied. A man kneeled to row with the double paddle. In these, one or two fished along the coast or in calm weather visited the islands. To prevent waterlogging and rot the balsas were stored on land (above drawings in Heizer and Massey, 1953).

preparation. Wheat noted that tule is tough when green but brittle after it dries. It was their pithy core that made them buoyant.

The Tachi Yokuts also used them green. Josefa Damián, a Tachi Indian interviewed by Harrington in the early years of the century, had traveled as a girl on tule boats with her mother, two sisters and stepfather. She told Harrington it was "green not dry, tules" from which the boats were built. And the boats looked green and stayed green long after, she said.

Bunching the Tule

Bautista's Tachi Yokuts boat was constructed from three tule bundles well over 16 feet long each, tapered toward both ends. The two bundles that would form the sides were around 9 inches to 11 inches thick when compressed and bound. The central bundle was 15 inches in diameter at the middle portion (Damián had remembered such bundles at around 1 foot). To achieve length the tules were undoubtedly overlapped but Harrington did not record how. Barker had written that the Yokuts lapped the butts of the tules at the center, causing a taper toward each end.

The Northern Paiute-style two-bundle boat tapered only slightly at the stern and sharply at the prow. Looking at Wheat's photographs, this appears to have been achieved in each of the two thick bundles used for the boat by enclosing an initial bundle, whose tips and butts were all aligned, with another aligned the same way. The tips of both bunches pointed in the same direction and the butts of the second were placed about 2 feet ahead of those of the first, fattening the bundle at that point to well over 1 foot and lengthening by about 2 feet the completed bundle (which was over 8 feet long).

Yoimut, the last full-blood survivor of the Chunut Yokuts from the northeast shore of Tulare Lake, dictated her story to Frank Latta seventy years ago. She spoke seven languages and could read and write in Spanish and English. The Chunut tule boat she knew well. It was formed of many small bundles each 6 inches thick at the middle and as long as the boat, about 25 feet; each bundle tapered to a point at the ends. Such dimensions indicate many tule lengths had to have been overlapped to form a single bundle, perhaps initially overlapping the butts of two bunches (the tips pointing in opposite directions) and then repeatedly adding bunches to each end in the fashion that the Paiute added a single bunch of tules to their much shorter bundle.

Binding Bundles into a Boat

Bautista tied each group of tules around the girth with cattail *(Typha latifolia)* leaves. Judging from photographs, a single tule bundle had seven cattail rope bindings in the middle portion. They were 18 inches apart, according to Harrington's note. The thin bundle ends remained unbound until the last, when the three bundles were joined together, the larger one placed in the center. The tips of the finished boat, trimmed of overextending or loose ends, would be 4 inches in diameter. Two feet from the tips the diameter was 15 inches. In the last 3 feet or so on each end were four bindings around all three bundles. These bindings became closer and closer together as the end of the boat was reached. They joined the bundles into a finished boat 16 feet long by 32 to 34 inches across at its widest.

Harrington noted that Bautista used a knife on the "straight across stern" to cut out the core so it would come to a point (the Tachi did not distinguish between prow or stern but used the same word for both). Harrington characterized bringing the two ends of the boat up high as an "afterthought." His photograph shows them propped on piles of loose tule to achieve the pleasing crescent shape. The deck appears flat, which would have made the larger middle bundle protrude somewhat below as a kind of keel. Josefa Damián had specified to Harrington the top of the tule boat was flat, not hollow.

But a question remained: How did one tie cattail rope tightly around a bundle of tule without breaking the rope? Anyone who has attempted a square knot in otherwise tough and seemingly flexible green stalks, vines, juncus, cattail leaves or blades of grass knows the problem. The first overhand knot works well, but the second on top of the first to form the square knot snaps as it is pulled tight. The material is simply too brittle to withstand the sharp bends imposed by a second knot.

Harrington found out the hard way. He had observed Bautista lay three cattail leaves one way and three the other, overlapping a little, and then simply twist them together to form a rope. (Wheat observed the Paiute thoroughly soaking the cattail leaves first to make them tough and pliable, then overlapping *the tips* before twisting them into rope for their balsa.) But Harrington failed to watch Bautista actually tie the tule bundles together. A few days later as they were leaving, he thought he knew how and tried himself.

He attempted to secure rolled-up tule mats with fresh cattail leaves, but all his double knots broke. A Yokuts lady named Josie took pity and showed him how to tie cattail rope Indian style.

First, she ran the leaves between her thumb and fingers "pinchingly" to break the cells inside the leaves and make them tougher. Then she twisted the leaves. Next she put them around the rolled-up tule mats and tied a *single* overhand knot. But instead of tying a double knot, she put the two ends together and twisted until it kinked once or twice. She laid the kinked section onto the strand of twisted cattail rope which encircled the mat and tied to the strand two or three *single* overhand knots in a series along the strand.

Wheat found that the Northern Paiute made no knots at all but after encircling the tule bundles with cattail rope merely twisted the two ends together and tucked them into the bundles. Five loops of cattail rope secured the central portion of each bundle. One heavy cattail rope held the two bundles together about 1 foot from the stern, toward which the taper was very slight. The thinner ends were brought together, curved up about 40 degrees as a prow and bound with four separate loops of cattail rope, the loops closer together than the others, very similar to the Tachi prow. A completed one-man craft was 8 feet long, but longer boats for two or more were built the same way.

Freshly cut willow withes were used to bind the huge Choinumne Yokuts balsas described by Thomas Mayfield who had been raised by the Choinumne in the 1850s. Sometimes they built small tule boats for one or two persons for deployment on Kings River just below their ranchería opposite Sycamore Creek. But for the long annual pilgrimage to Tulare Lake where they spent spring and summer among the Tachis, a boat which could hold many people and transport all of their belongings was made in a downstream slough. This boat was of three long bundles of tule, pointed and turned up at each end and bound with thin willow branches. There were two bundles of tule above and one at the bottom which made the boat keeled with a depression along the center of the deck where they piled mortars, pestles, baskets of acorns, acorn bread, seeds, meat and skins for bedding. Eight or ten Indians sat along the sides of the boat.

On Lake Tulare itself the Chunut Yokuts boat described by Yoimut was built up on the ground at the edge of the water from many small-diameter bundles of tule. Yoimut remembered it as thick, 8 feet wide, 25 feet long with turned-up pointed ends. Her description of the boat was consistent with Barker, who added that the bottom of such a boat had layer upon layer of tule bundles tied side by side, tapering to nothing at each end. Small green willow withes bound the bundles and bound them together and also securely bound two peeled fire-hardened willow poles, the same length as the boat, one to each side of the bottom platform of the boat. They were bound so they could not be seen and were bent so the ends met at the bow and stern. It made the boat stiff and unyielding when a great weight was placed at either end.

Finishing the Tule Boat

Strange as it may seem, tule balsas of Lake Tulare were equipped with fire. Indians often were out

Bob Bautista constructing a tule balsa for Ventura County Fair, October 1923. He is trimming the ends of the tules at the prow (or stern). Harrington's notes, likely meant for promotional purposes, read: "Made by Trehlawat, last surviving dancing man of the Tulare Indians who was brought to the Ventura County Fair by Mr. Harrington." Photographed by J. P. Harrington. (Smithsonian Institution National Anthropological Archives)

on the lake for days at a time and could cook fish or mud hens on hearths they built into their boats. Under Bautista's direction two Yokuts women made a tule mat. It was of small dimensions in width and length but thick, six or eight tules in each bundle instead of the usual three or four. A rim of bunches of tule was fastened on with pieces of cattail stuck through the mat. Bautista put the mat in the boat on one end and secured it with two willow twigs arched parallel to the length of the boat, one on either side, stuck into the tule of the boat. Over the mat he spread a 2-inch-deep layer of sticky mud. With leaves of carrizo and wood he made a fire on the mud. Josefa Damián recalled putting mud on the boat when they hunted mud hens and other game. They would take charcoal from an old fire with them and rub fire sticks to create a glowing hearth right on the boat.

Damián's mother told her they slept on the balsa. At night the lake was cold even in summertime and there were no mosquitoes. But they needed a blanket. To secure the blanket and other things while traveling, they arched slender twigs from the edge of one side of the boat to the other, sticking both ends into the tule. One arched twig was about 6 inches from the next and kept bundles from falling into the water.

Northern Paiute Jimmy George kept duck and mud hen eggs, game or weapons from sliding off his tule boat by constructing a gunwale of cattail leaves. A bundle 3 to 4 inches thick was tied at the middle about 2 feet from the tip of the prow (at the point it began to turn upward) and another about 1 foot from the stern. The ends of the two cattail bundles were brought along the sides and tied there and to each other with the twisted cattail leaves. To further deepen the hold of the boat, George stepped into the center of it while the boat was still on land.

The large Chunut Yokuts vessel described by Yoimut, made from many 25-foot-long, small-diameter bundles of tule, must have been somewhat flat bottomed for they also tied an extra bundle of tule along the top of each side so things would not fall off. In addition, near the stern a depression was cut and filled with mud for a fire to cook fish and ducks. In the middle of the boat an approximately 1-foot-diameter hole was made completely through for spearing fish. At the front of the boat a hole 3 feet in diameter and 1/2 foot deep, lined with tules woven like a basket, held the fish and ducks caught on the lake. A Choinumne boat briefly described by Mayfield, different from the one they journeyed in to reach the lake, seems to have been very similar to the Chunut boat known to Yoimut. It was wide and flat-bottomed and exclusively for use on the lake.

Yokuts singer Leon Manuel poles Bautista's tule boat, a bare-footed boy behind him. Background of tule. Harrington's notes indicate Manuel, just prior to setting out on the boat, had tied a single stem of tule around his head as he had tied a beaded band earlier when singing for Bautista's dance. Other relevant Harrington notes read: "Photographed on the Lake at the mouth of the Ventura River. Trehlawat is the last Indian who remembers how to make these boats." By J. P. Harrington, October 1923 (Smithsonian Institution National Anthropological Archives).

Deployment and Care of the Boat

Josefa Damián told Harrington her mother knew how to pole a tule boat. The pole had to be long, only willow could have worked, she believed, buttonwillow was too short. They went with only one pole. Sometimes it got stuck in the mud. She remembered the sound the water made as one poled, and Harrington recorded it: "tr'uq tr'uq."

Bautista poled kneeling or standing. When Harrington kneeled in the middle of Bautista's boat, he got his knees wet; the boat was low in the middle. Harrington judged from lifting the boat that it weighed between 75 and 100 pounds before launching and twice that after a few hours on the water. Damián could not remember the tule boats being taken out of the water, they were just tied up at the bank. They lasted a long time, she believed.

Jimmy George's Paiute boat was also propelled by a pole, but more often the hunter carried his weapons and game in the boat while he waded or swam, pushing the boat along. He said the tule boats never sank, but when not in use they were dried out on the shore.

Yoimut remembered that when their huge tule boat came in, they would all help pull it up on the bank to dry out. Once dry, it was very light. The men often had been out on Tulare Lake three days or more fishing. While still on the water they had cut the fish open, smoked them over the boat's fire and laid them on the raft to dry. They cut the meat from the ducks and dried it in the same way. Long poles moved the boat about the lake. She recalled the day when an American forced her family from their traditional village. They had to cross the entire lake in their tule boat, much of the way too deep to pole. Her stepfather waited three days for the north wind to blow and then set out. He piled the front of the boat high with tules which the wind caught like a sail and pulled them across the lake. On this occasion, however, winds turned to gales and the waves nearly drowned them. The tempest was followed by a great stillness, leaving them stranded over deep water. They made use of the time spearing fish through the fishing hole in the bottom of the boat. In that opening they could see nothing but fish. After two days a light wind came up, and with all-night poling by her mother and stepfather they reached their destination.

Mayfield described fishing on Tulare Lake. The Yokuts fisherman gigged fish lying on his stomach with his head and shoulders over the tule boat fishing hole which was covered with a tule mat. In this way, he saw into the water unseen by the fish.

The fishing hole could be used for hunting. Three or four Indians might be out on Lake Tulare for a week hunting ducks and geese. They made blinds of loose tules thrown over the boat and themselves. The Choinumne could call most any animal or bird—deer, rabbits, ducks or geese—but with a blind they approached within a few feet of the birds for an easy shot with bow and arrow. It was through the fishing hole they slowly, invisibly poled the boat up next to the birds. Ducks that flew overhead were taken in a net much like a modern angler's net for trout, about 2 feet across.

During the annual trip to Tulare Lake on the other, the three-bundle, tule balsa, hunters would leave the boat in the morning and rejoin the main group with game in the evening when they made camp. The boat drifted very slowly down the river and the journey took many days. Years later, Mayfield remembered it:

> When we were all aboard, the boats were poled out into the stream and allowed to drift with the current. Three or four of the men stood at the sides of the raft and kept it away from the snags and in the main current. In this way we boated along at about two or three miles an hour.
>
> At night the raft was moored to the bank in a quiet place and we camped on the shore. It was really one of the greatest experiences I have ever had, and certainly I ever had while living with the Indians. I believe that they, too, enjoyed these trips more than any of their other experiences. We traveled in style and in comfort. The river was lined with trees and wild blackberry and grapevines, and the whole trip was one beautiful scene after another. In after years I used to cross Kings River many times on the bridge south of Kingsburg, and the scene there always reminded me of our trips.

Tule Serving Tray

S. A. Barrett described it as one of the most characteristic features of Northeastern California Indian culture—the flat, triangular tule platter used by the Klamath Lake and Modoc for serving food. Broiled fish or roasted meat was presented on such a tray. The size varied greatly. The one pictured by Barrett measured 34 cm. in length. Although he gave no details of the actual process of manufacture, study of the twined tray makes the construction evident.

About 35 tule stems *(Scirpus)*, each approximately 70 cm. long, and of a very thin variety, were needed as warp. Just a few stems for the weft. (They could have been used green, but drying and remoistening would have prevented looseness in the construction which was often caused by shrinkage.)

The tules were formed into an even bundle, then folded over in half. A double tule stem weft wrapped around them just to one side of the point at which the bundle had been folded (this wrapping occurred in the middle of two overlapping tule wefts). The double weft was then twisted or "twined" to the opposite side of the bundle and drawn tight on the outer margin.

Here the two ends of the weft were twisted together for a short length and brought back into the bundle about 5 cm. from the outer part of the bend or vertex of the bundle.

The twisting in effect continued as the tules were twined across the bundle in a rough arc whose center was the bend of the bundle. There were approximately six twinings at this level, each taking in a fairly large number of the tule warp stems. The weft elements had been doubled through this stage but from this point they were apparently single.

Reaching the margin, the twisting of the weft strips together continued along the margin and again reentered the bundle about 5 cm. above the last row. In fact, all the courses of weft were separated each to the next by about 5 cm. The twinings in this row, however, equaled around 14. They progressively increased. Following courses approximated respectively 26, 34, 36, 38, and finally, 40. In the last couple of courses, some single tule stem warps were twined, though most were double. The wefts at the end of the last course were twisted together and brought back and tied off on the twisted weft to the side below it.

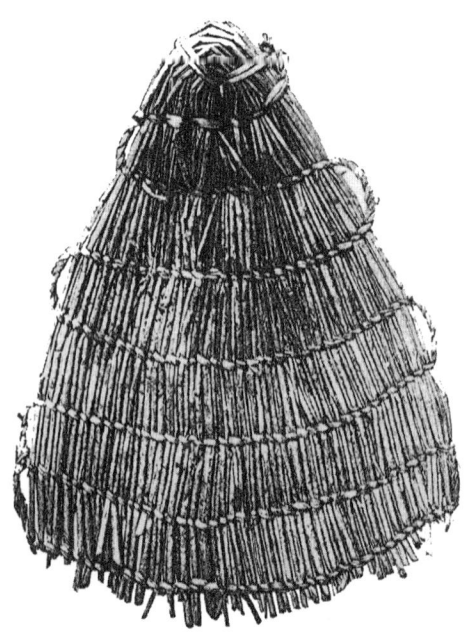

The serving platter (Barrett, 1910).

Twined Double Basket Pomo Fish Trap

The greatest variety of basketry sprang from the genius of the Pomo. Exquisitely coiled baskets covered completely in delicate feathers such "that the surface of the basket has almost the smoothness of the breast of a bird itself," S. A. Barrett observed nearly a hundred a years ago. The Pomo may have been the finest basket makers of all time. They could make baskets beautiful but they could also make them extremely functional, and one of the latter was a twined fish trap, a conical double basket with a funnel mouth. Many fish swam in but few swam out.

Fine craftsmanship in slender willow shoots, ingenious design, even the rolling curves of the thick braid-like rim on the old Pomo fish trap displayed at the Southwest Museum bespeak the beauty and wonder of this clever device. Surprisingly, a Pomo fish trap could be made rather quickly—in about a day—once the material had been gathered. The material consisted simply of the long slender shoots of the willow. Barrett mentioned no special preparation. The bark was left on. Willow shoots could be used green—the basket loosened little through shrinkage—or the withes were dried then dampened to the degree necessary to make them flexible before twining. This coarse, open-work basket depended more on effective design than on sheer skill of the maker, and once its construction was understood, other open-work twined baskets—burden baskets, storage baskets, other fish traps—could be easily constructed.

The Pomo set the trap in a twined brush weir built across a stream. The diameter of the mouth of the trap was about 19 inches. The fish would swim into the mouth and get channeled through the small 4-inch opening in the center of the inner conical basket (whose sides in the Southwest Museum example are slightly convex when viewed from within) and only rarely could find their way back out. The Yurok of northwestern California used double funnel traps in a willow weir to catch salmon ascending the stream. So effective were the weir traps that on occasion, according to Powers, they obstructed the salmon run and led to quarrels and bloodshed with Indians upstream.

The Karok made similar traps for eels. The Wiyot on the lower Eel River also captured eels in double funnel-shaped traps that they weighted down so that they would float below the surface. Then they tied them to stakes planted in the river bottom in such a way the trap would turn with the tide, the large open end always against the current. The driving of the stakes, as described by Powers, is a lesson in itself:

Wading out into the stream the fisherman grips the top of the stake firmly in one hand to prevent it from being splintered, and with a stone in the other softly and carefully beats it into the hard-packed shingle. He works and saws it about, tapping it gently the while; and in this fashion he labors sometimes for hours on one pile, but he drives it down at last so solid that nothing can root it out, where a white man with his impatience and his sledge-hammer, would have battered it into a hundred slivers and failed totally.

Simple basketry fish traps without the inner funnel seem to have been more common in Indian California. The Chumash made long conical fish traps of *guatamote* (or "mule fat," *Baccharis glutinosa*), a brittle wood compared to willow but also extremely common in stream-side southern California bush. Guatamote sprouts many long straight branches, especially after a torrential winter. The Chumash trap had no inner basket and was simply straight sticks of guatamote tied to a hoop of two or three branches twisted together, about 2 feet in diameter; the sticks tapered to an apex perhaps 7 feet or more from the hoop (to judge from J. P. Harrington's informants and very rough sketch), and were held together with native cordage twined around the cone every foot or so and tarred. They placed two or three of these in a rock weir tying the traps to some of the larger rocks. The mouths of the conical devices faced upstream. People would enter the pools above the weir and drive the fish downstream into the traps. They threw small fish back to grow bigger, the Chumash told Harrington.

In the mountain runs above Tulare Lake, Powers found that the Yokuts would drive trout, chub and suckers downstream into a trap set in the middle of a weir. They stretched a line of brushwood between the banks and dragged it downstream, driving the fish before them. Gayton described Yokuts weirs made from willow stakes about 3 feet long and a finger thick interwoven with willow-bark rope. As many as three cylindrical baskets, 12 to 18 inches in diameter and 6 to 10 feet long, were set into the weir facing upstream. For rapid results men, women and children would drive the fish down into the trap, but generally the traps were simply left overnight for a sufficient catch.

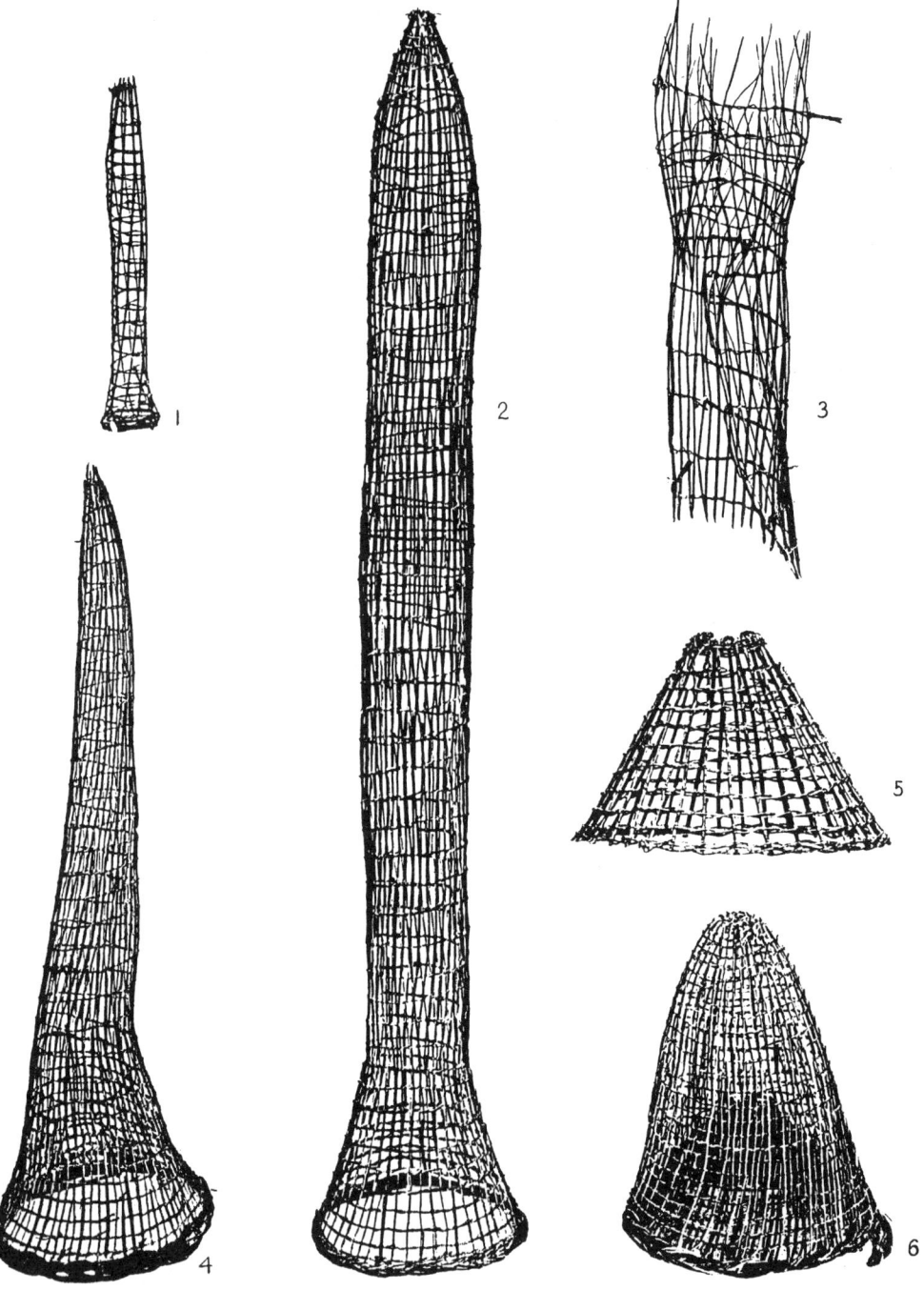

Twined openwork basket traps of the Pomo (scale 1 to 15): 1) Woodpecker trap; bound after dark over entrance to nest; birds entrapped as they left nest following morning. 2) Long, cylindrical fish trap, set in weir. The Chimariko made a similar trap of hazel shoots but, according to H.E. Driver, with a mouth 6' in diameter! They would set this at a narrow spot in the stream and hold it in place with stakes and stones, which partially damned the stream. The Wiyot placed such a trap in a weir with the mouth upstream and drove the fish into it. Once inside, the fish could not turn around nor could they back up because of the current. 3) Trap used in shallow streams for small fish. 4) Cone fish trap, set in weir. 5) Truncated cone trap, planted repeatedly here and there in shallow muddy water by wading fisherman; when he felt escaping fish strike side of trap, hand inserted in small opening above and fish removed. 6) Double basket fish trap with conical mouth. (Barrett, 1908)

The Tolowa possessed a cylindrical basketry trap up to 14 feet long whose function G. W. Hewes explained in extensive notes. The trap caught spring salmon from a double weir in water not over 3 feet deep. The lower weir was made of posts 3 inches in diameter and set 2 to 3 inches apart rising a foot above the water. The two flanks of the lower weir slanted in a V-shape toward the trap which was placed facing upstream. Fish easily jumped over this weir but hesitated jumping back because of the tight space created by the second upstream weir, about 3 feet beyond the first. It was constructed of stakes, some split, about 1 inch in diameter, fairly lightly intertwined with hazel withes. Considerable water pressure pushed against the fence which was reinforced with heavy upright posts driven into the stream bottom every 2 feet and banked with rocks. The posts rose 2 feet above the water and the woven fence 2 feet above that, creating a 4-foot barrier to discourage fish from jumping. The double weir was as much as a hundred feet long. When fish entered between the weirs, a fisherman waded in and drove them to the basket trap whose mouth was under-water but whose rear portion was just above the water where the trapped fish would soon find themselves stranded and helpless.

The Pomo too, in addition to their fine double trap, made the simple long conical fish traps set in a weir.

Pomo Basketry Trap Materials

Barrett, who conducted extensive investigations into basketry among the Pomo in the first years of the twentieth century, found that almost all Pomo baskets—coiled or twined—were built from a foundation of slender willow stems with or without the bark. The exception was in the northern Pomo area where hazel stems were similarly employed, probably as the result of contact with Athapascans to the north for whom hazel was the exclusive foundation material. In the coiled or tightly twined baskets various pliable dressed fibers formed the woof, or weft: roots of sedge, bulrush, bull pine, juniper, willow or bracken and branches of redbud. They were often treated to produce differing colors and from these an array of designs. The finer and ceremonial baskets were further ornamented with

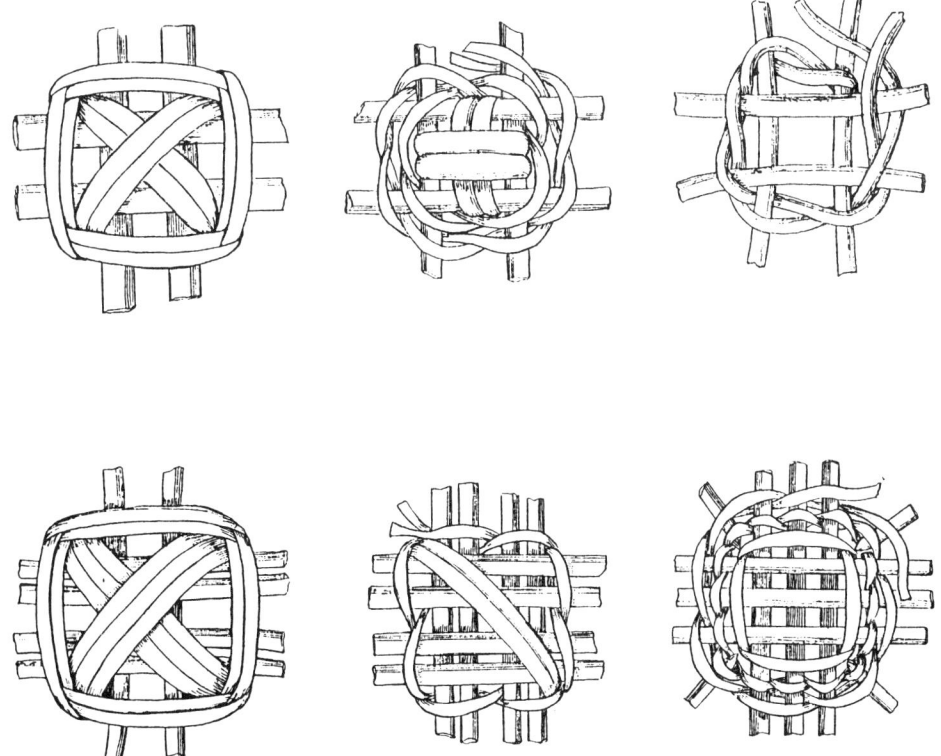

Pomo starting knots for twined baskets; knot at top right discussed in text. Note that in this particular example, seen from the interior perspective, the twining began counterclockwise, then shifted to a clockwise twist for a tightly woven woman's basket; the two strands in openwork fish traps, made by men, were twined counterclockwise (sketches from Barrett, 1908).

beads and bangles of shell as well as all variety of striking feathers. But in the simpler, coarser open-work twined baskets (which concern us here) only willow or sometimes hazel stems, very thin, around 1/16 of an inch in diameter, were used as woof. They were twined into the basket whole and unsplit, sometimes stripped of bark but often with the bark left on, giving an elegant but natural woodsy appearance to the finished piece.

One hundred years ago, Otis Mason, in drawing on an earlier Pomo basketry classification by J. W. Hudson and Carl Purdy, indicated that fish weirs could be twined of either undressed willow or hazel shoots and that hazel was thought to be the original material for this. Mason quoting Hudson's notes also identified hazel and willow species (and their Pomo names) used in basketry by the Pomo: stems of beaked hazel *(Corylus californica—pshû-ba')* and Hinds willow *(Salix sessifolia* or *hinds—bam)*, the prepared inner bark of black willow *(Salix nigra—ma-lóma-ló* and the prepared root of sitka willow *(Salix sitchensis—chi-ko)*. He specified that whole stems of sitka willow were used for fish weirs. The Pomo believed the best willow for coarse twined baskets (Mason followed Chesnut in this) was silver-leaved willow also known as white-leaved willow *(Salix argyrophylla—bam-kal-e)*, common along the Russian River. Much more recently Sandra Newman found it as a willow used in Pomo basketry. A long straight branch with buds few and far apart to minimize knots is best, she wrote.

Mason discussed roughly made willow baskets described earlier by N.J. Purcell among the Round Valley Indians, neighbors of the Pomo.

Willow sticks, while generally used green for basketry, were often gathered in quantities, allowed to dry, then soaked in water as they were needed to make a basket. Soaking branches to increase or restore flexibility was a widespread Indian technique.

Starting Knot

Various starting knots began baskets for the Pomo; some of the more common are shown here. The most frequently employed methods began by crossing pairs of warp sticks. Barrett found that all plain-twined, open-work baskets (except those single basket cylindrical fish traps which converge to a point but have no actual bottom) and most closely woven twined baskets began with a version of this knot. In its simplest form the pairs of crossed sticks were held together only by the regular twining of the incipient woof around each separate stick. I prefer this because of its simplicity. For the double-basket fish trap it would have been more open than other knots and offered less resistance to the flow of water that had to pass through it.

The inner basket of the double-basket Pomo fish trap, completely open at the bottom, started directly by looping the woof around a warp about 1 inch or so from the bottom and commencing to twine and add warp sticks. After a row equal to the circumference of the funnel entrance the warps were reversed and the twining continued just above the first row. The two rows lent stability to the warps before twining one side to the other in the start of a cone.

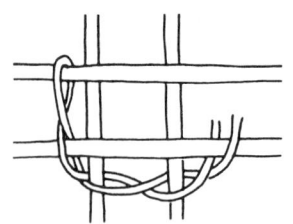 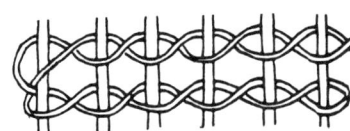 

On the left, starting knot for outer fish-trap basket seen from inside of basket—twined in counterclockwise twist (upward slanting), man's openwork style. In the center, diagrammatic sketch of beginning weave of inner basket. It would seem, from viewing the trap in the Southwest Museum, that after twining left to right a row equal to the circumference of the small funnel entrance, the warps were reversed, right side to the left and vice versa; and left to right twining continued just above the first row. This gave the appearance of an abrupt reversal in direction of twining. The two rows were probably meant to lend initial stability to the warps before twining one side to the other in the start of a cone. From that point, the twining would spiral upward and there would be frequent addition of warps. At right, the single strand, wrapped-twining method, likely used for attaching hoops to reinforce some fish traps. (Sketches adapted from Goodchild, 1984.)

Openwork Twining—Man's Work

The Pomo, recorded Barrett, had the greatest number of weaves in native California. For twining, they possessed five styles, not including special weaves for the borders of baskets. Simple plain twining, found on all forms of basketry, predominated. It was the only one employed on fish traps.

Plain twining is done with either with an upturning woof or a downturning woof. As the two woof strands are woven through the warp (one in front of or on the face of the warp stick, one behind, and then reversed for the next warp stick) they also revolve about each other completing a half revolution or reversal between the vertical warp sticks. If this revolving is clockwise, when the twining goes from left to right as it does in Pomo baskets, the woof is said to be downturning. If counterclockwise, it is upward turning. Upturning woof strands come from the lower side of the line of twining in front of one warp stick and pass up and behind the next warp stick.

Barrett reminds us that basketry among aboriginal peoples was essentially a woman's art and that the Pomo were no exception: Pomo women made all the coiled and almost all the twined baskets. Men made fish traps as well as coarse open-work storage and burden baskets, the latter sometimes also made by the women. Since all tightly woven baskets had downward turning woof strands and nearly all open-work baskets (those with open space between lines of twining) had upward turning strands, and since men made no tightly woven baskets and women very few open-work baskets; downward turning woof may be said to have been woman's weave and upward turning, the man's.

To keep the twining tight, the woof was held taut. The basket maker held one end of the woof in the mouth and the other in the right hand, exchanging the strand in the hand for the one in the mouth after the woof had passed around a warp. The twining proceeded in this rhythmic fashion.

Barrett did not find reinforcing hoops around the circumference on Pomo fish traps, but there are three hoops which over time have broken free and lie within the double-basket Pomo trap exhibited at the Southwest Museum (two were likely for the larger basket, one for the small opening of the funnel). Barrett did note the use of hoops on rims on other Pomo baskets such as conical burden and mortar baskets. These hoops were of willow and bound with sapwood of the grape *(Vitis californica)*, a general binding material used in house construction and in making brush fences for capturing game.

The Warp

From the starting knot the woof began to twine around and around in an upward spiral. The basket maker worked on the outside of the basket. New warp sticks were added almost at once. The first went in the four open corners of the knot. In analyzing the Pomo double-basket fish trap on display in the Southwest Museum, it was apparent that the larger end of each new warp stick was inserted first, pointing toward the bottom or knot. Besides giving the vortex of the basket—the area of severest wear and tear—greater strength, having the finer ends of the warp project from the rim facilitated the folding of these into the beautiful braid-like effect that was the hallmark of Pomo twined baskets.

Each new warp stick was allowed to meet the line of twining below; rarely, the end was pushed slightly *into* the line below, next to an adjoining stick. As the twining proceeded, sticks were added frequently to create the cone shape which gradually emerged under the control of the basket maker as he tightened the woof.

The warps varied from less than 1/8 to almost 3/16 of an inch in diameter. The Pomo double-basket fish trap shown by Barrett was about 2-1/2 feet long. Ideally, each new warp projected about 12 inches beyond the expected rim to provide material for the finishing border. However, in the Southwest Museum piece, a number of warps failed

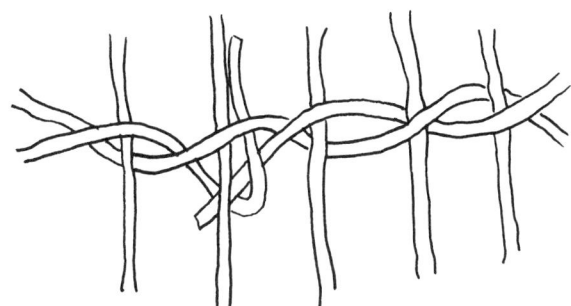

Pomo splice on plain-twined upturning woof.

even to reach the rim, and sticks of appropriate length were added and spliced. They were placed alongside the original warp stick and twined in by the weft for two or three rows next to the original stick. Distance between warps was about 5/8 of an inch, center to center, and between rows of twining about 5/8 to 3/4 of an inch. Available materials and intended use ultimately determined dimensions. Fingerlings caught in a tight trap could make the difference in a survival situation.

Splicing the Woof

The Pomo basket trap at the Southwest Museum revealed that as one of the old woof weavers came to its end, a new slender willow stem was begun next to the old weaver where it passed behind the last warp. The thin tail end of the old woof came down behind and under the new woof just past this warp, turned up over the new woof and slipped behind the other unspliced woof strand that passed above. Pulled snug, the old tail end would be

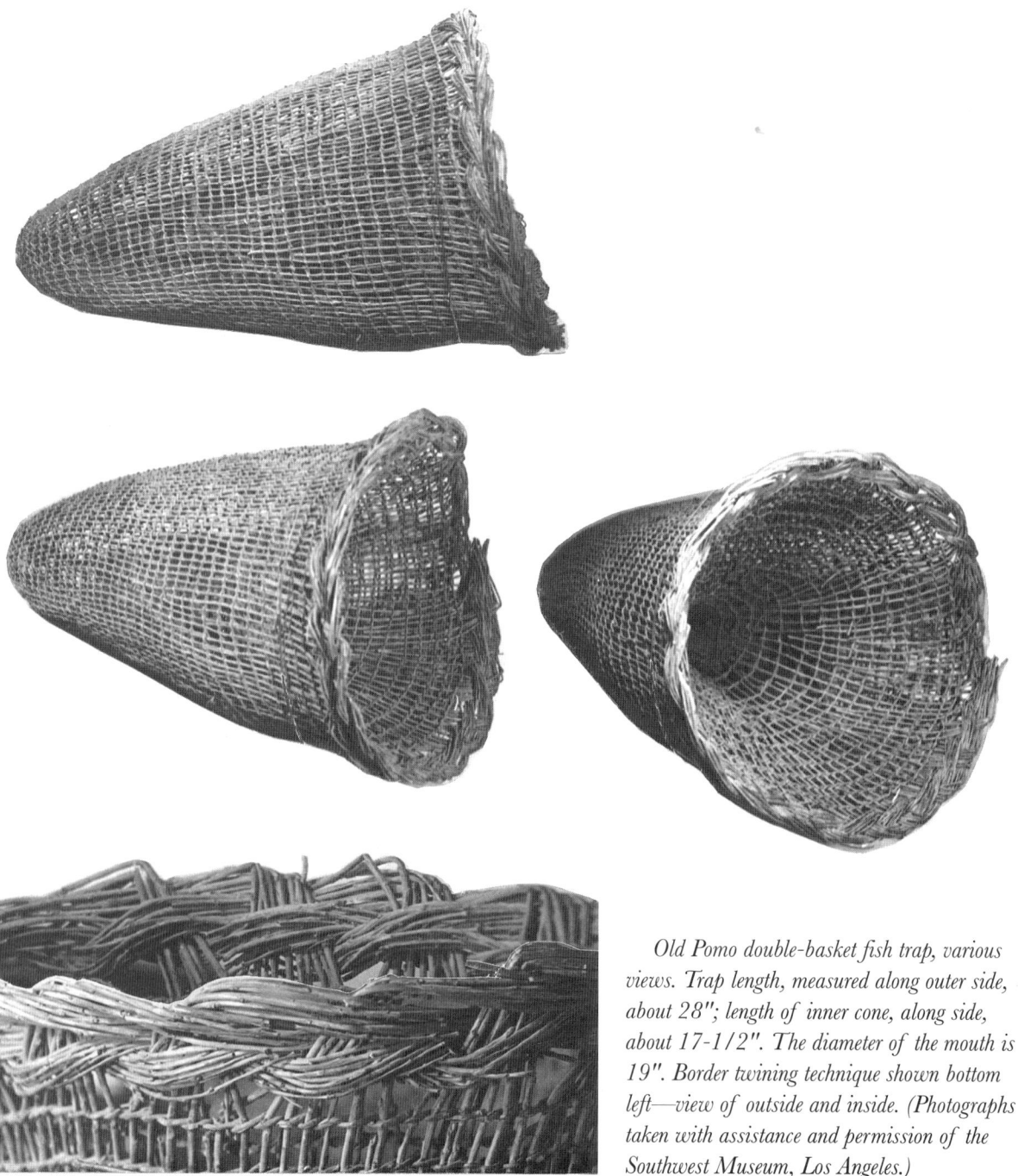

Old Pomo double-basket fish trap, various views. Trap length, measured along outer side, about 28"; length of inner cone, along side, about 17-1/2". The diameter of the mouth is 19". Border twining technique shown bottom left—view of outside and inside. (Photographs taken with assistance and permission of the Southwest Museum, Los Angeles.)

left jutting straight up next to the warp. Tension from the continued twining held the end of the new weaver in place. (See diagram.)

Borders and the Secret of How to Get the Fish Out

The fine tapering ends of the warp of Pomo fish traps were gathered in bundles, bent in the direction of the woof and twined together into a border that gave the appearance of a thick braid. The similarity to a braid came about from the manner in which each new bundle of warps entered the twining. As viewed from the outer surface of the basket, a freshly bent warp bundle came down and paralleled the twining on the outside of the following warp bundle. (The twining enveloped these bundles.)

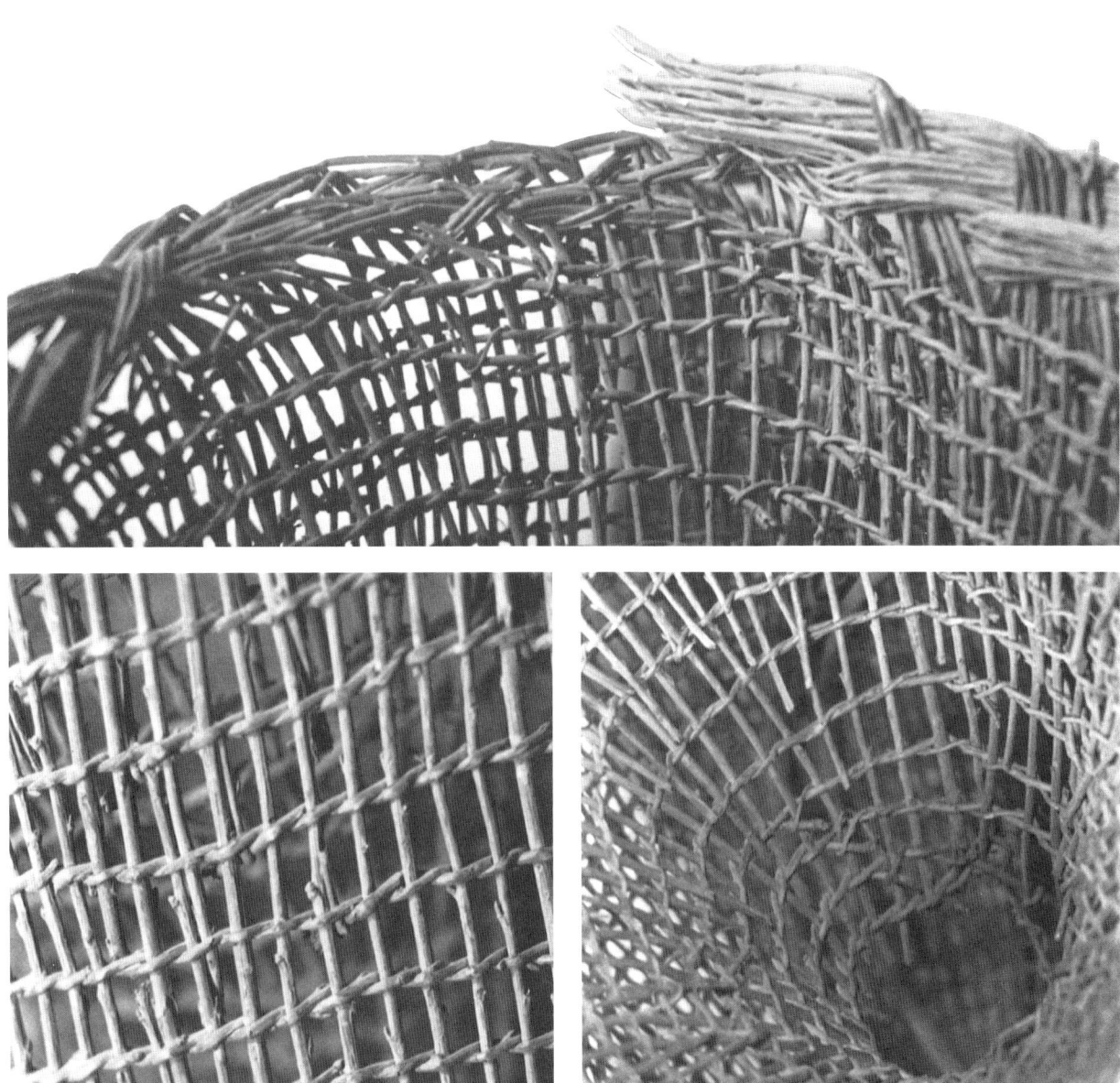

Close-ups of Pomo double-basket trap. Top: inside of inner basket where twining main body wefts meld (in top center of photo) with bent-over warps to begin twining of the rim, at first, of the inner basket rim and then after some inches (to the left) combining inner and outer rims; the termination of the border twining is seen as the raised border to the right. Bottom left: detail of outer basket shows splices of wefts (near center of photo) and warps and insertion of additional warps. New wefts as well as warps are begun with the thick end of the branch. Distance between warps is about 5/8", center to center, and between rows, a little over 5/8" to 3/4". Bottom right: the small mouth of the inner cone, slightly unraveled. Note frequent addition of warps as twining proceeds. (Photographs taken with assistance and permission of the Southwest Museum, Los Angeles.)

Next it folded into the previously gathered and twined bundles that together, as one woof element, passed diagonally downward to the inside of the third group of warps and continued as part of a thick, plain twined weave. The new bundle, as it paralleled the twining before integrating with it, added a rich third bundle strand over the line of twining and made the border look like a braid.

The effect of this border, done very tightly, on the double-basket Pomo fish trap in the Southwest Museum is striking. From four to nine adjacent thin warp ends were gathered from each basket, inner and outer, and combined as one very thick strand to enter the twining. This not only gave a beautiful and finished braid-like border to the trap but united the inner basket or funnel with the outer basket. The two mouth diameters were, of course, roughly the same.

In Barrett's account of such a double-basket trap, alternate warp sticks from each basket were cut off at the rim and two remaining sticks from each basket joined as groups of four sticks to enter the border twining as described.

When the end of the border twining was reached on most Pomo baskets, on a simple cone trap or other single baskets for example, the ends of the last warp sticks that remained were bound to the edge of the rim with a willow stem or string or braided together and the braid bound to the edge or passed in and out among the warp sticks just below the border twining. That was true, noted Barrett, except for the double fish trap just described.

In the double-basket fish trap the ends of the last warps were simply bound together but not fastened to the rim. In fact, for 8 or 10 inches after this the border was not woven in common but each had a separate border of warp bundles that had been twined together before they joined as one. This opening can be seen in the Southwest Museum example. It was to empty the trap of fish, wrote Barrett. It would have been next to impossible to get them out through the funnel opening. When set, the edges of the unsecured border and the projecting bundle of warps were temporarily bound together to keep the fish from escaping. To collect them, the temporary binding was simply cut and the trap turned bottom upwards.

Other Baskets

Simple storage or burden baskets in the plain twined, open-work Pomo style were essentially the same as the outer fish trap basket. Pomo burden baskets, for example, had a conical form but were generally not the near-perfect cone found in burden baskets among so many California Indians. The bottom of the basket was more rounded in the Pomo style and one side somewhat flattened to rest on the back where it was carried by means of a woven net. A band which passed over the forehead supported the weight. Sometimes a simple braided tumpline alone was looped around and attached to such a basket. Storage baskets had broad bottoms, softly convex sides and slightly constricted mouths.

On burden and storage baskets, more common than the false braided border was what Barrett called the plain twined bundle warp border. In its simplest form warp stems were bent sharply over in pairs and twined with a following pair. New pairs joined one of the two bundles on the inside surface of the basket as that bundle passed over and behind the other, thus camouflaging their entry and giving the basket, on the outside, the appearance of a continuous plain twined border.

Many Pomo baskets extended this principle of warp twining by gathering warp stems in groups of three or even four and from them creating three or four rows of twining. One stem from each warp group might be added to a strand on each row. Sometimes all the warp stems made only a second and top row where one or two strands might be incorporated, but in no case were all three incorporated in the top row; rather, one or two of each group were cut off even with the row.

Three-strand group border, second and top row, on twined Pomo basket collected by J.W. Hudson (Mason, 1904).

Fishing Nets

Harpoons and specialized nets for fishing characterized much of California Indian life. A detachable barbed head linked by a line to a spear shaft was an idea old as the European Paleolithic and a simple net to catch fish in a stream, undoubtedly ancient and enduring as well. When out hunting or for any purpose a Hupa man would carry a small conical net. It could quickly be strung around any pliable withe cut from the forest. The withe was bent into a hoop, the two ends were bound together to form a handle and the man was ready to net trout and crayfish from the nearest creek. Harpoons and fishing nets were basics of native California, especially in the northwest.

The lower courses of the large rivers were conducive to nets and there spears were little used. The depth and breadth also often precluded weirs. The downstream Wiyot respected greatly the spearing skill of the upstream Nongatl, for example, so complete was the Wiyot reliance on nets. California nets ran the gamut from small bag nets and hoop dip nets to large conical nets on frames held from scaffolds overlooking family-owned deepwater eddies to long rectangular gill nets and seines. The large conical nets took more salmon than any other kind.

While size and shape of nets varied, they all shared principles of construction. Before focusing on specific net designs and how they were used, it is well to understand California netting fundamentals.

Manufacturing Technique

Northwesterners made fishing nets from cordage of iris fiber *(Iris macrosiphon)*. Other Californians usually tied them of milkweed or Indian hemp. Strength of cordage and size and number of meshes depended on the weight and size of the fish sought. Nets came in just two basic forms—rectangular and cone-shaped. The universal netting knot was the sheet bend, tied as a kind of half hitch around the two sides of the bottom of a loop in the preceding row as the net maker made more loops working across the net from left to right.

The men of northwestern California made and repaired fishing nets in the evening or on rainy days in the sweathouse. Kroeber learned during extensive field work among the Yurok how they made salmon and sturgeon nets. A large hooked stick was rammed into the joint where the ridge pole rested on the upright timber in the middle of the wall, or a hole was made in a wall timber and a pole inserted. A smaller hook was used for nets for smaller species such as lampreys. From such a support the net was hung. The net maker moved farther and farther away from the support as the size of the net increased. He held a mesh measure of elk antler in his left hand and tied the knots with his right. He brought the cord wrapped on the shuttle down around the mesh measure. Then he passed it through the loop above from behind, circled around the back of the loop from right to left and brought it forward under itself, fastening the two sides of the loop in a half hitch. With the shuttle in his mouth, he adjusted the knot to the mesh stick and pulled it tight. He repeated the process with the next loop to the right.

Northwestern California shuttles, long, slender and slotted at each end, had been of elk antler in prehistoric times, the Yurok told Kroeber, who speculated that wood was probably a poor second choice. In historic times, at least, the Karok preferred the hard wood of manzanita. From the shuttle the cord was paid out as the net was tied.

Lark's head knot, formed by simply turning a loop back on itself and running a cord through the two loops thus formed; removing the cord removes the knot (Kroeber and Barrett, 1960).

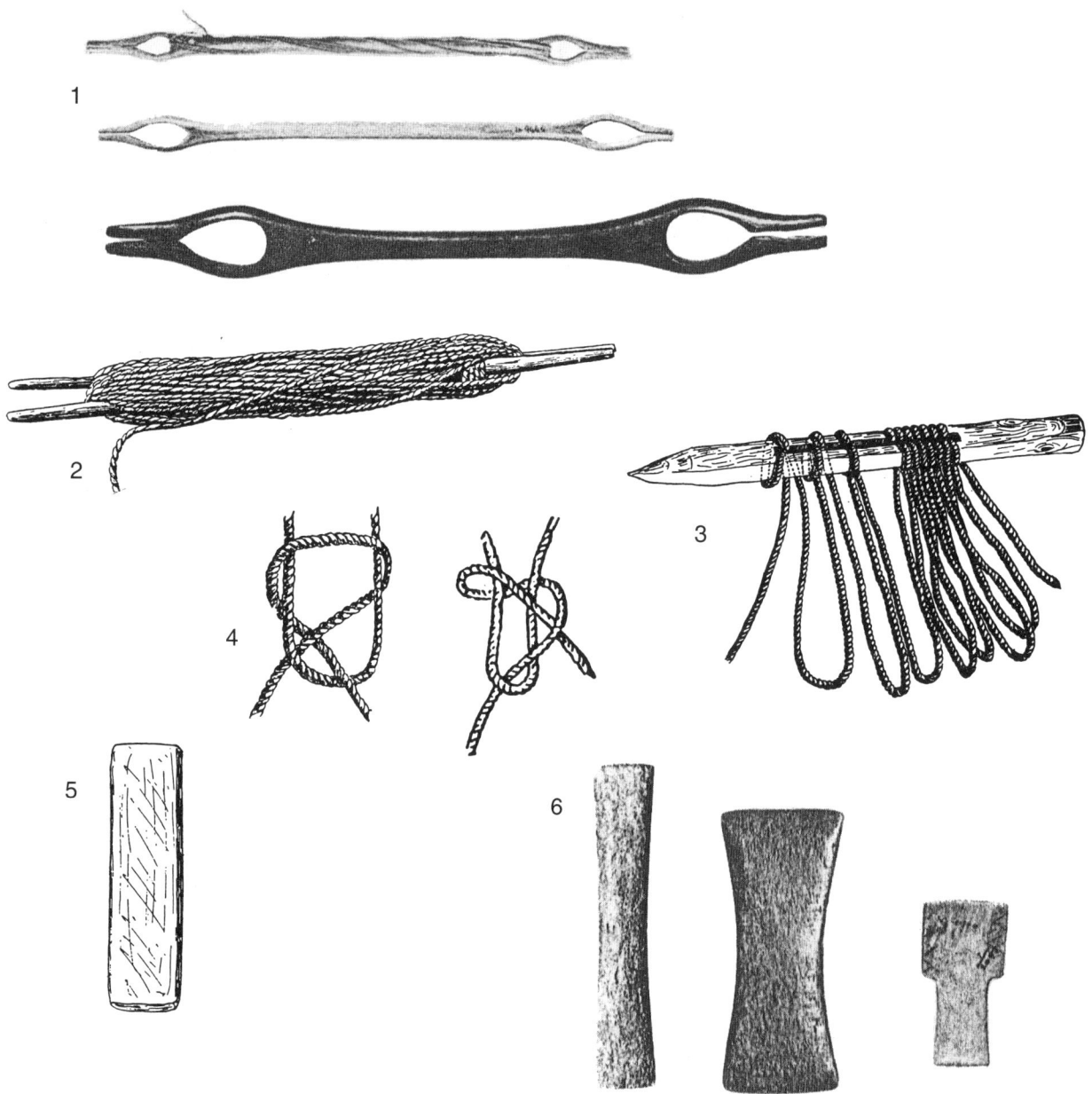

1. Net shuttle: top two of elk antler, probably Yurok, around 30 cm. long; below, likely of manzanita, Karok, around 40 cm. in length (Kroeber and Barrett, 1960).

2. Northern Maidu net shuttle (34.5 cm.) composed of two slender sticks. The only mesh measures used were the first two or three fingers of the hand (Dixon, 1905).

3. Wintu net shuttle. Flat wood, 7" long, sharpened at one end and slit cut in center; loops of cordage strung through the opening (Du Bois, 1935).

4. Sheet bend or mesh knots (first in Du Bois, 1935; second in Mason, 1889).

5. Wintu mesh measure, smooth flat wood, 5-1/4" long (Du Bois, 1935).

6. Northwestern California mesh measures, almost always of elk antler, sometimes of bone (likely from the ribs of large sea lions). Wood could be used for a temporary measure or by "shiftless men," wrote Kroeber and Barrett. They noted that many meshes had the high polish or the brown or rich old ivory look of having passed through the generations. Striations made in smoothing consistently remained on these measures, however, and suggest having been rubbed on a sandstone surface. Long slender measures were for sturgeon nets (for set nets, measures were around 6", for drag nets, 5" to 5-1/4"); shorter measures with more constricted middles were for salmon (around 4" for set nets, 3-1/2" for drag nets); unusual shapes, permitting different gauges on the same measure, were for smaller species. Specimens collected by Kroeber, early twentieth century (Kroeber and Barrett, 1960).

Flat rectangular nets were straightforward, simply a progression of loops and knots back and forth on a plain surface with numbers and size of meshes consistent throughout, 8 cm. square on the Yurok gill net discussed below for example. (For more graphic description of net making of this sort see chapter on carrying nets.)

In conical nets the mesh number and size increased from the bottom tip of the cone outward. The netting proceeded in an ever-expanding spiral of generally rectangular meshes. The original knot, wrote Kroeber, had three meshes originating from it, two of which were rectangular and one triangular. Apparently, the knot formed the first loop, and two subsequent knots each forming loops were tied to the circumference of the original loop, and the process of making knots and loops in a spiral continued. Thus, when one looked back, the original loop, which emanated from the original knot, was three-sided while the two others around the original knot were the standard four-sided (if more than one loop hung from one of these). As the tying of the cone-shaped net expanded outward, the number of meshes increased naturally, each round by about four, more rapid flare achieved by inserting extra meshes. Inserting extra meshes created some three-sided and five-sided meshes. The meshes themselves gradually increased in size by loosening the cord slightly as it passed around the mesh measure or by using net measures made with two or three gauges.

The edges of both kinds of nets, conical and rectangular, were frequently reinforced and finished with an added cord or cords knotted into or bound on the outside rows of loops to form a straight selvage. Large conical lifting nets mounted on A-frames, the much smaller, shorter landing nets also mounted on A-frames, and the small scoop net—all had extra cords on the two sides of the V against the frame and often across the front as well. Generally, the selvage of those nets was in fact two cords that had not been twisted together; they were knotted to the meshes and in turn bound every other mesh to much longer loops of heavier cordage. These long loops were knotted in a lark's head to an even stronger straight headline. Front meshes sometimes were attached directly to a headline with lark's-head knots.

Incidentally, the Yurok believed no one should pass behind a man knotting nets, nor speak loudly in his presence lest the salmon hear the noise and later avoid the net. Finished, the net was at once immersed in the river and considered ready for five to six years of service.

Scoop or Surf Net

In the roiling surf to his knees and higher, the Yurok fisherman anticipated the next wave. He grasped the net by the arched wooden crossbar and the juncture of the two long frame poles (over 3.3 m. each). With the silver of spawning surf fish, lampreys, candlefish or trout, he lowered the forward apron of the net to horizontal and below horizontal and caught the wave and the fish on the apron. The continuing force of the wave carried the fish back toward the pouch. He raised the net, and it hung heavy with fish. The bottom formed a bulging sack and the weight produced a natural constriction in the net above. The fisherman grasped this "neck" to prevent loss of his catch as he continued watching the waves and scooping

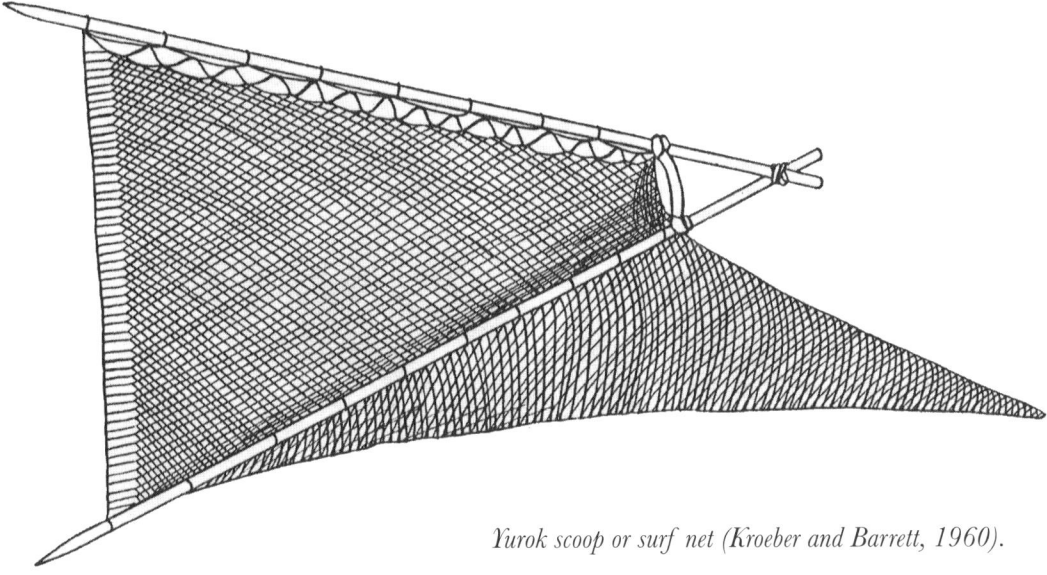

Yurok scoop or surf net (Kroeber and Barrett, 1960).

small fish from the surf. Releasing his grip on the neck, they slid back into the sack. With 20, 30, "even 50 wriggling pounds massed in the cone of his net," as Kroeber and Barrett described it, he finally staggered back up the beach.

To withstand the weight and added wear and tear, the cordage of the lower part of the cone was considerably heavier than the rest of the net, sometimes consisting of a doubled cord. Furthermore, to insure that no mesh opened too wide and allowed loss of the catch in this crucial area, meshes were made smaller. Kroeber and Barrett documented one net whose meshes were 13 by 13 mm. (1/2 inch square) at the tip of the pouch, 15 by 15 mm. square at the outer edge of the pouch and 24 by 24 mm. square on the front of the apron.

The apron itself was simply a flat rectangular extension on the circumference or top of the cone. In manufacture, the netting knots would stop following a spiral and switch to the common back-and-forth pattern. The apron would cover about one-half to two-thirds the circumference of the mouth of the 1-m.-deep cone. Kroeber and Barrett characterized the apron of the Yurok net shown as unusually long (almost 2 m.), increasing in width as it flared out mainly by progressively increasing the size of the mesh (the distance between knots made in this specimen on a 1 cm. standard) so that the back of the apron measured about 1.7 m. and the outer front 2.25 m.

Running along the front edge and both sides, a heavy buckskin thong served as headline. The last row of loops forming the meshes of the front edge were extended from the normal approximately 2 cm. between knots out 10 cm. to the headline where they were attached by a lark's-head knot. There were a total of 156 long meshes.

Along both sides of the apron, at every fifth to seventh mesh (of approximately 110 meshes), a line was knotted in the usual sheet bend and extended out about 12 cm. and tied in a lark's-head knot to the buckskin headline that was bound to the pole as shown. There were 18 points of attachment on each side. The edge of the net hung about 10 cm. from the headline.

The edge in the rear at the crossbar went 56 cm. and had a strong 3-ply cord headline to which the final loop of each mesh was attached with a lark's head. Of these knots, 108 crowded the short space. Though damage had occurred, remains and repairs suggested to Kroeber that loops of a stout cord had been joined to the headline and to the crossbar in a series of half hitches.

Lifting Nets

These A-frame nets, described by Kroeber and Barrett, were lowered into salmon-rich river eddies from ramshackle scaffolds jutting out over rugged banks or over the face of large boulders. Struts, braces, stringers— anything that might find a hold or support was lashed into the structure to secure

Trinidad Yurok man takes smelt with surf net. (Photograph by Edward S. Curtis circa 1923, courtesy of the Southwest Museum.)

a plank over the swirling water. On the plank, on a low solid cylindrical block sat the fisherman holding a signal button of bone or antler in his hand. A fisherman's club hung nearby.

Underwater fences to guide the salmon—horizontal poles with interwoven brush, barring passage of fish close to the bank—moved the fish into the faster water of the eddy and into the mouth of the net at the end of the platform. In some cases holes had been made during low water in the rock of the river bottom to seat the horizontal poles of the guide or fence.

The Yurok fisherman lowered the A-frame mouth of the net vertically into the water, slipping the rope ring tied near the bottom of one side of the frame over a short vertical pole in the riverbed near the scaffold. This side of the A-frame was notched so the net would not slip, according to Hewes. The other side, or the inshore pole of the frame, projected about a foot below the crossbar and came to a sharpened point that was pushed into the sand or gravel to anchor in place the lower edge of the net trap. Finally, to secure the net a guy line, usually of grapevine, ran from the pole to a tree, bush or rock on shore.

As the salmon, which swam close to the river bottom, entered the net through the large, lower openings between trigger cords, they would touch the cords or sides of the net near the cords or farther on and cause a vibration along the signal string to the signal button in the fisherman's hand. This was an alert to take in the net. Pulling up on the signal string, he partially closed the mouth of the net and entrapped the fish. The entire device was then lifted with the catch onto the scaffolding. A large wooden hook fastened to an upright often prevented the net from slipping back into the water. With his short wooden club he stunned the fish still in the net, then placed them safely on shore.

The cycle was repeated. At the height of the salmon run a winter's supply of fish might be taken in a few days, Kroeber and Barrett learned. Women generally did the cleaning, drying and storing of the fish caught by the men.

Hupa fishing platform on the Trinity River. Spring salmon were netted in quiet eddies where fish came to rest from raging waters. Projecting rocks turned the current around and allowed nets to be positioned with the mouth downstream. (Photograph by Edward S. Curtis, early twentieth century, courtesy of the Southwest Museum.)

Sturgeon lifting nets were larger and had larger meshes. Those for lampreys were much reduced in size. Smaller and shorter landing nets, mounted on an A-frame but without signal cords, the northwest California Indians used for dipping fish out of corrals or weir enclosures or from canoes in streams and lagoons. Lampreys, eulachon and other small species were taken with these small landing nets.

Dip or Plunging Nets

The so-called dip net the northwest California Indians and others in the northern part of California plunged into deep foaming waters at the foot of a fall or rapids or at the end of a roiling riffle where salmon congregated but could not be seen. Luck would usually bring up at least one fish but not always a salmon; trout, bullheads or even lampreys might be found struggling in the conical net strung at the base of two long poles which came together at the opposite end in an acute angle. Rarely more than a meter in diameter and the same in depth, the net looped over a bent withe lashed to the extremities of the side poles. Hewes' Yurok consultants said that these poles were of fir and the bent semicircular hoop, generally in two pieces, of oak, pepperwood or hazel. Farther back across the two long poles a heavy cord held the opposite side of the net. Informants told Hewes that formerly this had been a wood stick. Near the apex was the headbar.

The Karok told Gifford the headbar was about a foot from where the long poles came together and they described its function. At the foot of a fall or similar spot, especially in the heavy murky water of winter, the Karok thrust the net downward as deep as possible until it was stopped by the bar as it reached the *head* of the fisherman who was

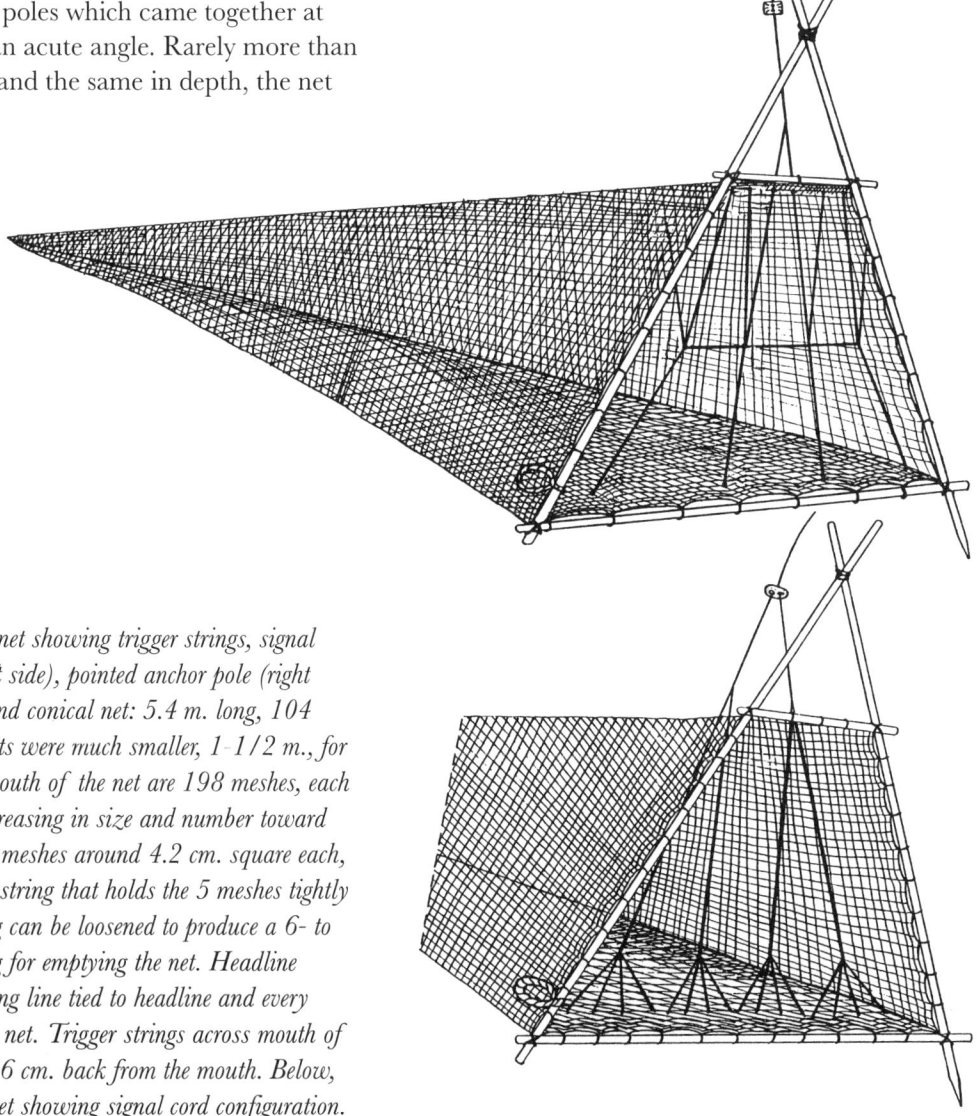

Above, Yurok lifting net showing trigger strings, signal button, rope ring (on left side), pointed anchor pole (right side), rest of A-frame and conical net: 5.4 m. long, 104 meshes. (Some lifting nets were much smaller, 1-1/2 m., for example.) Around the mouth of the net are 198 meshes, each about 7 cm. square, decreasing in size and number toward the tip, which ends in 5 meshes around 4.2 cm. square each, laced onto a heavy drawstring that holds the 5 meshes tightly together. The drawstring can be loosened to produce a 6- to 8-inch-diameter opening for emptying the net. Headline fastened to frame, stapling line tied to headline and every third mesh of mouth of net. Trigger strings across mouth of net are attached about 76 cm. back from the mouth. Below, front of Shasta lifting net showing signal cord configuration. (After Hewes, in Kroeber and Barrett, 1960.)

protected with a basketry cap. A woman's cap might be used, but men made one expressly for the purpose, twined from pineroot as carefully as the cap for women but without the usual xerophyllum overlay. Such a cap might also be used with a tumpline for carrying burdens. Hewes specified that the Karok fisherman stood *between* the poles when thrusting the net, which was stopped or prevented from flying out of his hands by the back of the head cushioned with a basketry hat. He hauled in the catch by lifting on the side poles, alternately, one after the other.

In shallower, faster water, the net was used differently. Kroeber and Barrett explained that the fisherman would cast his net out into the rapids almost horizontally as far as possible. He was not between the poles but behind them. It was the front of the basketry cap that now protected him as he hauled in his catch: first the apex of the frame rested on his forehead and then the poles rested on and slid over his head. Barrett, in the summer of 1957, witnessed a Karok using a plunge net in the rapids of Ishi Pishi Falls on the Klamath and secured motion pictures of the operation. The fisherman always cast his net somewhat upstream, but no matter how quickly he worked, the very turbulent fast-flowing rapids always carried the net downstream before it could be hauled out, making the fishing exceptionally strenuous.

In contrast, Hewes described the Yurok taking eulachon from a canoe with a dip net on lower reaches of the river where the water slowed. They pulled the net with a sidewise sweep. On bars at the mouths of streams or where shallow water ran slowly, the Yurok swung the frame sideways downstream with just enough speed to open the net. In a small eddy the net was plunged and held, the current sufficient to open the net for the fish.

Miscellaneous Uses of the Conical Net

Kroeber and Barrett described a Yurok conical net in the University of California collections. It had been catalogued as a "drag net for salmon." Two old slender sticks were still attached to the sides. With these it would have been held open in the stream. Each side of the trapezoidal mouth measured 47 cm., the top, 140 cm. and bottom, 200 cm. Its length was 250 cm.

Hewes recounted that on occasion the Yurok would splice two such conical nets together, side by side, and mount the double net at its two far flanks on poles, each about 12 feet long. The apparatus was intended for deep water and was held between two canoes by two men, one near the center of each canoe. Meshes were about 6 inches, suggesting large fish as the object. While Hewes found the nets sometimes used without sinkers, Kroeber described the Yurok double drifting bag net weighted with sinkers so that it could drag the river bottom. In the canoes, paddlers fore and aft, or sometimes only one paddler in each vessel, kept the canoes headed apart, counteracting the pull of the nets as they were swept downstream by the current. They paddled just enough to keep the nets open to take the salmon as they swam upstream. Slow waters or small eddies were best, and the conical drag net was especially

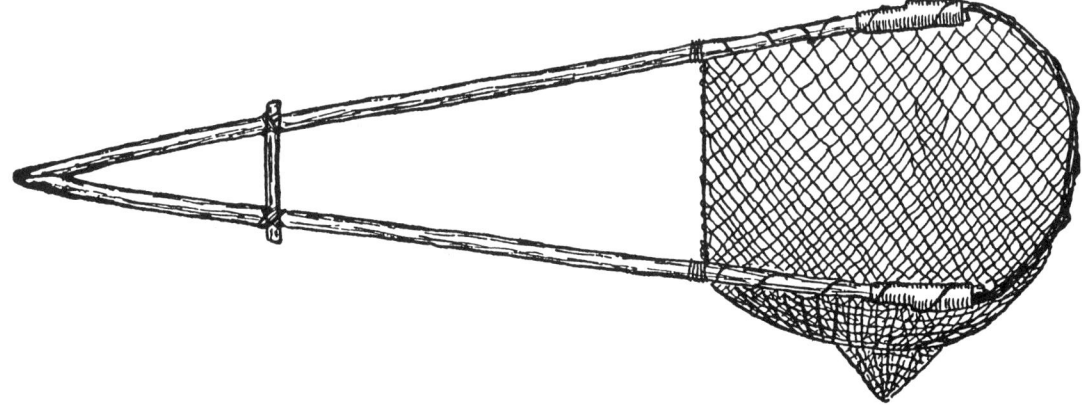

Wintu deepwater dip net, 6' to nearly 12' long, curved stick across 3' front wrapped to sides with cord, net also about 3' deep. Used in muddy water. Often accompanied by torchbearers who would drive the salmon as the Wintu fisherman scooped out the fish. This particular specimen was collected by Du Bois in 1929. It is 3.63 m. long, .81 m. across the mouth, 1.06 m. for length of the mouth, .68 m. across heavy cord at the rear of the net, and has a .28 m. headbar. The conical pouch is 83 cm. deep; the outer mesh, 3.5 cm.; mesh at cone tip, 2.5 cm. (Du Bois, 1935).

used in the low water of autumn on the Klamath. When they felt a fish, the pole was raised quickly and pushed upstream to close the net and entrap the fish.

The Hupa also employed the double bag net in the autumn, when the water would get muddy, they told Hewes. Strong women also participated as paddlers. Two conical landing nets were removed from their A-frames and fastened together with a 3-foot stick at their middle. Longer poles were placed at the two outer sides and held by men in the manner of the Yurok. When they felt a tremor on the poles, the canoes came closer together, the nets were hauled in, the fish clubbed and dropped into the boat. In muddy water the net was effective during the day; otherwise it was better at night.

The Wintu netted suckers with weirs during drives in the creeks and in the shallow waters of large rivers in August. Wings of brush weighed down with rocks or, in rocky creeks, wings of stone pointed diagonally downstream. Across the 2- to 3-foot opening in the center, a small conical net caught the fish that ran before the men who were wading the stream, throwing stones and shouting. Cora Du Bois noted that the drives, which were held in the morning, began with a race between the young men. They would dash naked to the net that would be used to seal the weir. After dividing the catch, everyone spent the day drying fish, feasting and gambling.

Barrett and Gifford recorded the use of a casting net among the Miwok. Its large circular mouth spread wide as it was cast on the water. A long rope drew it to shore while the mouth closed and entrapped the fish.

Flat Nets

In the quiet lower courses of rivers, on bays, estuaries and lagoons at river mouths; long narrow nets or seines were hauled by canoes to encircle fish. Thus trapped, the fish were taken out with dip nets. When set with sinkers and floats the long rectangular net became a gill net. In northwest California standard meshes took salmon and other fish, extra large meshes took sturgeon.

Hewes found that the Shasta seine measured 4 feet in width and 100 feet long. They tied one end ashore on a slow river where fish might be resting. The other end was held in a dugout canoe and taken in a wide arc to impound salmon and steelheads.

The Miwok seine described by Barrett and Gifford was from 6 to 8 feet high and as long as 40 feet. Placed across a river or lagoon, men drove all variety of fish, including salmon, into the net where

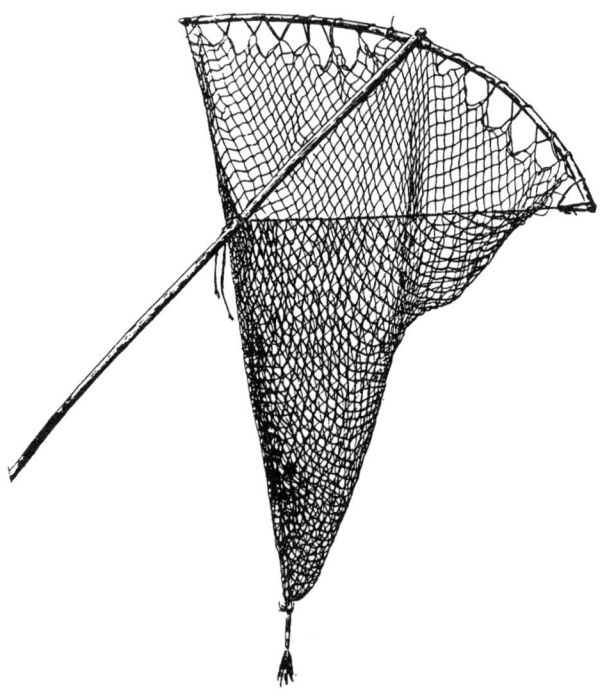

Northwestern Maidu bow net. Conical netting of milkweed or Indian hemp almost one meter long. While Maidu of the Sacramento Valley preferred seines, this net was the favorite of the mountains. Used chiefly for fish other than salmon on small streams. Mouth of net held open by flexible willow wand and straight pole tied to wand and middle of the opposite side of the net mouth. Bow was the upper side and the pole, stuck in the streambed, anchored the bottom. The net stretched completely across the streambed. After fish entered the net, raising the pole quickly caused the net to drape vertically over the mouth, entrapping the fish (Dixon, 1905). In another version T. Garth illustrated from the Atsugewi, the bisecting stick extended on the convex side of the willow bow where it was tied and made a handle; the cord connecting the two ends of the bow (and on which the net was strung) went straight across, 180 degrees, and was tied in its center to the end of the stick opposite the handle. The Atsugewi held the net facing upstream, the cord side of the mouth adapting nicely to an uneven bottom. Men would swim toward the net, driving the fish before them. The Sinkyone used the net in the surf. The straight edge was set in the sand with the mouth facing inland. Fish were caught in the net as the wave receded.

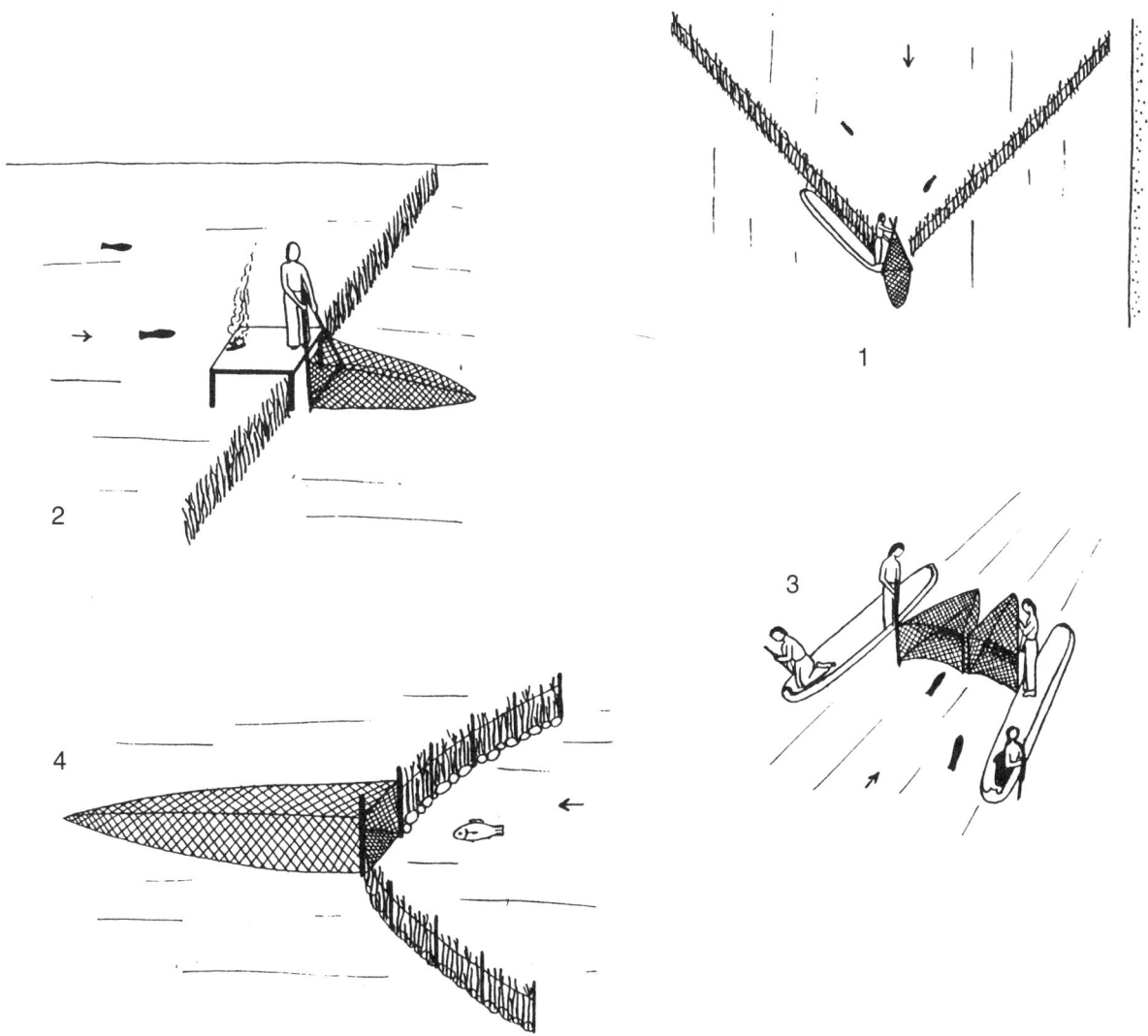

1. Wiyot weir set in fairly deep water of a stream or tidal slough, up to 60 feet in width (smaller weirs in depths of 4 feet of water were built across small streams in late spring or early summer by the Wiyot). An A-frame landing net was placed in the opening of two sharply converging wings for king salmon carried down with the ebb tide. Just below the trap a man in a canoe monitored the net to prevent escape of the fish and protect it from seals (after Hewes, in Kroeber and Barrett, 1960).

2. Chilula weir, a brush barrier built across a small stream such as Redwood Creek late in the season, especially to catch steelheads returning downstream after the spawn. The dip net was held on the downstream side of a 3'-wide opening. The fisherman stood on a redwood bark slab platform over which sand had been spread to hold a small warming fire during the night (after Hewes, in Kroeber and Barrett, 1960).

3. Hupa double drifting bag net for salmon (after Hewes, in Kroeber and Barrett, 1960).

4. Coast Yurok weir built in small creeks for salmon returning to downstream rivers. Some posts driven into the creek bed had brush piled against them in the form of two short wings pointing downstream. In the opening a bag net was fastened to side posts. Salmon and trout caught in the net were clubbed while still in the net and then removed. The Coast Yurok also built a dam of about ten stakes driven in a line across a 4-foot-deep and 20-foot-wide stream. No woven mats or leafy brush were used, but a log about a foot in diameter was fastened across the stakes and additional stakes were leaned against the upstream side of the log and rocks were placed along the bottom of the stakes. From the top of the dam or from the two or three 5-foot stagings built on the downstream side, the Yurok wielded a plunge net or double-pronged harpoon (after Hewes, in Kroeber and Barrett, 1960).

they were caught by the gills or trapped as the net was drawn ashore. In the slow water of the Sacramento Delta and among rushes or in marshes, the net had its lower edge weighted with mudballs wrapped in leaves. It was set out and taken up with the tule balsa.

In swifter, more upstream waters, a smaller set net with its bottom fastened to a wooden bow weighted with stones was set in a riffle or appropriate spot. The net was not drawn taut between the wooden bow at the bottom and headline that ran across the top. Rather, it was allowed to form a long

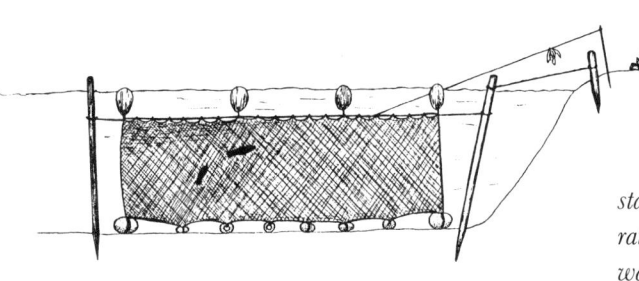

Yurok gill net with stone anchors and headline tied to stake and pole anchor. Line from net ran to a crab-claw rattle. Struggling fish sounded alarm for those on shore at a warming fire. Gill nets were often set out at night. Not only any kind of fish, but ducks and other species became trapped in the meshes of gill nets. Yurok gill nets generally ran from 6 to 7' wide by 50' to 60' long (after Hewes, in Kroeber and Barrett, 1960).

Weir built across Trinity River by Hupa each summer. Platforms, erected below openings, were used by fishermen with dip nets. (Photograph by Edward S. Curtis circa 1923, courtesy of the Southwest Museum.)

pocket by the moving water. Across the front of the long deep pocket, vertical trigger strings were tied and in the center of each of these ran a single long signal string attached on shore to a cocoon rattle or to the watcher himself; often the string was tied about his neck. A fish entering the net thus signaled the fisherman, who pulled up the net, caught the fish and replaced the net. Men upstream sometimes dove into the water to drive fish to the net.

DuBois learned that the Wintu undertook large communal fishing drives in midsummer on the McCloud and Sacramento rivers. A net was stretched across the river. Men waded toward the net downstream carrying torches, some even swam with the torches. Fish caught in the net were clubbed and strung on a grapevine that had been made pliable by warming and twisting.

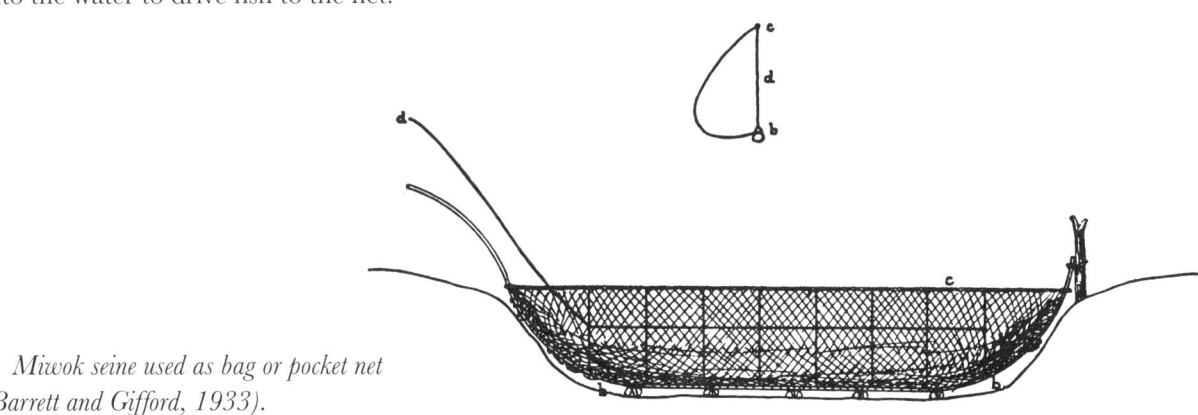

Miwok seine used as bag or pocket net (Barrett and Gifford, 1933).

Karok Indian Fritz Hanson chips a stone to make a sinker for a fishing net, 1926. Photograph by George W. Bayley, from the Harrington collection (Smithsonian Institution National Anthropological Archives).

Harpoons, Fish and Sea Mammals

The Karok knew that Chukchuk (Osprey) made the salmon harpoon for people who did not own a deep-water fishing spot, a hole on the river where salmon were easily netted in the countercurrent. The tale, collected by Kroeber in 1902, reflects the fact that harpooning was the manner for taking fish in the more extensive, less productive shallow waters, the numerous riffles where fish would at least be clearly visible and where anyone could fish without special rights.

Harpoons and nets complemented one another. In the spring, on the fast flowing augmented Kern River, the Tubatulabal used a harpoon with two deer-bone toggleheads, sharply pointed and barbed. As the year wore on, nets came into play higher up on the river and in mountain lakes. The fish grew sluggish in winter and then individuals harpooned or speared them from tule rafts on lakes along the South Fork Kern River. The fish spear was simply a long pole with two wooden points that had been sharpened by rubbing them on a rock.

Harpoons and nets could be used together during a communal fishing drive. Hewes learned that the Yurok would take a conical plunge net from its frame and set it in a small stream with the open end facing the current. While the net was tended by a couple of men or women, other men with harpoons would probe and spear under banks and around rocks and roots in the water above the net, scaring up salmon and steelhead. As they ran downstream, those with the harpoons called, "Going downstream!" And the net tenders raised the net with the fish.

Salmon and steelhead were the usual objects of the harpooners' thrust, especially in northwestern California. But other fish were taken with this two-pronged toggled harpoon, and sometimes fish and eels were impaled on simpler spears or gaffs of the California Indian. Against sea lions and related species a specialized vaned harpoon was hurled. Though they utilized the meat, they had no weapon at all for whales.

Fishing Harpoons of Northwestern California— Manufacture and Technique

The Karok told Hewes that they made both the single-pointed harpoon, with the head socketed directly onto the shaft, and the double-pointed harpoon which forked because of beveling where the foreshafts were bound. Mainshafts were 10 to 12 feet long. According to Gifford, shafts of the double-pointed Karok harpoon were made of fir. The foreshafts came from serviceberry *(Amelanchier alnifolia)*, a close-grained wood also used for Karok arrow foreshafts but one they felt especially good for holding the harpoon's deer-bone points, or toggleheads. Foreshafts were scorched to make them less noticeable. Sometimes the scorching was continued for part or the entire length of the mainshaft. Iris-fiber cords ran from the mainshaft to the toggleheads. Barbs on the points were hardwood, bone or antler, and were fastened to the points by wrapping them with iris-fiber string pitched with fir gum. They smoothed the wrappings with a hot stone.

The single-pointed harpoon was a rarity and usually confined to spearing steelhead from smaller streams. The double-pointed harpoon took salmon when the rivers ran low. Hewes learned from his Karok consultants that in earlier times, however, they infrequently employed harpoons for salmon. Fish weirs constructed across rivers and dip nets most effectively captured these fish. Steelheads ascending creeks in the spring to spawn were the proper targets of the harpoon.

Hupa man thrusts the double-pointed harpoon. (Photograph by Edward S. Curtis circa 1923, courtesy of the Southwest Museum.)

Kroeber observed a Yurok with a single-pointed harpoon at the mouth of the Klamath River in 1902. The weapon had a mainshaft 20 feet long. Hewes had been told the single-pointed harpoon was used upstream and the double-pointed in tidewater where spearing was difficult. At low tide, however, in pools or shallows or even stranded on the mud, fish were easily speared, perhaps explaining Kroeber's observation.

A Yurok informed Hewes that the best harpoon on the Klamath was double-pronged. It had one foreshaft more nearly parallel with the mainshaft and about 2 inches longer than the other. The longer prong was held over the other in use to avoid the lower from striking the bottom before the upper pierced the fish.

A double-pronged toggled harpoon thrust from boat or shore against salmon, steelheads, sturgeon or other fish had a number of advantages over a simple spear with a fixed point. It doubled the opportunity that at least one point would find a vulnerability and enter the quarry's body. If both points found the mark, the likelihood of holding a fish increased greatly. Further, barbed points made extraction unlikely. The Karok told Hewes that a togglehead might be thrust all the way through a salmon. To retrieve it the line was untied from the shaft and passed back through the fish. Even unbarbed Indian harpoon points held because the struggling of the speared fish pulled the toggle points off the wooden foreshaft prongs and, with the attachment of the toggle line somewhere in the middle of the point assembly, further struggle tended to pull them sideways, making escape almost impossible. Finally, the fish was literally on a line and could be played and weakened, a kind of fisherman's judo and a big advantage with a large fish whose energy and contortions at the outset would be enough to break a fixed point or wriggle free of a simple spear. Once exhausted, the fish could be clubbed or grasped by the gills. Even a single-pronged toggled harpoon had the advantage of allowing the fisherman to play and tire a fish before landing it. Skilled Sinkyone, Mattole and Bear River fishermen thrust the single-pronged harpoon. Old men and boys required the double-pronged.

The Yurok made harpoon points of deer leg bone and barbs of deer antler. We know from their neighbors, the Tolowa, that such materials, including wood, were ground with course sandstone

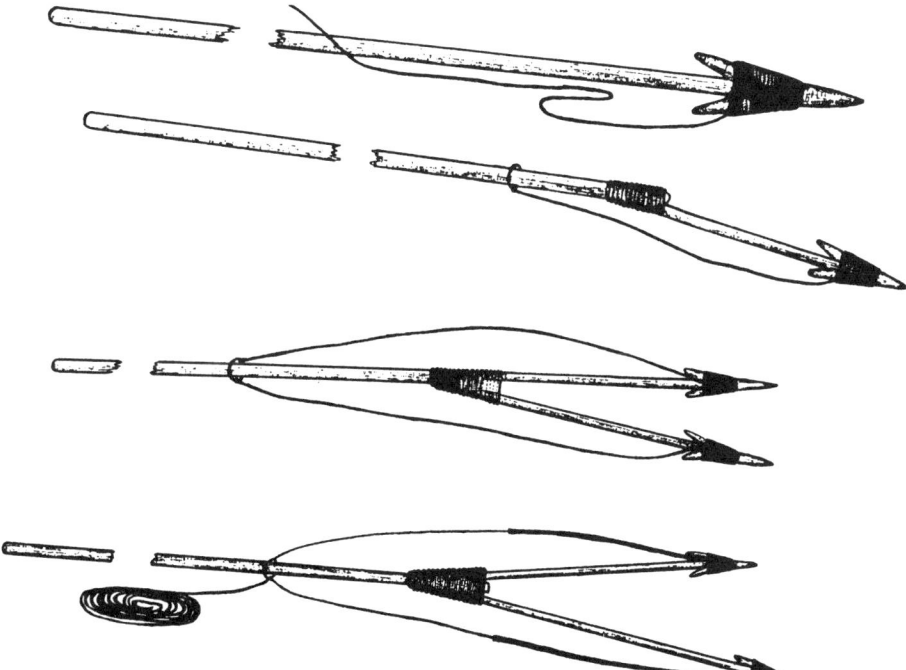

Various harpoons of northwestern California. Kroeber and Barrett's consultants said they ranged from 6 to 20 feet in length. The forward end was usually scorched for camouflage; sometimes the entire weapon was blackened. All wrappings were thoroughly pitched to waterproof them—a small heated stone rubbed the pitch smooth. The toggle line could be a heavy cord of iris fiber but because salmon teeth could cut it, a leader of buckskin, tanned elk hide, rawhide or seal hide was frequently used. Lines, too, were often pitched. The prongs of the harpoon, two beveled foreshafts from 1 to 3 feet long set at the double-beveled end of a mainshaft, could be of equal or unequal length (Kroeber and Barrett, 1960).

and polished with equisetum. Oiling prevented cracks and checks. Antler could also be soaked in water to make it more workable, steamed to shape it or cut with obsidian or flint. The Yurok ground the antler barbs as two separate pieces and bound them with a fine but strong cord to the base of the point. Immediately in front of the barbs at the side of the assembly, an end of the toggle line (generally consisting of a rawhide leader on a heavy cord) was bound at the same time, together with the point and barbs. The line emerged to the rear at the side of the point. The wrappings and attached end of the leader were heavily pitched. Toggle lines shown by Kroeber and Barrett collected around the turn of the century ranged from 62 to 106 cm. and each was a separate line. The smaller was exclusively of iris fiber, 54 cm. long with a bone point 4 cm. long, flanked by two wooden barbs 6.8 cm. long each. The fully assembled head measured 8 cm. in length. A Hupa leader they described was of rawhide 28 cm. with a 60 cm. iris cord. The bone point was 4 cm. and bone barbs 5.6 cm.; total length of head, 7 cm. Another Hupa rawhide leader measured 33 cm., the iris cord, 54 cm.; the bone point was again 4 cm. and the bone barbs, 5 cm.; the total length, 6 cm. A Yurok consultant described a combined-lined system where buckskin or sealhide leaders, about 20 inches long from each point, were attached to a single iris fiber toggle line of about 6 feet.

The Coast Yurok harpooned sturgeon from canoes in the shallows of the lower Klamath. The mainshaft of a two-pronged harpoon was about 15 feet long and the two toggleheads were attached by strings of iris fiber alone or combined with a buckskin leader. Around 3 feet up on the shaft the two lines joined a single cord which was fastened there by a slip knot with the remainder of the cord beyond this. Once the sturgeon was harpooned (below the dorsal plates) the fisherman laid the shaft in the boat and played the huge fish on the line held by the points. When he could get it close, he stunned it with a club.

Wintu Harpoon Fishing

The Wintu employed the harpoon when fishing alone for salmon on the McCloud River. The fisherman worked from the bank, Du Bois wrote, often at night with a torch to attract fish set near the water's edge or sometimes held by a partner. Some had special rights to a salmon house. Powers observed a Wintu fishing station during the nineteenth century: two stout poles tied in a cross and planted in deep water with a log laid out to it from shore. The harpooner would stand on the log, spear poised in the air. Some stations were more elaborate and included a conical spearing hut, a booth of boughs to block the sun so the harpooner could see the fish but remain unseen by them.

Redding gave a detailed 1881 account of their construction and use (quoted in Du Bois). Two stakes were driven into the bottom of a shallow spot near the shore where the salmon were running. They were fastened together with willow withes in the form of a St. Andrew's cross and two poles extended from the shore were set in the arms of the cross. On the poles over the channel where the fish passed, a wicker beehive-like structure was made, closely woven with branches and leaves to shut out the light. It had a small opening on the shore side, merely to allow for the admission of the head and arms of the harpooner, who would lie on the two poles with the remainder of his body and legs outside the shade. The hut extended to within inches of the running water and was open at the bottom. A small hole at the top allowed the shaft of the spear to pass. "Everything being ready, the Indian lies on the poles, his head and arms in the beehive.... No light comes to his eyes except that coming up through the water.... The Indian can see the bottom of the stream and all the fish that pass, while the fish cannot see him."

Many northern California Indian groups utilized the spearing scaffold, including the Chimariko, Karok, Yurok, Hupa and Nongatl. The Chetco, Tolowa, Wiyot, Mattole, Sinkyone, Kato, Coast Yuki and Yana had both scaffold and booth. The Pomo, Kato and Lassik are recorded as having built booths on weirs. Booths seem to have been most suited to the smaller rivers and streams. For even greater advantage the Wintu laid white stones

Hupa harpoon toggle-head. Collected by Lieutenant P. H. Ray in the nineteenth century (Mason, 1889).

on the bottom immediately below the booth so that fish passing over them could be easily seen; a torch might be added for night fishing. The Pomo, Wailaki, and Yuki used white stones in pools and the Yuki in weir openings as well. The Klamath and Atsugewi used them with scaffolds.

In addition to the salmon on the McCloud, the Wintu took steelheads in the upper Trinity. Less desirable suckers were usually netted in the openings of weirs on communal drives in the creeks and shallow waters of large rivers during August, but children on the McCloud were urged to spear suckers with miniature harpoons as the adults speared salmon. In Bald Hills, where fish were less common, Wintu adults also speared suckers.

Powers described the Wintu harpoon itself as long and slender, about 15 feet in length and the prong "with a joint of deer's bone at the end about 3 inches long, fashioned with a socket . . ." and fastened to the mainshaft "by a string tied around its middle." The Wintu Indian "aims to drive this movable joint quite through the fish, whereupon it comes loose, turns crossways, and thus holds the fish securely, flouncing at the end of the string. The construction of this spear shows a good knowledge of the gamey, resolute salmon; the string at the end allows him to play and exhaust himself, while a stiff spear would be broken or wrenched out of him." Powers noted the exceptional case of six Wintu Indians harpooning 500 salmon in a single night on the McCloud.

Fishing Arrows, Spears, More Harpoons and Gaffs

These were similar tools, cross fertilizing one another, and all could find their way to a fish. The use of arrows against fish seems to have been a marginal practice at best and was even proscribed by some groups. However, the Mattole made a very long arrow, as much as 8 feet—a veritable spear shot from a bow—blackened in the fire to decrease visibility, without feathering and with a sharpened wood point. The "arrow" was entered into a deep pool for about half its length and pointed below the fish, for it tended to shoot up, and thus positioned shot from a regular bow. Flounders, trout and bullheads were taken this way, wrote Hewes.

Loeb found that the Pomo made a fishing spear similar to their war spear which in turn was like their arrow. Ash or dogwood was used for the arrow and war spear. They were both heated then straightened in a device with a circular opening. The war spear was 6 feet long, split on the end and an obsidian point attached. It could be thrown but was generally thrust. The simple fishing spear was also made from ash (or young fir) and 1-1/4 to 1-1/2 inches in diameter at the larger extremity, tapering to a pencil-like point. A notch was cut near the lower end where milkweed lashings held a 3-inch-long bone point from the ulna of a deer. Fishing spears thrust from the banks of creeks were about 8 feet in length, those intended for lakes in the spring mea-

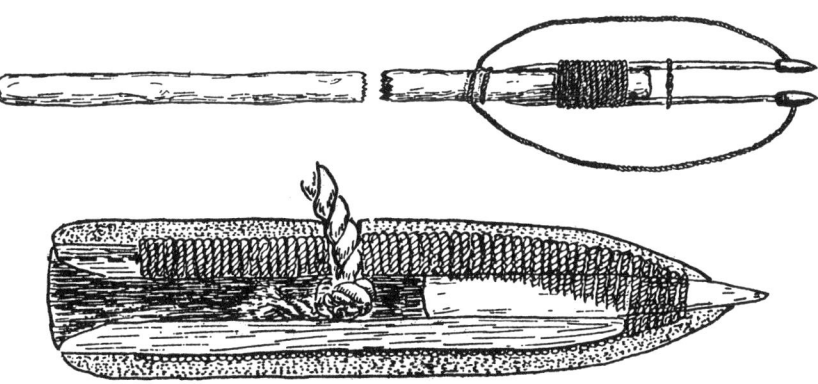

Thanks to Cora Du Bois we have a detailed description and sketch of the Wintu harpoon. A short one could be 10' to 12' long; for the salmon house they were around 15' to 20' in length. The main shaft was of fir; the two prongs, of hardwood painted black with pitch darkened by bark soot to make them less conspicuous. The toggles, each around 3-1/2" long, were fashioned from pieces of wood with a fairly wide pith channel in which deer-bone points were thrust to protrude slightly beyond the wood sheath. A hole was drilled in the middle on the side and a knotted toggle cord that ran to the shaft inserted. The toggle was then wrapped with twine and coated with pitch. It had no barbs; when the fish was speared the toggles pulled free of the prongs and lodged sideways in the fish. They remained fastened to the main shaft by the cord (Du Bois, 1935).

sured 12 to 14 feet. Harpoons made from fir were 10 feet long and 1 inch in diameter and had lashed to the tapered lower end two or three prongs of ash surmounted with bone points. With these they took large suckers or salmon in the lakes and rivers.

Central Miwok boys shot *sununu*, a 6- to 8-inch big-headed catfish-like species, with a bow and wood-pointed arrow—the only fish so taken because it could not be caught in a net. The boys would call, *yenene, yenene*, the same soft sound the fish made when removed from the water. The fish was eaten.

A spear of mountain mahogany tipped with obsidian was used by the Miwok against a whitefish in the shallow waters of the higher mountains. In the late spring the Miwok also speared salmon as they spawned in the shallow water. A fire built beside the river lured the fish for easy spearing at night. The fresh roe was boiled in a basket and eaten with a little salt or dried and preserved for the winter. It was reconstituted by soaking overnight and boiling for an hour or simply washed and cooked for an hour. Salmon and larger fish were commonly taken by the Miwok with a two-pronged harpoon, the detachable points made from a deer leg bone and attached with strong native string. The shaft itself, from 10 to 15 feet long, was of Oregon ash or mountain mahogany.

Barrett's Pomo informants told him of a fish spear with a single bone point bound to the pole at an angle of around 30 degrees—a gaff. The Coast Yurok gaffed fish from an artificial corral built at the first rapids up from the mouth of Little River. Hewes recorded that the corral was in the shape of a triangle with the apex pointed upstream and the third side reaching from shallow water to shallow water. An opening in the center of the third side allowed entry of fish swimming upstream. When the water had fallen to about 2 feet midstream, they constructed the 3-1/2-foot-high corral. Horizontal poles or logs spaced around 4 inches apart were bound with hazel withes between pairs of upright stakes pounded into the river bottom, like a rail fence. The fisherman stood in the water beside the opening and gaffed the fish as they entered the corral or climbed into the pen and hooked fish with his 5-foot gaff there. Gaffed fish were clubbed and thrown onto the bank.

The northern California lamprey ran from early spring through July. During the day lampreys hid in the crevices of artificial rock piles of the rivers or in the estuaries of the coast. The Karok took them with their gaff, an acute-angled bone or antler point lashed to a pole 3 feet or more in length. The Nongatl found it easier to pick lampreys by hand ("gloved" by a piece of buckskin grasped in the hand to prevent the lamprey from slipping away) from their artificial rock piles that stood about 1 foot high and extended nearly across a stream. Lampreys held onto the rocks by the suction of their mouths. The Nongatl plucked them in the early morning hours, though they too sometimes gaffed them, usually at night by torchlight. The Bear River people built their rock piles as big as 5 feet in diameter and nearly 21 inches high, within 2 inches of the stream's surface, and at the upper end of a riffle. The lampreys crawled in and attached themselves to the rock piles at night. In the morning the Indians removed the rocks in silence and with utmost care, one by one, and impaled the tails of the lampreys as they became visible on a small bone awl. They pulled out as many as eight to ten from a single pile. At various falls the lampreys would hang by their mouth down the face of the rock. Gifford found that the Karok would frighten them off and into a small-meshed dip net, normally meant for small fish, set below them. Or the net was placed in a narrows of the rocks while someone upstream moved his hands about the lampreys to release their hold and be carried by the current to the net. They were placed in a net bag. The Bear River people always cooked and ate them fresh and gave the surplus away. The Coast Yurok, Chilula and Tolowa preserved them by placing them in the sun, then hanging them over a fire.

Sea Harpoons

Kroeber and Barrett recorded Yurok Indian George Mahats' account of hunting sea lions with a harpoon. About six men went out in a boat to the rocks. Three or four disembarked wearing deerskin blankets or a bearskin, black like some sea lions. They acted like sea lions when they saw them coming—swaying, crawling, shouting—to bring them close. Then they readied their harpoons and they all threw at once. If a harpoon found the mark, the sea lion would drag it off into the water. The harpoon line was wound around the shaft. The single head made from elk antler had two barbs carved into it, one behind the other, on the same edge. The antler head was tipped with an obsidian or flint point. At the other end of the shaft was a vane that made the harpoon fly straight.

Men who had not disembarked stayed out of sight, perhaps landing and building a fire to keep warm. Later the men in the boat returned for the hunters and they all looked for the sea lion to emerge. Perhaps only the harpoon shaft rose to the top. They paddled to that and pulled on the line. Two positioned themselves with more spears while another held a spear crosswise in the boat ready to hand it to one of the two spearmen. The animal might have to be struck five times before it died. Big lions were taken in the morning because they might fight half a day. Some were too big to be taken into the boat. In those cases they made holes through the animals' lips and flippers and towed them back to land.

They were not skinned. Hair was singed off and the hide was left on the meat as the animal was cut up for distribution. The skin section of cut was usually kept as a reserve for lean times since it kept without spoiling. Oil was boiled out and stored in the stomach.

Hewes found that at times the Yurok harpooned sea lions and seals in the water or even on the beach at low tide. When one dove backwards somersaulting out of the water, an especially skillful hunter, believing the animal could not see him while it was belly up, ran quickly to the water and harpooned it. Several men got on the 30- to 60-foot line to hold and bring the sea lion to shore. But more commonly, Hewes learned, the sea lions were taken as described, on the rocks where they came to sun. This required great stealth and they always approached aware of the wind. Hewes noted that the target was the animal's thorax and sometimes the harpoon was hurled from as far as 30 feet. The sea lion would dive into the water. Men in the canoe held the harpoon line. A steersman kept the boat on an even keel as the animal pulled the boat toward the open sea. Many hours might pass before the quarry became exhausted and it could be towed back to shore, now perhaps enshrouded in fog with only a fire burning there to guide them.

It was difficult to club a harpooned sea lion, but hunters did wield a 6- or 7-foot-long heavy club and with both hands and two or three blows sometimes dispatched them on the rocks where they were clumsy and could be overtaken. Clubs were often tokens of a family's right to share in the hunting of specific rookeries and had been passed down in these families as heirlooms for generations.

A small dispatching dart might be used after the harpoon; it was similar but shorter. It had the vane at the butt to make it go straight and a long slender head that remained in the animal as the 25- to 30-foot line, attached just above the butt, was jerked to retrieve the shaft and replace the head for another thrust or throw. The hunter carried extra heads and sometimes even shafts. A spent animal could be brought up next to the canoe and killed with a short club. The Sinkyone harpooned seals and sea lions from redwood canoes and dispatched them with a cascara-wood club. The Coast Yuki made the clubs from tan oak or yew.

According to Hewes, the Yurok canoe carried at least two and as many as five hunters on a sea lion hunt. In the prow was the harpooner. Experienced, and frequently the leader, he alone had undergone ten days of singing special songs, abstaining from water, and eating only dried salmon and acorn foods. The success of the hunt depended on his adherence to the rituals and restrictions.

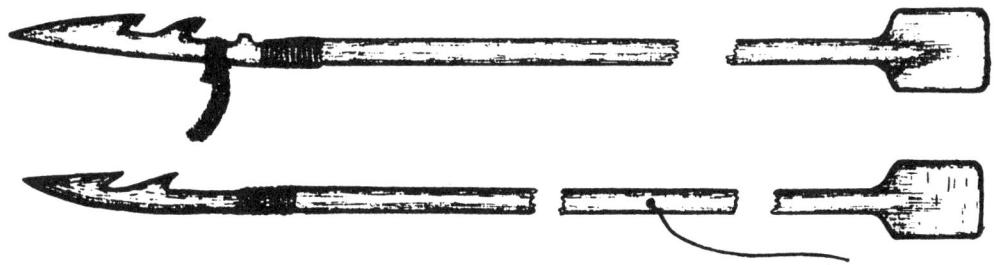

Yurok sea lion harpoons. Above, with detachable head socketed into a 4- or 5-foot-long shaft (note that this is opposite from salmon harpoon where the shaft is socketed into the head). Head was of bone or elk antler. Barbs were unilaterally placed. Behind the barbs was the guard, which prevented 70 to 80 feet of strong line from slipping off. A few turns were wound around the shaft and the rest, when hunting at sea, was coiled in the canoe. With the harpoon head lodged in the sea lion, men held the line as the animal towed the canoe. Below, fixed head harpoon, shaft much longer, about 10 feet. Line fastened midway. The fin or vane was 1" thick by 4-5" wide and as long as a foot. The fin stabilized the missile in flight and tended to stand out of the water in harpooned sea lions; it made following much easier. (After Hewes, in Kroeber and Barrett, 1960.)

The Tolowa lived on the sea coast and relied more than others on sea mammals. While the Mattole shot sea otters asleep on the rocks or on the surface of the ocean with bow and arrow and prized the animal for its fur, the Tolowa shot them with bow and arrow on the water or clubbed them on the shore for food. They hunted all the pinnipeds as well, including sea lions. In Hewes' account they used the harpoon from the canoe during the calm season of early spring through summer but when landing on the rookeries preferred the long club. Hunters often wore a sea-lion disguise, a skin covering from the waist up, even a sea-lion head as mask or at least charcoal-blackened faces. Several hunters went onto the rocks and corralled the younger more tender sea lions and clubbed them to death. They aimed just back of the nose or on the rear of the head. Stunned animals might roll off the rock into the sea where men in the canoe would try to get close enough to club them or within 20 or 30 feet for a harpoon shot. In another approach a single hunter would ascend the rocks and roar like a sea lion to attract them to the rocks and to within range of his club or occasionally his harpoon. The harpoon shaft was attached to one end of the line and the hunter made no attempt to hold the lion after the animal had been speared. The shaft acted as a float and marker, especially the vane. When the sea lion tired, the men seized the shaft and played the animal to exhaustion.

A small animal might be taken into the canoe or a larger one butchered alongside the canoe with a flint knife hafted with wood or bone. The skin, blubber and most of the meat were saved—the rest usually considered too heavy and discarded. If caught in a gale or heavy fog, the hunters followed the heavy swells or drift of the fog back to shore. After dark a beacon fire was lit. All had come down to await the return of the men and the feast that followed. Two fires were made, one where the women gathered, cooked and ate and another for warmth, surrounded by the men. Acorns and other foods accompanied fresh sea lion meat. Oils from the sea lion or from seals, if they had been taken, were stored in the paunches of the animals or in kelp bottles. The bulbous end of a "whip" kelp, partially dried, made a durable container.

Yurok dispatching dart (after Hewes, in Kroeber and Barrett, 1960).

The Wiyot especially enjoyed sea lion and seal meats for their fatness and fine flavor, recorded Hewes. The oil they stored in the sea lion paunch or bladder—carefully cleaned they became good storage receptacles. The bladder was blown up to a capacity of four or five gallons. Hewes' informants told him they ate the oil "like butter." Wiyot harpooners went out hunting sea lions from the mouth of the Eel River in dugouts. The harpoon, like some Yurok harpoons, had a small flint tip on its barbed bone head.

Whales

Whales were not hunted but when one washed ashore, after a lethal attack by a killer whale for example, it became the property of the village in control of that area. The dorsal fin, the choice piece of the animal, was the hereditary right of one family among the Yurok. They made a cut around the base with a flint knife and as someone pulled on an iris-fiber tumpline that had been attached to the fin, it was jerked free. After that, each family cut its own meat according to strict measurements (a bow and a half for a man). The tumplines tied into holes along the edge of a slice, as they had been for the fin, were pulled by the women to extract the meat.

Meat was cooked and dried at home (some said it could not be dried) or if people lived at a distance, cooked and dried in driftwood fires on the beach. It was eaten with many other foods. Pieces of whale skin with adhering dried blubber were preserved. Blubber came off with the skin while cleaning a whale. Chunks washed in the breakers were hung on four stakes over a very small fire. Where the piece sloped at one end, oil dripped into a steatite dish (large horse clamshells were also used by the Tolowa). A basket dipper transferred the oil to a bladder or paunch. (Paunch containers of the Tolowa were made by tying off the lower opening and plugging the upper with seaweed.) Oil in such a container would keep about one year. Whale oil was considered inferior to sea lion oil but used in the same way. Seaweed or the inferior meat of hookbill salmon or other foods were dipped in the oil for flavor.

The Mattole told Hewes that the slabs of whale were taken home and cured, the oil caught in the carapaces of land, river or sea turtles. (These also served as cooking vessels for stone boiling. The meat of land and river turtles was eaten but meat from the sea turtle was too strong.) The Mattole ate whale oil with dried fish and mussels or vegetable foods. The Sinkyone too dried whale meat and preserved the oil to enjoy with berries and other foods.

Indian Angling

In many ways the art of angling has changed little since the Stone Age. Theodora Kroeber expressed that thought when describing Ishi, a stone working Indian hidden until 1911 in the vastness of the California wilderness. For salmon Ishi used a double-pronged harpoon with detachable toggles. He understood the use of fish poison, the weir, seine and conical net but preferred taking trout and small fish with a hair snare or hook. He would have quickly understood our gear and we should not have had much difficulty with his. "No other occupation brings modern man so close to his Stone Age ancestors," Mrs. Kroeber concluded.

But let us step even closer. True, while the Indians of California customarily took fish with nets, weirs, traps, poison or harpoons; the line and hook were widely known. On the southern California coast where deep water may have restricted use of nets, circular hooks of mussel and abalone shell pecked into a near circle, bored and filed smooth with stone, became common. In the hinterland, on the rich lakes and mountain trout streams, a sharpened bone bound to a wooden shank made a hook, and with native twine and a sapling pole, the Indian Isaac Walton had only to find a grasshopper or grub to catch a fish.

It is in the use of hook and line we lovers of the outdoors retain something of our ancient selves. It is a small step to rid ourselves completely of metal reels, plastic lures and fiberglass poles. As a survival art along a remote brook or wild river, the making of hook, line and pole is fast and effective. And going fishing without the headache of store-bought gear, walking the seashore or the woods with *nothing* and coming home with a string of fish is, well, a pretty good fish story.

Circular Shell Hooks and Lines of the Southern California Coast and Offshore Islands

Around 1912 the Chumash Indian Fernando Librado told Harrington that patient women would cut off the shoulder of the abalone shell below the holes and give it to the men for a hook. (The women made breast pendants from the remainder.) Species of abalone were not mentioned by Librado but Heizer found that the blanks for hooks from San Nicholas Island in the de Cessac Collection were of red abalone, the largest California variety. The hookmaker would then break the shell with a rock until he had a piece about the size of the hook he wished to make. María Solares, an Ineseño Chumash, said the size depended on the kind of fish they wanted to catch.

With such a piece Librado would next grind the shell in order to shape and smooth it. After that, he used a stone of chert to cut a round hole in the shell. He ground the hole larger and larger and very round. Then he ground the edge to make a shank and point—the point very sharp. Finally, he made a groove on the shank for the fish line.

Fish lines were of nettle *(Urtica sp.)*, Spanish bayonet *(Yucca whipplei)*, surf grass *(Phyllospodix sp.)* or best of all Indian hemp *(Apocynum cannabinum)*. Librado said it could take a week or more to twist a nettle fish line. He saw old men in the dunes make them three-ply and color the cord with red ochre as they twisted it on the thigh. Cordlets for the hooks also had to be made; including the hook, they were 6 inches long and tied about 7 inches apart on the main cord. Hooks were attached by tarring the shank, laying the end of the string on and wrapping it with the remainder. A knot was tied, the ends twisted together and two half hitches made. The completed wrap was then tarred. Finally a spheroid rock, about 4 inches by 1 inch, was notched on each side and tied on the end of the fish line around 15 feet from the last cordlet. Fish lines were of several lengths and kinds for various fish. Librado said he used four hooks but some old people had as many as eight or ten. He described a line used by Felipe made of *tok* (Indian hemp) 150 feet long. The same line used in the surf could be used at sea from the *tomol*, the native plank boat.

They often fished from shore. Simplicio Pico said they never stood in water deeper than up to their knees. They baited the hook with clams and coiled the line. Then swinging the sinker about, they released their fingers and the fish line uncoiled and shot way out. They would leave it for awhile. If a fish nibbled, they might pull it but only a little. At last they brought it in.

Sharp Angled Hooks and Lines

Spines of cacti the Chumash "twisted like hooks" noted Father Juan Vizcaíno on a voyage through the Channel Islands in 1769. Much earlier in 1602 along the coast near San Luis Obispo, explorer Sebastián Vizcaíno had written of "hooks of cactus spines tied to some good lines like twine" and baited with sardines. The exact form of these hooks is unknown, although Harrington left notes, tantalizing in their brevity on this point, referring to Chumash hooks of cactus spine that were *sharp-angled*. According to Spier's studies during earlier years of this century, something as simple as the curved spines of the biznaga, or barrel cactus *(Echinocactus wislizeni),* heated and bent, served as hooks for Maricopa boys who fished with cotton string attached to the ends of long poles. They made a hole in the spine's end for the line and baited the hook with a worm. Crescent shaped floats of wood or pumice, drilled through the center so that the points stood vertically when in use on the water, completed their outfit.

The Chumash, at least in historic times, possessed the single hook, line and pole. Harrington consultant María Solares described one 10 feet long made from willow with the bark removed, 3/4 of an inch in diameter. It was used by a woman for trout. They also made poles of *guatamote* (mule fat). A collapsible pole of creek dogwood, each piece about 4 feet long, had the sections overlapped and wrapped with cord when in use. A 1- to 2-foot fish line fastened by means of a loop over a notch at the end of the pole was extended out from shore for bullheads under rocks. When not in use they disassembled the

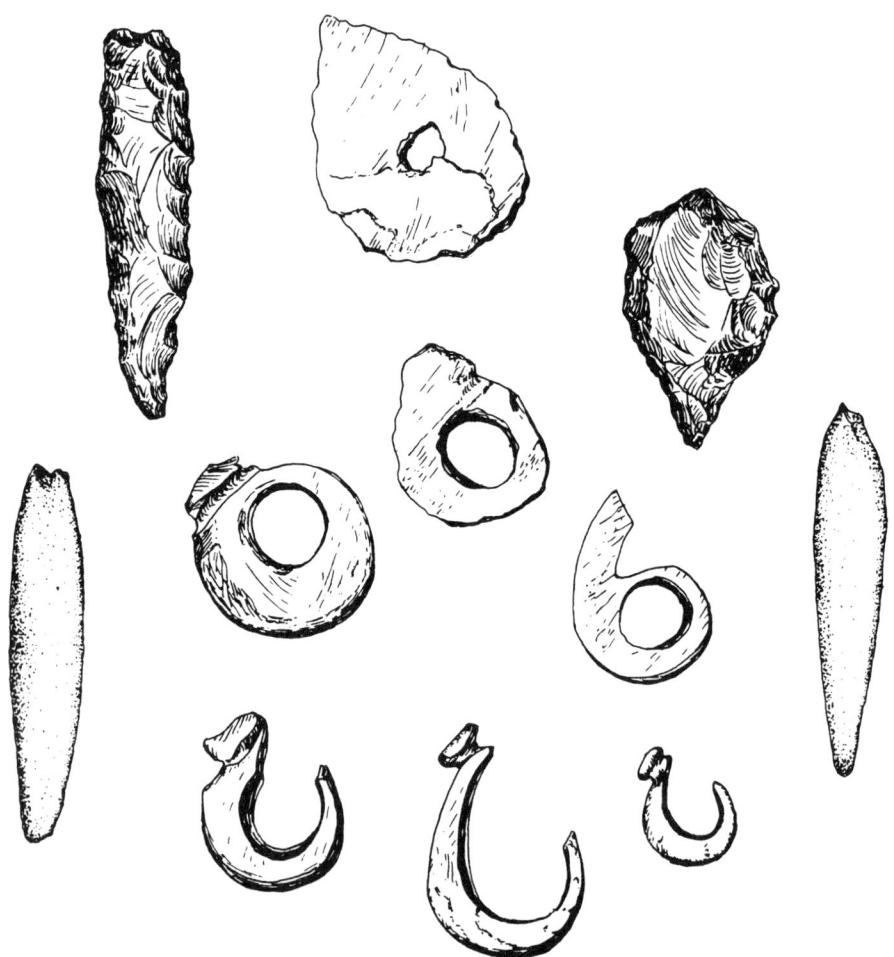

Along with large mortars and pestles, circular shell hooks (and the drills of chert and cylindrical stone files to make them) first appear at Level 3 in the stratified site of Malaga Cove, Los Angeles County. Artifacts of abalone shell from the site suggest the process by which the hooks were made. Completed hooks are actual size (Walker, 1951).

two pieces for carrying. A reel was fashioned from any wood, such as willow, 1 foot by 1 inch with the ends splayed in Ys. They strung the catch on a slender stick about 2 feet in length with a fork at the end to keep the fish from slipping off.

The Tubatulabal of the Kern River drainage were found by Vogelin to have used two-piece fish hooks. The barb came from the shank bone of a deer filed to a point on a rock. Wrapped with twine of asphalt-coated milkweed, it was attached at a 45 degree angle to the base of a longer piece, probably of wood. They tied the hook thus made to additional lengths of milkweed-fiber twine smeared with asphaltum and attached the line to the end of a long willow pole. Earthworms and grasshoppers served the Tubatulabal as bait. Often in preparing the catch to eat, the Tubatulabal selected four large fish, cleaned and tied them together in branches of "odorless willows"—sandbar willow *(Salix hindsiana and exigua)*, believed not to impart any odor to food—and cooked the wrapped fish in ashes at the fishing spot. They would carry the fish home in these willows as well.

Generally the Tubatulabal, like many California groups, harpooned fish from rocks, caught them in basket traps or corrals, in two- or four-man nets, or poisoned them. Driver, Kroeber and Barrett in discussing northwestern California made the point that groups living on large heavy-flowing streams found nets and weirs the efficient way for mass catches. Hooks, effective for individual, smaller fishes, were generally a waste of time for them and confined to peripheral groups in the smaller and more rapid streams.

There were many of these smaller streams and marginal groups however. Some Miwok made fish hooks of bone, according to Galen Clark, and fish lines from the silky fibers from the outer part of the stem of the showy milkweed *(Asclepias speciosa)*. Yurok of northern California bound an inch-long thorn from one of the briers to a wooden shank. They used the hook on a 6-foot line at the end of a pole and baited it with a grasshopper or hellgrammite or, more rarely, dried salmon. It was for catching trout from early spring into fall. Angleworms were used as bait in late winter for steelheads.

Chumash hooks, line and sinker (from Harrington and Librado, in Hudson and Blackburn, 1982).

Chumash stone sinker. Naturally shaped cobbles picked up on the beach or bank of a creek served the Chumash for sinkers. If necessary, they notched each side of the stone or pecked a groove across it. Alfred Kroeber recorded that the commonest type for all California was simply a flat beach pebble notched on opposite edges to hold a string (from Yates, 1890 in Hudson and Blackburn, 1982).

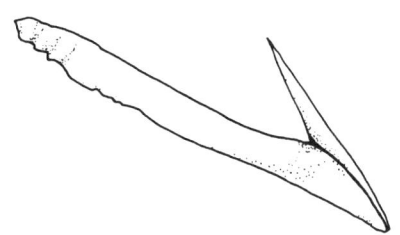

Compound fishhook of shell, wrapping gone, found on San Clemente Island (presently in Museum of American Indian—drawing based on photographs in Hudson and Blackburn, 1982).

During the summer the Nongatl of the Van Duzen in northern California used a sharp grass thorn that was naturally curved, about the size of a child's index finger, according to a consultant of Hewes. The grass in question was said to produce a rose-colored flower but little else could be determined. The needle-like hook had a 10-foot line attached to a notch cut in its base and was baited with a grasshopper. All the Nongatl used such a rig, effective for trout but too small for salmon.

The Mattole made a fish hook of the sharp claw of a chicken hawk; baited with meat and attached to a line, it worked on upstream riffles. Hewes reported that for salmon the Sinkyone, Mattole and Bear River made hooks from wooden shanks, bone points and lashings smeared with pitch. The Hupa employed a sharp bone of the sucker, according to one Hewes consultant, wrapped with cord (which was occasionally pitched) to a small wooden shaft. Any number up to 30 or 40 of these acute-angled hooks were attached by short leaders to a set line, anchored ashore and tied to a freely floating wooden block downstream. They used it in the fall for trout. Fish eggs or "gill rakes" served as bait. Goddard who did field work among the Hupa in the late nineteenth century described a miniature composite hook they used for trout and the other small fish of rivers and creeks. Between two small sticks, a sharp bone about half as long was placed at a 35-degree angle. Fine thread wrapped and bound them together and to a line of native string. Such trout hooks were usually used in bunches of ten or more on a set line.

To catch larger fish such as salmon or steelhead the Modoc and Klamath Lake Indians made a composite hook from a bone shank and two bone barbs or points wrapped in a 25-degree or 30-degree angle at the base with sinew and pitch. They baited it with minnows.

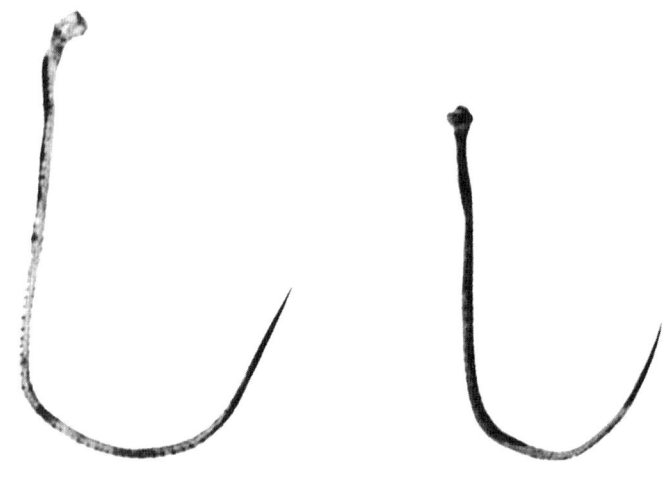

Biznaga (barrel cactus) spine fishhooks of the Cocopa, collected around 1900. Probably close to actual size (Smithsonian Institution).

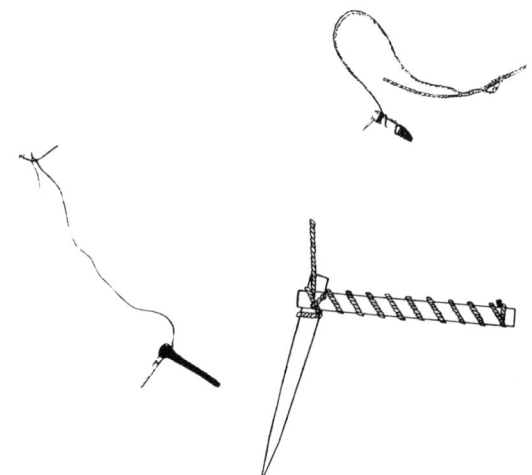

Lovelock Cave (near Great Basin lakes) compound fishhook (diagrammatic sketch and hook on left, from Loud and Harrington, 1931). Sharpened and polished bone 25 mm. long slivered from side of pelican ulna or humerus. A 2-mm.-diameter split twig folded over bone pinches a .7-mm. cord at its extremity; the cord circles the two halves and ends at the juncture with the bone in several half hitches. A set line with 12 hooks were found in the cave. Powers collected a similar set line and hooks from the Northern Paiute in 1875. It was 15 m. long with 75 tiny hooks of sharpened rabbit bone in split willow, about 1 cm. on a side, attached by small cords to a main cord with a rock sinker on the end and anchored to a cane shaft on the beach. Pitch covered line, rock and hooks. Baited with small white grubs, it took chub, dace and redsides (single hook from this set shown on right, in Fowler and Liljeblad, 1978).

Barbules were rare in Indian hooks. However, large acute-angled bone points bound to wooden shanks found in Humboldt Cave of northwestern Nevada had two barbules cut into them. One had both on the outer face, another had both on the inner side, and a third had one barbule toward the point on the outer side and another lower down on the inner surface.

Gorges

The simplest "hook" of all was the gorge. Likely also the most ancient of hooks, the fish gorge has been found throughout the world. It was merely a small bone or stick of wood sharpened at both ends and fastened in the middle to a line.

The Chilula used a gorge hook 1/2 to 3/4 of an inch long with a grasshopper bait attached to a 10- to 15-foot line on a pole. The Mattole had a bone gorge 3 inches long for steelheads mostly on riffles but also in deeper pools. In upriver pools the gorge took suckers. For ocean trout, perch and bullheads they used a smaller bone gorge (1-1/2 inches in length) with a 2-foot sinew leader. The gorge was baited with a "mussel worm" and floated on the surface. For other ocean fish the Mattole tied a sinker to the middle of the line. The fisherman used only one hook and fish line at a time. He threw it from the reef outside the bar at the Mattole River mouth, according to Hewes, or from rocks along the coast. The Sinkyone also angled the gorge hook from rocks for ocean fish. The Northern Paiute of Pyramid Lake baited a small bone gorge hook with grubs and used it on a set line for minnows. A larger one baited with sucker meat was for trout. The Northern Wintun made a gorge hook from a thorn, the San Clemente Islanders off southern California from the bones of birds. The Modoc and Klamath Lake Indians made a small bone gorge attached to the line with sinew and pitch. A small fish or fish eggs completely covered the bone as bait.

Fish Hook Theory

In some respects the Indian fisherman was more akin to the modern commercial fisherman than the weekend sportsman. Of course, Indian fishing was not a compartmentalized, commercial exploitation; fish were beings and fishing was a spiritual undertaking integrated into a complete way of life. It is the similarity of seriousness that strikes me: both groups exhibit tremendous sophistication.

Hupa trout hooks (Goddard, 1903).

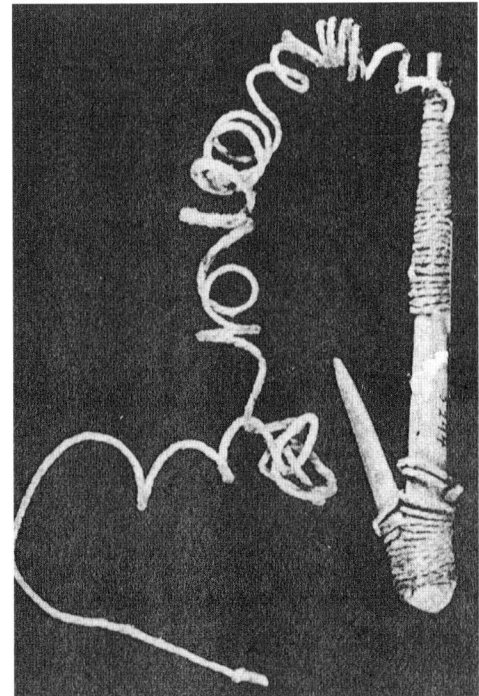

Large hook with greasewood barb and shank for trout (approximately 8.5 cm.). Collected from Northern Paiute on Pyramid Lake by Samuel Barrett in 1916. Concave socket on side held barb. Lashing continued 3/4 m. to main line which held 30 such hooks. Baited with minnows and anchored to shore, a swimmer took end out into lake—a large circular tule float as well as a stone sinker were attached. Some fishermen preferred gorge hooks baited with sucker meat for similar lines (photograph from Fowler and Bath 1981).

After extensive research and observation of the Indians of the Northwest Coast, Hilary Stewart wrote of the great skill of the fisherman in using his equipment and "the years of experience required to produce a hook, spear, net or trap that was exactly right for the fish and the environment from which it was taken. . . ." Archaeological studies of earlier, simpler techniques of the southern California coast reached the same conclusion. Each style of hook was crafted for a particular kind of fish in a special aquatic environment.

In his doctoral dissertation Louis James Tartaglia found that the bone gorge hook came first, uncovered in the earliest levels of Little Harbor, a temporary camp site occupied some 7,000 years ago on the seaward side of Catalina Island. The gorge works with fish that swallow their prey. Some cultures use it for birds and it may have evolved from a trapping tool on the land to its use in the water for fish. Baited with a mussel worm, which completely covered the deer-bone gorge and brought the gorge parallel to a line attached to a 7-foot pole, the Coast Yuki in northern California would dangle it in the water to take bullheads, black perch, rock cod and kelp fish. Once swallowed, tension on the line toggled the gorge, tearing through the bait and lodging the bone crosswise in the fish's throat.

  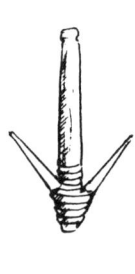

Left, tail bone of a sucker used on a hand or set line by the Klamath as a minnow hook. Liver of sucker or trout served as bait to catch minnows, which were eaten or employed as bait themselves (on the double-pointed hook, for salmon and steelhead). The barbs were natural spines on the bone (Spier, 1930).

Center, double-pointed Modoc and Klamath Lake hooks, barbs of bone secured to bone shank with sinew and pitch (photograph in Barrett, 1910).

Right, double-pointed Coast Salish hook, barbs of wild crab apple thorn, used for stream trout (drawing in Stewart 1977).

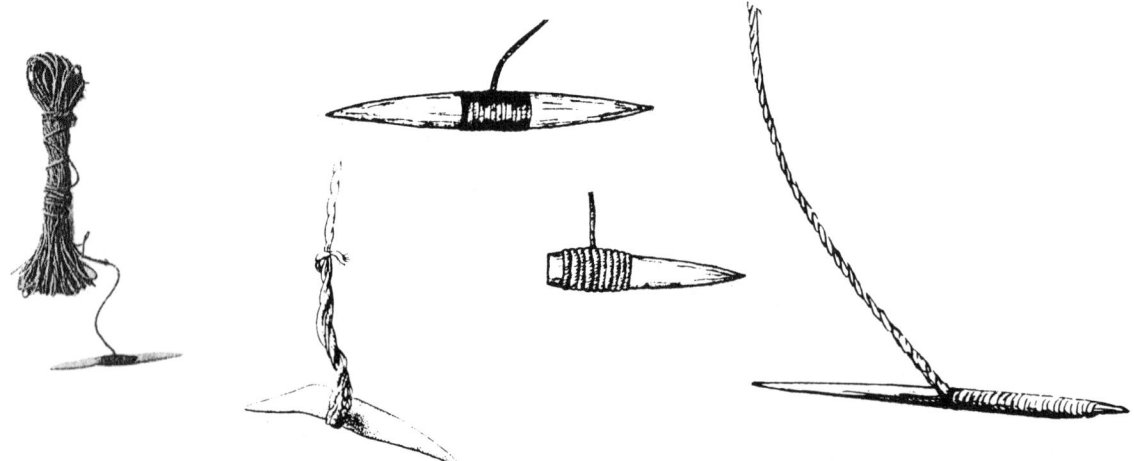

Gorges: left to right, Modoc and Klamath Lake, of bone, length 8 cm. (Barrett, 1910); Northern Paiute, of bone, collected on Pyramid Lake Reservation, 1934 (Fowler, 1978); Sinkyone gorge with iris-fiber line and Yurok single-pointed gorge used on a throw line from rocks along the seashore (Kroeber and Barrett, 1960); Kwakiutl bone gorge (Stewart, 1977).

Size of gorge limits size of take; large gorges would exclude smaller fish. Tartaglia studied the prehistoric occupation of the Chumash village of Malibu during the period from 80 B.C to 1000 A.D. and found that gorges from 2 to 3.4 cm. were associated with bones of mackerel, bonito and barracuda while those 3.5 to 6.4 cm. linked to yellowtail, albacore and skipjack. The gorge was not only the first hook but in some measure a specialized one and continued in use even after other hooks entered the life of early southern Californians.

Circular fish hooks at Malibu were linked to surfperch, rockfish (also true of later levels at Little Harbor), bass, sheephead, white croaker, halibut, and other bottom-dwelling species that commonly browse and nibble as they feed. Early ethnographic accounts of California fishing show mussel and abalone were often used for bait and the shells of these species were also used for the circular hooks of southern California. They were of convenient shape and their iridescence attractive to some species. Shell was a weak material, however, and shell hooks had to be fairly thick. Short shanks also compensated for this weakness by more evenly distributing the force applied to the hook and allowing the hook to rotate on the line. Bone, which was stronger, was sometimes employed especially for smaller hooks.

Shape and size of the hook were important for other reasons. The circular form with its incurving point and short shank rotated when suspended on a line. Pressured from a nibbling bite, the point would swing into the ideal angle for penetration of such a nibbling fish; and once penetration had occurred, pulling on the hook returned it to its original position, impaling the fish. This along with the close clearance between the point and the shank held the fish until the fisherman decided to raise his line. It was the perfect hook for catching bottom browsers, as experiments by researchers have proved.

Small curved bone fish hooks (1 to 2.4 cm.) with somewhat open points correlated prehistorically at Malibu with surfperch while larger (3.4 to 3.6 cm.) shell and bone circular hooks were used for rockfish. These had slightly more incurving points, thus increasing their holding ability, something one might expect since rockfish were caught in water over 200 feet deep and would have had more opportunity to escape.

  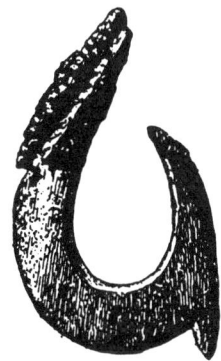

Shell fishhooks from southern California islands collected by M. León de Cessac during the nineteenth century (Hamy, 1885).

Short-shanked, circular shell hook turns markedly when pressure is applied to the point; it rotates into hooking position when nibbled. A long-shanked hook rotates less than the short-shanked hook because of the leverage effect of the longer shank. Considerable force is concentrated at the bottom of the shank during a strike from a fish. The longer shank does not give or rotate as the shorter and can easily snap if not made of stronger material. A longer shank is useful with acute-angle hooks to maintain the point in hooking position for fish that take the hook hard and quick (Tartaglia, 1976).

Interestingly, sixteen circular mussel-shell hooks, both small and large, with *extremely* narrow clearance between point and shank, along with eight gorges two or three times longer than the others (6.5 to 11.4 cm) had been burned in a shallow pit at the Malibu cemetery. Most of the circular hooks were broken. The tips, however, when found, remained sharp and complete. Tartaglia believed that these must have been purely ceremonial objects. It would have been nearly impossible for a fish to hook itself with such fine clearance of the point. The Chumash mourning ceremony, a commemoration held in late summer, included the deliberate breaking of offerings thrown into a pit and burned.

Few traces of highly perishable compound (wood-bone, cordage-wrapped) acute-angle hooks could be gleaned at Malibu. Those found were associated with Pacific bonito, yellowtail and albacore. On the ocean compound fish hooks generally caught medium-sized striking fish in open-water schools near the surface. They were caught by

Karok split-stick hook (in Driver, 1939).

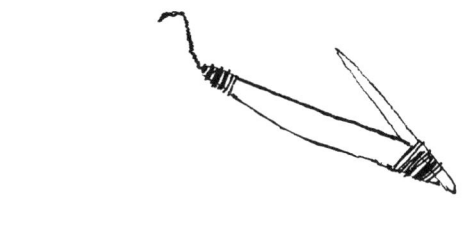

Typical southern California compound fishhook. It had a wood shank with a groove for a pinniped or whale-bone point, and was wrapped in Indian hemp, covered with asphaltum.

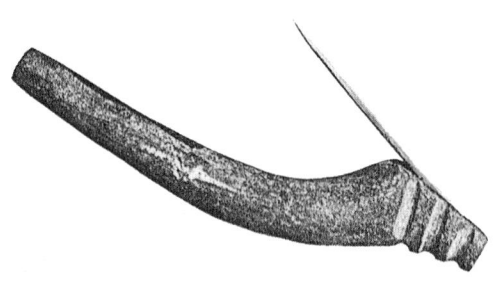

Notice the grooves to secure bone point on stone shank (which acted as its own sinker). Recovered from Ozette, Washington (photograph in Kirk, 1974).

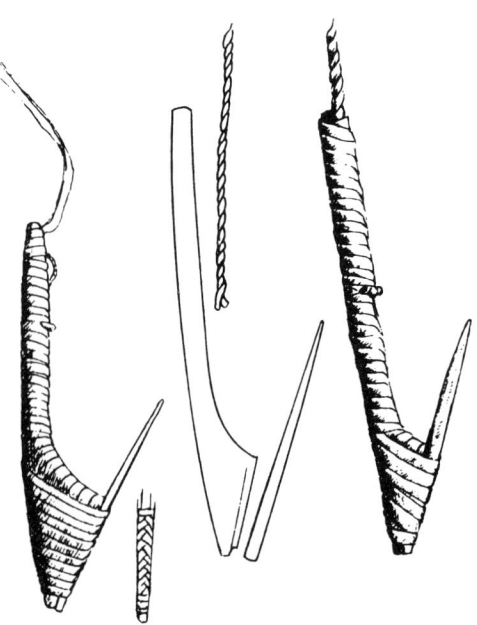

Tlingit salmon trolling hooks: bone barb lashed to wood shank with spruce root, leader of doeskin or cedar-bark twine (Stewart, 1977).

trolling. The material for manufacture of such hooks had to be more durable than the shell often used for bottom nibblers. Bone was the material of choice, at least for the point.

Since these hooks lacked the holding capability of the circular hook and were barbless, tension on the line had to be maintained once the fish was hooked in order not to lose it and landing the fish had to be done quickly. For this reason such hooks were usually used with poles. Also, if hook rotation occurred as with the short-shanked circular hook, the angle of point penetration would have been decreased markedly, not improved as in the round shell hook, and with it the likelihood of catching fish. This they overcame by *lengthening the shank* which reduced hook rotation.

The lesson from the Tartaglia study seems simple enough: hook design, size and manner of use proceeded with specific fish and environment in mind.

Wrapping the Acute Angle Hook

Remnants of acute angle hooks have been found on the islands off the southern California coast. Stone-sharpened pinniped or whale bone barbs apparently were fitted into a slight groove of a 30-degree bevel at the bottom end of a wooden shank. Where the barb and shank met they were wrapped with asphaltum-soaked Indian hemp. The same wrapping was used at the top of the shank to secure the leader. Much farther north the Karok and Van Duzen Nongatl made a split-stick hook (of which we have a sketch) bound at the apex of the split with native twine and held open by string inserted in the split to form the acute angle. Even a simple thorn or stone-sharpened sliver of wood or bone tightly wound with native thread or twine to a properly angled wooden shank with the wrappings daubed with pine pitch or asphaltum worked. But I felt there must be more. I searched for special cuts on shanks and secret ways of wrapping. Ethnographic accounts from most of the Californias are amazingly short on detail. I simply sought the best way to bind the acute-angled Indian hook.

Recent underwater and mudslide excavations of maritime Indians of the Northwest at Hoko River and Ozette on the Olympic Peninsula, home of the present-day Makah, brought to light hundreds of compound wood and bone hooks, perfectly preserved, and I naturally looked in that direction for help. Unfortunately, I found scant description of the techniques of manufacture. I began to believe I would have to receive a spirit message.

From the Tlingit of the Northwest Coast came the vision. After gazing at Hilary Stewart's drawing (reproduced here) of a compound, lashed, acute-angle Tlingit trolling hook, I understood. The thin abstracted edge showing the lashing pattern appeared in the drawing to belong to the front of the hook; actually it could only be of the back. The technique was amazingly simple and the best way to wrap a hook. How far it extended on the Pacific Coast of North America is difficult to know, but here is how it might be reproduced.

1) Hold the shank (a single groove in the 30-degree bevel helps) with the point to the right as shown. Place one end of the thread or twine upright on the lower portion of the shank and secure it with a couple of counterclockwise turns (left to right) 1/8 of an inch or so from the bottom. These turns go one above the other.

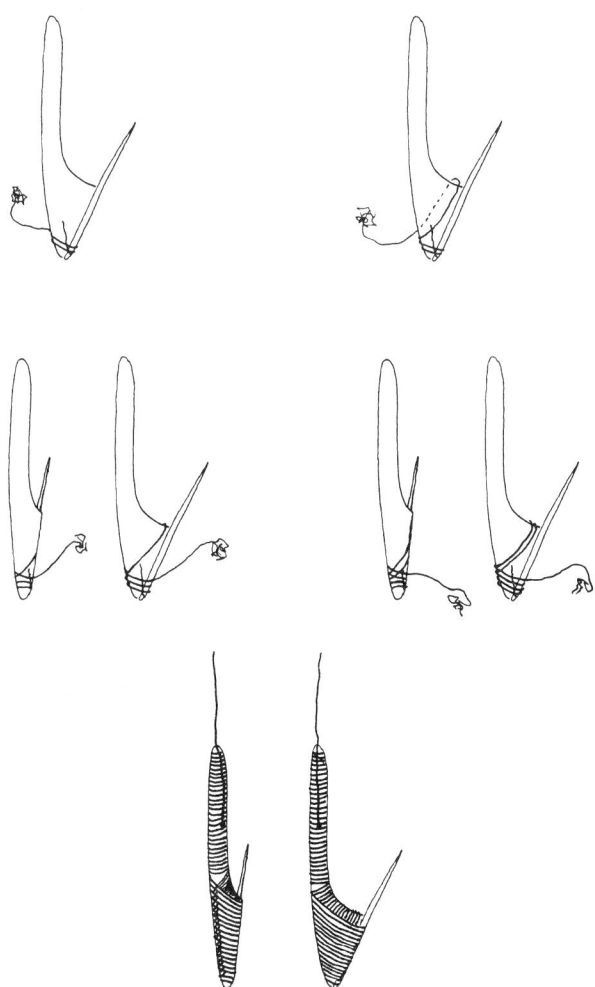

2) Continue by swinging up from the left edge and over the crotch of the shank, coming as close to the hook's barb as possible, and across the far or backside down to the first two turns at the bottom left, crossing the twine on the left edge (the back of the shank) and continuing with another turn around the bottom of the shank just above the first two.

3) Again, swing up from the left (having crossed the twine on the back side) over the crotch, parallel and just to the left of the first crotch wrap. Keep the wraps in place and prevent them from creeping up on the left edge by holding them in place with the left hand. Continue until the bottom of the shank has been fully wrapped.

4) Complete the shank with simple turns going over the leader which has been extended down the shank and which these turns secure. A knot tied at the lower end of the leader holds it fast. (A small loop shown in Stewart's sketch may be for attaching a stone sinker.)

5) Near the top of the shank tie a couple of half hitches or push the wrap under and through the last two turns and pull it tight. Cut off the excess.

6) I finish my hooks California style. If the twine has not already been smeared with viscous asphaltum, heated daubs of this or pine pitch are coated over and rubbed into the twine to secure and waterproof the lashings.

The Tlingit wrap anchors each of the crucial turns of the lower shank to the upper shank, thus preventing slippage, and secures the leader in one quick process. It adapts well to any size of compound hook. A few turns around the shank above as you work up from the base may be all that are necessary in some very small hooks. Most important, a finely wrapped, carefully engineered fishing tool looks good.

A final note. If you find yourself in a truly desperate survival situation unable to manufacture a hook and line, you can do as traditional Indians sometimes did: muddy the waters of a brook or river and catch fish with your hands. Trout will usually be found hiding under the banks. Come in slow, feel the fish, squeeze. The Miwok sometimes caught small rainbow trout with their hands. They said they found them in the holes along the banks. I have caught trout this way in their holes along the banks in the mountain streams above Los Angeles. I do not recommend it for the squeamish. Fingernails help.

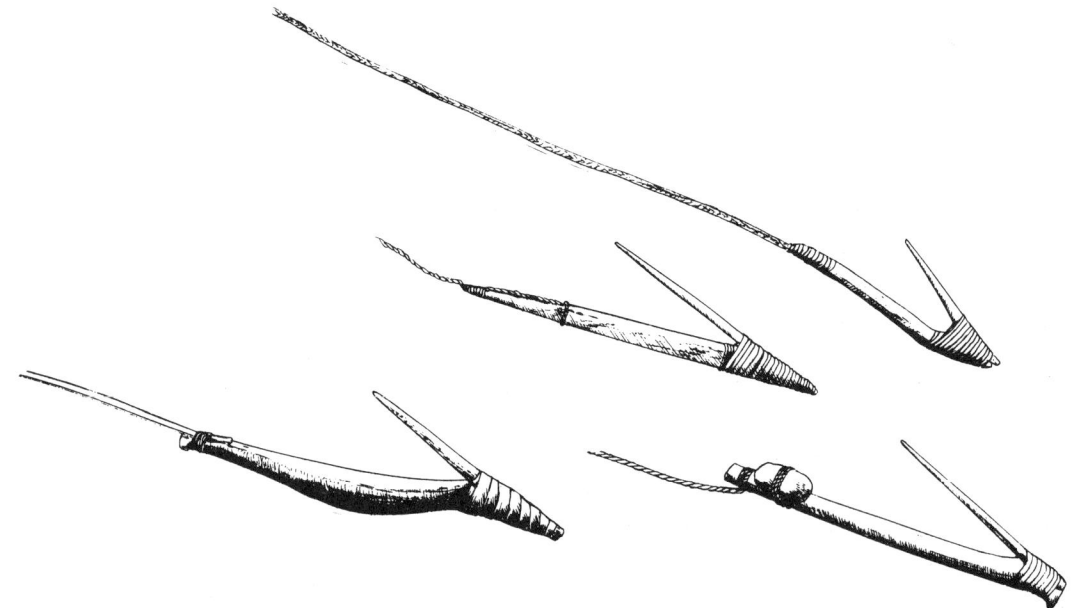

Northwest Coast salmon trolling hooks. Herring flesh was tied to the barb or it was baited with a fresh shiner, kept below the surface with a small sinker on the line. The Kwakiutl tied the fishline around their hand; the Nootka tied it to their canoe paddle. This gave the bait a life-like appearance as they plied a bay or inlet. A quick deft motion of the paddle landed the fish. Before baiting a hook, Northwest Coast Indians rubbed their hands with seaweed and held them in the water to remove the human scent. Top hook is Kwakiutl and has a braided leader of twelve long strands of woman's hair (Stewart, 1977).

Fish Poison

"Rather ignominious and un-Waltonian," Powers called the Wailaki practice of using poison to catch fish. Native Californians crushed or macerated certain parts of a variety of plants which they threw into quiet waters to kill or stupefy fish. Floating to the surface dead, or at least slowed by the narcotic effect, the fish were then easily scooped out or harpooned. Survival, not sportsmanship, was of course the concern of the California Indian. To put it into perspective: the effluent of a single modern household or careless camper—not to mention industrial waste, clearcut forests and agricultural water diversions—must kill more fish in a day than Indian poison ever did in a month.

The northern California Wailaki haunts were the upper reaches of little streams, especially in summer when the water slowed and stagnant pools appeared. They rubbed soaproot *(Chlorogalum pomeridianum)* in the water to stupefy the trout which, as a consequence, were easily scooped up. In southern California, after poisoning the pools with a plant when the water was low, the Luiseño took trout by hand or with a rush basket or dip net (for smaller fish) in the upper San Luis Rey River and its mountain tributaries. The larger, fast-flowing streams of northwestern California were not conducive to poisons, observed Kroeber and Barrett. Slow streams and still pools were needed to keep the poison concentrated. It was the peripheral and neighboring tribes of the big northwestern rivers who used fish poisons: the Chilula, Mattole, Sinkyone and Kato, for example.

The Chilula pounded soaproot with enough water to make suds and used the solution in creek holes for trout. The Nishinam of the Bear River pounded the soaproot fine and threw it into pools from which the fish had no exit; they roiled the bottom and made the water muddy. Galen Clark left us detail on the Miwok use of the soaproot in the waters of the South Fork of the Merced River at Wawona (where he had built a log cabin in 1857). For them it was a communal effort and not a matter of a simple stagnant pool. Every fish for a distance of three miles was caught in a few hours. The root worked in late summer when the water was low. Several bushels of soaproot bulbs were dug and pounded into a pulp on the bank of the river. They mixed in soil and water then spread the mixture in handfuls on boulders out in the stream, roiling the water. The soon stupefied fish rose to the surface where the Indians gathered them in scoop baskets.

The Mattole believed soaproot affected the viscera of the fish. The poisoned fish should not be allowed to float about but should be taken ashore and eviscerated as soon as possible, in their view. Soaproot, indeed, contains a poisonous saponin the Indian would sometimes remove by heating the bulb in an earth oven in order to make food. Most California Indians claimed, however, that the fish themselves, poisoned by whatever Native means, were not in turn poisonous to those who ate them.

Buckeyes *(Aesculus californica)*, hulled and pounded, could be used in much the same way as soaproot. Buckeyes contain prussic acid which was removed by heating or leaching when they were prepared as food. Kroeber recorded that the Yokuts ground buckeye nuts with earth stamped into them and threw the mixture into a small stream to bring the fish to the surface. They also crushed nademe leaves to stupefy fish and Gayton mentions two other plants used by the Yokuts to poison fish: *ta'dad*, which grew near streams, and *ya'oha*, which grew on the mountains. Unfortunately the plants were not further identified, but R.K. Beardsley included for the Yokuts soaproot, the most widely used of the California fish poisons; willow smartweed *(Polygonum lapathifolium)*; vinegar weed *(Trichostema lanceolatum*, a bluecurl), used by the Nomlaki and Maidu for the same purpose; and turkey mullein *(Eremocarpus setigerus*, also called dove weed or *yerba del pescado*), almost as widely employed in California as the soaproot for poisoning fish.

W. R. Goldschmidt found that the Nomlaki women poisoned stagnant holes with soaproot and turkey mullein. The mullein weeds were gathered, wetted and pounded on rocks at the edge of the water and then mixed into the water. The fuzz from the mullein got "into gills of fish and stifled them," they believed.

Many fish poisons were employed by Native Californians. In addition to soaproot, buckeye, and turkey mullein, Hewes listed pepperwood *(Umbellularia californica*, also known as the California bay tree) for the Miwok. It was the leaves of the pepperwood or the buckeye the Northfork Mono crushed to poison fish, but Barrett and Gifford found that the Miwok mashed the buckeye nuts to kill fish in small creeks or pools. Beardsley included the seeds and root of the Sierra manroot *(Marah horrida)* as a Miwok fish poison.

Hewes recorded that the Lassik and Wailaki took suckers and trout with the soaproot, turkey mullein and manroot *(Marah,* also known as squirting or wild cucumber). The Sinkyone used soaproot and manroot, either separately or together, pounded up and placed in deep holes of creeks when the water was low, good for trout and suckers, sometimes even steelhead. Wormwood (probably *Artemisia douglasiana*) and wild parsnip (probably cow parsnip, *Heracleum lanatum*) were also Sinkyone fish poisons. The Bear River people took trout, suckers and lamprey eels by pounding and mixing together soaproot, manroot and wild onion. It colored a pool purplish. In addition they used the turkey mullein plant and pounded buckeye nuts to poison fish. Ishi told Pope that the Yana used the beaten fruit of manroot (squirting cucumber) as a fish poison. For the Wintun it was soaproot, the turkey mullein and the root of the California manroot *(Marah fabaceus)*. The Wappo used soaproot, turkey mullein and *okali*. Driver wrote that soaproot or turkey mullein was pounded up by the Wappo and an amount equal to a full gunny sack dumped into a quiet pool. According to Heizer, the Maidu had horehound *(Lycopus sp.)*, the Washo, wild carrot *(Lomatium dissectum*, var. *multifidum)* and the Owens Valley Paiute, slim solomon *(Smilacina sessilifolia)*. The Kern River Tubatulabal also stupefied fish, wrote Voegelin, with slightly mashed roots, stalks and leaves of a solomon's seal *(Smilacina sp.)* that "looks like cane, grows in moist soil," and "has leaves that get reddish-yellow in fall," according to informant Steban Miranda. As they floated to the surface the Tubatulabal scooped the fish up in twined conical tule baskets.

For the Pomo, poisoning was a principal method of taking fish in streams. They even had a fishing chief who directed the communal undertaking in its entirety: gathering plants, making weirs and so forth. Soaproot bulbs and turkey mullein were used. Pomo consultants told Barrett the mullein was as effective as soaproot. The leaves were pounded up and put in the water. Sometimes they pulverized wild tobacco and mixed it with the turkey mullein. In small pools along the coast the Pomo placed the root of the California or coast manroot *(Marah fabaceus* or *oreganus)* to poison octopus, ocean eels and fish.

Barrett's informants denied that anyone ever became sick eating poisoned fish.

The Yuki, as described by George Foster sixty years ago, were especially fond of using poison for trout. Some of the best "weeds" had only native names such as *lilmil* (Hewes identified lilmil as probably manroot) and *kicilwoímuk*. Soaproot and tarweed *(Hemizonia sp.)* were also employed. Soaproot they deemed the least efficacious but because so common, it was often used. Tarweed they pounded between rocks to a moist pulp and dropped it in quiet pools in large quantities—it took about an hour to stun the fish that then appeared belly-up on the surface of the water. Poisons were used singly or together. The shoots and leaves of the buckeye poisoned fish for the Yuki, wrote Chesnut forty years before Foster's studies.

Garth found that the Atsugewi pulverized wild parsley root (also called Gray's lovage, *Ligusticum grayi*) and poured the powder into a quiet pool that they sometimes temporarily dammed off from the rest of the stream. It turned the water blue. Baskets dipped out the fish as they floated belly-up.

Angelica root, a Pomo charm, was also used as a fish poison but always in combination with another plant of known toxic properties, raising doubts about the biological effectiveness of angelica alone. The Cocopa dumped great quantities of willow leaves on small ponds bringing fish to the surface in two or three days. Apparently the astringent tannin slowly leached out and interfered with the fish's gills. This was, indeed, very slow acting in comparison to the fish poisons described for the other California groups.

Undoubtedly, there were poisons unremembered and unrecorded. Using poison to catch fish was already illegal in California and likely little practiced by the time early ethnographers began gathering their information. We should realize too, as Heizer discovered, that it was not the geographical occurrence of a poison plant alone that determined whether or not it would be employed as a piscicide. The awareness that a plant could be used for poison was invariably more restricted than the actual distribution of the species. In other words, not all Indians knew all of Nature's secrets.

Fish and Shellfish Preparation

The principles of California Indian cookery extended to the products of sea, stream, and lake. Indian foods could be eaten together but in preparing them they were not often mixed or seasoned. Simple drying for the purpose of preservation through the winter was ubiquitous, pulverizing and reconstituting by boiling common. Roasting or broiling meat on or near the coals of a fire, baking leaf-wrapped foods in an earth oven and boiling food fresh were the usual cooking techniques. When it came to fish, salmon exemplified California Indian cuisine. For millennia, salmon fed much of northern California.

Salmon and Other Fish

The clear-cutting of forests, building of dams and spreading of suburbia in the last fifty years has all but destroyed the once bountiful salmon fishery. It must be difficult for someone coming of age today to comprehend how great a resource this was and how important to the California Indian diet. Powers wrote over 100 years ago that the Winton harpooner "sometimes looks down on so great a multitude of black-backed salmon slowly warping to and fro in the gentle current, that he could scarcely thrust his spear down without transfixing one or more."

In the northwest of California the caught salmon was immediately split, the eyes removed and the flesh cured. The Karok spread ferns over the ground, laid the fish upon them and severed the tail at the small rear dorsal fin. The jaw was broken, the head snapped back and eventually along with the gills removed, according to Hewes. The back was cut down the full length. The viscera were taken out and discarded unless food was extremely scarce, but the eggs were always saved. Backbones, heads and tails were cooked and thoroughly dried on a scaffold placed about three feet over a small fire. Gifford learned how the Karok sliced fish the old way. A hafted knife of flint, kept sharp by retouching with a flaker, split the back of the fish and the spine was extracted. The resulting whole, wide slab was further widened by splitting the flesh of each side, leaving them attached along the back and folding the two sides out to create one very wide thin slab of four distinct sections. Such slabs were then draped over horizontal poles for a day and turned for a second day of preliminary drying. The curing fish were always shielded from the direct sun; a shade of boughs, usually pepperwood, was built if the curing was outdoors.

The slabs of salmon flesh were next flattened out and held by two or three cross sticks or bent-over withes, perhaps skewered through the fish. One informant told Gifford the sticks were of poison oak, others used willow. Two rows of stones about a foot high with poles between them constituted a grill. (Hewes found the Wiyot used a rack of green willow poles over a small fire that they said not only smoked the fish but also kept the flies from it.) A fairly hot fire of wood that was not pitchy burned within and over all was a shade. One Karok mentioned dead maple wood as the best for fuel because it gave heat without black smoke. Others preferred white alder, a wood that they burned for smoking eels and venison

Tom Willson, Yurok, at Weitchpec, July 1998.

as well. In fact, in aboriginal times Gifford's consultants told him they smoked not only salmon but sturgeon, lampreys, trout and many other species. Small fish or surf fish (smelt and eulachon, for example) were sun-dried or placed on small racks over smoldering fires when fog darkened the sun. Venison and other meats and even acorns were smoked. Rotten wood—dead dry limbs easily broken by striking them against the ground—of alder, madrone, oak, birch and others was burned, sometimes after dipping in water to slow the fire and produce more smoke.

The curing fire did not have to burn constantly. The sun's heat later in the day was sufficient to dry the fish. (As mentioned, they were kept out of the direct rays of the sun.) But in the morning a fire was always kindled. After about three days of this the fish were transferred to the regular drying racks well above but near the hearth fire of the home for an additional eight to ten days. They were hung about two inches apart to allow ample circulation of air. Hewes observed that a hole was made near the head end of the salmon slab. A pole passed through the hole and the slabs hung vertically.

It was during this stage of the curing a steatite bowl was set under the salmon to catch the rich oil that fairly trickled from the slab. Hewes recorded that the Mattole used the carapaces of land tortoises and sea turtles to catch oil. A large steatite bowl of gallon capacity with basketry cover, set in a hole at the edge of the Karok house floor, stored the oil. A kelp "bottle" was sometimes used. Seal, sea-lion and whale oils were stored in sea-lion bladders or stomachs also with a basketry cover.

Some groups only dried the salmon and did not use a curing fire. The eggs of salmon were hung outside on sticks and sun-dried. The Tolowa stored them in a seal-paunch lining.

Steelhead were cured much like salmon except head and tail were left on and the backbone was left in. Steelhead were smaller than salmon and they did not split the sides but flattened and skewered the fish after they had cut down its back and removed the viscera. Cured steelhead were eaten first because they did not keep so well as salmon.

The best storage for cured salmon, according to Hewes' Karok informants, was in a pine-needle-lined pit inside the back of the house. Sometimes the needles were mixed with maple leaves. The pit was covered with more pine needles. This preserved the fish from mold and insects and it kept its flavor better.

Large, covered, spheroid storage baskets, the same as for acorns, were a second choice. The layers of salmon in these were separated by maple-leaf mats and covered over all with madrone leaves.

To eat dried salmon the Karok usually simply broke pieces off the slab although sometimes they would boil it in a basket with hot stones. At times they would heat the slab slightly and if it was a piece with skin, initial light scoring on the skin with a knife allowed it to break more easily into smaller morsels. Acorn soup was considered the best accompaniment to dried salmon. Sun-dried salmon eggs were eaten as they were or first pulverized. Dried backbone, usually crushed, was boiled into soup or fed to the dogs.

To prepare and cook fresh salmon Karok-style, the fish was split lengthwise, the head, entrails and backbone removed but the tail usually left on one of the two sides. Hewes noted the Karok wiped out the interior with ferns, never cleansing it with water. Each half was cut across twice, making six pieces. Onto the middle of an 18-inch willow rod or maple stick each piece was skewered and the rod stuck in the ground slightly leaning toward a blazing fire, either indoors or out. The rod was turned end-for-end and adjusted to give an even broil and good flavor.

In contrast, dried salmon when skewered was usually hand held near the blaze. Unlike fresh salmon much oil dripped from the fish and was caught in a steatite dish. The oil quickly congealed and was eaten with a spoon as an accompaniment to acorn soup.

Pieces of fresh salmon were occasionally cooked by pushing the coals to one side and laying the fish directly on the hot rocks beneath. Salmon heads were broiled on a rack of four posts with crossbars about three feet above the coals for four to five hours. They ate the meat of the mandible and brains ("soft portions in the top of the head") and some even ate the eyes. (Karok hunters often removed and slit open the eyes of deer and ate the "eye jelly"—vitreous humor—raw for luck).

The Karok baked sturgeon head in a pit oven. They heated the pit, lined it with hot rocks, a layer of green leaves (preferably cottonwood), the head, another layer of leaves, a layer of sand and a final layer of coals and hot rocks. The head baked from morning until evening. Sturgeon eggs mashed with a pestle or wooden egg-masher were wrapped in maple leaves and cooked in the underground oven.

Hewes found among the Wiyot the same general methods for curing salmon applied to sturgeon, steelhead, perch and lampreys. Smaller species—herring, smelt, and suckers—the Wiyot ate fresh (Kroeber and Barrett suggested they may not have kept so well on the foggy Wiyot coast).

The Wintu did not dry the spring catch of Chinook salmon on the Sacramento and McCloud rivers at the time they were caught; they believed they were too rich in oil. Instead, the fish were baked in a stone-lined pit oven. The fish were laid on the heated stones in rows, head to tail, and covered with more hot rocks. After a few hours they were removed and the amount desired eaten. Those remaining were boned and flaked then dried out and pulverized into salmon flour.

The fall run was thought less greasy and these fish were immediately slit open, dried in the sun and stored for the winter. Heads, guts, tails and bones were also dried for the winter but, before storage, they were pounded into flour. Salmon flour was stored in wide baskets, recorded Du Bois; they narrowed at the top and maple leaves lined them. Salmon flour was mixed with dried roe and pine nuts for pemmican, a valuable Wintu item of trade with peoples to the south. The Nongatl pulverized dried backbone of salmon with dried meat or mixed the powder with dried roe.

Small fish, like trout and whitefish, that the Wintu caught with a fishhook of two thorns tied together in an acute angle or with the sharpened naturally curved nasal bone of a deer (or poisoned in isolated pools or small streams or caught in traps), were laid uncleaned on hot rocks. Slates were preferred. They salted and covered the fish with additional hot rocks. When done they scraped them off the stones and ate them. Leftovers were sun-dried and stored in baskets for the winter, when they were reconstituted by boiling.

The Wintu had another way of preparing small fish. They split them open along the backbone leaving the belly uncut then laid the flesh back and removed the bones and viscera. They roasted the flesh on chaparral brush.

Hewes reported that one of the few foods not dried by Bear River people was trout—surplus was merely given away. Those trout consumed were thrown whole and fresh on the hot coals to broil. Bullheads were also broiled and eaten this way.

Powers described the Yurok preparation of small fish in the 1870s. Smelt were dried whole on low wooden kilns with interstices allowing the smoke of a small fire to rise up freely. The fish were then further dried in the sun. The Yurok consumed them uncooked, often with a sauce of raw salal berries. "Let an Indian be journeying anywhither, and you will always find in his basket some bars of this silver bullion, or flakes of rich orange salmon," wrote Powers.

Lamprey

Yurok Robert Spott left us details of lamprey preparation (in Kroeber and Barrett). Heads were removed. Then with a small quartz flake, held between the fingers so that only one quarter to one third inches projected, the belly was slit (preventing the gall from being cut) to the anus and the insides removed. If being cleaned for drying, the cut continued around the anus to the tail end. Sixty or seventy were strung by the tails at this stage and the Yurok woman took them one by one and removed the notochord (sometimes these cords were left in). She dipped her left hand in ashes to better grip the doubled over lamprey tail. On a board across her knees and with her right hand she inserted the point of a bone awl or slitter under the notochord to work it loose, then with her right thumbnail beneath the cord she ran her thumb to the head end, opening up one side. The lamprey was laid on the other side and with the opposite hand she repeated the process. The notochord was loosened at the head end with the awl and stripped out. It was kept as reserve against famine or fed to the dogs. The lining of the inside was scraped with a flint knife or mussel shell. The flesh was cut in ribbons, left hanging from the skin, by repeatedly slitting the flesh lengthwise with the bone awl held short between thumb and finger so as not to reach the skin.

The lampreys were draped skin side down over the pole drying racks above the hearth fire and left for two or three days. This kept them from curling together. When they stayed flat they were again strung by the tails and hung in the house for final drying. They were eaten as they were. For the final drying the Chilula, according to Hewes, hung the lampreys by a hole in the tail over a small smoky fire and caught the oil that dripped out in a steatite dish.

Lamprey was also prepared fresh by the Yurok who described the procedure to Hewes. After having been slit down the belly with a bone awl and the notochord extracted from the tail upward to the head, they were laid about four at a time on hot coals away from the flames and turned from time to time to broil evenly. When done, the Yurok wound a turn of string around the lamprey and pulled it, cutting the soft buttery flesh into bite-size pieces.

Shellfish

The Sinkyone caught crabs and crayfish by hand, then cooked and ate them. Clams, mussels and abalone they collected, pounded and sun-dried, sometimes smoked. The Pomo gathered and ate mussels, barnacles and many other foods of the sea. They netted lobsters at low tide and caught snails. The Nomlaki dove for freshwater clams in rivers; the Wintu did the same for mussels and clams that they roasted, broiled or dried for future use. The Mattole ate limpets, raw or cooked. Many species of clams, mussels, abalone and other shellfish were collected and consumed at once with minimal preparation by the California Indians or dried as provisions for the winter or for barter with inland tribes.

The Tolowa, discovered Hewes, pried mussels off rocks with a sharp stick and roasted them fresh in their shells on hot coals. If there were many mussels and many to be fed, two or three baskets of unshelled mussels were spread over a rack of green sticks built over a fire and roasted. To preserve them, mussels were dried in the sun or over a fire. They were reconstituted by soaking during the night and stone boiling in a basket. The Mattole first cooked the mussels then sun-dried and strung them on strings that they hung up in the house for storage. Dried mussels were much-desired items of trade to those in the interior.

The Mattole told Hewes that mussels could be gathered and eaten at any time because around the mouth of their river "red water" or luminescence did not occur. Reddening of the water in the daytime and luminescence at night were signs to many Indians of the coast that mussels could be toxic. Driver found every coastal group from Tolowa to Coast Yuki knew about mussel poisoning. Some maintained that those of deep water were not affected. Kroeber and Barrett wrote that redness of the water and luminescence at night in summer was caused when a *Gonyaulax* plankton became numerous. Mussels concentrated the poison in their livers. They were not affected but it could be a paralyzing lethal poison to the warm-blooded animals who ate them. Pomo sentries watched for the luminescence

Tom Willson, Yurok from Weitchpec on the Klamath River, expertly roasts salmon he netted in the river and then soaked for some hours in a salt solution. The skewers he holds above are flat, pointed pieces of redwood. They are passed through the center of the salmon steaks. The somewhat wider bottom ends are stuck in one of the piles of earth, which has been excavated and pushed to either side of the long pit hearth. Chunks of madrone wood keep the fire hot. The skewers are revolved once, back to front, to evenly broil the fish—rich and succulent beyond imagination (July, 1998).

during very hot weather and when they saw it, shellfishing was suspended for two days.

The large mussel *(Mytilus californianus)* which grew to nine inches was also important for its shell: the butt served as a cutting blade on the stone-handled adze.

Many species of clams were eaten. The Tolowa roasted them in the coals and ate them fresh. If there was an abundance they were sun-dried on the shore where there were few flies or on the drying rack of the hearth fire protected by the smoke. Small white snails found on the beach especially in spring were boiled whole and the shells broken to extract the meat. The Mattole ate "water snails" after boiling or roasting in ashes but never raw. They cooked them in the shells then cracked the shells as they ate them.

The Mattole pried abalone off rocks with a chisel-shaped hard wood stick the length of one's forearm. The end was fire-hardened. They roasted the abalone in ashes or baked them in a shallow underground oven with a fire built over it. The abalone remained in the oven as long as it took to make them tender. They did not pound them. They were dried in quantity for winter.

According to R. E. Greengo, the Tolowa, Wiyot and Pomo ate the eggs or gonads of the sea urchin *(Strongylocentrotus purpuratus)* raw. The sea anemone *(Cribrina xanthogrammica)* was dried, soaked and warmed by the Pomo, cooked in hot ashes by the Coast Yuki or roasted on live coals by the Tolowa.

Loeb and Stewart recorded that the Pomo gathered barnacles and cooked them in the hot ashes of a fire. (According to Greengo those generally used in California were of the genuses *Balanus* and *Mitella*.) They also built fires on top of flat rocks where beds of barnacles were exposed at low tide.

Greengo added that the Yurok cooked pig's foot barnacles *(Mitella polymerus)* in hot sand.

The Tolowa cooked crabs in the sand and hot ashes of the fire. They told Hewes they plucked them from pools at low tide and used a torch if they hunted them at night; they threw them into a burden basket. Hewes' one report of a crab trap came from a still-water Wiyot. A shallow plate basket with strings attached to the edges in such a way as to keep it level was weighted with a stone or two, baited with meat or fish and lowered into the ocean near the shore. It was then raised carefully in order not to frighten the crabs, which were taken off by hand.

The inland Shasta trapped crayfish the same way. They lowered a flat basket into about four feet of water in the evening and pulled it gently to the surface after 15 minutes. They boiled the crayfish in another basket to eat them.

The Karok also used the flat basket trap but instead of strings they had a four-foot stick fixed to its center. Salmon gills served as bait and once the crayfish were aboard, according to Gifford, the device was quickly lifted. This was primarily an activity of children and old people. They roasted the crayfish in hot coals. The children strung the shells for toys. Alternately, the Karok held a pole and string baited with salmon gills to catch crayfish. The Yurok used the pole and string with a piece of salmon at its end, or they simply caught them by hand at the edge of a stream. The Tolowa caught them by hand under rocks while swimming and cooked them in ashes or in the earth oven.

The Wintu dove to the bottom of rivers for freshwater clams and either roasted or boiled them to open the shell. The meat was eaten at once or, if plentiful, dried in a flat basketry tray and stored for the winter.

Bibliography

Abrams, LeRoy and Roxana Stinchfield Ferris. *Illustrated Flora of the Pacific States, Washington, Oregon, and California* (in Four Volumes). Stanford University Press. Stanford, 1960.

Adovasio, J. M. *Basketry Technology.* Aldine Publishing. Chicago, 1977.

Allely, Steve. "Western Indian Bows." In *The Traditional Bowyer's Bible*, Vol. 1, Jim Hamm, ed. Bois d'Arc Press. New York, 1992.

———. "Great Basin Atlatls: Notes from the N.W. Corner." *Bulletin of Primitive Technology*, Vol. 1, No. 4. Society of Primitive Technology. Flagstaff, 1992.

Almstedt, Ruth Farrell. *Bibliography of the Diegueño Indians.* Ballena Press. Ramona, 1974.

Alvarez de Williams, Anita. *Primeros Pobladores de la Baja California.* Mexicali, Baja, California, 1973.

———. *Travelers Among the Cucapá* Dawson's Book Shop. Los Angeles, 1975.

Anderson, Kat. "At Home in the Wilderness." In *News from Native California.* Heyday Books. Berkeley, Spring 1992.

Baegert, Jacob. "An Account of the Aboriginal Inhabitants of the California Peninsula." In *Smithsonian Institution Annual Report, 1863.* Washington, D.C., 1872.

Baker, Tim. "The Causes of Arrow Speed." *Bulletin of Primitive Technology*, Vol. 1, No. 3. Society of Primitive Technology. Flagstaff, 1992.

Barco, Miguel Del. *Historia Natural Y Crónica de la Antigua California.* Miguel León-Portillo, ed. Universidad Nacional Autónoma de México. México, 1973.

Barrett, Samuel A. "Pomo Indian Basketry." *University of California Publications in American Archaeology and Ethnology*, Vol. 7, No. 3. Berkeley, 1908.

———. "The Material Culture of the Klamath Lake and Modoc Indians of Northeastern California and Southern Oregon." *University of California Publications in American Archaeology and Ethnology*, Vol. 5, No. 4. Berkeley, 1910.

———. "The Army Worm: A Food of the Pomo Indians." In *Essays in Anthropology in Honor of A.L. Kroeber.* R. H. Lowie, ed. University of California Press. Berkeley, 1936.

———. "Material Aspects of Pomo Culture." *Bulletin of the Public Museum, City of Milwaukee*, Vol. 20, Parts I and II. Milwaukee, 1952.

Barrett, S. A., and E. W. Gifford. "Miwok Material Culture." *Bulletin of the Public Museum of the City of Milwaukee*, Vol. 2, No. 4. Milwaukee, 1933.

Barrows, David Prescott. *The Ethno-botany of the Coahuilla Indians of Southern California.* University of Chicago Press. Chicago, 1900.

Barter, Eloise Richards. "Achumawi and Atsugewi Fishing Gear." *Journal of California and Great Basin Anthropology*, Vol. 12, No. 1. Malki Museum. Banning, 1990.

Bates, Craig. "The Reflexed Sinew-Backed Bow of the Sierra Miwok." *San Diego Museum of Man Ethnic Technology Notes*, No. 16. San Diego, 1978.

Baugh, Dick. "The Miracle of Fire by Friction." *Bulletin of Primitive Technology*, Vol. 1, No. 5. Society of Primitive Technology. Flagstaff, 1993.

Bean, Lowell John. "Cahuilla." In *Handbook of North American Indians, Vol. 8: California.* Smithsonian Institution. Washington, D.C., 1978.

Bean, Lowell John, and Katherine Siva Saubel. *Temalpakh: Cahuilla Indian Knowledge and Usage of Plants.* Malki Museum Press. Morongo Indian Reservation, 1972.

Beck, Beatrice M. *Ethnobotany of the California Indians*, Vol. 1: A bibliography and index. Koeltz Scientific Books. USA and Germany, 1994.

Belding, L. "The Pericue Indians." In *West American Scientist*, Vol. 1, No. 4. San Diego, 1885.

Benedict, Ruth F. "A Brief Sketch of Serrano Culture." *American Anthropologist*, Vol. 26. Menasha, 1924.

Blackburn, Thomas C. "Ethnohistoric Descriptions of Gabrielino Material Culture." *UCLA Archaeological Survey Annual Report.* Los Angeles, 1962–1963.

Bolton, Herbert Eugene, ed. *Spanish Exploration in the Southwest, 1542–1706.* (Includes translation of Sebastián Vizcaíno diary). Charles Scribner's Sons. New York, 1916.

Bowers, Stephen. *The Conchilla Valley and the Cahuilla Indians.* Santa Buenaventura, 1888.

Brooks, George R., ed. *The Southwest Expedition of Jedediah S. Smith: His Personal Account of the Journey to California, 1826–1827.* University of Nebraska Press. Lincoln, 1977.

Brown, Tom, Jr. *The Tracker.* Prentice-Hall. Englewood Cliffs, New Jersey, 1978.

Bryan, Bruce. "The Manufacture of Stone Mortars." *Southwest Museum Leaflets*, No. 34. Southwest Museum. Highland Park, Los Angeles 1970.

Callahan, Errett. "Medicine Bow Wickiup." In *Bulletin of Primitive Technology*, Vol. 1, No. 5. Society of Primitive Technology. Flagstaff, 1993.

Castetter, Edward F. "The Utilization of Yucca, Sotol, and Beargrass by the Aborigines of the American Southwest." *University of New Mexico Bulletin 372*. Albuquerque, 1941.

Castetter. Edward F., and Willis K. Bell. *Pima and Papago Indian Agriculture*. University of New Mexico Press. Albuquerque, 1942.

———. *Yuman Indian Agriculture*. University of New Mexico Press. Albuquerque, 1951.

Castetter, Edward F., Willis H. Bell, and Alvin R. Grove. "The Early Utilization and the Distribution of Agave in the American Southwest." *University of New Mexico Bulletin 335*. Albuquerque, 1938.

Caughey, J. *Indians of Southern California in 1852. (Report on Indians of Southern California by B. D. Wilson.)* Huntington Library. San Marino, 1952.

Chard, C. S. "Ethnographic Material Culture of the Napa Region." In *The Archaeology of the Napa Region, University of California Publications: Anthropological Records*, Vol. 12. R. F. Heizer, ed. Berkeley, 1953.

Chartkoff, Joseph L., and Kerry Kona Chartkoff. *The Archaeology of California*. Stanford University Press. Stanford, 1984.

Chase, J. Smeaton. *California Desert Trails*. Houghton Mifflin Company. New York, 1919.

Chesnut, V. K. "Plants Used by the Indians of Mendocino County, California." *Contributions to the National Herbarium*, VII. Washington, 1902.

Clark, Galen. *Indians of the Yosemite Valley and Vicinity: Their History, Customs, and Traditions*. Yosemite Valley, California, 1904.

Clavijero, Don Francisco Javier, S. J. *The History of [Lower] California*. Translated from the Italian and edited by Sara E. Lake and A. A. Gray. Stanford University Press. Palo Alto, 1937.

Collier, Mary E. T., and Sylvia B. Thalman, eds. "Interviews with Tom Smith and Maria Copa (Isabel Kelly's Ethnographic notes on the Coast Miwok)." *MAPOM Occasional Paper 6*. Miwok Archaeological Preserve of Marin. San Rafael, 1996.

Cook, Sherburne F. "The Mechanism and Extent of Dietary Adaptations Among Certain Groups of California and Nevada Indians." *Ibero-Americana 18*. University of California Press. Berkeley, 1943.

Cordell, Linda S. *Prehistory of the Southwest*. Academic Press. New York, 1984.

Cornett, James W. *Desert Palm Oasis*. Palm Springs Desert Museum. Palm Springs, 1989.

Cosgrove, C. B. "Caves of the Upper Gila and Hueco Areas in New Mexico and Texas." *Papers of the Peabody Museum of American Archaeology and Ethnology*, No. 2. Harvard University. Cambridge, 1947.

Costansó, Miguel. "The Narrative of the Portolá Expedition of 1769–1770." *Publications of the Academy of Pacific Coast History*, Vol. 1, No. 4. Berkeley, 1910.

Coyote Man, A recording of songs collected by. *Songs of the California Indian, Vol. I, Mountain Maidu*. Pacific Western Traders. Folsom, California, 1975.

Crabtree, Don E. "An Introduction to Flintworking." *Occasional Papers of the Idaho State University Museum*, Vol. 28. Pocatello, 1972.

Crabtree, Don E., and B. Robert Butler. "Notes on Experiments in Flint Knapping: 1, Heat Treatment of Silica Minerals." *Tebiwa*, Vol. VII. 1964.

Craig, Nathan. *Weaving the Web of Life: A Preliminary Report on Basketry Materials Used by Contemporary Native Americans Living in Proximity to the Cleveland National Forest*. Heritage Program, Cleveland National Forest. San Diego, 1994.

Craig, Steve. "Ethnographic Notes on the Construction of Ventureño Chumash Baskets." *UCLA Archaeological Survey Annual Reports*, Vol. 8. Los Angeles, 1966.

———. "The Basketry of the Ventureño Chumash." *UCLA Archaeological Survey Annual Reports*, Vol. 9. Los Angeles, 1967.

Cunningham, Richard W. *California Indian Watercraft*. EZ Nature Books. San Luis Obispo, 1989.

Curtin, L. S. M. *By the Prophet of the Earth: Ethnology of the Pima*. University of Arizona Press. Tucson and London, 1992.

Curtis, Edward S. *The North American Indian*, Vol. 15. Plimpton Press. Norwood, Massachusetts, 1926.

Davidson, G. "Remarks on a Boomerang from Los Angeles County, California." *Proceedings, California Academy of Sciences*, Vol. 4. San Francisco, 1873.

Davis, C. Alan, and Gerald A. Smith. *Newberry Cave*. San Bernardino County Museum Association. Redlands, California, 1981.

Davis, James T. "Trade Routes and Economic Exchange Among the Indians of California." *Reports of the University of California Archaeological Survey*, No. 54. Berkeley, 1961.

Dawson, Lawrence, and James Deetz. "A Corpus of Chumash Basketry." *UCLA Archaeological Survey Annual Report*, Vol. 7. Los Angeles, 1965.

Densmore, Frances. "Field-Work Among the Yuma, Cocopa and Yaqui Indians. Explorations and Field-Work—in 1922." *Miscellaneous Collections*, Vol. 74, No. 5. U.S. Smithsonian Institution. Washington, D.C., 1923.

———. "Musical Instruments of the Maidu Indians." *American Anthropologist*, Vol. 41. Menasha, 1939.

Dentzel, Carl Schaefer. *The Drawings of John Woodhouse Audubon: Illustrating his Adventures through Mexico and California 1849–1850*. The Book Club of California. San Francisco, 1957.

Devereus, George. "Amusements and Sports of Mohave Children." *The Masterkey*, 24(5). Southwest Museum. Highland Park, Los Angeles 1950.

Dixon, Roland B. "The Northern Maidu." *Bulletin of the American Museum of Natural History*, Vol. 17, Part 3. New York, 1905.

———. "The Shasta. The Huntington California Expedition." *Bulletin of the American Museum of Natural History*, Vol. 17, Part 5. New York, 1907.

Driver, Harold E. "Culture Element Distributions X: Northwest California." *Anthropological Records*, Vol. 1, No. 6. University of California. Berkeley, 1939.

Drucker, Philip. "The Tolowa and Their Southwest Oregon Kin." *University of California Publications in American Archaeology and Ethnology*, Vol. 36, No. 4. Berkeley, 1937.

———. "Culture Element Distributions V: Southern California." *University of California Anthropological Records*. Vol. 1, No. 1. Berkeley, 1937.

———. "Culture Element Distributions XVII: Yuman-Piman." *Anthropological Records*, Vol. 6, No. 3. University of California. Berkeley, 1942.

Du Bois, Constance. "The Religion of the Luiseño Indians of Southern California." *University of California Publications in American Archaeology and Ethnology*, Vol. 8, No. 3. Berkeley, 1908.

Du Bois, Cora. "Wintu Ethnography." *University of California Publications in American Archaeology and Ethnology*, Vol. 36, No. 1. Berkeley, 1935.

Ebeling, Walter. *Handbook of Indian Foods and Fibers of Arid America*. University of California Press. Berkeley, 1986.

Echlin, Donald R., Philip J. Wilke, and Lawrence E. Dawson. "Ord Shelter." *Journal of California and Great Basin Anthropology*, Vol. 3, No. 1. Malki Museum, Banning, 1981.

Edholm, Steven, and Tamara Wilder. *Wet-Scrape Braintanned Buckskin*. Paleotechnics. Boonville, 1997.

Elpel, Thomas J. "The Art of Nothing." *Bulletin of Primitive Technology*, No. 10. Society of Primitive Technology. Rexburg, 1995.

Engelhardt, Z. *The Missions and Missionaries of California, Vol. 1, Lower California* (2d ed.). Santa Barbara, 1929.

Essene, Frank. "Culture Element Distributions XXI: Round Valley." *Anthropological Records*, Vol. 8, No. 1. University of California. Berkeley, 1946.

Essig, E. O. "California Indians in Relation to Entomology." In *A History of Entomology*. The Macmillan Company. New York, 1931.

———. "The Value of Insects to the California Indians." *Scientific Monthly*, 38. 1934.

Fagan, Brian M. *Ancient North America: The Archaeology of a Continent*. Thames and Hudson. London, 1991.

Falk, Dean. "A Good Brain Is Hard to Cool." In *Natural History*, Vol. 102, No. 8. American Museum of Natural History. New York, August 1993.

Farmer, Justin F. *Indian Basketry Material Preparation*. Eagle Enterprises. Fullerton, 1991.

———. *California Indian Baskets: Their Characteristics and Materials*. Eagle Enterprises. Fullerton, 1993.

Farmer, Malcolm F. "The Mojave Trade Route." *The Masterkey*, 9. Southwest Museum. Highland Park, Los Angeles, 1935.

Faye, Paul-Louis. "Notes on the Southern Maidu." *University of California Publications in American Archaeology and Ethnology*, Vol. 20, No. 3. Berkeley, 1923.

Felger, Richard Stephen, and Mary Beck Moser. *People of the Desert and Sea: Ethnobotany of the Seri Indians*. University of Arizona Press. Tucson, 1985.

Fenenga, Gerrit L., and Eric M. Fisher. "The Cahuilla Use of *Piyatem*, Larvae of the White-lined Sphinx Moth." *The Journal of California Anthropology*, Vol. 5, No. 1. Malki Museum. Banning, 1978.

Font's Complete Diary. University of California. Berkeley, 1931.

Forbes, Jack D. *Warriors of the Colorado: The Yumas of the Quechan Nation and Their Neighbors*. University of Oklahoma Press. Norman, 1965.

Forde, C. Daryle. "Ethnography of the Yuma Indians." *University of California Publications in American Archaeology and Ethnology*, Vol. 28, No. 4. Berkeley, 1931.

Foster, George M. "A Summary of Yuki Culture." *University of California Publication: Anthropological Record*, Vol. 5, No. 3. Berkeley, 1944.

Fowler, Catherine S. "Subsistence." In *Handbook of North American Indians, Vol. 2: Great Basin*. Smithsonian Institution. Washington, D.C., 1986.

Fowler, Catherine S., and Joyce E. Bath. "Pyramid Lake Northern Paiute Fishing: The Ethnographic Record." *Journal of California and Great Basin Anthropology*, Vol. 3, No. 2. Malki Museum. Banning, 1981.

Fowler, Catherine S., and Sven Liljeblad. "Northern Paiute." In *Handbook of North American Indians, Vol. 11: Great Basin*. Smithsonian Institution. Washington, D.C., 1986.

Fowler, Don D., and David B. Madson. "Prehistory of Southeastern Area." In *Handbook of North American Indians, Vol. 11: Great Basin*. Smithsonian Institution. Washington, D.C., 1986.

Frémont, John C. "Report of the Exploring Expedition to the Rocky Mountains in the Year 1842, and to Oregon and North California in the Years 1843–44." *28th Congress, 2nd session, House Executive Document 166*. 1845.

Garth, Thomas R. "Atsugewi Ethnography." *University of California Anthropological Records*, Vol. 14, No. 2. Berkeley, 1953.

Gayton, Anna H. "Yokuts and Western Mono Ethnography; I and II." *Anthropological Records*, Vol. 10, No. 2. University of California Press. Berkeley and Los Angeles, 1948.

Gifford, Edward W. "Pottery-making in the Southwest." *University of California Publications in American Archaeology and Ethnology*, Vol. 23, No. 8. Berkeley, 1928.

———. "The Kamia of the Imperial Valley." *United States Bureau of American Ethnology*, Bulletin No. 97. Government Printing Office. Washington, D.C., 1931.

———. "The Cocopa." *University of California Publications in American Archaeology and Ethnology*, Vol. 31, No. 5. University of California Press. Berkeley, 1933.

———. "Californian Bone Artifacts." *University of California Anthropological Records*, Vol. 3. Berkeley, 1940.

———. "California Balanophagy." In *The California Indians*, R. F. Heizer and M. A. Whipple, eds. University of California. Berkeley, 1971.

Glassow, Michael A. "Prehistoric Agricultural Development in the Northern Southwest: A Study in Changing Patterns of Land Use." *Ballena Press Anthropology Papers 16*. Socorro, New Mexico, 1980.

Goddard, Pliny Earle. "Life and Culture of the Hupa." *University of California Publications in American Archaeology and Ethnology*, Vol. 1, No. 1. Berkeley, 1903.

Goldschmidt, Walter. "Nomlaki Ethnography." *University of California Publications in American Archaeology and Ethnology*, Vol. 42, No. 4. Berkeley, 1951.

Goodchild, Peter. *Survival Skills of the North American Indians*. Chicago Review Press. Chicago, 1984.

Goodrich, Jennie, Claudia Lawson, and Vana Parrish Lawson. *Kashaya Pomo Plants*. American Indian Studies Center, University of California. Los Angeles, 1980.

Goodstein, Carol. "Gary Paul Nabhan." In *The Amicus Journal*, Vol. 15, No. 3. Natural Resources Defense Council. New York, 1993.

Gould, R. A. "A Case of Heat Treatment of Lithic Materials in Aboriginal Northeastern California." *The Journal of California Anthropology*, Vol. 3. Malki Museum. Banning, 1976.

Grant, Campbell. "Chumash Artifacts Collected in Santa Barbara County, California." *University of California Archaeological Survey*, No. 63. Archaeology Research Facility. Berkeley, 1964.

———. "Rock Drawings of the Coso Range, Inyo County, California." *Maturongo Museum Publication* No. 4. China Lake, 1968.

———. "Eastern Coastal Chumash." In *Handbook of North American Indians, Vol. 8: California*. R. F. Heizer, ed. Smithsonian Institution. Washington, D.C., 1978.

———. "The Spear-thrower from 15,000 Years Ago to the Present." *Pacific Coast Archaeological Society Quarterly*, Vol. 15, No. 1. Costa Mesa, 1979.

Greengo, Robert E. "Aboriginal Use of Shellfish as Food in California." Master's thesis, University of California. University of California Library, Berkeley, 1951.

———. "Shellfish Foods of the California Indians." *Kroeber Anthropological Society Papers*, No. 7. 1952.

Grosscup, Gordon L. "The Culture History of Lovelock Cave, Nevada." *University of California Archaeological Survey*, No. 52. Archaeology Research Facility. Berkeley, 1964.

Hamy, E. "The Fishhook Industry of the Ancient Inhabitants of the Archipelago of California." *Reports of the University of California Archaeological Survey*, No. 59. Berkeley, 1963. (Reprint of article in French in *Revue d'Ethnographie*, Paris, 1885.)

Harner, M. J. "Potsherds and the Tentative Dating of the San Gorgonio Big Maria Trail." *Reports of the University of California Archaeological Survey*, No. 37. Berkeley, 1957.

Harrington, John Peabody. "Researches on the Archaeology of Southern California." *Smithsonian Miscellaneous Collections*, 78(1). Washington, D.C., 1926.

———. Unpublished field notes at the Smithsonian Institution. Washington, D.C., n.d.

Harrington, Mark Raymond. "Gypsum Cave, Nevada." *Southwest Museum Papers*, Number Eight. Highland Park, Los Angeles, 1933.

Haury, Emil W. *The Stratigraphy and Archaeology of Ventana Cave Arizona*. University of Arizona Press. Tucson, 1950.

Hedges, Ken. "A Rabbitskin Blanket From San Diego County." *Ethnic Technology Notes*, No. 10. San Diego Museum of Man. San Diego, 1973.

———. and Christina Beresford. "Santa Ysabel Ethnobotany." *Ethnic Technology Notes*, No. 20. San Diego Museum of Man. San Diego, 1986.

Heizer, Robert F. "A Complete Atlatl Dart from Pershing County, Nevada." *New Mexico Anthropologist*, Vol. 2. Albuquerque, 1938.

———. "The Use of Plants for Fish-poisoning by the California Indians." *Leaflets of Western Botany*, Vol. III, No. 2. California Academy of Sciences. San Francisco, 1941.

———. "Ancient Grooved Clubs and Modern Rabbitsticks." *American Antiquity*, Vol. 8. 1942.

———. "Preliminary Report on the Leonard Rockshelter Site. Pershing County, Nevada." *American Antiquity*, Vol. 17, No. 2. Salt Lake City, 1951.

———. "Aboriginal Fish Poisons." *Anthropological Paper No. 38 in Bureau of American Ethnology Bulletin 151*. Washington, 1953.

———. "A San Nicolas Island Twined Basketry Water Bottle." *University of California Archaeological Survey Report 50*. Berkeley, 1960.

———. "The Indians of Los Angeles County: Hugo Reid's Letters of 1852." *Southwest Museum Paper 21*. Highland Park, Los Angeles, 1968.

Heizer, R. F., and A. B. Elsasser, eds. "Original Accounts of the Lone Woman of San Nicolas Island." *Reports of the University of California Archaeological Survey No. 55*. Berkeley, 1961.

Heizer, R. F., and Alex F. Krieger. "The Archaeology of Humboldt Cave, Churchill County, Nevada." *University of California Publications in American Archaeology and Ethnology*, Vol. 47. 1956.

Heizer, R. F., and W. C. Massey. "Aboriginal Navigation off the Coasts of Upper and Baja California." *Bureau of American Ethnology*, Bulletin 151. Washington, 1953.

Hellweg, Paul. *Flintknapping: The Art of Making Stone Tools*. Canyon Publishing. Canoga Park, California, 1984.

Hewes, Gordon W. "Aboriginal Use of Fishing Resources in Northwestern North America." Ph.D. dissertation, University of California. University of California Library. Berkeley, 1947.

———. "Abstract of Aboriginal Use of Fishing Resources in Northwestern North America." *Kroeber Anthropological Society Papers*, No. 14. Berkeley, 1956.

Hickman, James C., ed. *The Jepson Manual*. University of California Press. Berkeley, 1993.

Hinton, Thomas B., and Roger C. Owen. "Some Surviving Yuman Groups in Northern Baja California." *American Indigenous 17*. 1957.

Hodge, Frederick Webb, ed. *Handbook of American Indians of North Mexico, Parts I and II*. Pageant Books Inc. New York, 1959.

Hooper, Lucille. "The Cahuilla Indians." *University of California Publications in American Archaeology and Ethnology*, Vol. 16, No. 6. Berkeley, 1920.

Hoover, Robert L. "Chumash Fishing Equipment." *Ethnic Technology Notes 9*. San Diego Museum of Man. San Diego, 1973.

Hough, Walter. "Fire-making Apparatus in the U.S. National Museum." *Annual Report of the Smithsonian Institution for 1888*. Washington, D.C., 1890.

———. "The Methods of Fire-making." *Annual Report of the Smithsonian Institution for 1890*. Washington, D.C., 1891.

Hudson, J. W. Unpublished manuscript of ethnographic field notes, 1899–1906. Field Museum of Natural History. Chicago, n.d.

———. Letter from J. W. Hudson to Dr. G. A. Dorsey, dated November 27, 1899. Field Museum of Natural History, Department of Anthropology. Chicago, 1899.

Hudson, Travis. "Chumash Wooden Bowls, Trays, and Boxes." *San Diego Museum Papers 13*. San Diego, 1977.

Hudson, Travis, and Thomas C. Blackburn. *The Material Culture of the Chumash Interaction Sphere. Vol. I: Food Procurement and Transportation*. Santa Barbara Museum of Natural History. Santa Barbara, 1982.

———. *The Material Culture of the Chumash Interaction Sphere. Vol. II: Food Preparation and Shelter*. Santa Barbara Museum of Natural History. Santa Barbara, 1983.

———. *The Material Culture of the Chumash Interaction Sphere. Vol. III: Clothing, Ornamentation, and Grooming*. Santa Barbara Museum of Natural History. Santa Barbara, 1985.

———. *The Material Culture of the Chumash Interaction Sphere. Vol. IV: Ceremonial Paraphernalia, Games, and Amusements*. Santa Barbara Museum of Natural History. Santa Barbara, 1986.

———. *The Material Culture of the Chumash Interaction Sphere. Vol. V: Manufacturing Processes, Metrology, and Trade*. Santa Barbara Museum of Natural History. Santa Barbara, 1987.

Hudson, Travis, and Ernest Underhay. "Crystals in the Sky: An Intellectual Odyssey Involving Chumash Astronomy, Cosmology and Rock Art." *Ballena Press Anthropological Papers*, No. 10. Santa Barbara Museum of Natural History. Santa Barbara, 1978.

James, George Wharton. *Indian Basketry*. Henry Malkan. New York, 1909.

Jamison, Richard L., comp. *Primitive Outdoor Skills*. Horizon. Bountiful, Utah, 1985.

Jamison, Richard and Linda, eds. *Woodsmoke: Collected Writings on Ancient Living Skills*. Horizon. Bountiful, Utah, 1997.

Janetski, Joel C. "Implications of Snare Bundles in the Great Basin and Southwest." *Journal of California and Great Basin Anthropology 1*. Malki Museum. Banning, 1979.

Johnston, Bernice Eastman. *California's Gabrielino Indians*. Southwest Museum. Los Angeles, 1962.

Johnston, Francis J., and Patricia H. Johnston. "An Indian Trail Complex of the Central Colorado Desert: A Preliminary Survey." *Reports of the University of California Archaeological Survey*, No. 37. Berkeley, 1937.

Kelly, Isabel T. "The Carver's Art of the Indians of Northwestern California." *University of California Publications in American Archaeology and Ethnology*, Vol. 24, No. 7. Berkeley, 1930.

Kelly, Isabel T., and Catherine S. Fowler. "Southern Paiute." In *Handbook of North American Indians, Vol. 9: Southwest*. Smithsonian Institution. Washington, D.C., 1978.

Kelly, William H. *Cocopa Ethnography*. University of Arizona Press. Tucson, 1973.

Kirk, Ruth. *Hunters of the Whale*. William Morrow and Company. New York, 1974.

Krmpotic, Msgr. M.D. *Life and Works of the Reverend Ferdinand Konscak S.J. 1703–1759*. The Stratford Company. Boston, 1923.

Kroeber, Alfred L. "Ethnography of the Cahuilla Indians." *University of California Publications in American Archaeology and Ethnology*, Vol. 8, No. 2. Berkeley, 1908.

———. "California Basketry and the Pomo." *American Anthropologist*, Vol. 11. 1909.

———. "Handbook of the Indians of California." *Bureau of American Ethnology*, Bul. 78. Washington, D.C., 1925.

———. "Arrow Release Distributions." *University of California Publications in American Archaeology and Ethnology*, Vol. 23 No. 4. Berkeley, 1927.

———. *Basketry Designs of the Mission Indians*. The American Museum of Natural History. New York, 1932.

———. "Elements of Culture in Native California." In *The California Indians*. R. F. Heizer and M. A. Whipple, eds. University of California Press. Berkeley, 1971.

Kroeber, Alfred L., and Samuel A. Barrett. "Fishing Among the Indians of Northwestern California." *Anthropological Records*, Vol. 21, No. 1. University of California Publications. Berkeley and Los Angeles, 1960.

Kroeber, Theodora. *Ishi in Two Worlds*. University of California Press. Berkeley and Los Angeles, 1969.

Latta, Frank F. *Handbook of the Yokuts Indians*. Kern County Museum. Bakersfield, 1949.

Laubin, Reginald, and Gladys Laubin. *American Indian Archery*. University of Oklahoma Press. Norman, 1980.

Lawton, Harry W., Philip J. Wilke, Mary DeDecker, and William M. Mason. "Agriculture Among the Paiute of Owens Valley." *The Journal of California Anthropology*, Vol. 3, No. 1. Malki Museum. Banning, 1976.

Lenihan, Daniel J., and James E. Bradford. "Ancient Indians Sought Shadows and Ice Caves." In *Natural History*, Vol. 102, No. 8. American Museum of Natural History. New York, August 1993.

Loeb, Edwin M. "Pomo Folkways." *University of California Publications in American Archaeology and Ethnology*, Vol. 19, No. 2. Berkeley, 1926.

Lothrop, Samuel Kirkland. *The Indians of Tierra del Fuego*. Museum of the American Indian, Heye Foundation. New York, 1928.

Loud, Llewellyn L., and M. R. Harrington. "Lovelock Cave." *University of California Publications in American Archaeology and Ethnology*, Vol. 25, No. 1. Berkeley, 1929.

Lowie, Robert H. "Notes on Shoshonean Ethnography." *Anthropological Papers of the American Museum of Natural History*, Vol. XX, Part III. New York, 1924.

Luomala, Katherine. "Tipai-Ipai." In *Handbook of North American Indians. Vol. 8: California*. Smithsonian Institution. Washington, D.C., 1978.

MacDougal, Daniel T. "The Desert Basins of the Colorado Delta." In *The Bulletin of the American Geographical Society*, Vol. 39. 1907.

Martin, Paul S. "The Bow-Drill in North America." *American Anthropologist*, Vol. 36, No. 1. 1934.

Martin, Paul S., et al. "Mogollon Cultural Continuity and Change: The Stratigraphic Analysis of Tularosa and Cordova Cave." *Fieldiana: Anthropology*, Vol. 40. Chicago Natural History Museum. Chicago, 1952.

———. "Caves of the Reserve Area." *Fieldiana: Anthropology*, Vol. 42. Chicago Natural History Museum. Chicago, 1954.

Martínez, José L. *California in 1792. The Expedition of José Longinos Martínez*. L. B. Simpson, trans. San Marino, California, 1938.

Mason, J. Alden. "The Ethnology of the Salinan Indians." *University of California Publications In American Archaeology and Ethnology*, Vol. 10, No. 4. Berkeley, 1912.

Mason, Otis Tufton. "The Ray Collection from Hupa Reservation." *Annual Report of the Board of Regents of the Smithsonian Institution, 1886*. Government Printing Office. Washington, D.C., 1889.

———. *Indian Basketry: Studies in a Textile Art Without Machinery* (2 vols.). Doubleday, Page & Company. New York, 1904.

———. "North American Bows, Arrows, and Quivers." *Smithsonian Report 1893. (Annual Report of the Board of Regents of the Smithsonian Institution*. Government Printing Office. Washington, D.C., 1894. (Reprinted by Carl J. Pugliese. Yonkers, New York, 1982.)

Massey, Lee Gooding. "Tabla and Atlatl: Two Unusual Wooden Artifacts from Baja California." *Pacific Coast Archaeological Society Quarterly*, Vol. 8, No 1. Costa Mesa, 1972.

Massey, William C. "Brief Report on Archaeological Investigations in Baja California." *Southwestern Journal of Anthropology*, Vol. 3, No. 4. University of New Mexico. Albuquerque, 1947.

———. "The Survival of the Dart Thrower on the Peninsula of Baja California." *Southwestern Journal of Anthropology*. Vol. 17. University of New Mexico. Santa Fé, 1961.

Massey, William C., and Carolyn M. Osborne. "A Burial Cave in Baja California, The Palmer Collection, 1887." *Anthropological Records*, Vol. 16, No. 8. University of California Press. Berkeley and Los Angeles, 1961.

Mayfield, Thomas Jefferson. *Indian Summer: Traditional Life among the Choinumne Indians of California's San Joaquin Valley*. Heyday Books and California Historical Society. Berkeley, 1993.

McLendon, Sally. "Rare California Feather Blanket." In *Terra*, Vol. 32, No. 5. Natural History Museum of Los Angeles County. Los Angeles, 1995.

Mead, George R. "The Ethnobotany of the California Indians: A Compendium of The Plants, Their Users, Their Uses." *Occasional Publications in Anthropology, Ethnology Series*, No. 30. Museum of Anthropology, University of Northern Colorado. Greeley, Colorado, 1972.

Meigs, Peveril, III. "The Dominican Mission Frontier of Lower California." *University of California Publication in Geography*, Vol. VII. University of California Press. Berkeley, 1935.

———. "The Kiliwa Indians of Lower California." *Ibero-Americana*, Vol. 15. University of California. Berkeley, 1939.

———. "Creation Myth and Other Recollections of the Nijí Mishkwish." *Pacific Coast Archaeological Society Quarterly*, Vol. 7, No. 1. Costa Mesa, 1971.

———. "Notes on the La Huerta Jat'am, Baja California Place names, Hunting and Shamans." *Pacific Coast Archaeological Society Quarterly*, Vol. 8, No. 1. Costa Mesa, 1972.

Meyer, Carl. "The Yurok of Trinidad Bay, 1851." In *The California Indians*. R. F. Heizer and M. A. Whipple, eds. University of California Press. Berkeley, 1971.

Michelsen, Ralph C. "Pecked Metates of Baja California." *The Masterkey*, 41(2). Southwest Museum. Highland Park, Los Angeles, 1967.

———. "Ethnographic Notes on Agave Fiber Cordage." *Pacific Coast Archaeological Society Quarterly*, Vol. 6, No. 1. Costa Mesa, 1970.

———. " 'Making It' in a Technologically Simple Society." *Pacific Coast Archaeological Society Quarterly*, Vol. 6, No. 1. Costa Mesa, 1970.

Michelsen, Ralph C., and Roger C. Owen. "A Keruk Ceremony at Santa Catarina, Baja, California, Mexico." *Pacific Coast Archaeological Society Quarterly*, Vol. 3, No. 1. Costa Mesa, 1967.

Michelsen, Ralph, and Helen C. Smith. "Honey Collecting by Indians in Baja California, Mexico." *Pacific Coast Archaeological Society Quarterly*, Vol. 3, No. 1. Costa Mesa, California, 1967.

———. "The Making of Paddle and Anvil Pottery at Santa Catarina." *Pacific Coast Archaeological Society Quarterly*, Vol. 8, No. 1. Costa Mcsa, 1972.

Mills, Elaine L., project editor. *The Papers of John Peabody Harrington in the Smithsonian Institution 1907–1957* (microfilm). Kraus International. White Plains, 1981–1991.

Mohr, Albert, and L. L. Sample. "Twined Water Baskets of the Cuyama Area, Southern California." *American Antiquity*, Vol. 20, No. 4. 1955.

Moratto, Michael J. *California Archaeology*. Academic Press, Inc., Harcourt Brace Jovanovich. San Diego, 1984.

Munz, P. A. *A California Flora*. University of California Press. Berkeley and Los Angeles, 1959.

Murdock, George Peter, and Timothy J. O'Leary. *Ethnographic Bibliography of North America*. Human Relations Area Files Press. New Haven, 1975.

Murphy, Edith Van Allen. *Indian Uses of Native Plants*. Mendocino County Historical Society. Ukiah, California, 1987.

Nabakov, Peter. *Indian Running*. Capra Press. Santa Barbara, 1981.

Newman, Sandra Corrie. *Indian Basket Weaving*. Northland Publishing. Flagstaff, 1974.

Niehaus, Theodore F. "A Field Guide to Pacific States Wildflowers." *The Peterson Field Guide Series*. Houghton Miflin. Boston, 1976.

Nomland, Gladys Ayer. "Bear River Ethnography." *Anthropological Records*, Vol. 2, No. 2. University of California Press. Berkeley, 1938.

North, Arthur W. *Camp and Camino in Lower California*. Baker & Taylor. New York, 1910.

Olsen, Larry Dean. *Outdoor Survival Skills*. Brigham Young University Press. Provo, Utah, 1973.

Ortiz, Bev. *It Will Live Forever: Traditional Yosemite Indian Acorn Preparation*. Heyday Books. Berkeley, 1991.

———. "Patient Tasks." In *News from Native California*. Heyday Books. Berkeley, Fall 1992.

Owen Roger C. "The Indians of Santa Catarina, B.C.: Concepts of Disease and Curing." Ph.D. dissertation, University of California. Los Angeles, 1962.

———. "Contemporary Ethnography of Baja California, Mexico." In *Handbook of Middle American Indians: Ethnology Part Two*. Evon Z. Vogt, ed. University of Texas Press. Austin, 1969.

Owen, Roger C., and Ralph C. Michelsen. "The Mountain People of Baja California." Unpublished. N.D.

Palmer, Edward. "Plants Used by the Indians of the United States." *The American Naturalist* 12. 1878.

Payen, Louis A. "A Spearthrower (Atlatl) from Potter Creek Cave. Shasta County, California." *University of California, Center for Archaeological Research at Davis Publication 2*. Davis, 1970.

Payen, Louis A., and R. E. Taylor. "Man and Pleistocene Fauna at Potter Creek Cave, California. *The Journal of California Anthropology*, Vol. 3, No. 1. Malki Museum. Morongo Indian Reservation, 1976.

Pepper, George H. "The Ancient Basket Makers of Southeastern Utah." *Journal of American Museum of Natural History II*, Guide leaflet No. 6. New York, 1902.

Perkins, William R. "Effects of Stone Projectile Points as a Mass Within the Atlatl and Dart Mechanical System." *Bulletin of Primitive Technology*, No. 10. Society of Primitive Technology. Rexburg, 1995.

Pope, Saxton T. "Making Indian Arrow Heads." *Forest and Stream*. Dec. 20, 1913.

———. "Yahi Archery." *University of California Publications in American Archaeology and Ethnology*, Vol. 13, No. 3. Berkeley, 1918.

———. "A Study of Bows and Arrows." *University of California Publications in American Archaeology and Ethnology*, Vol. 13, No. 9. Berkeley, 1923.

———. "Hunting With Ishi—The Last Yana Indian." *The Journal of California Anthropology*, Vol. 1, No. 2. Malki Museum. Banning, 1974.

Powell, John W. *The Exploration of the Colorado River and Its Canyons* (exact republication of *Canyons of the Colorado*, 1895 work published by Flood & Vincent). Dover. New York, 1961.

Powers, Stephen. "Tribes of California." *Contributions to North American Ethnology, Department of the Interior*. Government Printing Office. Washington, D.C., 1877.

Priestly, Herbert, ed. *A Historical Political, and Natural Description of California by Pedro Fages, Soldier of Spain*. University of California Press. Berkeley, 1937.

Redding, George H. H. "An Evening with Wintoon Indians." *The Californian*, No. 12, 2. December, 1880.

Reid, Hugo. *The Indians of Los Angeles County* (reprinted from his letters on "Angeles County Indians" in the *Los Angeles Star*). Los Angeles, 1926.

Reilly, P. T. "The Sites of Vasey's Paradise." *The Masterkey* 40(4). Southwest Museum. Highland Park, Los Angeles, 1966.

Richards, Matt. *Deerskins into Buckskins: How to Tan with Natural Materials*. Backcountry Publishing. Cave Junction, Oregon, 1997.

———. "Wood Ashes and Hide Tanning." *Bulletin of Primitive Technology*, Vol. 1, No. 15. Society of Primitive Technology. Rexburg, 1998.

Riddell, Francis A. "Maidu and Konkow." In *Handbook of North American Indians; Vol. 8: California*. Smithsonian Institution. Washington, D.C., 1978.

Riddell, F. A., and D. F. McGeerin. "Atlatl Spurs from California." *American Antiquity*, Vol. 34, No. 4. Salt Lake City, 1969.

Ritter, D. W. "Petroglyphs: A Few Outstanding Sites." *Screenings*, Vol. 14, No. 8. Oregon Archaeological Society. Portland, 1965.

Roberts, Helen H. *Form in Primitive Music*. New York, 1933.

Roberts, Norman C. *Baja California Plant Field Guide*. Natural History Publishing Company. La Jolla, 1989.

Robinson, John W. *The San Gabriels: Southern California Mountain Country*. Golden West Books. San Marino, 1977.

Rogers, Malcolm J. *Ancient Hunters of the Far West*. Union-Tribune. San Diego, 1966.

———. "Yuman Pottery Making." *San Diego Museum Papers*, No. 2. Ballena Press. Ramona, 1973.

Romero, John Bruno. *The Botanical Lore of the California Indians*. Vantage Press Inc. New York, 1954.

Rozaire, Charles. "Twined Weaving and Western North American Prehistory." Ph.D. dissertation, University of California. Los Angeles, 1957.

Schaad, Gerrianne, ed. *The Photograph Collection of John Peabody Harrington in the National Anthropological Archives Smithsonian Institution: A Catalog to the Microfilm*. National Anthropological Archives. Washington, D.C., 1994.

Schenck, Sara M., and Edward W. Gifford. "Karok Ethnobotany." *Anthropological Records*, Vol. 13, No. 6. University of California. Berkeley, 1952.

Schneider, Joan S. *The Archaeology of the Afton Canyon Site*. San Bernardino County Museum Association. Redlands, California, 1989.

Schumacher, Paul. "Methods of Making Stone Weapons." *U.S. Geographical and Geological Survey*, Vol. III, Bulletin 3, Article 17. 1877.

———. "The Method of Manufacture of Several Articles by the Former Indians of the Southern California." *Peabody Museum of Archaeology and Ethnology, 11th Annual Report*. Cambridge, 1878.

Schwartz, D. W., A. L. Lang, and R. de Saussure. "Split-twig Figurines in the Grand Canyon." *American Antiquity*, Vol. 23, No. 3. 1958.

Smith, Gerald A. "Split-twig Figurines from San Bernardino County, California." *The Masterkey* 37(3). Southwest Museum. Highland Park, Los Angeles, 1963.

———. "The Mohaves." *San Bernardino County Museum Association Quarterly*, Vol. 14, No. 1. 1966.

Sparkman, Philip Stedman. "The Culture of the Luiseño Indians." *University of California Publications in American Archaeology and Ethnology*, Vol. 8, No. 1. Berkeley, 1908.

Spier, Leslie. "Southern Diegueño Customs." *University of California Publications in American Archaeology and Ethnology* 20, No. 16. Berkeley, 1923.

———. "Havasupi Ethnography." *Anthropological Papers of the American Museum of Natural History* 29, Part 3. New York, 1928.

———. "Klamath Ethnography." *University of California Publications in American Archaeology and Ethnology*, Vol. 30. Berkeley, 1930.

———. *Yuman Tribes of the Gila River*. The University of Chicago Press. Chicago, 1933.

———. "Mohave Culture Items." *Museum of Northern Arizona Bulletin 28*. Flagstaff, 1955.

Squier, R. "The Manufacture of Flint Implements by the Indians of Northern and Central California." *University of California Archaeological Survey Reports*, No. 19. Berkeley, 1953.

Steward, Julian H. "Ethnography of the Owens Valley Paiute." *University of California Publications in American Archaeology and Ethnology*, Vol. 3, No. 3. Berkeley, 1934.

Stewart, Hilary. *Indian Fishing: Early Methods on the Northwest Coast*. University of Washington Press. Seattle, 1977.

Stewart, Kenneth M. "Mohave Hunting." *The Masterkey* 21(3). Southwest Museum. Highland Park, Los Angeles, 1947.

———. "Mohave Fishing." *Southwest Museum Masterkey*, 31(6). Southwest Museum. Highland Park, Los Angeles, 1957.

———. "Mohave Warfare." In *The California Indians*. R. F. Heizer and M.A. Whipple, eds. University of California Press. Berkeley, 1971.

Strike, Sandra S. *Ethnobotany of the California Indians, Vol. 2: Aboriginal Uses of California's Indigenous Plants*. Koeltz Scientific Books. USA and Germany, 1994.

Sutton, Mark Q. "Insects as Food: Aboriginal Entomophagy in the Great Basin." *Ballena Press Anthropological Papers*, No. 33. Thomas C. Blackburn, ed. 1988.

Tartaglia, Louis James. "Prehistoric Maritime Adaptations in Southern California." Ph.D. dissertation, University of California. Los Angeles, 1976.

Taylor, Alexander. "The Indianology of California, Col. 143." *The California Farmer and Journal of Useful Science*. July 24, 1863.

Taylor, Edith S., and William J. Wallace. "Mohave Tattooing and Face-painting." *Southwest Museum Leaflet*, No. 20. Highland Park, Los Angeles, 1947.

Teggart, Frederick, ed. "The Portolá Expedition of 1769–1770: Diary of Miguel Costansó." *Publications of the Academy of Pacific Coast History* 2(4). Berkeley, 1911.

Thwaites, Reuben G., ed. "The Personal Narrative of James O. Pattie of Kentucky." In *Early Western Travels, 1784–1846,* Vol. 18. Arthur H. Clark. Cleveland, 1905.

Treganza, Adam E. "Possibilities of an Aboriginal Practice of Agriculture Among the Southern Diegueño." *American Antiquity*, Vol. 12. 1947.

Treganza, A. E., and A. Bierman. "The Topanga Culture: Final Report on Excavations, 1948." *Anthropological Records*, Vol. 20, No. 2. University of California. Berkeley and Los Angeles, 1958.

Van Camp, Gena R. *Kumeyaay Pottery. Paddle-and-Anvil Techniques of Southern California.* Ballena Press. Menlo Park, 1979.

Voegelin, Erminie W. "Tubatulabal Ethnography." *Anthropological Records,* Vol. 2, No. 1. University of California Press. Berkeley and Los Angeles 1938.

Wagner, H. R. "Spanish Voyages to the Northwest Coast of America in the Sixteenth Century." (Journals of Cabrillo, Cermeno and Vizcaíno in 1542, 1595 and 1602.) *California Historical Society, Special Publication No. 4.* 1929.

Walker, Edwin. *Five Prehistoric Archaeological Sites in Los Angeles County, California.* Southwest Museum. Highland Park, Los Angeles, 1951.

Wallace, William J. "Hupa, Chilula, and Whilkut." In *Handbook of North American Indians, Vol. 8: California.* Smithsonian Institution. Washington, D.C., 1978.

———. "Music and Musical Instruments." In *Handbook of North American Indians; Vol. 8: California.* Smithsonian Institution. Washington, D.C., 1978.

Walsh, Jane MacLaren. *John Peabody Harrington: The Man and His California Indian Fieldnotes.* Ballena Press. Menlo Park, 1976.

Waterman, Thomas Talbot. "Native Musical Instruments of California." In *Out West*, Vol. 28. 1908.

———. "The Yana Indians." *University of California Publications in American Archaeology and Ethnology,* Vol. 13, No. 2. Berkeley, 1918.

———. "Yurok Geographical Concepts." In *The California Indians,* R. F. Heizer and M. A. Whipple, eds. University of California Press. Berkeley and Los Angeles, 1951

Watkins, Frances E. "Moapa Paiute Winter Wickiup." *The Masterkey* 19(1). Southwest Museum. Highland Park, Los Angeles, 1945.

Wescott, David. "An Introduction to the Atlatl." In *Woodsmoke: Collected Writings on Ancient Living Skills.* Richard and Linda Jamison, eds. Horizon. Bountiful, Utah, 1997.

Wheat, Margaret M. *Survival Arts of the Primitive Paiute.* University of Nevada Press. Reno, 1967.

Wheeler, S. M. "Split-twig Figurines." *The Masterkey* 13(1). Southwest Museum. Highland Park, Los Angeles, 1939.

———. *Archaeology of Etna Cave, Lincoln County, Nevada.* Nevada State Park Commission. Carson City, 1942.

Whitaker, John O., Jr. *The Audubon Society Field Guide to North American Mammals.* Alfred A. Knopf. New York, 1980.

Wilke, Philip J., et al. *The Cahuilla Indians of the Colorado Desert: Ethnohistory and Prehistory.* Ballena Press. Los Altos, 1975.

Wilken, Michael. "The Paipai Potters of Baja California: A Living Tradition." *The Masterkey* 60(4). Southwest Museum. Highland Park, Los Angeles 1987.

———. "Baja's Paipai Indians: People from an Ancient Time." *Baja Explorer.* November–December 1992.

Willis, W. H. *Early Prehistoric Agriculture in the American Southwest.* School of American Research. Santa Fé, 1989.

Winning, Hasso von. "The Tumpline In Prehispanic Figures." *The Masterkey,* 48(3). Southwest Museum. Highland Park, Los Angeles, 1974.

Woodward, Arthur, ed. *The Sea Diary of Fr. Juan Vizcaíno to Alta California, 1769.* Glen Dawson. Los Angeles, 1959.

Zigmond, Maurice Louis. "Ethnobotanical Studies Among California and Great Basin Shoshoneans." Ph.D. dissertation, Yale University. 1941.

———. *Kawaiisu Ethnobotany.* University of Utah Press. Salt Lake City, 1981.